Entering the Stream to Enlightenment

Entering the Stream to Enlightenment: Experiences of the Stages of the Buddhist Path in Contemporary Sri Lanka

Yuki Sirimane

Published by Equinox Publishing Ltd.

UK: Office 415, The Workstation,
15 Paternoster Row, Sheffield,
South Yorkshire S1 2BX

USA: ISD, 70 Enterprise Drive, Bristol, CT 06010

www.equinoxpub.com

First published 2016

British Library Cataloguing-in-Publication Data

A catalogue record for this book is available from the British Library.

ISBN 978 1 78179 203 2 (hardback)
ISBN 978 1 78179 204 9 (paperback)

Library of Congress Cataloging-in-Publication Data

Names: Sirimane, Yuki.
Title: Entering the stream to enlightenment: experiences of the stages of the Buddhist Path in contemporary Sri Lanka / Yuki Sirimane.
Description: Bristol, CT : Equinox Publishing Ltd, 2016. | Includes bibliographical references and index.
Identifiers: LCCN 2015031052| ISBN 9781781792032 (hb) | ISBN 9781781792049 (pb)
Subjects: LCSH: Religious life--Theraveada Buddhism. | Theraveada Buddhism—Sri Lanka.
Classification: LCC BQ7285.S57 2016 | DDC 294.3/444—dc23
LC record available at http://lccn.loc.gov/2015031052

Typeset by Queenston Publishing, Hamilton, Ontario, Canada

Printed by Lightning Source Inc. (La Vergne, TN), Lightning Source UK Ltd. (Milton Keynes), Lightning Source AU Pty. (Scoresby, Victoria).

Añño esa āvuso *gatakassa maggo nāma*
Friend, as for the Path, it is different for one who has trodden it!!

Venerable Mahā-Dhammarakkhita Thero
(Vism.III.53–55/Vism.97–98)

Contents

Acknowledgements xi

Foreword by Professor Asanga Tilakaratne xiii

Foreword by Professor Peter Harvey xvii

Abbreviations and Primary Sources xxi

1. Introduction 1

Research Methodology 7

Difficulties Encountered 9

About the Interviewer 18

A Note of Caution 18

Definitions of Key Technical Terms Used 20

The Path Related Sequence of States Leading to a Supramundane Fruit 23

Scheme of Study 24

2. Noble Persons and How to Recognize One 31

The References in the Pāli *Nikāyas* to the Four Supramundane Fruits of the Path 31

Declarations of Having Attained a *Phala* as Set Out in The Pāli *Nikāyas* 32

Declarations of Attainment of *Sotāpatti-Phala* (Stream-Entry) 33

Declarations of Attainment of *Anāgāmi-Phala* (Non-Returning) 35

Declarations of Attainment of *Arahatta-Phala* 36

The Possibility of Recognizing A Noble Person 38

Contemporary Difficulties in Recognizing Noble Persons 46

Conclusion 48

3. Does the Attainment of a Supramundane Fruit Necessarily Involve A Specific Experience? 53

References in the *Nikāyas* to Specific Places, Dates, Meditative Postures and Events During which Supramundane Fruits were Attained 55

References in Contemporary Sources to Supramundane Experiences of Meditators 56
The Findings of the Field Research of the Writer 57
Conclusion 62
4. "Path, Fetter-Breaking-Experience and Effect" 65
Definitions of the Word "*phala*" 65
References in the *Nikāyas* to "Path, Fetter-Breaking-Experience and Effect (of the Fetter-Breaking-Experience)" as Three Different Phenomena 67
Implications of the Thesis of "Path, Fetter-Breaking-Experience and Effect" 69
Conclusion 83
5. Noble Persons and the Nature of their Fetter-Breaking-Experience 87
The Types of Noble Persons 87
An Analysis of the "Fetter-Breaking-Experience" 90
Differentiating the Fetter-Breaking-Experience from Other Religious Experiences 102
Re-Experiencing the Fetter-Breaking-Experience: An Analysis of *Phala-Samāpatti* 105
Phala-Samāpatti and the Cessation of Perception and Feeling 114
Conclusion 117
6. The Stream-Enterer 121
The State of Mind of a Stream-Enterer 121
The Conduct of a Stream-Enterer 137
The Blessings and Strengths of a Stream-Enterer 148
The Possibility of Someone Having Become a Noble Person in a Past Life 151
Can a Stream-Enterer Commit Suicide? 154
To What Extent Does a Stream-Enterer See *Nibbāna*? 161
Lay Noble Disciples 164
Non-Humans Attaining Supramundane Fruits 167
Conclusion 168
7. An interview with a "Possible *Arahant*" 171
About the Interviewee 172
Mind-Set of an *Arahant* 173
Conclusion 192

8.	**Conclusion**	197
	Striking Commonalities	198
	Supramundane Fruits	202
	Reasons for Debates and Confusion	205
	A Simpler Approach to the Path	208
	Future Research	210
	The Essence of this Research	212
	Appendix I	215
	The Questionnaire Used For the Fieldwork and its Rationale	215
	Appendix II	221
	Interview Synopses and Analysis	221
	Interview No. 1	221
	Interview No. 2	227
	Interview No. 3	238
	Interview No. 4	249
	Interview No. 5	255
	Interview No. 6	260
	Interview No. 7	264
	Interview No. 8, with Venerable Ajahn Brahmavamso	270
	Appendix III	281
	Interview 1 (A Sample Interview)	281
	Bibliography	319
	Indices	323
	Subject Index	325
	Index of Proper Names	339
	Index for Findings of Field Research	343

Acknowledgements

This research would not have been possible without the sincerity, generosity and insight of many.

I am deeply indebted to the Most Venerable members of the Mahā *Saṅgha* who came forward to support this project despite the possibility of being victims of manifold criticism. Specifically, for the blessings and assistance of the Most Venerable Nāuyane Ariyadhamma Mahā Thero, the Chief Preceptor and Chief Abbot of the Nāuyana Aranya Senāsanaya, Malsiripura and Venerable Nāuyane Ariyananda Mahā Thero of Nauyana Aranya Senāsanaya; for the blessings of late Most Venerable Pānaduwe Khemānaṇda Mahā Thero, the former chief preceptor and chief abbot of NissaranaVana Aranya Senāsanaya, Meethirigala and for his support for this research even from his death bed; to Venerable Udueeriyagama Dhammajeeva Mahā Thero, the chief abbot and the chief preceptor of Nissarana Vana Aranya Senasanaya, Meethirigala; Venerable U Aggañña Māha Thero of the Pa-auk Forest monastery of Myanmar; Venerable Ajahn Brahmavanso Thero of the Bodhiyāna Monastery of Western Australia; all Venerable members of the Mahā *Saṅgha* and my *kalyānamitta*s who cannot be named here due to the need to safeguard anonymity, who reluctantly but agreed to be interviewed for the purposes of this field research and with compassion, bearing up and cooperating with a rigorous interview.

My gratitude is extended to my *kalyānamittas*: Harshana Bandara who spent months transcribing the Sinhala interviews and typing them; Mr. Sekara (Dharmasekara Perera) and Mrs. Beta Koswatta for their support and for the countless days spent accompanying me to forest monasteries and to Priyantha Gunawardena for extending the necessary technical support at the computer for preparing the book for publishing.

The findings of my doctoral research carrying a message of 'living Dhamma' from a group of forest monks committed to the practice, could never have been brought to the public domain if not for the kindness, generosity, commitment and insight of Professor Peter Harvey of University of Sunderland, UK, to whom I have no words to thank the long hours and months spent by him enriching and editing this book was indeed a gift of Dhamma. I also owe a debt of thanks to Keith Munnings, who initiated and so willingly coordinated the publishing of this book in UK, and Dr. Sunil Kariyakarawana for facilitating the same. Their patience and commitment towards the publishing of this book was an immense strength to overcome the challenges inherent in presenting research findings of this nature.

My gratitude to Equinox Publishing Ltd of UK and Janet Joyce for undertaking to publish this book; Vallerie Hall for the prompt support and cooperation extended to me throughout the production process and for the editorial support by Dr. Russell Adams.

I am also deeply indebted to the following. First, to my first Dhamma teacher Mr. Mithra Wettimuny, who introduced me to the Dhamma over 20 years ago and guided me through my meditation, without which I would not have had the courage to undertake a research project of this nature, knowing well the manifold consequences of this research. Secondly, to Venerable Dhammasunetta Thero of Nissarana Vana Aranya Senāsanaya, Meethirigala, for his unstinted support, guidance, patience and valuable time spent over the years, assisting in developing and fine-tuning this research. Thirdly, to Professor Asanga Tilakaratne of the University of Colombo, the mentor and teacher of my Buddhist academic studies and the supervisor of my doctoral research, for encouraging and guiding me throughout my studies, which I ventured into mainly out of curiosity–his guidance, assistance and understanding of the inherent difficulties of research of this nature helped me to complete a difficult and onerous task.

Finally my deep-felt gratitude to my husband, Maithri, is beyond words; without his patience, manifold sacrifices and support during the last 10 years in which I stepped down from my career, this research would have been only a dream. Also to my parents, the late Mr. Clifford Weerackody and Mrs. Felicia Weerackody and to all my *kalyānamittas* whose names are mentioned and unmentioned, who supported me in numerous ways in thought, word and deed—much merit to all of you!

Given the nature of some of the issues dealt with in this book, I am aware that at times I am expressing opinions contrary to the traditional Theravāda view point and also the field research may seem to be in breach of Theravāda *vinaya* rules. I beg for forgiveness from the venerable members of the Mahā *Saṅgha,* especially from those mentioned above who supported this research, for any uneasiness caused by being associated with this research. I take full responsibility for the short-comings and erroneous conclusions herein, if any. I sincerely believe that this kind of research has been long overdue, and despite the sensitivities associated with it, the spiritual experiences and the words of wisdom of the practitioners featured in the research will encourage those seriously treading this Path and will be of help to serious students of Buddhist studies.

May the wholesome *kamma* generated by conducting this research and bringing it to the public domain be for the benefit of all those who supported this venture, both seen and unseen and near and far, and to those seriously treading this Path.

Yuki Sirimane

Foreword by Professor Asanga Tilakaratne

Rune Johansson, Swedish psychologist turned Buddhist scholar, started his much praised work, *Psychology of Nirvana* (1969) with these words: "It is a well known fact that *nibbāna* is the *summumbonum* of Buddhism and that a person who has attained this ultimate goal is called an *arahant*. But here the agreement ends." Although more than four decades have passed since Johansson wrote these words, not much has changed in our understanding of some of the crucial aspects of *nibbāna* and the path leading to it. Unlike in Johansson's case, however, there is much in the state of stream-entry and in the other three states that is agreed upon by practitioners and scholars alike. Nevertheless, this does not mean that things are crystal clear or definitively settled.

Traditionally there are eight noble persons associated with the four noble paths and the four fruits. As the author of this book highlights, the point at which one ceases to be an ordinary worldling (*puthujjana*) and becomes a follower of the path of stream-entry, i.e. the first noble person, is not clear. Likewise not clear is the point when one ceases to be one who has achieved the fruit of stream-entry and becomes a follower of the path of once-returner. The same lack of clarity is there with regard to the fourth and fifth noble persons, and the sixth and the seventh noble persons. How to recognize a person who has attained a noble fruit, or one who has started on the next path, has always been problematic in the tradition. The difficulty of recognizing is not merely for others; more crucially, it has been a problem for the subjects themselves.

Pāli texts are unanimous in asserting that in one who has attained the state of stream-entry the first three fetters, namely, the view on personality, doubt, and grasping at rites and rituals, are no more. It is plain that others cannot know the exact state of mind not only of such a person but also of any person. The only possible exception is those who have achieved the knowledge of knowing others' minds. The more crucial problem, however, is that the subject herself may not be able to know the state of her mind definitively. That this is a difficulty common among practitioners is evident in the fourth "defeat" offence in the monastic *vinaya*, in that it leaves room for the exception of those who mistakenly are of the view that they have attained any particular noble fruit. Those with this deceived state of mind, which is called "over-measuring" (*adhi-māna*), are not considered guilty of the grave offence of making a false claim to a higher attainment.

In the Pāli commentarial literature there are stories about monks checking on their fellow monks to determine whether or not one has attained a higher attainment. One such story reports how an elder monk asked a younger one to go underwater and grab the feet of a fellow monk who was reputed to have attained higher fruits. When the latter started screaming out of fear that he had been attacked by a crocodile, it was taken as proof to that he was not an *arahant*. Another story with a somewhat different emphasis says how a senior monk was examined by his own pupil (*Visuddhimagga* XX.111–113). The pupil was an *arahant* who had the ability to read the mind of his teacher. The student asked his teacher, who himself had advanced mental faculties, to create a fierce elephant and make him run toward himself. The latter did so, and then started running for his life out of fear of his own creation. Then it became clear to the teacher himself that he was not an arahant as he had mistakenly thought himself to be, for *arahants* are not supposed to get stricken by fear. Perhaps the teacher was so deceived because he could not himself recollect an instance of any unwholesome thought arising in him for a very long time. The Pāli commentaries record many similar stories, and testify in this manner to a problem that has persisted throughout the Theravāda history—how to distinguish between true *arahants*, the genuinely misguided and the willful hypocrites. Apart from the social significance of distinguishing among these people, it is very important, for obvious reasons, for one who is treading the path to know their status on it.

Mapping out the path in its broad categories is already found in the discourses. Buddhaghosa, the main commentator on the Pāli canon, has contributed to it by introducing a fully systematized scheme into the path. The significant difference between Buddhaghosa and the Buddha is that, whereas the latter taught to specific individuals or groups with specific needs, the former created a comprehensive system meant for all in general. The enormous influence of Buddhaghosa in the Theravāda tradition is well known and has been largely positive. His influence, however, has not been solely positive, not due to some fault of Buddhaghosa, however, but due to the fault of others who took him as delineating a definitive path of purification applicable universally. Consequently there have been differences of opinions among practitioners as well as teachers on specific aspects of the path and its fruits.

The method that has been followed so far in order to settle such differences is to rely on the texts. But ultimately the textual method very often would lead to the dead-end of both parties appealing to the idea of the distinction between 'direct and indirect teaching' (*nīta-attha* and *neyya-attha desanā*) of the Buddha as it was the case with the debates from the *Kathāvatthu* of the 3rd century BCE to the contemporary scholarly monks of Myanmar and Sri Lanka debating, for example, on the necessity or otherwise of *samatha* for the practice of *vipassanā*. A more reliable method, although not without its own pitfalls, is to examine, as this book does, the practice and the experience of those who have been treading the path seriously.

The outstanding feature of the present work is that it seeks to substantiate the textual ideas through examining the practice and experience of living practitioners of the path. One may perhaps highlight various uncertainties associated with practice and experience and question the reliability of individual experience as a sufficient criterion for judging the text. Notwithstanding all such difficulties, it is heartening to see that the practitioners interviewed in this work are largely in accord on where they agree with the texts and where they disagree with the texts. Based on her field findings, the author questions the traditional *Visuddhimagga* view that the fruit-thought (*phala-citta*) immediately follows the one-instant path-thought (*magga-citta*), and proposes, in the place of path-thought and fruit-thought arising in quick succession, a triad, path, peak-experience and fruit which at least in some cases could have longer intervals in between.

The author's approach to the subject is basically that of an "observer participant": she is mainly a practitioner although her observer aspect is no less rigorous. Yuki Sirmane began her career as a corporate lawyer and she got into *vipassanā* meditation about two decades back. Meanwhile, joining academic life, she strengthened her knowledge in Buddhism by completing a Postgraduate Diploma and a Masters at the Postgraduate Institute of Pāli and Buddhist Studies of the University of Kelaniya. The present work is based on her doctoral research at the same institution. The author has been fortunate to have a group of practitioners who were willing to talk about their practice and its results, in spite of the fact that some of them, being the members of the monastic Sangha, had *vinaya* rules to observe which limit discussion of such matters. The readers too must feel fortunate that, in this book, they are meeting face to face some of the serious contemporary Theravāda practitioners, male and female, monastic and householder. The interviews alone may be considered a major contribution to our current understanding of the Buddhist soteriological practice and experience.

The author has brought experience back to the centre stage of the Buddhist debates over the nature of the soteriological path and its fruits. Through this method she has given answers to some important issues surrounding the nature of the Buddhist emancipatory practice and experience. The soundness of these answers remains to be judged by future practitioners and scholars. But what we can judge without waiting for the future is that the author has demonstrated that the Buddhist path is not a mere modern construction from textual studies but a truly living tradition across the Theravāda Buddhist world. Yuki Sirimane's work is in many ways, but not solely, an insider's work for insiders. It will no doubt renew hope within those increasing numbers across the world who are keen to follow the path and confirms that the "ancient path" taught by the Buddha is truly timeless.

Asanga Tilakaratne, PhD.
Professor of Pāli and Buddhist Studies
University of Colombo
Colombo.

Foreword by Professor Peter Harvey

This book arises from a fascinating doctoral research project by Yuki Sirimane. Her thesis was drawn to my attention by fellow Samatha Trust member, Keith Munnings, who had met Yuki in Sri Lanka. She was enthused by the research she had done and was hoping to be able to make it more widely available, as indeed it deserves to be.

The work explores, in both the Pali Buddhist texts, primarily the Suttas, and in contemporary experience, the stages of realization on the path of Theravāda Buddhism. In the Suttas, the Buddha speaks of the "worldling" or "ordinary person" who has not yet made any definitive spiritual change and will wander on in the round of rebirths until a break-through is made. Then there are the eight kinds of "noble" (*ariya*) person who have made such a break-though, or are on the brink of doing so: 1) one practising for realisation of fruit that is stream-entry (*sotāpatti-phala-sacchikiriyāya paṭipanno*); 2) the stream-enterer (*sotāpanna*); 3) one practising for realisation of the fruit that is once-returning; 4) the once-returner (*sakadāgāmin*); 5) one practising for realization of the fruit that is non-returning; 6) the non-returner (*anāgāmin*); 7) one practising for arahatship; 8) the *arahant* (e.g. *Aṅguttara Nikāya* IV 292).[1] Of these, 2, 4, 6 and 8 are the four kinds of people attained to a specific spiritual fruit, while the others are on a path of practice that will definitively lead to the relevant fruit. The *arahant* is the fully liberated saint, with no future rebirths, the non-returner will not return to rebirth as a human or lower god, but be reborn at a higher level, especially in the "pure abodes" where arahantship will be attained. The once-returner will only be reborn once more at the level of a human or lower god. The stream-enterer will have a maximum of seven lives, all at least of a human level, before arahatship is attained.

The stream-enterer is said to have destroyed three limiting spiritual fetters: 1) "view on personality" (*sakkāya-diṭṭhi*), that is, regarding any of the mental or physical processes making up a person as a permanent Self, possessed by a Self, containing a Self, or being contained in a Self (e.g. MN I 300); 2) "vacillation" /"uncertainty" (*vicikicchā*) concerning what is wholesome (DN III 49) or the teachings (*dhammas*) (SN III 106); 3) "clinging to rules and vows" (*sīla-bbata-parāmāsa*), based on the view that spiritual purification is by these alone, especially by brahmins and non-Buddhist renunciants (Vibh 365). The once-returner reduces attachment/lusting after (*rāga*), hatred and delusion so as to weaken the next two fetters: 4) "desire for sense-pleasures" (*kāma-cchanda*), and 5) ill-will (*vyāpāda*). These first five fetters are said to be those "binding to the "lower shore" i.e. rebirth in the realm of sense-pleasures, as a lower god, human, animal, ghost or hell-being. The non-returner is one who ends fetters 4) and 5), and so can only be reborn in the higher realms: those of pure/subtle/elemental form (*rūpa*) and the formless (*arūpa*). The non-returner is still bound by the five remaining fetters—those binding to the higher shore—which are destroyed on becoming an *arahant*. These fetters are: 6) "attachment to form" (*rūpa-rāga*); 7) "attachment to the formless" (*arūpa-rāga*); 8) "restlessness" (*uddhacca*); 9) "conceit" (*māna*); 10) spiritual "ignorance" (*avijjā*) (DN III 234).

In the Suttas, the most commonly described realizations are those of the attainment of stream-entry and arahantship, followed by becoming a non-returner. Instances of becoming a once-returner are hard to find, and there is a lack of clarity over what marks the start of a path of practice leading to one or other of the four "fruit" states. In the case of the path leading to stream-entry, it is said that a person on this is of one of two kinds: a Dhamma-follower (*dhammānusārī*), or faith-follower (*saddhānusārī*). These have not yet destroyed any fetters, but they have the faculties of faith, energy, mindfulness, concentration, wisdom, and for the first, "the teachings proclaimed by the *Tathāgata* are accepted with a measure of appreciative understanding (*mattaso nijjhānaṃ khamanti*) through his wisdom" and the second "has a (sufficient) measure of faith in and love for (*saddhā-mattaṃ ... pema-mattaṃ*) the *Tathāgata* (MN I 479).

In the commentarial tradition and the *Visuddhimagga*, the stages of "practising for realization of" one of the four fruit stages is seen, properly speaking, as lasting for one moment only, in which "path" (*magga*) state the relevant fetters are in the process of being quickly destroyed (or, for the once-returner, weakened). Such a moment is then immediately followed by several "fruit" (*phala*) moments which are the initial glow of now being a stream-enterer, once-returner, non-returner or arahant. These *phala* moments can later be returned to, and also reflected on. This perspective in effect makes noble persons types 1, 3, 5 and 7 last for only one moment. In the Suttas, though, they seem to last for a certain period of time.[2] Indeed SN III 225 says of 1 that "he is incapable of passing away without having realized the fruit that is stream-entry" implying a period of time as type 1. In effect, the Buddhaghosa takes as the path/practising phase as just the final moment of this phase according to the Suttas: the moment that immediately precedes the moment of becoming a stream-enterer, once-returner, non-returner or arahant.

The idea of an instant (whether literally one moment or a few) in which a crucial change occurs is borne out by the research on advanced practitioners that Yuki has carried out. She reports a number of instances of a sudden, transformative state, with various kinds of lead-up. One is here reminded of debates within Mahāyāna Buddhism over whether the path is gradual or sudden. It makes sense to say that it is both: there needs to be some kind of gradual build-up, but crucial changes of state then come suddenly: like a stone suddenly splitting after being repeatedly struck, or like the star-ship Enterprise, in the TV programme "Star Trek" suddenly zooming away in "warp-drive" after a period in which power builds up ready to enter this.

Of course a crucial question is how one tells, in oneself or another person, whether a sudden deep experience is that of, for example, becoming a stream-enterer. Might it be a genuine spiritual experience of a lesser nature, without permanent results, whether of deep *samatha* (a *jhāna*), or a side-effect of deep *vipassanā* known as a "defilement of insight"? Here the above list of fetters is relevant: to be a stream-enterer, for example, one has to have destroyed the first three fetters. So any genuine sign of their still existing in a person shows that they are not a stream-enterer; of course for this, the nature of the fetters and criteria for their existing need to be properly understood. Mindful and clear recollection of the relevant experience is also an aide.

Yuki's book explores textual material on the eight noble persons in a clear and helpful way. Its most original and helpful contribution, though, comes from her fieldwork material reporting on a range of meditators' deep experiences, seen by them and/or their teachers as signifying attainment of one or more of the noble states. She then reflects on these in the light of the textual material, canonical and commentarial. This allows textual descriptions and contemporary experiences to illuminate each other and poses and explores deep questions, of relevance for both practitioners and scholars of Buddhism and religious experience.

Peter Harvey, co-founder of the UK Association for Buddhist Studies, editor of *Buddhist Studies Review*, Emeritus Professor of Buddhist Studies at the University of Sunderland, UK.

Notes

1. Peter Harvey, "The *Saṅgha* of Noble *Sāvaka*s, with Particular Reference to their Trainee Member, the Person 'Practising for the Realization of the Stream-entry-fruit'." *Buddhist Studies Review* 30(1), 2013, 3–70.
2. Peter Harvey, "The Nature of the Eight-factored Ariya, Lokuttara Magga in the Suttas Compared to the Pali Commentarial Idea of it as Momentary," *Religions of South Asia* 8(1), 2014, 31–52.

Abbreviations and Primary Sources

References to Pāli texts are to the editions of the Pali Text Society of London, except for DN-a and Vism. as follows. Translations are broadly those listed in the bibliography, with adjustments where appropriate.

A.	Answer
AN	*Aṅguttara Nikāya*
I	edited by R. Morris.1885, revised by A. K. Warder, 1999
II	edited by R. Morris, 1888
III–V	edited by E. Hardy, 1897, 1899, 1900
AN-a	*Aṅguttara Nikāya Aṭṭhakathā*, II, edited by M. Wallesser and H. Kopp, 1967
DN	*Dīgha Nikāya*
I	edited by T. W. Rhys Davids and J. E.Carpenter, 1890, reprinted with corrections, 2007
II	edited by T. W. Rhys Davids and J. E. Carpenter, 1903
III	edited by J. E. Carpenter, 1911, reprinted with corrections, 2006, Lancaster
DN-a	*Sumangalavilāsinī - Dīgha Nikāya Aṭṭhakathā,* 1992, Colombo, Simon Hewavitarana Trust
Dhp.	*Dhammapada* , edited by O. Von Hinuber and K. R. Norman, 1994
Dhp-a.	*Dhammapada* commentary, edited by H. C. Norman
I	2nd edition, 1925
II–IV	1911, 1912, 1914
Dhs.	*Dhammasaṅgaṇī,* edited by E. Muller, 1885
It.	*Itivuttaka,* edited by E. Windisch, 1889
Miln.	*Milindapañha,* edited by V. Trenckner, 1880
MN	*Majjhima Nikāya*
I	edited by V. Trenckner, 1888
II	edited by R. Chalmers, 1886–1898, corrected by M. Wiltshire, 2004
III	edited by R. T. Chalmers, 1899–1902

MN-a	*Papañcasūdanī - Majjhima Nikāya Aṭṭhakathā*
I and II	edited by J. H. Woods and D. Kosambi, 1928, 1933
III–V	edited by I. B. Horner, 1933, 1937, 1938
n.	Note
Ps.	*Paṭisambhidāmagga*, edited by A. C. Taylor, 1905, 1907
PTS	Pali Text Society
Q.	Question
SN	*Saṃyutta Nikāya*
I	edited by G. A. Somaratne, 1998. 2nd edition
II–V	edited by L. Feer, 1881, 1890, 1890, 1898
SN-a	*Manorathapūranī - Saṃyutta Nikāya Aṭṭhakathā*
I and II	edited by J. H. Woods and D. Kosambi, 1928, 1933
III–V	edited by I. B. Horner, 1933, 1937, 1938
Sn.	*Sutta-nipāta,* edited by D. Anderson and H. Smith. 1913.
Thag.	*Theragāthā*
Thig.	*Therīgāthā - Theragāthā* and *Therīgāthā*, edited by H. Oldenberg and R. Pischel, 2nd edition with appendices, K.R. Norman and L. Alsdorf, 1999
Thag-a	*Theragāthā Aṭṭhakathā*, edited by F. L. Woodword, 1940
Ud.	*Udāna*, edited by P. Steinthal, 1885
v.	Verse
V.	*Vimanavatthu; Vimana Stories*, translated by P. Masfield,1989
Vibh-a	*Vibhangaṭṭhakathā*, edited by A. P. Buddhadatta Thero, 1923
Vin.	*Vinayapiṭaka*, edited by H. Oldenberg, 5 vols, 1879, 1880, 1881, 1882, 1883
Vism.	*Visuddhimagga—Visuddhimagga of Buddhaghosācariya*, Harvard Oriental Series, 1950. Edited by Henry Clarke Warren, revised by Dharmananda Kosambi, Delhi, Motilal Banarsidass

— 1 —

Introduction

> I pulled over my pillow and prepared to rest. As I lay down, my mind was still just as calm. As I was about to lay my head on the pillow, the mind inclined inwards—I didn't know where it was headed, but it kept moving deeper and deeper within. It was as if someone had turned on a switch and sent an electric current along a cable. With a deafening bang, the body exploded from the inside. The awareness inside the mind at that moment was at its most refined. Having passed beyond a certain point, it was as if the mind was cut loose and had penetrated to the deepest, quietest spot inside. It settled there in a realm of complete emptiness. Absolutely nothing could penetrate it from outside. Nothing could reach it. Having stayed in there for a while, awareness then withdrew. I don't mean to say that I made to withdraw; I was merely watching—just witnessing what was going on. Having experienced these things, the mind gradually withdrew and returned to its normal state.
>
> Once the mind had returned to normal, the question arose; "What happened?" The reply that came to it was, "These things are natural phenomena which occurred according to causes and conditions; there's no need to doubt about them"—I only needed to reflect a little like this and the mind accepted it. Having paused for a while, it inclined inwards again. I didn't make any conscious efforts to direct the mind, it went by itself. As it continued to move deeper and deeper inside, it hit the same switch like before. This time the mind shattered into the minutest and refined particles. Again, the mind was cut loose and slipped deep inside itself. Silence. It was at an even deeper level of calm than before—nothing could penetrate it. Following its own momentum, the mind stayed like that some time and then withdrew as it wished. Everything was happening automatically. There was no one influencing or directing events; I didn't try to make things happen, to enter that state or withdraw from it in any particular way. I was simply keeping with the knowing and watching. Eventually the mind withdrew to a state of normalcy, without stimulating any doubt. I continued to contemplate and the mind inclined inwards again. The third time I had the experience of the whole world completely disintegrating. The earth, vegetation, trees, mountains, in fact the entire planet appeared as ākāsa-dhātu (the space element). There were no people or anything else left at all. At this last stage there was complete emptiness. (Chah 1998, 17)

The above is an account of a set of religious experiences of the well known Venerable Ajahn Chah of the Thai tradition, widely believed to be one who has attained the supramundane fruits of the Path, as given in *The Key to Liberation*. On the other hand below is a religious experience of a non-Buddhist (R. Bucker), quoted by Ken Wilber in *No Boundaries*:

> All at once I found myself wrapped in a flame-colored cloud. For an instant I thought of fire, and immense conflagration somewhere close by in that city; the next I knew, the fire was within myself. Directly afterward there came upon me a sense of exaltation, of immense joyousness, accompanied or immediately followed by an intellectual illumination impossible to describe. Among other things, I did not merely come to believe, but I saw that the universe is not composed of dead matter, but is on the contrary, a living Presence; I became conscious in myself of eternal life. It was not a conviction that I would have eternal life but a consciousness that I possessed eternal life then; I saw that all men are immortal; that the cosmic order is such that without any pre-adventure all things work together for the good of each and all; that the foundation principle of the world, of all the worlds, is what we call love, and the happiness of each and all is in the long run absolutely certain. (Wilber 2001, 1)

The above quotes highlight the striking contrast between the understanding that is generated by the religious experience of a non-Buddhist and that of a Buddhist. Whilst both speak of a striking experience, the "intellectual illumination" that came about in one was, an awareness of "a living Presence; I became conscious in myself of eternal life ... I saw that all men are immortal," in the other, there was complete emptiness with the whole world completely disintegrating. To Ajahn Chah, the earth, vegetation, trees, mountains, in fact the entire planet appeared as *ākāsa-dhātu* (the space element). There were no people or anything left at all and he saw what had been experienced as natural phenomena which occurred according to causes and conditions. However, both had no doubt about their respective experiences as it was not a "belief" but a direct experience.

Ken Wilber is considered one of the most widely read and influential American theoreticians on the relationship of religions in recent times. His book *No Boundaries,* which is presented as a guide to the psychologies and therapies available in Western and Eastern sources, from Psychoanalysis to Zen, Existentialism to *Tantra*, concludes that:

> We should surely be making a grave error if we hastily conclude such experiences to be hallucinations or products of a mental aberration, for in their final disclosure, they share none of the tortured anguish of psychotic visions. (Wilber 2001, 1)

Based on accounts of religious experiences of diverse faiths similar to those quoted above, religious experience has become a subject discussed widely by both Western and Eastern philosophers. Generally it is believed that religious experience is transcendental and ineffable and belongs to a realm beyond ordinary human perception. Experiences similar to what is quoted above are used to support this claim.

Jack Engler, Daniel Brown and Ken Wilber's *Transformations of Consciousness—Conventional and Contemplative Perspectives on Development* is a book consisting of various closely related attempts to articulate a "full spectrum" model of human growth and development, a model that includes the stages of development typically investigated by conventional psychology and psychiatry as well as the stages of development apparently evidenced in the world's great meditative and contemplative traditions (Engler *et al.* 1986, Preface). In the said book, after systematic research, Daniel Brown concludes with a view that is the opposite of the stereotypical notion of mystical experience that perennial philosophers usually mean by the "transcendent unity of religions," that is, "There are many paths to the same end." Brown's in-depth analysis of meditation experiences suggests the opposite: there is one path which leads to different ends, different enlightenment experiences (Engler *et al.* 1986, 219).

Religious experiences of a Buddhist can vary, in terms of *samatha* or calm, from basic *samādhi* (concentration) such as the *upacāra samādhi* (access concentration), to *jhānas* (absorptions), up to *nevasaññānāsaññāyatana* (the sphere of neither-perception-nor-non-perception), and, in terms of *vipassanā* or insight, from *nāmarūpa pariccheda-ñāṇa* (knowledge of de-limitation of name-and-form) up to the experience of *Nibbāna*. The experiences at different mileposts of the Path have been expressed by noble persons (those who have attained a supramundane fruit of the Path, or are on the brink of doing so) in numerous ways, particularly in terms of their feelings and resultant knowledge, and descriptions of such experiences are scattered throughout the canonical texts. Further, the Buddha too has spelt out the mental states of various attainments of the Path.

Much has been said in the texts on the experience of an *Arahant*, *Nibbāna* being the ultimate goal. These statements are found as bold declaration by the disciples themselves such as in the *Theragāthā* and *Therīgathā*. In comparison, references to the experience or what is "felt" by a *sotāpanna* (stream-enterer) and *anāgāmī* (non-returner) are much less. Even scarcer or hardly any are the references in the texts to the experience of a *sakadāgāmī* (once-returner) in terms of their own pronouncements.

Today there is much intellectual debate about various aspects of both the Path and its fruits. These debates and controversies amongst equally knowledgeable and experienced authorities can give rise to confusion and undermine the confidence of novices seriously treading the Path or of serious students of Buddhist Studies. Set out below are some of the vital issues, relating to the Path and its fruits, under such discussion or debate.

Asanga Tilakaratne, in *Nirvāṇa and Ineffability*, suggests that the Buddhist religious experience is unique and not comparable with other religious experiences and that *Nibbāna is* neither transcendental nor ineffable (Tilakaratne 1993, 150). Bhikkhu Bodhi however, concludes that *Nibbāna* is a reality, which is transcendental and ineffable (Bodhi 1996, 163).

The texts refer to eight types of people on this Path [*aṭṭha purisapuggalā*]. They are those who have attained the four supramundane fruits of the Path and the four persons on the way (path) to these four fruits. However, the exact boundaries of each of the four Paths seem to be rather vague. Hence there is a need to locate and investigate any references or declarations in the texts about the experience of one who has "entered" the Path of any particular supramundane fruit.

Jack Kornfield's *Living Buddhist Masters* (1993) presents a spectrum of contemporary Theravāda Buddhist meditation masters from Burma, Thailand, Laos and Cambodia, together with their teaching techniques. In this and many other books, the Thai teacher Ajahn Mahā Boowa declares that wisdom develops *samādhi* (concentration) and Mahāsi Sayadaw and U Ba Khin, from the Burmese tradition, teach strict insight practice without preparatory concentration. Ajahn Chah and some other meditation masters accept either *samatha* (concentrative calm) or *vipassanā* (insight) as a starting point, depending on the inclinations of the practitioner. Venerable Pa Auk Tawya Sayadaw from the Burmese tradition, however, in *Light of Wisdom* (1993), teaches the attaining of very high stages of *samādhi*, reaching up to experiencing memory of previous births, as preparatory work for insight practice. Ajahn Brahmavamso, an English monk trained in the Thai tradition argues:

> I cannot see the possibility to penetrating to the full meaning of *anatta, dukkha, anicca* without the radical data gained in a *jhānic* experience. Yet there are some stories in the *Tipiṭaka* that suggest it might just be possible. (Brahmavamso 2004, 32)

He further suggests that this might be possible only in cases with very strong faith [*saddhā*] (33). Apart from the above different views of practitioners, much textual study on the Path to *Nibbāna* suggests that both routes are possible. Here it would be helpful to study the different approaches to the Path adopted by successful contemporary practioners.

Further, certain experiences relating to the Path referred to in the commentaries such as *phala-samāpatti* (fruition attainment) and the sixteen *vipassanā* knowledges referred to in the *Visuddhimagga* are rejected by some practitioners on the basis that they are not referred to in the canonical texts, whilst a significant number, including reputed meditation masters hold these to be essential experiences of the Path. *Light of Wisdom* by Pa Auk Tawya Sayadaw and *Vipassanā Shuni Kyan* (*The Method of Vipassanā Meditation*) by Venerable Mahāsi Sayadaw, the most venerated meditation masters of the Burmese tradition, explain in detail in terms of the *Visuddhimagga*, the attainment of *phala-samāpatti* by all those who have attained to supramundane fruits of the Path, and differentiate this experience from *nirodha-samāpatti* (cessation attainment). Hence there is a need to investigate whether or not, or to what extent, "*phala-samāpatti*" is in accordance with the *Suttas*; is it a concrete test of a person's supramundane attainments or experience, as believed by many contemporary meditation traditions?

There is much intellectual debate currently on the experience relating to the attainment of the *sotāpatti-phala* (fruit that is stream-entry), such as, in what sense a stream-enterer experiences or sees *Nibbāna*. The commentaries say they "see" *Nibbāna* in its fullest sense (but have not yet attained it). Bhikkhu Katukurunde Ñāṇananda refers to the *sotāpanna* (stream-enterer) as *diṭṭhadhammo, pattadhammo, viditadhammo, pariyogāḷhadhammo* etc.: he is one who has seen *Dhamma/Nibbāna*, reached *Dhamma/Nibbāna*, understood *Dhamma/Nibbāna*, and plunged into *Dhamma/Nibbāna* (Ñāṇananda 2003, I, 24; from, e.g., DN I 110). The *Kosambi Sutta* of the *Saṃyutta Nikāya* (SN II 118) however, refers to the experience of a trainee [*sekha*]—a noble person who is not yet an *Arahant*—as follows:

It is as if friend, there were in the desert path a well, and neither rope nor drawer of water. And a man should come by oppressed and afflicted by heat, weary, parched, and thirsty. He should look down in to the well. Verily in him would be the knowledge; "water!"—Yet he would not be in a position to touch it physically [*na ca kāyena phusitvā vihareyya*].

Even so friend I have well seen by right insight as it really is that ceasing of becoming is *Nibbāna* and yet I am not an *Arahant* in whom taints are extinct [*bhavanirodho nibbānanti yathā bhūtaṃ sammapaññayā sudiṭṭham na camhi arahaṃ khīṇāsavoti*].

Accordingly, the trainee does not "touch" *Nibbāna* with his meditative "body," but has knowledge of *Nibbāna* and sees it with right insight. Further it refers to "ceasing of becoming is *Nibbāna*." Based on these *Sutta*s there is much debate about whether or not a *sotāpanna* has a glimpse of *Nibbāna* and what is the kind of "cessation" above referred to: is it total cessation of *nāma-rūpa*, and if not, what exactly is this experience?

For the purposes of this study, the issue of whether or not the attainment of a supramundane fruit is marked by a specific experience is a vital factor. There are *Sutta*s which set out that one can declare that one has attained a supramundane fruit of the Path by examining oneself. This gives room for interpretation that one qualifies to do so without a specific religious experience which marks the attainment of the relevant fruit. One such passage is as follows:

> Ānanda I will teach you a Dhamma exposition called the mirror of the Dhamma, equipped with which, a noble disciple, if he wishes, could by himself declare of himself "I am one finished with hells ... animal realm, ... domain of ghosts ... plane of misery... the bad destinations ... the nether world, I am a stream-enterer no longer bound to the nether world, fixed in destiny, with enlightenment as my destination."
>
> And what Ānanda, is that Dhamma exposition, the mirror of the Dhamma ... Here, Ānanda, a noble disciple possesses confirmed confidence in the Buddha ... Dhamma ... *Saṅgha* ... He possesses the virtues dear to a noble one, unbroken leading to concentration. (SN V 356, as translated by Bodhi 2000, 1800)

The above quotation from the *Sotāpatti Saṃyutta* prima facie suggests that the Buddha's advice is, that one can declare oneself a stream-enterer, having looked within and found the aforesaid four qualities which are referred to as the "*sotāpattyaṅgāni,*" the "factors of stream-entry." There are many other *Sutta*s which set out that one can declare a supramundane fruit of the Path by examining oneself. Further, in the above passage there is no reference to the breaking the first three fetters, which are usually associated with becoming a stream-enterer. The three fetters eliminated on attaining the first fruit of the Path [*sotāpatti-phala*], or the fruit that is stream-entry are *sakkāya-diṭṭhi* (view on personality), *sīlabbata-parāmāsa* (clinging to rules and vows) and *vicikicchā* (skeptical doubt). If so, the issue arises as to whether all who *seem* to possess factors of stream-entry are *sotāpanna*s, even if they have not had a specific religious experience or broken any fetters.

In the passage quoted above, the virtue [*sīla*] of a *sotāpanna* is unbroken. There is however, much debate today about whether or not the *sotāpanna's sīla* (five precepts) is unbroken. Even during the time of the Buddha when the Buddha declared Sarakāni, the lay Sakyan disciple to be a *sotāpanna* immediately after his death, those who knew Sarakāni to have taken intoxicating drinks questioned the Buddha about his declaration about the attainments of Sarakāni (SN V 375). In discussing the same issue, William Hamilton, concluding his research about the enlightened persons in Theravāda tradition writes:

> For years I have had an opportunity to closely observe teachers and meditators whom I believe have attained at least the first level of enlightenment. They are mostly 1ay people and westerners, which is a fundamentally different situation for monks and nuns who have a primary duty of following precepts as a commitment to continuous mindfulness. In my opinion, they have a very strong tendency to be highly moral and many make a sincere effort to follow the precepts. Even

those who make no specific effort to follow the precepts are intuitively inclined to follow them. (Hamilton 1995, 110–111)

There is a need to investigate as to what is meant by "unbroken *sīla*" of a stream-enterer.

Apart from the above discussions on the attributes of a *sotāpanna*, there is also the issue of whether there are people alive today with a *phala* attained by them in their *previous* births. Venerable Kannimahara Sumangala Thero of Sri Lanka created history when he claimed publicly that he was born a *sotāpanna*.[1] In terms of the Buddhist philosophy it is a possibility that a *sotāpanna* or a *sakadāgāmī* without mastery of *jhāna* can be reborn in the human world and would strive to complete her mission here. There is however no systematic research on this topic.

Much of the debates referred to above are based on doubts and speculation that arise due to the limits of knowledge pertaining to deepest Buddhist religious experiences. The limits of knowledge on this has been dealt with comprehensively by K. N. Jayatilleke in *Early Buddhist Theory of Knowledge* (1963). There is a limit beyond which intellectual investigation cannot reach, but experiential knowledge can explore into this realm. The limitations of language also have added to the problem.

In the light of the above discussions and debates, there is a need to investigate into the true nature of the deepest Buddhist religious experiences with a view to finding answers to some of these questions. In this study, the term "religious experience" is primarily used to refer to the four stages of enlightenment referred to in the Pāli *Nikāyas*:

- the attainment of *sotāpatti-phala* (the fruit that is stream-entry),
- the attainment of *sakadāgāmi-phala* (the fruit that is once-returning),
- the attainment of *anāgāmi-phala* (the fruit that is non-returning),
- the attainment of *arahatta-phala* (the fruit that is Arahantship), or simply the attainment of *arahatta*. (A IV 292)

This study aims at both elucidating the various stages of religious experience referred to in the canonical texts and analyzing them and comparing them with the personal experiences of contemporary followers of the Path, with a view to establishing the essence of the experience at the four aforesaid mileposts of the Path. It also attempts to establish ways of recognizing and testing such mileposts, particularly in terms of the experience of contemporary followers of the Path who have a high probability of having attained a supramundane fruit of the Path, or who are believed, or believe themselves, to have such an attainment.

This study has a special focus on the experience at the stage of attaining *sotāpatti-phala* for two reasons. First, as it is the most significant to a follower of the Path, it being the point at which one gets confirmation that the path one has been following so far is correct, and the point at which one begins to tread the Path unreservedly. Secondly it can be reasonably expected that the opportunities to interview those who are believed to be or claim to be *sotāpannas* in contemporary society will be relatively more than those with higher fruits of the Path.

Research Methodology

Textual Analysis

The methodology of this research is twofold: textual analysis and fieldwork. A substantial part of the research has been based on textual analysis, mainly of the first four Pāli *Nikāyas*. Texts have been used specifically to determine the nature of the various stages of the Buddhist religious experience. Though the debate on "what is the original word of the Buddha?" may never be finalized conclusively in detail, A. K. Warder in *Indian Buddhism* presents a detailed analysis of the history and development of Buddhism, and concludes:

> Of the schools that preserved the philosophy of the Buddha, the Sthaviravāda (Theravāda), Bahusrutīya and Sautrāntika, among those known to us, appear the most faithful to his ideas. Where these three agree, as they usually do, we can say that we have authentic Buddhist tradition. Everything else is part of history and of religion, interesting in its own right and often derivable, with more or less distortion, from some aspects of the original teaching. (Warder 1980, Preface)

He further writes:

> If they preserved a very authentic body of original *Tripiṭaka* the Sthaviravāda certainly made substantial additions to this: these, however, took the form of new books rather than of insertions in the old ones, with the probable exception of the *Kṣudraka* texts (of the fifth *Nikāya*) which in all the schools seem to have grown gradually during a much longer period than the rest of the *Sūtra*. In fact it is likely that this "Minor Tradition" was for a long time not regarded as strictly canonical (in the sense of words of the Buddha himself), was thus a supplement to the *Tripiṭaka* in which interesting or useful texts which had been produced from doubtful sources, or composed by monks and nuns recently, could be handed down (Warder 1980, 297).

The secondary textual sources quoted herein are mainly books by reputed meditation masters and *bhikkhus* from the forest monasteries. Most of these books are those published for free distribution, published as aids to spiritual progress as opposed to being for academic purposes. Hence these books present various aspects of the Buddhist religious experience which is the subject matter of this research. The authors of these sources include Venerables Ajahn Chah and Ajahn Brahmavamso from the Thai tradition, Pa-auk Sayadaw and Mahāsi Sayadaw from the Burmese tradition, and Mātara Sri Ñāṇārāma Mahā Thero and Katukurunde Ñāṇananda Mahā Thero of Sri Lanka. Further, this study has also drawn on research findings of conventional psychology and psychiatry into the stages of development apparently evidenced in the world's great meditative and contemplative traditions. However, essentially the textual study is based on the Pāli *Nikāyas*. An attempt is made here to base the textual study (and the Path-related sequence of states leading to a supramundane fruit), exclusively on the four Pāli *Nikāyas*, to the exclusion of the commentaries and the *Visuddhimagga*. However, the *Visuddhimagga* has been quoted in the study to a bare minimum, only to highlight the controversies and debates about the nature of the religious experiences discussed here and also analogies have been drawn between the findings of our field research and certain passages from the *Visuddhimagga*.

Field Research

The textual analysis herein has been supplemented with fieldwork. It should be emphasized that this study does not depend solely on field research to substantiate our thesis. This research is primarily based on textual evidence which is supplemented by findings of the field research.

Interviewees

As fieldwork, I interviewed a selection of those seriously treading the Path: meditators and meditation masters of recognized meditation traditions, mainly from the forest tradition and forest monasteries of Sri Lanka. The group interviewed includes monks, a nun and a laywoman and includes a Malaysian monk and Chinese *bhikkhunī* who had been ordained as a Mahāyāna nun and is still in the attire of a Chinese nun. Out of the five Sri Lankan monks successfully interviewed, four are attached to well established, internationally renowned forest monasteries and two are meditation teachers. All the Sri Lankan monks who have been interviewed are personally known to the writer and she has associated with them as *kalyāṇa-mitta*s (spiritual friends and guides) and also associated with these forest monasteries for over 18 years. Also interviewed were two foreigners, with whom there was no prior association, who were presented for the purpose of this research by a monk whom the writer had already interviewed and also by their chief preceptor, these foreigners being students of both these monks. Whilst most of the monks interviewed lived in well established, well known forest monasteries, one lived alone in a cave. He too is attached to a well established forest monastery in Sri Lanka. The laywoman interviewed has also been closely associated with the writer for over 18 years as a *kalyāṇa-mitta* striving for common goals. Altogether I have successfully interviewed seven practitioners on their personal religious experiences. This number does not include the interviews that had to be given up half-way, and those who agreed to be interviewed, but did not co-operate with the interviewer. In addition to the above interviews on personal experiences, Venerable Ajahn Brahmavamso, being a renowned and experienced meditation teacher, was interviewed by me on Buddhist religious experiences in general, as an expert in the field of meditation.

Selection of the Interviewees

Though the candidates interviewed were close associates of the writer for many years, and lengthy discussions about meditative attainments is usually common amongst meditators and between students and teachers, their personal meditative attainments had never been discussed openly. Hence the initial selection of the subjects to be interviewed was done on a hunch that they had some relevant spiritual experiences. This was the first time in their practice that they had agreed to be subject to an interview of this nature.

Methodology

In general, none of those interviewed was interested in the outcome of a piece of academic research. The objectives of the research and its importance to the practitioner were also not their concern. However, having systematically prepared their minds for this purpose for over 18 months, and having sought to persuade them in numerous ways, such as through third parties who are *kalyāṇa-mitta*s, to cooperate with this research, some agreed to be interviewed and cooperate whilst others did not. The specific objectives of the research were explained in detail once more, immediately prior to the commencement of the interview.

All interviews have been presented here in a way that preserves anonymity, leaving out names of even the interviewees' teachers and places where the interviewees meditated. However, in order to establish the credibility of the person interviewed, personal data of the subject has been presented at the commencement of each interview, subject to the limits of preserving anonymity. The interviews were based on a standard questionnaire which gave general guidance to the interviewer as to the approach. However, though it was intended to pose the same questions to all, the questions differed depending on how the discussion evolved. All interviews were taped and transcribed word by word, checked and re-checked for accuracy and translated into English where necessary by the writer herself. One subject had a severe language barrier which was a serious obstacle for the interview and transcribing, and one was interviewed through a translator.

Pointed questions were asked aiming at resolving specific issues in addition to discussing the religious experience in general. In interviews where there was no direct confirmation about attainment of a specific *phala*, the issue was approached from a different angle using "fetters" overcome as the benchmark, rather than using technical terms assigned for the supramundane fruits of the Path. At times, when things were obvious but not expressed clearly enough, leading questions had to be asked in order to get confirmation. Leading questions were also asked to exclude other possibilities and narrow things down to the relevant issue. Technical terms in the sense they are used in the canonical texts were used to standardize the interviews. The question "could you describe your first significant religious experience on this Path?" was posed as a convenient starting point. As the specific objective of the interviews was to conduct "research into the nature of the supramundane fruits of the Path," interviewees were reminded of this immediately prior to the start of the interview. Irrespective of whether the interviewees admitted an attainment of a supramundane fruit or not, most who agreed to be interviewed cooperated with me and responded to the said question by describing the experience relating to "their attainment of stream-entry."

The same question was asked in different ways and the same issue was addressed through many different angles, as clarity and coherence in the answers to all questions with regard to a particular issue was needed in order to establish credibility of the knowledge claimed. Particularly when 200 to 400 questions are posed within a short time span such as 1 ½ to 3 ½ hours, to someone unprepared, there is a good chance of gaining clarity or highlighting doubts on the relevant issues. Moreover, under these conditions, there is a greater chance for a consistent pattern of answering and the true state of mind of the interviewees being revealed, though their wish might be to play down or avoid revealing their religious attainments.

Difficulties Encountered

Needless to say, this type of research is always subject to the difficulty of recognizing noble persons. This issue of how to recognize a person who has attained one or more supramundane fruits of the Path, and factors posing problems for this, has been dealt with in detail in Chapter 2, and it will not be discussed in this chapter.

Fieldwork of this nature largely depends not only on gaining access to the right people but also on their willingness to cooperate and share or divulge their spiritual experiences. Buddhist monks of Theravāda tradition with higher ordination [*upasampadā*] are reluctant to discuss or divulge their spiritual attainments mainly due to two disciplinary rules applicable to the *upasampadā* monk.

I set out below the relevant disciplinary rules.

Pārājikā Rule IV (Rule Leading to Defeat)

This disciplinary rule, one of those leading to "defeat" in the monastic life, if broken, is set out in the disciplinary code as follows:

> Should any *bhikkhu*, without direct knowledge, claim a superior human state, a truly noble knowledge and vision, as present in himself, saying, "Thus do I know, thus do I see," such that regardless of whether or not he is cross-examined on a later occasion, he—being remorseful and desirous of purification—might say, "Friends not knowing, I said I know; not seeing, I said I see—vainly, falsely, idly," unless it was from over-estimation, he also is defeated and is no longer in affiliation.[2]

In terms of the *Suttavibhaṅga*, Volume I of the *Vinaya Piṭaka*, the above *pārājikā* rule was enacted under the same or similar conditions under which *pācittiya* rule VIII (rule requiring confession) was enacted which is discussed under the next sub-heading (p. 11). The latter rule sets out a series of incidents in which the Buddha gives a ruling whether or not a particular statement of a monk entails that he has committed a *pārājikā* offence, a minor offence [*dukkhata*] or not an offence [*anāpatti*]. This series of incidents is an aid to interpret the above *pārājikā* rule. I do not intend to undertake a detailed analysis of the *Vinaya* rules set out above. However, from the incident that lead to the enactment of the rule [*Nidāna*] set out in Volume I and II of the *Suttavibhaṅga* of the *Vinaya Piṭaka*, it is very clear that the *motive* or *intention* and the *circumstances* under which a statement of a monk relating to his religious experiences are made, is a material factor to be considered in determining whether or not the statement constitutes an offence, and, if so, its gravity.

Several cases have been reported in the *Suttavibhaṅga* where Venerables Moggallāna and Anuruddha are accused by other monks of being guilty of the fourth *pārājikā* offence. On one occasion Moggāllana has made a statement about what he saw through his psychic powers, such as:

> I saw a skeleton going through the air, and vultures, crows and hawks were following hard, striking it ... while it uttered a cry of distress. Indeed it is wonderful, indeed it is marvelous that a being will become like that, that a *yakkha* will become like that, that one having existence will become like that.

On all such occasions the Buddha declares "Monks Moggāllana spoke truly; there is no offence for Moggallāna"(Vin. III 105). Similarly a monk through undue estimate of himself [*adhimāna*], declared attainment of *arahatta-phala* [*aññā*] and later he was remorseful and was worried whether he had fallen into an offence of defeat. The Buddha declared "there is no offence monk, (merely) because there was an undue estimate of yourself" (Vin. III100).

Pācittiya Rule VIII (Rule Requiring Confession)

Should any *bhikkhu* report (his own) superior human state to an unordained person, when it is factual, it is to be confessed.[3]

The Buddha declared this to be an offence when he was in Vajjī during a famine. At this time, a group of monks thought they would persuade laypeople in the village to give them alms food by saying that they were monks among them who had higher religious attainments such as *jhānas*, higher knowledges such as psychic powers and fruits of the Path such as stream-entry. They thought this would enable them to comfortably obtain their alms food. The above *pācittiya* rule was enacted as a result of this incident. The Buddha on this occasion censured the monks thus:

> How can you, monks, for the sake of your stomachs, speak praise to householders concerning this or that superhuman quality? It is not monks, for pleasing those who are (not yet) pleased ... And thus, monks, this rule of training should be set forth. (Vin. IV 25)

Jotiya Dhirasekere comments on this issue:

> Apart from considerations of truthfulness and honesty of a monk in the mode of obtaining his requisites from the laymen, there seems to be yet another associated idea in this *sikkhāpada* (disciplinary rule). To our mind it is the unscrupulous exploitation of the regard and the respect which the lay people of the time had for these "super-human achievements" which were generally associated with those who had renounced the household life ... These hint at fraud and artful conversation as means of gaining easy livelihood in an unworthy manner.
>
> (Dhirasekere 1964, 86–87)

Despite the spirit and the objective of these two disciplinary rules, the Theravāda tradition seems to be generally following this *Vinaya* rule "to the letter." Moreover, It seems to have gone beyond the spirit of the rule and developed to a custom of not discussing one's attainment at all except however with one's teacher.

In the backdrop of the above two disciplinary rules, first let us discuss the difficulties encountered by the writer in the field research. Most of those interviewed were closely known to the writer for many years and recognized the commitment of the writer to the practice. Under these circumstances, having explained the importance of this research to a practitioner as well as to academics, some had a reasonable appreciation of the need for a study of this nature, though most of those approached refused to even entertain the idea of a discussion. Some believed that as monks with higher ordination they should not be talking to a lay person about their spiritual attainments, irrespective of the motive.

Some monks who agreed to be interviewed, in principle had no problems discussing this subject with the writer for this purpose, despite her being a laywoman, yet refused to identify any of their deep experiences as attainment of a specific *phala*. This was so even when, in terms of the text, an experience and the understanding it generated had all the ingredients of attainment of a *phala*, (i.e. breaking of the first three fetters would correspond to attainment of the first fruit of the Path- *sotāpatti-phala*). Some refused to "label" their experience on the basis that, as *Nibbāna* was their ultimate goal, an interim *phala* is immaterial to them and is also a concept like any other concept. Some others, though initially agreeing to speak out and intending to cooperate, in the process of the interview had natural inhibitions to opening up, such that the interviews had to be curtailed. Some interviews had to be given up half way as the monks concerned felt too uncomfortable to answer at the depth that was needed by the writer. The writer could not even get started with some interviews; the file was merely opened and closed as the monk concerned felt it was "suicidal" to answer even the very first question, "what is your most significant religious experience?." Some interviews had to be totally disregarded as the monk concerned only spoke in very general terms or as an experience of a third party, and not as his own personal experience. There were some others who didn't deny that a particular experience marked the attainment of a specific *phala*, but who stated that *vinaya* precluded them from answering a pointed question. Such interviewees ended up answering in phrases such as "yes it is possible that it is the attainment of *sotāpatti-phala,*" or "it may or may not be," or "according to the text it is so" etc.

I set out below some extracts from this fieldwork to enumerate more specifically the difficulties encountered by the writer:

In one of the interviews (Interview No. 5) that had to be given up half way, the interviewee's response at one point was as follows:

> Is it alright if I say this? (laugh) I feel the questions are going too far. Do you understand? (not clear) You are laypeople. You can delete this and take it (referring to the recording). Then I will have to answer these questions to the last. Whatever I have realized is not for this kind of purpose. When you ask these, there is a limit to what we can answer. Otherwise we commit transgressions. Do you understand? That is, there is limit to what we can declare with regards to these. So my conscience is pricking me as to why I am answering these. You understand? If we talk like this to a conclusion in this fashion, if anyone listens to this, he will even blame me for this. Therefore I cannot discuss this. I can talk on these in some other way. I can speak through my knowledge, meditation experiences or else according to what I have learnt. You understand? Because this subject doesn't agree with us. Why? Because as a monk with higher ordination. This is the problem. Do you understand? You don't understand this. In short, if I knew the type of questions I wouldn't have consented to this (laugh). Do you understand? This is not the way to ask these questions. Though an individual engages in the meditation the questions should be directed in a different way. It is useless my telling you this now, things have already been told. The way you can discuss about meditation experiences for your own needs and ... This style is different. Here I always have to draw on my own realization. Isn't it? So when we talk like this it's difficult for me to answer in accordance with my conscience. Not because someone will find out who I am and I will be accused or that they will look for my weaknesses. Do you understand? You have to understand (laugh).You don't understand these issues. There should be a limit to these questions. You have to ask within this limit. It is good that I got to know these things from within. But if I am to answer you in this style, I have to be pulling out all my meditation. Do you understand? So actually I don't like it (laugh).

In Interview No. 2, the monk doesn't admit directly that he has attained *sotāpatti-phala*. However he admits that the first three fetters have been eliminated by him and that they have been eliminated "relative" to a particular experience. Having reflected on this experience, he realized that he is on "track," on the Path, in the stream, that "cessation of becoming" has begun. The first three fetters are eliminated at the stage of attaining *sotāpatti-phala*. In addition he admits that the hallmarks of a *sotāpanna*—unshaken confidence in the Buddha, Dhamma and *Saṅgha* and strong commitment to *sīla*—are present in him and that they were sparked off "relative" to this experience. Furthermore, much later in the interview there are indications of possible higher fruits of the Path by way of indirect admissions of a higher fruit, (i.e. *anāgāmi-phala*) (Q.25, 29–36). In this interview the relevant discussion goes as follows:

Q.29 So what you are saying is, the first three fetters are no more in you?
A. Exactly I agree with you.
Q.30 So, aaah, that means, that is, you are a *sotāpanna*!
A. You can label it as the way you want. But yes, of course I am following the Path, exactly the Noble Eightfold Path, *sotāpanna*, if you mean that, that is the way you are in the stream, yes.

In Interview No. 3, too, the monk doesn't directly admit that the relevant experience triggered off the attainment of a supramundane fruit (i.e. *sotāpatti-phala*). When he was questioned whether such experience triggered off the attainment of *sotāpatti-phala,* he says he doesn't know, "cannot say for sure," "according to the texts it has to be either a *jhāna* or a *phala.*" But he realized that this is an important event on the *vipassanā* side. This is an indirect admission that it is not a *jhāna* but a supramundane fruit.

When he was asked whether, immediately after this experience, he realized that he had attained a supramundane fruit, his response was:

> I don't know that. I don't know that. But I realized a big quake, a big difference, a big transformation, a big explosion, that a big release occurred. These were classified into various things much later after I was ordained (Q.17).

Responding to the question of if he had a *phala* he further states:

> That is actually a conceptual thing that comes about through both, the fundamental principles and the practical experiences. But no one can deny the experiences that occur. So I can only say that I cannot deny the experience but no teacher whom I practised under encouraged me or asked me to classify these, nor do I ask those meditating under me to do it. "If you came up to this stage now proceed further" was all that these teachers told us. (Q.18)
>
> I cannot say that for sure. According to the books, to go on with this experience for years it has to be a *jhāna* or a *magga-phala.* At that time I had no idea about *jhāna* not even about *samatha vipassanā.* Later when I started to read and also when I consider what I normally experience as *jhāna,* I realized that this is a hundred times bigger fireworks display and not a small thing like that. Therefore I realized that this is an important event on the *vipassanā* side. I am talking on a comparative note because this is very similar to an abiding in a *jhāna.* Yet in terms of its intensity, if in *jhāna* the bursting is thirty percent so to say, in that its hundred percent. Therefore there is no need to refer to this by technical terms. But I can say that this is an important event in the spiritual life. (Q.15)

This monk however admitted that subsequently he trained under the guidance of a teacher to abide in *phala-samāpatti* (Q.16). *Phala-samāpatti* is abiding in the "fruition" relevant to a particular supramundane fruit already attained by the person concerned, that is, re-experiencing the fetter-breaking-experience relating to the attainment of a fruit (though without breaking any further fetters). So there is indirect admission that he has already attained a fruit. Further, he states that immediately after this experience he started to "refine" this experience (meaning to master the *phala-samāpatti*) according to the instructions given in the book which he read. He was surprised when he realized that it confirmed his "profound state of mind" and referred to this "profound state of mind" according to the texts as needing a teacher and *sīla* (five precepts). In general, according to the texts a teacher and abiding in *sīla* is considered pre-conditions for attainment of a supramundane fruit.

When asked whether he realized with this incident or immediately after this incident that certain fetters were gone, he says this is exactly what happened and certain clear cut changes took place in him, a "chemical change" took place (Q.20–21). He says with these he felt enormously indebted to the Buddha and to the Dhamma (Q.19) and wanted to surrender to a teacher. Further, in him who was up to that time ridiculing *sīla*, there was an irreversible change in morality to such an extent that the *sīla* that he ridiculed became the sole purpose of his life (Q.19–21). The above is a confirmation of *saddhā* or *avecca pasāda* in the Buddha Dhamma and the *Saṅgha* and the "unbroken *sīla*" which are widely described in the text as the hallmarks of a *sotāpanna*.

When asked whether the first three fetters broke with this incident, his answer is "there is no necessity to declare in terms of three out of ten" (Q.22). The first three fetters are broken only at the stage of attaining *sotāpatti-phala*. If he identified the fetters broken relative to the "10 fetters" [*dasa saṃyojanāni*] which are the fetters to be broken progressively in order to attain Arahantship, it would have been a direct admission of having attained a supramundane fruit. Hence he avoids references to the "first three" fetters. His understanding of the Dhamma confirms the absence in him of the first three fetters, though, and both this and the fact that he will not seek another teacher for his salvation are hallmarks of a *sotāpanna* (Q.29–39).

It is also noteworthy that although these monks do not admit having attained supramundane fruits they also do not deny it outright as they are also prohibited by the same disciplinary code to make false or misleading statements.

Michael Carrithers, in *Forest Monks of Sri Lanka—An Anthropological and a Historical Study*, writes about the difficulties he had in obtaining an interview from a monk about his meditative life:

> I turn now to illustrate the teaching and practice of meditation as it is actually carried out in the *samsthāva*. I obtained this circumstantial account of a monk's life in meditation in a remarkable interview. I could not have got the information—monks are prohibited by *vinaya* from claiming higher attainments, and are therefore properly reluctant to discuss such matters in personal detail—had Jinavamsa not been present. He gave the monk permission to speak to me freely.
>
> (Carrithers 1983, 243)

Carrithers in this book reports extracts from the interview with the interviewee referred to by a pseudonym, yet there is nothing in it relating to the religious experiences of the monk concerned. Carrithers in this book reports his experience with Sri Lankan forest monks to be the same as the writer's experience.

My field research is essentially centred round the forest tradition of Sri Lanka. I came across similar resistance to discuss about the practice even in the case of monks who are not Sri Lankan, for example, those from the Burmese or Thai tradition, including from Western monks. In Sri Lanka however there have been a few monks who seem to be discussing spiritual attainments more openly such as the late Pallekele Amitha Gavesi Thera (December 1918–June 2003) and Arapola Vipassi Thera (Sugatha Sasana Meditation Centre, kotte). The late Venerable Kannimahara Sumangala Thero, as referred to earlier in this chapter, claimed that he was a "*jāti sotapanna,*" a stream-enterer by birth. We did not undertake a study on any of these monks, their conduct, nor their understanding of the Dhamma. Hence we cannot comment on the statements made by them.

A similar piece of field research was conducted by William Hamilton[4] and is reported in *Saints and Psychopaths* (1995). This research too highlights how difficult it is to get a monk or a layperson to speak about their religious experiences. Referring to it as the "Embarrassment of Enlightenment" in the Theravāda tradition, he writes:

> The number of people who are enlightened, but are embarrassed because they do not want to say that they are enlightened, is larger than the group that do not know if they are enlightened ... I want to say something about the feeling of embarrassment. The feeling of embarrassment seems to come from at least, these reasons: 1) there is an expectation that people will have arbitrary expectations for them to live up to. 2) It is difficult for them to describe what enlightenment is like. 3) People tend to regard enlightenment as something that has been acquired, when, in fact, nothing has been acquired. (Hamilton 1995, 122)
>
> Fortunately, Buddhist etiquette makes enlightenment a private, personal matter. Many teachers will not even directly discuss with their students whether or not they have attained enlightenment. However, it seems common all over the world that people who have done long periods of practice together, and have been successful, will have an intuitive awareness of which of their friends have been successful. They will discretely discuss their attainments with close friends that they are sure having had similar experiences. (114)

One of the ways of acknowledging attainments is silence. Hamilton reports the Enlightenment of Tungpulu Sayadaw of Burma, whom he says was one of the most widely recognized *Arahant*s of the twentieth century:

> I heard the following story about how it became known that he was an *Arahant.* While he was meditating in his cave for thirty-nine years, he would be visited by an old friend who had practiced with him under the guidance of the same teacher. At first, he asked Tungpulu if he had become a Once-Returner, Tungpulu said "No I have not become a Once-Returner." After a few years, he again asked Tungpulu if he had become a Once-Returner, and he remained silent. Then he asked him if he had become a Non-Returner, and Tungpulu said, "No, I have not become a Non-Returner." After a few more years, he asked him whether he had become a Non-Returner, and Tungpulu remained silent. Then he asked him if he had become an *Arahant*, and he said "No, I have not become an *Arahant.*" Finally, after many years he asked him if he had become an *Arahant*, and Tungpulu remained silent. Once a woman asked him in public if he was an *Arahant.* Tungpulu raised up his hand to her indicating that she should not ask that question. (Hamilton 1995, 126)

We attempted to identify the possibility of a specific historical or a cultural reason for the "blanket reticence" in South and Southeast Asian forest monastic traditions to discuss or divulge one's spiritual attainments. Whilst we could not identify a specific reason, in general, this custom of restraint in discussing or divulging one's attainment is considered as a protection for the practitioner, for others, and for the teaching itself, and has been perceived as an important safeguard within these regions. It is considered as a protection for the practitioner in the sense of avoiding undue attention and exposure to undue scrutiny, both by those who accept and reject such a claim, thus ensuring one's inner peace. It is considered a protection for others in the sense of, not providing an opportunity for unwholesome action by those who would reject such a claim by a genuine *aryan* (noble person). It is a protection for the teaching itself, as references to attainments too freely would result in the genuine *aryans,* the mistaken and the imposters equally claiming attainments freely and casually, thus degrading such a lofty and a scarce attainment and also creating confusion amongst genuine practitioners.

Particularly with regard to the situation in Sri Lanka, Ven. Ñāṇavīra in *Clearing the Path—the Writings of Ñāṇavīra Thero,* reports the uncomfortable situation that developed subject to the news of his stream-entry (p. 155). Also our Interviewee No. 1 refers to the situation he faced in his forest hermitage due to the attitude of his brother monks towards him, consequent to the news of his attainment of *arahatta-phala* despite his teacher's acceptance of such a possibility (Appendix III,Q.328, p. 310).

Further, in *Aṅguttara Nikāya Aṭṭhakathā* it is reported that once king Saddhatissa inquired from the monks whether there is a noble [*ariya*] monk whom he could pay homage to. King having heard from them that Maṅganavāsī Khujjatissa thera was an *ariyan*, travelled a long distance with a large retinue to pay homage to him. The thera having heard that the king is visiting him and wanting to discourage the king, when the king was approaching, lay down on a bed and was drawing lines on the ground. King having seen this, thinking "Arahants cannot have such misconduct with hands" [*hatthakukkuccaṁ*] turned back and went away without paying homage to him. Subsequently, having seen the psychic powers displayed by the monk at the time of his passing away, the king came back to pay homage to the monk and cremated the relics with reverence (AN-a II 247).

Also the *Majjhima Nikāya Aṭṭhakathā* refers to two brothers who were elders at *Cetiyapabbata* one of whom was practising the ascetic practice [*dhutaṅga*] called the sitter's practice [*nesajjikaṅga*], that is, restricting himself to a sitting posture and not lying down at anytime of the day or night. Though the two were sharing the same residence, he hadn't revealed his ascetic practice to the other. But one night the other saw through the flash of lightening, him sitting up on bed and asked him whether he was a "sitter." As he did not wish to reveal his practice to the other, he responded to the other, immediately lying down in bed, pretending not to understand the question. Afterwards he had undertaken the practice a fresh, which shows he would rather break his practice than reveal it (Vism.62/ MN-a II 140). The same *Aṭṭhakathā* also refers to Sosānika Mahā Kumara thera who had undertaken the ascetic practice called the charnel-ground-dweller's practice (*sosānikaṅga*) for sixty years, but he had not revealed to a single *bhikkhu* that he was a charnel-ground- dweller (MN-a II 140). It also refers to Sāketa Tissa thera who had adopted the practice of *pariyatti appicchatā* (fewness of wishes relating to learning), who didn't wish to reveal his learnedness (*bahussutabhāva*). As a result the thera did not leave any opportunity for him to expound the dhamma and for the rest of the monks living with him to question him on the dhamma. However having attained Arahantship, he delivered a discourse which amazed the entire village, and went away that night itself before the dawn of the morning (MN-a II 140). The said commentary specifically refers to the practice of "*adhigama appicchatā*" (fewness of wishes relating to attainments of fruits of the Path), that is, not wishing to reveal one's spiritual attainments (MN-a II 140–141).

Though the latter stories are not directly relating to supramundane fruits, but to ascetic practice, the above stories in general indicate a historical background to the attitude of Theravāda monks towards revealing spiritual attainments and practices. It seems to be specifically influenced by the practice of "*adhigama appicchatā.*" However there is an emerging trend of publication of biographical or autobiographical information of forest monks of South and Southeast Asia, which are often freely distributed books published as meritorious acts, that includes references to meditative states of such monks. This is very much a late twentieth-century phenomenon starting from the famous biography of Ajahn Mun (1870–1949) by his disciple Ajahn Maha Boowa (1913–2011) followed by his (own) autobiography. In fact the latter was the subject of much criticism by those who rejected his claim to Arahantship. Of the Northeast Thai tradition, Ajahn Chah too has been more "upfront" in the references to his spiritual experiences as presented at the commencement of this chapter. But his disciples are not: Ajahn Sumedho, Ajahn Dhammavaro and of course Ajahn Tate in his autobiography (written only, he says, to prevent others doing it for him), do not discuss personal attainments.

It has been observed that in general, the tendency in Sri Lankan society today, with regard to declarations of fruits of the Path, is either blindly accepting or rejecting same with prejudice. The "negativity" associated with such declarations seems to be influenced significantly by the notion of "disappearance of the teaching" [*sāsana antardhāna*]. That is, the statements "attributed" to the Buddha regarding the eventual disappearance of the teaching (Vin. II 256, see also DN II 151) seems to have been fast-tracked out of context, leading to the notion that attainment of supramundane fruits of the Path is not possible in this day and age. The degradation of the state of Buddhism in Sri Lanka due to foreign invasions, (to the extent of having to bring back higher ordination from Thailand) seems to have had an impact on such a notion. So much so that in this research, the writer came across a book written in Sinhala language in 1960 (Udita 1960), by an erudite monk who undertakes a very critical analysis of certain traditional Theravāda viewpoints, however written on the underlined premise that fruits of the Path are not possible anymore. However with a significant revival of the practice in the last three decades, with monks and laypeople equally undertaking the practice seriously, as of today, the attitude towards supramundane attainments seems to have changed. Today there are forest monks who are serious practitioners conducting regular meditation programmes in Colombo, which are focused on attaining supramundane fruits of the Path "in this very life" and are attended by large numbers. Particularly as of today, open and frank discussions about supramundane attainments by serious practitioners are not uncommon even in the electronic media. This is quite a contrast with the environment that prevailed when the writer commenced her practice two decades ago.

The interviews with the laypeople were relatively less complicated. However, even some of those who were approached for an interview, despite having a fair acquaintance with the writer, turned the request down on the grounds that they would be uncomfortable discussing their experiences, as they were of very personal nature.

About the Interviewer

The interviews were done personally by the writer, who has herself been a serious practitioner of *vipassanā* meditation for over twenty years. She has closely associated with the leading forest monasteries and leading contemporary meditation masters, both *bhikkhus* and laypeople, in Sri Lanka. Further, as of the date of the interviews, she has known most of the Sri Lankans interviewed for this research, for over 12 years. In fact the interest in this field of research came about as a personal interest in resolving some of the controversies and debates amongst the practitioners with regard to the Buddhist religious experience. To that extent, as a research strategy, the interviewer's role is more of a "participant observer" rather than an "observer participant."

The writer is an Attorney-at-Law with a First class degree from the Sri Lanka Law College (1987) and a Solicitor of England and Wales; she has been a corporate lawyer for over twenty years. She holds a Doctorate in Buddhist Studies from the Postgraduate Institute of Pāli and Buddhist Studies, University of Kelaniya, Sri Lanka and was awarded the Gold Medal for obtaining the highest marks for the Masters Degree in Buddhist Studies (2004). Amongst her contributions towards facilitating the communication of knowledge to practitioners is Beyond-the-Net, (www.beyondthenet.net), a widely known website on Theravāda Buddhism which was designed and administered by her (1997–2012). She also set up and managed the official web site for the Buddhist Publication Society, Sri Lanka, for seven years under the guidance of Bhikkhu Bodhi. She is also one of the founders of Damrivi Foundation (www.damrivi.net), a group of Buddhist professionals committed to Buddhist social work which she steered as its Director Operations from its inception. The present book is based on research that was done for her Doctorate in Buddhist Studies.

A Note of Caution

In terms of the conclusions of Chapter 2 about the difficulties in recognizing noble persons and as to who is qualified to pass judgment on this issue, it should be specifically stated that this is no attempt by the writer to pass judgment or to award "certificates" on whether or not a particular interviewee is a noble person. Knowing the yardsticks given by the Buddha to identify one, as stated in Chapter 2, and having a long and close association, as *kalyāṇa-mittas*, with all whose interviews are presented here and used as source material, it should be emphasized that first, in terms of their conduct, the writer has not observed anything contrary to the state of mind established in the interviews. Secondly, what is claimed by the interviewee or established by the writer can be established logically in terms of the interview. Similarly few interviews that were done but not presented here, have been excluded only on the basis that the interviews lack certain vital information which are material enough to logically form a "fool-proof" conclusion. These deficiencies in the interviews were due to various reasons such as memory lapses, language barrier, omissions on the part of the interviewer to pose a relevant question, lack of clarity in the answers etc. As to the two foreigners presented here with whom the writer has had no prior association, apart from the logical conclusions that can be drawn from the interviews, they have been included due to the writer having confidence in the judgment of their teachers who recommended them, one of their teachers himself having been interviewed by the writer for this purpose.

It could be argued that anyone well read and well exposed to discussions on meditation experiences could reproduce book knowledge to answer the questions posed in the interview very convincingly, and that the interviewee need not necessarily be a noble person. However, when the same issue is approached from numerous angles, the coherence in the answers supports credibility of the state of mind claimed. For example it is often found that scholars of Buddhist philosophy who can give perfect conceptual answers to questions such as "what is *sakkāya-diṭṭhi?*," when it comes to their own views on issues such as Buddhist cosmology (e.g. are there divine beings, or lower beings such as *peta*s and *bhūta*s), or deep understanding of the concepts of *anicca*, dependent origination, *kamma* etc., they may make pronouncements totally contrary to the concept of *sammādiṭṭhi* (right view) set out in the same texts that they have mastered their understanding of *sakkāya-diṭṭhi* (view on personality) from. For instance, it is not uncommon to find eminent Buddhist scholars claiming that there are no divine beings or that the lower beings, the *deva loka*s and hells are all "on this earth itself." Hence mastery of texts alone would not ensure a display of "right view" or "right knowledge."

Further, with regard to these interviewees, the writer is personally aware that they hold *sīla* (moral virtue, guided by precepts) as an essential ingredient in their chosen Path. Given their commitment to *sīla*, having agreed to participate in this research after much persuasion, having agreed to do so more "for the cause" rather than for personal relationships, with anonymity being a fundamental condition of the research, there is no reason for the interviewees to intentionally make false claims. However, someone could be genuinely mistaken about his attainments. This issue can be addressed only through "logical conclusions" that can be drawn from the interviews about their state of mind and understanding of the Dhamma. Further, in most cases the experiences focused on have occurred many years ago, giving sufficient time for any doubts to arise in their minds about the reality of their attainment or attainments.

Similarly one can question as to how a particular incident, a common occurrence such as lightning or thunderbolt or an encounter with snakes etc. could trigger off attainment of a *phala*, as highlighted in some interviews presented here. We should not lose sight of the fact that these are practitioners who have, up to such time, put in an exceptional effort to practise the Path recommended by the Buddha. It is not the *incident* that brings about the attainment of the fruit of the Path, but the overall practice that culminates in the fruit, triggered off by such an incident, just as much as common occurrences such as the extinguishing of an oil lamp (Thig.115–116), breaking of an alms bowl, tripping and falling on the ground (Thig.17) etc. have triggered off Arahantship during the time of the Buddha.

When 200 to 400 questions are posed to someone unprepared within a short time span such as one and a half to three and a half hours, slips of the tongue are inevitable. Though these can initially pose a seeming difficulty, the overall trend and consistency and the final outcome of the interview is what has been relied on.

At the end of the day, there can still be reasonable doubts about the credibility of the claims made in the interviews. However, this is as far as an academic study can go and a final assessment is to be made by each one for him or herself through actual practice. Even the monks of the calibre of Venerable Katukurunde Ñāṇananda Mahā Thero (Bhikkhu Ñāṇananda) who is well-known both as practitioner and an academic, having a long and close association with the writer as a *kalyāṇa-mitta* over 18 years, who was initially appreciative of the writer undertaking academic studies in the field of Buddhist Philosophy, finally refused to participate in the research, not only on his personal religious experiences, but even for expert comments, as in the interview done with Ajahn Brahmavamso. He was of the view that the gap between the Buddhist academic and the practitioner is unbridgeable, and therefore research of this nature is a waste of valuable time for the writer, given the need to proceed with her own practice in the limited time available to her.

Definitions of Key Technical Terms Used

Path [*magga*]

The Noble Eightfold Path as part of *sīla, samādhi, paññā* (moral virtue, meditative concentration and wisdom) and includes both the elementary practice of the Path and practice at an advance, intensified or supramundane level. The term "Path" in this work does not mean the "momentary supramundane path" as referred to in the *Visuddhimagga* (Vism.XXII.11/Vism.787). According to the *Visuddhimagga*, the supramundane path lasts only for a fraction of a second, as a supramundane consciousness arising immediately prior to several moments of a supramundane "fruit" consciousness that indicates the attainment of stream-entry, once-returning, non-returning or Arahantship. But in the *Sutta*s the Noble Eightfold Path, at both, an elementary level and advanced level, lasts over a period of time and is not momentary.[5] Its precise nature at a supramundane level is not clear in the *Nikāyas*.[6]

Fruit [*phala*]

One of the four supramudane fruits or noble fruits of the Noble Eightfold Path i.e. the fruit that is stream-entry, once-returning, non-returning or Arahantship [*sotāpatti-phala, sakadāgāmi-phala, anāngāmi-phala, arahatta-phala*]. "Fruit" in this work means the general state of mind of the relevant noble person, (i.e. the kind of knowledge and the absence or state of the relevant fetters in their minds), and does not mean the moments of supramundane consciousness which immediately follows the supramundane path, as referred to in the *Visuddhimagga*. According to the *Visuddhimagga*, a fruit of the Path is a moment of signless [*animitta*] supramundane consciousness, with *Nibbāna* as its object, which flashes a few times immediately after the moments of "path consciousness" (Vism.XXII.15–16/Vism.788, Vism.XXIII.4/Vism.820). However in the *Sutta*s the word "fruit" has been used in a much broader sense, as fruits of *samaṇahood* [*sāmaññaphalāni*, SN V 25) and as fruits of brahminhood [*brāhmaññaphalāni*, SN V 25]. Final knowledge [*aññā*] and the state of non-returning [*anāgāmitā*] are referred to as fruits of developing the faculties of faith and wisdom (SN V 236). Two types of *Arahant*s and five types of non-returners are referred to as fruits and benefits [*satta phalā sattānisaṃsā*] of developing the spiritual faculties (SN V 237). It is also notable that while *arahatta-phala* is often listed as the fourth fruit (e.g. at DN III 255), it is sometimes, as at AN IV 292, replaced simply by *arahatta*, Arahantship. This strongly indicates that the four fruits are not something additional to stream-entry or Arahathood, but are identical with them. Realization of the four supramundane fruits are listed amongst the seven manifestations that arise due to the arising of a *Tathāgata*, the other manifestations being various types of special knowledge that arise on this Path, (i.e. penetration of various elements-*anekadhātu paṭivedo hoti*) and of the diversity of elements [*nānādhātu*], realization of the four branches of logical analysis [*paṭisambhidā* etc.—AN I 23]. A declaration on possessing the four factors of stream-entry, i.e. unwavering confidence in the Buddha, Dhamma and *Saṅgha* and possessing unbroken virtue is referred to by the Buddha as "declaring the stream-entry-fruit" (SN V 397 and 387). Hence in the *Sutta*s the word "*phala*" indicates a general state of mind encompassing, the state of fetters, knowledges acquired, benefits etc. and not a supramundane momentary state as in the *Visuddhimagga*.[7]

Words such as "*phala*," "*magga-phala*," were used in our interviews, in the sense of the general state of mind of a person who has attained to a supramundane fruit. But there is a possibility that some interviewees understood it to be "*phala*" as used in *Visuddhimagga*, meaning, "a momentary, signless experience." However the discussion as a whole was focused on the impact of such experience, that is, to determine the fetters overcome and the general state of mind which evolved as a consequence of such experience, and our conclusions on whether a particular interviewee has attained a supramundane fruit or not has been based on the general state of mind which emerged from the interview. Therefore, misunderstandings if any, with regard to the usage of the term "*phala*" has no impact on our conclusions. Furthermore, none of the interviewees had based their practice on the *Visuddhimagga* per se or on any meditation system that is based on the *Visuddhimagga*. Hence the room for such misunderstandings is very small.

Noble Person [*ariya puggala*]

Any one of the eight types of persons referred to in the *Sutta*s as members of the *sāvaka-Saṅgha* (e.g. AN IV 292). Accordingly a noble person is either a) one who has attained any of the supramundane fruits of the Path, so as to be the second, fourth, sixth or eighth noble persons, i.e. stream-enterer, once-returner, non-returner, or *Arahant,* or b), anyone seriously practising to become one of them, i.e. first, third, fifth and seventh noble persons, being those who are intently striving to become the second, fourth, sixth or eighth noble persons respectively.

Stream-enterer [*sotāpanna*]

2nd Noble Person, one who is free from the first three of the lower fetters (SN V 357).

Once-returner [*sakadāgāmī*]

4th noble person, the one who is free from the first three of the lower fetters and has weakened the next two (SN V 357).

Non-returner [*anāgāmī*]

6th noble person, one who is free from all five lower fetters (SN V 357).

Arahant

8th noble person, one free from all ten fetters (SN V 357).

Religious Experience

A religious experience or a series of them which occur in association with a person's practice of the Noble Eightfold Path, in the build-up towards the attainment of a supramundane fruit. The nature of such an experience or the series relating to a noble state varies from person to person, depending on their practice of the Path, state of spiritual faculties etc. The intensity of the experience too varies from person to person and it could be overwhelming, severe, gentle, mild or calm. Whatever its overall flavour may be, it can still be singled out as a striking mental phenomenon or a series of them and it includes a peak-point.

Fetter-breaking-experience

The peak-point of a specific, striking religious experience through which one breaks through to, or which marks the dawn of, a supramundane fruit of the Path. It is a striking experience because it can be singled out from the adjacent mental phenomena. Irrespective of the variety of religious experiences reported in contemporary books quoted by us and by all our interviewees, the crucial fetter-breaking-experience is reported by such contemporary books, and our interviewees, to be a sudden, momentary one and a signless, wishless or empty [*animitta, appaṇihita, suññata*] experience at which point one ceases to experience the five sense objects—one does not see, hear, smell, taste nor physically feel anything whatsoever. Hence at this point, one feels as though one has become cut off from the rest of the world. It is signless because, at such moment the mind is free of any kind of worldly object [*nimitta*] whatsoever. It is wishless because, there is no sign for the mind to hanker after, the mind is absolutely desireless, and it is empty in the sense of being completely empty of anything and everything, especially greed, hatred and delusion, including the notion of self.

Signless [*animitta*] States

The *Sutta*s refer to a range of signless experiences such as: the signless deliverance of mind [*animitta cetovimutti*];[8] cessation of feeling and perception[9] [*saññā-vedayita-nirodha-samāpatti*], an experience that an *Arahant* and non-returner who have mastered the *arūpa jhāna*s (formless *jhāna*s) can attain (MN I 302); signless concentration of mind [*animitta cetosamādhi*], a state having the potential to mature in to the final fruit (AN III 397, AN IV 78–79); and *animitta samādhi* as "path that leads to the unconditioned" (SN IV 360). In the range of *samatha* experiences referred to in the texts such as the four *jhāna*s, the four *arūpa* (formless) attainments (MN I 41), the eight liberations [*vimokkha*, MN II 12], the eight bases for transcendence [*abbhibhāyatana*, MN II 13], the eight attainments, (MN II 14) etc., the mind is unified with the chosen *samatha* object. Hence in all these a conceptual sign [*nimitta*] is present and what is known is not fully signless, wishless or empty in the sense of the fetter-breaking-experience of the Path. The fetter-breaking-experience originally comes about as a result of a mind-state with strong *vipassanā* (insight) into impermanence, *dukkha* or non-Self.[10]

Though at first sight these *animitta* states look alike, such states of mind differ qualitatively from each other depending on the underlying tendencies or fetters remaining in each state. Every signless experience is not a fetter-breaking-experience in terms of our definition because every signless experience is not associated with a supramundane fruit. The fetter-breaking-experience as reported in our field research is *prima facie* closest to the signless concentration of mind [*animitta cetosamādhi*] mentioned in the text. However it would differ from all other signless experiences discussed above depending on the state of the underlying tendencies and fetters in such a mind or the understanding or knowledge it has generated.

Phala-samāpatti

This is a term drawn from the *Visuddhimagga* (Vism.XXIII.3–11/ Vism.819–822) and commentaries and refers to the re-experiencing, from time to time, of the fetter-breaking-experience of a supramundane fruit (except, of course, that on this re-visiting of the experience, no further fetters are broken). This is experienced only by those noble persons who have already attained a *phala*. *Phala-samāpatti* is described by practitioners to be an experience which is identical to the fetter-breaking-experience of a *phala* they have already attained, that is, signless, wishless and empty. In the *Suttas*, such a state seems to be referred to at SN IV 269, though it is not named "*phala-samāpatti*" there.

The Path Related Sequence of States Leading to a Supramundane Fruit

The sequence of states leading up to the attainment of a supramundane fruit and there onwards, which evolved from our research (textual and fieldwork together), are as follows:

1) The ordinary [*lokiya*] Path,

2a) Then an intensified form of Path,

Or

2b) An intensified form of Path as experienced by the first of the eight noble persons (perhaps also by the third, fifth and seventh); the person practising for the fruit that is stream-entry, which is marked by a specific religious experience and includes a peak-experience very similar to a fetter-breaking-experience. During this period, the person continues to re-experience the peak-experience (however, the majority of the noble persons do not seem to go through this stage, but proceed to the next stage) (2b is triggered by a specific peak-experience and 2a is intensified practice in general),

3) Then, the culmination of the Path which is a fetter-breaking-experience,

4) Then, immediately following the fetter-breaking-experience, reviewing the experience and the state of mind,[11]

5a) And immediately thereafter, realizing the absence of certain fetters and understanding the consequent state of mind,

Or

5b) After the fetter-breaking-experience, continuing to review the state of mind over a period of time and on a subsequent day, realizing that certain fetters have been already broken and understanding the consequent state of mind,

6) Subsequently, (any time after 4), re-experiencing the fetter-breaking-experience and periodically re-experiencing it until the attainment of the next fruit.[12]

Scheme of Study

In this introductory Chapter I have set out some current debates and controversies relating to the Buddhist religious experiences and identified some of the issues which are dealt with in this study. This study depends on both textual analysis and findings of field research based on reports of religious experiences of practitioners of the Path. Hence the issue of identifying those with attainments of the Path particularly for the purpose of the field research is a vital factor for the success of the study. Hence Chapter 2 discusses the topic "Noble persons and how to recognize one." In this chapter, this subject has been dealt with under four sub-topics:

1) The references in the Pāli Nikāyas to the four supramundane fruits of the Path: linking them to the corresponding fetters that are eliminated on the attainment of each fruit.
2) Declarations of having attained a *phala* as set out in the Pāli Nikāyas: This includes the various expressions used by those who claim to have attained a fruit of the Path, and highlights the various ways in which the attainment of a fruit of the Path is signaled: i.e. with references to the types or the number of fetters broken, knowledge acquired, consequences [*ānisaṃsa*] in terms of future rebirths, and lists out a spectrum of such expressions.

   It further examines as to by whom these claims have been made and concludes that the declarations have been made only by the person who attained the *phala* or by the Buddha, excluding a teacher or any third party bestowing such status.
3) The possibility of recognizing a noble person: This sub-topic sets out the possibilities of and limitations for recognizing a noble person as set out in the texts and who, if any, can recognize one. It concludes that one with the same or a higher attainment may recognize another with the same or lower attainment, or certain gross behaviours may be indications of not having a particular supramundane fruit, if such behaviour has been categorized in the text as impossible at the level of a particular attainment. In general, none other than the Buddha (or one equal to him) and the person who attained himself would know for sure about the attainment of a supramundane fruit.
4) Contemporary difficulties of recognizing a noble person: Presented in terms of the field research of the writer and other recent research and contemporary books such as research by psychologists, psychiatrists and meditators.

By the above discussion, subject to these limitations and difficulties, I establish a reasonable yardstick to evaluate the authenticity of the claims made by those interviewed in the field research of this study. Under these limitations we can make a judgment of an attainment only through a logical analysis. That is, if the first three fetters—"view on personality" [*sakkāya-diṭṭhi*], which sees the factors of body and mind as in any way related to a permanent self, clinging to rules and vows [*sīlabbataparāmāsa*] as sufficient for attaining liberation, and skeptical doubt [*vicikicchā*] as regards what is truly wholesome—clearly seem to be absent in a person, logically it can be concluded that such a person is at least a stream-enterer [*sotāpanna*], especially if there is a specific religious experience which has led to this state and such experience is a result of following the Noble Eightfold Path.

On the other hand, this chapter also excludes or limits the space available for outright rejection or dismissing of any claims of an attainment by those who are *not qualified* to do so and without *reasonable grounds.*

Having established this yardstick to identify an authentic claim of an attainment, in Chapter 3 we study in depth whether attainment of a *phala* really does involve a specific experience. This issue is vital to this study and the following chapters are based on this foundation. It concludes that attaining a *phala* entails a specific, striking experience with a peak-point which I refer to as a "fetter-breaking-experience," and the intensity of the experience may vary from person to person. The fetter-breaking-experience has been articulated in the secondary sources quoted herein and in this field research as a "strange experience," "a fine point," "a tapering off," "cessation," "emptiness," "a breaking of a boundary," "a going beyond," "an oceanic experience" etc. Hence for the purposes of this study, attainment of a *phala* has been defined as a specific, striking experience of a person treading or making an effort to tread the Noble Eightfold Path, resulting in the understanding or knowledge which leads to breaking of the corresponding fetters [*saṃyojana*s].

The conclusion that attainment of a *phala* entails a specific experience has been made based on:

1) References in the *Nikāya*s to specific places, dates, meditative postures and events during which supramundane fruits were attained
2) References in contemporary sources to supramundane experiences of meditators
3) The findings of the field research of the writer

Having established that attainment of a *phala* entails a specific experience, the ensuing chapters use this thesis as a springboard, as a base for the discussion on the nature of the Buddhist religious experiences and also to resolve some of the contentious issues that this study addresses.

Based on the conclusion that attainment of a *phala* entails a specific, fetter-breaking-experience, in Chapter 4 we proceed to establish that a supramundane "*phala*" in the *Sutta*s is a fetter-breaking-experience *together* with its ongoing effects, as opposed to the Pāli commentarial usage in which a "*phala*" of the Path is just a "peak-experience" that lasts only a few moments following the fetter-breaking "path" moment. This chapter includes:

1) Definition of the word "*phala*": This extracts the various meanings attributed to the word "*phala*" in general.
2) References in the *Nikāyas* to Path, fetter-breaking-experience and the effect (of the fetter-breaking-experience) as three different phenomena: This extracts evidence from the *Nikāyas* to highlight references to fetter-breaking-experiences and their effects as distinctly different phenomena.
3) Implications of the thesis of "Path, fetter-breaking-experience and effect": Having highlighted that *Suttas* recognize the series of "Path, fetter-breaking-experience and its effect" as against "four path-moments, each followed by several *phala*/fruit moments," it highlights the implications of this thesis of "Path, fetter-breaking-experience and its effect" on some long-standing debates on the nature of the ultimate Buddhist religious experience (i.e. "*Nibbāna,* transcendence and ineffability" etc.). This chapter concludes that references to *Nibbāna* in the text as "a not born, not become, not made, not compounded,"[13] or "the sphere wherein there is neither earth, nor water, nor fire, nor air, neither the sphere of infinite space, nor the sphere of infinite consciousness, nor the sphere of nothingness, nor the sphere of neither perception nor non-perception, neither this world, nor the world beyond, nor the sun and the moon"[14], which are usually produced in support of the thesis that *Nibbāna* is a transcendent reality, are references to the fetter-breaking-experience. In contrast, references such as, "I have become cool, quenched" (Thig.15), "The three knowledges have been realized, the Buddha's teaching has been done" (Thig.30), or "I have attained peace of mind" (Thig.91) etc., which are usually produced in support of the thesis that *Nibbāna* is neither transcendental nor ineffable, are a reference to the *effect* of the fetter-breaking-experience. It highlights that many of the debates amongst scholars on issues such as the transcendence of *Nibbāna* are a result of not recognizing the significance of the fact that a supramundane fruit includes both, the fetter-breaking-experience and its effect. Even amongst them who recognize this difference, they differ as to which one of these two they take as *Nibbāna*.

This chapter also discusses the implications of the findings of this study about the nature of the fetter-breaking-experience, on the traditional Theravāda view that *Nibbāna* is a transcendental reality and the debate amongst scholars whether it is so or not. Similarly this chapter, based on the thesis "Path, fetter-breaking-experience and effect," proposes a definition of the noble person practising for the fruit that is stream-entry.

Having established in Chapter 4, the significance of the fact that there is a distinction between the fetter-breaking-experience and its effect, Chapter 5, "Noble persons and the nature of their fetter-breaking experience" proceeds to analyze the nature of different types of fetter-breaking-experiences and their respective effects. It sets out in detail:

1) Types of Noble persons
2) Analysis of the "fetter-breaking-experience" both in terms of the Pāli *Nikāyas* and *Visuddhimagga* and in terms of the expressions found in the field research such as "cessation," "complete emptiness" "a strange experience" "tapering off" etc. It explains the experience to be "*animitta, appaṇihita* and *suññata*" (signless, wishless, empty), and differentiates this from "experiencing the world" and substantiates this experience with reference to the *Nikāyas*. It also compares and distinguishes the fetter-breaking-experience at the attainment of each of the four fruits of the Path and distinguishes between the general state of mind of a stream-enterer, once-returner, non-returner and *Arahant*. Particularly in the light of little evidence in the texts as to the experience when a person becomes a *sakadāgāmī*, it distinguishes between the experiences relating to becoming a *sakadāgāmī* and *anāgāmī* based on field research.
3) Differences between the fetter-breaking-experience and other religious experiences: Differentiating the fetter-breaking-experience from similar Buddhist and non-Buddhist religious experiences such as *turiya* in the *Upaniṣads* or the *Islamic sufi* experiences, this section concludes that though these experiences prima-facie seem to be almost identical with the Theravāda Buddhist experience of attaining a *phala*, the Theravāda experience sees the true nature of worldly, conditioned existence to be subject to dependent arising, impermanent, unsatisfactory and non-self and consequently sees that nothing is worth clinging to [*sabbe dhammā nābhinivesāya*], whilst these non-Theravāda Buddhist religious experiences generate a sense of identity or oneness with Brahman or God.
4) An analysis of the re-experiencing of the fetter-breaking-experience [*phala-samāpatti*]: This includes implicit or explicit references to a *phala-samāpatti* in the Pāli *Nikāyas* and the *Visuddhimagga*. Contrary to various opinions expressed about *phala-samāpatti* by scholars and practitioners, this concludes that the re-experiencing of the fetter-breaking-experience of a supramundane fruit is real and is also a signless state, though we can not conclude for sure whether it is identical to the state designated as *phala-samāpatti*. This is experienced by noble persons whether they believe in the technicalities as mentioned in the *Visuddhimagga* or not. Yet it is not a concrete test of a *phala*. Though the term *phala-samāpatti* does not occur in the *Suttas*, some of the signless [*animitta*] states referred to in numerous occasions in the *Nikāyas* seem to correspond to this state.
5) Differences between *phala-samāpatti* and cessation of perception and feeling [*nirodha-samāpatti*]: This includes a comparison of these two states and it contrasts them with the fetter-breaking-experience. It highlights that the fetter-breaking-experience and *phala-samāpatti* seem to be identical states of mind (except that in the latter, no further fetters are actually broken) and both are technically different to the cessation of perception and feeling.

Chapter 6 is a comprehensive and a detailed analysis of the attainment of the *sotāpatti-phala*, it being the most vital milepost on this Path. This chapter includes a discussion on the following:

1) The state of mind of a stream-enterer
2) The conduct of a stream-enterer
3) The blessings and strengths of a stream-enterer
4) The possibility of someone having become a noble person in a past life
5) Can a stream-enterer commit suicide?
6) To what extent does a stream-enterer see *Nibbāna*?
7) Lay noble disciples
8) Non-humans attaining supramundane fruits

The chapter concludes that the experience of attaining *sotāpatti-phala* becomes the most significant experience one ever encounters up to such time in *saṃsāra*. It makes one a Buddhist by conviction. It makes one a "*born-again*" Buddhist. A stream-enterer is (DN III 84): "a legitimate son of the Buddha [*oraso putto*], born from his mouth [*mukhato jāto*], born of the Dhamma [*dhamma-jo*], created by the Dhamma [*dhamma-nimmito*], heir of the Dhamma [*dhamma-dāyādo*]." From this turning point in *saṃsāra*, the vision one acquires about the true nature of existence, together with the degree of mindfulness appropriate to a stream-enterer which has an inherent tendency to look back, reflect, look into the mind, and to have attention that is alert to causes and conditions [*yoniso manasikāra*], pushes one up-stream against the tide of *saṃsāra* so that within a maximum of seven more births the stream-enterer makes the final exit from *saṃsāra*, never again to be subject to the unsatisfactoriness and the dangers of existence. A stream-enterer, however, is not a flawless floating saint as most people would imagine, and has the potential to commit or engage in anything except for what has been expressly set out in the Suttas as impossible for a stream-enterer. However a stream-enterer based on his ability to look back, reflect and to apply *yoniso manasikāra*, is continuously refining his moral virtues.

Chapter 7 presents an analysis of an interview with a possible *Arahant*. In terms of the Buddha's invitation for a fair inquiry, with a view to accepting or rejecting the declared state of mind of this interviewee, it sets out the relevant extracts from the interview under a given topic and compares these with available textual evidence which sets out the mindset of an *Arahant*. Contrary to the popular belief that an *Arahant* is buoyant and jubilant, denoting "supreme bliss," this chapter concludes that an *Arahant* seems to spend the rest of his life happy and contended but "though not dull" but without a sense of excitement in life and bears with equanimity, the inevitable ills of the rest of the short stay in *saṃsāra*. What the "supreme bliss" of *Nibbāna* seems to denote is the fact that an *Arahant* has gained freedom all round including from *saṃsāric* woes, never to be subject to birth and death ever again. The predominant mind-set of an *Arahant* though, seems to be one of equanimity.

In Chapter 8, this study concludes that the Buddhist religious experience is unique and it is impossible to draw adequate conclusions about it based on a mere textual study alone. Many debates, controversies and confusions are due to overlooking the experiential aspects and teachers and preachers introducing new elements, terminology and analyses to Dhamma over and above what the Buddha declared, at times even against the advice of the Buddha. Even amongst the successful practitioners there are varied views depending on the route each one followed personally up to their goal and they take it that that alone is the Path and all others are not-the-Path. However, despite these debates amongst successful practitioners, a common ground can be established with regard to the fundamentals of their transforming experience on the Path. These fundamentals also correspond to what has been laid down in the texts. Further, many current trends of thought relating to supramundane fruits and noble persons and even public claims made by certain individuals with regard to the Path and attainment of its fruits, can at least be evaluated technically against the texts. In fact there is ample room to do so without having to accept them blindly or reject them outright, or even getting confused about contradictory views and opinions expressed by equally knowledgeable and known authorities.

It also concludes that, despite rampant distortions, myths and wrong views professed publicly, the true Dhamma is not limited to the texts. It is still very much alive, taught generously and is practised diligently, though discretely or even silently. Finally, it is fitting to encapsulate the essence of this entire research with the statement of Venerable Mahā Dhammarakkhita Thero: *Añño esa āvuso gatakassa maggo nāma*—"Friend, as for the Path, it is different for one who has trodden it" (Vism.III.53–55 / Vism.98).

Notes

1. Two of our interviewees referred to this incident. See Interview No. 2, Q.139 and Interview No. 3, Q.111.
2. *Yo pana bhikkhu anabhijānaṃ uttaramanussadhammaṃ attūpanāyikaṃ alamariyañāṇadassanaṃ samudācareyya iti jānāmi iti passāmīti, tato aparena samayena samanuggāhiyamāno vā asamanuggāhiyamāno vā āpanno visuddāpekkho evam vadeyya: ājānaṃ evaṃ āvuso avacaṃ jānami, apassaṃ passāmi, tucchaṃ musā vilāpin ti, aññatra adhimānā, ayampi pārājiko hoti asaṃvāso'ti,* (Vin. III 91, as translated at Ṭhānissaro 2007, vol. I, 93). See Ṭhānissaro 2007, 93–108 for a detailed discussion on this subject.
3. *Yo pana bhikkhu anupasampannassa uttarimanussadhammaṃ āroceyya, bhūtasmiṃ pācittiyan ti,* (Vin. IV 25, as translated at Ṭhānissaro 2007, vol. I, 318).
4. William L. Hamilton has been engaged in extensive meditation in meditation centres and monasteries since 1971. He has studied under some of the greatest meditation masters in the world. He has been teaching Buddhist *Vipassanā* meditation since 1985 (Hamilton 1995).
5. See *Sāmañña-phala Sutta* (DN I 47–86), *Subha Sutta* (DN I 204–210), *Mahācattārīsaka Sutta* (MN: 117).
6. The *Mahācattārīsaka Sutta* (MN: 117) indicates that the path exists at two levels, the ordinary [*lokiya*] level and the supramundane [*lokuttara*] level. However its nature at the supramundane level is not clearly spelt out. Peter Harvey concludes that: "The *Suttas* seem to see the noble *magga* as a whole as lasting some time, as experienced by the faith-follower and *Dhamma*-follower who are those who are

"practising for the realisation of the fruit that is stream-entry" (first of the eight kinds of noble persons). As this is a state in which a person is wholly taken up with *Dhamma*, it seems that the noble *magga* is a persistent state, rather than one that is periodically re-entered, such that it will not be left until stream-entry is attained. Thus suggest that, while it may not be momentary, it may well not last a very long time" (Harvey 2014).

7. Also the word "fruit" has been used in *Milindapañha* (*Questions of King Milinda*) in the simile of the Buddha's fruit shop to mean the fruits which are stream-entry, once-returning, non-returning and of Arahantship and also, as separate items, attainment of the empty, signless or wishless fruits (Miln.334).
8. MN I 296/Ñāṇamoli and Bodhi 1995, 393.The commentaries explain this as fruition attainment (See n. 449, 1238).
9. See Chapter 5 for a detailed discussion on this topic.
10. The commentaries add the mind-states of the four supramundane paths [*magga citta*], four supramundane fruitions [*phala citta*], *Nibbāna* etc. as *animitta* states. See Chapter 5 for a discussion. For an analysis of the range of signless experiences, see Chapter 5 (pp. 102–114) and also Harvey 1986.
11. 3 seems to be what the *Visuddhimagga* refers to as momentary "*magga*"and "*phala*" moments and 4, 5a and 5b seems to be similar to the "reviewing-knowledge" [*paccavekkhana-ñāṇa*] referred to in the *Visuddhimagga*.
12. What the *Visuddhimagga* refers to as "*phala-samāpatti.*"
13. Ud.81, see Tilakaratne 1993, 74 for more details.
14. Ud.80, and see Ñānananda 2003, IV, 373.

— 2 —

Noble Persons and How to Recognize One

In this chapter I propose to discuss the possibilities and difficulties in recognizing a noble person.[1] For the purposes of this study, I define attainment of a supramundane fruit [*phala*] to be a specific striking experience of a person treading or making an effort to tread the Noble Eightfold Path, resulting in the understanding or knowledge which leads to breaking of a set of spiritual fetters [*saṃyojanas*]. The key elements of this phenomenon being:

- Path
- Experience
- Arising of knowledge
- Breaking of fetters

The issue of whether attainment of a *phala* entails a specific experience is dealt with in detail in Chapter 3. In this chapter, the proposed theme has been discussed under four sub-topics:

1) The references in the Pāli *Nikāyas* to the four supramundane fruits of the Path: linking them to the corresponding fetters that are eliminated at the attainment of each fruit.
2) Declarations of having attained a *phala* as set out in the Pāli *Nikāyas*: This includes the various expressions used by those who claim to have attained a fruit of the Path, and highlights the various ways in which the attainment of a fruit of the Path is signalled: i.e. with references to the types or the number of fetters broken, knowledge acquired, consequences [*ānisaṃsa*] in terms of future rebirths, and lists out a spectrum of such expressions.
3) The possibility of recognizing a noble person: This sub-topic sets out the possibilities of and limitations for recognizing a noble person as set out in the texts and who, if any, can recognize one.
4) Contemporary difficulties of recognizing a noble person: Presented in terms of the field research of the writer and other recent research and contemporary books by psychologists, psychiatrists and meditators.

The References in the Pāli *Nikāyas* to the Four Supramundane Fruits of the Path

The texts refer to attainment of supramundane fruits very freely. There are references to attainment of four main classes of supramundane fruits of the Path in the texts. They are: attainment of fruit that is stream-entry, the fruit that is once-returning, the fruit that is non-returning, and the fruit that is Arahantship [*sotāpatti-phala, sakadāgāmi-phala, anāgāmi-phala, arahatta-phala*] (e.g. SN V 25).

Setting out the ranking of the main supramundane fruits of the Path, the Buddha says:

> Bhikkhus there are these five faculties. What five? The faculty of faith, energy, mindfulness, concentration and the faculty of wisdom. One who has completed these five faculties is an *Arahant*. If they are weaker than that, one is a non-returner; if still weaker, a once-returner; if still weaker a stream-enterer; if still weaker a Dhamma-follower; if still weaker a faith-follower. (SN V 200/Bodhi 2000, 1674)

These noble persons are further classified in the *Eka Bīja Sutta* of the *Indriya Saṃyutta*. It refers to 12 types of individuals. An *Arahant*, five types of non-returners, a once-returner, three types of stream-enterers, a Dhamma-follower and a faith-follower (SN V 204), the last two being the first kind of noble persons, those practising for realization of the fruit that is stream-entry (See pp. 75–82).

These noble persons are classified depending on the state of the fetters remaining in them. Fetters [*saṃyojanas*] are deep-rooted faults that bind one to the cycle of birth and death. Altogether there are 10 fetters. With the destruction of the first three of the lower fetters, one attains the fruit that is stream-entry [*sotāpatti-phala*]. With the destruction of these three fetters and the diminishing of greed, hatred and delusion, one attains the fruit that is once-returning [*sakadāgāmi-phala*]. With the destruction of five lower fetters (the first five of the 10 listed below) one attains the fruit that is non-returning [*anāgāmi-phala*] and with the destruction of all 10 fetters, the fruit that is Arahantship [*arahatta-phala*] (SN V 357).

The ten fetters are:

1) *sakkāya-diṭṭhi* (view on personality)
2) *vicikicchā* (sceptical doubt)
3) *sīlabbata-parāmāsa* (clinging to rules and vows)
4) *kāmacchanda* (desire for pleasures of the senses)
5) *vyāpāda* (ill-will)
6) *rūpa-rāga* (lust for pure form existence)
7) *arūpa-rāga* (lust for formless existence)
8) *māno* (conceit)
9) *uddhacca* (restlessness)
10) *avijjā* (ignorance)

The first three are called "*tīni saṃyojanāni*" (the three fetters) and the last seven, "*satta saṃyojanāni*" (the seven fetters). Also the first five are called "*orambhāgiyāni saṃyojanāni*" (lower fetters or the fetters that bind to the lower existence: rebirth in the realm of sense-desires) and the last five are called "*uddhaṃbhāgiyāni saṃyojanāni*" (the higher fetters or the fetters that bind to the higher existence: rebirth in the pure form or formless realms).[2]

Declarations of Having Attained a *Phala* as Set Out in The Pāli *Nikāyas*

We will first examine the various expressions used by those who claim to have attained fruits of the Path as set out in the texts. In the texts, there are various ways in which the attainment of a fruit of the Path is signalled: i.e. with references to the types or the number of fetters broken, knowledge acquired, consequences [*ānisaṃsa*] in terms of future rebirths, and lists out a spectrum of such expressions. Here we will also examine as to by whom these claims have been made.

Declarations of Attainment of *Sotāpatti-Phala* (Stream-Entry)

1) In the first sermon of the dispensation of Gotama Buddha, the *Dhammacakkappavattana Sutta*, it is reported as follows:

> This is what the Blessed one said. Elated, the bhikkhus of the group of five delighted in the Blessed One's statement. And while the discourse was being spoken, there arose in the Venerable Koṇḍañña the dust-free, stainless Dhamma-eye [*virajaṃ vītamalaṃ dhammacakkhum udapādi*]: "Whatever is subject to origination is all subject to cessation" [*yaṃ kiñci samudayadhammaṃ sabban taṃ nirodhadhamman' ti*]
>
> ... Then the Blessed One uttered this inspired utterance: Koṇḍañña has indeed understood! Koṇḍañña has indeed understood!. In this way the Venerable Koṇḍañña acquired the name "Aññā Koṇḍañña—Koṇḍañña who has understood" [*Aññāsi vata bho Koṇḍañño aññāsi vata bho Koṇḍañño ti. Iti hidam āyasmato Koṇḍaññassa Aññāta-Koṇḍañño tveva ñāṇam ahosī ti*]. (SN V 423–424)

The words "*virajaṃ vītamalaṃ dhammacakkhum udapādi, 'yaṃ kiñci samudayadhammaṃ sabban taṃ nirodhadhamman' ti*" form the stock phrase to describe the attainment of stream-entry. (Though this phrase is usually associated in the texts with the attainment of stream-entry, it could also be directed at higher fruits). Here attainment of the fruit is declared in terms of the knowledge acquired: all that is of the nature to arise [*dukkha*] is of the nature to cease. This declaration of the attainment of stream-entry of Venerable Koṇḍañña is made by the Buddha.

2) In the *Nidāna Saṃyutta* the Buddha tells Anāthapiṇḍika that when five fearful animosities have subsided in a noble disciple (i.e. with regard to the present and future life, arising on account of breach of the five moral precepts), and he possesses the four factors of stream-entry, and he has clearly seen and thoroughly penetrated with wisdom the noble method [*ariyo cassa ñāyo paññāya suddhiṭṭo hoti suppaṭividdho*—SN II 68], if he wishes, he could by himself, declare of himself as follows:

> I am one finished with hell, finished with the animal realm, finished with the domain of ghosts, finished with the plane of misery, the bad destinations, and the nether world. I am a stream-enterer no longer bound to the nether world, fixed in destiny, with enlightenment as my destination. [*khīṇānirayomhi khīṇātiracchānayoniyo khīṇāpettivisayo khīṇāpāyaduggativinipāto, sotāpanno ham asmi avinipātadhammo niyato sambodhiparāyano*]. (SN II 68)

This is a declaration in terms of future births and is meant to be made by the person who attained to stream-entry himself.

3) When a group of monks visited Ugga the householder to inquire about the astonishing and amazing qualities he is supposed to possess as referred to by the Buddha, Ugga declares to them:

> While I sat in that same seat, the dust-free, stainless Dhamma-eye arose in me: "Whatever is subject to origination is all subject to cessation." I saw the Dhamma,

> attained the Dhamma, understood the Dhamma, fathomed the Dhamma, crossed over doubt, got rid of bewilderment, attained self-confidence, and became independent of others in the teaching of the Teacher [*diṭṭhadhammo pattadhammo viditadhammo pariyogālhadhammo tiṇṇavicikiccho vigatakataṃ katho vesārajjapatto aparappaccayo Satthu sāsane*]. Right there I went for refuge to the Buddha, the Dhamma, and the *Saṅgha* and undertook the training rules with celibacy as the fifth [*brahmacariyapañcaimāni*]. (AN IV 210)

This declaration of the attainment of stream-entry is made in terms of the knowledge acquired and the declaration is made by Ugga himself.

4) Venerable Udāyi declares to the Buddha:

> Then, venerable sir, whilst I was staying in an empty hut, following along with the surge and decline of the five aggregate subject to clinging, I directly knew as it really is [*yathā bhūtam abbhaññāsiṃ*]: "This is suffering," I directly knew as it really is: "This is the origin of suffering," I directly knew as it really is: "This is the cessation of suffering," I directly knew as it really is: "This is the way leading to the cessation of suffering." I have made the breakthrough to the Dhamma, venerable sir, and obtained the path [*Dhammo ca me bhante abhisamito maggo ca paṭiladdho*] which, when I have developed and cultivated it, will lead me on, while I am dwelling in the appropriate way [*yo me bhāvito bahulīkato tathā tathā viharantam tathattāya upanessati*], to such a state that I shall understand: destroyed is birth, the holy life has been lived ... there is no more for this state of being. (SN V 89–90)

This too is a declaration made by the person who attained to the fruit himself and made in terms of knowledge acquired.

5) Prince Abhaya having climbed up the Mount Vulture Peak to meet the Buddha and having heard the Dhamma and understood declares to the Buddha:

> The bodily fatigue, and the mental fatigue that I experienced from climbing Mount Vulture Peak have subsided. I have made a breakthrough to the Dhamma [*dhammo ca me abhisameto*]. (SN V 128)

Bhikkhu Bodhi concludes that this is a declaration that he has attained stream-entry. Here the bodily fatigue has subsided due to happiness born of the breakthrough to the Dhamma. This declaration is made in terms of the knowledge acquired by him and is made by Prince Abhaya himself (Bodhi 2000, 1913, n. 116).

6) In the *Indriya Saṃyutta* the Buddha declares:

> So too bhikkhus, the Brahmin Unnābha has gained faith in the Tathāgata that is settled, deeply rooted, established, firm [*Tathāgate saddhā niviṭṭhā mulajātā patiṭṭhitā dalhā*]. It cannot be removed by any renunciant or brahmin or *deva* or *māra* or by anyone in the world. If, bhikkhus, the brahmin Unnābha were to die at this time, there is no fetter bound by which he might come to this world. (SN V 219)

This is a declaration relating to the attainment of the fruit that is stream-entry of brahmin Uṇṇābha. The declaration is in terms of fetters abandoned and his destination after death and the declaration is made by the Buddha.[3]

7) The Buddha addressing the Chamberlains Isidatta and Purāṇa confirms that they are stream-enterers as follows:

> Chamberlains, you possess confirmed confidence in the Buddha ... in the Dhamma ... in the *Saṅgha* ... Moreover whatever there is in your family that is suitable for

> giving, all that you share unreservedly among those who are virtuous and of good character. What do you think, carpenters, how many people are there amongst the Kosalans who are your equals, that is in regard to giving and sharing? (SN V 352)

This is a declaration that Isidatta and Purāṇa are stream-enterers. This declaration is made in terms of the fundamental qualities of a stream-enterer and is made by the Buddha.

8) A conversation between Venerable Ānanda and Anāthapiṇḍika in the *Anāthapiṇḍika Sutta* is reported as follows. Ānanda says "for the instructed noble disciple who possesses these four things there is no fright, trepidation, or fear of imminent death." In response Anāthapiṇḍika says:

> I am not afraid, Venerable Ānanda. Why should I be afraid? For, Venerable sir, I possess confirmed confidence in the Buddha ... in the Dhamma ... in the *Saṅgha*. And as to these training rules for the laity taught by the Blessed one, I do not see within myself any that has been broken.
>
> Then Ānanda says "It is a gain for you, householder! It is well gained by you, householder! You have declared, householder, the fruit that is stream-entry." (SN V 387)

This declaration is made in terms of the fundamental qualities of a stream-enterer. As to who makes the declaration, it should be noted that Ānanda merely re-phrases what Anāthapiṇḍika has already declared by himself.

9) The Sakyan woman Kāligodhā declaring the fruit that is stream-entry is reported as follows. First the Buddha says:

> "Godhā, a noble disciple who possesses four things is a stream-enterer, no longer bound to the nether world"

the Buddha goes on to explain the four factors of stream-entry. Then Godhā says:

> "Venerable sir, as to these four factors of stream-entry taught by the Blessed One, these things exist in me, and I live in conformity with those things." Then the Buddha responds "It is a gain for you, Godhā! It is well gained by you, Godhā! You have declared the fruit that is stream-entry." (SN V 397)

Here is an instance where a person declares attainment of a fruit of the Path by herself, but with guidance from the teacher to recognize the constituents of the fruit. Nevertheless it is Godhā, the person who attained to the fruit herself who declares the fruit.

10) A similar instance is reported in the case of Dhammadinnā. It is reported that with the guidance of the Buddha, Dhammadinnā together with five hundred lay followers all declared stream-entry (SN V 408).

Declarations of Attainment of *Anāgāmi-Phala* (Non-Returning)

1) The householder Sirivaḍḍha declares the attainment of *anāgāmi-phala* to Venerable Ānanda as follows:

> Venerable sir, as to these four establishments of mindfulness taught by the Blessed One—these things exist in me, and I live in conformity with those things. I dwell, venerable sir, contemplating the body in the body ... feeling in the feeling ... mind in mind ... phenomena in phenomena, ardent clearly comprehending, mindful, having removed covetousness and displeasure in regard to the world. And as to these five lower fetters taught by the Blessed One, I do not see any of these una-

bandoned in myself [*Yāni cimāni bhante Bhagavatā pañcorambhāgiyani saṃyojanāni desitāni, nāhaṃ tesaṃ kiñci attāni appahīnaṃ samanupassāmi ti*]. (SN V 177)

This declaration is made in terms of fetters eliminated and is made by Sirivaḍḍha himself.

2) Venerable Ariṭṭha declares that he has attained the *anāgāmi-phala* as follows:

I have abandoned sensual desire for past sensual pleasures, venerable sir [*Atītesu me bhante kāmesu kāmacchando pahīno*], I have gotten rid of sensual desire for future sensual pleasures, and I have thoroughly dispelled perceptions of aversion towards things [*dhammesu paṭighasaññā*] internally and externally. (SN V 315)

This is a declaration in terms of the fetters abandoned and is made by Ariṭṭha himself.

Declarations of Attainment of *Arahatta-Phala*

Some of the most commonly found expressions of attainment of *arahatta-phala* are:

1) Destroyed is birth, the holy life has been lived, what has to be done has been done, there is no more for this state of being [*khīṇā jāti, vusitam brahmacariyaṃ, kataṃ karaṇīyaṃ, nāparam itthattāyā' ti pajānāti*] (SN IV 140).

All sets of verses in the *Theragāthā* and *Therīgāthā* include declarations of attainment of fruits of the Path. We set out below some of such expressions:

2) I am grown cool, extinguished [*sītibhūto'smi nibbuto*] (Thag.298).
3) The three knowledges have been attained; The Buddha's teaching has been done [*tisso vijjā anuppattā, kataṃ buddhassa sāsanan ti*] (Thag.224).
4) All lust is abandoned; all hatred has been rooted out; all my delusion has gone. I have become cool, quenched [*sītibhūto' smi nibbhuto' ti*] (Thag.79).
5) Whatever action was done by me, whether small or great, all that is completely annihilated. There is now no renewed existence [*Yaṃ mayā pakataṃ kammaṃ appaṃ vā yadi vā bahu sabbam etaṃ parikkhīṇaṃ, n' atthi dāni punabbhavo' ti*] (Thag.80).
6) Truly I was able to draw myself from the water to dry land. As if being borne along on a great flood, I comprehended the truths [*Asakkhiṃ vata attānaṃ, uddhātuṃ udakā thalaṃ,vuyhamāno mahoghe va saccāni paṭivijjh' ahan ti*] (Thag.88).
7) The muds and mires are crossed, the chasms are avoided. I am released from flood and tie. All conceits are exterminated [*Uttiṇṇā paṅkā palipā, pātālā parivajjitā, mutto oghā ca ganthā ca, sabbe mānā visaṃhatā 'ti*] (Thag.89).
8) Come, Nandaka, let us go into the presence of the preceptor. We shall roar the lion's roar face to face with the best of the Buddhas [*sīhanādaṃ nadissāma buddhaseṭṭhassa sammukhā*]. We have now attained that goal for which, in compassion for us, the sage made us go forth—the annihilation of all fetters (Thag.175).
9) Having received ordination at the age of seven, I bear my last body [*dharemi antimaṃ dehaṃ*]. Hail to the essential rightness of the Dhamma (Thag.486).
10) The teacher has been waited on by me; the Buddha's teaching has been done. The heavy load has been put down; that which leads to renewed

existence has been rooted out [*Paricinno mayā satthā, kataṃ buddhassa sāsanaṃ, ohito garuko bhāro, bhavanetti samūhatā*] (Thag.604).

11) In the *Saṃyutta Nikāya* is a passage where, as a response to a report from *bhikkhu* Kālāra that Venerable Sāriputta has declared final knowledge by saying "Destroyed is birth, the holy life has been lived, what has to be done has been done, there is no more for this state of being," the Buddha questions Sāriputta so as to get him to declare final knowledge in different ways. He explains that he understands that birth is dependent on becoming, down to craving being conditioned by feeling, and then says:

> there are three feelings ... pleasant ... painful ... neither painful nor pleasant ... these are impermanent; whatever is impermanent is painful; When this was understood, delight in feeling no longer remained present in me. (SN II 53)

The Buddha commends Sāriputta: "Good Sāriputta this is another method of explaining in brief that same point: 'whatever is felt is included within the painful [*yam kiñci vedayitaṃ taṃ dukkhasminti*]'."

In this *Sutta*, some of the other ways in which Sāriputta declares Arahantship are:

> I have no perplexity, friend
> But as to the future, friend?
> I have no doubt, friend. (SN II 50)[4]

> Through an internal deliverance [*ajjhattam vimokkhā*], through the destruction of all clinging [*sabbhupādānakkhayā*], I dwell mindfully in such a way, that the taints do no flow within me and I do not despise myself [*āsavā nānusavanti attānaṃ ca nāvajānāmīti*]. (SN II 54)

12) In the *Vinaya Piṭaka* Venerable Sona declares Arahantship as follows:

> Venerable sir, that monk who is one perfected, who has destroyed the taints, lived the life, done what was to be done, shed the burden, won his own goal, destroyed utterly the fetter of becoming and is wholly freed by profound knowledge, he comes to be intent upon six matters; he comes to be intent upon renunciation, ... upon aloofness, ... upon non-harming, ... upon the destruction of grasping ... Upon the destruction of craving, ... upon non-confusion. (Vin. I 183)

Even if forms cognizable by the eye come very strongly into the field of vision of a monk whose mind is wholly freed, they do not obsess his mind, for his mind comes to be undefiled, firm, won to composure and he notes their passing.

Sona makes similar statements in relation to sounds, smells, tastes, touches, mental objects. He states further:

> It is as if, venerable sir, there were a rocky mountain, a slope without a cleft, without a hollow, of one mass, and as if wild wind and rain should come very strongly from the eastern quarter—it would neither tremble nor quake nor shake violently; and ... from the western quarter... from the northern quarter, ... from the southern quarter—it would neither tremble nor quake nor shake violently. Even so venerable sir, if forms cognizable by the eye come very strongly into the field of vision of a monk who is wholly freed, or if sounds..., scents, ... tastes ..., touches ..., mental objects ..., they do not obsess his mind, for his mind comes to be undefiled, firm, won to composure and he notes its passing [*n' ev' assa cittaṃ pariyādiyanti, amissikatam ev' assa cittaṃ hoti ṭhitaṃ āneñjappattaṃ vayañ c'assānupassati*]. (Vin. I 184)

Here the Buddha praises Sona for the manner in which the declaration is made as follows: "Thus monks do young men of family declare profound knowledge [*aññaṃ*]. The goal is spoken of but self is not obtruded [*atto ca vutto attā ca anupanīto*]. But then it seems to me that there are some foolish men here who declare profound knowledge for fun; these afterwards come to disaster" (Vin. I 185).

All the above declarations have been made with reference to knowledge, feelings experienced, fetters broken, status after death etc., and they have been made by the person who attained Arahantship himself.

So far we have examined the range of declarations made in respect of attaining supramundane fruits of the Path. There are many other such declarations scattered throughout the texts. As to the question, "who can make such declarations?," from examining these it can be concluded that declarations of attainment of supramundane fruits have been made always either by the person who attained such a fruit himself or by the Buddha. Hence there is no room in these passages for recognizing or even conferring of fruits of the Path by a third party such as by a teacher, divine being such as a *brahmā* or a *deva* or by anyone else. There *is* however a possibility of recognizing a noble person by a third party. Next we will examine such possibilities in terms of the texts.

The Possibility of Recognizing a Noble Person

Once when a carpenter (Dārukammika) visited the Buddha, he was asked by the Buddha whether his family gave alms to monks. He replied that his family gave alms to monks who were "forest-dwellers, alms food collectors, wearers of rag robes, *Arahants* or on the path to Arahantship" [*āraññakā, piṇḍapātikā, pāṃsukulikā arahanto vā arahantamaggaṃ vā samāpannā*]. Then the Buddha replies:

> Since householder, you are a layman enjoying sense-pleasures, living in a house full of children, using sandal-wood from Kāsi, wearing garlands, scents, and unguents, and receiving gold and silver, it is difficult for you to know: "These are *Arahants* and on the path to Arahantship." (AN III 391/Bodhi 2012, 945)

This spells out that as a general rule, those enjoying sense pleasures are not qualified to make a judgment on the attainment of Arahantship of others.

A similar incident is reported regarding an encounter between King Pasenadi of Kosala and the Buddha. Once when the king was with the Buddha and a group of ascetics passed by, the King rose up and worshiped in that direction and once they were gone he turned to the Buddha and said, "Those, venerable sir, are to be included among the men in the world who are *Arahants* or who have entered upon the path to Arahantship." The Buddha on this occasion advises the king that being laymen enjoying sense pleasures, dwelling in a home etc, it is difficult for him to know who are *Arahants* or who have entered upon the path to Arahantship. Then the king admitted that these "ascetics" who passed by were merely his spies, undercover agents returning after spying out the country (SN I 178).

A further incident is reported in the *Aṅguttara Nikāya*. Once Migasālā, a female lay disciple, questioned Venerable Ānanda as to how to understand the Dhamma taught by the *Tathāgata*, as it seems that both one who lives a *brahmacāri* (celibate) life and one who doesn't, may after death take similar births. She said:

> My father, Purāṇa, was celibate, living apart, abstaining from sexual intercourse, the common person's practice. When he died, the Blessed One declared: "He

attained to the state of once-returner and has been reborn in the Tusita group (of *devas*)." My parental uncle Isidatta was not celibate but lived a contended married life. When he died, the Blessed One also declared: "He attained to the state of once-returner and has been reborn in the Tusita group (of *devas*)." Bhante Ānanda, just how should this teaching of the Blessed One be understood, where one who is celibate and one who is not celibate, both have exactly the same destination in their future life? (AN III 347/Bodhi 2012, 911)

This incident was reported to the Buddha by venerable Ānanda, seeking an explanation. Here the Buddha comes out very strongly against the dangers and limitations of the ability to pass judgment about the attainments of others:

Who indeed is the female lay-follower, Migasālā—a foolish, incompetent woman with a woman's intellect? And who are those (who have) the knowledge of other persons as superior and inferior? [*kā c' Ānanda Migasālā upāsikā bālā avyattā ambakā ambakasaññā ke ca purisapuggala-paropariya ñāṇe*]. (AN III 347/Bodhi 2012, 911)

The Buddha explains that there are six types of people in this world, as follows:

1) There is one person who is mild, a pleasant companion, with whom his fellow monks gladly dwell. But he has not listened (to the teachings), become learned (in them), and penetrated (them) by view [*diṭṭhiyā pi appaṭividdhaṃ hoti*], and he does not attain temporary liberation [*sāmāyikam pi vimuttiṃ na labhati*[5]]. With the breakup of the body, after death, he heads for deterioration, not for distinction, he is one going to deterioration, not to distinction [*hānagāmī yeva hoti no visesagāmī*]. (AN III 349)
2) There is one person who is mild, a pleasant companion, with whom his fellow monks gladly dwell. But has listened (to the teachings), become learned (in them), and penetrated (them) by view, and he attains temporary liberation. With the breakup of the body, after death, he heads for distinction, not for deterioration, he is one going to distinction, not to deterioration.

Then the Buddha says:

Ānanda, those who are judgmental will pass such judgment on them [*pamāṇikā pamiṇanti*]: "This one has the same quality as the other. Why should one be inferior and the other superior?" That judgment of theirs will indeed lead to their harm and suffering for a long time. (AN III 349)

The Buddha explains that out of these two, the person who has listened to the teaching, learnt the teaching and penetrated them by view and who attains temporary liberation, surpasses the other and excels because the Dhamma-stream carries him forward. He asks "who can know this difference except a Tathāgata?"

Similarly in this *Sutta* the Buddha sets out four more types of people:

(3) and (4): A person in whom anger and conceit are found, and from to time states of greed arise in him. [*kodhamāno adhigato hoti, samayena samayañ c'assa lobhadhammā uppajjanti*], and he has not listened (to the teaching), become learned (in them), and penetrated (them) by view, and he does not attain temporary liberation. With the breakup of the body, after death, he heads for deterioration, not for distinction, he is one going to deterioration, not to distinction.

Another likewise, but has listened to the teaching, learnt them and penetrated them, by view and attained temporary liberation: he surpasses the other and excels.

> (5) and (6): A person in whom anger and conceit are found, and from time to time he engages in an exchange of words [*vacīsaṅkhārā*]. And has not listened (to the teaching), become learned (in them), and penetrated (them) by view, and he does not attain temporary liberation. With the breakup of the body, after death, he heads for deterioration, not for distinction, he is one going to deterioration, not to distinction.

Another likewise, but he has listened to the teaching, learnt them and penetrated them, by view and attained temporary liberation: he surpasses the other and excels.

Thereafter the Buddha gives a strong warning against attempts to pass judgment on others spiritual attainments:

> Therefore, Ānanda, do not be judgmental regarding people [*mā puggalesu pamāṇikā ahuvattha*]. Do not pass judgment on people [*mā pugglesu pamāṇaṃ gaṇhittha*]. Those who pass judgment on people harm themselves. I alone or one like me, may pass judgment on people. (AN III 351)

Against the backdrop of the general rule against attempting to pass judgment on the attainment of supramundane fruits of others, let us see to the possibilities of recognizing a noble person.

Five Types of Declarations of Arahantship

The Buddha refers to five types of declarations of final knowledge [*aññā*], or Arahantship. One makes a declaration (AN III 119);

1) because of one's dullness and stupidity [*mandattā momūhattā aññaṃ vyākaronti*].
2) because one has evil desires and is motivated by desire [*pāpiccho icchāpakato*].
3) because one is mad and mentally deranged [*ummādā cittakkhepā*].
4) because one overrates oneself [*adhimānena*].
5) or one correctly declares final knowledge [*samma-d-eva aññaṃ vyākaroti*].

Accordingly, claims of Arahantship can be made by a person due to any of the above reasons. Not only Arahantship, the other three fruits of the Path too can be declared due to any one or more of these reasons. Hence the question arises as to how to recognize a genuine noble person. First we can follow an elimination process based on what the texts set out as what is impossible for a particular class of noble persons.

What is Impossible for an *Arahant*

The *Navaka Vagga* of the *Aṅguttara Nikāya* sets out nine acts which are impossible for an *Arahant* to commit [*abhabbo so nava ṭhānāni*] (AN IV 371–372). A monk in whom taints are destroyed cannot:

1) deliberately take the life of any living being.

2) with intention to steal, take what is not given.
3) indulge in sexual intercourse.
4) intentionally tell a lie.
5) storing things up in order to enjoy sensual pleasures [*sannidhikārake kāme paribuñjituṃ*].
6) act improperly through desire [*chanda*].
7) act improperly through hate [*dosa*].
8) act improperly through delusion [*moha*].
9) act improperly through fear [*bhaya*].

Similarly the *Suttas* set out what is impossible for a stream-enterer or what he is incapable of. A detailed discussion on how to recognize a stream-enterer is given in Chapter 6 (pp. 142–145).

If what is given above as impossible for an *Arahant* or what is impossible for a stream-enterer is transgressed, you can be sure that such a person is not an *Arahant* or a stream-enterer respectively. For example if they have no respect for the *Saṅgha* (AN III 439), or if they do not believe in the deva worlds, as "there are no other worlds and there are no beings who are born spontaneously" being wrong view (SN III 207), or if they hold the view that the mind [*citta*] or mentality [*mano*] or consciousness [*viññāṇa*] is everlasting (being wrong view no. 8 in the *Brahmajāla Sutta*) (DN I 21), then in each case one can know for sure that they are not stream-enterers. Similarly at the attainment of *anāgami-phala* one eliminates the fetters of *kāma-rāga* (desire for pleasures of the senses) and *vyāpāda* (ill-will). Hence if a person is sexually active you can be sure that he is not a non-returner.

Though certain gross acts of transgressions could be visible as transgressions, at times it may be difficult for a third party to determine conclusively whether all mental factors for a particular transgression have been fulfilled or not. That is, whether a particular act was motivated by ill-will or not or whether or not the intention of a particular statement is to mislead or to deceive etc. Hence this judgment too is subject to certain limitations. In determining whether a person has committed what is impossible for someone who has attained a particular fruit of the Path, we have to go by what is cognizable through the eye or the ear. In the *Vīmaṃsaka Sutta* the Buddha invites an inquiry even into the Buddha's state of mind, as "are there found in the *Tathāgata* or not any defiled states cognizable through the eye and through the ear?" (MN I 318). Bodily actions are states cognizable through the eye and words are states cognizable through the ear. Just as one infers the presence of fish from the rippling and bubbling of water, so from a defiled action or utterance one infers that the mind originating it is defiled (Ñāṇamoli and Bodhi 1995, 1243, n. 483).

Having inquired based on "what is impossible," next we can adopt questioning and discussion as a tool for recognizing a noble person.

Questioning a Monk Who Has Declared Arahantship

The *Chabbisodana Sutta* of the *Majjhima Nikāya* sets out how to verify the truth of a declaration made by a *bhikkhu* if and when he declares final knowledge (Arahantship). It says his words should neither be approved nor disapproved of.

Rather he should be questioned in the following manner:

> Friend there are four kinds of expressions rightly proclaimed by the Blessed One, who knows and sees, accomplished and fully enlightened. What four? Telling of the seen as it is seen [*diṭṭhe diṭṭhavāditā*]; telling of the heard as it is heard, telling of the sensed as it is sensed; telling of the cognized as it is cognized. This friend, are the four kinds of expressions rightly proclaimed by the Blessed One ... How does the venerable one know, how does he see, regarding these four kinds of expressions so that through not clinging his mind is liberated from the taints? [*Kathaṃ jānato pan' āyasmato kathaṃ passato imesu catusu vohāresu anupādāya āsavehi cittaṃ vimuttan ti*?] (MN III 29)

If the *bhikkhu* is one with taints destroyed he would answer thus:

> "regarding the seen, I abide unattracted, unrepelled, independent, detached, free, disassociated, with a mind rid of barriers [*Diṭṭhe kho ahaṃ āvuso anupāyo anapāyo anissito appaṭibaddho vippamutto visaṃyutto vimariyādikatena cetasā viharāmi*]."

If the same is said about the heard, sensed and the cognized, one may then delight and rejoice in the answer saying "good." However one should continue to ask him further questions, one after the other as set out as follows with the appropriate answers:

1) "How does he know and see the five aggregates subject to clinging, so that through not clinging his mind is liberated from the taints?"

and the nature of the answer would be:

> Having known material form ... feeling ... perception ... volitional activities ... consciousness to be feeble, fading away and comfortless [*āvuso abalaṃ virāgaṃ anassāsikaṃ*], with the destruction, fading away, cessation, giving up and relinquishing of attraction and grasping regarding material form etc., (and) of mental standpoints, adherences and underlying tendencies regarding them [*rūpe upāyupādānā cetaso adhiṭṭhānābhinivesānusayā tesaṃ khayā virāgā nirodhā cāgā paṭinissaggā*], I understand that my mind is liberated [*vimuttam me cittam ti pajānāmi*]. (MN III 30)

2) "How does he know and see regarding the six elements so that through not clinging his mind is liberated from the taints?"

and the answer would be:

> Friends, I have treated the earth element as non-self [*paṭhavīdhātuṃ kho ahaṃ, āvuso, anattato upagacchiṃ*], with no self based on the earth element [*na ca paṭhavīdhātunissitaṃ attānaṃ*]. And with the destruction, fading away, cessation, giving up and relinquishing of attraction and grasping based on the earth element, (and) of mental standpoints, adherences, and underlying tendencies based on the earth element, I have understood that my mind is liberated. Similarly for the water element, fire element, air element, space element and consciousness element. (MN III 31)

3) "How does he know and see the six internal and external bases [*ajjhattikāni bāhirāni āyatanāni*], i.e. eye and forms, ear and sounds, nose and odours, tongue and flavours, body and tangibles and mind and mind objects, so that through not clinging his mind is liberated from the taints?"

The answer would be:

> ...with the destruction, fading away, cessation, giving up, and relinquishing of desire, lust, delight, craving, attraction and clinging and of mental standpoints, adherences, and underlying tendencies regarding the eye, forms, eye-consciousness and things cognizable (by the mind) through eye-consciousness, I have understood that my mind is liberated.

4) "How does he know and see, so that in regard to his body with its consciousness and all external signs [*saviññāṇake kāye bahiddhā ca sabbanimittesu*], I-making, mine-making, and underlying tendency to conceit have been eradicated in him [*ahiṃkāramamiṃkāramānānusayā susamūhatā ti*]?" (MN III 32).

To this question he explains the path followed by him from the commencement of his practice to the end, that is, how he was ignorant before, and then the *Tathāgata* or his disciple taught him the Dhamma through which he acquired faith. Thereafter he considered that the household life is with obstacles so that he went forth to homelessness. Thereafter he purified his *sīla* and entered the first to fourth *jhāna*s and when his concentrated mind was purified, bright, unblemished, rid of imperfections, he directed it to knowledge of destructions of the taints. Then he would say: "I directly knew as it actually is "This is suffering"... "This is the origin of suffering" ... "This is the cessation of suffering"... "This is the way leading to the cessation of suffering" ... "These are the taints"... "This is the origin of the taints"... "This is the cessation of the taints"... "This is the way leading to the cessation of the taints."

He further states:

> When I knew and saw thus, my mind was liberated from the taints of sensual desires, from the taint of being, and from the taint of ignorance. When it was liberated there came the knowledge "It is liberated," I directly knew "Birth is destroyed ..." It is knowing thus, seeing thus, friends, that in regard to this body with its consciousness and all external signs, I-making, mine-making, and the underlying tendencies to conceit have been eradicated by me. (MN III 36)

The commentary (MN-a IV 95) say that if the above questions are answered satisfactorily, the *bhikkhu* should be questioned further as follows (Khemānanda 2007, 16–19).

1) *kiṃ te adhigataṃ?*—(What have you realized?), (i.e. if he has attained *arahatta-phala* he will say so).
2) *kinti te adhigataṃ?*—(How did you realize?), this refers to the strategy he has adopted for his attainment, (i.e. whether he used the mark of impermanence, suffering or non-self, or practised concentration or *vipassanā* etc.)
3) *kadā te adhigataṃ?*—(When did you realize?) (i.e. was it in the morning, afternoon etc.)
4) *kattha te adhigataṃ?*—(Where did you realize?), (i.e. was it under the root of a tree, monastery etc.)
5) *katame te kilesā pahiṇā?*—(What are the defilements destroyed by you?), (i.e. *sakkāya-diṭṭhi* (view on personality), *vicikiccā* (skeptical doubt) etc.)

6) *katamesaṃ tvaṃ dhammānaṃ lābhī?*—(What states have been gained by you?), (i.e. whether he is a stream-enterer, once-returner etc.)

Though the above questions referred to in the commentaries are meant to question one who has declared Arahantship, they are equally applicable to all four fruits of the Path. The commentaries further say that different strategies should be used to test the state of the mind, to see whether a person is actually free of certain defilements, such as, if he claims to be an *Arahant* who is free of fear, a fearful image could be created to see his reflexes, or some temptations could be created to see the arising of craving.[6]

Discussion

It is also possible to recognize a noble person through a process of elimination by discussion. The Buddha says that the wisdom of another can be gauged by discussion, however only by an equally wise person and by engaging in discussion for a long period of time and also having been attentive. He says:

> It is by discussion with someone, great king, that his wisdom is to be known [*sākacchāya kho mahārāja paññā veditabbā*], and that (too) after a long time, not after a short time; by one who is attentive, not by one who is inattentive, by one who is wise, not by a dullard [*manasikarotā no amanasikarotā paññavatā no duppaññena*]. (SN I 179)

On this occasion the Buddha also advises that it is by living together with someone, that his virtue is to be known, it is by dealing with someone, that his honesty is to be known, and in adversities that a person's fortitude is to be known. In all these instances it is possible only if such dealing, discussing etc. has persisted for a long time, not after a short time and by one who is attentive, not by one who is inattentive, and by one who is wise, not by a dullard.

The elimination process discussed above can be undertaken within limits when a person makes an open declaration about his attainments. But often the question is raised is: how do we know whether there are *Arahant*s, or for that matter even stream-enterers living today? This is raised through good faith or lack of faith or mere curiosity. Often having associated with a meditating monk or a layperson or a Dhamma-teacher, people, based on their own judgment, begin to label them as having one or more supramundane fruits or debate amongst themselves whether or not a particular person is a noble person or not, or whether he is a stream-enterer or a non-returner, etc. Let us see what the texts offer us in this regard.

The Buddha gives yardsticks to judge another's wisdom as follows:

> Judging from the way this venerable one initiates, formulates, and poses a question, he is unwise [*duppañño*], not wise. For what reason? This venerable one does not speak about matters that are deep, peaceful, sublime, beyond the sphere of reasoning, subtle, comprehensible to the wise [*gambhīraṃ atthapadaṃ udāharati santaṃ paṇītaṃ atakkāvacaraṃ nipuṇaṃ paṇḍitavedanīyaṃ*]. When this venerable one speaks on the Dhamma, he is not able to explain, teach, describe, establish, reveal, analyze, and explicate the meaning either briefly or in detail. This venerable one is unwise, not wise.
>
> Just as if a man with good sight, standing on the bank of a pond, were to see a small fish emerging, he would think: "judging from the way this fish emerges, from the ripples it makes, and from its force, this is a small fish, not a big one."

So too, when conversing with a person, one comes to know: "judging from the way this venerable one initiates, formulates, and poses a question, he is unwise, not wise." (AN II 189)

In all above *Sutta*s the reference is to an "unwise person." In the *Sacca Saṃyutta* the Buddha says that those renunciants or brahmins who do not understand as it really is; "This is suffering," "This is the origin of suffering," "This is the cessation of suffering" and "This is the way leading to the cessation of suffering," they look up at the face of another renunciant or brahmin, thinking: "This worthy is one who really knows, who really sees. For what reason? Because they have not seen the four True Realties for the Noble Ones [*ariya-saccānaṃ*] (SN V 444).

To directly and experientially understand the four True Realties for the Noble Ones, one has to attain at least the first fruit of the Path [*sotāpatti-phala*]. Only such a person will be able to recognize another who "knows and sees," and that too after long and close association and through intense discussions. Based on these a *sotāpanna* will be able to recognize another *sotāpanna*. Similarly a noble disciple with higher fruits of the Path will be able to recognize their counterparts or those with lesser fruits of the Path.

The Vaṇgīsa Saṃyutta reports that once the Buddha was dwelling in Rājagaha on the Black Rock of the Isigili Slope, together with five hundred *bhikkhu*s, all of whom were *Arahant*s. Then Venerable Moggallāna searched their minds with his own mind and saw that they were released, without acquisition (SN I 419/Bodhi 2000, 291). Moggallāna was an *Arahant* and one with the eight *samāpatti*s (abidings). Therefore with his wisdom coupled with his concentration levels being at the highest level, he was able to recognize other *Arahant*s.

Can Gods Recognize a Noble Person?

There are references in the texts to certain gods recognizing noble persons. Once a group of monks visited Ugga of Hatthigāma, a householder, to inquire about the "astonishing and amazing qualities" possessed by him as declared by the Buddha. Addressing them, Ugga the householder declares that, amongst the astonishing and amazing qualities is that, when he invites the *Saṅgha*, it is not out of the ordinary for *devas* to come and tell him, that such and such monk is one freed-in-both-ways [*ubhato bhāgavimutta*], such and such a person is wisdom-freed [*paññāvimutta*], seer-in-body [*kāyasakkhī*], view-winner [*diṭṭhipatta*], faith-freed [*saddhāvimutta*], Dhamma-follower [*dhammānusārī*], faith-follower [*saddhānusārī*], virtuous [*sīlavā*] and not virtuous [*dussīla*] (AN IV 215).

Similarly in the *Devatā Saṃyutta* there is a reference to certain *devatā*s recognizing an assembly of *Arahant*s when the Buddha was surrounded by five hundred *Arahant*s at Kapilavatthu. On this occasion the *devatā*s from 10 world systems had assembled in order to see the Blessed One and the *bhikkhu Saṅgha*. Then the thought occurred to four *devatā*s from the Pure Abodes that all the monks there were *Arahants* (SN I 55).

This indicates that there is a possibility that gods have the ability to recognize noble persons. If so the question arises as to whether *all* gods have the ability to recognize noble persons. The above *devatā*s are reported to be from Pure Abodes [*suddhāvāsa brahmā* worlds], where all inhabitants are either *Arahants* or non-returners.

Once two *devas*, who were "radiant, lighting up the whole of Gijjakuta," approached the Buddha after the night had passed away. One said to the Buddha "Venerable sir, these *bhikkhunīs* are liberated! [*etā bhante bhikkhuniyo vimuttā ti*]." And the other said "Venerable sir, these *bhikkhunīs* are well liberated without residue remaining! [*etā bhante bhikkhuniyo anupādisesā suvimuttā ti*] Seeing that the Buddha approved this, they saluted the Buddha and disappeared (AN IV 76).

At this point of time Venerable Moggallāna was seated there and the thought crossed his mind as to what *devas* would know one who has residue remaining as "one with residue remaining" and one who has no residue as "one without residue." Then he saw that the monk Tissa had recently died and had arisen in one of the *brahmā* worlds and there they knew him as *brahmā* Tissa, the mighty, the very powerful. Moggallāna vanished from there and appeared in that *brahmā* world in the presence of *brahmā* Tissa and questioned him as to which *devas* would know who is partly attached and who is wholly unattached.

Brahmā Tissa replied that it is the *devas* of *brahmā*'s company [*brahma-kāyika*] who have this knowledge. Then Moggallāna questions whether all *brahmā devas* have this knowledge. *Brahmā* Tissa replies that those who have this knowledge are those *brahmās* who are not satisfied with *brahmā* life, *brahmā* beauty, *brahmā* happiness, *brahmā* glory, *brahmā* authority and who understand as there really is an escape higher than this [*uttariṃ nissaraṇaṃ yathābhutaṃ pajānāti*—AN IV 77], which here reflects a *brahmā* who is an *Arahant*. A *brahmā* who is a non-returner with the said qualities would be able to recognize a non-returner or one with the attainment of a lesser fruit.

This *Sutta* sets out six kinds of persons who can be recognized by such a *brahmā*. They are: *ubhata bhāgavimutta* (one freed-in-both-ways), *paññāvimutta* (wisdom-freed), *kāyasakkhī* (seer-in-body), *diṭṭhippatta* (view-winner), *saddhāvimutta* (faith-freed) and *dhammānusārī* (Dhamma-follower). The Buddha confirms the truth of this statement of *brahmā* Tissa and adds a seventh to this list who can be recognized by such a *brahmā*. That is one who dwells in "*animitta ceto samādhi*" (one who abides in signless mental concentration).[7]

Once again, even in terms of the above *Sutta*, a divine being who can recognize an *Arahant* is only a *brahmā* who is an *Arahant*, one who has the highest wisdom and also the highest *jhānas*.

Hence considering the above *Suttas* of the *Aṅguttara Nikāya* and the *Saṃyutta Nikāya* and Ugga's statements discussed before, it can be concluded that a divine being who is a noble person can recognize another noble person, whether human or divine, with the same or a lower fruit of the Path.

Contemporary Difficulties in Recognizing Noble Persons

So far we discussed the possibility of recognizing a person who has attained supramundane fruits of the Path as set out in the texts. In Chapter 1 I presented the possibilities and difficulties in recognizing them in terms of the field research of the writer (pp. 9–18). Now I will present another recent research by psychologists, psychiatrists, and meditators.

A systematic study into meditative traditions done by Ken Wilber, Jack Engler, and Daniel P. Brown is reported in their *Transformations of Consciousness—Conventional and Contemplative Perspectives on Development* (Engler *et al.* 1986). This book consists of various closely related attempts to articulate a "full spectrum" model of human growth and development, a model that includes the stages of development typically investigated by conventional Psychology and Psychiatry as well as the stages of development apparently evident in the world's great meditative and contemplative traditions.

The methodology for the aforesaid research included textual, intensive interviews with practitioners and teachers, a quantitative measure they developed and titled "A Profile of Meditative Experience" (POME),[8] and the Rorschach inkblot test used as a measure of cognitive and perceptual change. The sample of "Advanced meditators" used for the research were eight subjects, including two teachers and were nominated by two masters. The masters themselves also agreed to participate in the study, making a total number of ten: eight women mostly mothers and housewives, and two men. All were middle-aged. All practised the same type of Burmese *satipaṭṭhāna-vipassanā* or mindfulness insight meditation in the lineage of Venerable Mahāsi Sayadaw of Yangong. According to teacher-rating, five subjects had attained the first stage of enlightenment [*sotāpatti-phala*], four had attained the second [*sakadāgāmi-phala*], and one had attained the third [*anāgāmī-phala*] (Engler *et al.* 1986, 171).

Although the Rorschach test[9] was originally used as a personality measure, Brown and Engler found that "practitioners at different levels of the practice gave records that looked very distinct. In fact, the Rorschach records seemed to correlate with particular stages of meditation. Common features were more outstanding than individual differences at each level of practice." Using the Rorschach inkblots as a measure of cognitive and perceptual change, Brown and Engler found that the specific qualitative features of the Rorschachs for each group are consistent with the classical descriptions of the psychological changes of that stage of practice (Engler *et al.* 1986, 161). The single Rorschach of the master representing the advanced meditators [*anāgāmi-phala*] was unusual (Engler *et al.* 1986, 212–213).

This unexpected observation raised the further question of whether perhaps there were qualitative features (and quantitative variables) in the Rorschach that discriminated between the major divisions or stages of the practice. If so this would be an initial step towards establishing the possible validity of the stage-model of meditation (Engler *et al.* 1986, 164). In terms of the results of this test, prima facie there seems to be a possibility that the Rorschach could be used as an instrument to recognize a noble person. However the concrete test of having attained a supramundane fruit is the wisdom generated in such a mind or the absence of the fetters and the underlying tendencies in it and not merely perceptions. In their study, the Rorschach was used as a measure of cognitive and perceptual change, not as a personality measure. Here it served as a stage-sensitive validation instrument by administering it to criterion groups defined according to their level of practice (Engler *et al.* 1986, 164). Brown and Engler themselves write:

The objective of a validation study is to establish independent empirical measures of the alleged cognitive changes described in the traditional texts and in the subjective reports and questionnaires of contemporary practitioners. The Rorschach may not seem to be a likely choice for such a validation study (Engler *et al.* 1986, 164).

We conclude that this is not a concrete test to recognize a noble person.

Conclusion

This chapter examined as to who could declare attainment of supramundane fruits of the Path and saw that it is only the person who attained such a fruit himself and the Buddha alone who had made such a claim. This excludes a teacher, *deva* or a *brahmā* bestowing such status on another directly or indirectly. As this is a process of "letting go," there is no room for these attainments to be considered one's qualifications, status or to be added as a title behind one's name for purposes of recognition or for identification, nor to be awarded by way of a certificate.

As to the possibility of a third party recognizing a noble person, one with the same or a higher attainment may recognize another with the same or lower attainments, at least after a long and close association and much discussion. For this purpose, the one attempting to make such a judgment ideally has to be at least a stream-enterer. Certain gross behaviours may be indications of not having attained a particular supramundane fruit, if such behaviour has been categorized in the text as "impossible" at the level of a particular attainment.[10] However the first fruit of the Path (fruit of stream-entry) is about acquiring a view, right view. To this extent, by discussion and questioning we could establish whether or not knowledge and understanding of a particular *yogī* (meditator) corresponds to the right view provided such *yogī* conforms to the rest of the essential ingredients of a supramundane fruit, (i.e. he is able to point to a day and a place of a specific religious experience, an attempt on his part to develop the Noble Eightfold Path etc).

When those noble ones with fruits of the Path wish to remain silent or are so very reluctant to admit their state, and those without any noble *phala* tend to declare fruits of the Path through stupidity, evil desires, insanity and confusion or over-estimating themselves [*adhimāna*], as a general rule, none other than a Buddha himself or someone equal to him would know for sure about the attainment of a supramundane fruit of the Path of another. It is not surprising that the Buddha gives such a strong warning against attempts to pass judgment on spiritual attainments of a third party, whether in favour of or against such attainment.

By virtue of his exclusive knoweldges such as *indriyaparopariyatte ñāṇa* (knowledge of penetration of spiritual faculties of beings) and *anāvarana ñāṇa* (unobstructed knowledge)[11] the Buddha is qualified to make this judgment as he is able to examine another's mind and determine the state of his spiritual faculties and the defilements remaining. Hence the common curiosity to definitively ascertain the level of spiritual attainments of another would be a vain exercise to say the least. However some of the *Arahant*s during the time of the Buddha, with taints destroyed, with mighty super-natural powers, with the ability to read others minds including the minds of even *brahmā*s such as Venerables Moggallāna, Kassapa, Kappina, Anuruddha (SN I 315) ought to have the ability to make such judgement though not to the extent of the Buddha.

By the above discussion, subject to the limitations and difficulties discussed in this chapter and also in Chapter 1, we also establish a reasonable yardstick to evaluate the authenticity of the claims made by the subjects interviewed in the field research of our study. Under these limitations we can make a judgment of an attainment only through a logical inference. That is, if the first three fetters of *sakkāya-diṭṭhi, sīlabbata-parāmāsa* and *vicikiccā* are absent in a person, and such state of mind or such knowledge has been a consequence of a specific experience gained by following or attempting to follow the Noble Eightfold Path, logically it can be concluded that such a state of mind corresponds to *sotāpatti-phala*, provided there is credibility on the part of the person making such declaration. The supramundane field, however, is far beyond "logic."

On the other hand, this chapter also excludes or limits the space available for outright rejection or dismissal of any claims of an attainment made in our field research by those who are "not qualified" to do so and without reasonable grounds. Who is qualified to do so is, ideally, one who is at least a stream-enterer. Under these circumstances, in terms of the Buddha's invitation for a fair inquiry, one is compelled to evaluate the claims made in our field research without prejudice, with an open mind.

Notes

1. The term "noble person" [*ariya puggala*] has been used here in the sense of "a disciple who is noble (i.e. any one of the eight types of persons referred to in the *Suttas* as members of the *sāvaka-Saṅgha*) as against "the disciple of the noble one." See p. 21 for the definition of "noble person" and Harvey 2013 for a discussion on the "noble person."
2. *Pāli English Dictionary*, T.W. Rhys Davids, William Stede 2001, 656.
3. The above is usually the declaration of *anāgāmi-phala*. However in this case the commentary says that he was a "*jhāna*-non-returner," meaning that he was a stream-enterer who has abandoned the five hindrances by the first *jhāna*. If he were to die without having fallen away from *jhāna* he would be reborn in a higher world and attain final *Nibbāna* there. However, he did not fall from the *jhāna* at the time of his death and therefore his destiny was determined (Bodhi 2000, 1936, n. 22). However Uṇṇābha had already met Venerable Ānanda and their discussion generated a high degree of *saddhā* and insight (SN V 272). The questions directed at the Buddha shows that he had already developed insight. The Buddha says that "those who have sufficient faith in me, sufficient love for me are all headed for *deva* worlds" [*yesaṃ mayi saddhāmattaṃ pemamattaṃ sabbe te saggaparāyanā*] (MN I 142). Therefore I feel what the Buddha meant was that given the *saddhā* Uṇṇābha had, he would be reborn in the *deva* worlds and proceed to higher fruits from there, not having to come back to this world.
4. In response to being asked whether he had attained solace in the Dhamma and the Discipline.
5. The commentary explains this as occasional joy from listening to the teachings, while Ps. II 40 explains *samayavimokkho* as the four *jhānas* and formless attainments (Bodhi 2012, 1760, n. 1443).
6. See Rahula 1993, 220–222 for a series of strategies adopted in ancient Ceylon to test the mindset of possible noble persons.
7. See Chapter 5 (classification of persons based on religious experience) for a description of these seven persons, and the "faith-follower," who is usually listed after the "Dhamma-follower."
8. The research covered different meditative and contemplative traditions such as Tibetan *Mahāmudrā*, The Hindu *Yogāstras*, and Theravāda *Vipassanā* (this cartog-

raphy was subsequently cross-checked with other contemplative texts, Christian, Chinese, etc.). The method of investigating the texts of each tradition began with the identification of the place of meditation along the relevant path as well as the technical terms used to express the experiences at each stage. In order to increase the reliability, authoritative commentaries and related texts were also used. For cross-cultural validity of the study, the *Yogaāstras*, *Visuddhimagga* and key *Mahāmudrā* texts were compared synoptically, stage by stage to test whether there was an underlying sequence (Engler *et al.* 1986, 223).

9. The Rorschach inkblot test is a method of psychological evaluation. Psychologists use this test to try to examine the personality, characteristics and emotional functioning of their patients. The Rorschach is currently the second most commonly used test in forensic assessment and is the second most widely used test by members of the Society for Personality Assessment. It has been employed in diagnosing underlying thought disorder and differentiating psychotic from non-psychotic thinking in cases where the patient is reluctant to openly admit to psychotic thinking.

   There are ten official inkblots. Five are black ink on white paper. Two are black and red ink on white paper. Three are multicoloured. After the individual has seen and responded to all the inkblots, the tester then gives them to him again one at a time to study. The test subject is asked to note where he sees what he originally saw and what makes it look like that. The blot can also be rotated. As the subject is examining the inkblots, the psychologist writes down everything the subject says or does, no matter how trivial.

   The Rorschach scoring systems have been described as a system of pegs on which to hang one's knowledge of personality. The most widely used method in the United States is based on the work of John E. Exner. In the Exner system, responses are scored with reference to their level of vagueness or synthesis of multiple images in the blot, the location of the response, which of a variety of determinants is used to produce the response (i.e. what makes the inkblot look like what it is said to resemble), the form quality of the response (to what extent a response is faithful to how the actual inkblot looks), the contents of the response (what the respondent actually sees in the blot), the degree of mental organizing activity that is involved in producing the response, and any illogical, incongruous, or incoherent aspects of responses. (Rorschach inkblot test—Wikipedia—http: // wikipedia.org).

   However this test has been criticized as inherently problematic. It is considered "projective" because the patient is supposed to project his or her real personality into the inkblot via the interpretation. The inkblots are purportedly ambiguous, structureless entities which are to be given a clear structure by the interpreter. In criticizing this test it is said:

   > For one thing, to be truly projective the inkblots must be considered ambiguous and without structure by the therapist. Hence, the therapist must not make reference to the inkblot in interpreting the patient's responses or else the therapist's projection would have to be taken into account by an independent party. Then the third person would have to be interpreted by a fourth ad infinitum. Thus, the therapist must interpret the patient's interpretation without reference to what is being interpreted. Clearly, the inkblot becomes superfluous ... In other words, the interpretation must be examined

as if it were a story or dream with no particular reference in reality. Even so, ultimately the therapist must make a judgment about the interpretation, i.e., interpret the interpretation. But again, who is to interpret the therapist's interpretation? Another therapist? Then, who will interpret his? (The Skeptic's Dictionary—Robbert Todd Caroll—http: // skepdic.com)

Quite apart from its validity, the test's reliability is also questioned on the basis that the results can depend substantially on details of the testing procedure, such as where the tester and subject are seated; any introductory words; verbal and nonverbal responses to subjects" questions or comments; and how responses are recorded. Further the actual cards used for the test are meant to be kept a secret so that the answers are spontaneous. However now the testing materials are publicly available. (Rorschach inkblot test—Wikipedia—http: //wikipedia.org)

10. A parallel could be drawn with Karl Popper's Theory of Falsification as against the Logical Positivists" Theory of Verification, which holds that the truth content of theories, even the best of them, cannot be verified by scientific testing, but can only be falsified. (Wikipedia—http: //wikipedia.org/Karl Popper). Karl Popper was one of the greatest Philosophers of Science in the twentieth century. Popper takes falsifiability as the criterion for demarcating science from non-science. He argues that for a theory to be scientific it should be possible to test it with empirical observations. As Popper represents it, the greatest problem in the Philosophy of Science is that of demarcation between science and "non-science" under which heading he ranks, inter-alia, logic, metaphysics and psychoanalysis. For Popper, however, for an unscientific theory, it is not necessary to hold that it is unenlightening, still less that it is meaningless, for it sometimes happens that a theory is unscientific (because it is unfalsifiable) at a given time may become scientific because it becomes falsifiable with the development of technology (http://plato.stanford.edu/entries/popper).
11. For a detail list of the Buddha's special knowledges, see "Wisdom and Seventy three knoweldges of mundane and supramundane knoweldges," by Bhikkhu Ñāṇadassana, www.beyondthenet.net

— 3 —

Does the Attainment of a Supramundane Fruit Necessarily Involve a Specific Experience?

In Chapter 2 we examined how to recognize a noble person. We also defined an attainment of a supramundane fruit to be a specific striking experience of a person treading or making an effort to tread the Noble Eightfold Path, resulting in the understanding or knowledge which leads to breaking of the corresponding fetters [*saṃyojanas*]. One of the key elements of this definition is a specific striking religious experience. Not recognizing that an attainment of a supramundane fruit entails a specific religious experience, or not appreciating the implications of such an experience has resulted in many controversies and debates about the nature of Buddhist religious experiences. Some of these controversies and debates will be discussed in detail in Chapter 4. In this chapter we will examine whether an attainment of a supramundane fruit must in fact involve a specific experience. For this purpose we will examine:

1) References in the *Nikāyas* to specific places, dates, meditative postures and events, during which supramundane fruits were attained
2) References in contemporary sources to supramundane experiences of meditators
3) The findings of the field research of the writer

There are a few *Suttas* in the *Sotāpatti-Saṃyutta* which suggest that one can declare having the *sotāpatti-phala* merely by examining the defilements in one's mind or the qualities of one's mind. There is room in these *Suttas* to conclude that one could declare a supramundane fruit at any time, without a specific religious experience marking such attainment. Set out below are some of such instances.

The Buddha advised Venerable Ānanda on the "mirror of the Dhamma," equipped with which, one can make a declaration about one's attainment of the fruit that is stream-entry. According to this *Sutta*, prima facie, if one has unshaken confidence in the Buddha, the Dhamma and the *Saṅgha* and has unbroken *sīla* dear to noble ones [*ariyakanta sīla*], one can declare oneself to be a stream-enterer at any time whether or not one has had a specific religious experience heralding the attainment of a supramundane fruit. It says:

> Here, Ānanda, a noble disciple possesses confirmed confidence in the Buddha [*Buddhe aveccappasādena samannāgato*]... Dhamma ... *Saṅgha* ... He possesses the virtues dear to the noble ones—unbroken, untorn, unblemished, unmottled, freeing, praised by the wise, ungrasped, leading to concentration [*Ariyakantehi sīlehi samannāgato hoti akhaṇḍehi acchiddehi asabalehi akammāsehi bhūjissehi viññūpasatthehi aparāmaṭṭhehi samādhisaṃvattanikehi*]. This Ānanda is that Dhamma exposition, the

mirror of the Dhamma, equipped with which a noble disciple, if he wishes could by himself declare of himself: "I am one finished with hell." (SN V 355–356)

Similarly in the *Aṅguttara Nikāya* Buddha advises Anāthapiṇḍika that if the fivefold perils and enmities [*pañca bhayāni verāni*] have been eliminated by a noble disciple and she possesses the four factors of a stream-enterer [*sotāpattiyaṅgas*], she may declare herself to be a stream-enterer, one free from bad rebirths and bound for enlightenment (AN IV 405).

In the *Kāligodhā Sutta* of the *Sotāpatti Saṃyutta,* addressing Kālighodā, the female noble disciple, the Buddha points out that the noble disciple who possesses four things is a stream-enterer. That is, a noble disciple who possesses unshaken confidence in the Buddha, the Dhamma, and in the *Saṅgha* and one who dwells at home with a mind devoid of the stain of stinginess, freely generous, open handed, delighting in relinquishment, one devoted to charity, delighting in giving and sharing (SN V 396).

On this occasion, Kālighodā having recognized the qualities in herself, declared herself to be a stream-enterer and the Buddha praises her for declaring stream-entry in terms of these four qualities. This *Sutta* too might be interpreted to support the argument that one can declare the attainment of the fruit of stream-entry by merely examining one's state of mind without having had a specific religious experience.

There are similar references to *arahatta-phala*. In the *Aṅguttara Nikāya* the Buddha asks Venerable Sāriputta, "When a *bhikkhu*'s taints have been destroyed, how many powers does he possess by reason of which he can claim "My taints have been destroyed'?" [*yehi balehi samannāgato khīnāsavo bhikkhu āsavānaṃ khayaṃ paṭijānāti*], Sāriputta replies saying eight and goes on to set out the eight:

1) When the *bhikkhu* with taints destroyed has clearly seen all conditioned phenomena as they really are with correct wisdom, as impermanent,
2) When he has clearly seen sensual pleasures as they really are, with correct wisdom, as similar to a charcoal pit,
3) When the mind of a taint-free *bhikkhu* slants, slopes and inclines to seclusion, it is withdrawn, delighting in renunciation and is entirely finished with all things that are the basis of taints,
4) When he has developed and well developed the four establishments of mindfulness,
5) The four bases of psychic power,
6) Five spiritual faculties,
7) Seven factors of enlightenment, and
8) The Noble Eightfold Path. (AN IV 224–225)

According to the above *Sutta*, it is possible that someone who thinks that she is equipped with these attributes may decide to declare herself as having the *arahatta-phala* at any given time, without having had a specific religious experience.

On the other hand there are countless *Suttas* in the *Nikāyas* in which attainment of supramundane fruits have been declared with reference to a date, place, in a particular meditation posture, during a particular incident, at the time of death etc. Based on these many *Suttas*, I propose that attainment of a supramundane fruit necessarily involves a specific religious experience with a peak-point (a fetter-breaking experience), which can be identified as to time and place. In support of this proposition, I will begin by highlighting various declarations from the *Saṃyutta* and the *Aṅguttara Nikāyas* and the *Theragāthā* and *Therīgāthā* which suggest that a fruit involves a specific experience that can be identified as to time and place.

References in the *Nikāyas*, to Specific Places, Dates, Meditative Postures and Events, During which Supramundane Fruits were Attained

References to Attainments of Fruits at the End of or During a Specific Sermon

There are countless *Suttas* which report that at the end of a *Sutta*, the listeners had attained supramundane fruits. Some of those are as follows:

1) It is said that when the *Anattalakkhaṇa Sutta* was being delivered by the Buddha to the five ascetics, at its end all five, who were already trainees [*sekhas*], attained Arahantship.[1]
2) The *Rāhula Sutta* of the *Saḷāyatana Saṃyutta* reports that whilst this discourse was being spoken, the Venerable Rāhula's mind was liberated from the taints by non-clinging and in those many thousands of *devas* who were present, there arose the dust free, stainless vision of the Dhamma; "Whatever is subject to origination is all subject to cessation." That means, at this point, Rāhula attained Arahantship and the others became stream-enterers (SN IV 107, and Bodhi 2000, 1415, n. 112).

References to Attainment of Fruits During a Specific Event or at a Specific Place

Ugga the householder of Vesālī relates about the occasion of his stream-entry to a group of monks who visited him to inquire about the "astonishing and amazing qualities" he is supposed to possess. He says he attained *sotāpatti-phala* when the Buddha was preaching the Dhamma to him during his very first meeting with the Buddha.[2] Venerable Vītasoka refers to his attainment of Arahantship which took place whilst he was at the barber:

> I thought "I shall shave my hair"; the barber approached. Then taking a mirror I considered my mortal body [*sarīraṃ paccavekkhisaṃ*].
>
> My body seemed empty [*tuccho kāya adissittha*]. In my state of (mental) blindness the darkness of (ignorance) disappeared. All top knots have been cut off; there is now no renewed existence. (Thag.169–170)

Similarly there are references to attaining Arahantship: whilst a monk was entering a village on an elephant's back, on an alms round[3], whilst the former wife approached a monk with his child on her hip,[4] whilst getting up from a fall and pacing up and down,[5] and whilst a monk was attempting suicide by cutting his throat with a razor.[6]

Rajadatta Thera refers to attaining Arahantship when he was at a burial ground.[7]

Further there are references to attaining fruits of the Path by a person on his death bed. In the *Dighāvu Sutta* of the *Sotāpatti Saṃyutta*, the Buddha visited the gravely ill householder Dighāvu and the conversation between the Buddha and Dighāvu suggests that Dighāvu possessed only the factors of stream-entry at that point in time. However immediately upon the departure of the Buddha, Dighāvu died and upon being queried by the monks as to the destiny of Dighāvu, the Buddha declared that he, with the destruction of the five lower fetters, had become one of spontaneous birth and was due to attain *Nibbāna* there without returning from that world (SN V 344). This means that he attained the fruit that is non-returning at the death bed.

References to Specific Days and Time at Which Fruits Had Been Attained

The following are some references to attainments of fruits on a specific day or at a specific time:

1) Venerable Mahā Kassapa recalling his attainment of Arahantship says, the Buddha having given him an exhortation, and then rose from his seat and departed, thereafter for seven days he ate the alms food as a "debtor," but on the eight day, final knowledge arose (SN III 221).
2) Uttama Therī declares that having heard the Dhamma from a *bhikkhunī*, she sat for seven days in one and the same cross-legged position, consigned to joy and happiness. On the eight day she stretched her feet, having "torn asunder the mass of darkness of ignorance" (Thig.44).
3) Bhaddā Therī recalls her final release as "having sent me forth, the teacher, the conqueror, entered the monastery. The sun had not yet set; then my mind was released" (Thig.477).
4) Sunīta Thera recalls:

> For the first watch of the night I recalled my previous births; for the second watch of the night I purified my *deva* eye; in the last watch of the night I tore asunder the mass of darkness. (Thig.627)

Further, in the *Aṅguttara Nikāya* it is said that though a monk engaged in developing the mind [*bhāvanaṃ anuyuttassa*] does not know to what extent taints [āsavas] had been worn away that day, or the previous day or at any given time, yet when they are worn away, he knows that they are worn away. This is then compared to a carpenter or a carpenter's apprentice inspecting the handle of his adze. He sees the impressions of his fingers and thumb on the adze, but does not know how much of the adze-handle had been worn away that day, nor the previous day, nor at any time, yet when it has worn away, he knows that it has worn away. I propose that the words "when they are worn away" here refer to the point which manifests as a specific experience [the fetter-breaking-experience], this being recognised at the end of the period of review of the state of mind, after such experience (AN IV 127).

References in Contemporary Sources to Supramundane Experiences of Meditators

So far we examined the relevant material in the *Nikāyas* and the *Theragāthā* and the *Therīgāthā*. The spiritual experience of well known Venerable Ajahn Chah of the Thai tradition, widely believed to be one who has attained supramundane fruits of Path, was quoted by us in the introductory chapter (Chapter 1, p. 1). He has described his experience as a "disintegration of the whole world," "The earth, vegetation, trees, mountains, in fact the entire planet appeared as ākāsa-dhātu (the space element)," or "There were no people or anything left at all, at this last stage there was complete emptiness." He describes the undefiled mind he touched at the peak of this as the "pure mind." The result of this experience is that his "sense of reality" changed completely. Scrutiny of all his expressions shows that he has had a striking experience if not an overwhelming one, and it had occurred at an identifiable point of time.

The *Transformation of Consciousness* reports on the findings of more recent field research on this subject. Based on the field research done on Theravāda Buddhist meditation, Brown and Engler report on the culmination of the Theravāda religious experience and the mental build up towards an attainment of a supramundane fruit. This research reports that in the process of the meditation, there comes a "moment" at which all conceptual distinctions fall away and the mind experiences "supreme silence" which is said to be referred to by meditators as a "cessation experience." There is reference in this book to a "moment" at which a "profound shift" takes place which can be identified as an "extraordinary experience." With this experience enduring trait changes are said to occur (Engler *et al.* 1986, 205).

The Findings of the Field Research of the Writer

Next we will compare the above findings with the findings of our field research.

Interview with Ajahn Brahmavamso

Ajahn Brahmavamso is a Western monk of the Theravāda tradition, who is internationally renowned as an experienced meditation teacher and practitioner. On the issue of whether attaining a supramundane fruit necessarily involves a specific experience which can be located in terms of time and place, he says that it is a "discernible event" which takes place at a specific place and a time. He says:

> The attainment of stream-winning is a discernible event. You know the time, you know the place. The last piece of evidence (is) in the *Aṅguttara Nikāya* (AN I 107), (where) the Buddha actually says, "there are three places monks which you should revere for the rest of your life." The first place is the place where you went forth as a *sāmaṇera*, the first stage of ordination, where you first wore the brown robes. The second place, where you should revere for the rest of your life is the place where you attained the stream. And the last place is the third place where you defeated all the defilements and became an *Arahant*. Buddha certainly agreed that it was (at) a specific place, a specific time. (Interview No. 8)

All our other interviewees, whether they admitted that they had attained a supramundane fruit or not, recognized a specific experience based on which fetters were destroyed. Irrespective of the intensity of the experience, they were able to relate it to a specific day, time, place, and a specific meditation posture or to associate it with a particular event. Set out below are some of our findings.[8]

Interview No. 3

This was with a 54 year old Sri Lankan monk who lives in a well-known forest hermitage on the outskirts of Colombo. He is currently the chief preceptor of the hermitage and is known as a teacher locally as well as internationally.

His experience relating to the attainment of stream-entry as a layperson is expressed as follows; It was a difficult period in his life; at that time he had been thrown out of his job and he was facing many uncertainties. He was serving as a staff member in a meditation centre, at the same time devoting a few hours to meditation. But he didn't have a teacher, did not have a specific meditation object, did not know whether he was doing *samatha* or *vipassanā* and was not "consciously" abiding in *sīla* (the five precepts). But he badly felt the need for meditation. A book *Sattavisuddhi* written by a well known meditation teacher, on the seven stages of purification caught his attention.[9] He started reading this book chapter by chapter. Each time he read a chapter, he closed the book and tried to practise what he had read. He felt that what was written in it "repeated within him," "got activated in him" as a spiritual experience. This way he went on reading and experimenting from chapter to chapter and he felt that what was read unfolded within him like a "curled up coil opening up." At one point he felt a very clear "going beyond," "a breaking of a boundary," like "a river gushing into the sea," "an opening up," " a river bund breaking and water gushing over the river bank," "fever going down," or like a "festered boil bursting and pus being released." He felt a huge spiritual awakening. He felt that he had got caught up in a "huge operation with some fundamental principles." He felt that, whilst all his problems—such as not having a job, the issue of whether or not to marry, and the rest of the uncertainties in life—remained unresolved, yet there was a definite solution to all his problems. He felt that his personality had gone through a change. He says:

> What triggered it was the word called "*Sattavisuddhi*"... The "*Sattavisuddhi*" was very clear in this. I didn't read the whole book. What I did was I read one chapter, closed the book and meditated (laugh). Nobody would believe. Because of the situation that I was in, when I read one chapter, I felt I have already finished doing it. Then I really understood that the Path has been laid for a long journey ahead of me. Because I had a lot of space in my timetable, there was complete room for it in the meditation centre. When I read the next chapter, I had already got accustomed with what I had read before. When I sit again in meditation, it works. When I was leaping like this from one chapter to another, at a point there was a very clear "going beyond," "breaking a boundary." Or else it was like a big river gushing into the sea. I think that huge mental pressure or the issue of responsibility I had due to being without a job, likewise the issues such as, "Should I marry?" or "Should I enter the robes?," "What am I going to do next?," "If I am to enter the robes whom should I choose as my teacher?," there were a number of problems like this, while all these problems remained unresolved, there was a huge breakthrough from another side ... On the one hand it's a big spiritual awakening on other hand it was unbelievable (Q.5). ... Like a "breaking up" [*kadaagenayaamak*] breaking of a bund and the water gushing over the river bank. But it's not a harmful flood. This serious mental strain, no, you cannot call it even a mental strain, I didn't have a mental strain at that time, even if I say a bursting of a balloon, that too is something that'll bring unhappiness to a baby, it's more like a festered boil bursting and the pus being released (Q.12). ... I realized a big quake, a big difference, a big transformation, a big explosion, a big release occurred (Q.17). ... It's like a fever going down. Or else I still say I felt that it was a definite solution to my problems in the lay life.

> Yet not a single problem was solved. But I knew that I am no more at that level, that it is not a problem to me anymore. Yet the problem was unresolved (Q.6) ... I don't know, I can only say that when I was reading this [book], what was in that book repeated within me, it got activated in me. It's after that I realized that I was caught up in a "huge operation" with some fundamental principles. Or else that such a thing was expressed through me. But at that time I realized that my likes and dislikes, my personality had gone through a change (Q.4).

Interview No. 2

This was with a Sri Lankan monk who lives alone in a shrub jungle on the outskirts of Colombo. This monk is known for his austere living. He lives under very rough conditions, in a cave without doors, windows and walls which is exposed to wild animals and serpents day and night, with no electricity, his *kuṭī* (abode) having only a raised plank as his bed with a mosquito net. He lives on one meal a day from his alms round to the closest village, which is a few kilometers away from the cave. As of the date of the interview, he had been treading the Path for 20 years and had ordained in 1994.

His experience relating to the attainment of stream-entry as a layperson is expressed as follows; His meditation system at first was "labeling": whatever he felt or the mind focused on, was noted by him and a label was assigned to it, for example "sitting," "standing," "feeling," "thinking." One day when he had been labelling in this manner for some time, the mind then refused to label any more. It was tired of labelling in this manner. At one point he experienced a "cessation," a "gap," a "gulf" a "total blankness" in his consciousness, everything stopped, he didn't feel consciousnesses any more for a short while, and then it appeared again. This way the "consciousness" appeared and disappeared in quick succession within a short period for a couple of times, so much so that he realized he experienced something special, though at that time the mind refused to accept it as an attainment of a supramundane fruit of the Path. Much later he realized that it was "non- becoming" that he experienced. He says:

> Something strange thing happened. I was meditating according to my teacher's instruction, but, aaah, that really I didn't accepted as, aaah, the way I want, but anyway I did whatever they asked me to do and I realized something like I was falling asleep while meditating, everything stopped, and, aaah, my ... (Q.3). ... yes that experience is, it's like total blank, it's like dead or slept, it's a big gap (Q.8). ... It's a gulf, something like that; I mean I couldn't label any more (Q.9). ... I was seated. They asked me to put label as much as possible, but thoughts are coming, sensations are coming, at that time so much going on picture, the only thing I can say "knowing knowing" that much, and something I can't put the exact label, but so much coming in. But after some time I couldn't do that even, then stopped somewhere, I don't know what happened, it's like the sleep, then again it came, then again it died (Q.11). I looked back and thought I was sleeping ... the mind refused to accept it as something special but still I went and reported it to the teacher (Q.3). ... I don't think I, I still think that I slept. I couldn't label that's the thing. I, I couldn't label (Q.18). ... But later, then I realized this is something like, if it is not sleeping, it is "non-becoming" (Q.4).

His next significant spiritual experience is expressed as follows and it is possible that this experience triggered off the attainment of the fruit of once-returning. He was doing walking meditation in his *kuṭī* one rainy night during thunder and lightning. Lightening struck the floor of his *kuṭī* and the floor cracked right in front of him, by his foot. For a moment he was frightened and shocked but immediately as he has trained himself to do, he looked into his mind. The mind went totally blank for a moment, just like his experience which triggered off *sotāpatti-phala*. After a while he realized that he was not walking any more but standing, and then he gave his mind the command to continue with his walking meditation: "what are you doing? You are supposed to be doing walking meditation." As he started to walk there was another thunderbolt, but this time he realized that there was no shock and no fear in his mind. Again the mind went into a "blank." This way the mind experienced the "blankness," a "gap" in consciousness or "not feeling the consciousness" two to three times in quick succession. When he looked within, he realized that the mind was "not reacting" any more, he realized that there "was no fear in his mind or that fear has faded away." He says:

> Well I don't know the, whether next two fetters were breaking away or fading away ... much later, while I was walking alone, aaah, in thundering shower, inside the *kuṭī* there was a thunderbolt, I think I was petrified, I because of the lightning, petrified or shocked I don't know, I can't really remember, and immediately I thought I'm dead already and but my mind was trained to look in, it was trained. When it looked in, I didn't know where I was or standing or sitting, I can't remember the ... [not clear] It was totally blank, after some time, I can't say the period, a thought arise "aaah, what are you doing? You are supposed to be walking." But in spite of mind's wish I tried to raise the leg, another thunderbolt blasted. So (laugh) then I thought no shock this time, no fear neither, when I look into the mind, but it's still and very reluctant to act for the first command, to walking meditation, ... I walked, another thunder blasted, nothing happened, I usually, normally, usually about 2–3 hours I walk and I got wet also because for the first thunderbolt it was cracked [the roof]. (Q.61)

His third significant spiritual experience is expressed as follows. It is very likely that this experience triggered off *anāgāmi-phala*. When he was washing some dishes outside a monastery, in broad daylight at around 1 p.m., suddenly someone in his vicinity told him that there was a huge snake coming their way. The interviewee told him to let it be, that he was not concerned about it. The man, despite protests by the monk, took a stone and threw it at the snake saying, "if you are not concerned, I will show you." The snake hissed, put his hood up and came forward but stopped two metres away in front of him. Just then the monk heard the sound of some dry leaves moving behind him and then he realized that there were two more snakes coming in his direction at lightning speed. He was surrounded by three snakes, two on either side and one in front of him. Now the training he had been practising was to look within, to look into his mind. After some time a man came and shook him saying, "what are you doing? Here there are serpents and they have gone away" Then he realized that for some time his mind was totally "blank"[10], he was standing but had stopped his work, his eyes were fully open and he was conscious, fully aware, but he didn't see or hear the commotion of people shouting and the snakes going away. Others thought that he was frightened and was suffering from shock, and as a result couldn't move. But he realized that one defilement had gone forever, he got confirmation that fear was no more; "reacting power" had gone forever, there was no fear of death, so that the "mind is now bold enough to face death" (Q.82–89).

He says:

> Now I was surrounded by on either side two and in front one, three. Then what I trained was not to identify the snake but identify what is happening inside my mind. When I checked, I mean I looked in, now it is very conscious, totally blank and I didn't know I have already stopped my work what I was, I was washing some dishes outside and, aaah, I was not doing that. I think someone came after some time and shook me "what are you doing? Here there are serpents and they have gone away." They thought that I was panicky and I can't move my legs, really not so. I knew, awareness totally there but I was watching my mind, its blank (Q.84). ... I got the confirmation that I have no more fear for the death or protect anything, it's gone completely. (Q.86)

Interview No. 5

This was with a 66 year old monk who lives in a well known forest hermitage in Sri Lanka. He had been treading this Path for 12 years and it was nine years since he had entered the *Saṅgha*. His preceptor is well known and was most respected for his realized knowledge and knowledge of the *Tipiṭaka* and was considered one of the best Sri Lanka had in recent history.

His experience relating to the attainment of *sotāpatti-phala* is described as follows:

> When you commence the meditation, when you take your mind along the [meditation] object, right along the object, normally you experience various feelings. When you take the mind along these feelings further and further, on this object itself, along the object itself, there arises a very strong feeling. At this point when you go along contemplating this feeling, following this feeling, then thereafter you come across a fine experience, you realize that this is a "fine point"... (Q.8) generally like a "tapering off" [*gevaadameemak*] ... (Q.9) at this point in time you don't feel the oppressive nature of these five aggregates, "feeling" got nullified [*vedanava ahosiveemak*] (Q.10). ... With this experience, having enjoyed it for a short time, for a while, thereafter again when the mind follows the object, the mind returns to that former state again [the painful nature of the five aggregates] (Q.14).

In the interviews done by us the intensity of the religious experience relating to the attainment of a supramundane fruit varied from an overwhelming one—like an "explosion," a "big quake," a "breaking of a boundary," or a "huge operation"—to one with a moderate intensity, such as a "gap" or a "gulf" in consciousness, blanking of consciousness etc. to a very mild experience such as a "fine point ... a tapering off of feeling [*vedanaava gevaadameemak*]," nullifying of feeling [*vedanaava ahosi veemak*]. Nevertheless, all interviewees reported a specific religious experience. In Chapter 5 we will discuss the nature of this experience in detail.

Conclusion

At the commencement of this chapter we examined the two possible positions relating to the attainment of a supramundane fruit, that is, as one necessarily involving a specific experience or as a state of mind that could be declared without such experience, but by merely examining the mind to see the defilements remaining. Having set out the two possibilities, diverse evidence in support of the proposition that a supramundane fruit involves a specific religious experience was presented by us. To sum up, supramundane fruits of the Path have been declared with reference to a specific event, day, place, time, a meditation posture, or as an overwhelming feeling or experience. I conclude that a supramundane fruit entails a specific striking experience with a peak-point which I refer to in this study as the "fetter-breaking-experience."

The *Sutta*s quoted at the commencement of this chapter which leaves room for a different interpretation, (i.e. that supramundane fruit does not or does not necessarily entail a specific religious experience), refer to reflection on the state of mind which flows from such specific religious experience. Such reflection is merely to recognize the state of mind which resulted from such experience.

The said *Sutta*s (such as the *Mirror of the Dhamma Sutta*), at a glance suggest that a monk can examine at any point of time whether these qualities are within him and decide to declare, for example, Arahantship without having had a specific religious experience. However, it is noteworthy that in the *Sutta*s discussed at the commencement of this chapter, the words used are "the *bhikkhu* whose taints have been destroyed [*khīnāsavassa bhikkhuno*]" (AN IV 224) or "to the noble disciple [*ariyasāvakassa*]" (AN IV 405), For example, "When a *bhikkhu*'s taints have been destroyed, how many powers does he possess by reason of which he can claim "My taints have been destroyed?'" (p. 54) or "when a noble disciple possesses noble confidence in the Buddha, the Dhamma and the *Saṅgha*, ... if he wishes, he could by himself declare stream-entry (p. 53)." By the use of the word "taint-free *bhikkhu*" or "noble disciple," the said passages pre-suppose a *"khīnāsava"* or an *"ariyasāvaka"* status before the declarations are made about their attainment. This *khīnāsava* or *ariyasāvaka* state pre-supposes an actual destruction of the relevant taints or fetters (except for the first of the eight noble persons) which entails a specific experience. This is further confirmed by the use of the word "*paṭijānāmi*" in the said *Sutta* referring to the taint-free *bhikkhu* (p. 54). "*Paṭijānāti*" means acknowledge, to agree, approve, and consent.[11] This word suggests that here, one only acknowledges an existing situation, rather than determining the arising of a supramundane fruit afresh.

Elucidating this point further, I wish to conclude by analyzing the following two types of stanzas which are commonly found in the *Sutta*s:

1) He understands as it really is: "This is suffering" [*So idaṃ dukkhan ti yathābhutaṃ pajānāti*], ... "this is the origin of suffering," ... "this is the cessation of suffering," ... "this is the way leading to the cessation of suffering." He understands as it really is "These are the taints," ... "this is the origin of the taints," ... "the cessation of the taints," ... "the way leading to the cessation of the taints."

   When he knows and sees thus, his mind is liberated from the taint of sensuality [*Tassa evaṃ jānato evaṃ passato kāmāsavā pi cittaṃ vimuccati*], the taint of existence, the taint of ignorance. When it is liberated there comes the knowledge: "It's liberated." He understands: "destroyed is birth, the holy life has been lived, what has to be done has been done, [*vimuttasmiṃ vimuttaṃ iti ñāṇaṃ hoti, khīṇā jāti vusitaṃ brahmacariyaṃ kataṃ karaṇīiyaṃ*] there is no more for this being" (AN I 165).

2) Seeing thus, *bhikkhus*, the instructed noble disciple experiences revulsion towards contact [*phasse nibbindati*], revulsion towards feeling, revulsion towards perception ... volitional activities ... consciousness. Experiencing revulsion he becomes dispassionate. Through dispassion his mind is liberated. When it is liberated there comes the knowledge "It's liberated" [*Nibbindaṃ virajjati. virāgā vimuccati, vimuttasmiṃ vimuttamhīti ñāṇaṃ hoti*]. He understands: "destroyed is birth, the holy life has been lived, what has to be done has been done, there is no more for this being" (SN II 97).

The above sequence is a build-up towards the attainment of a supramundane fruit, in this case, towards *arahatta-phala*. That is, "his mind is released/liberated," by release comes "the knowledge that he is released/liberated." The words "mind is released" or "liberated" [*cittaṃ vimuccati*] in the above series are significant and denote the "specific striking experience" which is associated with the attainment of a supramundane fruit. However understanding the consequent state of mind comes by reviewing the state of mind and this understanding is denoted by the word "knowledge" [*vimuttasmiṃ vimuttaṃhīti ñāṇaṃ hoti*].

I conclude that a supramundane fruit necessarily invloves a specific striking experience with a peak-point, which is designated herein as the "fetter-breaking-experience."

In the next chapter we will discuss the significance of recognizing that a supramundane fruit involves a specific experience with a peak-point, on some current debates and controversies about the nature of the ultimate Buddhist religious experience.

Notes

1. "Elated, those *bhikkhus* delighted in the Blessed One's statement. And while this discourse was being spoken, the minds of the *bhikkhus* of the group of five were liberated from the taints by non-clinging [*anupādāya āsavehi cittāni vimucciṃsū ti*]" (SN III 68).
2. "While I sat in that same seat, the dust-free, stainless Dhamma-eye arose in me: 'Whatever is subject to origination is all subject to cessation'" (AN IV 210).
3. "Putting over my shoulder a robe the colour of the mango sprout, seated on an elephant's neck I entered a village to beg. Descending from the elephant's shoulder, then I felt great spiritual agitation [*saṃvegaṃ*]; I was agitated, then calm. I gained the destruction of the taints" (Thag.197–198).
4. "Covered with silver (ornaments), attended by a crowd of servant women, taking her child upon her hip, my wife approached me. And seeing her coming, the mother of my child adorned, and well dressed, like a snare of death spread out, Then wise attention [*manasikāro yoniso*] arose in me ... Then my mind was released ... The three knowledges have been obtained, The Buddha's teaching has been done" (Thag.295–298).

5. "I went forth from my cell overcome by torpor. Stepping up on to the terrace I fell on to the earth on that very spot. Rubbing my limbs, stepping up on to the terrace again, I paced up and down on the terrace. I was well concentrated inside. Then wise attention arose in me; the peril became clear, disgust with the world was established. Then my mind was released; see the essential rightness of the Dhamma. The three knowledges have been obtained; the Buddha's teaching has been done" (Thag.271–274).
6. "It is twenty-five years since I went forth. Not even for the duration of a snap of the fingers have I obtained peace of mind. Not having obtained intentness of mind, afflicted by desire for sensual pleasures, wailing with outstretched arms, I went out from the cell. Shall I ... or shall I take up a knife?. What need have I of living? How indeed should one such as I, rejecting the training die? Then taking a razor, I sat on the couch. The razor was placed around to cut my own vein. Then wise attention arose in me, the peril became clear... Then my mind was released ...The three knowledges have been obtained; The Buddha's teaching has been done" (Thag.405–410).
7. "I, a bhikkhu going to a burial ground, saw a woman cast away, thrown away in the cemetery, being eaten, full of worms. Seeing her dead and evil, some men were disgusted. (But in my case) Desire for sensual pleasure arose. Truly I was as though blind with regard to the flowing (body). Quicker than the cooking of rice I left that place. Possessed of mindfulness, attentive, I sat down on one side. Then wise attention arose in me, the peril became clear ... Then my mind was released ... The three knowledges have been obtained, the Buddha's teaching has been done" (Thag.315–319).
8. For the basis on which we conclude that these experiences resulted in the attainment of a supramundane fruits, see synopsis of each interview given in Appendix II.
9. "*Sattavisuddhi*" is a simple book based on *Rathavinīta Sutta* (MN: 24). The *Visuddhimagga* too uses the seven purifications mentioned in this *Sutta* as its basic framework; however *Visuddhimagga* has expanded this framework to include all relevant commentaries to form a comprehensive compendium of the Buddha's doctrine. Thus all books based on the idea of the seven stages of purifications of this *Sutta* cannot be considered to be a counterpart of the *Visuddhimagga*. In fact this interviewee who is a well-known meditation teacher is rather critical of the meditation practices directly based on the *Visuddhimagga*.
10. See Chapter 5 (pp. 90–102), analysis of the fetter-breaking-experience, for an analysis of the state of the mind referred to by him as a "blank mind."
11. Davids and Stede 1921–1925/2001, 395.

— 4 —

Path, Fetter-Breaking-Experience and Effect

In Chapter 3 we established that attainment of a supramundane fruit involves a specific striking religious experience with a peak-point which is referred to herein as a "fetter-breaking-experience." Based on this premise, this chapter proceeds to establish that there is a "Path, fetter-breaking-experience and effect (of the fetter-breaking-experience)" rather than "Path and its fruits." For this purpose we will consider:

1) Definitions of the word "*phala*"
2) References in the *Nikāyās* to Path, fetter-breaking-experience and effect (of the fetter-breaking-experience) as three different phenomena.
3) Implications of the thesis of "Path, fetter-breaking-experience and effect"

Definitions of the Word "*Phala*"

We will first consider the various shades of meaning attributed to this word in the dictionaries which seem to be mainly based on the commentarial understanding and usage.

Definitions Given by the Dictionaries

1) Venerable Nyānatiloka in Buddhist Dictionary—Manual of Buddhist Terms and Doctrines defines "*phala*" as:
   a) Result, effect (often together with cause [*hetu*]); e.g. the results or benefits of recluseship as in *Sāmañña-phala Sutta* (DN: 2).
   b) Path result or fruition, which denotes the moments of supramundane consciousness which flashes immediately after the moment of "path-consciousness" of a noble person. This may recur innumerable times during the practice of insight, till the attainment of the next higher path. If thus repeated they are called the "attainment of fruition" [*phala-samāpatti*] which is explained in detail in the *Visuddhimagga* chapter XXIII (Nyānatiloka 1946, 141).[1]
2) Rhys Davids and William Stede in *Pāli English Dictionary* attribute the following meanings (1921–1925/ 2001, 477):
   a) (lit.) fruit (of trees etc.) ... At Miln. [*Milindapañha*] 333, a set of 7 fruits is used metaphorically, in simile of the Buddha's fruit shop, i.e. *sotāpatti-phala, sakadāgāmi-phala, anāgāmi-phala, arahatta-phala, suññata-phala samāpatti* (Cp. Cpd.[2] 70) *animitta-phala samāpatti, appaṇihita-phala samāpatti.*
   b) A testicle ...

c) (fig.) fruit, result, consequence, fruition, blessing. As technical term with reference to the Path and the progressive attainment (enjoyment, fruition) of Arahantship, it is used to denote the realization of having attained each stage of the *sotāpatti, sakadāgami* etc. (the four supramundane fruits of the Path).

It further illustrates that:

i. in the phrase "*magga, phala, nibbāna*" used frequently in exegetical literature, it immediately precedes *Nibbāna.*

ii. as "*agga-phala*" it is almost identical with Arahantship.

iii. frequently it is combined with "*vipāka*" to denote the stringent conception of "consequence" e.g. at DN I 27 and 58; III 160.

iv. as "profit" almost synonymous with "ānisaṃsa" in the sense of fruition, benefit (at DN III 132).

v. "*phalaṭṭha*" (stationed in fruition) i.e. enjoying the result or fruition of the Path (Cp. Cpd. 50) Miln.342.

In addition:

vi. "At Dhp-a I.110 "*magga-phala*" (the fruit of the Path i.e. attainment of the foundation or first step of Arahantship), is identical with *sotāpatti-phala* on p.113." (Rhys Davids,William Stede, 1921–1925/2001, 512)

Reference to "*Phala*" in the *Visuddhimagga*

According to the *Visuddhimagga,* the fruit is a moment of signless supramundane consciousness which flashes a few times immediately after the moment of path consciousness (Vism.XXII,15–16/Vism.675 and XXIII.4/Vism.820).

In general both in *Sutta*s and the commentaries, when not referring to a kammic result, the term "*phala*" has been used to denote an attainment at a crucial juncture or end of the noble Path, consequences or benefits of the Path [*ānisaṃsa*], a fruition of the Path and in the commentaries, in addition to the aforesaid, it denotes the supramundane moments of consciousness of a noble person.

The Term "*Phala*" as Used in this Work

The term "*phala*" or "fruit" has been used in this work to mean one of the four supramundane fruits or noble fruits of the Noble Eightfold Path, i.e. the fruit that is stream-entry, once-returning, non-returning and Arahantship [*sotāpatti-phala, sakadagāmi-phala, anāngāmi- phala, arahatta-phala*]. In this work it specifically means the *general state of mind* of the relevant noble person, i.e. the knowledge attained by such a person, the qualities and powers developed in such a mind and the state of the fetters (whether fetters are reduced or eradicated) in such a mind which are the benefits or consequences of the Path or the fruition of the Path. By the term "*phala*" or "fruit" as used in this work, we do not mean the moments of "supramundane consciousnesses" referred to in the *Visuddhimagga* as stated above. In the introductory chapter I have already justified in terms of the *Sutta*s, my definition of the word "*phala*" as the general state of mind (Chapter 1, p. 20), however we hold that this state necessarily involves a momentary "fetter-breaking-experience."

Accordingly, "fruit that is stream-entry [*sotāpatti-phala*]" means the general state of mind of the second noble person. The scope of this word includes the absence of the three lower fetters and the knowledge appropriate to a stream-enterer such as the knowledge of impermanence, dependent origination etc.,[3] qualities and powers that arise in a stream-enterer's mind such as the unshaken confidence in the Buddha, the Dhamma and the *Saṅgha* and the virtue dear to a noble one etc.[4] Similarly, the fruit that is once-returning [*sakadāgāmi-phala*], means the general state of mind of the fourth noble person and means the absence of the first three fetters and the reduction of desire for sense pleasures and ill-will. The fruit that is non-returning [*anāgāmi-phala*] means a mind devoid of the five lower fetters and the fruit that is Arahantship [*arahatta-phala*] means the general state of mind of an *Arahant*, that is, a mind devoid of all ten fetters, and the respective knowledge, qualities and powers appropriate to these noble persons (SN V 356).

References in the *Nikāyās* to "Path, Fetter-Breaking-Experience and Effect (of the Fetter-Breaking-Experience)" as Three Different Phenomena

Based on the premise that a supramundane fruit includes a specific religious experience with a peak-point, in this section we proceed to establish that the *Nikāyas* recognize the series "Path, fetter-breaking-experience and effect" as against "Path and its fruits." For this purpose let us examine some common occurrences in the *Suttas*. By the term "effect" we mean the general state of mind of the noble person. The *Visuddhimagga* refers to "reviewing knowledge," in which a person looks back and understands what they have attained (Vism.XXII.19–20/ Vism.789), that is, a stream-enterer looks back and understands that the first three fetters have been destroyed in him. By the term "effect" here, we do not mean the said "reviewing knowledge" in the same sense as in the *Visuddhimagga;* here it means simply the *general state of mind* which ensues subsequent to a fetter-breaking-experience, which *includes* reviewing.

Liberation and the Knowledge and Vision of Liberation [*Vimutti* and *Vimutti-Ñāṇadassana*]

There are references in the *Suttas* to "liberation" [*vimutti*] and the "knowledge and vision of liberation" [*vimutti-ñāṇadassana*]. These two have been listed as two different qualities out of five qualities that a gift worthy monk is endowed with (AN III 134). The other three are *sīla, samādhi and paññā.* Here "knowledge and vision" need not have been specifically spelt out as they are necessarily the result of "liberation." This distinction has been made because these two are distinctly different phenomena. I propose that here "*vimutti*" denotes the fetter-breaking-experience and "*vimutti-ñāṇadassana*" denotes the effect of *vimutti,* that is, the state of mind which flows from such fetter-breaking-experience. Based on this passage we can conclude that the *Suttas* recognize the series "Path, fetter-breaking-experience and effect" as against "Path and its fruits."

A Fruit and its Benefit [*Phala* and *Phalānisaṃsa*]

Similarly there are references in the *Suttas* to "*phala*" and "*phalānisaṃsa*" as follows:

> Bhikkhus, these five things, when developed and cultivated, have liberation of mind as their fruit (*cetovimutti-phalā*], liberation of mind as their fruit and benefit [*cetovimutti-phalānisaṃsā*]; they have liberation by wisdom as their fruit [*paññāvimutti-phalā*], liberation by wisdom as their fruit and benefit [*paññāvimutti-phalānisaṃsa*]. (AN III 84)

There is a similar reference to "*cetovimutti-phala* and *cetovimutti-phalānisaṃsa*" and "*paññāvimutti-phala* and *paññāvimutti-phalānisaṃsa*" in the *Mahāvedalla Sutta* of the *Majjhima Nikāya* (MN I 294). These passages make a distinction between "*phala*" and "*phalānisaṃsa*," the fruit and the benefits of the fruit. One might wonder why such a distinction is made by the Buddha when *ānisaṃsa*, benefit or advantage could have easily been included in the "fruit" [*phala*]; after all, such advantages are essentially a fruit of following the Path. Tradition takes it that these are different ways of saying the same thing. However it is also possible that by using two different terms, the Buddha meant two different phenomena as given in the earlier passage (AN III 134), that is, "liberation and knowledge and vision of liberation." I propose that this distinction is made because in this passage the "fruit" [*phala*] refers to the fetter-breaking-experience which heralds the dawn of a supramundane fruit, and "benefits of the fruit" [*phalānisaṃsa*] refer to the effect of the fetter-breaking-experience. Given our definition of "*phala*" to mean the general state of the mind, what this interpretation means is that, there is a "fruit" (fetter-breaking-experience) which is part of and the start of a "fruit" that is the general state of a person. On the face of it, this sounds rather awkward. But the term "*phala*" has been used here to denote the fetter-breaking-experience as the fetter-breaking-experience is the culmination of the path leading up to a supramundane fruit. However *Sutta*s such as these are few in number, but particularly AN III134 is clear enough to highlight that the fetter-breaking-experience and the knowledge that ensues are two different phenomena. It seems that whilst in general the word "*phala*" has been used in the *Sutta*s to mean the *general state of mind* of a noble person (Chapter 1, p. 20), on a few occasions the same term has been used to refer to the fetter-breaking-experience. Perhaps it is based on these, that the *Visuddhimagga* developed the idea of a "momentary" *phala* as against *phala* as the general state of mind.

There are a few other such references in the *Sutta*s which denote a "fetter-breaking-experience and effect." The following passage too suggests such a sequence:

> Having contacted with the body
> The deathless element, which is asset-less
> And realized the relinquishment of assets
> Being taint-free, the perfectly enlightened one
> Proclaims the sorrow-less, stainless state.[5]

Here, "the deathless element" [*amata-dhātu*] seems to mean the fetter-breaking-experience which marks the dawn of the supramundane fruit that is Arahantship, and "the relinquishment of assets and being taint-free," are the effects, that is, the general state of mind of the *Arahant*.

From the *Sutta*s discussed above I conclude that the *Sutta*s recognize the sequence of "Path, fetter-breaking-experience and effect" (the resultant state of mind), as against "Path and its fruits."

Implications of the Thesis of "Path, Fetter-Breaking-Experience and Effect"

The significance of this sequence of "Path, fetter-breaking-experience and effect" in relation to some of the longstanding debates on some aspects of the Buddhist religious experiences cannot be ignored. Below, we will examine its implications on the debate amongst scholars on whether or not *Nibbāna* is a transcendent reality and whether *Nibbāna* is ineffable.

Nibbāna, Transcendence and Ineffability

Theists believe that the ultimate experience in religion is the union with God which transcends phenomenal reality. Due to his transcendent nature, God is considered ineffable. That is, it is not possible to express such experience in words: words are completely inapplicable to it (Tilakaratne 1993, 142). The parallel claim in Buddhism says that the ultimate religious experience in Buddhism is to attain *Nibbāna* which transcends phenomenal reality. In other words this claim says that *Nibbāna* is the transcendent in Buddhism. The difference between the two is that the former is personal and the latter is impersonal. There is a tradition of Buddhist scholars who maintain that *Nibbāna* is the Buddhist Transcendent.[6]

The following statement is quoted by almost all who think *Nibbāna* is a transcendent reality in support of their claim:

> Monks there is a not born, not become, not made, and not compounded. Monks if that not born, not become, not made, not compounded were not, no escape from the born, become, made, compounded would be known here. But monks since there is a not born, not become, not made, not compounded, therefore an escape from the born, become, made, compounded is known.[7]

The significance of the above statement is in the adjectives that have been used to describe *Nibbāna*, particularly the adjective "uncompounded" [*asaṅkhata*] which means that *Nibbāna* is not a compounded or conditioned phenomenon [*asaṅkhata*]. The compounded phenomena or *saṅkhāras* are causally conditioned and dependently originated. To say that *Nibbāna* is *asaṅkhata* has been taken to mean that this law does not apply to everything, but only to what is impermanent and *dukkha*. If Buddhism holds that *Nibbāna* is over and above the ordinary reality, this automatically amounts to holding that *Nibbāna* is a transcendent reality (Tilakaratne 1993, 75). This particular statement has been taken by some as providing conclusive evidence in support of the transcendent interpretation.[8]

Further, many passages describing the after-death status of an *Arahant* is often quoted in support of interpreting *Nibbāna* as a transcendental reality. The after death status of Venerable Bāhiya is described as follows:

> Where water, earth, fire, and air do not find a footing
> There the stars do not shine and the sun spreads not its lustre
> The moon does not appear resplendent there
> And no darkness is to be found there.
> When the sage, the Brahmin with wisdom understands by himself
> Then is he freed from form and formless
> And from pleasure and pain.[9]

Another passage often used in favour of this argument is as follows:

> The Tathāgata is liberated from reckoning in terms of material form ... feeling ... perception ... volitional activities ... consciousness, Vaccha, he is profound, immeasurable, hard to fathom as is the ocean. [*gambhīro appameyyo duppariyogāho seyyathā pi mahāsamuddo*]. (MN I 487–488)

The two concepts, transcendence and ineffability are closely related. In the sense that if something is unknowable, it has to be ineffable, that is, one cannot say anything at all about it. The same passages quoted in support of "transcendence" are quoted in support of the argument that *Nibbāna* is ineffable.[10]

Of the scholars who have entered this debate on *Nibbāna*, transcendence and ineffability, K.N. Jayatilleke thinks that such a metaphysical reality exists and it is realizable. He says that what is transempirical cannot be empirically described or understood but it can be realized and attained.[11] He cites the Buddha's answer to the question "is there anything else after complete detachment from and cessation from the six spheres of experiences?" (*channaṃ ... phassāyatanaṃ asesavirāganirodhā atth'aññaṃ, kiñcī ti*]" (AN II 161), which is, "do not ask thus" [*mā h'evam*]: the question is to be set aside [*ṭhapanīya pañha*]. This is not an outright rejection of the question with a "no," and Jayatilleke explains that it is because the question imputes to the transcendent reality, the characteristics of existence, non-existence etc. which have a valid application only within the realm of experience (Jayatilleke 1963, 292–293).

Asanga Tilakaratne in *Nirvāṇa and Ineffability* writes:

> It is noticeable that the general trend in comparative studies of religion has been to identify a meeting point common to all religions. It is believed that this meeting point is transcendence. Accordingly God, undifferentiated unity, *nirvāṇa*, sūnyatā and satori etc. are grouped together and claimed to be similar in being transcendental. (Tilakaratne 1993, 76)

Tilakaratne concludes that (the highest) Buddhist religious experience is unique and cannot be compared with the religious experience of the theist or the monist, as in the popular classification of religions, in the sense that the ultimate Buddhist religious experience can be explained rationally, conceptually defined and analyzed. Analyzing the experience of "*Nirvāṇa*" he suggests that Buddhist religious experience is neither transcendental nor ineffable. Citing the doctrine of dependent origination he argues that there cannot be an independent transcendent reality and that the same philosophical assumption applies to Buddhist religious experience (Tilakaratne 1993, 21–26). His attempt in *Nirvāṇa and Ineffability* is to highlight the "non-mystical" character of the Buddhist Path and religious experiences (i.e. it highlights that the experience is not a strange, mysterious, or an unexplainable one). In support of his argument he falls back on the definitions of *Nibbāna* such as "*Nibbāna* is the extinction of greed hatred and delusion (S V 251)." He further argues that the feelings of the person who is freed from suffering have been described with the metaphor of being cool [*sītibhūta*] and pacified [*nibbuta*] (as in Thig.16 and 34). Thus *Nirvāṇa* is basically characterized as the calm, cool, serene and pacified mentality versus the heat and the fire of defilements (Tilakaratne 1993, 57). He cites the following simile given in the *Sāmaññaphala Sutta* in support of his argument that *Nibbāna* is not a mystical experience:

> Just as if, in the midst of mountains there were a pond, clear as a polished mirror, where a man with good eyesight standing on the bank could see oyster-shells ...

> And he might think: This pond is clear ... there are oyster shells... Just so with the mind concentrated ... he knows: "Birth is finished, the holy life has been lived, done is what had to be done, there is nothing further." (DN I 84/Tilakaratne 1993, 64)

Comparing this with the theistic type of experience, Tilakaratne argues that there is no revelation or grace here, the follower is fully aware of what is taking place. When the mind is liberated from defilements, he has the knowledge that his mind is liberated (MN I 249). Based on these non-mystical lines and on declarations such as "*sītibhūtasmi nibbuto*" of *Arahant*s he concludes that *Nibbāna* is not ineffable.[12]

However Bhikkhu Bodhi in a review of Tilakaratne's *Nirvāṇa and Ineffability* writes:

> Even within the Pāli tradition alone interpretations of *Nibbāna* are bewildering in their diversity, ranging from postulations of a metaphysical absolute to a conviction of personal annihilation. Despite vast differences, however, most expositors of Buddhist thought would probably concur on two propositions concerning the final Buddhist goal: (i) *Nibbāna* is transcendental, a reality in some way beyond the phenomenal world and (ii) this reality is ineffable, inexpressible in words.
>
> (Bodhi 1996, 163)

Bhikkhu Bodhi concludes that *Nibbāna* is indeed a distinct object of knowledge on the basis of which defilements are destroyed and to which *Arahant* has special access in an extraordinary sphere of contemplation that the unenlightened person can hardly think of without bafflement. Further, that from the standpoint of the Pāli commentaries, *Nibbāna* is neither the simple act of destroying the defilements nor the purified condition of mind that results from their destruction, but the undefiled reality, the deathless element [*amata-dhātu*], in dependence on which the destruction of defilements comes about (Bodhi 1996, 166). In the opinion of Bhikkhu Bodhi, though texts dealing with the "metaphysical" aspects of *Nibbāna* are certainly few in number, such texts are straightforward enough to leave little doubt that *Nibbāna* is a transcendental reality which serves as a distinctive object of meditative knowledge (Bodhi 1996, 170).

Venerable Ñāṇananda, commenting on the passage at Ud.9 discussed above, rejects the commentarial interpretation of this verse, as a description of the "place" [*yattha āpo ca paṭhavī tejo vāyo na ghādati*] where Venerable Bāhiya who was an *Arahant* "went" after *parinibbāna*. Ñāṇananda says, that this is a reference to "non-manifestative consciousness" [*anidassana viññāṇa*] which Bāhiya has realized here and now, in his concentration of Arahantship, or it is the *arahatta-phala-samādhi* (Ñāṇananda 2005, III, 334–335). Referring to the Ud.80 passage which is quoted in support of *Nibbāna* as a transcendent reality, "monks there is a not born, not become, not made, not compounded ...," Ñāṇananda says:

> The commentator, the Ven. Dhammapala, pays little attention to the word *"idha"* "here," in this passage, which needs to be emphasized ... The prospect of stepping out from decay and death here and now in this very world has to be asserted for its novelty, which is why the declaration opens with the word *"atthi"* "there is." However most of the scholars who tried to interpret this passage in their discussions on *Nibbāna*, instead of laying stress on the word *"idha"* "here," emphasize the opening word *"atthi"* "there is," to prove that *Nibbāna* is some form of reality absolutely existing somewhere. (Ñāṇananda 2005, III, 311)

Further answering the question, "is *Nibbāna* an absolute, *paramattha*?," he says it is not a *paramattha* in the sense of an absolute. It is *paramattha* only in the sense that it is the highest good, *paraṃa attha.* This is the sense in which the word was used in the discourses, e.g. Sn. v. 219 [*aññāya lokaṃ paramatthadassiṃ*—him that has realized (the nature of) the world, visioning the highest weal], Thag.748 [*ko so pāraṃgato loke*—he who has gone to the far show in the word], and as in "*āraddhaviriyo paramatthapattiyā*" (Sn. v. 68), "with steadfast energy for the attainment of the highest goal," the *Sutta* speaks of highest good to be attained (Ñāṇananda 2005, III, 285).

Quoting "*rāgakkhayo dosakkhayo mohakkhayo—idaṃ vuccati nibbāna*" (SN IV 371), "the destruction of attachment, hatred and delusion—this is called *Nibbāna*" from the *Nibbāna Sutta* of the *Asaṅkhata Saṃyutta*, Ñāṇananda says that the destruction of craving itself is *Nibbāna*. Criticizing the commentarial interpretation to this phrase "*Nibbānaṃ āgamma rāgādayo khīṇāti ekameva Nibbānaṃ rāgakkhayo dosakkhayo mohakkhayo ti vuccati,*" "It is on coming to *Nibbāna* that attachment etc. are destroyed," it is the same one *Nibbāna* that is called the destruction of attachment, the destruction of hatred, the destruction of delusion" (Vibh-a 53), i.e. that destruction of craving alone is not *Nibbāna* [*khayamattam na Nibbānaṃ*], Ñāṇananda says:

> It seems that the deeper connotations of the word *Nibbāna* in the context of *paṭicca-samuppāda* were not fully appreciated by the commentators. And that is why they went in search of a new etymology. They were too shy of the implications of the word "extinction." Probably to avoid the charge of nihilism they felt compelled to reinterpret certain key passages on *Nibbāna*. They conceived *Nibbāna* as something existing out there in its own right. They would not say where, but sometimes they would even say everywhere. With an undue grammatical emphasis they would say that it is on coming to that *Nibbāna* that lust and other defilements are abandoned ... To project *Nibbāna* into a distance and to hope that craving will be destroyed only on seeing it, is something like trying to build a stair—to a palace one cannot yet see. (Ñāṇananda 2003, I, 13–14)

He further quotes in support of his argument that when the holy life [*brahmacariya*] is lived to the full, it culminates in *Nibbāna* (SN III 189), is merged in *Nibbāna*, its consummation is *Nibbāna*. Based on this *Sutta*, comparing it to a river merging in the sea, he concludes that where the holy life is lived out to the full, *Nibbāna* is right there (Ñāṇananda 2003, I, 17). In general Ñāṇananda's view is that *Nibbāna* is transcendental only in the sense that it transcends defilements. In other words his stand is that *Nibbāna* is not a "transcendental reality" existing out there in its own right as argued above by Bhikkhu Bodhi. I agree with Ñāṇananda's view that *Nibbāna* is not a "transcendental reality" existing "out there" in its own right. It is a state "relative" to the conditioned objects, i.e. *absence* or *cessation* of conditioned objects, which reflects the application of the term "*idappaccayatā,*" specific conditionality or relatedness between cause and effect (See pp. 96–99 for the explanation of the fetter-breaking experience).

The Findings of the Field Research

Against the backdrop of the above arguments for and against *Nibbāna* as having a transcendental nature, our fieldwork has highlighted both a fetter-breaking-experience with an apparent mystical nature (in the sense of a mysterious or a strange experience) and also the non-mystical, naturalistic nature of the "effect" of such a fetter-breaking-experience. This is so, not only in relation to the fetter-breaking-experience of *arahatta-phala,* but even in relation to the lower fruits of the Path. In the following two excerpts, the fetter-breaking-experience has been referred to as the mind going "to a different place" and as a "mystery" to the world of senses.

Interview No. 1

Describing the nature of the fetter-breaking-experience of the attainment of the fruit of stream-entry as experienced by him, the interviewee says "for a second, for a minute my mind got cut off," the mind "went in" to a different place, the mind "didn't continue," he couldn't see anything, he didn't feel the consciousness. Describing the fetter-breaking-experience relating to his attainment of *arahatta-phala* he says, his mind "went in for one second then arose and stopped." He realized that all defilements got cut off.[13] Despite describing his fetter-breaking-experience as a "mystical" one, this interviewee describes his concept of *Nibbāna* as "fully no more defilements," (i.e. as destruction of all defilements).

Interview No. 3

Referring to the nature of the fetter-breaking-experience of the attainment of stream-entry, the interviewee says that it is not something that can be explained in terms of the five physical sense-bases, as several stages before you come to this experience the mind escapes from these sense-bases. When asked whether there was sight, sound, touch, smell etc. or whether he experienced feeling, perception, volitional activities, he says there was all these, but it is not something that can be explained in terms of (physical) sense bases as several stages before you come to this experience, the mind escapes from these (Q.8) and goes on to say that this experience is the "biggest mystery to the world of senses."[14]

In general all our interviewees have described the fetter-breaking-experience as "beyond the sense-bases." To our specific question as to their concept of *Nibbāna,* whilst most have talked in terms of the "effect" such as knowledge gained or consequences, i.e. "Fully understanding the reality with regard to the aggregates" (Interview No. 5), "Permanent cessation (of becoming)" (Interview No. 2), "Finished with *saṃsāra,* not being reborn" (Interview No. 6) etc., one talked in terms of the fetter-breaking-experience as "*avedayita,* cannot be experienced with the body and it is some sort of a non-human experience" (Interview No. 3). These interviewees being *aryans* though not *Arahants,* ought to understand *Nibbāna* in terms of principles (See p. 163). Hence the question "what is your concept of *Nibbāna?*" highlights the variation in the responses, some thinking in terms of the fetter-breaking-experience and some others in terms of its effect.

In Chapter 5, I have substantiated the fetter-breaking-experience in terms of the *Sutta*s and highlighted that it has validity in terms of the texts (See pp. 96–100). Hence I will not undertake a discussion on it here. The nature of the fetter-breaking-experience at different stages of the Path and the subsequent re-experiencing of it will be discussed in detail in Chapter 5. The fetter-breaking-experience is reported by the interviewees of this study to be momentary at the time of attaining a supramundane fruit, however when it is re-experienced (the *phala-samāpatti* described in the *Visuddhimagga*), it lasts for a much longer period. Both at the momentary stage and the re-experiencing stage, the nature of the fetter-breaking-experience is reported by these interviewees as identical, in that, for example, the five sense-bases are not active.[15] Hence it appears to be a mysterious, unexplainable experience. Perhaps this has led to *Nibbāna* being interpreted as a transcendental reality.

This debate amongst academics on issues such as "transcendence and ineffability" of *Nibbāna* is, I hold, a result of not recognizing the significance of the sequence "Path, fetter-breaking-experience and effect" as against "Path and its fruits," or not recognizing at all that a supramundane fruit involves both a fetter-breaking-experience and its effect. Based on the above thesis of "Path, fetter-breaking-experience and effect," I propose that the references in the texts to *Nibbāna* as "a not born, not become, not made, not compounded" (Ud.80), or "sphere wherein there is neither earth, nor water, nor fire, not air ..." (Ud.9),which are quoted above in support of the thesis that *Nibbāna* is a transcendent reality, is a reference to the fetter-breaking-experience at the dawn of a supramundane fruit of *arahatta-phala.* In contrast, references such as "Having plucked out craving root and all, I have become cool, quenched" (Thag.15), "The three knowledges have been realized, the Buddha's teaching has been done" (Thag.30), or "I have attained peace of mind" (Thag.91), or the definition of *Nibbāna* as "extinction of lust, hatred and delusion" etc. which are cited in support of the thesis that *Nibbāna* is neither transcendental nor ineffable, are references to the "effect," the state of mind that flows from such fetter-breaking-experience.

Those who argue that *Nibbāna* is ineffable or a transcendental reality beyond the phenomenal world do so taking the fetter-breaking-experience of *arahatta-phala* as *Nibbāna* and those who conclude that *Nibbāna* is not ineffable and not transcendental phenomenon do so taking its "effect," the knowledge, qualities, powers etc. that flow from such fetter-breaking-experience as *Nibbāna.*[16]

I conclude that a supramundane fruit essentially comprises of two elements, the fetter-breaking-experience and its effect, the latter being the living experience of the *Arahant*. Therefore *Nibbāna* being a supramundane fruit, its nature cannot be explained based on only one of these components of *arahatta-phala* leaving out the other, but both elements have to be combined.

Further the Theravāda tradition takes it that the four paths and the four fruits take as its object, the timeless unconditioned *Nibbāna.*[17] For this study, in effect this means that the signless fetter-breaking-experience takes the timeless unconditioned *Nibbāna* as its object or the fetter-breaking-experience is that which sees the timeless unconditioned *Nibbāna.*

However this study has highlighted another possible scenario. That is, at the point of the fetter-breaking-experience (of all four fruits), all conditioned phenomena cease to manifest and the consciousness takes as its object, the *absence* or the cessation of conditioned phenomena, that is, the signless state.[18] This state of mind is reflected in the stanza "not attending to any sign and attending to the signless element [*sabba-nimittānaṃ ca amanasikāro, animittāya ca dhātuyā manasikāro*]" (MN I 296). Having become an *Arahant*, when the fetter-breaking-experience is re-experienced by the *Arahant* subsequently, he "perceives" or "understands" this experience as "This is peaceful ... sublime ... *Nibbāna* [*etaṃ santaṃ etaṃ panītaṃ... Nibbānaṃ*]"(AN V 318–319).[19]

But when the *Visuddhimagga* says the four paths have *Nibbāna* as their object (Vism. XXII.5/Vism.785), it holds that at this point, the consciousness of all noble persons (from stream-enterer onwards), takes an object over and above the said "signlessness" reflected in the consciousness and that state is understood as "*Nibbāna.*" However nowhere in the *Suttas* do we find that the Buddha has said "not attending to any sign and attending to the *Nibbāna* element" [*sabba-nimittānaṃ ca amanasikāro, Nibbānāya ca dhātuyā manasikāro*]. Therefore I conclude that at this point (at the point of the fetter-breaking-experience), the consciousness takes the "signlessness" as its object and not any other object over and above the signless state.

Nibbāna has been defined by the Buddha in its ultimate sense as destruction of craving [*taṅhakkhayo*] (SN V 421) or security from bondage [*yogakkhemaṃ*] (MN I 167) which is a general state of mind. The *Sutta* passages such as that on *Nibbāna* and *paṭicca-samuppāda* being beyond the sphere of reason (MN I 167) should be understood as, for those who are delighting in attachments [*ālayaramā ālayaratā*], it is difficult to understand *Nibbāna* by *mere reasoning,* (i.e. it has to be personally experienced, not to be intellectually debated or defined). Further, although *Nibbāna* is not dependently originated and consequently not subject to change, the cessation aspect of dependent origination or "specific conditionality" [*idappaccayatā*], a term which is seen to accompany the words "dependent origination" (SN II 65) applies to *Nibbāna* equally, with reference to the "cessation" aspect of it, in the sense of "when that does not exist, that does not come to be; with the cessation of this, that ceases [*imasmiṃ asati, idaṃ na hoti, imassa nirodhā idaṃ nirujjhati*]" (SN II 65) that is, with the destruction of craving, hatred and delusion, there is cessation of suffering [*dukkha-nirodho*] (*Nibbāna*), or with the end of suffering, there is cessation of being [*bhava-nirodho*] (*Nibbāna*). We conclude that *Nibbāna* is not a "transcendental reality" in the sense of "existing out there" in its own right, independent of the person who experiences it.

So far we discussed that, based on *Sutta* passages such as Ud.9/Ud.80 etc. and the *Visuddhimagga,* that the Theravāda tradition takes *Nibbāna* to be timeless unconditioned transcendent reality, which exists independent of the person who realizes it. However, the *Sutta* passages quoted in favour of this viewpoint concern what we hold as the "fetter-breaking-experience." We also discussed that Tilakaratne's conclusion is that *Nibbāna* is the destruction of craving, hatred and delusion itself, which we hold as the "effect" of the fetter-breaking-experience. However we conclude that *Nibbāna* encompasses both, the fetter-breaking-experience of *arahatta-phala* and its effect, (i.e. the general state of mind of an *Arahant*) and it is not a transcendent reality lying "out there" in its own right, independent of the experiencer.

Eight Types of Persons [*Aṭṭha Purisa Puggalā*]

The sequence of "Path, fetter-breaking-experience and effect" has a bearing on the issue as to who is a "person practising for a supramundane fruit" as referred to in the texts. The texts refer to eight types of persons as follows (AN IV 292):

1) The one who is practising for the realization of the stream-entry-fruit and the stream-enterer [*sotāpatti-phala-sacchikiriyāya paṭipanno* and *sotāpanno*]

2) The one who is practising for the realization of the once-returning-fruit and the once-returner [*sakadāgāmi-phala-sacchikiriyāya paṭipanno* and *sakadāgāmī*]
3) The one who is practising for the realization of the non-returning-fruit and the non-returner [*anāgāmi-phala-sacchikiriyāya paṭipanno* and *anāgāmī*]
4) The one who is practising for the realization of *arahatta* and the *Arahant* [*arahattāya paṭipanno* and *Arahā*].

The question arises as to whether these eight types are found in the Buddha's dispensation in different people or whether all eight are found in one and the same person in his practice on the way towards Arahantship. The general understating is that all eight are found in the same person in the sense that one may pass through all eight stages gradually.

In Chapter 3 we discussed the attainment of the four supramundane fruits as being marked by specific experiences. Therefore attainment of the four supramundane fruits can be identified in terms of time and place. If the Buddha has spelt out eight types of persons making up the *sāvaka-Saṅgha* as above, we should be able to identify the attainment of the states of all eight of them in terms of time and place. The texts however are not clear as to the exact point at which one becomes a "person practising for the stream-entry-fruit" or once- returning-fruit etc.

Attempting to explain this first kind of person, the *Visuddhimagga* defines a person who is practising for the first noble fruit, that is, *sotāpatti-phala-sacchikiriyāya paṭipanno,* as one who has attained the *sotāpatti-magga* and the path is defined in the *Visuddhimagga* as a "momentary path." According to the *Visuddhimagga*, the path lasts only an instant, and is a signless momentary supramundane consciousness which arises immediately prior to the arising of a supramundane fruit (Vism. XXII.11/Vism.787). We do not agree with the *Visuddhimagga* that what is meant in the *Suttas* by "Path" is a momentary state. As defined in our introductory chapter, our position is that the Noble Eightfold Path as included in *sīla, samādhi, paññā* is developed over a period of time and includes the practice at an advance, intensified or supramundane level.[20] Hence the question arises as to who is a "person practising for the fruit"?

The general understanding is that a noble person practising for the realization of the once-returning-fruit is simply the stream-enterer who is moving towards the fruit of once-returning. If this is the case, considering our position that the fruit of stream-entry or once returning is the "general state of mind" of such stream-enterer or the once-returner[21] and not a momentary state, there would be no difference between a stream-enterer and a "person practising for the realization of once-returning." This would be because, having entered the Path and being endowed with the spiritual faculties (SN V 196–197), every stream-enterer would immediately and naturally commence moving towards the fruit that is once-returning and thus becomes a person "practising for the fruit that is once-returning." However until the attainment of the next supramundane fruit, the "general state of mind" of such person is only that of a stream-enterer. If so, such a person, in addition to becoming "one practising for the once-returning-fruit" would also be a stream-enterer. Hence this argument in effect reduces the number of noble persons to five and not eight, as some of the stages would overlap as aforesaid. The five would be: a) one practising for the stream-entry-fruit, b) the stream-enterer and one practising for the once-returner-fruit, c) the once-returner and the one practising for the non-returner-fruit, d) the non-returner and one practising for the Arahantship-fruit, and e) the *Arahant.*

For the Buddha to have specifically spelt out eight types of noble persons, the eight ought to actually be different from each other, that is, the underlying tendencies have to be different from each other. Hence there has to be something that distinguishes a stream-enterer from a noble person practising for the stream-entry-fruit.

Harvey in a recent study on noble *sāvakas* concludes that first of the eight persons is a "trainee" noble person (Harvey 2013). Further Harvey, in a detailed study on the nature of the *ariya magga* [*lokuttara magga*] in the *Suttas* as against the momentary *magga* in the commentaries (Harvey 2014), concludes that the *ariya magga* is a state when a person is "wholly taken up with the Dhamma," it is "a basic orientation in a state of open readiness that is certain to bring the relevant noble fruit sometime in the current life." Explaining the way a "person practising for stream-entry" conducts himself, amongst other teachings, Harvey refers to the four factors for stream-entry [*sotāpattiyaṅgas*], i.e. association with genuine people [*sappurisas*], hearing the true Dhamma [*sadhamma*], wise attention [*yoniso manasikāra*], and practice in accordance with the Dhamma [*dhammānudhamma-paṭipadā*] (SN V 347), and the description of one who is "practising in accordance with the Dhamma" [*dhammānudhamma-paṭipanna*] is one who "speaks only of Dhamma when he speaks, thinks only of Dhamma when he thinks [*vitakketi*] so as to have equanimity, mindfulness and clear comprehension" (It.81).

I agree with Harvey's conclusion that the *ariya magga* is a state in which a person is wholly taken up with the Dhamma. Yet the issue of identifying the beginning of the noble path remains unanswered. A person becomes a stream-enterer with the breaking of the first three fetters and becomes a once-returner having reduced the next two fetters. Is there a point of time at which one passes from the status of a stream-enterer to the status of a noble person practising for the realization of the once-returning-fruit, or one passes from the status of an ordinary worldling to the status of the one practising for the realization of the stream-entry-fruit?. The fact that a distinction has been made in the texts between the ordinary worldling, one person practising for the stream-entry-fruit, the stream-enterer and one practising for the once-returning-fruit suggests that there has to be a point at which one passes from one status to the other.

In our search for an answer to this question, the definition of two more types of people mentioned in the texts, namely, "faith-follower" [*saddhānusārī*] and the "Dhamma-follower" [*dhammānusārī*] offers a clue (MN I 479). These two types of people are said to have "gone beyond the plane of the worldling" and "entered the fixed course of rightness." They are incapable of doing any deed which will lead them to the four woeful states and passing away without realizing the stream-entry-fruit. They are described as those who have entered the "*sappurisa-bhūmi,*" the plane of superior people or the good people, or righteous people [*okkanto sammatta-niyāmaṃ sappurisa-bhūmiṃ okkanto vītivato puthujjhana-bhūmiṃ*] (SN III 225). So they have not yet realized the stream-entry-fruit. But they have gone beyond the plane of the ordinary people and also are certain of realizing the fruit that is stream-entry during the current life. Therefore they are persons who have entered the noble path [*ariya magga*]. This makes them "noble persons practising for realization of the stream-entry-fruit."

The words "entering" [*okkanto*] the plane of the superior people [*sappurisa-bhūmi*], suggests a time and place at which one enters the *ariya magga*. One way of explaining this entry point is that the *ariya magga* is triggered by a specific experience, or one enters the *ariya magga* with a specific experience.

In Chapter 3 we concluded that a supramundane fruit is characterized by a specific experience. The fieldwork of this study has highlighted another scenario in which the practitioner reports a peak-experience which is very similar to the fetter-breaking-experience, that is, an experience the practitioner reports as signless, wishless and empty and at which point the five physical sense-bases are not active and it keeps recurring until they understand fully what it points to, and which has ultimately resulted in them attaining the fruit that is stream-entry (See Interview Nos. 2 and 3). When we examine the texts, the majority of the practitioners found in the texts seem to realize that they have attained a supramundane fruit immediately after the fetter-breaking-experience, that is, they realized that the relevant fetters broke and they acquired the knowledge appropriate to such a fruit almost immediately after such experience. For instance there are references to attaining supramundane fruits whilst listening to a sermon, whilst at the barber, entering a village on an elephant's back, attempting suicide etc. which suggest that they understood that they attained a supramundane fruit immediately after the fetter-breaking-experience.[22] However there seem to be exceptions to the rule who may take time to investigate "an experience" to come to terms with it, or to fully realize the significance of such an experience. This variation from the general rule is obviously based on the state of one's spiritual faculties. The said period of investigation can vary depending on how sharp the spiritual faculties of such person are.

The *Mirror of the Dhamma Sutta*[23] says that when a noble person [*ariya-sāvaka*] possesses the four factors of stream-entry i.e. unshaken confidence in the Buddha, Dhamma and the *Saṅgha* and the virtues dear to a noble person, if he wishes to, he could by himself declare the stream-entry-fruit. For one to know that he possesses these factors he has to reflect on his state of mind over a period of time until he is sure or fully confident that he is in fact endowed with these. Similarly the Buddha's advice to Anāthapiṇḍika says "when for the *ariyan* disciple the fourfold moral shame and hatred has ceased and he is endowed with the four factors of the stream-entry... he may, should he wish, by himself declare himself a stream-enterer" (AN IV 405). In these two instances, this person may not immediately realise that these fetters have broken, but come to understand this later. Based on this understanding, he may then declare that he is a stream-enterer. But in fact he would have been a stream-enterer from the time his three fetters broke, not from the later time that he came to realise that these fetters had been broken.

The *Sabbāsava Sutta* (MN I 6) gives a sequence different to the above two *Suttas*. It refers to the path to destruction of taints. It says "the destruction of the taints is for one who knows and sees [*jānato passato*]. ... Knows and sees what? Wise attention and unwise attention [*yoniso manasikāraṃ ca ayoniso manasikāraṃ*]" (MN I 7). *Yonisomanasikāra* is attending to something in a manner that one sees the conditions on which phenomena arises. In other words, in its ultimate sense it means, seeing the arising and ceasing of the five aggregates subject to clinging (suffering). Thereafter this *Sutta* says the "well-thought noble disciple [*sutavā ariyasāvako*)" (MN I 7–9) attends wisely "This is suffering," "This is the origin of suffering," "This is the cessation of suffering," "This is the way leading to the cessation of suffering'." When he attends this way, his first three fetters are abandoned. In other words, this "noble disciple" [*ariyasāvaka*] becomes a "stream-enterer" after having attended to suffering wisely, before which he had already "known and seen" *yoniso manasikāra* (that sees the arising and the ceasing of the aggregates subject to clinging, i.e. the arising and ceasing of suffering). We conclude that this practitioner was already a "noble disciple" before he became a stream-enterer, that is, he was already the first of the eight noble persons and for him to become the first noble person, he had already "known and seen" "*yoniso manasikāra*" (the arising and the ceasing of the five aggregates subject to clinging). The words "knowing and seeing" denotes a direct experience. Therefore we conclude that he came to "know and see" through a direct experience which converted him to the first of the eight noble persons.

The above *Sutta*s refer to two possible scenarios as follows:

1) A person has already attained the fruit that is stream-entry, that is, already had a fetter-breaking-experience and the three fetters had broken, but the person concerned has not yet recognized that they are broken and that he is a stream-enterer. Therefore he keeps reviewing his state of mind and subsequently realizes that he had already broken the three fetters (SN V 356/AN IV 405), or
2) A person has had a "peak-experience" and due to its striking nature he keeps reflecting upon it more and more [*yoniso manasikāra*], consequently his understanding about what the experience points to gets deeper and deeper and ultimately it leads to the breaking of the three fetters, resulting in the attainment of the fruit that is stream-entry (MN I 6).

During such period of reflection and attending wisely as envisaged in situation 2, such person would be "wholly taken up with the Dhamma" as referred to by Harvey, since such person would be engrossed in the practice to understand in terms of the Dhamma, a very striking experience he has had. Hence it could be that this heightened state of practice during which one reviews and analyses a "specific experience together with the resultant state of mind," later leads to the understanding of the four Noble truths. Such person, during such period of reviewing would be a "noble person practising for the realization of the stream-entry fruit." In such a situation as 2 above, practically it would be difficult to pinpoint the exact time of the breaking of the fetters.

Our field research too has highlighted the practical difficulties encountered by practitioners in understanding fully a particular experience. Whilst the majority understood the fetter-breaking-experience and realized that they attained a supramundane fruit immediately after the fetter-breaking-experience, two out of seven persons interviewed took time to fully understand a "peak-experience" which they report as very similar to the fetter-breaking-experience i.e. signless, wishless, and empty experience. When the said peak-experience kept on recurring, over a period of time, after reviewing it over and over again, at a point they realized that the first three fetters were no more in them. Whether these are cases where these practitioners had already broken the three fetters but took time to realize it (as in situation 1 above) or whether the fetters broke subsequently as a result of reflecting and investigating the "peak-experience" is a vital issue to be considered here.[24]

Our Interviewee No. 2 had very good technical knowledge to recognize whether he was a stream-enterer or not (i.e. he knew what the first three fetters were and knew that the absence of those was a state of mind of a stream-enterer). Nevertheless, even after being told by his teacher that he had attained the fruit that is stream-entry, he refused to accept it and went on for nearly one year, investigating a peak-experience very similar to a fetter-breaking-experience i.e. a signless, wishless and empty experience.[25] All he knew was that it was a significant experience but couldn't fully fathom it. Finally when the same kind of signless experience kept recurring, at a point he understood it as "the process of cessation of becoming has begun"[26] and that the first three fetters were now no more in him, meaning he understood the experience in such a way, that at such point, he overcame the first three fetters. Until such time he was not sure that cessation of *saṃsāra* was possible and he didn't think the first three fetters were broken by him. The knowledge that it is possible to end *saṃsāra* is also a fundamental knowledge of a stream-enterer. Apart from the fact that he didn't think that the fetters were absent in him, he was also not a stream-enterer until such time such knowledge about the possibility of ending *saṃsāra* arose in him, as until such time he would not have the mindset of a stream-enterer. A stream-enterer has no doubt that she will be putting an end to *saṃsāra* in the near future. So this is not a case of him not knowing that he was already a stream-enterer, but he was in fact not one. He became a stream-enterer much later, after having investigated what seems to be the recurring of the original experience. Subsequently, over a period of 20 years, his practice had progressed, so that he attained higher fruits, up to the fruit that is non-returning. Unlike the fruit that is stream-entry, the fruit that is once-returning and non-returning were attained by him immediately after the relevant fetter-breaking-experience without any difficulty, without an apparent time gap.

In the second case (Interview No. 5),[27] the interviewee understood that it was a supramundane fruit only after about two months from the relevant peak-experience which he reports as signless, wishless and empty. At the time of the experience he had very little knowledge about supramundane fruits. After one day from the experience, based on a discussion with his teacher he came to the conclusion that he had attained a "supramundane fruit." However he was convinced that the first three fetters were no more in him only when such a "peak-experience" kept on recurring over a period of time. It took him two months to confirm that the fetters were "completely eliminated." Whether this case falls within (1) or (2) above is hard to say, as he did not have sufficient technical knowledge to understand his state of mind with the very first peak-experience.

It looks like during the period of the heightened investigation of the "peak-experience" (i.e. the period of one year in the case of Interview No. 2), the interviewee was a "person practising for the fruit" and at the time when he concluded that the first three fetters were no more and that he was definitely on his way to ending *saṃsāra,* he became a stream-enterer. It is noteworthy that during this period of the heightened investigation, the "peak-experience" kept on recurring many times which helped him to understand the experience fully. It seems that the original peak-experience over a period of time developed in to a deeper and more powerful experience, increasing the level of understanding, thus ending up in a fetter-breaking experience.

The reported experience of Interviewee No. 7 of this study is also noteworthy in this regard. This is a *bhikkhunī* of Chinese nationality in the attire of a Chinese *bhikkhunī*, residing in a forest hermitage in Sri Lanka. She first undertook the Theravāda meditation practice in a country other than Sri Lanka under one teacher and later went to another meditation centre in the same country to practise a different meditation system under another teacher. Her first significant experience came in the second centre (Q.21, 55). It appears that at such time she was practising what was taught by her first teacher and not the system practised at the second centre. She describes a significant experience which she had on a specific date, time and place on which occasion she entered a "vast emptiness" which is also described to have occurred at the "end of the *vipassanā* practice whilst contemplating ceasing." With this experience she gained 100% confidence in the triple gem (Q.45). Immediately after this experience, she realized that she had broken the first three fetters (Q.56, 69) and had no doubt that the three fetters were gone.

Though she says that the first three fetters are no more in her, still she is not sure whether she has attained the first fruit of the Path, the fruit that is stream-entry. Since a stream-enter is a person who has destroyed (only) the first three fetters, if she was sure she had done this, she should have been sure she was a stream-enterer. And if she was not sure of this, she could not be sure she had destroyed the first three fetters. There cannot be confusion in her about Buddhist terminology, as she displayed very good technical knowledge of the first three fetters (Q.17, 32). Explaining the reason for her not being able to conclude whether this is the first fruit, she says, once she described this experience to the teacher at the second meditation centre referred to above, he wanted her to do the practice all over again, according to the meditation system practised at that centre, to see whether she can reach it through that system too (Q.20). Ever since then she has been bent on mastering that meditation system which includes mastering deep *samādhi*. Hence ever since then she has devoted her total practice to master this meditation system, without reflecting on her original experience. This is her reason for not being sure whether she was a stream-enterer or not.

Although she does not consider herself a stream-enterer, her understanding of non-self, the place and role of rites and ritual on the Path to liberation and the confidence in the Buddha Dhamma and the *Saṅgha*, (showing she was without the three fetters broken at stream-entry), theory of dependent arising and *Nibbāna* is in line with the understanding of a stream-enterer as given in the texts. Her right view is also apparent by her views on Buddhist cosmology, the existence of other planes of lives, *Arahant*s and other noble persons. Her previous deep experience has also recurred in her a few times as longer spells of "vastness." However despite this understanding and though she feels the first three fetters have been eradicated by her and she feels she "saw the reality," the very fact that she is putting so much time and effort to mastering yet another meditation system to test whether that too gives the similar results shows an element of doubt in her about what she saw. As once a person "knows and sees" the reality, there is no need to test it out through different systems as the reality does not depend on meditation systems. It is very likely that this is a noble person "practising for the fruit that is stream-entry" who mistakenly believes she has already broken the first three fetters. Again this is a case where one could argue that this is a stream-enterer but for various reasons does not recognize it. However as with Interviewee No. 2 discussed before, she has sufficient technical knowledge about the first three fetters and knows that the absence of these three fetters is a state of mind of a stream-enterer. But she needs time not to "review" her state of mind, but to "test it out and confirm" through yet another meditation system. A stream-enterer is one who has overcome doubt about the experience and the consequent state of mind, being unsure about her state of mind shows doubt. The day she develops sufficient understanding to overcome all doubt about what she originally experienced and the recurring similar experiences, she would be considered a stream-enterer. This could be a noble person practising for the stream-entry fruit, the first noble person.

In contrast to Interview No. 2 and 7 discussed above, Interview No. 1 realized that he had had a fetter-breaking-experience, which "reduced his defilements by 30%," and that he had became a stream-enterer, only two months later, when he had the fetter-breaking-experience relating to his attainment of the fruit that is once-returning. Comparing the two experiences and the resultant states of mind, he realized that the earlier experience he had had two months previously was one in which he attained the first fruit. Immediately after the attainment of the first fruit he only realized that 30% of his defilements had reduced. This is a clear case of a noble person recognizing that he had attained a supramundane fruit two months after the fetter-breaking-experience.

Further, in another reported case, Ñāṇavīra Bhikkhu, an English monk who lived in the jungles in the south of Sri Lanka, committed suicide having declared himself a stream-enterer. This case has been discussed by me in details in Chapter 6 under the sub-heading "Can a stream-enterer commit suicide?" We have also examined the possibility of him being a stream-enterer. Ñāṇavīra Bhikkhu in his declaration of stream-entry writes as follows:

> Then to Ñāṇavīra *bhikkhu* who was pondering, investigating and reviewing with the mind, on the teaching as had been heard and learnt, the dustless stainless eye of the *dhamma* arose, "whatever is of the nature to arise, all that is of the nature to cease." Having been a *dhammānusāri* [*dhamma* investigator] for a month (he) became a *diṭṭhipatto* (view attainer).[28]

In the above declaration he identifies a specific time period during which he was a noble person practising for the fruit of stream-entry, (i.e. a period of one month), which ought to be marked or signalled by a specific experience. This is yet another case which supports our proposition that a noble person practising for a noble fruit of the Path is one who investigates a specific experience until such time as he or she fully realizes the significance of that experience resulting in a supramundane fruit.

This textual research and field research as discussed above highlight the possibility of identifying a noble person practising for the fruit that is stream-entry. Nevertheless, the research has not been able to identify cases of the noble persons practising for attaining the rest of the three supramundane fruits.

Conclusion

Based on the conclusion in Chapter 3 that a supramundane fruit involves a specific experience marked by a peak-point (a fetter-breaking-experience), this chapter first extracted the various meanings attributed to the word "*phala*" in the texts, such as, an attainment at the end of the Path, consequence or benefit of attainment [*ānisaṃsa*] of the Path, fruition [*samādhi/samāpatti*] of the Path and the supramundane moments of consciousness. It also highlighted that the term "*phala*" has been used in this work to specifically mean, along with the fetter-breaking experience, the general state of mind of a noble person particularly with regard to the state of the fetters in such a mind and the relevant knowledge, qualities, power etc. acquired, being the consequences or benefits of the Path. Next it extracted evidence from the *Nikāyas* to highlight that the *Nikāyas* recognize the sequence of "Path, fetter-breaking-experience and effect (of the fetter-breaking-experience)" (which are three distinctly different phenomena) as against "Path and its fruits." Next based on our definition of a supramundane fruit to include both the fetter-breaking-experience and the effect, we discussed the implications of the sequence of "Path, fetter-breaking-experience and effect" on the current debates such as "*Nibbāna,* transcendence and ineffability" and definition of the eight persons making up the *sāvaka Saṅgha.*

I conclude that references to *Nibbāna* in the texts as "a not born, not become, not made, not compounded..." or "sphere wherein there is neither earth, nor water, nor fire, not air...,"which are usually cited in support of the thesis that *Nibbāna* is a transcendent reality, as a reference to the fetter-breaking-experience. In contrast, references such as, "I have become cool, quenched," "The three knowledges have been realized, the Buddha's teaching has been done" or "I have attained peace of mind" etc., which are usually cited in support of the thesis that *Nibbāna* is neither transcendental nor ineffable, as a reference to the "effect" (of the fetter-breaking-experience). I conclude that many of the debates amongst scholars on issues such as whether *Nibbāna* is a transcendent reality or whether or not *Nibbāna* is ineffable are a result of not recognizing the sequence of "Path, fetter-breaking-experience and effect" and that *Nibbāna,* is a "supramundane fruit" which ought to entail both, the fetter-breaking-experience that initiates the *arahatta-phala* and its effect, the latter being the living experience of an *Arahant* which includes the knowledge, qualities, powers etc. that flow from such fetter-breaking-experience. Even if some of these scholars recognize these two aspects as different phenomena, they differ on which one of them they take as *Nibbāna* or whether they say neither is *Nibbāna,* but the fetter-breaking experience is "that which knows *Nibbāna* as a timeless unconditioned reality."

The traditional Theravāda view is that the four paths and the four fruits take as their object, the timeless unconditioned *Nibbāna.*[29] However we conclude that, at the point of the fetter-breaking-experience, no conditioned phenomena manifest and the consciousness takes as its object, the absence or the cessation of conditioned phenomena, that is, the signless state. This state of mind is reflected in the stanza "not attending to any sign and attending to the signless element [*sabbanimittānaṃ ca amanasikāro, animittāya ca dhātuyā manasikāro*]" (MN I 296). Further we conclude that at the point of the fetter-breaking-experience, the consciousness does not take any object over and above the "signlessness," that is, it does not take *Nibbāna* as its object and *Nibbāna* is not a "transcendent reality" existing "out there" in its own right.

Discussing the relevance of the thesis of "Path, fetter-breaking-experience and effect" on the issue of the definition of the eight types of persons, I conclude that a "person practising for the fruit that is stream-entry" is a person treading the Noble Eightfold Path, who has had a impactful signless, wishless or empty experience, but yet not fully understood same, but such experience has led to intensified practice, which finally leads to the breaking of fetters in this current life. The knowledge or the understanding that is necessary for eliminating fully, the respective fetters, will eventually flow from such experience itself or through its recurrence. Such experience may need to recur many times before the level of understanding necessary to break fetters finally arises. Findings of this research have not been able to define conclusively the nature of the persons practising for the rest of the supramundane fruits.

Notes

1. The most common usage of the word *"phala"* in other contexts besides that of Path attainments is *kamma-phala*, a kammic fruit/result.
2. Cpd. = *Compendium of Philosophy*, S.Z.Aung and C.A.F.Rhys Davids translation of the *Abhidhammattha-saṅgaha* 1910, Pali Text Society /Cp= Cariyā Piṭaka 1882, Pali Text Society.
3. The "level"of knowledge which causes the destruction of fetters would belong to the Path.
4. SN V 347, SN V 356. Also see Chapter 6 for a comprehensive discussion on the state of mind of a stream-enterer.
5. *Kāyena amataṃ dhātuṃ,*
   phusayitvā nirūpadhiṃ,
   Upadhipaṭinissaggaṃ,
   Sacchikatvā anāsavo
   Deseti sammāsambuddho
   Asokaṃ virajaṃ padaṃ. (It.62)
6. "Transcendence" here has been used in the sense of transcending ordinary human experience (and also many forms of spiritual experiences of a non-ultimate nature) and which cannot be comprehended by the rational faculty of the human mind, but has to be felt. This means the experience is non-rational and cannot be conceptually defined, presented or analyzed (Tilakaratne 1993, 1). See Tilakaratne 1993, 74 for a comprehensive discussion on this topic.
7. *Atthi bhikkave ajātaṃ abhūtaṃ akataṃ asaṅkhataṃ. No ce taṃ bhikkhave, abhavissa ajātaṃ abhūtaṃ akataṃ asaṅkhataṃ, naidha jātassa bhūtassa katassa saṅkhatassa nissaraṇaṃ paññāyetha.Yasmā ca kho bhikkave atthi ajātaṃ abhūtaṃ akataṃ asaṅkhataṃ, tasmā jātassa bhūtassa katassa saṅkhatassa nissaraṇaṃ paññāyati.* (*Tatiya-nibbāna-paṭisaṃyutta Sutta,* Ud.80, as translated by Tilakaratne 1993, 74).
8. Some of these are Stace, Zeahner, and John Hick. For details see Tilakaratne 1993, 75.
9. *Yattha āpo ca paṭhavī tejo vāyo na ghādati*

na tattha sukkā jotanti ādicco nappakāsati
na tattha candimā bhāti tamo tattha na vijjati
yadā ca attanāvedi muni monena brāhmaṇo
atha rūpā arūpā ca sukhadukkhā pamuccatī ti.
(Ud.9, as translated at Ñāṇananda 2005, III, 334)

10. See Tilakaratne 1993, (chapter vi), 55–82 for a detailed discussion on *Nibbāna* as ineffable.
11. Tilakaratne 1993, 77/K.N. Jayatilleke 1963, 476.
12. Two other scholars who do not agree with the transcendental interpretation of *Nibbāna are* Johansson (1969, 51) and Kalupahana (1976, 74). See Tilakaratne 1993, 76 for a detailed discussion on this issue.
13. See synopsis, Interview No. 1.
14. See synopsis, Interview No. 4.
15. Which is different to the experience of *jhāna* and formless states, as in *jhāna* and formless states there is a *nimitta.* The sphere of infinite space, has space as its *nimitta.* Similarly in the other three formless states, a person gets absorbed in the respective *nimittas;* it is *by* taking such a *nimitta* that meditators enters upon it. i.e. with non-attention to perception of diversity, being aware that "space is infinite" they enter upon and abide in the base of infinite space [*ananto akāso ti ākāsānañcāyatanaṃ upasampajja viharati*—MN I 456]. Here the mind is absorbed in the chosen *nimitta* to the exclusion of all other *nimittas.* Usually in the sequence of formless *jhānas* appearing with the signless state, the signless state is listed after the four formless *jhānas.* However the fetter-breaking-experience is *animitta.* See Chapter 5 (p. 90–100) for detailed discussion about the nature of the fetter-breaking experience.
16. See Chapter 5 for an analysis of the fetter-breaking-experience and its object.
17. The *Visuddhimagga* states that "the four paths and the four fruits take timeless unconditioned *Nibbāna* as its object" (Vism.XXIII.4/Vism.820).
18. See Chapter 5 for an analysis of the fetter-breaking-experience.
19. Every signless experience is not a fetter-breaking-experience. See Chapter 5 for details. Also see Chapter 5 for a discussion on re-experiencing the fetter-breaking-experience.
20. See definition of Path, Chapter 1, p. 20.
21. See definition of *phala*, Chapter 1, p. 20.
22. See Chapter 3, pp. 55–56 for more examples.
23. SN V 356. See also SN V 396.
24. See Path related sequence of states leading to the attainment of supramundane fruits discussed in Chapter 1, pp. 23–24.
25. See Interview No. 2, Q.5, 19, 20, 51–53, 55 and also based on further discussions with the interviewee.
26. Amongst Sri Lankan practioners the term "cessation" is loosely used to mean that the sense-bases or aggregates subject to clinging "ceased" temporarily. It does not mean that they have attained *Nibbāna.* What this refers to is the signless experi-

ence in which sense objects, feelings etc. did not manifest. Two interviewees have used this term in this same sense. See Interview No. 4, Q.5–6. 9.

27. See Interview No. 5 Q.34–35, 37, 39–40.
28. *Ekaṃ samayaṃ Ñāṇavīro bhikkhu Bundalagāme viharati arraññakuṭikāyaṃ.Tena kho pana samayena Ñāṇavīro bhikkhu rattiyā pathamaṃ yāmaṃ cankamena āvaraniyehi dhammehi cittaṃ parisodheti, yathāsutaṃ yathāpariyattaṃ dhammaṃ cetasā anuvitakketi anuvicāreti manasānupekkhati. Atha kho* [Ñāṇavīrassa] *bhikkhuno evaṃ yathāsutaṃ yathāpariyattaṃ dhammaṃ cetasā anuvitakkayato anuvicārayato manasānupekkhato virajaṃ vītamalaṃ dhammacakkhuṃ udapādi, yam kiñci samudhaya dhammaṃ sabbaṃ taṃ nirodhadhammanti. So dhammānusari māsaṃ hutva diṭṭhipatto hoti.* (Ñāṇavīra 2002, II, Introduction, 1)
29. The *Visuddhimagga* states that "the four paths and the four fruits take timeless unconditioned *Nibbāna* as its object" (Vism.XXIII.4/Vism.820).

— 5 —

Noble Persons and the Nature of their Fetter-Breaking Experience

In Chapter 4 I differentiated between the fetter-breaking-experience and its effect and defined an attainment of a supramundane fruit to include both. In this chapter we will analyze the "nature" of different types of fetter-breaking-experiences and their respective effects. It sets out:

1. The types of noble persons
2. An analysis of the fetter-breaking-experience: both in terms of the Pāli *Nikāyas* and the *Visuddhimagga* and the expressions found in our field research and a comparison of the "fetter-breaking-experience" at the attainment of each of the four fruits of the Path
3. The difference between the fetter-breaking-experience and other religious experiences
4. An analysis of the re-experiencing of the fetter-breaking-experience [*phala-samāpatti*]
5. The difference between *phala-samāpatti* and cessation of perception and feeling.

The Types of Noble Persons

Due to differences in the spiritual faculties, there are differences in the fruits. Due to differences in the fruits, there are differences amongst persons (SN V 201). The five spiritual faculties are: the faculty of faith, effort, mindfulness, concentration and wisdom. In Chapter 1 we discussed the four supramundane fruits of the Path and the respective fetters eliminated at the attainment of each fruit. The four noble persons who attain these fruits have been classified depending on the state of their spiritual faculties.

Altogether there are eight types of persons [*aṭṭha purisa-puggala*] making up the *Saṅgha* refuge: the *sāvaka-Saṅgha* who are referred to as being worthy of veneration (AN IV 292), that is, those who have attained the four supramundane fruits of the Path and those practising for the realization of such fruits.[1] These eight came to be known as the eight kinds of noble persons [*ariya-puggala*]. They have been further classified as follows.

Two Types of *Arahants*

First, there are two types of *Arahants*: the *ubhato-bhāga-vimutta* (one liberated in both ways) and *paññā-vimutta* (one liberated by wisdom). The *Kitāgiri Sutta* of the *Majjhima Nikāya* describes these two types as follows.

The *ubhato-bhāga-vimutta* person "contacts with the body and abides in those liberations that are peaceful and formless, transcending forms, and his taints are destroyed by his seeing with wisdom."[2] He is said to have finished his work. He is no more capable of being negligent.

The liberations are, any of the eight liberations (DN II 70–71). The commentary to this passage says *ubhato-bhāga-vimutta* includes those who attain Arahantship after emerging from one or another of the four formless attainments [*arūpa jhānas*] and the one who attains it after emerging from the attainment of cessation of perception and feeling [*saññā-vedayita-nirodha-samāpatti*] (Ñāṇamoli and Bodhi 1995, 1272, n. 702).

The *paññā-vimutta* "does not contact with the body and abide in those liberations that are peaceful and formless, transcending forms. But his taints are destroyed by his seeing with wisdom." He is said to have finished his work. He is no more capable of being negligent (MN I 477). The commentary here explains that these include those who attain Arahantship either as dry-insight meditators [*sukkha-vipassaka*] or after emerging from one or another of the four *rūpa jhānas* (Ñāṇamoli and Bodhi 1995, 1272, n. 703). Unlike the *ubhato-bhāga-vimutta*, he has not attained the formless *jhānas* or cessation, but he has nevertheless destroyed all the taints.[3]

The Body Witness [*Kāya-Sakkhī*]

Of the remaining noble persons, the *kāya-sakkhī* (body witness) has attained the four formless [attainments] [*arūpa jhānas*], while the others have not. Some of the *kāya-sakkhī*'s taints are destroyed by his seeing with wisdom, but he still has work to do (MN I 478). The commentary explains that this includes the six types of individuals, from the one established in the fruit that is stream-entry to the one on the path of Arahantship who first contacts the formless [*jhānas*] and subsequently realizes *Nibbāna* (Ñāṇamoli and Bodhi 1995, 1272, n. 704).

One Attained to View [*Diṭṭhi-Patta*] and One Liberated By Faith [*Saddhā-Vimutta*]

With the *diṭṭhi-patta*, "some of his taints are destroyed by his seeing with wisdom, and he has reviewed and examined with wisdom the teachings proclaimed by the *Tathāgata*," but he still has work to do (MN I 478). These are the same six types of persons as in the case of the *kāya-sakkhī*, from the stream-enterer to the one practising for the fruit that is Arahantship, but without attaining the formless *jhānas*.

With the *saddhā-vimutta*, "some of his taints are destroyed by his seeing with wisdom, and his faith is planted, rooted and established in *Tathāgata* [*Tathāgate c' assa saddhā niviṭṭhā hoti mūlajāta patiṭṭhitā*]" (MN I 47). The commentary says that this type includes the same six persons from stream-enterer to one who has attained to the Path of Arahantship [*arahanta-maggā-panna*] but he has not reviewed and examined the teachings of the Buddha with wisdom as much as the *diṭṭhi-patta* has (Ñāṇamoli and Bodhi, 1995: 1272, n. 706).

The Dhamma-Follower [*Dhammānusārī*] and Faith-Follower [*Saddhānusārī*]

The lowest ranking two noble persons are the Dhamma-follower and the faith-follower. These two persons have not eliminated any taints or fetters at all but are considered as noble persons as they are those who are seriously "practising for the fruit that is stream-entry." These two types of persons are said to have gone "beyond the plane of the worldling" and "entered the fixed course of rightness" (SN III 225).They also understand the four noble truths (SN V 229).

The stream-enterer has been defined as one who is "endowed with [*samannāgato*]" the Path (SN V 348). However, one who is "rightly practising [*sammā-paṭipanno*] has been defined as one having right view through to right concentration (SN V 23) which is the Noble Eightfold Path and "right practice" (SN V 23–24). Further, *samaṇa*-hood [*sāmañña*] is described as the Noble Eightfold Path (SN V 25) and its goal is given as stream-entry-fruit up to the Arahatship-fruit. As the Path leads not only to the three higher fruits, but also to the first one, stream-entry, those engaged in the Path ought to include the first kind of "practising" [*paṭipanna*] person. Such a person ought to be endowed with the eight factors to some degree, though not as fully as a stream-enterer.

The Dhamma-follower is one who "with wisdom has sufficiently gained a reflective acceptance of the teachings proclaimed by the Buddha [*Tathāgatappaveditā c' assa dhammā paññāya mattaso nijjhānaṃ khamanti*]" (MN I 479). He has developed the five spiritual faculties. That is, he has sufficiently understood by wisdom (Anuruddha 2004, 508).

The faith-follower is one who "has sufficient faith in and love for the *Tathāgata* [*Tathāgate c'assa saddhā-mattaṃ hoti pemamattaṃ*]" (MN I 479) He has also developed the five spiritual faculties, though SN V 204–205 says that these faculties are weaker in him than in the Dhamma-follower.

In the Dhamma-follower the wisdom faculty is predominant and in the faith-follower the faith faculty is predominant. When they attain the fruit, the Dhamma-follower becomes the *diṭṭhipatta* (attained to view) and the faith-follower becomes the *saddhā-vimutta* (liberated by faith) (Ñāṇamoli and Bodhi 1995, 1211, n. 273).

Similes for the Seven Types of Persons

The same classification of seven types of persons referred to above is found in the *Sattaka-Nipāta* of the *Aṅguttara Nikāya*. Here people have been classified into seven types comparing them to those in water (AN IV 11).They are:

1) One who has gone under and remains under [*nimuggo nimuggo' va hoti*]: He possesses exclusively black, unwholesome qualities [*ekantakālakehi akusalehi dhammehi samannāgato*].
2) One who has risen up and then goes under [*ummujjitvā nimujjati*]: He accepts faith, moral shame, concern for consequences, energy, wisdom as wholesome qualities but his qualities do not become stable but diminish. This way he goes under.
3) Having risen up he stays there [*ummujjitvā ṭhito hoti*]: He accepts faith, moral shame, concern for consequences, energy and wisdom as wholesome qualities, but they do not grow or diminish, he stays there.
4) Having come up, he sees clearly and looks around [*ummujjitvā vipassati viloketi*]: Breaking the first three fetters he becomes a stream-enterer.
5) Having risen up he crosses over [*ummujitvā pātarati*]: Breaking the first three fetters and diminishing attachment, hatred and delusion he becomes a once-returner.

6) Having risen up he finds a firm foothold [*ummujjitvā paṭighādapatto*]: Breaking the five lower fetters he becomes a non-returner.
7) Having risen up he crosses over and goes beyond, a brahmin who stands on high ground [*ummujitvā tiṇṇo hoti pāragato thale tiṭṭhati*]: Breaking all fetters he becomes an *Arahant*.

Sub-Types of Non-Returners and Stream-Enterers

There are references in the texts to five types of non-returners [*anāgāmīs*] (SN V 201). They are:

1) *Antarā-parinibbāyī*—attainer of *Nibbāna* in the interval; this type is interpreted in the Theravāda as being born in the pure abodes as an *anāgāmī*, and as attaining *Nibbāna* during the first half of his life span (Bodhi 2000, 1902, n. 65). Other early schools see this kind of person as attaining *Nibbāna* in a between-lives period.
2) *Upahacca-parinibbāyī*—one who attains *Nibbāna* cutting short, interpreted by the Theravāda as attaining Nibbāna in the second half of his life-span.
3) *Asaṅkhāra-parinibbāyī*—an *anāgāmī* who attains *Nibbāna* in the new abode without effort. Such a person becomes completely cool naturally without any effort (Anuruddha 2004, 144).
4) *Sasaṅkhāra-parinibbāyī*—an *anāgāmī* who attains *Nibbāna* in the new abode with much effort.
5) *Uddhamsota akaniṭṭhagāmī*—an *anāgāmī* who takes life in successive pure abodes, and finally attains *Nibbāna* in the fifth one, the Akaniṭṭhaka realm, the highest *brahmā* realm.

The *Ekabīja Sutta* of the *Aṅguttara Nikāya* refers to three types of stream-enterers based on how many rebirths they may still have (AN I 233).They are:

1) A seven-times-at-most attainer [*satta-kkattuparaṃ*], who after roaming and wandering on amongst *devas* and humans seven times at most, makes an end of suffering.
2) A family-to-family attainer [*kolankola*], who after roaming and wandering on amongst good families two or three times, makes an end to suffering.
3) A one-seed attainer [*ekabījin*], who being born once more in the human existence, makes an end of suffering.

An Analysis of the "Fetter-Breaking-Experience"

The above classification of noble persons provides the background for examining the nature of the fetter-breaking experience that marks entry to the main noble states. What makes an attainment of a supramundane fruit of the Path is the fetter-breaking-experience together with its effect, particularly the right understanding of the true nature of things generated by this experience. Now we will investigate whether the fetter-breaking-experience differs from person to person and whether it differs for different fruits within the same person. We will also investigate the role of the five aggregates (form, feeling, perception, volitional activities and consciousness) and the six sense-bases (eye, ear, nose, tongue, touch and the mind) in this experience.

The fetter-breaking-experience has been articulated in the secondary sources and in our field research as "complete emptiness," a "strange experience," "a fine point," "a tapering off," "cessation," "a breaking of a boundary," "a going beyond," "an oceanic experience" etc. Below we first set out the ways in which it has been articulated by our interviewees and make a comparison between these various experiences.

Findings of our Field Research

Ajahn Brahmavamso (Interview No. 8) describes the fetter-breaking-experience which marks the dawn of a supramundane fruit as a "different state of consciousness for a while," "a powerful experience," like a "big explosion going off in one's mind." He says when an explosion goes off, we know that some things have been destroyed, but we have to wait until the smoke clears and the dust settles before we can see what fetters or defilements remain standing (Q.10). On the issue of whether and to what extent the five aggregates subject to clinging are active during the fetter-breaking-experience, he says:

> In the experience of stream-entry one is fully conscious. It is not a time of suspension of consciousness. The consciousness only terminates properly after the fourth *arūpa* [*jhāna*]. You have to go through that first of all. And you should know from the *Suttas* it's only those *Arahants* who are liberated both ways (who) have experience of those *arūpas*. Many *Arahants* haven't experienced cessation at all.[4] (Q.27)

On the issue of whether the transforming experience in general including the fetter-breaking-experience differs from person to person and from the attainment of one fruit to another within the same person, Ajahn Brahmavaṃso says it is different for different fruits for the same person. He says:

> These are completely different. Remember these are not *samādhi* experiences. It's not cessation. Note the fact that some people think if you experience this twice then you are *sakadagāmi*, thrice you are *anāgāmī*, four times you are *Arahant*. That's not true. (Q.26)

Comparing the attainment of the four fruits, Ajahn Brahmavamso feels that the attainment of the fruit that is stream-entry, non-returning and Arahantship entail powerful experiences that they are "events." However, the attainment of the fruit that is once-returning is hard to define. So much so that he would not take it to be an event (Q.38–39).

Now let us consider some of the other expressions from the field research of this study, on the fetter-breaking-experience:

1) Interview No. 6: The experience relating to the attainment of her first fruit of the Path is described as the "body falling apart, part by part, reducing to a skeleton and to a heap of ash" and finally at its peak (fetter-breaking-experience), for a "moment," for a "second," "within a wink of an eye," "like striking a match stick," the "disappearance" of even the dust, meditation posture and everything around and "losing awareness of feeling" (*kshanayakin daneema nathiwuna*). At this moment, for a short while, there was no form, feeling, perception, volitional activities, sound, smell, touch etc. Not even consciousness (Q.75–79). She says "the feeling that something was happening was there (Q.31) ... most probably consciousness came up subsequently" (Q.77).

2) Interview No. 5: The fetter-breaking-experience relating to the attainment of his first fruit is described as a "fine point" in meditation with a "tapering off of feeling" [*gevaadameemak*], "not having the feel of the vedanā" [*vedanava ahosiveemak*], "not feeling the [oppressive nature of the] five aggregates subject to clinging" (Q.9–13, Q.16–18). For him, in this state there was no form, feeling, sound, smell, touch etc. However he feels there was consciousness. He says "there you can say, it is only consciousness ... because you get to know it with the consciousness, isn't it?" (Q.75–78).
3) Interview No. 4: The fetter-breaking-experience relating to the attainment of his first fruit is described thus: "I have been able to see that whatever *rūpa, vedanā, saññā, saṅkhāra, viññāṇa* that are experienced in the meditation, these five aggregates subject to clinging are subject to cessation completely, without remainder" (Q.4) (meaning he saw cessation within this experience itself)[5], or as seeing the release from all these for a short while (Q.4–8). At this point, for him, there was no sound, taste, touch, form, perception, feeling, volitional formations etc. As to the query on whether there was consciousness, the answer was "not even consciousness ... usually when a person experiences cessation, he experiences the cessation of all these. Apart from this, one cannot see form or anything else" (Q.73–75).
4) Interview No. 3: He described the fetter-breaking-experience relating to the attainment of his first fruit of the Path as a "going beyond," "a breaking of a boundary," "like a river gushing into the sea," "an opening up," "like a river bund breaking and water gushing over the river bank," "a fever going down," or "a festered boil bursting and pus being released." He felt a huge spiritual awakening. He felt that he had got caught up in a "huge operation" with some "fundamental principles." He says:

> On the one hand it's a big spiritual awakening on other hand it's unbelievable (Q.5) ... like a "breaking up" [*kadagenayaamak*], breaking of a bund and the water gushing over the river bank, but it's not a harmful flood. This serious mental strain, no, one cannot call it even a mental strain, I didn't have a mental strain at that time, even if I say a bursting of a balloon, that too is something that'll bring unhappiness to a baby, it's more like a festered boil bursting and the pus being released (Q.12) ... I realized a big quake, a big difference, a big transformation, a big explosion, that a big release occurred (Q.17).

As to whether the sense-bases were active at this point of time, he says that it is not something that can be explained in terms of the (physical) sense-bases, as several stages before you come to this experience, the mind escapes from these (Q.8). When asked whether there was sight, sound, touch, smell etc. or form, feeling, perception, volitional activities, he says:

> There is all this, yet you don't experience these through the sense-bases or from outside ... If you penetrate this, there is even a light perception. Therefore this is the biggest mystery to the world of senses (Q.45)... It is like you draw two lines across and you see the point at which they cross each other and seeing that such point has no substance, no worldly importance (Q.54).

5) Interview No. 2: The fetter-breaking-experience relating to the attainment of the fruit that is stream-entry was described by him as a "cessation," a "gap," a "gulf" a "total blankness" in his consciousness. Everything stopped for him, he didn't feel the consciousnesses anymore for a short while. Again it appeared. This way the "consciousness" appeared and disappeared in quick succession within a short period for a couple of times (Q.3–4, 8–9). The fetter-breaking-experience relating to the attainment of his second most significant religious experience on the Path (the fruit that is once-returning) also was felt as a "gap" in the consciousness (Q.61–72). Similarly the third most significant religious experience on the Path (relating to the attainment of the fruit that is non-returning) was also felt the same way, as a "blanking out" of consciousness (Q.82–89). Referring to the circumstances in which he experienced the third fruit of the Path, which was an encounter with three snakes, he said he realized that for some time his mind was totally "blank," he was standing but had stopped his work, his eyes were fully open and he was conscious, fully aware, but he didn't see or hear the commotion of people shouting and snakes going away (Q.82–89).Which means his five sense-bases were not active, just the same way the fetter-breaking-experience was described in the rest of the interviews quoted above.

Comparing the fetter-breaking-experiences relating to the attainment of the fruit that is stream-entry and once-returning with the experience relating to the attainment of the third fruit, he says, the mind was "blank," there was "no feeling"[6] just as during the earlier two experiences, but he thinks this third experience was stronger (Q.93–94). With regard to the earlier two experiences, initially there were doubts about its nature and significance, however this was a "contrast," a "vivid experience" as it was in broad daylight, amidst a lot of commotion, his mind being fully energetic, and he got immediate confirmation of the breaking of the next two fetters (Q.95). With regard to the attainment of the first fruit of the Path, it took him nearly one year from the original peak-experience to conclude that the first three fetters were no more in him and that "the process of cessation had begun for him."

The fruit that is once-returning is a stage where the next two fetters that is, *kāmacchando* and *vyāpādo* (desire for the pleasures of the senses and ill-will) reduce but do not break completely. To that extent, the experience relating to this attainment is "hazy" compared to the experience relating to the attainment of the other three fruits of the Path at which stages, the relevant fetters break away completely. This feeling of haziness can be seen in the choice of words used in the above interview to explain the understanding that arose from the general experience relating to the attainment of the second fruit compared to the experience relating to the attainment of the first fruit. The interviewee says "I can't tell you in black and white whether this is a fruit or not." Though even in the case of the other two fetter-breaking-experiences (relating to the stream-entry and once returning fruits), he does not admit directly whether they are in any way related to supramundane fruits or not, the choice of words describing the second experience is relatively mild and hazy. He only knows something happened and thereafter certain defilements were "almost gone." Whereas soon after he had the fetter-breaking experience relating to the third fruit, he knew that the next two fetters broke completely.

6) Interview No. 1: This is an interview through which the attainment of all four fruits of the Path can be compared. At the attainment of the first fruit of the Path (stream-entry), he felt that "for a second, for a minute, his mind got "cut off," the mind "went in" to a "different place," the mind "didn't continue," he couldn't see anything, he didn't feel the consciousness (Q.114–116, 119). He felt that the defilements in him were reduced by 30%. He felt 30% of the "heavy duty" was no more. He felt very comfortable as though a "30% of heavy weight on his back has been thrown away."

After about two months, in the same hermitage, whilst doing walking meditation, he says he attained the second fruit, the fruit that is once-returning. His mind experienced a similar moment of "going in" like the experience relating to the attainment of the fruit that is stream-entry, but the feeling was different from the first experience. He felt that this time he cut off 60% of the defilements. Immediately after this second experience, he understood that he had attained the second fruit and it was only at that time he realized that his earlier similar experience marked the attainment of the fruit that is stream-entry (Q.160–164). This experience, though similar, was stronger than the experience relating to the first fruit. Subsequent to this experience he understood that his greed and anger reduced significantly, so did delusion. His *sīla* got stronger; "right view" and the view of impermanence were stronger. The "feeling" was "more enjoyable, more comfortable" than the earlier experience, relating to the first fruit of the Path (Q.165, 166, 149).

He revealed that he attained the fruit that is non-returning after about four months from the second fruit. He experienced a similar state of "going in" of the mind. Immediately after the experience he understood that he attained a supramundane fruit. This time he felt as if "99% of the defilements were destroyed." So much so that at first he thought there were no defilements at all remaining. His teacher had to remind him that altogether there are four stages on the Path, then on his own he realized that he attained only the third and not the fourth fruit of the Path (Q.193–195). Afterwards he realized that "1–2%" defilements were still remaining in him. This experience relating to the third fruit was felt as a deeper experience than the earlier two but the experience was a similar "going in" of the mind (Q.178, 181, 188, 192).

Revealing the attainment of the fruit that is Arahantship, he says that, whilst he was walking he focused on his mind and realized that his mind "went in" for one second, then "arose and stopped." Immediately he realized that all defilements got cut off, he felt "he has no more duties to fulfill." Comparing this with the attainments of the previous supramundane fruits, he says here the right view is stronger, understanding of impermanence is stronger and *sīla* became stronger (Q.153). He describes *Nibbāna* as "fully no defilements."

Accordingly, comparing the experiences relating to the different stages of the fruits of the Path, he says that at each stage the defilements reduce very differently and from the attainment of the first fruit onwards he felt a "gap" between the mind and the defilements. Elaborating this further, he says he felt that the "gap" was different at each stage and increased at each stage. In other words, the "distance" between the defilements and his mind increased with the attainment of each fruit of the Path. Our discussion goes as follows:[7]

Q.165 What made you think that it is the second fruit, it could have been the first fruit?

A No, no, because the difference is, I already told you, because the defilements reduced very differently.

Q.178 Third stage?

A Third stage go in, *anāgāmī* go in, because more different is, because more deeper, is more different, defilement very destroyed.

Q.204 So when you "go in" those days, after the third, when you go in, what is the difference between that "going in" and earlier two "going in"?

A The difference is, I always say, when the second stage, first stage, I destroy because my something, to me my front is little bit far one foot only, look like one foot first stage, second, little bit far already, defilements come from, third stage, already come from 3 feet, nothing impact to me directly, so I understand that "going in" that stage is different stage.

Differentiating the fetter-breaking-experience relating to the different fruits of the Path in terms of percentages by which the defilements reduced, this interviewee seems to be clear regarding the qualitative difference of the fetter-breaking-experience at each stage.

Secondary Sources

Ajahn Chah refers to the peak of his most significant religious experience as "ākāsa-dhātu (the space element) ... there was complete emptiness." He describes the "undefiled mind" he touched at the peak of this experience as the "pure mind." He says:

> Having passed beyond a certain point, it was as if the mind was cut loose and had penetrated to the deepest, quietest spot inside. It settled there in a realm of complete emptiness. Absolutely nothing could penetrate it from outside. Nothing could reach it. Having stayed in there for a while, awareness then withdrew. ... Having experienced these things, the mind gradually withdrew and returned to its normal state. (Chah 1998, 17)

The phrase "absolutely nothing could penetrate it from outside. Nothing could reach it" shows that his five sense-bases were cut off at this point of time through which signals could reach him. Further "the mind gradually withdrew and returned to its normal state" shows that the mind was in an "unusual" level of consciousness.

From the above descriptions of the fetter-breaking-experiences, it is clear that all interviewees report that the five sense-bases were cut off at this point of time. They did not see, hear, smell, taste and didn't feel the touch of anything. There were no ideas or thoughts. They reported a signless experience. Whilst some expressed this in terms of the absence of sense objects, some expressed it in terms of the aggregates subject to clinging, such as "not feeling the five aggregates subject to clinging, and some by expressions such as "the mind got cut off," "a gap in the consciousness" which covers both the state of the sense objects as well as the aggregates subject to clinging. However, as to the role of the five aggregates subject to clinging, while one of the interviewees felt that it is through the aggregate of consciousness that one understands the state of the mind at this point of time, all others felt a "total cessation" of all five aggregates including the consciousness even at the stage of attainment of stream-entry. Under the next sub-heading we have examined what may be the true state of affairs in relation to the aggregate of consciousness at this point (see pp. 96–100).

The *Nikāyas*

Now we will examine what the *Nikāyas* offer to explain the fetter-breaking-experience of a supramundane fruit as reported in our field research.

In the *Nalakalāpi Sutta* of the *Nidāna Saṃyutta,* Venerable Sāriputta compares consciousness and name-and-form [*nāma-rūpa*] to two bundles of reeds. When two bundles of reeds stand with one supporting the other and first one of these is drawn out, the second would fall, and if the second is drawn out, the first would fall [*ekan ākaddheyya, ekā papateyya, aparam ce ākadheyya, aparā papateyya*] (SN II 114). Similarly depending on name-and-form, consciousness comes "to be" and with consciousness as a condition name-and-form comes "to be" and in the absence of one, the other does not arise (SN II 104 and 114).

Consciousness is an endless process of identifying itself with name-and-form, i.e. form, feeling, perceptions and volitional activities, or sights, sound, smell, taste, touch, ideas. SN II 3–4 explains the name-and-form conditioned by consciousness as, in effect the first four aggregates, including contact and attention. Consciousness arises depending on these. The identifying with name-and-form is driven by craving, conceit and views [*taṇhā, māna, diṭṭhi*]. Suppose there comes a point at which there is no tendency in the mind to identify with or cling to any of these external or internal signs—meaning-laden objects—(i.e. form, feeling, perceptions and volitional activities or sights, sound, smell, taste, touch, ideas), so that the mind lets go of these through the process of developing insight, at such a point, there would be no "manifestation" of consciousness too.

The fetter-breaking-experience can be explained in terms of this simile. Suppose the two bundles, name-and-form and consciousness, stand leaning on each other in the shape of "V" turned upside down. When one is pulled, the other would fall too; they would fall apart in the sense of not leaning on each other anymore (not as extinguishing). At such time name-and-form would not "manifest" in the consciousness, it would not register in the consciousness. This is due to non-identification of conscuiousness with name-and-form. The traditional Theravāda view is that at this stage the mind takes as its object a timeless, unconditioned transcendent realm, *Nibbāna*[8]—meaning at this stage one directly experiences *Nibbāna*. However I hold that at this stage, as the person is conscious and not unconscious, although there are no conditioned objects manifesting, which means it is a signless experience, the consciousness takes as its object the "absence of conditioned phenomena," that is, the signless state or signlessness.[9] This state of mind is reflected by the phrase "non-attention to any sign and attention to the signless element" [*sabbanimittaṃ ca amanasikāro animittāya ca dhātuyā ca manasikāro*—MN I 296]. Though this state is empty of conditioned phenomena (including ideas), it still has the perception of "the signless" [*animitta*] and is attentive to this state.

The point of the "fetter-breaking-experience" as reported in our fieldwork where a person feels that the "whole world stopped for him," or the "whole world fell apart" or he "ceased to experience the world" or "the consciousness ceased" can be explained in terms of this simile of the two bundles of reed. That is, this is the point at which name-and-form does not manifest and consequently the consciousness does not manifest. Therefore one does not experience the "world" internally or externally.

Explaining this further, let us consider a conversation between Venerable Ānanda and the Buddha regarding the arising of contact. The Buddha asks "If, Ānanda, all those modes, characteristics, signs, indications by which there comes to be a designation of name-and-form were absent, would there be manifest any contact?" for which Ānanda answers "there would not." Then the Buddha concludes "wherefore Ānanda, this itself is the cause, this is the origin, this is the condition for contact, that is to say, name-and-form" (DN II 62). So if name-and-form does not arise, one does not contact the "world" internally or externally, one gets cut off from the "world."

This comes out very clearly from the description of the fetter-breaking-experience in our Interview No. 2, quoted previously. This interviewee's meditation system initially was "labelling." Whatever he felt or mentally focussed on was noted by assigning a label to it such as "sitting," "standing," "feeling," "thinking" etc. One day when he was labelling in this manner for some time, the mind refused to label any more, it was tired of labelling, and at one point he experienced a "cessation," a "gap," a "gulf," a "total blankness" in his consciousness, everything stopped, he didn't feel consciousnesses any more for a short while, then it appeared again. This way consciousness "appeared and disappeared in quick succession" within a short period, for a couple of times, so that he realized he experienced something special. Though at such time he refused to accept it as having attained a fruit of the Path, much later he realized that it was "non-becoming" that he experienced momentarily and consequently he understood that he had broken the first three fetters.

In our Interview No. 3, to the question "what was the nature of this experience, was there sight, sound, taste, touch, smell, in this?" the answer was:

> There is all this, yet you don't experience this through the senses or from outside. If you penetrate this, there is also a light perception. There is a sound perception and a bodily, tactile sensation also. There is everything in this. But you don't experience this in any sense through the eye, ear, nose, tongue etc. Therefore this becomes the biggest mystery to the world of senses. The sense-bases cannot deny this. Yet none of the sense-bases such as the ear or nose comes forward to claim that "I saw, I heard" etc. (Q.45)

He compares this phenomenon with a passage in the *Caṅki Sutta, "kāyena c'eva parama- saccaṃ sacchikaroti' paññāya ca taṃ ativijjha passati"*: "he realized with the body, the ultimate truth and sees it by penetrating it with wisdom" (MN II 173). He says; "here, there is some rūpa; in terms of *vedanā*, it is referred to as "*avedayita*"*;* in terms of *saññā* it is said "*na asaññā saññī no pi visaññī*" [referring to Sn. v. 874, see p. 98], there is *saññā* yet no *saññā*; there is a "*visaṅkhāra*" nature in the *saṅkhāra*; *viññāṇa* is *"anidassana,"* "non-manifestive." So when you get there you will ask "where is the five?," but by using these words what is indicated is that the five aggregates have got extinguished" (Q.45–46). Perhaps what he means is that all aggregates subject to clinging are around including form, but do not come into "contact" with the consciousness, so the sense bases don't claim "I saw," "I heard."

Further the following passage which was cited by us before, gives the mental build up towards attaining a supramundane fruit. It gives the progressive stages of insight which develops on this Path:

> Seeing thus, *bhikkhus*, the instructed noble disciple experiences revulsion towards contact ... feeling ... perception ... volitional activities ... consciousness. Experiencing revulsion he becomes dispassionate. Through dispassion [his mind] is liberated. When it is liberated there comes the knowledge "It's liberated." He understands: Destroyed is birth, the holy life has been lived, what has to be done has been done, there is no more for this being.[10]

Accordingly, by investigating the aggregates in the prescribed way, and through the process of developing revulsion [*nibbidā*], dispassion [*virāga*] etc., the mind experiences liberation [*vimuccati*]. At the point of "*vimuccati*" the mind has stopped identifying with any of the external or internal signs, meaning-laden objects. It is because to the mind so developed, all these "signs" become stressful objects. Hence the mind lets go of all signs and the two bundles of reed fall apart and you experience a signless [*animitta*] state. It's not that one is unconscious, and nor does the consciousness come to cease. Since the whole world seems to cease at this point of time, the person who experiences this tends to think that consciousness too ceases. This is further supported by the fact that even at the fetter-breaking-experience relating to *arahatta-phala*, there is no cessation of consciousness. The following stanza from the *Kalahavivāda Sutta* (Sn.v. 874) reflects the state of the perception of an *Arahant* at the point of the fetter-breaking-experience. For perception to operate in some form or the other, it has to be accompanied by consciousness. The state of mind described in this stanza corresponds to the fetter-breaking-experience relating to the *arahatta-phala* and also to other fruits as reported in our fieldwork:

> *Na saññasaññī na visaññasaññī*
> *No pi asaññī na vibhūtasaññī*
> *Evaṃ sametassa vibhoti rūpaṃ*
> *Saññānidānā hi papañcasaṅkhā*

This verse discusses a state of mind where form as well as pleasure and pain have ceased. A person in this state is not one with normal perception [*sañña-saññī*], nor is he someone with abnormal perception [*visañña-saññī*]. He is not non-percipient [*asaññī*] nor has he rescinded perception [*vibhūta-saññī*]. It is to one constituted in this manner that (perceived) form ceases to exist (Ñāṇananda 2003, III, 233–234). That is, the person referred to is not one with the ordinary worldling's perception, which is deluded, nor has he fainted and become unconscious [*na saññasannī na visaññasaññī*]. He is not in the kind of trance that is devoid of perception [*no pi asaññī*), nor has he put an end to perception [*na vibhūtasaññī*]. Venerable Ñāṇananda says what these four negations highlight is what he calls the "vacant gaze" of one who is emancipated through wisdom.[11]

Ñāṇananda explains this "vacant gaze" with the following simile. Suppose one is in a cinema hall enjoying a matinee show (a film show screened in the afternoon), where the hall is dark due to heavy curtains and closed doors and windows. There is a beam of light directed at the screen, and one is entranced and deluded by the show. Suddenly the doors and windows are flung open and the curtains are pulled aside. Then immediately one steps out of the cinema world. The film may go on, but because of the light coming in from all sides, the limited illumination on the screen fades away, the film thereby loses its enjoyable quality. One undergoes such an internal transformation that it becomes questionable whether one is still seeing the film show. This is because one's perception of the film show has undergone a change. Hence one doesn't "see" a film show anymore. But one has not put an end to consciousness. One's gaze is actually a "vacant gaze."

In our day-to-day experience, there are many instances where a particular sound keeps disturbing us, but with non-attention to it, at a point we stop hearing it though the sound continues outside. Or we keep gazing at something with our mind elsewhere and as a result the mind does not actually visually register it. This is because the object has not made an impression on our eye consciousness. This is simply because we stop focusing on the sound or sight, as we do not see it as significant: we do not grasp at it as a significant "sign" [*nimitta*], we do not identify with it. In this instance, though one sense-base is not active (i.e. the ear or the eye), the other bases are at work. For example, though we do not hear the particular sound which has been disturbing us, we still could be thinking of something or seeing something. In contrast to this, at the fetter-breaking-experience we stop identifying "signs" through all six sense-bases, all at once. Hence it becomes an unusual experience.

If we are to compare this situation with someone who has fainted, fainting is described as "a brief loss of consciousnesses" caused by temporary lack of oxygen to the brain.[12] This is a medical condition and consciousness is restored immediately upon the blood supply to the brain being restored. At the fetter-breaking-experience, however, as discussed earlier, one is fully conscious yet perceptual signs do not get registered in the mind.[13]

However in AN V 318–319 the Buddha says that it is possible that one will not be percipient of the six sense bases, yet will have the perception as follows:

> This is peaceful this is sublime that is, the stilling of all activities, the relinquishing of all acquisitions, the destruction of craving, dispassion, cessation, *Nibbāna* [*etaṃ santaṃ etaṃ panitaṃ ... Nibbānaṃ*].

Similarly AN V 321 says when one is not percipient of the six sense bases, it is still possible for one to be attentive as given above. I hold that these are references to the re-experiencing of the fetter-breaking-experiences of an *Arahant* and not that of the lesser nobles.[14] For an *Arahant*, every time the fetter-breaking-experience is re-experienced, he perceives it as "peaceful ... destruction of craving ... *Nibbāna*." However this perception is based on his prior knowledge that he has already attained the destruction of craving, *Nibbāna*. The fetter-breaking-experience of an *Arahant* is also a signless experience. But the fetters are actually eliminated not by the signless experience by itself, but based on rightly understanding it, that is, the right view yoked with it.[15] An *Arahant* has already rightly understood this state of mind to be *Nibbāna*. So he perceives in the re-experience of the signlessness, what he has already understood as *Nibbāna*.

So far we discussed the fetter-breaking-experience in general to be signless, wishless and empty. Let us assess whether the fetter-breaking-experience relating to all four supramundane fruits are the same. The fetter-breaking-experience of the first three fruits can be compared in our Interview No. 2. Accordingly all three experiences were felt by this interviewee as a "gap" in the consciousness. However at each stage the experience was felt as a stronger experience than the previous one, the last being the most vivid experience. However all experiences were felt as signless, wishless and empty. The fetter-breaking-experiences of all four fruits can be compared in our fieldwork in Interview No. 1.The interviewee describes all four experiences by the same words, that is, as the "mind going in." He describes all four experiences as fundamentally the same, i.e. as signless, wishless, and empty. However as he progressed on the Path, each fetter-breaking-experience was felt as a deeper experience than earlier ones, with his last experience being the deepest of all. Here he says "the mind went in, arose and stopped." However the basic nature of all four experiences is reported by him to be the same, i.e. signless, wishless and empty.[16]

The description by our Interviewee No. 1 of the fetter-breaking-experience relating to the attainment of the fourth fruit, that is, "the mind went in, arose and stopped," as against "the mind went in" being the description for the remaining three fruits, warrants an explanation. Immediately after the fetter-breaking-experience of the rest of the three fruits, when the sense bases get re-activated, as delusion [*moha*] is yet to be eradicated, "the name and the form" [*nāmañ ca rūpañ ca*[17]] is joined again by the consciousness to form what appears to be "I." In the *Arahant*, once the name and the form fall apart, at the fetter-breaking-experience, and subsequently when the sense bases get re-activated, the name and the form do not get "entangled" ever again, in such a way as to form "I." Thereafter Interview No. 1 reports his perception to be "coming stop, coming stop," which means that though "the name and the form" arises in the sense bases, as they arise he realizes that "this is the name, this is the form" (i.e. this is not someone nor something). This change of perception came for him with the understanding that arose subsequent to the fetter-breaking-experience, in effect, immediately after the sense bases got activated. The same situation with regard to the change of perception is articulated by Ajahn Chah when he uses the phrase "still flowing water." He refers to the mind of one who understands things as impermanent, stressful, and non-self as "still flowing water." That is, the mind is still, yet can discern, discern all around. Whilst discerning, yet it is peaceful. He compares a peaceful mind (a mind not entertaining pleasure and pain) to still water and the discerning mind to flowing water (Chah 2013, 26–44).

I conclude that in the fetter-breaking-experience, the five sense bases are cut off totally i.e. there is no sight, sound, taste, smell, touch. As for the mind base, no ideas arise through the mind door. However the consciousness continues and hence perception and attention. Aggregates such as feeling, mental formations do not manifest at this point. But perception and attention continues taking the signlessness as its object. Hence the mind as a sense base is not totally cut off, though not fully functional. Comparing the fetter-breaking-experiences of all four fruits, I conclude that the basic nature of all four fetter-breaking-experiences are the same, i.e. signless, wishless and empty, though the experience at each stage gets deeper as one progresses on the Path and the underlying tendencies are different at each stage.

The Triple Gateway

The *Visuddhimagga* recognizes all four "momentary supramundane fruits" of the Path to be either signless, wishless or empty [*animitta, appaṇihita* or *suññata*]. Referring to these three as the "triple gateway to liberation" [*tividha-vimokkha-mukkha*], the *Visuddhimagga* considers these as three different gateways, which are outlets from the world. It says after the "knowledge of equanimity" about formations one might experience liberation through any one of these gateways as follows (Vism. XXI.70/Vism.768):

1) When one with great resolution brings formations to mind as impermanent, he acquires the signless [*animitta*] liberation.
2) When one who has great tranquillity, brings to mind formations as painful [*dukkha*] he acquires the wishless [*appaṇihita*] liberation.
3) When one who has great wisdom brings to mind formations as non-self, he acquires the empty [*suññata*] liberation.[18]

Our field research investigated into this classification of "gateways." It was found that all who attained a supramundane fruit understood their "fetter-breaking-experience" as signless, wishless and empty [*animitta, appaṇihita* and *suññata*] and these three were understood to be different facets of the same thing and not as three different phenomena.

One of the Interviewees (No. 2), explaining his fetter-breaking-experience in terms of "*animitta, appaṇihita* and *suññata*," says:

> Mind has no object to hang on, it has no craving to identify, I think that's what happened. It was so fed up, it couldn't label it. So that means he didn't never identify the object and no craving for that because of the tiredness (Q. 56) ... That is void of any self, there is nothing no essence there, always flowing, coming and going down, coming and going down, so what is there to label? (Q.57) ... I think different facets of the same thing. It's not three different things (Q.59) ... It's not three different paths or like that, same thing, but different perspectives of your own view (Q.60).

Another Interviewee (No. 3) explains it as follows:

> From a *lokuttara*[19] angle there is no breaking up into three. It has a unitary nature. In the *lokuttara* there is no distinction as those who have experienced this and not experienced, or Buddhists and non-Buddhists or those developing the Path and those who have attained the fruit. These differences are only in this world. If you look at it from a worldly angle, *appaṇihita* is that it has no value whatsoever to a man who has worldly desires. *suññata* means empty. [*Animitta*?] *animitta* means he cannot point at anything. That means it's not worth a penny. If I am to explain in my words, it means that it is not worth a penny (Q. 61)... Different facets of the same thing (Q. 62).

The *Rahulovāda Sutta* (MN III 277) and many other *Sutta*s set out that what is impermanent [*anicca*] is painful [*dukkha*] and therefore is non-self [*anatta*]. To take something as a sign [*nimitta*] is to take it as substantial and permanent. When the mind realizes that there is nothing permanent in the world, that everything is unstable, it refuses to cling on to anything, it doesn't hanker on anything. Therefore the mind is wishless [*appaṇihita*]. To know things as *suññata* is to realize that everything is empty of self. Therefore these three are three different "gateways" only to the extent of the "focus" of the mind. The focus of the mind at the point of attainment of a supramundane fruit could be any one of these, i.e. signless,wishless and empty. Once the mind comes to realize one of these three realities, it simultaneously experiences the other two. They are three facets of the same *dhamma*, the unconditioned. Therefore these differences in the "gateways" or the "liberations" seem to have no real significance in the experience of a practitioner.

With regard to the nature of the "fetter-breaking-experience," I conclude that though the experience as a whole differs from person to person and within the same person, i.e. body parts falling apart and ending up as dust (Interview No. 6), blanking out of the consciousness (Interview No. 2), tapering off of feeling (Interview No. 5), breaking of a river bund or a boundary (Interview No. 3) etc., and within the same person, it differs from the attainment of one supramundane fruit to another, the basic nature of the fetter-breaking-experience is common to all, and is common to all four supramundane fruits of the Path, that is, it is signless, wishless and empty [*animitta, appaṇihita* and *suññata*]. The intensity of it differs from one supramundane fruit to another, that is, the experience is felt with greater impact and consequently with greater clarity as one attains the higher fruits of the Path. Depending on the training and wisdom developed, the knowledge that results from such experience varies. It is based on this knowledge that arise consequent to the fetter-breaking-experience, that the noble persons are classified in terms of the four fruits of the Path.

Differentiating the Fetter-Breaking-Experience from Other Religious Experiences

Buddhist Experiences

The *Aṅguttara Nikāya* relates an incident where Venerable Mahā Koṭṭhita rejects the state of mind attained by Venerable Citta Hatthisāriputta which was considered by Citta's colleagues as wisdom (AN III 397). When Mahā Koṭṭhita was engaged in a conversation with some senior monks, Citta together with his friend came there and kept on interrupting the conversation of the senior monks. When he was censured by Mahā Koṭṭhita for interrupting their conversation, Citta's friend responds to Mahā Koṭṭhita by saying that Citta should not be censured in that manner as Citta is a "wise man who is able to talk to the elders on *abhidhamma*." In response to this statement, Mahā Koṭṭhita goes on to set out the progressive states of spiritual attainments which are possible, from first to fourth *jhāna* and the "signless mental concentration" [*animitta cetosamādhi*] which is attained by non-attention to signs, and emphasizes that even having attained a signless concentration, yet the mind may not be permanently released from defilements. He predicts that with time defilements do flow into such a mind and such a person ends up leaving the noble life. As predicted, Citta left the robe before long, though he got re-admitted subsequently and attained the final goal.

On this occasion Mahā Koṭṭhita says, supposing a king or his minister with the four hosts of the army were to come up a high road and pitch their camp for one night in the forest, and the sound of the cricket in the forest be drowned by the sound of elephants, horses, chariots and foot soldiers etc., it would be wrong for anyone to say "never now in this forest shall the cricket be heard again," for when the king and his ministers leave the forest, the cricket will be heard again. Even so, when a person with paying no attention to all signs, enters and abides in the signless concentration thinking "I have gained the signless concentration," but "keeps company, untrammelled, rude, given to gossip, passion corrupts his heart and he gives up the training and returns to the lower life."

Let us consider the state of mind referred to in the above *Sutta* which is as follows:

> Consider a person paying no attention to all signs, who enters and abides in the signless concentration thinking "I have gained the signless concentration."[20]

The state of mind referred to above sounds very similar to the fetter-breaking-experience of a supramundane fruit, to the extent that it is signless. However this person grasps such state of mind, thinking "I have gained signless concentration"; he grasps it with craving and conceit. In other words, in this person there is no right view about this state of mind and as a result, for him such experience has not led to breaking of fetters or elimination of underlying tendencies. Hence though this experience sounds almost identical with the fetter-breaking-experience of a supramundane fruit, it is accompanied by an underlying wrong view. In whom there is no right view, there is no way that the experience will lead to fully comprehending *idappaccayatā* (relatedness between cause and effect), *anicca, dukkha* and *anatta* (impermanence, unsatisfactoriness, non-self) being the true nature of reality. Hence with time, when conditions are conducive for same, the defilements return to such a mind. However, if an experience as quoted above is accompanied by right view, it would lead to the breaking of fetters.[21]

This *Sutta* proves that every signless experience is not a fetter-breaking-experience. A signless experience of a worldling would lead to the breaking of fetters only if right view is developed sufficiently, prior to the experience and the experience itself is yoked with such right view.

The *Cūlasuññata Sutta* (MN: 121) refers to one progressing to higher states of concentration in dependence on the lower states of concentration and attains the base of neither-perception-nor-non-perception. Thereafter, by not attending to the base of neither-perception-nor-non-perception, attending "in dependence on" the signless concentration of mind [*animitta cetosamādhi*].[22] The *Sutta* highlights that thereafter one has to understand this signless concentration of mind as being "conditionally and volitionally produced [*abhisaṅkhatam abhisañcetayitam*] and therefore impermanent and liable to cessation" (MN III 108). When he knows and sees thus, his mind is liberated from taints. In other words the signless state has to be yoked with "right view" for taints to be destroyed and the signless state by itself does not result in the breaking of fetters.[23] Accordingly, the signless state here is still the Path, though the best of conditioned [*saṅkhata*] states (AN II 34). Further this *Sutta* refers to two steps, that is, not attending to neither-perception-nor-non-perception and attending to the signless concentration. Yet this signless state is not *Nibbāna* as one is urged to do something more (i.e. attend to it as impermanent) in order to attain *Nibbāna*. This *Sutta* too highlights that every signless experience is not a fetter-breaking-experience.

Other Religious Experiences

There are states of mind reported in other religious experiences too which are similar to the fetter-breaking-experience. Venerable Ñāṇananda, comparing the concept of *papañca* in the Pāli *Nikāyas* and the Brahmanical *Upaniṣads*, notes that the similarity between the Upaniṣadic passage describing the experience of the "*turiya*" state and v.874 of the *Sutta-nipāta* cannot be ignored:

> *turiya* is not that which is conscious of the internal (subjective) world, nor that which is conscious of the external (objective) world, nor that which is conscious of both, nor that which is a mass of all sentiency, nor that which is simple consciousness, nor that which is insentient. (It is) unseen (by any sense-organ), not related to anything, incomprehensible (by the mind), uninferable, unthinkable, indescribable, essentially of the nature of consciousness, constituting the self alone, negation of all phenomena, the peaceful, All bliss and the non-dual. This is what is known as the fourth [*turiya*]. This is the ātman and it has to be realized [*Māṇḍuka Upaniṣad*]. (Ñāṇananda 1976, 131)

Further we have already discussed v.874 of the *Sutta-nipāta,* from the *Kalahavivāda Sutta,* with regard to the nature of the fetter-breaking-experience (p. 98). In the *turiya* state, the person is not conscious of the external or the internal world, or of both. He is not unconscious, nor is it simple consciousness. It is "non-dual consciousnesses." This state of mind is understood as *turiya.*

A similar state of mind is reported in Islamic Sufism by Master Sufi Ali Ghizali, as follows:

> He who is invoked by prayer takes possession of the mind of him who prays and the mind of the latter is absorbed in God whom he addresses, his prayers ceasing and no self-consciousness abiding in him, even to this extent that a mere thought about his prayers appears to him a veil and a hindrance. This state is called "absorption" by the doctors of mystical lore, when a man is so utterly absorbed that he perceives nothing of his bodily members, nothing of what is passing without, nothing of what occurs to his mind—yea, when he is, as it were, absent from all these things whatsoever, journeying first to his Lord. But if the thought occurs to him that he is totally absorbed, that is a blot; for only that absorption is worthy of the name which is unconscious of absorption. (Sirdar Ikbal Ali Shah 1933, 219)

The above is a total absorption, without "self-consciousness," perceptions nor thoughts. These spiritual experiences prima-facie seem similar to the fetter-breaking-experience discussed in our study. However the view these experiences generate completely differ from the view that the fetter-breaking-experience in Theravāda Buddhism generates, which it naturally regards as the truly right view. Whilst the Theravāda Buddhist, consequent to the fetter-breaking-experience and its effect, sees the true nature of conditioned existence to be subject to dependent arising, impermanent, unsatisfactory and non-self and consequently sees that "nothing is worth while holding on to [*sabbe dhammā nābhinivesāya*]," all other religious experiences generate a sense of identity or oneness with God or the Universe. Ken Wilber, referring to other religious experiences, writes:

> The most fascinating aspect of such awesome and illuminating experience is that the individual comes to feel, beyond any shadow of a doubt that he or she is fundamentally one with the entire universe, all the worlds, high or low, sacred or pro-

> fane. The sense of identity expands far beyond the narrow confines of the mind and body and embraces the entire cosmos. (Wilber 2001, 3)

R.M. Bucker referred to this as "cosmic consciousnesses" (Wilber 2001, 3). Muslims call it "supreme identity," Wilber refers to it as "unity consciousness," a loving embrace with the universe as a whole (Wilber 2001, 3). For the Theravāda Buddhist, such experiences, while having sublime aspects, is still conditioned and does not lead to an exit from *saṃsāra* and an ending of the ten fetters; the underlying tendencies of the mind remain intact. What makes the difference in the final outcome of the fetter-breaking-experience of Theravāda Buddhism is the right view [*sammā-diṭṭhi*] which Theravāda Buddhists see as unique to their path.

Daniel Brown, in his study of the stages of meditation in cross-cultural perspective, judges that a Hindu and a Buddhist meditator progress through the same eighteen stages of meditation and yet have different experiences along the way because of the difference in "perspectives" which are taken. Brown's conclusion is the opposite of the stereotypical notions of mystical experiences that perennial philosophers have usually meant by the "transcendent unity of religions." These philosophers conclude that there are many paths to the same end. Brown concludes the opposite: there is one path which leads to different ends, different enlightenment experiences (Engler *et al.* 1986, 219–220). The difference in the "perspective" as referred to by Brown, of a Theravāda meditator is the "right view," the very first factor of the Noble Eightfold Path which is the foundation of this Path and which is unique to this Path. In general the difference is not so much in the religious experience, but the special way in which one sees (*vi + passanā*) one's experience. However, opposed to Brown's conclusion that "there is one path which leads to different ends, different enlightenment experiences," I conclude that these are different paths that lead to different enlightenment experiences.

Re-Experiencing the Fetter-Breaking-Experience: An Analysis of *Phala-Samāpatti*

Those who have had a specific experience which resulted in attaining a supramundane fruit, continue to experience a similar state of mind from time to time, either naturally or consequent to resolving for such an abiding. This is referred to in the *Visuddhimagga* as "fruition attainment" [*phala-samāpatti*], and some contemporary meditative traditions consider this to be a concrete test of having attained a supramundane fruit.

Here we will analyze the implicit and explicit references to *phala-samāpatti* in the Pāli *Nikāya*s and the *Visuddhimagga* and compare these with the findings of our field research, with a view to examining its true nature and relevance to actual experience: whether it is a concrete test of an attainment of a supramundane fruit.

The Visuddhimagga

The *Visuddhimagga* says, just as a king experiences royal bliss and a deity experiences divine bliss, so too, the noble ones think "we shall experience the noble supramundane bliss" [*ariyaṃ lokuttarasukhaṃ anubhavissāma*]. It says that they attain this for comfortable living in this life [*diṭṭhadhamma-sukha-vihāratthaṃ*] and after deciding on the duration, they attain the "fruition attainment" whenever they choose (Vism. XXIII.8/Vism.821).

Phala-samāpatti is described in the *Visuddhimagga* as:

> An absorption in the cessation in which the noble fruition consists. No ordinary people attain it, because it is beyond their reach. But those who have reached a higher path do not attain a lower fruition because the state of each successive person is more tranquilized than the one below. And those who have reached a lower path do not attain a higher fruition because it is beyond their reach. Each one attains his appropriate fruition. (Vism.XXIII.6/Vism.820)

Accordingly, a stream-enterer will only be able to attain the fruition relating to the attainment of stream-entry and not the fruition attainment relating to the fruit of once-returning. Nor can a once-returner attain the fruition relating to the fruit of stream-entry. Each one can attain absorption only in their respective fruition attainments and not in an attainment higher or lower.

As to the process of attaining *phala-samāpatti*, the *Visuddhimagga* says:

> A noble disciple who seeks the attainment of fruition should go into solitary retreat. He should see formations with insight according to rise and fall and so on. When that insight has progressed, then comes change-of-lineage-[*gotrabhū*-] knowledge with formations as its object. And immediately next to it consciousness becomes absorbed in cessation by way of the attainment of fruition (*phala-samāpatti-vasena nirodhe cittaṃ appeti*). (Vism. XXIII.10/Vism.822)

According to the *Visuddhimagga* (Vism.XXIII.12/Vism.822), this is a signless attainment which is sustained by three conditions: by not attending to sign (any object other than *Nibbāna*), attending to the signless element [*Nibbāna*], and prior volition, as given at MN I 296. Prior to attaining the fruition, by prior volition (to abide in the fruition) for a pre-determined period of time, one can make it to last for this time.

The *Visuddhimagga* differentiates *phala-samāpatti* from attainment of the cessation of perception and feeling [*saññā-vedayita-nirodha-samāpatti*]. In the latter, one experiences total cessation of consciousness. This latter state of mind is discussed in detail in this chapter (pp. 114–116). Venerable Pa-auk Sayadaw of the Burmese tradition differentiates *phala-samāpatti* from *nirodha-samāpatti* by the fact that all mental factors cease without remainder in the latter, but in the former there is not only consciousness present, but also volitional activities (Pa-auk Tawya Sayadaw 1993, 242).

Venerable Mahāsi Sayadaw of the Burmese tradition is of the opinion that one should be reassured of one's own real attainment only if one could absorb oneself repeatedly in *phala-samāpatti*. He says that since it has been stated in the *Visuddhimagga* that determination should be made without any doubt and if a person is a genuine *ariya*, he can without fail absorb himself in the fruition he has attained. For this reason, if a person is incapable of absorbing himself in a "trance of *phala*" despite the fact that he is an *ariya*, it only remains to make a presumption that the failure to absorb is due to lack of vigour and keenness in *samādhi* and also in the remaining faculties [*indriya*]. Therefore *vipassanā* should be repeatedly practised and developed to make that *samādhi indriya* etc. fully strengthened and vigorous (Māhāsi Sayadaw 1980, 413).

In general it seems that the Burmese tradition considers the "fruition attainment" [*phala-samāpatti*] as a concrete test of the attainment of a supramundane fruit.

Implicit References in the *Nikāyas* to *Phala-Samāpatti*

The term "*phala-samāpatti*" does not occur in the Pāli *Nikāyas*. However states of mind similar to what is described in the *Visuddhimagga* as "*phala-samāpatti*" can be found in the *Suttas*. It is based on these *Suttas* that the *Visuddhimagga* has dedicated sections 5 to 15 of chapter XXIII to this state of mind. Let us consider some of these passages.

In the *Mahāvedalla Sutta* of the *Majjhima Nikāya*, in a conversation between Venerable Sāriputta and Venerable Mahā-koṭṭhita, there is a reference to entering, sustaining and emerging from a signless state of mind which is referred to as "signless liberation of mind" [*animitta cetovimutti*]. It says there are two conditions for the attainment of signless deliverance of the mind: "non-attention to any sign and attention to the signless element [*sabba-nimittānaṃ ca amanasikāro, animittāya ca dhātuyā manasikāro*]" (MN I 296). Sustaining this state is by these two conditions plus the prior determination of its duration [*pubbe ca abhisaṅkhāro*] and two conditions for emergence [*vuṭṭhānāyāti*] from it are attention to any sign and non-attention to the signless element (MN I 296).

In *Sutta* 7 of the *Cittasaṃyutta* of the *Saṃyutta Nikāya*, Venerable Godatta refers to a "signless liberation of mind" [*animitta cetovimutti*]. Here, the process of attaining it is simply given as "non-attention to any sign" (SN IV 296).

When the Buddha was ill towards the last days of his life, he addressed Venerable Ānanda as follows:

> Whenever, Ānanda by non-attention to any sign and by the cessation of certain feelings, the Tathāgata enters and dwells in the signless concentration of mind [*animittaṃ cetosamādhiṃ*], on that occasion Ānanda the body of the *Tathāgata* is more comfortable. Therefore Ānanda dwell with yourself as your own island, with yourself as your own refuge, with no other refuge.[24]

This is a state of mind apparently similar to the *animitta cetosamādhi* of Venerable Citta Hatthisāriputta (AN III 397) discussed in this chapter (pp. 102–103). However unlike Citta Hatthisāriputta, Venerable Ānanda was an *aryan* prior to the *parinibbāna* of the Buddha, though not an *Arahant*. The Buddha could not have asked Ānanda to dwell in the cessation of perception and feeling, as cessation of perception and feeling could be attained only by non-returners and *Arahants*. It is possible that the Buddha on this occasion was advising him to dwell in the "fruition attainment" of the fruit that is stream-entry. For him who has experienced the fetter-breaking-experience relating to the fruit that is stream-entry, the mind has a tendency to revert to the most comfortable place it has ever experienced, in this case, the fetter-breaking-experience of the fruit that is stream-entry.

Bhikkhu Bodhi, commenting on this passage, explains:

> The expression used is *animitta cetosamādhi*. But this concentration must be different from the one with the same name mentioned in *sutta* 9 of *Moggallāna Saṃyutta* (*sutta* 40:9 (SN IV 268–69). The commentaries explain the latter as deep insight concentration, the present one as fruition attainment [*phala-samāpatti*]. This would then make it identical with *animitta cetovimutti* of 41:7 (*sutta* 7 of *Cittasaṃyutta*).
> (Bodhi 2000, 1921, n. 142)

In *Sutta* 9 of the *Moggallāna Saṃyutta*, with reference to the practice of Venerable Moggallāna, it is said that the following thought occurred to Moggallāna: "here by non-attention to all signs, a *bhikkhu* enters and dwells in the signless concentration of the mind [*animitta cetosamādhi*]. This is called the signless concentration of mind." Here Moggallāna says:

> Then, friends, by non-attention to any sign I entered and dwelt in the signless concentration of mind. Whilst I dwelt therein my consciousness followed along with signs [*nimittānusāri viññāṇaṃ hoti*]. Then, friends, the Blessed one came to me by means of his spiritual power and said "Moggallāna, Moggallāna, do not be negligent, Brahmin, regarding the signless concentration of mind. Steady your mind in signless concentration of mind, unify your mind in the signless concentration of mind, concentrate your mind in the signless concentration of mind." Then on a later occasion, by non-attention to all signs, I entered and dwelt in the signless concentration of the mind. (SN IV 269)

At this time Moggallāna was an *ariyan* established in right view and yet not an *Arahant*. Therefore this is not *arahatta-phala-samādhi*. Nor is this state referred to in this *Sutta* as "*nirodha-samāpatti*." It is possible that the Buddha was advising Moggallāna to attain the re-experiencing of the fetter-breaking-experience of the last supramundane fruit attained by him, though the above shows that good concentration is needed for this, probably so as to attain the second condition needed for sustaining it: attention to the signless element.

Further, the *Sutta*s differentiate between the attainment of cessation of perception and feeling and a signless state of mind accompanied by consciousness as follows. In the *Cittasaṃyutta* of the *Salāyatanavagga*, there is a passage which differentiates between cessation of perception and feeling and a signless [*animitta*] state of mind. Answering the question raised by Citta the householder on cessation of perception and feeling, Venerable Kāmabhū says "householder when a *bhikkhu* has emerged from the attainment of the cessation of perception and feeling, three kinds of contact touch him: empty contact, signless contact, wishless contact" [*suññata-phassa, animitta-phassa, appaṇihita-phassa*] (SN IV 295). This shows that having emerged from cessation of perception and feeling, in a state where consciousness is functional, one "contacts" a signless state. It is through consciousness that one understands the signless state.

Again in the *Cūlavedalla Sutta*, when Visākha asks, "when a *bhikkhu* has emerged from the attainment of cessation of perception and feeling, how many kinds of contact touch him?," Bhikkhuni Dhammadinnā says, three kinds of contact "touch" [*phusanti*] him: empty contact, signless contact, and wishless contact (MN I 302). Hence this passage too, like SN IV 295, distinguishes between the cessation of perception and feeling and a signless state, that is, a signless state accompanied by consciousness.

As discussed earlier, according to the *Visuddhimagga*, *phala-samāpatti* is a state of mind which can be attained by a noble person who has attained a supramundane fruit. During it, the mind attends to the signless, "*Nibbāna*," and is free from any sensory "sign" as object; it can be attained for a predetermined period of time. This state of mind referred to in the above *Sutta*s on the face of it seems to be very similar to the fetter-breaking-experience of the religious experience which marks the dawn of a supramundane fruit which was discussed in this chapter (pp. 90–102) to the extent that they are both signless states. Here one does not experience the objects from the sense-bases, one does not experience form, sound, smells, taste, touch nor ideas, and also feelings, and volitional activities do not manifest at this point of time though one is percipient of and attentive to the "absence of" conditioned phenomena, (i.e. the signless state). It is also noteworthy that all monks referred to in the above *Suttas* in relation to whom the said state of mind has been discussed, are *aryan* disciples. Whilst the Burmese tradition and the commentaries take the ability to attain *phala-samāpatti* as a concrete test of having attained a supramundane fruit, some contemporary meditation masters reject this as wishful thinking as people create in their mind what they want to experience (Interview No. 8, Q.18).

Ajahn Brahmavamso rejects "*phala-samāpatti*" as he is of the opinion that it is a commentarial, *abhidhamma* term, which has no justification in the *Suttas*, no justification in real life (Interview No. 8, Q.15). He is of the opinion that this is only a memory of a very powerful experience such as the fetter-breaking-experience of a supramundane fruit and not a "re-experience." He justifies his position on the basis that "once a person eradicates fetters at the time of the dawn of the relevant supramundane fruit, you cannot eradicate them again by pre-determination." He says:

> A person who attained to be a stream-enterer can always reflect on that experience and realize that he is a stream-enterer again. It's a memory of that experience which the commentary calls it a re-experience of a supramundane fruit. It's just the memory of the most powerful experience of one's life which you can recall at will. But it's a memory rather than an abiding. That's because, the attainment of stream-entering is a purification of a view; the memory is always the re-experiencing of that view. When it comes to the fruit of *anāgāmī*, you have eradicated sensual desire and ill-will; this is an eradication of a tendency of the mind. Once you eradicate it, you don't eradicate it again. Once you blow up the twin towers, you don't blow it up a second time. They are gone once and for all. But what you can do is, recall that they are no longer there and have been eradicated. (Interview No. 8, Q.16)

However, as discussed earlier, a signless experience by itself does not break fetters, it is the understanding generated relative to such an experience that leads to breaking of fetters and makes it the "fetter-breaking-experience." Re-experiencing the signless experience based on which the fetters broke would lead to developing of wisdom as it helps to develop better understanding of suffering arising through the sense bases and the aggregates subject to clinging. The peace experienced due to the absence of *nimittas* would also encourage one to pursue higher fruits of the Path. Unless and until the degree of wisdom necessary to eradicate the next set of fetters (relating to the attainment of the next fruit) is developed by one, mere re-experiencing the signless experience which led to eradicating the earlier set of fetters would not lead to breaking of the next set of fetters. Moreover, as the Path followed by one is the same as the Path followed by one for the attainment of the previous fruit, it ought to lead to the same result (i.e. letting go of conditioned objects, the two bundles of name-and-form and consciousness falling apart, and the mind experiencing a signless state). For the same reason, perhaps the intensity of the re-experiences relating to the attainment of the same fruit ought to be the same. As discussed above, Ajahn Brahmavamso feels that it is at most only a memory of a very powerful experience such as the attainment of a supramundane fruit and not a re-experience, as once a person eradicates fetters at the time of dawn of a relevant supramundane fruit, he cannot eradicate them again. However, referring to people who are born in the human world, having already attained a fruit that is stream-entry in a previous birth, Ajahn Brahmavamso says that such a person would "re-experience" such experience in the current birth (Interview No. 8, Q.31). If an experience relating to an attainment of a supramundane fruit can be carried forward to a future birth, there is no reason why one cannot re-experience it in this very life, whether it is designated as "*phala-samāpatti*" or by any other term.

Ajahn Brahmavamso, in rejecting *phala-samāpatti,* seems to be doing so on the basis that some practitioners at times report on *phala-samāpatti* as though it involves a "blanking out of consciousness" and that they equate it to some sort of a cessation. He argues that, if so, it is possible only by those who are non-returners and *Arahants* and with the four formless absorptions (*arūpa jhānas*). He says:

> Very often what I sometimes heard is that people attain some degree of stopping of consciousness for some reason even though it is not a nirvāṇic state. It is just like blanking out the mind. It's like something wonderful and amazing. But it is not the attainment of the path and fruit of stream-entry nor attaining of Arahant[ship]. They have not attained to a blanking out of consciousness or some sort of cessation that is gained as a result of a *samādhi* experience or a *jhāna* or even the *arūpa jhāna.* Emerging afterwards and reflecting that as an insight experience. And what that experience [attainment of a supramundane fruit] really is, it is again a powerful letting go which has always been associated with an enormous happiness and bliss. It is a bliss knowing that a huge amount of suffering is taken away from you and that itself is overcoming of hindrances. But it is not a *samādhi* state in the sense of a *sammā samādhi* or *jhāna*. It is the commentaries which have actually tried to equate *samādhi* with a supramundane fruit that is not really good. (Q.17)

Considering the full interview, Q.17–24, Brahmavamso's view seems to be:

1) The attainment of a supramundane fruit (the fetter-breaking experience) is not a state of *samādhi*, as *samādhi* pertains to the *jhānas* and formless states of *samatha*.
2) At times when reporting the re-experience of the fetter-breaking-experience people use the phrase "blanking out of the consciousness" or "cessation of consciousness." (However when questioned in detail, what they mean is not cessation of consciousness, but a signless state of mind). Brahmavamso, mainly based on the words "stopping of consciousnesses," seems to assume that they are reporting an attainment of "cessation of consciousness" meaning *nirodha-samāpatti*. Hence he denies the possibility of this experience without mastery of the four *jhānas* and the four formless *jhānas* and also without being at least a non-returner.

However, as discussed above, we saw that in terms of the *Visuddhimagga*, *phala-samāpatti* is not a state of mind in which consciousness ceases. Both the *Suttas* and the *Visuddhimagga* differentiate this experience from "cessation of perception and feeling" [*saññāvedayitanirodhasamāpatti*], that is, in the latter, consciousness ceases totally and consciousness is present in the former.

Findings of the Field Research

Whatever the differences of opinion may be on *phala-samāpatti*, the findings of our field research point to the occurrence of a state of mind which is very similar if not identical to the "fetter-breaking-experience" experienced at the dawn of a supramundane fruit. Whilst some have experienced this state with prior determination, some others experience it naturally, and some can attain it both ways and some have mastered this attainment. I found that some interviewees who do not believe in the "*phala-samāpatti*" as set out in the *Visuddhimagga* do actually continue to experience a state similar or identical to the "fetter-breaking-experience" experienced by them at the dawn of the supramundane fruit they have attained. Set out below are some of our findings:

1) Interview No. 3: Throughout the interview, this interviewee refers to re-experiencing of the spiritual experience relating to the attainment of the fruit that is stream-entry and he also says that subsequently he practised for *phala-samāpatti* under the guidance of a teacher. He describes *phala-samāpatti* as an "oceanic experience," as "an escape from the sensory world." He could switch between abiding in *phala-samāpatti* and a normal state of mind, like switching between sunshine and cloudiness (Q.7, 8, and 11). He says:

> I just let it go freely [the mind]. Like a kite having gone high up having broken off the thread. So I was just watching the kite flying, limitless, that is, there is nothing done, there is no knowledge of anything done, at that time it was so oceanic"[cool] and enjoyable that it was like taking me up to and showing me the *deva* world or the *brahmā* world. It was like opening me to a dream world. It was like telling me "now you are in a dream world, enjoy it," it's such a thrill. So I stayed there for a long time. Even subsequently, at any time, I was able to go back to the sensory world, again do some walking and sitting, again to go back there. When I could switch between these two speedily, I knew that now there was some control. But in order to go there, you need some initial preparation. Having gone there, it was possible to go back to the usual things in the normal world (Q.7). ... clearly it is not something that can be explained in terms of the eye, ear, tongue, nose (Q.8). ... At any given time, from time to time, it gets cloudy, again the sun shines, again it gets cloudy, again the sun shines. Although there is this darkness around, now there is no doubt whether the sun has vanished. (Q.11)

When asked whether *phala-samāpatti* is a concrete test of the attainment of a supramundane fruit, this interviewee, who is a chief preceptor of a well-known forest hermitage and an experienced teacher, says:

> Whether anybody does it or not, the Buddha has stated that if someone has attained something there is a tendency to turn and look back at it. Even the eagle that snatches a prey, having risen up to the sky, has a tendency to look back. After the catch he looks back to see "from where did I aim at the prey?, from where did I choose it?, how did I catch it?" etc. This is the nature of the human mind too. Therefore, this is a matter based on which you can form a theory. But this cannot be made a criterion for it. (Q.94)

2) Interview No. 2: On several occasions after attaining the fruit of stream-entry, when his teacher asked him to do so, this interviewee by prior determination experienced a state of mind similar to the fetter-breaking-experience relating to the fruit that is stream-entry, for almost the exact period of time he resolved for it (Q.22). The variation in time period for which he resolved and what he actually abided in, was seconds (Q.22). This is an interviewee who doesn't believe in the concept of *phala-samāpatti* as stated in the *Visuddhimagga.* Yet on the instructions of his teacher when he attempted to abide in it, he was successful in experiencing a state similar to the fetter-breaking-experience relating to his attainment of stream-entry.
3) Interview No. 4: After his attainment of stream-entry, from time to time, this interviewee has experienced a state similar to the "cessation" he experienced with the attainment of stream-entry. He accepts that it is *phala-samāpatti* (Q.34). But he experiences it not by resolving for it, but only as a natural outcome of his meditation (Q.23–28). He doesn't believe in attaining this by prior determination as stated in the *Visuddhimagga.* Further, he also feels that in this state, though the rest of the sense objects have ceased, the mind base is still active as it is focused on a "state of liberation like a state of *Nibbāna.*" To the question on whether he can experience it by prior determination, he says "I cannot accept it. Because often when you wish for something the mind loses its equanimity. But when you forget about it for some time and continue to work, it is possible that it can happen naturally. But resolving is not necessary for it" (Q.26–28). He refers to experiencing this state of mind, a state similar to the fetter-breaking-experience relating to the fruit that is stream-entry, on two occasions, i.e. whilst meditating and also whilst reflecting on the "earlier experience." He says this state of mind is like a state of *samādhi*, and it can be experienced through reflection, when there is good mindfulness and when the mind is free from hindrances (Q.25).
4) Interview No. 5: After the attainment of the fruit that is stream-entry, from time to time, this interviewee has experienced a state similar to the "non-occurrence of feeling" he experienced at the dawn of the attainment of the fruit that is stream-entry. He experiences it both ways, with a resolve for it and also as a natural outcome of his meditation (Q.26–27, 39). He admits that it is *phala-samāpatti* (Q.30). He experiences it with both types of meditation (i.e. when engaged in *vipassanā* as well as *samatha* meditation) (Q.50).

In another reported case,[25] we found that the person concerned experiences a state of mind similar to the fetter-breaking-experience of her fruit of stream-entry when listening to an inspiring sermon on insight. She finds that she loses awareness of a few successive words in the midst of a sentence or losing awareness of a few letters within a word. That is, in the word "*vipassanā*" she hears the sound "*vi*" and next she knows is "*nā*" and in between these sounds, she loses track of the "world" and she feels the "coming back to the world" prominently through hearing. During this time she clearly experiences a signless state and the experience is very similar to the fetter-breaking-experience relating to the attainment of her fruit that is stream-entry. This happens a few times in quick succession, whilst listening to an inspiring sermon and quite unexpectedly. She has also experienced it for a longer period of about 20–30 minutes, both whilst meditating and whilst listening to an inspiring sermon. During this time she feels she is "dead to the world." This is a case where the fetter-breaking-experience is re-experienced for seconds or minutes, and happens naturally, when the mind is inclined towards *vipassanā*. However, her mind is not inclined to sit and master it as given in the *Visuddhimagga* as she does not believe in attaining it with prior determination.

It is noteworthy that these people who were interviewed began to experience a state of mind similar to the state referred to as "*phala-samāpatti*," only after their attainment of a supramundane fruit and never have they experienced it before, even though during the course of their practice there would have been many occasions where the mind may have experienced significant levels of *samādhi*. It is natural that a mind inclines towards the most comfortable state it has ever experienced before, especially when the conditions are conducive for it and the fetter-breaking-experience relating to one's current supramundane fruit ought to be the loftiest state that a person's mind has ever experienced.

Further there are references in the *Suttas* to *Arahants* dwelling in the state of mind realized by them at the time of their attainment of Arahantship, that is, an *Arahant* who realized for himself the taintless liberation of mind, liberation by wisdom, can enter upon it and dwell in it [*upasampajja viharati*] (AN IV 119). Another *Sutta* says an *Arahant* should attend to the five aggregates subject to clinging as impermanent ... non-self, which leads to pleasant dwellings [*diṭṭhadhamma-sukhavihāra*] (SN III 168).

I conclude that, contrary to Ajahn Brahmavamso's opinion discussed above (i.e. that *phala-samāpatti* has no justification in the *Suttas*, no justification in real life), the re-experiencing of the fetter-breaking-experience relating to a supramundane fruit is real and is experienced as a signless [*animitta*] state. But we cannot conclude for sure whether it is the same state that *Visuddhimagga* designates as "*phala-samāpatti*." This is experienced by noble persons whether they believe in the technicalities as mentioned in the *Visuddhimagga* or not. Though the term "*phala-samāpatti*" does not occur in the *Suttas*, certain signless states referred to in the *Nikāyas* as highlighted by us in this chapter as implicit references to *phala-samāpatti* (see pp. 107–108), correspond to this state of mind. Both the *Suttas* and the *Visuddhimagga* differentiate this state from "cessation of perception and feeling," as *phala-samāpatti* is accompanied by consciousness and cessation of perception and feeling is a state where consciousness is wholly suspended. For some, this re-experience may be more prominent than for some others. Some attain it with prior determination, those who do not believe in it still experience a similar state naturally, and some experience it both naturally and with prior determination.

As to the mode of attaining this state, most attain it whilst engaging in *vipassanā*. A few others feel they experience this whilst engaged in *samatha* too. It could also be attained by reflecting on the fetter-breaking-experience of a supramundane fruit as, at such a time, the mind gets focused on the memory of the signless nature of the fetter-breaking-experience, which would serve as the preparatory work for *phala-samāpatti* according to both the *Suttas* and the *Visuddhimagga*,(i.e. "non-attention to any sign and attention to the signless element").

Further, it could be concluded that, when one re-experiences this fetter-breaking-experience soon after the attainment of a supramudane fruit, it is experienced as a striking phenomenon, but with time, it loses its vigour and settles as a natural phenomenon of the mind or as the true nature of the mind.

Of the *Suttas* we considered above (pp. 107–108) as having implicit references to *phala-samāpatti*, some *Suttas* refer to two conditions needed for attainment of this, that is, non-attention to any sign and attention to the singless element (MN I 296), whilst some other *Suttas* refer to only the first condition, (i.e."by paying no attention to any sign") and not the second condition (SN IV 269).The variation found in our field research with regard to the process of attaining the re-experiencing, i.e. some attaining this naturally in the process of insight practice and some others with prior determination, and some both ways, reflect the variation in the conditions mentioned in the *Suttas*. Those who attain the state with prior-determination fulfil the second condition namely, "by attention to the signless element."

However, as discussed in this chapter (pp. 102–105), it is possible that similar signless states of mind could be experienced by *non-ariyans* as well, as in the case of Citta Hattisāriputta. These states experienced by *non-ariyans*, though apparently similar, would in fact be qualitatively and technically different, as the state of fetters and underlying tendencies in the mind of a *non-ariyan* and the *ariyan* are different and outwardly one might not know the difference. Therefore we conclude that though the re-experiencing of the fetter-breaking-experience is real, it is not a concrete test of an attainment of a supramundane fruit, as another signless state might be mistaken for it. The concrete test of an attainment of a supramundane fruit is the absence of the relevant fetters, which is reflected through the insight, attitudes and behaviour of the person concerned.

Based on our field research, we find that the duration of the attainment of the re-experience differed from a few seconds or minutes to around half an hour or even longer.

Phala-Samāpatti and the Cessation of Perception and Feeling

Cessation of perception and feeling [*saññā-vedayita-nirodha-samāpatti*] is a state of mind technically different to *phala-samāpatti,* though one may feel that *phala-samāpatti* is an experience in which everything ceases. In fact at times the term "cessation" is used to describe the fetter-breaking-experience relating to a supramundane fruit or to the *phala-samāpatti* experienced by one subsequently, as various states do cease in this state. In the *Visuddhimagga,* the cessation of perception and feeling is also referred to as "attainment of cessation" [*nirodha-samāpatti*] and it is defined as the "non-occurrence of consciousness and its concomitants owing to their progressive cessation" [*anupubba-nirodha-vasena citta-cetasikānaṃ dhammānaṃ appavatti*] (Vism.XXIII.18/Vism.824). The *Cūlavedalla Sutta* reports a discussion between Dhammadinnā Therī and the lay follower Visākha, which highlights the details with regard to this state of mind (MN I 302).

According to the *Visuddhimagga*, "no ordinary person ("worldling"—*puthujjana*), no stream-enterer or once-returner, and no non-returner and *Arahant* who are bare insight workers attain it. But both non-returners and those with taints destroyed, who are with the eight attainments, attain it" (Vism.XXIII.18/Vism. 824, cf. AN III 194).Therefore for attainment of cessation, the four *arūpa jhānas* (formless *jhānas*) are essential. *Phala-samāpatti* can be experienced even without mastery of the formless *jhānas*. In *phala-samāpatti*, as discussed earlier in this chapter, consciousness does not cease and all noble persons who have attained the four supramundane fruits can attain it. But cessation of perception and feeling is experienced only by non-returners and *Arahants*, that too, by those amongst them who have mastered the four formless *jhānas*.

How and Why Do They Attain and Emerge from the Cessation of Perception and Feeling

According to the *Visuddhimagga*, being wearied by the occurrence and dissolution of formations (or conditioned states, *saṅkhāras*), they attain it thinking "Let us dwell in bliss by being without consciousness here and now and reaching the cessation that is *Nibbāna*" (Vism.XXIII.30/Vism.828).

The *Cūlavedalla Sutta* says that when attaining the cessation of perception and feeling, it does not occur to a person, "I shall attain the cessation of perception and feeling" or "I have attained the cessation of perception and feeling"; but rather his mind has previously been developed in such a way that it leads him to such a state. Similarly when emerging from cessation of perception and feeling, it does not occur to him "I am emerging or I have emerged" rather the mind has previously been developed in such a way that it leads him to that state (MN I 302).

According to the *Visuddhimagga*:

> It comes about in one who performs the preparatory tasks by striving with *samatha* and *vipassanā* and causes the cessation of [consciousness belonging to] the base consisting of neither-perception-nor-non-perception. One who strives with *samatha* alone reaches the base consisting of neither-perception-nor-non-perception and remains there, while one who strives with *vipassanā* alone reaches the attainment of fruition [*phala-samāpatti*] and remains there. But it is one who strives with both *samatha* and *vipassanā*, and after performing the preparatory tasks, cause the cessation of [consciousness belonging to] the base consisting of neither-perception-nor-non-perception, who attains it. (Vism.XXIII.31/Vism.828)

So we can see that this is a state that needs a lot of preparatory work, it needs both the *arūpa jhānas* and a process of insight, together with pre-determination to attain it. This cessation lasts only for the predetermined duration (Vism.XXIII.48/Vism.708). It has been recommended that one abides in this only for a maximum of seven days. One should attain this only after resolving that "my own vital formations should go on occurring for seven days" (Vism.XXIII.42/Vism.832).

Further, when a person is emerging from the cessation of perception and feeling, what arises first is mental formation (*citta-saṅkhāra*, in the form of feeling and perception), thereafter bodily formation (*kāya-saṅkhara*, in the form of breathing) and lastly verbal formation (*vacī-saṅkhāra*, in the form of mental application and examination). Having emerged, three kinds of contacts touch him, empty [*suññato phasso*], signless contact [*animitto phasso*] and wishless contact [*appaṇihito phasso*], and the mind inclines leans and tends towards seclusion (MN I 301 and 302), this seclusion being Nibbāna (Vism.XXIII.50/Vism.832). According to the *Visuddhimagga*, the emergence from it comes about by means of fruition of non-return in the case of a non-returner or by means of the fruition of the Arahantship in the case of an *Arahant* (Vism.XXIII.49/Vism.832). Accordingly, when a person emerges from this state, he first experiences a *phala-samāpatti*: in the case of an *anāgāmī*, the *phala-samāpatti* of *anāgāmī-phala* or in the case of an *Arahant*, the mind will touch *arahatta-phala-samāpatti*.

How Does it Help to Eradicate Defilements?

When emerging from cessation of perception and feeling, as the mind is fully concentrated and sharp, particularly in the context of the empty, signless and the wishless state, the newly arisen formations become a very striking experience. Therefore at such time, the mind turns inwards and it is possible to observe these formations as they arise and cease as when re-appearing after a period of complete absence, their nature is clearly seen and strong insight into them arises. The mind does not get entangled with these newly arisen formations at this point, there would be only pure awareness. Subsequently, for a non-returner, but not an *Arahant*, the mind begins to experience some craving and conceit and begins to get entangled with the formations. However, at this point of emerging, the mind can observe these newly arisen formations as impermanent, unsatisfactory and non-self or even if defilements arise, it has an opportunity to then and there, one by one, with wisdom already developed, extirpate them. That is, the mind could apply *yoniso manasikāra*, wise attention, and can go back to the root point where the mind got entangled with the arisen formations. Once the mind identifies the root cause as "conceit and craving" through "wisdom already developed" the mind cuts off the identified defilements. This way one attains the final goal as an *ubhato-bhāga-vimutta*, with the mind released both ways (Ñāṇamoli and Bodhi 1995, 1272, n. 702).

One who fails to eradicate all defilements in this way, who is not yet an *Arahant*, as he has experienced the "peace" of transcending of perception through *saññāvedayitanirodhasamāpatti*, his mind would incline towards it more and more. The more he attains it, emerging from it, the more such a mind will be inclined to observe the newly arisen formations as aforesaid and he would apply *yoniso manasikāra* and by wisdom previously developed, would cut off the remaining defilements.

The Difference Between the Cessation of Perception and Feeling and Death

The *Mahāvedalla Sutta* of *Majjhima Nikāya* differentiates between the cessation of perception and feeling and death. In one who is dead, his vital formation [āyu saṅkhāra] are ceased and subsided so is bodily formation, verbal formation and mental formation (perception and feeling). His vitality is exhausted [*usmā vūpasantā*] and his life has dissipated [*āyu parikkhīno*] and his faculties are fully broken up [*indriyāni viparibhinnāni*]. However, in one who is abiding in this *samāpatti*, while his bodily, verbal and mental formations are ceased and subsided, his vitality is not exhausted, his heat is not dissipated and his faculties become exceptionally clear [*indriyāni vippasannāni*] (MN I 296).

This *Sutta* also states that, *āyu-saṅskāra* (vital formation) and "states of feeling" [*vedanīya dhamma*] are two different states as, if both were one and the same, once one abides in cessation of perception and feeling, it would not be possible for him to emerge from it alive.

Conclusion

In this chapter we first examined the nature of the fetter-breaking-experience relating to a supramundane fruit and the types of noble persons related to such experiences. I conclude that, though the liberating religious experience in general differs from person to person, and within the same person it differs from attaining one supramundane fruit to another, the basic nature of the peak-point of such experience (the fetter-breaking-experience) is common to all, and is common to all four supramundane fruits to the extent it is signless, wishless and empty [*animitta, appaṇihita* and *suññata*]. The intensity of the fetter-breaking-experience differs from one supramundane fruit to another and the intensity increases as one attains the higher fruits. I found that at the fetter-breaking-experience, due to the mind not identifying with any perceptual signs, name-and-form does not manifest in consciousness, it would not register in it. However at this stage, as the person is conscious and not unconscious, although there are no conditioned objects manifesting as it is a singless experience, the consciousness takes as its object the "absence of conditioned phenomena," (i.e. the signless state). At this stage, the signless state is the object of consciousness and not that the signless state takes itself as an object—it is the consciousness that takes objects. Though this state is empty of conditioned phenomena, it still has the perception of "the signless" [*animitta*] and is attentive to this state. Having become an *Arahant*, the fetter-breaking-experience is perceived and understood by an *Arahant* as "This is peaceful, sublime ... *Nibbāna*." It is based on the knowledge that arises consequent to the fetter-breaking-experience, and especially the fetters that have been destroyed, that the noble persons are classified in terms of the four fruits of the Path.

Differentiating the fetter-breaking-experience from similar Buddhist and non-Buddhist religious experiences, this chapter concludes that a signless experience by itself does not result in breaking fetters and for it to result in the breaking of fetters it has to be yoked with right view. For the same reason, though some of the non-Buddhist experiences at first sight seem to be almost identical with the fetter-breaking-experience relating to a supramundane fruit of Theravāda Buddhism discussed in this study, the knowledge these other experiences generate completely differs from the knowledge the Theravāda Buddhist experiences generate, (i.e. the latter generate "right view"). Whilst the Theravāda Buddhist, further to such experiences, sees the true nature of existence to be subject to dependent arising, impermanent, unsatisfactory and non-self and consequently sees that "nothing is worth while holding on to" [*sabbe dhammā nābhinivesāya*], these non-Theravāda Buddhist experiences generate a sense of identity or oneness with God or the universe. Hence, though some of these non-Buddhist religious experiences sound similar to the fetter-breaking-experience, they are qualitatively and technically different from the fetter-breaking-expereinces found in Theravāda Buddhism.

Contrary to various opinions expressed about *phala-samāpatti*, this chapter concludes that the re-experiencing of the fetter-breaking-experience of a supramundane fruit is real and is also a signless state though we cannot conclude for sure whether it is identical to the state designated as "*phala-samāpatti*" by the *Visuddhimagga*. This is experienced by noble persons whether they believe in the technicalities as mentioned in the *Visuddhimagga* or not, yet it is not a concrete test of an attainment of a supramundane fruit. Though the term "*phala-samāpatti*" does not occur in the *Suttas*, certain signless [*animitta*] states referred to in numerous places in the *Nikāyas* correspond to this state of mind and this is a state technically different to cessation of perception and feeling. Whilst in the fetter-breaking-experience, the five sense-bases together with ideas are cut off, in the cessation of perception and feeling, all six sense-bases and all five aggregates subject to clinging including consciousness cease for a pre-determined time period.

Notes

1. See p. 75 for the list of eight types of noble persons.
2. *ekacco puggalo ye te santā vimokhā atikkamma rūpe āruppā te kāyena phassitvā viharati, paññāya c' assa disvā āsavā parikkhīṇā honti* (MN I 477)
3. For a discussion on *ubhato-bhāga-vimutta and paññā-vimutta*, see De Silva 1978.
4. According to the *Visuddhimagga* (Vism.XXIII.18/Vism.824), non-returners and Arahants with eight *jhānas* can attain cessation of perception and feeling. See this chapter (pp. 114) for more details on attaining cessation of perception and feeling.
5. See Chapter 5 (pp. 96–100) for our final analysis of the fetter-breaking-experience.
6. This statement has been analyzed in this study to mean that the feeling didn't manifest, i.e. the interviewee did not notice any feeling.
7. This was done in Englsh, though the interviwee's English was very poor.
8. The *Visuddhimagga* states that "the four paths and the four fruits take timeless unconditioned *Nibbāna* as its object" (Vism.XXIII.4/Vism.820).
9. We hold that this signless state by itself is not *Nibbāna.* Also see pp. 102–103 for examples of where signless states are not *Nibbāna.*
10. *Evaṃ passaṃ bhikkhave sutavā ariyasāvako phasse nibbindati, vedanāya pi nibbindati, saññāya...viññāṇasmiṃ pi nibbindati, Nibbindam virajjati. virāgā vimuccati, vimuttasmiṃ vimuttaṃ īti ñāṇaṃ hoti. khīṇā jāti vusitaṃ brahmacariyaṃ kataṃ karaṇīyaṃ.* (SN II 97)
11. For a discussion on this topic, see simile of the cinema, Ñāṇananda 2006, IV, 359 and also 2004, II, 147.
12. http://medical-dictionary.thefreedictionary.com/fainting.
13. Chapter XXII of the *Visuddhimagga* gives the lead up to the point of fruition of the supramundane Path (Vism. XXII.5/Vism. 785) and refers to a signless state. It is so with regard to all four fruits of the Path. According to the *Visuddhimagga,* states of mind referred to as "path moments" are said to arise immediately prior to the states referred to as "*phala* moments," which state is also given as "emerging from all signs" (Vism.XXIII.4/Vism.820). The said para. 4 reflects the point of time which we refer to as the "fetter-breaking-experience" at which point one feels that one "got cut off from the whole world," or the mind "went in to a different place." However we differ from the *Visuddhimagga* in our definition of "Path" and its "fruits" (see pp. 20).
14. See Chapter 5 (pp. 105–114) for a discussion on re-experiencing of the fetter-breaking-experience.

15. See Chapter 5 (pp. 102–103) for the need to yolk right view with a signless experience for eliminating fetters.
16. In the *Visuddhimagga* too, the passages referring to the point of fruition relating to the attainment of the fruit of once-returning, non-returning and Arahantship is identical (Vism. XXII.23/Vism.790, Vism. XXII.26/Vism. 791, Vism. XXII.29/ Vism. 791), suggesting that there is no difference in the experience at the point of attaining the fruit of once-returning and non-returning, from that of *arahatta-phala*, and that they are also the same as the experience relating to stream-entry (Vism.XXII.5/Vism.685–686). However the *Visuddhimagga* refers to this stage still as the path and not fruit. The relevant passage is as follows:

    At the end of equanimity about formations, conformity and change-lineage-knowledge have arisen in a single adverting in the way already described, then the path of once-return/non-return/Arahantship arises next to change of lineage.

17. As given in the stanza "*yattha nāmañ ca rūpañ ca asesam uparujjhati... ettha esā chijjate jaṭā*" (SN I 354).
18. *The Paṭisambhidāmagga* (II.59 and 65), which the *Vism.* often quotes, says that of the signless, wishless and empty liberation, only one is dominant in a particular experience, but the others are also there in a secondary sense and can be more fully developed later (Harvey1986, 45).
19. "*lokuttara*" means supramundane (i.e. transcending the world).
20. *Idha panāvuso ekacco puggalo sabbanimittānaṃ amanasikārā animittaṃ cetosamādhiṃ upasampajja viharati, so lābhī' mhi animitassa cetosamādhissa' ti samsaṭṭho viharati* (AN III 397).
21. For the nexus between arising of right view/understanding and the fetter-breaking-experience, see Chapter 6, sub-sections on "Right view" and "Knowledge of Dependent Arising" (pp. 121–129).
22. *amanasikarivā nevasaññā nāsaññāyatanasaññaṃ animittaṃ cetosamadhiṃ paṭicca manasikaroti.*
23. Similarly MN: 106 says one delighting in equanimity would not attain *Nibbāna*, but would end up in the realm of neither-perception nor non-perception.
24. *Yasmiṃ Ānanda samaye Tathāgato sabbanimittaṃ amanasikārā ekaccānaṃ vedanaṃ nirodhā animittaṃ cetosamādhiṃ upsampajja viharati phāsutaraṃ Ānanda tasmiṃ samaye Tathāgatassa kāyo hoti. Tasmā ti hānanda attadīpā viharanta attasaraṇā anaññasaranā dhammadīpā dhammasaranā anaññasaraṇā.* (SN V 154)
25. Unrecorded discussion with an interviewee.

— 6 —

The Stream-Enterer

In Chapter 5 we discussed the various types of noble persons [*ariya-puggala*] in the dispensation of the Buddha. We saw that every noble person enters the plane of an *ariyan* through an experience which marks such entry. The entry to the noble plane is through the Noble Eightfold Path and such entrant is referred to as a "stream-enterer" [*sotāpanna*]. The first of the eight noble persons being the one practising for stream-entry is endowed with the eight factors of the Noble Eightfold Path to some degree (see p. 89), though not fully. A stream-enterer is defined as one who possesses the Noble Eightfold Path (SN V 348). "*Sota*" means stream. It denotes the Noble Eightfold Path. "āpatti" means "entering upon" the stream. So "*sotāpatti*" means fully entering upon the stream of the Noble Eightfold Path, or the Path that leads to *Nibbāna*. "*Sotāpanna*" means one who has entered upon the stream (David and Stede 1921–1925, 725).

The fruit that is stream-entry is the first supramundane fruit of the Path. What is most significant at the point of this attainment is destruction of the three lower fetters, i.e. view on personality [*sakkāya-diṭṭhi*], clinging to rules and vows [*sīlabbata-parāmasa*], and skeptical doubt [*vicikicchā*],[1] and the arising of the right view.

This is the most significant milepost on the Path next to attaining Arahantship. The expression "fruit that is stream-entry" as used in this work specifically means the general state of mind of the stream-enterer. The scope of this term includes the absence of the said three fetters and the resultant knowledge, qualities and powers that arise in such a mind.[2]

In this chapter we will examine the following:

1) The state of mind of a stream-enterer
2) The conduct of a stream-enterer
3) The blessings and strengths of a stream-enterer
4) The possibility of someone having become a noble person in a past life
5) Can a stream-enterer commit suicide?
6) To what extent does a stream-enterer see *Nibbāna*?
7) Lay noble disciples
8) Non-humans attaining supramundane fruits

The State of Mind of a Stream-Enterer

Right View

What is most significant at the point of the attainment of stream-entry is that this noble person abandons the "view on personality" [*sakkāya-diṭṭhi*] and acquires right view [*sammā-diṭṭhi*].

Right view is twofold. There is the "right view that is affected by taints, partaking of merit, ripening on the side of attachment" [*sāsavā, puññābhāgiyā, upadhivepakkā*] and there is "right view that is noble, taintless, supramundane, a factor of the Path" [*ariyā, anāsavā, lokuttarā, maggangā*] (MN III 72). The latter is called in the commentaries (MN-a IV,131 and AN-a II,24 and 162) the "supramundane right view" [*lokuttara sammā-diṭṭhi*]. The former is called the "mundane right view" [*lokiya sammā-diṭṭhi*], in the form of the right view of the ownership of kamma [*kammassakatā*], which is a meritorious factor that conduces to a favourable rebirth but cannot by itself transcend conditioned existence (Ñāṇamoli and Bodhi 1995,1322, n. 1102).

Mundane right view is believing in the following:

1) There are fruits and results of giving, and of good and bad actions,
2) Both this world and the next world are real.
3) Mother and father should be respected.
4) There are beings, in the heavens, who are born spontaneously,
5) There are in the world, good and virtuous renunciants and brahmins who have realized for themselves by direct knowledge and declare this world and the other world.

Supramundane right view is the right view found in a noble person. That is "wisdom, the faculty of wisdom, the power of wisdom, the investigation-of-states enlightenment factor, the path factor of right view found in a noble person who possesses the Path and who is developing the Path" [*paññā, paññindriyam, paññābalam, dhammavicayasambojjhango, sammā-diṭṭhi maggangā*] (MN III 72).

The *Cūḷavedalla Sutta* of the *Majjhima Nikāya* sets out 20 modes of views on personality which an uninstructed worldling [*assutavā puthujjana*] could hold, as follows:

1) Self is material form [*rūpa*]
2) Self is possessed of material form
3) Self is in material form
4) Material form is in self

Similarly he regards feeling, perception, volitional activities and consciousness [*vedanā, saññā, saṅkhāra, viññāna*] in the above four modes making up to twenty modes of views on personality (MN I 300).

The commentary on this passage illustrates these four modes in terms of material form as follows (Ñāṇamoli and Bodhi 1995, 1239, n. 462). One may regard "material form" as (a permanent) "self," in the way a flame of a burning oil lamp is identical with the colour of the flame; one may regard self as "possessing material form," as a tree possesses a shadow; one may regard material form as "in self," as the scent in the flower; one may regard self as "in material form," as a jewel is in a casket.

A range of wrong views and perplexities a stream-enterer abandons are set out in the *Diṭṭhi Saṃyutta* of the *Saṃyutta Nikāya* and includes the following:

1) He abandons perplexity about suffering, the cause of suffering, the cessation of suffering and the Path leading to the cessation of suffering (SN III 203).

2) He abandons perplexity as regards the following six: form, feeling, perception, volitional activities, consciousness, and the sixth group being collectively referred to as "what is seen, heard, sensed, cognized, sought after and ranged over by the mind" (SN III 203).The sixth group here is explained to include the visible form base [*diṭṭhaṃ*], the sound base [*sutaṃ*], the sensed [*mutaṃ*]—meaning smell, taste and touch—the cognized [*viññātaṃ*] and the "attained, sought after and ranged over by the mind" [*pattam pariyesitam anuvicaritam manasā*], the last being explained as a reference to views (Bodhi 2000, 1095, n. 250).

The above description encompasses the entire universe of an individual. If so, upon stream-entry one abandons wrong view about the entire universe. Nothing in the universe does he see as permanent, pleasurable and as self. No perplexity arises in such a mind about the true nature of any of these.

3) He does not cling to form, feeling, perception, volitional formation or consciousness as "this is mine, this I am, this is myself" (SN III 203).
4) By clinging to the five aggregates subject to clinging, he does not adhere to the view "that which is the self is the world, having passed away, I shall be permanent, stable, eternal, not subject to change" (SN III 204).
5) By clinging to the five aggregates subject to clinging he does not adhere to the view that "I might not be, it might not be for me, I will not be and it will not be for me" (SN III 205).
6) No perplexity arises in him with regard to the views in the ten unanswered [*avyākruta*] questions (SN III 213–217) i.e:
    a) The world is eternal.
    b) The world is not eternal.
    c) The world is finite.
    d) The world is infinite.
    e) Life-principle and mortal body are the same [*taṃ jīvaṃ taṃ sarīram*].
    f) Life-principle and mortal body are different.
    g) The *Tathāgata* exists after death.
    h) The *Tathāgata* does not exist after death.
    i) The *Tathāgata* both exists and does not exist after death.
    j) The *Tathāgata* neither exists nor does not exist after death.
7) No perplexity arises in him with regard to the eight varieties of eternalism with regard to the after death condition (SN III 218–220) i.e.:
    a) Self consists of form and is unimpaired after death.
    b) Self is formless and is unimpaired after death.
    c) Self consists of both form and formless.
    d) Self neither consists of form or formless.
    e) Self is exclusively happy.
    f) Self is exclusively miserable.
    g) Self is both happy and miserable.
    h) Self is neither happy nor miserable.
8) The *Brahmajāla Sutta* sets out 62 wrong views and a noble disciple abandons all these (DN I 1–46). Some of these wrong views are as follows:

a) The nihilistic doctrine [*natthikavāda*] or annihilationism [*ucchedavāda*] ascribed to Ajita Kesakambalī: "There is nothing given, nothing offered, nothing offered as charity, no fruit or result in good or bad action, no this world, no other world, no mother, no father, no beings who are reborn spontaneously, no renunciants and brahmins faring and practising rightly in this world [so far, the precise opposite of mundane right view]... the persons consists of four great elements and upon death merges and returns to the four great bodies; earth body, water body, heat body and air body" (SN III 206).

b) The doctrine of the inefficacy of action [*akiriyavāda*] ascribed to Purāṇa Kassapa: "When one acts or makes others act, when one mutilates or makes others mutilate, when one tortures or make others torture, when one plunders, kills, ... no evil is done by the doer. If one goes down the Ganges giving gifts and making offerings and making others give gifts and make offerings ... there would be no merit or no outcome of merit" (SN III 208).

c) The doctrine of non-causality [*ahetukavāda*] ascribed to Makkhali Gosāla: "There is no cause or condition for the defilement or purification of beings, there is no action by self, by others, there is no power, no energy, manly endurance, manly power, all living beings are without mastery" (SN III 210).

d) The doctrine of seven bodies [*sattakāyavāda*] ascribed to Pakudha Kaccāyana: "There are seven bodies unmade, uncreated, barren, steady as mountain peak, pillars. They do not move or obstruct each other. Nor are they able to cause pleasure or pain to others. If one cuts off another's head with a sharp sword, it does not deprive anyone of his life, the sword merely passes through the space between these seven bodies" (SN III 211).

The *Sammmādiṭṭhi Sutta* sets out a series of right views a noble disciple is endowed with as follows (MN I 46–55). He understands: 1) What is wholesome and the root of the wholesome and what is unwholesome and the root of the unwholesome; 2) What is nutriment (for continuing in *saṃsāra*), the origin of nutriment, the cessation of nutriment and the path leading to the cessation of nutriment; 3) Similarly he understands the following, their origin, their cessation and the path leading to their cessation: a) The four noble truths, b) aging and death, c) birth, d) being, e) clinging, f) craving, g) feeling, h) contact, i) the sixfold sense-bases, j) name-and-form k) consciousness, l) volitional activities, m) ignorance, and n) taints.

A stream-enterer understands as they really are, the gratification, the danger, and the escape, [*assāda, ādinava, nissarana*] as regards the five spiritual faculties i.e. the faculty of faith, energy, mindfulness, concentration, wisdom (SN V 193).

In short a stream-enterer has no doubts about the Buddha, the Dhamma, the *Saṅgha*, the Noble Eightfold Path, past, present, future, dependent origination [*paṭicca-samuppāda*], the world, *kamma*, rebirth, *kusala* and *akusaka dhamma* (wholesome and unwholesome things), *devas* and *bhūtas*, divine worlds and hells and other places of woe and *Nibbāna*. It is through "knowledge of Dhamma" [*dhamme ñāṇa*] and "knowledge of entailment" [*anvaye ñāṇa*] that the stream-enterer overcomes doubt about all these phenomena. (Bodhi 2000, 754, n. 103) That is, having understood dependent origination, he applies it to the past and to the future and overcomes doubt about the true nature of all phenomena whether conditioned or unconditioned, including *Nibbāna*. The Buddha explaining this says:

> When bhikkhus, a noble disciple thus understands aging-and-death, its origin, its cessation, and the way leading to its cessation, that is his knowledge of the principle [*dhamme ñāṇa*]. By means of this principle that is seen, understood, immediately attained, fathomed, he applies the method to the past and to the future thus; "Whatever renunciants and brahmins in the past directly knew aging-and-death, its origin, its cessation, all these directly knew it in the very same way that I do now. Whatever renunciants and brahmins in the future will directly know aging-and-death, its origin, its cessation, and the way leading to its cessation, all these will directly know it in the very same way that I do now. This is the knowledge of entailment [*anvaye ñāṇa*]. (SN II 57)

The Knowledge of Dependent Arising

The Buddha says that it is impossible that a stream-enterer does not understand *paṭiccasamuppāda* (dependent origination) (AN III 440). Therefore the knowledge of dependent origination is an essential knowledge of a stream-enterer.

The *Dhammacakkappavattana Sutta*, the first sermon of the Buddha's dispensation records the attainment of stream-entry of the first noble disciple of the dispensation of Gotama Buddha, thus:

> And while this discourse was being spoken there arose in the Venerable Koṇḍañña, the dust free, stainless vision of the *Dhamma* [*virajaṃ vītamalaṃ dhamma-cakkhum udapādi*]: "Whatever is subject to origination is all subject to cessation" [*yaṃ kiñci samudaya-dhammaṃ sabban taṃ nirodha-dhamman ti*]. (SN V 423)

Further, for a noble person, the "noble method has, through wisdom, been well seen and well penetrated" [*ariyo cassa ñāyo paññāya sudiṭṭho suppaṭividdho*]. The noble norm is the law of dependent arising (SN II 68).

Based on the "signless, wishless and empty" fetter-breaking-experience at the point of fruition, with an awareness that passes beyond *nāma-rūpa*, for the first time a stream-enterer understands by direct knowledge the heart of dependent arising: that "whatever is of the nature to arise, all that is of the nature to cease." The well known words of Venerable Sāriputta, "*yo paṭiccasamuppādam passati so dhammam passati*" (MN I 190–191), "one who sees *paṭiccasamuppāda* sees the Dhamma," signifies that one who penetrates the pattern of *paṭiccasamuppāda*, penetrates to the core of the Dhamma. He understands that if anything is to arise due to causes or conditions, it ceases upon the cessation of such causes or conditions. This insight is called the "dustless stainless Dhamma eye." The following passage explains the connection between the knowledge of dependent origination and right view:

> When bhikkhus, a noble disciple has clearly seen with correct wisdom as it really is this dependent origination and these dependently arisen phenomena, it is impossible that he will run back into the past thinking: "did I exist in the past?," "did I not exist in the past?," "what was I in the past?," "how was I in the past?," "having been what, what did I become in the past?"; or that he will run forward into the future: "will I exist in the future?," "will I not exist in the future?," "what will

> I be in the future?," "having being what, what will I be in the future?"; or he will not be inwardly confused about the present thus: "do I exist?," "do I not exist?," "what am I?," "how am I?," "this being, where has it come from, and where will it go?." (SN II 26)

Hence for the stream-enterer there will be no doubt that "I" is not part of the true nature of existence.

Also the stream-enterer is endowed with "wisdom directed to the rise and fall of phenomena which is noble and penetrative leading to the complete destruction of suffering" [*udayattha-gāminiyā paññāya samannāgato ariyāya nibbhedikāya sammā-dukkha-kkhaya-gāminiyā*] (DN III 237). This is wisdom which penetrates through two extreme dogmatic views in the world, i.e. the "world exists" and "does not exist." This penetration comes through seeing the rise and fall of phenomena. When one sees arising, it is impossible to conclude that "nothing exists," and when one sees cessation, it is impossible to conclude that "everything exists." To the one who sees in this manner, the right view that the world is dependently arisen gets established (SN II 17).

Now let us examine the connection between the transforming experience of a person treading the Path and the arising of right view. Ajahn Brahmavamso explains the significance of the experience at the point of fruition of stream-entry as follows:

> There occurs a tremendous paradigm shift. Just like the shifting of the earth's tectonic plates produces a massive earthquake, so the shifting of fundamental standpoints for views is like a terrific earthquake in the mind. Many ancient and cherished constructions of concepts and views come crashing to the ground. Such high powered deep insight feels like an explosion in the mind. For a while one does not know where to stand. One is sure one has not gone mad. In fact the mind feels saner than it has ever felt before. (Ajahn Brahmavamso 2004, 24)

At the dawn of the fruit that is stream-entry, right view is oriented towards cessation [*nirodha*] as against the mundane right view which is oriented towards arising [*samudaya*] and which takes *kamma* as one's own. When all necessary conditions are fulfilled, this mundane right view breaks through to the level of supramundane right view. Let us consider the findings of our field research to understand the mechanics of this.

Findings of Our Field Research

Let us examine some of the reported experiences from the field research of this study and the knowledge that arose based on them. Though some of these experiences have already been quoted in Chapters 4 and 5, for easy reference and comparison, I set them out below once again.

Interview No. 6

The Experience

> At that time my whole body... all my flesh dissolved and the whole body became a skeleton. When I was watching this skeleton for a long time, even that started to fall apart, disjointed, it became like a powder and settled right at the bottom. At that time I felt it like a heap of ash. Even this heap of ash scattered all over.

For a second, within the wink of an eye, the meditation object and the feeling that it became like dust also disappeared, and immediately after that the posture re-appeared, I felt it again (Q.3–12). It was like "striking a match stick suddenly, where it lights up and extinguishes, like flaring up suddenly" (Q.122). I continued to stay on; again to focus on that same meditation object. Then gradually I began to come back to my normal state (Q.5).

The Knowledge That Arose

"If anything is of the nature to arise, all that is of the nature to cease." [Also] the stanza "*ye dhammā hetuppabhavā tesam hetuṃ tathāgato āha*" ("those dhammas which proceed from a cause, the Tathāgata has told the cause") came to my mind (Q.88)... That moment itself, after a little while after seeing it, it struck me that what I felt is indeed the meaning of this stanza (Q.91). ... From this I felt that this is what happens to this body too. It is difficult for me to retain this. This is not a necessary thing; this is not a thing I can sustain. This is the feeling I got at that time (Q.3) ... that there is nothing here that I can hold onto, this is what I understood at that time (Q.13) ... I saw impermanence there, very strongly. When I was seeing this impermanence so strongly, the idea or feeling "I" never occurred there. It was the feeling that we are trying to grasp something that does not belong to us, the idea of "non-grasping" is what was felt (Q.36). ... Because of these experiences I was able to go through the rest of the time with much ease. Why, because if there were any hurtful feelings etc. I was able to accept those with ease. In everything, the feeling that things ought to happen this way and in no other way, was not there anymore, there was the ability to take things as it comes (Q.167).

Interview No. 4

The Experience

I remember when I was meditating in 1992, when I was developing the meditation objects such as *kāyanupassanā, ānāpānasati* (mindfulness of the body, mindfulness of breathing) etc. from time to time, it has been possible to see, I have been able to see that whatever *rūpa, vedanā, saññā, saṅkhārā* or *viññāṇa* that are experienced in the meditation, these five aggregates subject to clinging are subject to cessation completely, without remainder...(Q.7) That is, by meditating, through developing the four foundations of mindfulness, i.e. either as *kāyānupassanā, vedanānupassanā, cittānupassanā or dhammānupassanā* we are able to see with wisdom, the impermanent nature of that object or its conditioned nature and mentally, you see the release from that object. That is, by meditating on *vedanā* etc. according to the four foundations of mindfulness, you are able to see the *nirodha* (cessation).You can see this cessation very clearly (Q.5)... this cessation is experienced for a very short while (Q.8).

Knowledge That Arose

I have been able to see that whatever *rūpa, vedanā, saññā, saṅkhārā* or *viññāṇa* that are experienced in the meditation, these five aggregates subject to clinging are subject to cessation completely, without remainder (Q.7)... the mind arises having the five aggregates subject to clinging such as *rūpa* etc. as its object. Then it is the nature of the mind to arise having those as objects. Then at a given point through our meditation, if we experience the impermanence of all these with wisdom, if we realize it, at such moment we feel the release from all these. Then you see that this realization is not neither *rūpa, vedanā, saññā, saṅkhārā* nor *viññāṇa* (Q.9) ... The view, the right view got purified (Q.80)...you know that "all" is cause and effect and the fact that "all" that ceased (Q.56).

You get an understanding about suffering. You get the understanding that before there was suffering due to that, now that suffering doesn't arise in you any more. If you did anything, any unwholesome deeds under a delusion, taking it as self, now you don't commit those. (Q.83). ... If I had any kind of *dukkha* or a difficulty, a problem, this understanding has sufficed as a solution to such a problem. Why? Because it solved my problem. I am not interested in solving the problems of others. If I had any delusion about the five aggregates subject to clinging, that it is me, I have been able to be liberated from that. Because after this, my wisdom is "it is not so, this problem has arisen because of my wrong understanding" (Q.16). ... Therefore you know that there will never arise any sorrow and lamentation due to that reason any more (Q.38).

Interview No. 2

The Experience

His meditation system at first was "labeling": whatever he feels or that gets focused in the mind are noted by assigning a label to it such as "sitting," "standing," "feeling," "thinking" etc. One day when he was labelling in this manner for some time, the mind refused to label any more, and was tired of labelling, and at a point he experienced a "cessation," a "gap," a "gulf" a " total blankness" in his consciousness, everything stopped, he didn't feel the "consciousness" anymore for a short while, again it appeared. This way the "consciousness" appeared and disappeared in quick succession within a short period for a couple of times that he realized he experienced something special. Though at such time the mind refused to accept it as a fruit of the Path, much later he realized that it was "non-becoming" that he experienced (Q.72.)

The Knowledge That Arose

Much later having read books, discussed and reflected on this experience he understood that what he experienced, though "temporarily," was "cessation of becoming." He realized that the "process of cessation" has begun for him. He realized that he is on track, on the Path, stream [to *Nibbāna*]. He realized that his "Path is very correct." He realized that he is not the same person anymore, his attachments were less, his mind started to reject "entertaining" various extraneous objects and thought processes what he had entertained up to such time. He cut down on reading, listening to music etc. for entertainment; he restrained himself by himself without anybody's prompting. Earlier he undertook *sīla* as something "enforced" on him, but now he realized the need for it. He realized that "becoming" is the source, there is nothing called "I am," there is nothing that is not subject to change, nothing in this world that he can rely on, depend on as permanent, there is no such thing as soul or self, that the whole world system consist of projections of the mind including God and the Buddha. With this realization, the first three fetters were broken; there was no doubt about the Path, *Nibbāna* and in the triple gem (Q.24, 28). He realized that relative to the temporary cessation he experienced, he could "project" what *Nibbāna* is, *Nibbāna* being permanent cessation. He got confidence that he can attain *Nibbāna*, he got the "assurance of *Nibbāna*" (Q.48–51).

All the above accounts illustrate that the understanding, without an iota of doubt, that the true nature of existence is impermanent, unsatisfactory and non-self [*anicca, dukkha, anatta*] has come about in these interviewees based on the understanding of the relationship between cause and effect [*idappaccayatā*], dependent arising [*paṭiccasamuppāda*]. Since at such time, they experienced directly, the non-appearance of *nāma-rūpa* and consequently the non-manifestation of the "world," they understood dependent arising. This indeed is the Dhamma one breaks through to, at the dawn of stream-entry.

View on personality is the wrong view that the aggregates are somehow related to a supposed permanent self. The stream-enterer understands in principle that there is no such permanent entity in his core, though he still-has the vague "I am conceit"; what a stream-enterer lacks is any view which identifies any aggregate subject to clinging as self, or related to self. He understands that there are only conditioned phenomena internally and externally and that with the cessations of such conditions, the effects too cease. He understands that there exists in him, only a chain of psycho-physical phenomena (name-and-form) which is arising and ceasing so rapidly that it appeared to him as a permanent entity called "self." He further realizes that rules and vows are not something to cling to as sufficient for liberation but only, in some cases, *part* of the path to liberation. Thereafter he observes and vows, precepts and rituals knowing their limitations. Having experienced with direct knowledge the truth of the Dhamma, he overcomes all doubts regarding the Buddha as the supreme teacher, the Dhamma as the only Path to liberation and the noble *Saṅgha* as those who have trod the Path and reaped its fruits.

In the *Mahāmālunkyaputta Sutta,* the Buddha says when in an ariyan disciple the view on personality and the rest of the relevant fetters are abandoned, it is abandoned together with the respective "underlying tendencies" to these fetters. He says that though a young tender infant lying on his back does not even have the notion "personality," the underlying tendency towards view on personality lies within him (MN I 434). This underlying tendency raises its head the moment conditions are conducive for this. However in one who is established in right view, not only the fetter, but all mental standpoints and adherences [*adhiṭṭhānam abhinivesānusayam*] in relation to the fetter are also abandoned or destroyed (SN II 17).

The Stream-Enterer and the God Concept

Experiences similar to the fetter-breaking aspect of a religious experience discussed above is often interpreted by a non-Buddhist as the unification with God. One of the hallmarks of an *ariyan* disciple is that the understanding of dependent arising [*paṭiccasamuppāda*] replaces the concept of a Creator God, if he had any. To the questions "Could this be the experience of the Creator God or the soul?" and "Why not?," the following were some of the responses of our interviewees:

Interview No. 2

The interviewee says what he experienced was the undefiled nature of the mind, if one can penetrate what he called the "norm" of dependent arising, then he can experience the undefiled nature of the mind, not God or *Brahmā.*

> I think God is gone long time ago (laugh) because God, Buddha and everyone is our creation, the whole world. Mind is so tricky that it can create any damn thing if you give it a value. Even *Nibbāna* you can create. It's a concept (Q.120)... To understand this you have to go back to what Buddha has preached about it, that is dependently arising. If you penetrate to that norm then you can see the pure nature of the mind, undefiled, that's what you experience. Relative to that only you can judge. You can achieve to that undefiled nature [of] mind that is not God or *Brahmā*. If you cling to it you are finished because that is another subtle ego trick. Very subtle, but you are attached. You entertain that as "my" *Nibbāna*... (Q.122).

Interview No. 4

> There is no such thing for us who are Buddhists (Q.71). We know through our own experience that it cannot be so. The Creator God is none other than these five aggregates subject to clinging (Q.72).

Interview No. 6

> It can't be. It is something you see from within you, not something that happens due to the influence of a third party (Q.73–74).

Interview No. 3

> That depends on how you define the word "God." Now according to Vivekananda, Ātman and *Brahman* is the ultimate truth. We know that we have realized the ultimate truth by experiencing it. If you personify this, it becomes the God. If you take it without personifying, it becomes the ultimate truth (Q.43). ...personifying this is the meanest thing that man can do to mankind. Having personified, they teach others also to personify. Therefore it is a dangerous thing ... But the Buddha has declared in the *Brahmajala Sutta* that he arose to tear this apart. He showed a method for it. Therefore there is no point in explaining this in terms of theory or by way of principles to one who has not reached it, it's like calling a lunatic a lunatic. It is meaningless. Therefore from our angle, if you put a piece of apple in your mouth you know the taste of apple. To the one who hasn't eaten, however much I say, it doesn't work. In other words, once you have an experience your skills don't diminish. It doesn't get limited. If he wants to, he can call this "God," or call it "Soul," but he doesn't get caught up in these, he is not obliged to prove this or to prove that this is a Catholic God or he is ten or fifteen feet tall. If you want you can call it even "ice cream" or "chocolate." The fact that you don't get caught up in designations is the biggest gain from this insight or from this leap (Q.44).

However a stream-enterer is accepting of the existence of *devas*. The concept of Creator God is not to be confused with the Buddhist cosmology. Accepting the reality of different planes of life including the celestial and the planes of woe is an essential part of right view. A noble disciple contemplates on the qualities and the virtues of the *devas;* "there are *devas* ruled by the four great kings, there are the *devas* of the *Tāvatiṃsa* ..." [*devatānussatim bhāveti "santi devā Catummahārājika, santi devā Tāvatiṃsa* ..."] and that they had previously, as humans, been endowed with certain good qualities that had led to their rebirth in their present states (AN III 287). In our field research it was found that though the interviewees were not looking forward to the help of the *devas* for their salvation, or whether they have had personal experiences of any interaction with *devas* or not, all of them believed in the existence of *devas*. Most offered merit to them at the end of a religious ceremony as is customarily done.

The Unshaken Confidence of a Stream-Enterer

People are declared by the Buddha to be stream-enterers on account of possessing four qualities. They are: he possesses unshaken confidence [*aveccappasāda*] in the Buddha, the Dhamma and the *Saṅgha* and he possesses unbroken, unblemished virtue dear to the noble ones. These qualities are called "*sotāpatti-aṅga,*" the factors of stream-entry.[3]

Aveccappasāda in the Buddha, the Dhamma and the *Saṅgha* is yet another hallmark of a stream-enterer: "*bhikkhus* all those who have *aveccappasāda* in me are stream-enterers" [*Ye kechi bhikkave mayi aveccappasannā, sabbe te sotāpannā*] (AN V 120). Bhikkhu Bodhi translates the term "*aveccappasāda*" as "confirmed confidence" and K. N. Jayatilleke as "appreciation born of understanding" (Jayatilleke 1963, 386). This term has been translated in F.L.Woodward's 1936 translation (AN V 81) as "unwavering faith." The term "*saddhā*" which is commonly translated as "faith" has been the focus of many debates. Having first considered the opinions expressed by some scholars about the nature of *saddhā*, thereafter we will proceed to examine how it has been expressed in our field research. The term "faith" as used in religious parlance in general means, belief in something that cannot be explained. K.N. Jayatilleke in *Early Buddhist Theory of Knowledge* (1963) has undertaken a detailed analysis of the concept of *saddhā* in Buddhism.

According to Jayatilleke (1963, 382–899) there are three main aspects of *saddhā*, namely, cognitive, conative and affective and there are at least two strata in the evaluation of *saddhā* within the Pāli canon. In the earlier stratum, *saddhā* was quite in accordance with the rational attitude detailed in the *Kālāma Sutta* (AN I 188–189). Comparing the earlier stratum of *saddhā* with the attitude reflected in the *Kālāma Sutta,* Jayatilleke says in the earlier stratum this word represents an attitude of "neither accepting nor rejecting" a statement of authority, but should be tested before deciding to reject or accept (1963, 390–391). In the later stratum, the situation changes towards a more "sentimental state" (affective) (Tilakaratne 1997, 594). Asanga Tilakaratne, undertaking a detailed analysis of *saddhā* and commenting on K. N. Jayatilleke, says that it is clear that Jayatilleke considers the cognitive aspect of *saddhā* to be the most significant of the three aspects mentioned here, and that Jayatilleke holds that:

1) *saddhā* or faith in the Buddhist religious practice is not groundless faith [*amūlika saddhā*] but a rational faith [*ākāravatī saddha*] and
2) once the practitioner becomes enlightened, his *saddhā* will be completely replaced by *paññā* (wisdom) (Tilakaratne 1997, 594).

3) Quoting the *Kālāma Sutta* (AN I 188), *Caṅkī Sutta* (MN: 95) and the *Vīmaṇsaka Sutta* (MN: 47), Jayatilleke concludes that there are three stages of *saddhā* (faith or belief) depending on how this term has been used (Jayatilleke 1963, 393–394) i.e.:
   a) accepting the doctrine for the purpose of testing (provisionally accepting),
   b) "safeguarding the truth" [*saccānurakkhanā*], the stage in which one reposes faith in a person after realizing that he was honest, unbiased and wise,
   c) partial and personal verification of the doctrine; it is at this stage that one is said to have a "rational faith."

Jayatilleke says that, if we take the *Kālāma Sutta* to be saying that one should not accept anyone on authority or nor even seriously consider the views of others in order to test their veracity, but rely entirely on one's own experiences in the quest and discovery of truth, then this would be contradictory to the concept of *saddhā* in the Pāli *Nikāyas*. But if, on the other hand, we interpret the *Kālāma Sutta* as saying that, while we should not accept statements as true on the grounds of authority, we should test the consequences of statements in the light of our own knowledge and experience, in order to verify whether they are true or false, it would be an attitude which is compatible with s*addhā* as understood at least in one stratum of Pāli canonical thought (1963, 391).

The above stages of verification are given in the *Caṅkī Sutta* of the *Majjhima Nikāya*. Accordingly a statement may be accepted provisionally, for the purpose of verifying its truth so long as we do not commit ourselves to the view or claim that such statement is true or false prior to verification. The actual provisional acceptance is made only after ensuring the honesty, unbiased nature and intelligence of the person making the statement. That is, such a person should be first examined in respect of three things. He should be examined to see whether he is making such statement with selfish motives [*lobhanīyehi dhammehi pariyādinnacitto*], whether his mind is obsessed with malevolent motives [*dosanīyehi dhammehi*] or whether his mind is obsessed with delusion [*mohanīyehi dhammehi*]. Only if we are satisfied that these are not the case can we accept a teacher's statement even for verification (MN II 171–173).

The *Vīmaṇsaka* Sutta gives a more stringent test for accepting the truth of a statement. It is only after a partial but personal verification of the truth that it can be accepted. Here it is said that "a monk who is an inquirer, who cannot read another's mind should investigate the *Tathāgata* to determine whether he is enlightened or not." In this *Sutta*, the Buddha is to be examined in respect of two things, i.e. through what is cognizable through the eye and the ear, that is, through observation and through listening to what he says. Therefore having doubts about the Buddha is not condemned but plays a central role in the process of inquiry.[4]

However in the lists of qualities necessary for liberation where *saddhā* and *paññā* are listed, *saddhā* is always listed as the first factor and *paññā* the last. K. N. Jayatilleke says this sequence cannot be accidental and probably reflects the fact that *saddhā* is a preliminary requirement, it finally leads to understanding which is reckoned to be the greatest value (Jayatilleke 1963, 397). The faith of a *saddhānusarī* (faith-follower) who is the lowest ranking *ariyasāvaka* cannot be of the same degree of that of a *saddhāvimutta* (faith-released) and could not be considered to have reached the stage of "rational faith" [*ākāravatī saddhā*]. The *saddhānusarī* is defined as one having "sufficient faith in and love for *Tathāgata*" [*tathāgate c'assa saddhā-mattaṃ hoti pemamattaṃ*] (MN I 479).

Gethin (1992) is of the opinion that *saddhā* is best understood as a positive mental attitude of trust or confidence (1992 [2002], 110) and is essentially affective in nature. Terms such as *pema* (affection) and *bhatti* (devotion) which are often juxtaposed and associated with *saddhā* in the *Nikāyas*, only seem to reiterate its essential affective nature. He says that Jayatilleke's assumption that one can understand *saddhā* as having a straightforward cognitive value leads him to some serious misunderstandings (i.e. it is misleading to talk of it as being replaced by *ñāṇa*). Gethin's view is that *saddhā* is the instigator of a process which culminates in *paññā*, which in turn reinforces *saddhā*. Gethin feels that "*pasāda*" denotes a more developed stage of *saddhā*, and that it conveys a notion of mental composure, serenity, or purity. Accordingly "*pasāda*" as used in "*aveccappasāda*" means full trust that results from a certain degree of understanding (p.113). According to him, *saddhā* is the confidence in the heart of what motivates and spurs on spiritual activity and it ends up in *aveccappasāda*, trust based on understanding (p.116).

Asanga Tilakaratne (1997, 608) concludes that *saddhā* is a pre-requisite for religious action which ultimately leads to religious knowledge. He argues that knowledge is hard to come by without action and action is impossible without *saddhā* in the Buddhist religious practice. Distinguishing it from the philosophical use of the term "belief" to mean a proposition accepted as true, he considers the earliest stage of *saddhā* in a psychological sense to mean a "believing mentality." In this sense belief, justified or unjustified, marks a stage prior to knowledge. Whether the belief will turn out to be true or false is largely beyond the control of the believer. He compares it to choosing a new dentist based on information gathered about the dentist and believing that he is good. Similarly based on what is cognizable about the Buddha through the eye and the ear (i.e. what is observed and heard about him), one decides to experiment with his teaching. Tilakaratne's view seems to be that initially *saddhā* is of an affective nature (believing mentality) accompanied by a cognitive element.

In terms of the *Vimaṇsaka Sutta,* having been satisfied with the inquiry on the Buddha through the states cognizable through the eye and the ear, one should proceed to question the Buddha. *Saddhā* established in this manner is called "rational or reasoned faith [*ākāravatī saddhā*]" which is "indestructible by anyone in the world."

The conversation between Nigaṇṭha Nātaputta and Citta the householder brings out the place for *saddhā* in Buddhism. Nigaṇṭha Nātaputta asks a question from Citta with the motive of ridiculing the Buddha, that is, "Do you believe in the statement of the recluse Gotama that there is a *jhānic* state in which there is no discursive or reflective thought and that there is cessation of discursive and reflective thought?" [*saddhāsi tvaṃ samaṇassa Gotamassa atthi avitakko avicāro samādhi atthi vitakkavicāranaṃ nirodho ti*]. Citta, who has himself experienced such a state, answers "... knowing and seeing thus why should I accept this on the grounds of faith in any renunciant or brahmin, that there is a *jhānic* state in which there is no discursive and reflective thought ..." (SN IV 298). This passage shows that if you know something directly, you do not need to go on trust in someone else's word about it. However one could still have *saddhā*/trust in the Dhamma in general and the Buddha as the teacher.

Again Sīha the general tells the Buddha, "Bhante I do not go by faith in the Blessed One concerning those four directly visible fruits of giving declared by him, I know them too" [*nāham ettha bhagavato saddhāya gacchāmi, ahampi etāni jānāmi*] (AN III 39). The Buddha tells Venerable Ānanda on one occasion "you speak out of confidence Ānanda, but I know this for a fact" [*pasāda kho tvam ... vadesi ñāṇaṃ eva h'ettha Tathāgatassa*] (AN II 80).

In the above passages "*saddhā*" (faith) and "knowledge" has been used as mutually exclusive qualities. This would be true only of the cognitive aspect of *saddhā*, not its affective aspect.

Arahant is described as "*assaddho*" (Dhp.97). It is pointed out that this is because an *Arahant* is in a position to claim the highest knowledge without having to rely on faith [*aññatreva saddhāya ... aññaṃ vyākareyya*-SN IV 138] (Jayatilleke 1963, 399).

In the cases of Sīha, Citta and Venerable Ānanda above, the term *saddhā* has been used in the sense of a "believing mentality." However to take the term *saddhā* to mean only justified belief connected with the cognitive progress seems to ignore the emotional and the affective aspects of *saddhā*. In the early discourses *saddhā* has been coupled with emotion-related qualities such as *pasāda* (appreciation), *bhatti* (devotion) and *pema* (affection) (Tilakaratne 1997, 603).

On Jayatilleke's conclusion that once the practitioner becomes enlightened his *saddhā* will be completely replaced by *paññā*, Asanga Tilakaratne comments:

> The persistence of justified belief is a requirement in the pursuit of knowledge. Although it disappears once the knowledge is achieved, we can imagine that the effective element of *saddhā*, namely the conviction and the appreciation, could continue to exist, having become firmer and more established. When knowledge arises the conviction reaches culmination and the resultant appreciation of the teacher not only continues but also reaches culmination. As a result an *Arahant* can be the one who has the highest *pasāda* in the Buddha and his teaching, for he enjoys the highest degree of conviction. (Tilakaratne 1997, 607)

However, the term used to denote the distinguishing mental constituent of a stream-enterer more specifically is "*aveccappasāda*" and not "*saddhā*." As referred to at the commencement of this discussion on *saddhā*, this term "*aveccappasāda*" has been translated as "confirmed confidence" or "appreciation born of understanding." In the book referred to above, K. N. Jayatilleke has undertaken a detailed etymological study of the term "*aveccappasāda*." In our field research we enquired into the concept of *saddhā* of each of our interviewees with a view to getting a first-hand account of the meaning of the term "*aveccappasāda*."

Findings of the Field Research of the Writer

Interview No. 2

This interviewee is a monk who is a very untraditional person, who is very critical of contemporary Buddhist practices, meditation systems and rites and rituals. He had no or very little "faith" in the triple gem when he started his practice. Though he had no faith, he followed the meditation instructions given to him very diligently by his teacher who was a well-known meditation master from the forest tradition of Sri Lanka. Even after a significant religious experience which subsequently led to the fruit that is stream-entry, he refused to accept its significance though according to his teacher, such experience satisfied the criteria for an attainment of a supramundane fruit. After nearly one year of investigating, he on his own concluded that what he experienced before was "non-becoming" and with such understanding he concluded that he had entered the Path towards "complete cessation."

Today he has no doubt about the triple gem and has hundred percent confidence in the Buddha, in *Buddhahood* and has gratitude towards the Buddha for showing the Path. To the question "Do you have gratitude to the Buddha?" and "What is *aveccappasāda* in the Buddha Dhamma and the *Saṅgha?*," he says:

> I know certain defilements are no more in my mind. It never comes. I am very sure about it. So therefore I know the Buddha has been following this Path, he has totally extirpated, rooted out all defilements—whatever defiles your mind, colourful and I mean prejudice, bias and all these things, he hasn't got. Now I have 100% confidence in Buddha, what *Buddhahood* is (Q.42). ... I'll do anything not for Buddha, (but for) who is trying to follow this Path, yes I sacrifice my whole life on behalf of them, that is my gratitude to Buddha, for the *sāsana* (Q.41).

In response to the query about his gratitude to the Buddha, this interview recalled an incident which took place during his stay in one of the jungles. When he was returning from his alms round from the village through the jungle track, he got caught to a heavy rain. He was approaching an intersection in the middle of the jungle, where someone had kept a small, old Buddha statue, which was getting drenched in the rain. He recalled how he was so moved to see the "Buddha getting drenched in the middle of nowhere," that he immediately removed his robe, folded it and placed it on the head of the Buddha statue as a shelter, and walked away to his cave, bare-bodied, himself getting drenched in the rain. Despite this monk's usual disposition being very critical of conventions, for him to be moved to this extent over a "clay statue," shows the degree of gratitude and respect in him for the teacher.

Interview No. 3

This monk is also very untraditional and a radical, particularly during his youth. At the time he attained the first fruit, he was not "consciously" abiding even in a minimum *sīla* (five moral precepts) as widely expected to be undertaken, and in fact was ridiculing those who were abiding in *sīla*. He had the mindset of a radical, wanting to break all norms and practices, including those conducive for attainment of supramundane fruits of the Path. However after his experience which marked the attainment of the fruit that is stream-entry, he says he felt enormously indebted to the Buddha and to the Buddha *sāsana*, wanting to serve the Dhamma unreservedly, so he ordained as a monk. For the last eighteen years he has been totally committed to the practice and to the teaching of the Buddha, surrendered to the monkhood (Q.19), and has no doubt in the Buddha Dhamma and the *Saṅgha* (Q.31). To the question "Do you have *saddhā* in the Buddha?" he says:

> I am not a person who has faith. But when we meditate, when we see that causes produce effects and these effects again form causes etc. and that the Buddha has

> seen these two thousand five hundred years ago and seen this comprehensively, there arises a *saddhā* through your own experience. That *saddhā* of course increases by the day, the more you sit for meditation, the more you meet noble friends, and the more you proceed in monkhood. I don't know whether it is towards the Buddha. But it's something that comes from right within. A greater part of it naturally gets set off towards the Buddha like paying off taxes, because there has been no-one who could explain this to me so well in a palatable way. With regard to this *saddhā*, I think I am still at a preliminary level, there is a long way to go ... when I think of how the Buddha preached this conditional origination, about causes and effects, my *saddhā* that arises towards the Buddha and the teachers (compared to the *saddhā* there should be) is still very much low in the scale. The lower it is, the higher the marks to the nobleness of the Buddha (Q.37).

Interview No. 6

Explaining why she has *saddhā* in the Buddha, this interviewee says:

> As the teacher who showed us the Path, *saddhā* develops through the Dhamma. We develop this *saddhā* when we listen to the Dhamma. It is because of this that we have been able to experience this. That is, based on what the Buddha preached. (Q.67–68).

Interview No. 5

This interviewee expresses his *saddhā* in the Buddha as:

> Gladness that doesn't change. The faith in the triple gem that doesn't change under any condition whatsoever (Q.67) ... it is in the teaching of the Buddha that we are established in. That is what we follow. We have gladness about it that does not change nor shake. (Q.69)

In all the above expressions, we can see that "*aveccappasāda*" is the unwavering and unshaken confidence in the triple gem based on wisdom coupled with gladness and gratitude. This also includes an unwavering commitment to serve and safeguard the Dhamma. These expressions include both cognitive and affective elements of *saddhā*.

A careful examination of both interviews No. 2 and 3 shows that at the commencement of the practice the practitioner had no "*saddhā* or faith" in the Buddha and the teaching in the sense of "accepting as true," one of the meanings people attribute to the term *saddhā* or faith. However both of them had a "believing mentality" as a pre-requisite to religious action when they decided to experiment with the practice. This is "provisionally accepting for the purpose of verification." This has led to "partial and personal verification" of the doctrine. This has in fact led both these practitioners to renounce the lay life and commit themselves totally to the practice. Today they have "100% confidence in the Buddha and the teaching," would "sacrifice their whole life" for this cause, and *saddhā* is increasing by the day as they progress on the Path.

The field research of this study, on the mindset of an *Arahant*, shows that an *Arahant* can do nothing but serve the dispensation of the teacher, which he does with gratitude. On the question on whether the interviewee No. 1 has *saddhā* as an "*Arahant*," he says he has a lot of *saddhā* in the triple gem. He doesn't engage in Buddha-*vandanā* but when he sees a Buddha statue when he is passing it in the hermitage, he pays homage to it (Interview No. 1, Q.315–322).

In the *Cūlasaccaka Sutta* the Buddha says that even if a person's mind is fully liberated, by becoming an *Arahant*, she still honours, reveres and venerates the Buddha (MN I 235). This *Sutta* shows that the veneration is not only for guiding a person to attain enlightenment, for crossing over, for attaining *Nibbāna*, but also in appreciation for the fact that the Buddha teaches having himself attained enlightenment, crossed over and attained *Nibbāna*. Further, in the *Bhaddāli Sutta* the Buddha says that an *Arahant* would become a plank for the Buddha to walk across the mud, if the Buddha asked him to do so (MN I 439). These are expressions of gratitude.

We conclude that a stream-enterer is one who has experienced with direct knowledge the truth of the teachings of the Buddha, which she had previously followed with an "inquiring mind" but not with certainty. Stream-entry brings confirmation that the Buddha is in fact fully enlightened, the Dhamma is well proclaimed, and the *Saṅgha* is practising the proper way (MN I 320). His confidence in the Buddha as the unparalleled teacher, in the Dhamma as the only Path to liberation and in the noble Saṅgha as those who have reaped the benefits of the Dhamma having followed the Noble Eightfold Path, gets established fully. Hence *aveccappasāda* reflects a state which is unshakable confidence and trust in the Buddha, the Dhamma, and the *Saṅgha* based on understanding, fortified by gladness in and gratitude to the Noble Triple Gem.

The Conduct of a Stream-Enterer

Ariyakanta Sīla (Virtue Dear to the Noble Ones)

A stream-enterer is said to possess virtue dear to the noble ones or loved by the noble ones [*ariyakantehi sīlehi samannāgato*] (SN V 394). That is, he keeps the five precepts. In the *Sotāpatti Saṃyutta* it is also described as abstaining from killing, stealing, sexual misconduct, false speech, divisive speech, harsh speech, frivolous speech and idle chatter (SN V 353).

A noble disciple's sīla is described as a *sīla* "unbroken, flawless, unblemished, unblotched, freeing, praised by the wise, ungrasped, leading to concentration" [*akhaṇḍehi acchiddehi asabalehi akammāsehi bhūjissehi viññupasatthehi aparāmaṭṭhehi samādhisaṃvattanikehi*] (SN V 343, AN III 213). AN I 231–232 explains that stream-enterers and once-returners have "completely fulfilled" [*paripūrakārī*] *sīla*, so as to re-establish their adherence to the monastic training rules after any small lapses from them, and have "some measure" [*mattaso kārī*] of *samādhi* and wisdom.

The concept of *ariyakanta-sīla* of a stream-enterer has been the subject of much debate even at the time of the Buddha. In the *Sarakāni Sutta* of the *Sotāpatti Saṃyutta,* when Buddha was residing in Nigrodharamaya in Kapilavatthupura when Sarakāni the Sākyan died, the Buddha declared him to be a stream-enterer. However the people who knew Sarakāni to have taken intoxicating drinks thought his training was too weak to become a stream-enterer and went to the Buddha and questioned him as to the attainment of stream-entry of Sarakāni. The Buddha explains his position thus:

1) if a person is endowed with the five faculties—faith, energy, mindfulness, concentration and wisdom—and the teachings of the Buddha are

accepted by him after being pondered to a sufficient degree with wisdom or

2) a person endowed with the said five faculties has sufficient faith in the *Tathāgata,* sufficient devotion to him, then he is one who does not go to hell, the animal world, domain of ghosts, to planes of misery, bad destinations. Explaining further he says:

> Even if these great Sal trees, Mahānāma, could understand what is well spoken and what is badly spoken, then I would declare these great Sal trees to be stream enterers, no longer bound to the nether worlds, fixed in destiny, with enlightenment as their destination. How much more then ... Sarakāni the Sakyan undertook the training at the time of his death. (SN V 377)

The qualities referred to by the Buddha in (a) and (b) above are respectively those of a *saddhānusārī* (faith-follower) and a *dhammānusārī* (Dhamma-follower), the lowest ranking noble disciples and they are assured of attaining stream-entry before their death.

Bhikkhu Bodhi concludes that though during his lifetime Sarakāni may have indulged in strong drinks, before his death he undertook the observance of the precepts and thereafter attained stream-entry (Bodhi 2000, 1958, n. 347). He says, Sarakāni was one who had attained to the "Path of stream-entry," *sotāpatti magga* during his association with the Buddha and before his death he attained the fruit (1958, n. 346).

The impact of the fruit that is stream-entry could be assessed through the words of our Interviewee No. 2:

> I who was poking fun at or ridiculing *sīla* began to worship the virtuous. There was an irreversible change in [my] morality to such an extent that *sīla* that I ridiculed became the sole purpose of my life (Q.19–21). ... Later for years I examined myself: can I kill, can I steal, can I engage in sexual misconduct etc. and shame, fear, disgust arise towards these (Q.21). ... Before this experience, I had the desire to investigate into lust, therefore I had distorted ideas about it, that I need to experience everything about it. Similarly with hatred, to chop a creature alive knowing well that its alive and struggling, to steal from the most heavily guarded place, to taste all the possible intoxicating drugs in the world, in cheating, to cheat even my mother and father etc. Having done all this I have been fairly successful. But there was nothing achieved. Then when I came on to this side, the opposite happened. I wanted to stay away from even thinking of lust and hatred ... this kind of transformation took place. (Interview No. 3, Q.69)

The concept of *ariyakanta sīla* is not directly defined in the *Nikāyas* other than spelling out the types of precepts included in it as aforesaid. However the sense in which a stream-enterer's five moral precepts are "unbroken," as given in the *Suttas* above, has been the subject of debate for a long time. In fact there is a tendency to make conclusions about the attainment of a supramundane fruit solely based on the criterion of whether or not a person in question transgresses one or more of the five precepts. In our field research we attempted to extract some ideas on this subject from our interviewees and also the specific question "wouldn't a stream-enterer say even a white lie?" was posed to each of these interviewees. The responses are as follows.

Interview No. 2

> The concept of *ariyakanta sīla* can be understood only by another *ariyan* disciple and not by a *puthujjana* (worldling). It's a moral attitude against engaging in acts which are blamed by one's own mind, one's own consciousness ... a stream-enterer can break his *sīla* but he would be very mindful, he watches his mind and knows when it is broken. What is meant by "*akhaṇda*" (unbroken) is at a mental level, that is, he is fully aware of what is happening in the mind. Therefore he will not repeat the breach unless he would break one to safeguard against a more blameworthy situation. (Q.43–47)

This interviewee admits that he says a white lie.

Interview No. 3

This interviewee described it as the *sīla* that is protected naturally, from within, to which ariyan disciples have a magnetic attraction. He elaborates further as follows:

> According to the text, the *aveccappasāda* (unshaken confidence) in your *sīla* turns into *ariyakanta sīla*. If there is no *aveccappasāda,* there won't be anything called "*ariyakanta sīla,*" *sīla* that the monks have a magnetic attraction to. In other words, the day *sīla* is protected from within oneself, from that day the *sīla* is *ariyakanta*. As long as someone says I undertake to abide in *sīla*, it is a bluff. But I am not saying that these people are on the wrong track. Because sometimes they may come to the stage of "*sīla* being protected from within." They may or may not reach that. If they don't, it becomes *sīlabbata-parāmāsa* ... Besides this, there is nothing "to do" in it. When one reaches it, one appreciates it, great joy arises when one thinks "I don't break *sīla*, *sīla* is not broken by me, there is no need for me to break *sīla*." I can tell you, practically this is what *ariyakanta sīla* is. (Q.40)

As to whether the stream-enterer's *sīla* is unbroken he says a stream-enterer's abiding in the five precepts cannot be placed within a frame and pin-pointed. That is, it is not a fixed, cut-and-dry thing. A stream-enterer keeps questioning himself as to whether his *sīla* broke. Yet he doesn't place himself on the other shore (place himself on a pedestal as a saint) like the way the *puthujjana* (worlding) classifies a stream-enterer. He says: "It's fifty fifty. From a *puthujjana*'s point of view, a stream-enterer may seem to break all five precepts. But the interpretation of *sīla* of each one is different, it can be ten different things. This is a hundred percent open issue." He says:

> The Buddha clearly says in the *Sarakāni Sutta* that the *sīla* is flawless. Here the Buddha scans the person hundred percent. Because the *sīla* that the Buddha sees in the stream-enterer is after he himself reached Buddhahood. The *Arahant* doesn't see it this way, he sees only according to the route he took. There is no problem for an *Arahant* to recognize a stream-enterer. But he sees that there are shortcomings in them. Yet the Buddha has said that there cannot be shortcomings. So the *Arahant* doesn't mess up, (or) be fussy. Whatever people may say, though people may say that a stream-enterer can have shortcomings, the *Arahant* doesn't blunder on this issue. There is more room for an *anāgāmi* to get confused about this. If a stream-enterer looks into himself, it could be about fifty percent. "Did my *sīla* break?, was it intentional?," "didn't I say a lie?, was it intentional or not?,"

"I took alcohol with my medicine, did I take alcohol?, was it as a medicine?," "did I engage in sexual misconduct?," a stream-enterer keeps questioning this way. Yet he doesn't place himself on the other shore like the way the *puthujjana* does. It's fifty fifty. But what is hilarious is from the angle of an ordinary *puthujjana*, all five can be broken by a stream-enterer. I don't know whether it is right for me to say this. But it can appear to be broken. Because the interpretation of *sīla* of each one is different, it can be ten different things. This is a hundred percent open issue. (Q.42)

Interview No. 4

This interviewee feels that a noble disciple has sufficient mindfulness not to commit a breach of *sīla*. As to the meaning of "unbroken *sīla*," he says that though an outsider may feel that a precept is broken, it may not be so from the point of view of the noble disciple concerned, as the *factors* necessary to constitute a breach might not have come together within. He says:

Often the world may see it as a lie or as something or other. But you know, the person who has mindfulness knows that it has not been committed by you. ... Now often there are certain factors that have to come together to make it a lie. Even in the case of killing a being, only if all these factors get fulfilled that it becomes a killing in that sense. It could be something like this. (Q.70)

Interview No. 6

Ariyakanta sīla was described by this interviewee as the virtue that goes hand-in-hand with the triple gem. That is, following these precepts having the Buddha, the Dhamma and the *Saṅgha* in the forefront, taking refuge in the triple gem (Q.70–71). As to the issue of whether the five precepts of a stream-enterer are unbroken, she says "more than by anything else, it can get flawed by a minor thing like a white lie. But he does not hide those. If a *sīla* breaks or he commits a wrong, he declares it without concealing it. It is not kept in hiding. There is a tendency to openly accept the fault and ask for forgiveness" (Q.72).

Interview No. 5

This interviewee says *ariyakanta sīla* is the virtue which has been purified by a disciple of the Buddha, the purest virtue (Q.71). As to the issue of whether the five precepts of a stream-enterer are unbroken, he says "this is a very complex issue, it can happen knowingly and unknowingly. A stream-enterer never breaks the five precepts knowingly. It is possible that these precepts can get blemished unknowingly" (Q.72).

To my question "Is a stream-enterer's *sīla* unbroken?" Venerable Ajahn Brahmavamso categorically says: "a stream-enterer can break their precepts, but they would always be able to know it, to make amends to it afterwards" (Interview No. 8, Q.46).

William Hamilton in *Saint and Psychopaths* writes:

For years, I have had an opportunity to closely observe teachers and meditators whom I believe have attained at least the first level of enlightenment. They are mostly laypeople and westerners, which is a fundamentally different situation for monks and nuns who have a primary duty of following precepts as a commitment to continuous mindfulness. In my opinion, they have a very strong tendency

> to be highly moral and many make a sincere effort to follow the precepts. Even those who make no specific effort to follow the precepts are intuitively inclined to follow them.
>
> However, I have also observed that there have been occasions when, because of neuroses, personality characteristics and cultural conditioning, they would violate all or some of the five basic precepts. At the Insight Meditation Society[5] it was decided that overwhelming infestations of cockroaches and flies were to be dealt with by poisoning. Many would take a glass of wine at a party and some would take psychedelic drugs on occasion. Some have failed to report income on their tax returns. Some have answered questions falsely in meditation interviews. Many have had sex with people they were not married to. Some have taken food from the kitchen, that was offered and eaten it after the noon meal, while on retreat. Some have consciously or unconsciously swatted mosquitoes. According to the commentaries, it would be impossible for a stream-enterer to do any of these.
>
> (Hamilton 1995, 110–111)

We do not have sufficient evidence to come to conclusions whether or not the meditators whom Hamilton refers to above are in fact noble disciples. Therefore we cannot conclude whether or not a stream enterer's *sīla* can be breached to the above extent. However, our field research set out above indicates that there can be breaches of the five precepts to some extent though it may not be to a gross level. Whilst some directly admit that a stream-enterer's *sīla* is "not unbroken" most others including monks who are long standing members of the *Saṅgha* community who are well versed in the Dhamma and experienced teachers agree that there can be breaches. We conclude that a stream-enterer has the potential to commit a breach of morality though he will not commit what is listed as impossible [*abbhabbo kātum*] for a stream-enterer. However he would be continuously reflecting on his *sīla*, *yoniso manasikāra* (wise reflection) being an inherent tendency of the mind of a stream-enterer thus continuously refining his sīla. This potential for lapses in morality is also supported by the fact that though a majority of the *Sutta*s have spelt out the four qualities necessary for declaration of the fruit that is stream-entry to include *ariyakanta sīla*, there are a few *Sutta*s in the *Sotāpatti Saṃyutta* (SN V 397, SN V 352, see p. 147) which give a different criterion for such a declaration i.e. the unshaken confidence in the Buddha, the Dhamma and the *Saṅgha* and the fourth being living in generosity. In these *Sutta*s generosity has been substituted for "unbroken *sīla* dear to a noble one" [*ariyakanta sīla*]. However these are *Sutta*s addressing lay people and not monks. Hence we can conclude that with regard to *lay people*, unbroken *sīla* is not an essential criterion to be a stream-enterer, although a stream-enterer whether lay or renunciant is hundred percent committed to following the five moral precepts.

This is further supported by the passage of the *Ratana Sutta* of the *Suttanipāta* (v. 232) which says of one without the first three fetters (i.e. a stream-enterer), even though he may commit an evil action [*kiñcāpi so kammaṃ karoti pāpakaṃ*] by body word or thought, he is incapable of concealing it [*abhabbho so tassa paṭicchādāya*] and this is called an incapacity of him who has seen *Nibbāna* [*diṭṭha padassa*]. This stanza refers to the state of mind of a stream-enterer and clearly admits that evil action [*pāpa kamma*] by a stream-enterer is a possibility. AN I 231–232 also says that stream-enterers can at least have minor lapses from the monastic code, even if these are immediately regretted and made good.

Hence with regard to *ariyakanta sīla* of a stream-enterer we conclude that whilst a stream-enterer has an extra-ordinary sense of mindfulness about safeguarding the five precepts, it is possible that there can be breaches particularly with regard to lay people. But he would not cling even to *sīla*. This mindset towards *sīla* arises due to the absence of the fetter of clinging to rules and vows [*sīlabbataparāmāsa*] which is eliminated at stream-entry. However he would be very mindful about a breach of *sīla*. Breaking a precept would hit a stream-enterer hard, much harder than it would hit an ordinary worldling. Hence he would make a conscious effort to rectify the situation even though he may not be successful in the initial few attempts. Further it would be harder for a stream-enterer to make up his mind to break a precept in the case of the inevitable. A stream-enterer may even consciously adopt strategic measures to avoid falling into the framework of a breach "technically." In the *Sarakāni Sutta* though Sarakāni was seen by others to be "blameworthy" the Buddha declared him "blameless." It is possible that due to the strong mindfulness of the stream-enterer, the mental constituents (such as full intention, and no regret) that are necessary to make up such a breach do not come together in the mind of a stream-enterer although outwardly an act may appear to be a breach of a precept. Hence I conclude that *ariyakanta sīla* is the purity of mind appropriate to a noble disciple who is accompanied by virtual "unbroken mindfulness" about its state of purity and triggered off by an unshaken confidence in the Buddha, the Dhamma and the *Saṅgha*. What is "unbroken, flawless, unblemished" etc. is the mindfulness about the "state of the *sīla*" rather than the *sīla* itself. This degree of mindfulness about the morality coupled with wise reflection [*yoniso manasikāra*] would lead a stream-enterer to continuously refine his *sīla*.

Noble Use of Language

A noble disciple is endowed with noble language [*ariya-vohāra*; AN IV 307]:

1) They do not declare as seen what has not been seen nor declare as not seen what has been seen.
2) They do not declare as heard what has not been heard nor declare as not heard what has been heard.

Their practice is the same towards (3) what is sensed [*mute*] and (4) for what has been cognized [*viññate*]. The above qualities of a noble disciple flow from *ariyakanta sīla* of a stream-enterer.

What is Impossible For A Stream-Enterer

There are many *Sutta*s in the *Nikāya*s which list out what is impossible for a stream-enterer. It is said that, being "fully released from the four woeful states, he is incapable of committing the six grievous offences" [*catuh' payehi ca vippamutto cha cābhiṭhānāni abhabbo kātuṃ*] (Sn.41, v. 231). These six are the five *ānantariyakamma* and the *aññāsatthār' uddesa;* seeking a teacher other than the Buddha for his salvation (Jayawickrama 2001, 93, n. 231). The five *ānantariya kammas* are: killing one's mother, father, or an *Arahant*, causing physical harm to the Buddha and causing disunity amongst the *Saṅgha*. The sixth impossibility is following a teacher other than the Buddha for one's liberation.

These impossibilities are also set out in the *Chakka Nipāta* of the *Aṅguttara Nikāya* (AN III 438–440), along with others:

1) Accepting conditioned thing as permanent [*nicca*] or pleasurable [*sukha*], accepting anything as self [*atta*] and resorting to the belief that purity comes from superstitious and auspicious acts [*kotūhala-maṅgalena suddhiṃ paccāgantuṃ*],
2) Seeking a person worthy of offering, outside the order [*bahiddhā dhakkhiṇeyyam gavesituṃ*],
3) Dwelling without reverence and deference towards the Buddha, [*satthāri agāravo viharitum appatisso*], the Dhamma and the *Saṅgha* and towards the training, and resorting to anything that should not be relied upon [*anāgamaniyam vatthum paccāgantuṃ*] (such as the heretic views and breach of the precepts leading to a bad rebirth: Bodhi 2012, 1770, n. 1439) and to taking an eighth birth,
4) Having the view on personality [*sakkāya-diṭṭhi*], clinging to rules and vows [*sīlabbata-parāmāsam*], skeptical doubt [*vicikicchā*], lust, aversion and ignorance leading to planes of misery [*apāyagāminiyam rāgam, apāyagāminiyam dosam, apāyagāminiyam moham*],
5) Not understanding *paṭicca-samuppāda*.

I conclude that a stream-enterer has the "potential" to commit any action by thought word or deed, over and above what has been listed above as impossible or incapable of being committed.

Seeking Another Teacher

One of the things a stream-enterer is incapable of is seeking another teacher [*aññāsatthār' uddesa*] (Sn.41, v. 231) other than the Buddha for his liberation. Not only does he turn away from seeking liberation or solace through other teachings, she would also not seek refuge in anything other than in the triple gem. A stream-enterer, though at times may be seen participating in customary rites and rituals concerning divine beings or *petas* and *bhūtas* (types of beings in lower realms) etc., would not seek refuge in beings such as *devas*, *brahmās*, *yakkhas* even in a limited sense. This is one easy way of recognizing who is not a stream-enterer.

To the question "Would you seek a teacher other than the Buddha for your salvation?" the answer from all our interviewees was a categorical "No. " However our Interviewee No. 3 has the following to say:

> No, that is something I can't even think of. When you consider the word "salvation from suffering" the bold answer is "No." But I would be happy if I had the opportunity to associate with Jesus Christ, Prophet Mohamed and some of these recent Hindu Rishies. From the books I have read, I can see that they have pointed at "nirvana" in terms of principles, logic or as a line of teaching but *Nibbāna* is something that cannot be shown in terms of principles. None of them have realized it. But I respect each of their theory. But I feel very sorry for them. Having been able to explain this so well they have not been able to taste this. Therefore I cannot make them my teacher nor revere them. But I bow my head for what they have done for me. For this I don't discriminate in terms of religion or race. Similarly the teachings in the Vedānta have struck me hard. Again I must refer

> to Mahāyāna Buddhism, the declarations and the sacrifices of Jesus Christ, what Prophet Mohamed, the Sufi leaders have done, when I look at all these there is no reverence in me, but I say that these are people who should be protected and worshipped, they are not to be ridiculed. I consider them to be nobler than I am.
> (Interview No. 3, Q.39)

Clinging to Rules and Vows [*sīlabbata-parāmāsa*]

One of the three fetters [*saṃyojana*] that are eliminated at the attainment of the fruit that is stream-entry is *sīlabbata-parāmāsa*, which is attachment or clinging to rules and vows. A stream-enterer, having directly experienced the true nature of existence, knows precisely the Path he followed up to such attainment, (i.e. the Noble Eightfold Path). With this he knows the limited role of rules and vows in attaining the final goal and does not cling to mere rules [*sīla*] and vows [*vata*].

In our field research, in investigating into the fetter of *sīlabbata-parāmāsa*, I probed into the practices of rites and rituals of a stream-enterer, but omitted to probe into "*sīla*" in relation to this fetter. However from the flexibility displayed by all interviewees in relation to the issue of whether or not or how a stream-enterer's *sīla* is unbroken, it is highly improbable that they would cling even to their own *sīla*, including *upasampadā sīla* (discipline relating to higher ordination) as a complete means to liberation; rather, they would see it as only part of the path to liberation. If their *sīla* becomes in any way flawed, they would be much inclined to declare it and accept the lapse in the true spirit of a noble person. I inquired about the attitude of *aryan* disciples towards Buddhist rites and rituals and whether they totally abstain from engaging in rites and rituals. The findings of our field research are as follows.

Interview No. 2

The interviewee used to engage in many rites and rituals before he attained the fruit that is stream-entry but stopped doing all that upon stream-entry. He realized that there is no point in engaging in rites and rituals because he understood that there is nothing within and without worthwhile to safeguard (Q.28, 38–39). He says "even Buddha is not a reality, that is what the Buddha found as far as I am concerned. It is not his body, neither feeling, nothing, that is his Enlightenment. There is nothing essence inside or outside, so then if there is nothing, what is there to doubt? Buddha is Buddha that is right, what is there to save? Therefore what's the use of doing rituals?." This is an interviewee who is a forest monk living alone in the jungles and is not compelled to participate in Buddha *pūjā* and *vandanā* (offerings to and worshipping of the Buddha) which is an essential group activity of the daily routine of a Buddhist temple or even in a forest hermitage.

Interview No. 3

This interviewee's concept of *sīlabbata-parāmasa* extends beyond what is described in the texts to include "any act which doesn't realize in *Nibbāna* this birth itself even if done with proper understanding." Before his experience of the fruit that is stream-entry, he did not engage in any rites and rituals and used to ridicule rites and rituals (i.e. Buddha *vandanā* and *bodhi pūjā* etc.). However after the attainment of stream-entry, he can engage in them particularly if he has to carry them out as a monk and in fact he spends a considerable amount of time in the shrine room of the hermitage. He says:

> Those days I looked at this with contempt. For years, we have discussed for hours finding fault with various religious rituals ... After I got ordained, I thought I must try out all these that I rejected before. If I want I can do all those rites and rituals which are meaningless. I am capable of doing it. In fact I do these. Therefore however meaningless it may be and irrespective of my likes and dislikes, if I have to do it, I am capable of doing these rites and rituals merely for the sake of rites and rituals ... What the sitting meditation does is breaking the "spirit" gathered from the rites and rituals. But while it's there you can engage in this "spirit" also. Then you can balance the two extremes. Only when you do this you realize that there is an "awakening" in my life ... on the face of it rituals and insight meditation are contradictory. It is hundred percent contradictory. But when you can look at rituals through insight and laugh it off it becomes a very special type of amusement. (Q.34)

Interview No. 4

This monk used to engage in rites and rituals before the attainment of stream-entry, but now engages in them very little (Q.61–62). His concept of *sīlabbataparāmāsa* is:

> The belief that you can search for *Nibbāna* through undertaking all kinds of wrong practices, wrong restraints. It is there to some extent in a worldling, in a person who has not fully understood *Nibbāna*. But once you see *Nibbāna* such a person understands, he does not accept that you can realize *Nibbāna* through these wrong practices and restraints, it is because of your own realization (Q.60).

Interview No. 6

This interviewee engages in Buddhist rites and rituals, but not as much like previously. She says, "I spend a little time for rites and rituals and more time for meditation" (Q.62). Her concept of *sīlabbataparāmāsa* is "wrong practices, to grasp wrong things that is, we grasp rites and rituals, we get addicted to rites and rituals, beliefs etc." (Q.61).

I found that the general attitude of a stream-enterer towards Buddhist rites and rituals such as *Buddha pūjā* (offerings), *Buddha vandanā* (worshiping), *bodhi pūjā*, etc. is very flexible. Whilst they do not cling to these, if they want to or are compelled to engage in them for whatever reason, their mind is open to do so with *saddhā*. They are neither attached to them nor have aversion to them. Some who had no faith at all in the Buddha before their attainment of the stream-entry, started engaging in it to a considerable extent after stream-entry, motivated by *saddhā* and gratitude towards the Buddha. Some others who had been engaging in these rituals to a great extent, reduced the degree of involvement in them considerably, but nevertheless continued to do them. Some others, especially those who are living a solitary life without community obligations, generally gave up such rituals. However all of them engage in them to some extent, having well understood the limited value they played in their Path towards attainment of stream-entry and their contribution towards the higher fruits of the Path.

Not Dependent on Another to Complete the Path

A stream-enterer is described as "*apara-paccayo satthu sāsane*" (DN I 110). That is, he is not dependent on another for his understanding of the teachings of the Buddha. A stream-enterer, having seen with direct knowledge the true nature of existence and having certitude of the Path, is not dependent on another to reach his final goal. He has full confidence in the Path to be followed up to *Nibbāna* with or without a teacher. In our field research we found that almost all our interviewees who are stream-enterers and beyond, had no teacher at the time of our interview and felt that a teacher is not essential to complete the Path. All of them in fact were fiercely independent, without being guided by another, whether a human or a divine being and are faring alone like "a horn of a rhinoceros," which is a hallmark of a stream-enterer (Sn. 9, v. 55/Jayawickrama 2001, 20). The tendency to seek instructions on the practice from divine beings who are believed to have listened to the Dhamma from the Buddha himself, which seems to be an increasing current trend amongst meditators, goes against the grain of this distinct quality of a stream-enterer.

As regards to not having a need for a teacher, in our field research comparing the experience at different stages of the fruits of the Path, one of the interviewees (No. 1) says that at each stage the defilements reduced very differently and from the first fruit onwards he felt a "gap" between the mind and the defilements. The word "gap" reflects a state of mindfulness which has got prominent after the first fruit. Elaborating this further, he says that he felt that the "gap" was different at each stage and the gap began to widen at each stage. The gap or the distance in the mind between defilements and the "mind" felt by him is because wisdom has reduced "grasping" in general. The gap in turn gives room to further "cut" the defilements by applying wisdom. The mindfulness only restrains defilements. It is the wisdom that cuts off defilements (Sn.198, vv. 1034–1035). The more one cuts defilements, the more one develops *sīla* and wisdom. This is the way the mind of an *ariyan* proceeds to higher stages of development without the need for a teacher. When the said interviewee says that wisdom occurs all the time in his mind, and this wisdom cuts off defilements, this is faster than a teacher's guidance and his mind is his teacher (Q.141–144), it is in line with Sn.198 above.

In the mind of a noble disciple, what is most prominent is the tendency to look back at the point of origin of a thought process and understanding causes and conditions for same. This is referred to as "*yoniso manasikāra*," probing attention, wise reflection, which includes reflecting on the cause or point of origin of such mental phenomena. By this he understands that it is dependently arisen and also that if such causes are eliminated such mental phenomena would cease and consequently that such phenomena are impermanent unsatisfactory and are devoid of self. For a noble disciple, the balance of his practice until the final goal is guided by this principle. The Buddha says, "Bhikkhus I do not see even one other thing on account of which unarisen sensual desire arises and arisen sensual desire increases and expands so much as the mark of attractive [*subha-nimitta*]. For one who is attending carelessly [*ayoniso manasikaronto*] to the mark of the attractive, unarisen sensual desire arises and the arisen sensual desire increases and expands" (AN I 3). The Buddha says that careless attention (i.e. attention only to the surface appearance of things), is also involved in the arising of the second and fifth hindrances: ill-will and sceptical doubt. This is in effect what occurs in the mind of this interviewee, when he says "my mind is my teacher."

The Generosity of a Stream-Enterer

As much as a stream-enterer is defined in terms of possessing four qualities, namely, unshaken confidence in the Buddha, the Dhamma and the *Saṅgha* and virtues dear to a noble one [*ariyakanta sīla*] as discussed above, there are a few *Suttas* in which the fourth quality of a stream-enterer is being:

> one who dwells at home with a mind devoid of the stain of stinginess, freely generous, open handed, delighting in relinquishment, one devoted to charity, delighting in giving and sharing.[6]

Here when the Buddha pointed out this and the other three qualities above, the disciple Kālighodā, having recognized them in herself, declared herself to be a stream-enterer.

In the *Sotāpatti Saṃyutta*, the Buddha addressing the chamberlains Isidatta and Purāna, gives the same criteria as above for declaring fruit of stream-entry. The Buddha says:

> chamberlains, you possess confirmed confidence in the Buddha, the Dhamma and in the *Saṅgha* ... Moreover, whatever there is in your family that is suitable for giving, all that you share unreservedly among those who are virtuous and of good character. What do you think carpenters, how many people are there among the Kosalans who are your equals, that is in regard to giving?

With this statement Isidatta and Purāna recognized that they are stream-enterers (SN V 352).

From the above we can see that a stream-enterer is endowed with the quality of giving [*dāna*] to an exceptional degree. Again it is mindfulness together with right view that sparks off this quality. Having seen the true nature of things, it is natural for a stream-enterer to loosen the grip on his possessions. Absence of mindfulness or negligence [*pamāda*] is a cause of stinginess. With right view and good mindfulness, one will be naturally inclined towards giving and sharing. This includes a mental attitude of relinquishing [*cāga*]. A stream-enterer is mindful to continue to develop on the Path and to continue to eliminate stinginess [*lobhanīya dhamma*] from his Path. The quality of generosity could be best judged in the case of lay stream-enterers to whom material possessions are available for giving. However we found that even the forest monks we interviewed easily parted with the bare minimum of the four basic requisites that they are offered.

Giving includes not only donating material things, but also the giving of time and effort and making sacrifices for the benefit of others. Contrary to the common belief that to advance on the Path one has to "selfishly sit in meditation," we found in our field research that most stream-enterers are exceptionally committed towards helping others and have a natural inclination towards making sacrifices. It is this generosity together with unshaken confidence in the triple gem that make a stream-enterer totally committed to helping others to tread the Path. This was so, even during the time of the Buddha as illustrated by the lives of stream-enterers such as Visākhā, Anāthapiṇḍika etc.

The Blessings and Strengths of a Stream-Enterer

Better than sole sovereignty over the earth,
Or better than going to heaven,
Better than even lordship over all worlds,
Is the fruit that is stream-entry.
(Dhp.v.178)

The above stanza of the *Dhammapada* uttered by the Buddha to Anāthapiṇḍika confirming that his son had attained the fruit that is stream-entry amply demonstrates the significance of stream-entry. The status of a universal king [*cakkavatti rāja*] appears in the text to be the most powerful on earth, as an "unparalleled supreme status" which is the culmination of all one's accumulated good kamma. He is blessed with seven extraordinary treasures that enhance and secure his power (DN II 172–177). However even a universal monarch, at the break-up of the body is not assured of freedom from rebirth in the planes of misery, hells and bad destinations.

Incalculable Merit, and Little Suffering Remaining

A stream-enterer's "streams of merit [*puññābhisandā*], streams of the wholesome [*kusalābhisandā*], nutriments of happiness" are incalculable and immeasurable like the water in the great ocean which cannot be measured as "there are so many gallons of water" or "there are so many hundreds of gallons of water"... thousands of gallons etc. The merit of a noble disciple is incalculable (SN V 400 and 402).

The suffering a stream-enterer has eliminated compared to the trifling of suffering still remaining for her in *saṃsāra* has been described by the Buddha as follows:

1) The suffering left to be experienced is like a bit of soil on a fingernail and the suffering eliminated is like the soil in the great earth (SN V 459).
2) or it is like seven little balls of clay of the size of jujube kernels placed on earth compared to the size of the great earth (SN V 462).
3) or it is like two or three drops of water drawn from the ocean compared to the water in the great ocean (SN V 463).
4) or it is like seven grains of gravel of the size of mung beans compared to the size of mount Sineru (the king of all mountains) (SN V 457).

It is said that if a man who is to live for hundred years is offered to be struck by hundred spears each morning, noon and night, but that at the end of the 100 years he will make a breakthrough to the four noble truths to which he had no breakthrough earlier, it is good for such man to accept such an offer. The Buddha says it is because *saṃsāra* is without discoverable beginning, a first point cannot be discerned of blows by spears, blows by swords, blows by axes. And even if this may be so, he says "bhikkhus I do not say that the breakthrough to the four noble truths is accompanied by suffering or displeasure. Rather the breakthrough to the four noble truths is accompanied only by happiness and joy" (SN V 441).

Fixed in Destiny

The supreme blessing of the stream-enterer is that she possesses "wisdom that is directed to arising and passing away which is noble and penetrative leading to the complete destruction of suffering" [*udayatthgāminiyā paññāya samannāgato ariyāya nibbhedikāya sammā-dukkha-kkhayā-gāminiyā*] (SN V 392). Having traversed the beginningless *saṃsāra* a stream-enterer at last sees a light at the end of the tunnel. Due to the newly gained insight he declares with unwavering confidence "I am fixed in destiny, with enlightenment as my destination" [*niyato sambodhiparāyano*] (SN V 358). Even though a stream-enterer may be extremely negligent she does not take an eighth birth (Sn. 40 also AN III 439). Within a maximum of seven births, a stream-enterer attains *Nibbāna* and ends the *saṃsāric* journey with all its woes. So naturally the suffering she has eliminated is incalculable and immeasurable.

The Destination of a Stream-Enterer

As much as a stream-enterer's final destination is assured within a maximum of seven more births, during the remaining journey in *saṃsāra*, a stream-enterer will never be reborn in states of woe and will always be reborn in the human or the celestial realms (SN V 365, SN V 342). Often the after-death status of a stream-enterer is expressed as follows:

> I am one finished with hell, finished with the animal realm, finished with the domain of ghosts, finished with the plane of misery, the bad destinations, and the nether world. I am a stream-enterer no longer bound to the nether world, fixed in destiny, with enlightenment as my destination.[7]

Assuring the future destination of a stream-enterer, the Buddha says:

> Bhikkhus there may be alteration in the four great elements—in the earth element, water element, heat element and the air element- but there cannot be alteration in the noble disciple who possesses confirmed confidence in the Buddha. Therein this is alteration: that the noble disciple who possesses confirmed confidence in the Buddha might be reborn in the hell, in the animal realm, or in the domain of ghosts. This is impossible. (SN V 356)

Even a wheel turning monarch, if he is not a stream-enterer, at the break-up of the body is not freed from rebirth in the planes of misery, bad destinations and the nether world, i.e. the hells, animal world, the worlds of ghosts (SN V 342). Even beings passing away from *brahmā* worlds, if they are not noble disciples, could be born in planes of woe (AN II 126).

Further, it is said that a stream-enterer slants, slopes and is inclined towards *Nibbāna* just as a tree which slants, slopes and inclines towards a particular direction would, upon it being cut down at its root, fall towards the direction it was slanting or sloping (SN V 371).

The destination of a stream-enterer after death is explained further as follows:

> *Bhikkhus* just as when rain pours down in thick droplets on a mountain top, the water pours down along the slope and fills the cleft, gullies, and creeks; these being filled fill up the pools; these being filled fill up the lakes ... the streams ... rivers ... and the great ocean; so too for a noble disciple, these things—confirmed confidence in the Buddha Dhamma and the Saṅgha and the virtues dear to the noble ones—flow onward and having gone beyond they lead to the destruction of the taints. (SN V 396)

Upon being questioned as to how he is so certain about the destination of a stream-enterer, the Buddha says, "suppose a man were to submerge a clay pot of ghee or oil in water and break it; the fragments of the pot would sink downwards but the oil or ghee would rise upwards." Similarly one whose mind has been fortified by the relevant qualities would go upwards and not downwards (SN V 370). The right view of the stream-enterer, coupled with his *ariyakanta sīla* and mindfulness, makes it difficult for him to commit unwholesome thoughts, words and deeds which slants towards states of woe after death. Venerable Ñāṇananda, explaining this, says that once the view on personality is abandoned, the "assets" [*upadhi*] on which the sense of "self" depend (i.e. the five aggregates subject to clinging) begin to get liquidated. Naturally such a person's inclination is towards *Nibbāna* (Ñāṇananda 1974, 38–39).

The Strengths of a Stream-Enterer

The following are some of the powers that a stream-enterer acquires on entering of the Path:

1) A stream-enterer is endowed with a long life span, beauty, happiness, fame and sovereignty whether celestial or human [*āyu, vaṇṇa, sukha, yasa, adhipateyya*] (SN V 390).
2) He possesses the five powers of faith, moral shame, concern for consequences, energy and wisdom [*saddhā, hiri, ottappa, viriya, paññā*] (AN III 1).
3) When confronted by the eight vicissitudes of life—gain and loss, fame and disrepute, praise and blame, pleasure and pain– a stream-enterer can reflect "these are impermanent, subject to suffering and subject to change," hence these don't engross her mind. Such a mind does not get overly elated or dejected by these (AN IV 157).
4) A stream-enterer is considered rich with much wealth and property (SN V 402).
5) A stream-enterer grows in ten ways which include growth in both the material and spiritual spheres. The ten fields are: fields and land, wealth and grain, wives and children, slaves, workers and servants, livestock, faith and virtue, learning, generosity and wisdom (AN V 137). Some of these obviously refer to the lay ariyan disciple and to the cultural practices during the time of the Buddha.
6) The *devas* are elated with a stream-enterer and they speak of her as being similar to them (SN V 394).
7) For a stream-enterer there is no fright, trepidation or fear at death (SN V 386).
8) A stream-enterer is an unsurpassed field of merit for the others, is worthy of gifts, of hospitality, of offerings and of reverential salutation (AN IV 292).

Despite the above attributes of stream-enterers, they also have limitations, as can be seen from the conduct of Venerable Ānanda upon the *Parinibbāna* of Venerable Sāriputta and the Buddha himself. With the news of Sāriputta's demise, Ānanda tells the Buddha, "Venerable Sir, since I heard that the Venerable Sāriputta has attained final *Nibbāna*, my body seems as if it has been drugged, I have become disoriented, the teachings are no longer clear to me." And the Buddha asks him:

> Why Ānanda when Sāriputta attained final *Nibbāna* did he take away your aggregate of virtue, ... concentration, ... wisdom, ... liberation ...aggregate of knowledge and vision of liberation? Have I not already declared Ānanda that we must be parted, separated, severed from all who are dear and agreeable to us? (SN V 162–163)

He is then advised by the Buddha to be an island unto himself and take refuge only in the Dhamma (SN V 162–163). The *Mahāparinibbāna Sutta* relates how Ānanda wept upon the *Parinibbāna* of the Buddha (DN II 157). Nevertheless the Buddha has declared that though Ānanda was only a stream-enterer, his wisdom was second to none.

The Possibility of Someone Having Become a Noble Person in a Past Life

The commentaries report the account of Sirimā the courtesan of Rājagaha who had attained stream-entry. When she died, the Buddha, with the help of king Bimbisāra auctioned her rotten dead body with a view to driving a point of wisdom to a love-sick young monk. There being no bidders for the corpse, the Buddha finally gave the funeral oration as a practical lesson highlighting the impurities of the body. On this occasion Sirimā, being reborn as a *devatā*, attended her own funeral and responding to a query from another *deva*, she declares that she had been established in stream-entry in her just ended human birth (Nyanaponika and Hecker 1997, 306–309, from Dhp-a III 103–109 and V.v.137–149). There are also a few other accounts of noble persons immediately after their demise, being reborn in the divine worlds and visiting the human world to pay homage to the Buddha (e.g. Anāthapiṇḍika) (SN I 71).

It is possible for noble persons who are stream-enterers and once-returners to take re-birth in the human world. The *Nikāyas* do not record any account of such a rebirth in the human world, though there are many accounts of noble persons being reborn in the divine worlds. This study investigates the possibility of recognizing such a noble person who has been reborn in the human world.

When asked whether he has come across noble persons by birth and how one could recognize them, Ajahn Brahmavamso confirms that he has come across people who have attained stream-entry in a previous birth. He says:

> The only way you know that, is to re-experience that *phala* in this life. In other words if you were, say, a stream-enterer in your previous life, you would not know that as a baby, you would not know that as a young man, or a young girl. There'll come a time in your life when you re-experience the same thing and you say you are a stream-enterer again. (Interview No. 8, Q.30–37)

Accordingly, at a certain point in their life they re-experience the experience that had previously led to the first three fetters being broken or, which marked the dawn of their stream-entry, as if they are experiencing it for the first time. Still they would recognize it on their own as a repeated experience, only if they have the ability to recollect their past births and see for themselves that they have had this experience in a previous life too and not otherwise.

Two of our interviewees referred to a case where a Sri Lankan monk, Venerable Kannimahara Sumangala Thero, claimed publicly that he became a stream-enterer in his previous birth and urged the chief preceptor of their forest hermitage, who was a leading and experienced meditation master in Sri Lanka, not to overlook this possibility when dealing with meditation students (Interview No. 3, Q.111 and Interview No. 2, Q.139).

The following two cases were recorded by us in our interviews[8] which could be possible cases of individuals who had become noble persons in a past life.

Case 1

This is a case of an American young man of around 26 years whom our interviewee No. 2 (a monk) met in his forest hermitage in Sri Lanka. The boy had two degrees and has been born to a very rich family. At the age of 16 years he had a very strange experience. Whilst he was in the bathtub he felt his "body dissolving" in the water. Whilst he was watching it, he found his mind too "getting dissolved" the same way, and he experienced a total blankness, he felt his mind went to "some other place." When he "regained his consciousnesses" he realized that it was a very blissful experience. Ever since he tried to get into that "blankness" but he couldn't. Much later, he saw a Vietnamese monk and went to Japan in search of Buddhism. By that time he had stopped his studies to go in search of this experience. At the time of this experience he was preparing for a higher degree. When he went to Japan, he found that what he was looking for is not available there and came back and proceeded to Korea and was guided by a Korean monk. Later he found out about Theravāda Buddhism and that it was available in Sri Lanka and came to Sri Lanka. In Sri Lanka, he saw Buddhist monks, he liked them and the environment so much that he purchased a robe and wrapped it round by himself and "became a monk" on his own and lived alone in the hill country. One day he was told by a villager that there are formalities to be followed to be ordained as a Buddhist monk and he was directed to the forest hermitage where our interviewee was living.

When the monk (interviewee) met him, he was 26 years. He strongly believed in *kamma* and re-birth. He understood the experience he had as a "temporary cutting down of *saṃsāra*." And he never wanted to be reborn ever again. He did not believe in God or the Soul. He strictly observed the five moral precepts. In his whole life he had killed only one animal, that too accidentally. He did not know Buddhism but for him Buddhism was what he saw outwardly such as the rites and rituals, monks and the temples.

As to my question on whether he re-experienced this state of mind subsequently in this life, apart from his original experience in the bathtub, it was reported that once he was trying to experience it the whole day, but was unsuccessful. That particular night he was compelled to drive his vehicle to the town. While driving the vehicle his mind was very concentrated, and suddenly, unexpectedly, he got absorbed in this blankness which he was trying to experience the whole day. His vehicle went out of control and met with an accident. He suffered a permanent scar on his shoulder which was very visible. In fact this story was related by him as a response to our monk's query as to what was wrong with his shoulder.

However at that time, no teacher in Sri Lanka investigated into these experiences nor recognized the possibility that a person being reborn is already a noble person. At such time the monk who was talking to us, with whom his story was discussed also was inexperienced to identify this. So the teachers in Sri Lanka wanted him to start his practice all over again, as though he was a complete novice. The youth was dissatisfied with the guidance of the teacher and disrobed and went back to Korea, to his Korean teachers. Thereafter his whereabouts were not known.

Case 2

This is a report of a youth of around 18 years whom the monk referred to in case 1 above met at the same monastery. The youth was a Swiss national. Both his parents were Professors of Theology. He was born to a wealthy family and he was the only son. When he was about 16 or 17 years old, he saw a Buddha statue for the first time in a shop and he got totally absorbed in it. He couldn't move from that place. At that time his mind "went blank" totally. He didn't know what had happened to him. When he came back to his senses he felt "I must follow this Path, this is the only solution." Then immediately he set off to Jerusalem in search of a person like the one he had seen portrayed in the statue. He was so rich, he could afford to stop everything and go in search of such a person. His parents, being Theologians, told him that what he saw in the statue and Jesus were one and the same. So he looked for it in Jerusalem and didn't find what he was looking for. Then someone told him that it is available in India. He proceeded to India and ended up at a Goenka Centre. In the Goenka Centre too, nobody spoke to him or investigated his background and he was instructed to start meditation as a beginner. Though he was initially happy, later he became dissatisfied with the practice. After six months he left India to reach Sri Lanka as he had heard that what he sought was available in Sri Lanka. He went to the Island Hermitage of Polgasduwa, but the meditation there was not to his satisfaction and he finally ended up in the forest hermitage where the monk interviewee then lived.

At the time this interviewee met him, this youth was a layman but later he got ordained as a Buddhist monk. As a young boy he had observed the five moral precepts strictly. He had never killed in his whole life. He never took alcohol in his life nor womanized though he had enough opportunities being so rich and young. What was prominent in him was his understanding of *anatta*. At the time our interviewee (monk) met this youth, the interviewee was inexperienced and was still a layman. He did not have a deep understanding of Buddhism. But this youth insisted that what is most prominent in Buddhism is *anatta*. The interviewee says:

> "There is no soul, I am very sure," he insisted with me. I said I can understand *anicca*, yes I can; I can understand *dukkha*. But I don't know what is *anatta*. He repeatedly told me "there is nobody here to hold, why can't you understand *anatta*?— it is very prominent in Buddhism." He is 18 years, I can't understand, he is far from my age. He said this is *anatta*, there is no control. There isn't any essence, ever changing. That much he understood. He strongly believed in rebirth and *kamma*.

He did not believe in a God though born to parents who were both Professors of Theology. In fact he was feeling very sorry for his parents.

He was looking to re-experience this strange experience but he couldn't. Here again no teacher discussed with him about his background, nobody investigated into this experience. But he was directed to practise meditation as a beginner. Later he disrobed and left Sri Lanka. His whereabouts were not known thereafter.

The above two cases sound strangely too close to a person re-experiencing the fetter-breaking-experience of the specific religious experience relating to the attainment of a supramundane fruit that is commonly known as "*phala-samāpatti.*" Although no one investigated deeply to assess their "right view" [*sammā-diṭṭhi*], their non-belief in a creator God and the Soul, together with strong belief in rebirth and *kamma* coupled with strong inclination to observe the five moral precepts from their childhood, particularly given their family, religious and social background, and above all the fact that this experience when experienced for the first time triggered off a relentless search for the meaning of existence rather than an anxious visit to the doctor or a psychiatrist, together with experiencing it more than once, makes it highly probable that it is a case of a person being reborn in the human world as already a noble one. It is also noteworthy that in both these cases, the two men have been born to extremely wealthy families and were enjoying a luxurious living. As discussed earlier, a stream-enterer is supposed to grow in wealth and also the exceptional generosity of a stream-enterer would naturally result in this level of luxury and comfort if reborn in the human world.

Can a Stream-Enterer Commit Suicide?

Venerable Ñāṇavīra (1920–1965) an Englishman who was ordained as a Buddhist monk and was living in meditation in a *kuṭī* in the jungles of Bundala, in the south of Sri Lanka, declared himself to be a stream-enterer but ended his life by committing suicide. He was suffering from an acute amoebic condition for which he was given medication which gave rise to erotic feelings. Ñāṇavīra, being unable to cope with the discomfort of the sickness aggravated by the erotic feelings caused by the medication, after a long struggle contemplating suicide, finally ended up committing suicide. He was a prolific writer. As he was unable to put in long hours of meditation due to his sickness, he was in the habit of writing letters to his close supporters [*dāyakas*] about the Dhamma that arose in his mind and about the controversy of him contemplating suicide. After his death the letters he wrote to his *dāyakas* were published as *Clearing the Path—the Writings of Ñāṇavīra Thero*.

The introduction to *Clearing the Path* says:

> This formerly well-to-do Englishman, residing in a hut at the edge of a Ceylonese jungle, (was) visited by elephants, snakes, tarantulas and by curious people who were unsure whether he was a saint or mad man ... (Ñāṇavīra 2002 II, Introduction, i). Ven. Ñāṇavīra plainly tells us why he no longer wanted to live. First of all he suffered from great physical distress. In addition to amoebiasis, the gut wrenching bowel disorder he discusses in detail, he was afflicted by diarrhoea, insomnia, bursitis, and damage to his sciatic nerve from sitting cross-legged all night on hard floors. His doctors could not cure him. During the last years of his life he endured constant and severe pain ... and since as he saw it, the unswerving pursuit of *Nibbāna* was the only justifiable purpose of his existence, he could not in good faith return to lay life. With no hope of ever again practising intense concentration, he was in effect condemned to serving a life sentence, which after long deliberation he decided to terminate. (Ñāṇavīra 2002, II, Introduction, ix)

It is reported that Ven. Ñāṇavīra handed over a letter to a Colombo Thera, with the envelope saying, "In the event of my death, this envelope should be delivered to and opened by the senior *bhikkhu* of the Island Hermitage, Dodanduwa—Ñāṇavīra *Bhikkhu*, 20th September 1960." Apparently the letter was kept till 1964, when it was handed over already opened and its contents were then discussed. This discussion became then known to others, and thus the author's attainment of stream-entry came to be known (and accepted by some and rejected by some others) even before his death (Ñāṇavīra 2002, II, 376).

The envelope contained the following message, in Pāli:

> At one time Venerable Ñāṇavīra was living in a small *kuṭī* in the village of Bundala.
>
> At that time, Ñāṇavīra *bhikkhu*, was walking up and down in the first watch of the night, cleansing the mind of the *dhammas* that cloud the mind and was pondering, investigating and reviewing with the mind, on the teaching as had been heard and learnt. Then to Ñāṇavīra *bhikkhu* who was pondering, investigating and reviewing with the mind, on the teaching as had been heard and learnt, the dustless stainless eye of the *dhamma* arose: whatever is of the nature to arise, all that is of the nature to cease.
>
> Having been a *dhammānusāri* (*dhamma* investigator) for a month (he) became a *diṭṭhipatto* (view attainer). (Dated 27. 6. 1959)[9]

The above is a declaration on his attainment of stream-entry. On this matter he subsequently wrote:

> It was not originally my intention to speak about this matter at all, but I found myself more and more at cross-purposes with various people, and the increasing strain of trying to provide a plausible account of my behaviour without mentioning the most important item eventually persuaded me that I am perhaps not justified in perpetuating false situations in this way. Whether my decision was right I am not sure (it is not the sort of thing about which one can consult someone else), but I feel that my situation is much simplified since this rather awkward cat is out of the bag and is semi-public property for which I am no longer solely responsible. This seems to make living easier for me (though of course, it also makes it easier to die). (Ñāṇavīra 2002, II, 229)

During his remaining journey in *saṃsāra*, a stream-enterer will never be reborn in states of woe and will always be reborn in the human or the celestial realms (SN V 342–343). A stream-enterer declares: "I am one finished with hell, finished with the animal realm, finished with the domain of ghosts, finished with the plane of misery, the bad destinations, and the nether world. I am a stream-enterer no longer bound to the nether world, fixed in destiny, with enlightenment as my destination" (SN V 343). This destiny of a stream-enterer seems to have given the confidence to Ñāṇavīra to carry out his thoughts on suicide.

The introduction to the said book further says:

> Critics have been appalled by the correspondence with his physician and his Publisher wherein he contemplates putting an end to his life. They have used it as a weapon to attack him personally and to discredit his *Notes on Dhamma*. Supposedly one who could commit such a desperate act was surely *non compos mentis* and could not possibly perceive the *dhamma* correctly; those morbid thoughts prove his ideas are flawed or worse deluded ... (viii). Clearly, the real question is whether Venerable Ñāṇavīra's ideas on *dhamma* hold up to scrutiny. It is a pity to spend even a few words refuting *adhominem* arguments, but as he would say,

> although the "seasoned thinker" will be wise to them, they could deceive readers with logical fallacies. (ix)

Before we deal with the possibility of a stream-enterer committing suicide, we need to deal with the issue of whether Ñāṇavīra belongs to the category of a stream-enterer as declared by him. The criteria for recognizing a noble person have been discussed in detail in Chapter 2. We defined an attainment of a supramundane fruit to be a specific striking experience of a person treading or making an effort to tread the Noble Eightfold Path, resulting in the understanding or insight-knowledge which leads to breaking of the corresponding fetters [*saṃyojana*].The key elements of this phenomenon being: 1) Path, 2) a specific experience, 3) arising of insight-knowledge, and 4) breaking of fetters.

A specific experience which marked the attainment of his stream-entry has been declared by him in his note as quoted above, with reference to a specific date, place and a meditation posture. Further, the understanding that arose has been declared as "*virajam vītamalam dhamma-cakkhum udapādi, yam kiñci samudaya-dhammam sabbam tam nirodha-dhammanti*": "the dustless stainless eye of the *Dhamma* arose: whatever is of the nature to arise, all that is of the nature to cease." Though some yardsticks for recognizing a noble person such as long and close association and careful observation etc. are not available to us, there is ample opportunity to examine his understanding of the *Dhamma* through his letters published in *Clearing the Path*.

The essence of the understanding at stream-entry is acquiring right view and gaining direct insight into the principle of dependent origination. Throughout his letters we see nothing lacking in his understanding of *dependent origination*. This is further demonstrated by the confidence with which he dismisses the interpretation of the 12 linked formula of *paṭiccasamuppāda* as given by Ñāṇamoli in the *Visuddhimagga* translation. Ñāṇavīra writes:

> I admit that I have not investigated these. But by all accounts they are unsatisfactory. In any case, the *paṭiccasamuppāda* formulation (as I see it) does not admit of alternative interpretations. There is one and one only. I do not see that anyone offering a number of interpretations as equally valid can possibly be right in any of them. (It is quite possible that someone actually reaching *sotāpatti*, and therefore seeing *paṭiccasamuppāda* himself, might still hesitate before deciding on the meaning of the expanded—twelve term—formulation, since what he sees for himself is "*imasmim sati idam hoti*" etc. and not its expansion in terms—*avijjā, saṅkhāra*, and so on—whose meaning he may not know. But one thing is certain: whatever interpretations he gives will be in conformity with his private knowledge, *Imasmin sati* ... and since he has already grasped the essence of the matter he will not look around for alternate interpretations). But the Ven. Thera may have had something else in mind when he spoke. (Ñāṇavīra 2002, II, 13)

Responding to certain criticism about his writing by a third party Ñāṇavīra writes:

> The thing is that I have a source of information (my own experience) that he does not know about: and when I say that a certain thing is true without giving the *Sutta* backing he will always get the impression that I am imposing arbitrary views. (Ñāṇavīra 2002, II, 243)

His understanding of *sīlabbata-parāmāsa* and Buddhist cosmology can be seen when he writes:

> About spirits in the East, one of the reasons for their being here may be that (as) given in the *Ratana Sutta*, second verse (Sn. 223), where it is said that human beings bring them offerings [*balim*] day and night. The Buddha in certain *Sutta* passages encourages laymen to make offerings to spirits who are capable of receiving them. This I think is more than just the offering of merit. (I never advise anyone not to make material offerings to spirits, but to be quite clear in their mind what they are doing. Gifts given to anyone human or not, bring merit, but do not lead to *Nibbāna*. And spirits certainly do, upon occasion, give protection (I am not in agreement with the modern skeptical tendency). (Ñāṇavīra 2002, II, 165)

The confidence that he has in the Buddha, the Dhamma and the *Saṅgha* can be assessed when he writes:

> And the Buddha himself warns (in the *Māhāsuññata sutta*—M.122: iii 109–118) that one who becomes a layman after following a teacher may fall into the hells when he dies. It is hard for a layman (and even, these days, for the majority of *bhikkhus*, I fear) to understand that when a *bhikkhu* devotes his entire life to one single aim, there may come a time when he can no longer turn back—lay life has become incomprehensible to him. If he cannot reach his goal there is only one way for him to do—to die (perhaps you are not aware that the Buddha has said that "death" for a *bhikkhu* means return to lay life—*Opamma Saṃyutta* 11: ii, 271).
>
> (Ñāṇavīra 2002, II, 124)

Distinguishing an ordinary worldling from a noble disciple, he writes:

> A *puthujjana* does not see or know that "all things are *dukkha*." The *puthujjana* has no criteria or norm for making any such judgment and so he does not make it.
>
> The *puthujjana*'s experience is *saṅkhāra dukkha* (the suffering related to conditioned states) from top to bottom, and the consequence is that he has no way of knowing *dukkha* for himself; for however much he "steps back" from himself in a reflective effort, he still takes *dukkha* with him. ... The whole point is the *puthujjana*'s non-knowledge of *dukkha* is the *dukkha* that he has non-knowledge of; and this *dukkha* that is at the same time non-knowledge of *dukkha* is the *puthujjana*'s (mistaken) acceptance of what seems to be a "self" or "subject" or "ego" at its face value (as *nicca/sukha/attā*). (Ñāṇavīra 2002, II, 326)

Although we cannot pass judgments conclusively about another's spiritual attainments, given the commitment of Ñāṇavīra to tread the Path, there is no reason to doubt the genuineness of his claim. With regard to the issue of whether he could be mistaken or over estimating his state of mind, the writings of Ñāṇavīra display the hallmarks of a stream-enterer as claimed by him. Furthermore, the writings display a mood of detailed reflection, humour and confidence rather than a mood of depression, anxiety, fear or being emotional, which are hallmarks of a psychopath.

Venerable Ñāṇavīra writes on his suicidal thoughts:

> I find that under the pressure of affliction, I am oscillating between two poles. On the one hand, if I indulge the sensual images that offer themselves, my thoughts turn towards the state of a layman; if, on the other hand, I resist them, my thought turns towards suicide. Wife or knife, as one might say. For the time being, each extreme tends to be checked by the other, but the situation is obviously in unstable equilibrium (mental concentration what offers relief, is difficult for me on

> account of my chronic digestive disorders, as you already know; and I cannot rely on it for support). I view both these alternatives with distaste (though for different reasons); and I am a faintly nauseated, but otherwise apathetic spectator of my oscillations between them. Sooner or later, however, unless my condition much improves, I may find myself choosing one or the other of these unsatisfactory alternatives; and a fresh attack of amoebiasis, which is always possible, might well precipitate a decision. (Ñāṇavīra 2002, II, 64)

> But the absence of a reason for living is not necessarily a condition for dying (though the visiting psychiatrist was assuming the contrary, hence his panic at the suggestion that the purpose of life might be questionable). Absence of a reason for living simply makes the decision to die easier. The reason for ending one's life is the discomfort and difficulty of one's situation and this is why any medical help that can be given is welcome. It is perhaps possible that my secondary complaint might improve in the course of time and the situation would then become easier. Well and good if it does. On the other hand, I might get re-infected with amoebiasis; and this possibility raises a question. If this should happen, would it be possible to treat the infection without again provoking the erotic stimulation? Can you answer this question for me? If the answer is negative, it at once becomes evident that I cannot afford to get the infection again; for I should have to choose between erotic stimulation and untreated amoebiasis, either of which would almost certainly upset the apple cart. (Ñāṇavīra 2002, II, 72)

In line with the qualities of a stream-enterer, admitting his weaknesses he writes:

> Do not think I regard suicide as praiseworthy—that there can easily be an element of weakness in it, I am the first to admit (though the stoic regards it as a courageous act)—but I certainly regard it as preferable to number of other possibilities. (I would a hundred times rather have it said of the Notes that the author killed himself as a *bhikkhu* than that he disrobed; for *bhikkhus* have become *Arahants* in the act of suicide, but it is not recorded that anyone became an *Arahant* in the act of disrobing. (Ñāṇavīra 2002, II, 127)

Commenting on the implications of his suicidal thoughts as regards *Vinaya* he writes:

> As regards *vinaya* and *dhamma* I am well aware of the situation and do not need to seek the advice of others. Suicide, though a fault, is not (contrary to a widespread opinion) a grave offence in *vinaya* (it is a *dukkata*) and as regards *dhamma* I know better than anyone else how I am placed. Taking all these matters into consideration I do not find, at least as far as my own personal situation is concerned, any very strong reason (though I regret the *dukkata*) to restrain me from taking life (naturally I am speaking only of my own case); for others there may be, and most probably are, very grave objections of one kind or other to suicide ... (Ñāṇavīra 2002, II, 119)

In the *vinaya*, or the monastic code, offences are grouped according to seriousness, the most serious being *pārājikā*, involving expulsion from the order and *sānghādisesa*, involving confession and temporary suspension of certain privileges. *Dukkata* (lit meaning "wrongly done") is the least offence except for *dubbaca* (wrongly said) (Ñāṇavīra 2002, II, 360).

In this chapter we discussed what is impossible for a stream-enterer (pp. 142–143). Given the said impossibilities expressly set out in the *Nikāyas* and the fact that suicide is not included as an impossibility, I conclude that anything over and above these is a possibility, depending on the circumstances of each case.

The intentional destruction of human life has been classed among the *pārājikā* offences, the four most serious offences under the monastic disciplinary code involving expulsion and complete loss of monastic status. *Pārājikā* rule 3 (Vin. I 73), which covers this subject of homicide, also regards other conditions such as aiding and abetting which would contribute to the commission of suicide as being equally reprehensible and leading to defeat as a monk (Dhirasekara 1964, 82). However there is no mention of the legal consequences of suicide per se.

The Māra Saṃyutta reports Venerable Godhika's suicide (SN I 264–268). Godhika was practising resolutely but, being frustrated with his lack of progress in his practice, used a knife across his throat and committed suicide. However, just before he died he had become an *Arahant*. Minutes before his *parinibbāna*, Māra visits the Buddha and addresses him:

> O great hero who has vanquished death,
> Your disciple is longing for death.
> He intends to [take his own life]:
> Restrain him from this, O Luminous One!
> How, O Blessed One, can your disciple,
> One delighting in the Teaching,
> A trainee seeking his mind's ideal,
> Take his own life, O widely famed?

On this occasion the Buddha, having seen that Godhika had just committed suicide but knowing that he had become an *Arahant* before passing away, and also knowing that this is Māra who is addressing him, answers:

> Such indeed is how the steadfast act:
> They are not attached to life.
> Having drawn out craving with its root,
> Godhika has attained final *Nibbāna.*

The Buddha visited the scene where Godhika was lying with his jugular vein cut immediately after the act of suicide and confirmed that Godhika passed away as an *Arahant.*

A similar incident is reported about *bhikkhu* Vakkali (SN III 119–124). Here Vakkali, who was suffering from a grave illness, decides to end his life by using a knife across his throat. Upon his request, the Buddha visited him, gave him an exhortation and went away. The next morning, just before this *bhikkhu* left to the site where he committed suicide, the Buddha sent a message to him through some other *bhikkhus* informing him that on the previous night two *devatās* had told him about the intention of Vakkali. This *Sutta* reports that whilst one *devatā* said to the Buddha, "Venerable sir, *bhikkhu* Vakkali is intent on deliverance [*vimokkhāya ceteti*]," the other said, "surely venerable sir, he will be liberated as one well liberated [*vimutto vimuccissatīti*]. Further, the Buddha sends the message to Vakkali, "Do not be afraid, Vakkali, do not be afraid! Your death will not be a bad one [*apāpakaṃ te maraṇam bhavissati*]; your demise will not be a bad one" (SN III 122). At this point Vakkali requests the messengers to pay homage to the Buddha on his behalf and pass on his statement that he knows without doubt [*vicikicca*] that the five aggregates are impermanent, and hence painful, so that he has "no desire, lust [*rāga*] or affection for them," implying he was at least a stream-enterer. Soon afterwards, he was taken to the Isigili slope where he committed suicide using a knife across his throat. The Buddha visited the site the next day and confirmed that he had passed away as an *Arahant*. The commentary to this passage takes it that Vakkali over-estimated himself if he thought he was already an *Arahant*, though he became an *Arahant* just before he passed away. Venerable Anālayo in a trilogy of research papers on the issue of whether it is possible for an *Arahant* to deliberately end his or her life, contrary to the said Pāli commentary, concludes that Venerable Vakkali and Venerable Channa whose case is discussed below, were in fact *Arahants* at the time they decided to end their life and not that they became *Arahants*, in the act of suicide (Anālayo 2012, 165). However, in the case of Vakkali, for Buddha to have sent the message "Do not be afraid, your death will not be a bad one," indicates that Vakkali was not an *Arahant* up to such time, because, if he was already an *Arahant*, there would not have been an issue about "fear" and about his death being a good or bad one. The Buddha's message to him seems to be an assurance to Vakkali that he would die as an *Arahant*. However, Vakkali's final message to the Buddha, "form is impermanent, I have no perplexity about it" etc., indicates that he was at least a stream-enterer at this point in time.[10] We conclude that this is a case where an *ariyan* disciple who is not an *Arahant* has decided to commit suicide.

The Buddha under *these* circumstances does not condemn suicide, nor does he condemn it unconditionally, as one would expect him to do.

The case of Channa reported in the *Channovāda Sutta* of the *Majjhima Nikāya* (MN: 144) is somewhat different. Here Channa, who was grievously sick, is visited by Venerable Sāriputta and Venerable Mahā Cunda to inquire about his illness and Channa expresses his intention of committing suicide due to the condition of his sickness. When he is discouraged from doing so by Sāriputta, Channa says "Friend Sāriputta remember this; the *bhikkhu* Channa will use the knife blamelessly [*anupavajjam*[11]]." Then both of them ask Channa certain questions to assess the state of mind declared by Channa as "blameless." Sāriputta asks: "do you regard the eye, eye-consciousness, and things cognizable [by the mind] through eye consciousness thus: "This is mine, this I am, this is my self," to which Channa says that he does not consider any of these like this. The Sāriputta asks "what have you seen, what have you directly known in the eye, eye-consciouness, things cognizable by the eye-consciousness for you to not regard them as "This is mine, this I am, this is my self?" Channa replies, "it is through seeing cessation [*nirodham*], through directly knowing cessation [*nirodham abhiññāya*] in the eye, in eye consciousness and in things cognizable by the eye-consciousness that I regard them thus." At this point Mahā Cunda gives him instructions as to how he should proceed with his practice "for the end of suffering [*anto dukkhassāti*]"; "Therefore friend Channa, this instruction of the Blessed One has to be constantly given attention ...." Immediately after they walked away Channa committed suicide. When Sāriputta heard this he went to the Buddha and inquired about Channa's future birth [*Tassa kāgati ko abhisamparāyo ti*].Then the Buddha asks Sāriputta "Sāriputta didn't the Venerable Channa declare to you his blamelessness? Sāriputta when one lays down his body and clings to a new body, and then I say one is blameworthy. There was none of that in the *bhikkhu* Channa. The *bhikkhu* Channa used the knife blamelessly" (MN III 263–266). Here the Buddha confirms that Channa passed away as an *Arahant.*

The commentary to this passage says that Channa made this statement about his blamelessness thinking that he was an *Arahant* and that was an overestimation. Further, that Mahā Cunda gave the advice regarding the future practice assuming that Channa was an ordinary man [*puthujjana*] (Ñāṇamoli and Bodhi 1995, 1351–1352, n. 1308–1314). I cannot agree with the commentator on this explanation. When Channa declared that "it is through seeing and directly knowing cessation of the eye" etc., what he declares is, at least the fruit that is stream-entry. Though Sāriputta was unable to understand the state of mind of Channa, Cunda, having understood him to be an *ariyan,* but yet not an *Arahant*, gave him the instructions for the completion of his practice without discouraging him from suicide, which Cunda could have done and one would expect him to have done. This is further confirmed by the statement of the Buddha to Sāriputta, "Sāriputta didn't the Venerable Channa declare to you his blamelessness?," that is, almost saying "why are you disbelieving Venerable Channa when he declared his blamelessness to you?" For the Buddha to refer to him as "blameless" at the time the declaration was made to Sāriputta, Channa ought to have been at least a stream-enterer, but there is no mention or indication that he was an *Arahant* at such time.

Moreover there are reported cases in the texts where *Arahants* have passed away using the heat element [*tejo dhātu*] as in the case of the *Arahant* Dabba (Ud.92–94), or the Buddha deciding to relinquish his "life-activity" [*āyu-saṅkhāra*] at a predetermined time (DN II 106) which might appear to the outside world as "suicide," though did not involve "using the knife." Rather, they have passed away by falling back on their mental power developed as an *Arahant.* Venerable Anālayo, commenting on the possibility of *Arahants* committing suicide and the Buddha himself giving up his life deliberately (deciding to relinquish *āyu-saṅkhāra*), says, the tradition envisaged that such a decision could be taken without defilements (Anālayo 2012, 153–157). He says that killing oneself seems to be blameworthy only if one is reborn after death. In other words, suicide of an *Arahant* or one on the brink of such attainment does not seem to be blameworthy. Commenting on the "approving attitude" towards the suicide of an *Arahant*, quoting Lambert Schmithausen,[12] he points out that, in contrast to ordinary living beings, *Arahants* do not regard their biological life as something valuable and are indifferent to it, since for them, the ultimate value is not biological life but *Nibbāna* (Anālayo 2012, 167).

Accordingly, I conclude that it is possible for a stream-enterer to commit suicide. Considering that they cannot be reborn at less than a human level, but if grievously ill might hope for conditions more supportive of attaining a higher fruit in another human life, we can understand their quest for the final goal taking precedence over even their life.

To What Extent Does a Stream-Enterer See *Nibbāna*?

Whether a stream-enterer experiences *Nibbāna* or not has been a longstanding debate. Even in our field research, some of our interviewees explaining their experience of attaining stream-entry understood it to be the experience of *Nibbāna* whilst some others understood *Nibbāna* "relative" to the fetter-breaking-experience of the attainment of stream-entry.

In the *Ambaṭṭha Sutta* a stream-enterer is described as one who had "seen the Dhamma, had mastered it, understood it, dived deep down into it, who had passed beyond doubt and put away perplexity and gained full confidence, who had become dependent on no other man for his knowledge of the teaching of the master" [*diṭṭhadhammo pattadhammo viditadhammo pariyogāḷhadhammo tiṇṇavicikiccho vigata-kathaṃkatho vesārajjapatto aparapaccayo satthu sāsane*] (DN I 110).

Venerable Ñāṇananda, explaining this passage, says:

> *Diṭṭhadhammo:* one who has seen the *dhamma*, that is *Nibbāna*. It is said in the *Ratana Sutta* that along with the vision of the first Path, three fetters are abandoned ... Some might argue that only these fetters are abandoned at this stage, because it is a glimpse of *Nibbāna* from a distance. But then there is second epithet, *pattadhammo*, which means that he has reached the *dhamma*, that he has arrived at *Nibbāna*. Not only that, he is *viditadhammo*, he is one who has understood the *dhamma*, which is *Nibbāna*. He is *pariyogāḷhadhammo,* he has plunged into the *dhamma*, he has dived into the *dhamma*, which is *Nibbāna*. He is *tiṇṇavicikiccho,* he has crossed over the doubts. *Vigatakathaṃkatho*, his waverings are gone. *Vesārajjapatto*, he has attained to proficiency. *Aparapaccayo sathusāsane*, in regard to the dispensation of the teacher, he is not dependent on others. And that is to say that he could attain to *Nibbāna* even without another's help. (Ñāṇananda 2003, I, 25)

Clearly Ñāṇananda takes it that a stream-enterer experiences *Nibbāna*. The traditional Theravāda view is also that the four paths and the four fruits take the timeless, unconditioned *Nibbāna* as its object, meaning that one at these states directly experiences *Nibbāna*.[13] The extent to which, or sense in which a stream-enterer sees *Nibbāna* could be understood by examining the difference between a *sekha* and an *asekha* (a trainee and an *Arahant*) as given in the texts. The texts are very clear about the difference of the trainee and an *Arahant*. There are differences between them with regard to the four foundation of mindfulness (SN V 175), their degree of knowledge [*abhijānati* as against *parijanāti*] (SN IV 125 and 83), the strength of their spiritual faculties (SN V 230), the degree to which the five hindrances are abandoned (SN V 327), their relationship with the five aggregates subject to clinging (SN III 161) etc. From the above differences it is clear that the state of mind of a stream-enterer and an *Arahant* is distinctly different. These differences originate "based on" or "relative to" the religious experience that ensues at the dawn of their respective supramundane fruits of the Path and the knowledge it generates. For the knowledge to be so different, the religious experience in general, on attaining the two stages ought to be different.

The *Kosambi Sutta* of the *Nidāna Saṃyutta* sets out the difference between a trainee and an *Arahant* and the connection between the transforming experience and the knowledge that arises from this. Here a Saviṭṭha asks a fellow monk, Nārada, "apart from faith, apart from personal preference, apart from oral tradition, apart from reasoned reflection, apart from accepting a view after pondering it, does the venerable have personal knowledge on the condition for each of the links of dependent origination and that "*Nibbāna* is the cessation of being'?" Nārada answers "yes, apart from faith, apart from personal preference, apart from oral tradition, apart from reasoned reflection, apart from accepting a view after pondering it, I know this, see this, "*Nibbāna* is the cessation of being'."

Then Saviṭṭha concludes "Then Venerable Nārada is an *Arahant* whose taints are destroyed." But Nārada replies:

> Friend, though I have clearly seen as it really is with correct wisdom, "*Nibbāna* is the cessation of being," I am not an *Arahant*, one whose taints are destroyed [*bhavanirodho nibbānanti kho me āvuso yathā bhūtam sammapaññāya suddiṭṭham na camhi araham khīṇāsavo*]. Suppose friend there was a well along a desert road, but it had neither a rope nor bucket. Then a man would come along, oppressed and afflicted by the heat, tired, parched and thirsty. He would look down into the well and the knowledge would occur to him, "There is water" but he would not be able to make bodily contact with it. So too friend, though I have clearly seen as it really is, with correct wisdom, "*Nibbāna* is the cessation of being," I am not an *Arahant* one whose taints are destroyed. (SN II 115–118)

Bhikkhu Bodhi comments that Saviṭṭha drew a wrong conclusion that the defining mark of an *Arahant* is the understanding of dependent origination and the nature of *Nibbāna*. This understanding is shared by both *Arahants* and trainees. Bhikkhu Bodhi says that what distinguishes an *Arahant* from the trainee is not his insight into dependent origination but the fact that he has used his insight to eradicate all defilements and has thereby gained access to a unique meditative state (the fruition attainment of Arahantship) in which he can dwell "touching the deathless element with the body" (Bodhi 2000, 783, n. 204).

To our question "Is it *Nibbāna* that you experienced?," meaning whether they "saw" *Nibbāna* in the fetter-breaking-experience relating to stream-entry, one of our interviewees (No. 4) felt that even though for a moment, his mind experienced *Nibbāna*. One felt that "that is what ought to be experienced in *Nibbāna*" (No. 6) and two other responded; "That is temporary cessation, *Nibbāna* is permanent cessation" (No. 2), and "Stream-entry as short term extinguishing and *Nibbāna* as long term extinguishing" (No. 5).

We have already discussed that a stream-enterer is described as "*aparapaccayo sathusāsane,*" not dependent on others for understanding the teaching of the Buddha, that is, he can attain *Nibbāna* even without another's help. Here what the stream-enterer is not dependent on another for is to attain *Nibbāna*. This clearly shows that there is a "path yet to tread" to attain *Nibbāna* for which he is not dependent on others. Hence there is a distance between stream-entry and *Nibbāna*. A stream-enterer has only a "vision" of *Nibbāna* but has not attained *Nibbāna*. He now knows the Path to *Nibbāna* but is yet to attain *Nibbāna*.

The issue here is what is meant by "clearly seen *Nibbāna* as it really is with correct wisdom" as stated above in *Kosambi Sutta*, that is, whether *Nibbāna* is experienced directly or as a "clear possibility." In our field research we saw that every noble person including the first noble person[14] enters the plane of the *aryan* through a specific experience, the peak of which is signless, wishless and empty, at which point the "experience of the world" ceases. A stream-enterer "relative to" this fetter-breaking-experience understands the principles of arising and the ceasing of the aggregates subject to clinging and the six sense-bases; he understands that it is possible to attain a state where the five aggregates and the six sense-bases cease completely, forever, that a complete cessation of these is a clear possibility.[15] He understands the "possible complete cessation" as *Nibbāna*. Also he understands that just as much as the first three fetters have been destroyed, by following the Path, it is possible to eliminate the rest of the fetters too. Also relative to the peace experienced consequent to the fruit that is stream-entry, he could project the peace and the excellence of *Nibbāna*.

In other words, at stream-entry, one understands the principle of dependent origination. Having understood the norm of dependent origination, then the stream-enterer applies it with wisdom, to the past and to the future and thereby understands *Nibbāna*. A stream-enterer understands *Nibbāna* only through *anvaye ñāṇa*, (knowledge by entailment) (SN II 58), and not that he directly experiences *Nibbāna*. The knowledge of entailment relates to extending knowledge of the present into knowledge of the past and future. Based on the fetter-breaking-experience, the "present knowledge" is of the impermanent nature of the five aggregates subject to clinging. He extends this knowledge to the future to understand the possibility of complete cessation of the five aggregates of clinging (i.e. *Nibbāna*). In other words, relative to his fetter-breaking-experience of the fruit that is stream-entry, he understands *Nibbāna* as a reality. He understands that the process of cessation of *saṃsāra* has begun for him. Therefore a stream-enterer has been compared to a person walking along a mountain path who catches a "distance glimpse" of a splendid city, but must walk across several more mountains to reach his destination. An *Arahant* is like one who has arrived at the city and now dwells comfortably within its bounds (Bodhi 2000, 847, introduction). The distant city is actually "seen" but as a "glimpse" (with wisdom only) but one has not reached it physically.

I conclude that as illustrated in the *Kosambi Sutta* above, a stream-enterer based on direct knowledge, with wisdom, clearly "sees" *Nibbāna*, but does not make "bodily contact" with *Nibbāna*. Seeing is only as a "projection," it is "through wisdom," nevertheless based on his direct experience (direct knowledge) of the attainment of the fruit of stream-entry. In the passage *diṭṭha-dhammo patta-dhammo vidita-dhammo pariyogāḷha-dhammo* quoted from *Ambaṭṭha Sutta* on p. 162, the word *"dhamma"* refers to dependent origination [*paṭicca-samuppāda*] and not to *Nibbāna*. The *Ariyaparyesana Sutta* (MN: 116), differentiates between *Nibbāna* and dependent origination and what a stream-enterer experiences with direct knowledge is dependent origination.

Lay Noble Disciples

In the *Mahāvacchagotta Sutta* of the *Majjhima Nikāya* (MN: 73), Vacchagotta the wanderer, being pleased with the discourse given by the Buddha, questions him as follows:

> Apart from Master Gotama and *bhikkhus* and *bhkkhunīs*, is there any one male lay follower, Master Gotama's disciple, clothed in white leading a life of celibacy, who with the destruction of the five lower fetters will reappear spontaneously and there attain final *Nibbāna* without ever returning from that world!

The Buddha answered:

> There are not only one hundred, two hundred ... five hundred but far more male lay followers, my disciples, clothed in white leading a life of celibacy who, with the destruction of the five lower fetters will reappear spontaneously and there attain final *Nibbāna* without ever returning from that world.

The Buddha goes on to say the same of female lay followers. The above question refers to non-returners. Similarly, Vacchagotta continued to question about once-returners and stream-enterers that may choose to remain in lay life and continue to enjoy sense pleasures. For all these questions, the Buddha's answer was "not one hundred, two hundred ... five hundred but far more ..." (MN I 490).

The above *Sutta* indicates beyond doubt that the lay male and lay female disciples who attained the fruits of the Path were many at the time of the Buddha and that lay people are certainly capable of attaining supramundane fruits of the Path, not just renunciants.

The *Sotāpatti Saṃyutta* refers to a countless number of householders by name, both men and women, who had attained stream-entry and some higher fruits who yet continued in lay life some enjoying sense pleasures, some leading a celibate life. Some of the notable lay disciples who attained supramundane fruits of the Path as mentioned in the texts are as follows.

1) Nandamātā (Nanda's Mother) from Velukanda, Rājagaha, having served alms to the retinue of monks headed by Venerables Sāriputta and Moggallāna and upon Sāriputta questioning her, she declares her close encounter with the *deva* Vessavana who had informed her the previous night that the retinue of monks would be approaching Velukanda early the next morning. Thereafter, in the presence of the retinue she very proudly declares her spiritual attainments to include her ability to attain to the four *jhānas* and that she is a non-returner having destroyed the five lower fetters. At the end of this episode Sāriputta responds "It is astounding and amazing Nandamātā" (AN IV 65–67). She has been declared by the Buddha as the foremost amongst lay female meditators.
2) The female disciple Visākhā attained stream-entry at the age of seven years. She got married at the age of 15 or 16 years. In the course of time she gave birth to 10 sons and 10 daughters and all of them had the same number of descendants down to the fourth generation. Visākhā herself lived up to the remarkable age of 120 years. She was strong as an elephant and worked untiringly throughout the day looking after her large family. She found time to feed the monks every day, to visit monasteries, and to ensure that none of the monks lacked food, clothing, shelter, bedding and medicine. Above all, she still found time to listen to the Dhamma again and again. She wore her valuable bridal jewellery even when she went to listen to the Dhamma. She was declared by the Buddha as the foremost among women lay supporters who serve as supporters of the *Saṅgha* (Nyanaponika and Hecker 1997, 247).
3) Anāthapiṇḍika, a happily married successful businessman, was a stream-enterer. His wife Puññalakkhaṇa (One with Mark of Merit) lived up to her name and was devoted to the Dhamma. He had four children, three daughters and a son. Two of the daughters were immersed in the Dhamma like the father and had attained stream-entry. And just as they took after their father in spiritual matters, so did they in worldly affairs. They were both happily married. The youngest daughter surpassed the rest of the family in deep wisdom; she was a once-returner. His son

too, though he at first did not want to listen to the Dhamma, having immersed himself completely in business affairs, and later attained stream-entry. He too, just like his father, became a major benefactor of the Buddha and was known as "little Anāthapiṇḍika" (Nyanaponika and Hecker 1997, 345).

4) Ugga, a householder of Vesāli, was referred to by the Buddha as one possessing astounding and amazing qualities. Hearing this, once some monks approached Ugga to clarify the Buddha's comments on him and Ugga declared that he was a non-returner having destroyed the five lower fetters. At the time he attained stream-entry, he had four wives, young daughters and much wealth. He also declared his close encounters with the *devas*. When the monks returned to the Buddha and reported their conversation with Ugga, the Buddha confirmed that all that was declared by Ugga was true (AN IV 211).

5) Ugga of Hatthigāma, in a similar episode as in the case of Ugga of Vesāli, was referred to by the Buddha as having astounding and amazing qualities. The monks approached Ugga to verify what the Buddha said and Ugga confirmed that if he died before the Buddha, he would be declared as not having fetters to come back to this world, which indicate that he had attained the fruit that is non-returning. Here Ugga describes his first encounter with Buddha and declares that when he first saw the Buddha he was sporting in a *nāga* glade and that he was drunk. However upon seeing the Buddha his drunkenness vanished. The Buddha later confirmed these declarations to be true. Ugga declared that it was not uncommon for *devas* to come and try to talk to him on Dhamma but that he was not elated about it and did not encourage it. The Buddha praised this as one of the eight amazing qualities that Ugga was endowed with. Further, when Ugga visited monks, if they did not preach to him, he preached Dhamma to the monks (AN IV 212).

6) Sīha an army General attained stream-entry (AN IV 186) and continued to serve in the army.

7) Amongst kings who were stream-enterers are King Bimbisāra of Magadha (Bodhi 1989, 55, n. 1).

8) Isidatta and Purāna, two chamberlains of King Pasenadi of Kosala, were declared by the Buddha as stream-enterers. They are seen complaining to the Buddha about the onerous nature of their duties in the palace which is a burden to their mind such as having to prepare elephants for riding, having to carry and place the royal ladies "heavily scented and with a bodily touch like cotton wool" on the elephants and having to guard them and in addition having to guard their own minds against lust, but they declared "yet we do not remember having an evil state of mind with regard to those ladies." Here the Buddha declares that the householder's life is a confinement and a path of dust and the going forth is like the open air. The commentary says that at the time of their death the Buddha declared them both once- returners, Purāna was then celibate and Isidatta lived contented with his wife (SN V 348–352).

9) It is said that in the village called Ñātika, many had died on account of a plague; the commentary says 24 thousand had died. Amongst those who died, the Buddha says that 50 male lay followers were non-returners, 90 were once-returners, and 506 were stream-enterers. Even if the number may be inflated in the commentary, this account shows that there were many lay noble disciples in this place (SN V 358).
10) Jivaka, the personal physician of the Buddha, is said by the *Dīgha Nikāya* commentary to have become a stream-enterer (Bodhi 1989, 52).
11) Sarakāni the Sākyan layman who died in Kapilavattupura was declared by the Buddha to be a stream-enterer even though he had been a drunkard before going for refuge to the Buddha, the Dhamma and the Saṅgha and undertaking the training (SN V 375).
12) Citta the householder of Macchikāsanda, near Sāvatthi, was a non-returner and was declared by the Buddha to be the foremost lay male disciple amongst the speakers on the Dhamma. Citta and Hatthaka of Ālavaka, both lay noble disciples, were declared by the Buddha to be the standard to be followed by lay male disciples. Many of Citta's Dhamma-encounters with *bhikkhus* are reported in *Citta Saṃyutta* where he questions *bhikkhus* and upon their failure to answer, expounds the Dhamma to them. The commentaries explain that he was capable of attaining *nirodha-samāpatti*. On his deathbed, *devas* surrounded him and asked him several times to wish to be reborn as a universal monarch but he refused, reminding them of impermanence (SN IV 301–304).
13) Dhigāvu the householder of Rājagaha was a stream-enterer but attained the fruit that is non-returning on his deathbed (SN V 344–346).
14) Nakulamātā, wife of Nakulapitā, was a stream-enterer. Nakulamātā and Nakulapitā (Mother of Nakula and Father of Nakula) are mentioned by the Buddha amongst his foremost lay disciples, and their unfaltering faithfulness to each other has been highlighted in the text. The Pāli Canon depicts their relationship with each other as exemplary and a conjugal love of divine stature accompanied by absolute trust based upon their common faith in the Blessed One. An old couple by the time they met the Buddha, the wife and husband declared to him that though married to each other at a very young age, they had not even once broken faith with each other throughout the years, not even by thought let alone by deed. They had not deviated for a moment from their mutual fidelity. In their devotion to each other, both of them expressed to the Buddha their longing to be together in future births and asked him for advice on how to achieve this; they were advised by the Buddha accordingly (AN III 295).

Non-Humans Attaining Supramundane Fruits

There are many references in the *Nikāyas* and their commentaries to *devas* who are noble persons. In the *Sakka Pañha Sutta*, the god Sakka is seen attaining the Dhamma-eye together with a retinue of 80 thousand *devas* (DN II 288).

The *Rāhulovāda Sutta* records that when Venerable Rāhula was established in *arahatta-phala* many thousands of *devas* who were following the discourse given by the Buddha to Rāhula attained the Dhamma-eye (SN IV 109), with the commentary saying that with this, some became stream-enterers, some once-returners, some non-returners, and some *Arahants* (Bodhi 2000, 1415, n. 112).

The commentary on the *Dhammacakkappavattana Sutta* says that, at the end of this discourse, not only Venerable Koṇḍañña, but also innumerable *brahamās* attained stream-entry (Bodhi 2000, 1962, n. 383).

The *Devatā Saṃyutta* reports a conversation between Venerable Samiddhi and a *devatā* who asked him a question. Being unable to answer, Samiddhi goes with the *devatā* to the Buddha. The commentary to this passage says that, having heard the Dhamma from the Buddha, she attained stream-entry (SN I 8–12/Bodhi 2000, 357, n. 39).

Again the commentary to a *Devatā Saṃyutta* passage (SN I 69) reports that a *devatā*, on being born in the Tāvatiṃsa heaven and being disgusted at the sensual pleasures enjoyed there and seeing their danger, returns to earth immediately to meet the Buddha to look for a way out of conditioned existence. At the end of the Buddha's discourse to him, the *devatā* attained stream-entry (Bodhi 2000, 375–377, n. 100–102).

There are also some references to *yakkhas* attaining stream-entry. In the *Yakkha Saṃyutta, yakkha* Sūciloma who came to harass the Buddha ended up listening to a discourse from him (SN I 445). The commentary says he attained stream-entry, and that as stream-enterers do not live in monstrous bodies simultaneously with this attainment, his needle-like hair all fell out and he obtained the appearance of an earth deity (Bodhi 2000, 478, n. 569).

Again Punabbasu's Mother, a female *yakkha* who heard the Buddha delivering a sermon developed deep affection for Dhamma and reverence to the Buddha and at the end of the discourse, she "saw" the Noble Truths (SN I 452) (i.e. became a stream-enterer), with the commentary saying that her son also attained stream-entry then (Bodhi 2000, 481, n. 583).

Seeing Āḷavaka the *yakkha*'s potential to be a noble disciple, the Buddha paid an unwelcome visit to him in his haunt. After a fierce encounter with the Buddha, Āḷavaka challenges the Buddha, saying that if he could not answer the questions posed by him, he would drive the Buddha insane and split his heart, grab him by his feet and hurl him across the Ganges. After the Buddha answers his 3 questions to his satisfaction, the *yakkha* was tamed (SN I 460) and he attained stream-entry, ("attained the good pertaining to the future life") and became a follower of the Buddha (Bodhi 2000, 485, n. 598 and 488, n. 603).

Conclusion

In this chapter we examined the state of mind of a stream-enterer, the knowledge acquired by him and his powers, qualities and blessings. The significance of stream-entry is emphasized by the Buddha when he says that the three things a monk should remember all his life [*yāvajīvam saranīyani bhavanti*] are: i) the place where he went forth as a monk; ii) the place where he gained insight into the Noble Truths (understanding "This is *dukkha*" etc.) that is, became a stream-enterer; and iii) the place where he attained *arahatta-phala* (AN I 107). Similarly the Buddha says that the three persons to whom it is not easy to repay, by paying homage, by rising up for them, by reverential salutation, presenting them with robes, food, lodging and medicine etc., are: i) the person through whom one went for refuge to the Buddha, Dhamma and *Saṅgha*; ii) the person through whom one gained insight into the Noble Truths [*idam dukkham ti yathābhūtam pajānati...*- i.e. entered the stream] (Bodhi 2012, 1638, n. 362); and the person through whom one attained Arahatship (AN I 123). The Buddha warns that if a person reviles and abuses one "accomplished in view" [*diṭṭha-sampanna*], (i.e. a stream-enterer) with an evil mind, she generates much bad *kamma*, much more than reviling and abusing "an outsider," a "non-believer" [*titthaka*] (AN IV 136).

Based on the foregoing discussion, I conclude that the attainment of stream-entry becomes the most significant event one ever encounters in *saṃsāra* up to such time. It makes one a Buddhist by conviction. It makes one a "*Born-again*" Buddhist. The *Aggañña Sutta* describes one with settled faith in the Tathāgata, (i.e. a stream-enterer), as: "a legitimate son of the Buddha [*oraso putto*], born from his mouth [*mukhato jāto*], born of the Dhamma [*dhamma-jo*], created by the Dhamma [*dhamma-nimmito*] heir of the *Dhamma* [*dhamma-dāyādo*]" (DN III 84). In the *Saccavibhanga Sutta* the Buddha equates Venerable Sāriputta to a mother as he guides others to stream-entry [*sotāpatti-phale vineti*] by revealing the four Noble Truths, so giving birth to them as stream-enterers (MN III 248).

From this turning point in *saṃsāra*, the vision one acquires about the true nature of existence together with a degree of mindfulness appropriate to a stream-enterer, which has a inherent tendency to look back and reflect, to look into the mind and understand the reasons behind phenomena, to have attention that is alert to causes [*yoniso manasikāra*], pushes one up-stream against the tide of *saṃsāra* so that within a maximum of seven more births the stream-enterer makes the final exit from *saṃsāra* never again to be subject to the unsatisfactoriness and the dangers of conditioned existence. However a stream-enterer is not a flawless floating saint as most people would imagine and has the "potential" to commit or engage in anything except what has been expressly set out in the *Suttas* as "impossible" for a stream-enterer. However a stream-enterer based on his tendency to look in to the mind, reflect and to apply *yoniso manasikāra*, continues to refine his moral virtues. Also it is possible for laypeople to attain stream-entry and continue in lay life until at least the stage of non-returning.

Notes

1. SN V 357. Also see Chapter 2, p. 32 for the list of the ten fetters.
2. For the definition of the words "*phala*" and "*sotāpatti-phala*" see Chapter 1, p. 20.
3. *idhāvuso ariyasāvako buddhe aveccappasādena samannāgato hoti. Iti pi so Bhagavā ... Dhamme ... Saṅghe ... ariyakantehi sīlehi samannāgato hoti akhaṇḍehi samādhisaṃvattanikehi* (SN V 347).
4. *vīmaṇsakena bhikkhunā parassa cetopariyāyam ājānantena Tathāgate samannesanā kātabbā, sammāsambuddho vā no vā iti viññāṇāyā ti.* (MN I 317. See also Jayatilleke 1963, 392).
5. At Barre, Massachusetts.
6. *vigatamalamaccherena cetasā agāram ajjhāvasati muttacāgo payatapāni vosaggarato yācayogo dānasaṃvibhāgarato* (SN V 397 and 401).

7. *...khīṇāṇirayomhi khīṇātiracchānayoniko khīṇāpettivisayo khīṇāpāyaduggativinipāto, sotāpanno ham asmi avinipātadhammo niyato sambodhiparāyano* (SN V 356).
8. Related by Interviewee No. 2.
9. *Ekam samayam Ñāṇavīro bhikkhu Bundalagāme viharati arraññakuṭikāyam.Tena kho pana samayena Ñāṇavīro bhikkhu rattiyā pathamam yāmam cankamena āvaraniyehi dhammehi cittam parisodheti, yathāsutam yathāpariyattam dhammam cetasā anuvitakketi anuvicāreti manasānupekkhati. Atha kho* [Ñāṇavīrassa] *bhikkhuno evam yathāsutam yathāpariyattam dhammam cetasā anuvitakkayato anuvicārayato manasānupekkhato virajam vītamalam dhammacakkhum udapādi, yam kiñci samudayadhammam sabbam tam nirodhadhammanti. So dhammānusari māsam hutva diṭṭhipatto hoti.* (Ñāṇavīra 2002, II, 1)
10. His claim to lack *vicikicca* indicates that he saw himself as having overcome the first three fetters. Venerable Analayo notes that, contrary to the commentary on *Saṃyutta Nikāya*, other Theravāda commentaries point out that Vakkali had become an *Arahant* or at least a non-returner on a previous occasion (Analayo 2011, 28.2).
11. The commentary glosses this by *anuppattika* meaning "without further arising" (MN-a V 82). The possible implications of this are discussed by Damien Keown (1996, 22–24).
12. 2000. "Buddhism and the Ethics of Nature — Some Remarks." *The Eastern Buddhist* 32(2): 26–78, 36 and 38.
13. The *Visuddhimagga* states that "the four paths and the four fruits take timeless unconditioned *Nibbāna* as its object" (Vism.XXIII.4/Vism. 820).
14. See Chapter 4, pp. 75–82 for a discussion on the first noble person.
15. See pp. 126–129 for connection between the fetter-breaking-experience and the right view.

— 7 —

An Interview with a "Possible *Arahant*"

In Chapter 6 we discussed in detail the state of mind of a stream-enterer. What is most significant in the attainment of stream-entry is that a stream-enterer is assured of his ultimate goal, Arahantship, within a maximum of seven more births. A stream-enterer declares "I am ... fixed in destiny, with enlightenment as my destination" [*niyato sambodhiparāyano*] (SN II 68).

However, we live in an era where the majority, at least in Sri Lanka, does not believe that there are living *Arahants* or any other noble persons. The fruits of the Path have been shelved as monuments or glories of the past. The slightest hint of a possible noble person raises so much curiosity and skepticism. But this is what the Buddha said to his last disciple Subhadda, just before his *parinibbāna*:

> In whatsoever *Dhamma* and discipline there is found the Noble Eightfold Path, there is found a true renunciant of the first, second, third and fourth (noble) kind. Now in this *Dhamma* and discipline, Subhadda is found the Noble Eightfold Path and in it is found a true renunciant of the first, second, third and fourth kind. Devoid of true renunciants are the systems of other teachers, but if, Subhadda, the *bhikkhus* live rightly, the world will not be empty of *Arahants* [*sammā vihareyyum, asuñño loko arahanteti assa*]. (DN II 151)

Hence so long as there are monks and nuns treading the Noble Eightfold Path, there can be *Arahants* even today. The problem is in recognizing one. In Chapter 2 we examined the possibilities of and difficulties in recognizing a noble person.

In this chapter we will examine the final destination of a stream-enterer. We will examine the state of mind of an *Arahant* in terms of the texts and with reference to the content of the interview done as a part of our field research, with a "possible *Arahant*." For this purpose I first set out the relevant extracts from the interview under a given topic and compare it with the available textual evidence which sets out the mind-set of an *Arahant*. Given the limits for recognizing and confirming the state of Arahantship as discussed in Chapter 2, and in terms of the Buddha's invitation for a fair inquiry, with a view to accepting or rejecting the declared state of mind of this interviewee, such a comparative analysis with the texts is all we could do in an academic study of this nature.

The attainment of a supramundane fruit was defined herein to be a specific striking experience of a person treading or making an effort to tread the Noble Eightfold Path, resulting in the understanding or knowledge which breaks the corresponding fetters [*saṃyojanas*]. The key elements of this phenomenon are: a) Path, b) an experience, c) arising of knowledge, and d) breaking of fetters.

The interviewee concerned has been treading the Noble Eightfold Path untiringly and relentlessly for three years under the guidance of one of Sri Lanka's greatest contemporary meditation masters. He has got ordained in 2001, five years prior to our interview and completed the Path in three years. During this time, other than talking to his teacher, the monk observed complete silence for three consecutive years and was totally engrossed in the practice. Before entering the *Saṅgha* in Sri Lanka he has been practising as a Mahāyāna monk.

A specific religious experience which marked the apparent attainment of his *arahatta-phala* has been declared by him in the interview, with reference to a specific date, place and a meditation posture: on 28th March 2004 when he was walking up to the *kuṭī* of the chief abbot of the hermitage to attend to the duties assigned to him, half way through, on the walk-way to that *kuṭī*, he attained the fruit that is Arahantship. He distinctly remembers this date. There is no mention of a specific date with reference to the attainments of the rest of the supramundane fruits. It was after about one year from the fruit that is non-returning. He was meditating on the thirty-two impurities of the body and on the four elements, continuously observing his silence for altogether three years. Whilst he was walking he focused on his mind and realized that his mind "went in" for one second then "arose and stopped." Immediately he realized that all defilements got cut off, he felt he had "no more duties to fulfil."

Hence the Path and specific religious experiences have been declared by the interviewee. The knowledge and understanding that arose from the experiences and whether they led to breaking of, ultimately, all his fetters is what we will investigate in this chapter.

Arahatta-phala requires the destruction of all taints [*āsavas*] and all ten fetters.[1] An *Arahant* is defined as one "whose taints are destroyed, who has lived the holy life, done what had to be done, laid down the burden, reached his own goal, utterly destroyed the fetters of existence, one completely liberated through final knowledge, usually dwells with a mind well established in the four establishments of mindfulness.[2]

About the Interviewee

Before we analyze the content of the interview, the background of the interviewee is as follows. He is a 43 year old monk who is a Malaysian by nationality, who lives in a well established and well known remote forest hermitage of Sri Lanka. The interviewee is not personally known to the writer. He was introduced to the writer for this purpose by his teacher who is the chief preceptor of the hermitage, who is closely known to the writer for over 12 years. The monk has not obtained higher ordination [*upasampadā*], hence was free to speak out about his spiritual attainments, particularly after being requested by his teacher to have a discussion with the writer for this purpose.

The interview was severely hampered by a language barrier of the interviewee and a strong accent, difficult to understand. Hence certain issues, though raised, were not followed up by the writer and certain other issues were never raised at all as the writer felt that there wouldn't be clarity. Due to the same reason, transcribing too was enormously difficult, time consuming and frustrating and to that extent could have an impact on accuracy levels. However it is possible to follow the general trend of his thought process and knowledge and understanding.

As the interview proceeded from stage to stage, the interviewee said that he had attained Arahantship. However, as the writer was unaware of this at the early stages of the interview, answers to certain questions may be obscured by the knowledge gained by higher supramundane fruits of the Path. That is, responses relating to the issues on *saddhā*, right view etc. at the stage of stream-entry may be obscured by the knowledge from his higher attainments, and responses to questions on states of mind such as fear and anger etc. at the stage of *anāgāmi-phala* may be obscured by the knowledge from the fruit that is Arahantship.

It is noteworthy that in the interview his references to the four fruits of the Path are in terms of the "percentages" (the degree) by which the defilements reduced at each stage. Further, throughout the interview, the monk refers to his mind as "he." In observing his gestures, there was a regular hand movement of his bent arm stretching out in the "forward direction," indicating a "going in" of the mind, as he explained the fetter-breaking-experiences relating to his attainments. His main meditation object was on the thirty-two impurities of the body [*asubha* meditation], subsequently combined with meditation on the four-elements. He declares that he is a *sukkha-vipassaka*, one who practises "dry insight"; he says he has no *jhāna*, hence no psychic powers or higher knowledges such as the ability to see previous births, and that he cannot attain *nirodha-samāpatti* (cessation). The writer found him to be calm and collected, unassuming, pleasant and gentle in his disposition and with no barriers to smiling and laughing. Despite a severe language barrier throughout the long and tedious interview process, which to him may have been of little interest, he displayed a high level of mindfulness and equanimity.

The interview was done by the writer in English in the said forest hermitage on 27th July 2006 (Interview No.1). Two years later, when the writer again met this interviewee at this hermitage, he was spending most of his time in a cave in a well known rain-forest in Sri Lanka with abundant wildlife. He was happy to be away from people and was quite at peace with the elephants and snakes.

The extracts quoted here may not be sufficient to draw conclusions about the intention of the interviewee or our interpretation of the statements made by him. I invite the readers to go through the bare interview (in Appendix II) in order to understand the context in which these statements have been made.

Only content relevant to the state of mind of Arahantship has been extracted in this chapter. I draw the attention of the readers to the synopsis of the interview with a view to getting an understanding about the state of mind declared by the interviewee, with regard to the lower supramundane fruits attained by him.

The Mind-Set of an *Arahant*

In this section we will analyze the statements made by the interviewee and compare it with available textual evidence which sets out the mind-set of an *Arahant* during the time of the Buddha.

No Defilements and Only Phenomena Arising and Ceasing

To my question on whether there are any defilements remaining in him, the interviewee says there are no more defilements in him and whatever phenomena that arise in the mind all cease then and there. He describes his mental process as "coming, stop, coming, stop." Our conversation goes as follows:

Q.212 Are there any defilements remaining in you now?
A No, I all the time clear only, coming, stop, coming, stop.
Q.213 Defilements come?
A No no, no defilements come, no defilements. In me I think don't want this thing. Because I all the emptiness, air only, cannot saw anything, my mind cannot saw anything even I close the eye this world is emptiness.

The above description of his mental process as "coming, stop, coming, stop" reflects a state in which the name and the form (sense objects) arise at the sense bases, however the consciousness does not join them in such a manner to form "I," they do not get "entangled" to form defilements as discussed earlier in Chapter 5 (p. 100).[3] No sooner objects arise, the *Arahant* identifies it as "the name and the form" and it stops right there, before being entangled.

The interviewee's description of his thought process as "coming, stop, coming, stop" as stated above also highlights the observational sharpness of his mind. It also reflects the following state of mind referred to by the Buddha in the *Mahāsakuludāyi Sutta*:

> Udāyin I have proclaimed to my disciples the way whereby realizing for themselves with direct knowledge, they here and now enter upon and abide in the deliverance of mind and deliverance by wisdom that are taintless with the destruction of the taints. Just as if there were a lake in a mountain recess, clear, limpid, and undisturbed, so that a man with good sight standing on the bank could see shells, gravel, and pebbles and also shoals of fish swimming about and resting. He might think, "There is this lake, clear, limpid and undisturbed, and there are these shells, gravel and pebbles and also these shoals of fish swimming about and resting." So too I have proclaimed to my disciples the way whereby by realizing for themselves with direct knowledge, they here and now enter upon and abide in the deliverance of mind and deliverance by wisdom that are taintless with the destruction of the taints. (MN II 22)

Just as the man who stands by the lake can see the lake together with its contents right down to its bottom, an *Arahant* can see his mind very clearly, as a whole, as a sense organ, together with the whole of its mental accompaniments and objects.

Ajahn Chah's famous simile of the still forest pool also reflects precisely this state of mind where one can see clearly the arising and ceasing of mental phenomena within oneself. Ajahn Chah says:

> Try to be mindful, and let things take their natural course. Then your mind will become still in any surrounding, like a clear forest pool. All kinds of wonderful, rare animals will come to drink at the pool, and you will clearly see the nature of all things. You will see many strange and wonderful things come and go, but you will be still. This is the happiness of the Buddha. (Chah 1987, vi)

A Perception of Emptiness

After this experience the interviewee sees life as empty, wherever he looks he sees things only as "particles of air" arising and ceasing like a television screen before the transmission. Though he can see things when he is with his eyes open, when he closes his eyes, the whole world for him is nothing but "emptiness," he cannot even visualize his own face. There is emptiness 24 hours a day. During the day, all the time he sees emptiness, when he goes to bed he watches emptiness, when he gets up in the middle of the night too what he sees is emptiness. So he sees the world as "dull." He says:

> I all inside cannot saw anything but good is 24 hours is emptiness but is dull only, little bit dull ... The mind is very dull (Q.263–264) ... yeh very dull because this world all the particles (laughter) sometimes I cannot accept this world, I that time "how come, this world, this world what I saw previous, still I enjoyed that *deva* anything still, after that no more," but my mind don't have no desire, dull, what is that, how to describe, I don't know how to describe the thing, like air only, you cannot see say that air is, have feeling (laughter) (Q.293).

It is said that "To the one who knows and sees, there is not anything (to hold on to)" [*jānato passato natthi kiñcanam*] (Ud.80). The idea is that when craving is penetrated through with knowledge and wisdom, one realizes the emptiness in the world. The *Arahant* sees everything as "substance-less" or empty of a self, therefore there is nothing to hold on to.

The interviewee feels that he cannot relate to this world any more. He says: "this world look like not related to me, ... my body or anything I only particle only, I don't think particles is me also (Q.295–296), the mind *kiriya kiriya* the mind *javana-kiriya* only, nothing" (Q.301). Here "*kiriya*" is the purely functional mode of the mind that *Arahants* respond to the world with, without generating any new kamma, good or bad, in the active phase of responding to the object called *javana*. Our conversation goes as follows:

Q.281 While you were walking up there you experienced this "going in," now from time to time do you experience that?

A. Yeh I all the time, like a even I saw, I hear, I think—sixth (sense) or anything I no defilements. Even they talk anger to me, even now describe as, even the woman take up all the thing (referring to stealing) I sometime describe something all the time it takes out all because previous I greedy, very strong this thing attachment, after that now I imagine all the thing they do something the bad thing in my face imagine only, I don't have this feeling or anything, my thought, hear only, saw only, I imagination anything not this world look like not related to me.

Q.282 You feel this world is not related to you?

A Aaah, related to me, my body or anything I only particle only, I don't think particles is me also. So I don't think about now also, I don't think now.

Q.283 So the crux of that experience, if I put it to you, is like you don't feel a part of this world is that correct?

A. What that?

Q.284 You said just now this body, sorry, that you don't feel a part of this body, is that what you said?

A. yeh yeh, anything when it cut it off or anything this world doesn't belong to me.

Q.285 Oh! this world doesn't belong to you?

A. Aha, anything nothing because all the 24 hours saw particles only, cannot saw anything (24hours hour?), aaah, 24 hours, all the time emptiness, the mind *kiriya kiriya* the mind *javana-kiriya* only, nothing.

An *Arahant*'s perception of the "world" is completely different to that of a worldling. What the worldling sees as bliss, is not bliss to them any more, what is meaningful to the worldling is meaningless to an *Arahant*. In the *Dvayatānupassanā Sutta* of the *Devatā Saṃyutta*, a *devatā* recites the following in a conversation with Venerable Subhuti:

> Forms, sounds, odours, tastes, tactile objects and all objects of mind—desirable, lovely, agreeable, as long as it's said "They are" [*yāvat'atthī ti vuccati*].
>
> These are considered pleasurable by the world with its *devas*; but when they cease, that they consider *dukkha*.
>
> The ceasing of personality [*sakkāyassa*[4]] is seen by the noble ones as pleasurable. This (view) of those who see (properly) is contrary to (that held) by the entire world.
>
> What others speak of as pleasurable, that the noble ones say is *dukkha*; what others speak of as *dukkha*, that the noble ones know as pleasurable. See a Dhamma that is hard to understand. Here the ignorant are confused.
>
> Murk it is to those enveloped, as darkness unto the undiscerning,
>
> But to the Good wide open it is, as light is unto the discerning,
>
> So near, and yet they know not,—Fools!—unskilled in the Dhamma.
>
> (Sn. vv.759–765)

Accordingly what is pleasurable to the worldling is *dukkha* to an *Arahant* and what is *dukkha* to the worldling is pleasurable to an *Arahant*. This is because *Arahant*s know that pleasant sense-objects are impermanent and insubstantial, and bring pain and disappointment if clung to, and they also know the sublime relief of non-clinging.

In the *Brahmanimantanika Sutta* of the *Majjhima Nikāya* it is said that thirteen concepts of the world have no relevance to an *Arahant*.

> Consciousness which makes nothing manifest, infinite and all lustrous: this does not partake of the earthiness of earth, the wateriness of water, the fieriness of fire, the airiness of air, the creaturehood of creatures, the *deva*-hood of *devas*, the *pajāpati*-hood of Pajāpati, the *brahmā*-hood of Brahmā, the radiance of the Radiant Ones, the *subhakiṇha*-hood of the Subhakiṇha *brahmās*, the *vehapphala*-hood of the Vahapphala *brahmās*, the overlord-ship of the overlord, and the all-ness of the all.[5] (As translated at Ñāṇananda 2004, II, 42)

The above passage shows the non-manifestive consciousness [*anidassana* viññāṇa] of an *Arahant*. Venerable Ñāṇananda, criticizing the commentarial interpretation of the term "*anidassana* viññāṇa" to mean that this is a state that doesn't come within the range of the eye-consciousness (Ps. II 413) (meaning that it is restricted to the fetter-breaking–experience of *arahatta-phala* or the re-experiencing of it) and emphasizing the context in which this *Sutta* was delivered, that is to challenge a wrong view of permanence self by Baka, the *brahmā*, and to assert that the non-manifestive consciousness of an *Arahant* has "transcended" the worldly concepts such as elements, divinity etc., concludes that the above stanza reflects the ordinary consciousness of an *Arahant*.[6] Substantiating his interpretation of this term, he also falls back on a previous statement of the Buddha in this *Sutta*, that is, "having directly known earth as earth, and having directly known what is not partake of the earthness of earth, I did not claim earth to be 'mine'..."—meaning having directly understood by a special kind of knowledge, not by ordinary perception (i.e. through the fetter-breaking-experience or the re-experience of it), an *Arahant* does not attribute an inherent nature to concepts that the worldling takes as real. Ñāṇananda says that the worldling's distortions in his perceptions are such that even in the concept of "all" there is an "all-ness." An *Arahant*'s ordinary consciousness does not register perceptions of permanence regarding the concepts of the world. He argues that it is in this sense that the *Arahant*'s consciousness is called "non-manifestive." I conclude that an *Arahant*'s consciousness is non-manifestive in the above manner both at the level of the fetter-breaking-experience and the re-experiene of it as well as therafter, at the level of the ordinary consciousness.

When the interviewee visualized taking a knife and cutting off his head, the feeling in the third fruit [*anāgāmi-phala*] was different from when he visualized the same thing in the fourth fruit [*arahatta-phala*]. In the third, he was still cutting off "elements," there were elements within, still there was "body," the feeling was "I cut my body." However in the fourth, he was cutting only air, there was nothing inside, only emptiness. He says:

> I using I imagination, I using one knife, you try put your head cut it off, how you feeling, in the 3rd path I still had little bit, little bit, fear ... little bit not fear but little bit different because he still inside have elements ... After 4th stage the difference is, I using the knife cut it off, I cut air only, nothing already, inside all emptiness (Q.223–225, 276).

When he says that he sees his body as elements and air, what it means is that he has transcended the perception of body. His responses to this issue are as follows:

Q.294 Sorry! air?

A. Like air, air no feeling, my air, my body is like air only, I imagination. I use my hand, go to here he out come out behind already (he is showing with his fist that when he presses the hand against the chest it comes out from the back of the body), air only.

Q.295 So you feel your body is like air?

A. Emptiness all the time. Particles only, cannot saw anything.

The perception of emptiness articulated by the interviewee reflects the following stanza uttered by *Arahant* Adhimutta when he got caught to a band of robbers who were getting ready to offer him as a human sacrifice:

> It does not occur to me "I was,"
> Nor does it occur to me "I will be,"
> Mere preparations get destroyed,
> What is there to lament?
> To one who sees as it is,
> The arising of pure *dhammas*,
> And the sequence of pure preparations,
> There is no fear O' headman! (Thag.715–716)

As to his feelings towards his parents, he says in the third fruit he had the feeling "he has parents," that he has to do something for his parents, for his family, but in the fourth fruit whilst he still knows that he has parents, he knows that "they have to die and separate." In other words there was no attachment to family (Q.246–248).

It has been said that the world for the most part rests on a dichotomy, such as that between the two views "it (substantially) exists" and "it does not exist (at all)" (SN II 17, *Kaccāyanagotta Sutta*). The worldling's way of thought ends up in one extreme or the other within this framework. The *Arahant* transcends it; his consciousness is therefore, endless, *ananta*. It is said:

> Hard to see is the endless
> Truth is not easy to see.
> Pierced through is craving
> And for him who knows and sees, there is not anything (to hold on to).
> (*Dutiya Nibbānapaṭisaṃyutta Sutta*)[7]

Happy and Contented

The interviewee says he is happy and contented in life all the time because there are no defilements remaining in him.

> Q.322 If I may ask you again, do you have joy and happiness and contentment in you as an *Arahant*: ... now as an *Arahant* do you have joy, happiness and contentment?
> A. What that meaning, contentment?
> Q.323 Are you happy with what you are?
> A. Oh! If you say I happy, I happy, I happy all the time. If I say I con ... (contented) I con ... .(contented) All the time but I happy, I not attachment anything because the mind no defilements, because happy.

The joy, happiness and contentment of release from the fetters and defilements have been expressed by *Arahant*s of the time of the Buddha as reported in the *Theragāthā* and *Therīgāthā* in phrases such as "My body is light, touched by much joy and happiness" (Thag.104). Some other of these expressions are set out in Chapter 2 (pp. 36–37).

The interviewee expresses similar sentiments about the lower supramundane fruits attained by him. Referring to *anāgāmi-phala*, he says that even when people blame him, his mind does not produce anger but he remains calm and happy all the time and can be smiling. He says:

> Even if someone blame me, anger me, I only smile, only calm and peace only, I don't say anything, my mind not produce anger. So that stage even anything also I saw, I smiling already but attach, still little bit attachment. Ah! I would go to heaven, at this stage I was thinking, I thinking at this stage, I still go to heaven but all the time very happy, it produce happy many and no anger anything no anger (Q.174). ... I saw that anything that someone hatred me, I, I calm and peace only ... (Q.225).

Expressing his feelings as a stream-enterer the interviewee says, he enjoyed the cutting off of defilements as though one enjoys the fruits of a tree after planting and nurturing it (Q.121–122). He says:

> Actually like a person, when you plant a tree after that you can enjoy the tree, aaah, enjoy the fruit, mmm, that that enjoy the fruit, fruit is like a enjoy, earlier, I aah, enjoy the 30%, 30% is no more defilements, cut off 30% only (Q.19).

An *Arahant* is referred to as one who has "laid down the burden" [*ohitabhāro*]. Referring to the reducing of defilements "by 30%" at the point of stream-entry, he felt 30% of the "heavy duty" was no more. He felt very comfortable as though a 30% of heavy weight on his back has been put down (Q.14). He says "the feeling is, aaah, like the person you put down the 30% the heavy duty."

Expressing his feelings when he is re-experiencing the fetter-breaking-experience of a supramundane fruit [*phala-samāpatti*], he says it is like having fresh water when he is very thirsty or like a place where he can enjoy and relax. He says:

> In there you feel, look like now I am very thirsty, in that place had the water very fresh, that you can go to be relax, relax and really enjoy that place. Before I can't enjoy this these thing (the monk is pointing at his body), now after I go there, I can enjoy all the time, enjoy because I don't have this thing (Q.45).
>
> I, previous I cannot, I didn't know how to throw out the defilements, now I cut but he not come back again. So I very happy, very enjoy this thing because I all the time can enjoy (Q.50).

Dull

What comes out prominently in this interview is that though the interviewee is happy, at the same time, life is very "dull" for him. Our conversation goes as follows:

Q.226 So, aaah, Bhante now as an *Arahant*, how do you feel? Is there happiness and joy?

A. Maybe I what I say, I attainment this, I attainment some I saw the *Sutta* some attainment they are very happy all the time. Actually I am very happy, but I am very dull. (Very?) Very dull, dull, dull, very boring, dull (laugh), very dull this world, because don't like this world, because I all the time I cannot saw this world anything empty only.

Q.227 You can see only emptiness in this world?

A. when I, yeh I, my mind, I eye open, I can see, but I close my eyes this world is nothing. I cannot imagine how is my face look like, how is my parents, how is anything, emptiness only because like air particles only, cannot see anything.
... I all inside cannot saw anything, but good is 24 hours is emptiness but is dull only, little bit dull ... The mind is very dull (Q.263–264). ... yeh, very dull because this world all the particles (laughter).

Once a deity asks the Buddha "Do you rejoice [*nandasi*] renunciant?" And the Buddha responds "On getting what friend?" Then the deity asks "Well then do you grieve?" And the Buddha answers "On losing what friend?" The deity remarks "So then, renunciant you neither rejoice nor grieve?." The Buddha confirms "That is so friend" (SN I 124).

In the *Mūlapariyāya Sutta* of the *Majjhima Nikāya*, it is said of an *Arahant* that he does not rejoice even in *Nibbāna*. It says:

> A bhikkhu who is an *Arahant*, fully liberated ... completely liberated through final knowledge, directly knows *Nibbāna* as *Nibbāna*, having directly known *Nibbāna* as *Nibbāna*, he does not conceive [*maññati*] (himself as) *Nibbāna*, he does not conceive (himself as) in *Nibbāna*, he does not conceive [himself apart] from *Nibbāna*, he does

> not conceive *Nibbāna* to be "mine," he does not delight [*abhinandati*] in *Nibbāna*. Why is that? Because he is free from lust through the destruction of lust. (MN I 5)

Venerable Sāriputta declares about himself in the *Theragāthā* as follows:

> Having attained the perfection of wisdom, having great discernment and great thought, not dull (but) as though dull [*ajaḷo jaḷasamāno*], he always wanders quenched [*sadā carati nibbuto*]. (Thag.1015)

The meaning of the term *jaḷo* is "dull" or "stupid." An *Arahant* is certainly not stupid, but he may appear this way to a worldling as he is far beyond worldly concerns. An *Arahant* does not "go up and down" with success and failure, pleasure and pain. The *Arahant*'s seeming "dullness" seems to reflect more an equanimous state of mind. As for the interviewee, what he meant by the word "dull" seems to be also that, while he is happy, there is "no excitement" in his mind, the mind is in equanimity all the time.

Nothing to Do

One of the main reasons for the feeling of "dullness" in the interviewee is that he feels there is nothing more for him to do in life. He has "done what has to be done." Subsequent to the attainment of *arahatta-phala*, the interviewee asked his teacher when he would die and he was told that he would have to wait till around 80 years. He felt it was too long a wait. Perhaps the question about his passing away crossed his mind as he was dull and had nothing to do in this world. He was unable to abide in *nirodha-samāpatti* (Q.381), which would have helped him to while away time to some extent.

Our conversation goes as follows:

Q.291 In the night, how much do you sleep?
A. Normally I follow the here, 9 plus 10, after that 12 o'clock, 1 o'clock wake up already, but wake up nothing to do, focus again, sleep again.
Q.292 Focus where?
A. Focus particles only, nothing to do, no work to do, so he wake up, he self sometimes to fresh the mind wake up nothing to do, all emptiness also, lay out there tired, sleep again, wake up sometime.
Q.293 Aaah, you must be, no wonder you say you are very dull.
A. eh, very dull, because this world all the particles (laughter) sometimes I cannot accept this world, I that time "how come this world, this world what I saw previous, still I enjoyed that *deva* anything still, after that no more," but my mind don't have no desire, dull, what is that, how to describe, I don't know how to describe the thing, like air only, you cannot see say that air is, have feeling (laughter).

An *Arahant* is referred to as one who has "done what has to be done" [*kata karaṇīyo*] with nothing more to do. It is recorded that Venerable Dabba Mallaputta Thero attained Arahantship at the age of seven years. One day the following thought occurred to him when he had risen up from meditation:

> Perfection was realized by me seven years after birth. Whatever has to be attained by a disciple, all this has been fully attained by me; for me there is nothing further to be done, to be added to that which has been done. What now if I should render a service to the Order?

Then Dabba thought he should assign lodging to the Order and should distribute the meals. Then he went to the Buddha and informed him of his thought; the Buddha approved it and Dabba was officially appointed for that purpose (Vin. III 158).

The above story shows that the young *Arahant* Dabba found himself having "nothing to do" to while away time. He goes and asks the Buddha to serve the Buddha-*sāsana*. It is further recorded that Dabba passed away before the *parinibbāna* of the Buddha. On that occasion, he came to see the Buddha, saluted him, sat down at one side and said, "Now is the time for my utter passing away, Welfarer" [*parinibbanakālo me dāni sugatā' ti*]. The Buddha said "Do what you deem it time for, Dabba" [*yassa dāni tvam Dabba kālam maññāsi'ti*]. Accordingly Dabba "rose from his seat, saluted the Buddha with his right side, rose into the air and, sitting cross-legged in the sky, attained the sphere of heat, and rising from it attained *parinibbāna*. His body ... was consumed, burnt up utterly, so that not an atom of ash or soot was to be seen. Just as, for instance, when ghee or oil is consumed and burnt utterly, not an atom of soot is to be seen" (Ud.92–93).

> The Buddha, seeing this, uttered the following *Udāna*:
> Broken is body, perception has ceased,
> All feeling is cooled, volitional activities have subsided,
> And consciousness has reached its end. ...
> Just as the bourn of a blazing fire
> Struck from the anvil, gradually fading,
> Cannot be known—So in the case of those
> Who've rightly won release and crossed the flood
> Of lust that binds, and reached the bliss unshaken,
> The bourn they've won cannot be pointed to. (Ud.93)

Dabba became an *Arahant* at the age of seven years and passed away before the *parinibbāna* of the Buddha. The Buddha taught for only 45 years. Even if Dabba had entered the *Saṅgha* at its very start, he would have still been no more than 52 years (45 +7) at the time of his passing away. Perhaps the feeling of having "nothing to do" may have had an influence on his decision to pass away so young. However, this cannot be compared with "suicide," which is fuelled by greed, hatred or delusion [*lobha, dosa, moha*] as *Arahants* have fully transcended the concept of self, thereby over-coming *bhava-taṇhā* and *vibhava-taṇhā*, the craving "to be" and the craving to "not be." If this were not so, the Buddha would not have spoken in the above tone with regard to the mode of passing away of Dabba. The Buddha's tone above amounts to praise of Dabba's spiritual attainments and approval of his choice of the mode of passing away, which to the ordinary worldling amounts to "suicide by setting himself alight."[8]

Venerable Sāriputta in the *Theragāthā* (Thag.1002–1003) says:

> I do not long for death; I do not long for life;
> I shall lay down this body attentive and mindful.
> I do not long for death; I do not long for life;
> But I await my time, as a servant his wages.

The *Arahant* does not delight in death, but nor does he yearn for life; he bears with life equanimously until the time of his passing away like a worker awaiting his wages. In the *Devatāputta Saṃyutta*, too, the Buddha describes Sāriputta as one who "awaits the time [*kālaṃ kaṅkhati*]." The commentary to this passage says that what Sāriputta meant was that he awaited the time of his *parinibbāna*.

> Here a young *deva* describes Sāriputta as follows:
> He is widely known to be a wise man,
> Sāriputta who is free of anger
> Of few wishes, gentle, tamed,
> The seer adorned by the Teacher's praise

The Buddha responds to the young *deva* as follows:

> He is widely known to be a wise man,
> Sāriputta who is free of anger
> Of few wishes, gentle, tamed,
> Developed, well tamed, he awaits the time. (SN I 151)

Sāriputta was known as the "marshal of the Dhamma," who was relentlessly engaged in the propagation of the Dhamma, having no time for boredom. Yet the above *Theragāthā* verses indicate that he too waited patiently for the time of his *parinibbāna*, just as a wage-earner awaits his monthly wages until the end of the month. Hence the mindset of an *Arahant* awaiting the final passing away seems to be an inevitable consequence of the wisdom generated, that is, "there is nothing worthwhile to look forward to" and such thought is not propelled by *vibhava-taṇhā*.

The Language of an *Arahant*

Most of the time during the interview, this interviewee refers to his mind as "he," for example, "he goes in" or "he arising and stop" and at times as "my mind." He even makes statement such as "I don't like this world." He says:

> I half way, I go to do my duty Mahā Thera there, after that half way focus. He go in one second, he arising and stop again. I understand ah! No more already. All stop already, I understanding because I, I, I in my mind. I told my teacher because I understand my teacher know my mind, I told my teacher, teacher my duty no more, I already finished ... (Q.220)

or

> very dull this world, because don't like this world, because I all the time I cannot saw this world anything empty only (Q.226).

With regard to the language of an *Arahant*, it is said:

> If a bhikkhu is an *Arahant*, consummate with taints destroyed,
> One who bears his final body,
> He might still say "I speak,"
> And he might say "They speak to me,"
> Skilful knowing the world's parlance,
> He uses such terms as mere expressions.[9]

Arahants have higher knowledge and full comprehension with regard to worldly concepts. As such they are not carried away by the worldling's grammatical structure. Venerable Ñāṇananda compares it to the "child language" that parents use when speaking to their children. Although they use such language, they are not swept away by it. There is no inner entanglement in the form of imagining. There is no attachment, entanglement, and involvement by way of craving, conceit and views, in regard to those concepts (Ñāṇananda 2005, III, 278).

The Sense Bases as "Demagnetized"

The sense-bases of an *Arahant* can be said to be "demagnetized," in that there is no attraction to their objects. We already saw the responses of an *Arahant* towards the in-coming sense-objects as given in the *Dvayatānupassanā Sutta* of the *Devatā Saṃyutta* which is as quoted above in the section on "A perception of emptiness" (pp. 174–178): the world wants pleasant sense-objects to continue, but Noble Ones see their complete cessation as bliss.

We will now examine the interviewee's responses towards the in-coming sense objects.

Sight

When he opens his eyes, he sees visual forms just like any other person. But sometimes he sees such forms as particles of air, just like a TV when it is switched-on but has no signal from an aerial. But when he closes his eyes what he feels is only emptiness. As a result he sees the world as empty. Our conversation goes as follows:

Q.227 You can see only emptiness in this world?
A. When I, yeh, I, my mind, I eye open, I can see, but I close my eyes this world is nothing. I cannot imagine how my face looks like is, how is my parents how is anything, emptiness only because like air particles only, cannot see anything.
Q.228 You can see only as air particles?
A. Yeh, particles.
Q.229 When you close your eyes?
A. Yeh.
Q.230 When you open your eyes?
A. When open I sometime, I saw particles particles there but he not gaining not reduce, not gaining not reduce, all look like, like what is it, like that television before the channel, without channel, they are seeing particles, particles, all the time this world is like that.
Q.231 So do you see me like that?
A. I see you, I understanding, but sometimes have small small particles.

Sound

He says he is not attached to sound, not even to the sound of the Dhamma. His mind produces Dhamma. His responses are as follows:

Q.205 Do you, are you attached, aah, to the sound of Dhamma, Dhamma, you like to listen to Dhamma (previously?) Now, now in the third fruit, is there attachment to Dhamma, sound of pirith (blessing chants), sound of ...
A. Actually, anything not very attachment anything.
Q.206 Not even for Dhamma?
A. Even anything look like mind is Dhamma understanding. (Sorry?) mind is produce Dhamma already.

Q.207 Mind produces Dhamma?
A. Aaah.

Taste

Since he sees only emptiness and particles, the question was raised of whether, when he eats, he feels like he is eating "air" and whether he feels the taste. He says he feels the taste but he is not attached to it (Q.247–248). For him, eating is more habitual, not done through desire. Our conversation goes as follows:

Q.232 ... I eat air only.
Q.233 You eat air?
A. Aaah.
Q.234 No taste?
A. Taste have, (taste have!) but understanding but he not attachment anything.

Smells

He says when he smells even faeces, even if it is brought right up to his nose, no anger or disgust arises in him, unlike before. When he hears anything, whether good or bad, praise or blame, it stops at that (Q.375).

In general with regard to his responses towards the five sensual pleasures, he says there is no attachment to them but there is an inclination to "habitual" things. Given a choice, mind would reach for something he is used to before but it is not "likes or dislikes" as, if it is not available it does not matter to him (Q.191–195).

Ideas

With regards to mind objects, the interviewee says that when he has to think, he only thinks; he does not rejoice in the past or plan for the future with attachment. With regard to sleeping and thinking, the attitude to both is the same: no attachment, only "*kiriya*," a neutral response. He expresses the following ideas about his mind-set in general:

> Actually what I thinking is the way is very different in the third stage and the fourth stage. Sometime I show this thing, because very different, different is, some day very difficult to believe, like *Arahant* stage in, when he saw he only saw, he don't have attachment one second attachment also, he saw, stop already, *kiriya*, when he heard anything, he blame or anything, good or anything, he don't think about this thing, he will hear stop already, smell only very interesting, I describe sometime the faeces, some thinking faeces there, they are very anger, very disgusting will arising, but he now even from give to my front how, very long time I don't have anger, I don't have smell, I have smell, but don't have attachment, don't have this type thing, so eat only eat only, but they will eat the thing, may be habitual, little bit but he not attachment to eat anything, he because his mind no desire, sleep also, thinking also, when he thinking, he think only, when he thinking, ah! Good past he, thinking only, he want to consider something thinking something he do thinking only, future also he don't have planning, this thing. But he want to think, he think only, but he not attachment anything (Q.375).

As to the question on whether he plans for the future, he says he plans only if he has to plan to execute something which is his duty, such as, if the *Saṅgha* assigns some task to him. Otherwise he doesn't plan anything for the future. He doesn't think about the future or the past. The mind does no planning (Q.376, 380). More specifically, his responses are as follows:

Q.376 So *Arahants* do plan for the future?

A. Actually not planning unless he wants to do something, have planning to some thing, normally he don't have planning, even I now all the time I don't think about previous, I not properly do it, *anāgāmi* thinking by this way, but when I think, that Path, all time, previous time, I don't think about yesterday is what, a *deva*, I don't think future how I can be, how I did, now I don't think also.

Q.377 (When you were an) *Anāgāmi*, did you think about the past? (yeh,yeh) You thought about the past?

A. Yes, because delusion have.

Q.378 Right, you planned for the future?

A Yes.

Q.379 Right, now there is no planning?

A. No planning future.

Q.380 I mean if your teacher tell you tomorrow you have to do this, don't you plan for it?

A. I plan it, but I my treat it like duty only, my duty not because my, I want to body, I want to planning, keep many thing, not this type thing, this because *Saṅgha* want, I member here, I have to do my duty.

The above state of mind declared by the interviewee shows that he lives in the present. It reflects the much quoted Buddha's exhortation to Bāhiya "well then Bāhiya, you should train yourself thus: "In the seen, there will be just the seen; in the heard, there will be just the heard; in the sensed, there will be just the sensed; in the cognized, there will be just the cognized'."[10]

The "demagnetized" state of his sense-bases is further confirmed by the description of his mind as "coming, stop, coming, stop," as discussed at the commencement of this chapter (Q.212–213). When we examine his responses above we can see that whatever sense data arise in his mind, all of that ceases right there.

Is an *Arahant* Free from All Suffering?

To my question on whether he feels pain, the interviewee says that he is not a robot, he is not wood, he still has the body, so he still senses through it. He says if someone else burns himself or cuts himself that person will be angry, but no anger will arise in this interviewee and he could smile. For him pain is more "habitual" (Q.235–236). His responses are as follows:

Q.235 Bhante with your new experience of Arahantship, do you have feeling? Do you have painful feeling?

A. Actually painful and what I mean is I, I can describe something painful, pain. We have the body, because I am still have this body, so he has the sense, if I am not robot. I am not wood, I still have sense or anything. So he has sense like the next (person), habitual only, habitual.

Q.236 Habitual?

A. Habitual like this thing, we have our life but he cut off already 90%, 99% already the feeling anything. Normally, normally the person he cut, burn something or fire burn something, he will anger will arising our, but even when I burn maybe I will smile, don't have difference of this type.

As to the question on whether *Arahants* are free from all suffering, Ajahn Brahmavamso says the answer comes as a surprise to all is; "no! *Arahants* are not free from all *dukkha* yet." In order to explain the difference between an *Arahant* and all others, the Buddha taught the following simile of the dart:

> For most people when they experience a painful bodily feeling, it's followed immediately by a painful mental feeling like being struck by two darts in quick succession. But for the *Arahant*, when they experience a painful bodily feeling, it is not followed by a painful mental response. It is like being struck by only one dart. The Fully Enlightened ones have removed the "dart" of mental suffering, but they still must experience the "dart" of bodily suffering (SN 36.6). (Brahmavamso 2004, 62)

Carrying the Body Around with Forbearance

The interviewee's attitude towards his body is one of "duty." The interviewee feels that his body has no "connection" to him, it is not related to him any more. Even if parts of his body are cut off one by one, there wouldn't be even one word of anger arising in his mind. There is no more attachment, no anger, and no fear. He sees his "body" only as his "duty." He says:

> In that time, my teacher, I come to my teacher, my teacher asked me, one word only "how is your non-self?" I respond, my non-self, if the person take out my eye, cut it off my head piece by piece, my anger is not arise, even one word come from my mind. I don't have this thing. So I describe it to my teacher. I no more no more anger, no more anything, no more fear, that from that no more this thing (Q.278) ... I saw that anything that someone hatred me I, I calm and peace only, I understand this person is hatred, hate me anger me because why, but I don't understanding there I but don't anger to him anything, all the time understanding only, because very far, anger for anything, attachment very far already, look like not this [the monk pointing at his body] will not connection anything, not related to me, hatred or anything same only (Q.225) .... have this thing [pointing at the body], I after, I now I cut anything is not my thing, I, my duty only, if no more, no more my duty only, no more my duty only (Q.280).

An *Arahant* sees his body as a group of dependently originated phenomena and bears with it and carries it around equanimously. Once Venerable Sāriputta was the victim of a false accusation. A monk complained to the Buddha about him, "Lord, Venerable Sāriputta, doubtless thinking to himself "I am the chief disciple," struck me a blow that almost damaged my ear. And having done that, without so much as begging my pardon, he set out on his journey." The Buddha summoned Sāriputta to his presence for an explanation. In the mean time Venerables Mahā Moggallāna and Ānanda, knowing, that a great "lion's roar" would take place, assembled all the monks in the Jetavana Monastery where this incident took place. When the Buddha questioned Sāriputta in the presence of all these monks, without expressly denying the accusation, he goes on to declare his state of mind as: "vast, exalted and measureless, without enmity and ill-will."

Sāriputta, comparing the disgust he feels at his own body to the disgust arising from contact with the carcass of a snake or human and the fatty excrescence of the body, declares:

> Just as a woman or a man—young, youthful, and fond of ornaments, with head bathed—would be repelled, humiliated and disgusted if the carcass of a snake, a dog, or a human being were slung around her or his neck; so too Bhante, I am repelled, humiliated and disgusted by this foul body. ...
>
> Just as a person may carry around a cracked and perforated bowl of liquid fat that oozes and drips; so too Bhante, I carry around this cracked and perforated body that oozes and drips. (AN IV 376)

So the *Arahants*, while seeing the body as "humiliating and disgusting," yet carry it around with forbearance, without such "disgust" disturbing their equanimity.

No Amassing of Possessions

This interviewee says he does not amass things, he no more has possessions. He has no problem in anyone taking away what is around him. He could also "bear up" whatever is offered to him. The interviewee, referring to his mind as "he," says:

> but he not attachment anything, if you like the thing you take the thing, doesn't matter. If the Path and fruition, that Path very different. Anything you like, OK you want to take, doesn't matter. I don't like more thing I like less thing, less better but not attachment. If you give me anything doesn't matter but I like very less thing only (Q.234).

In Chapter 2 we discussed the things that an *Arahant* cannot do (pp. 40–41). Storing things up in order to enjoy sensual pleasures is one of them (AN IV 370). Ajahn Brahmavamso writes about an experience with his teacher, Ajahn Chah as follows:

> Since there is no longer any idea of "mine" an *Arahant* does not store up possessions like other people do. For instance when my teacher, Ajahn Chah, was at the height of his fame and still very active he asked me to go up to his room for something. It was the first time that I had seen his living quarters and I will never forget the experience. Even though Prime ministers, powerful generals and wealthy business people were presenting all sorts of gifts to Ajahn Chah, he kept nothing for himself. His room was empty, but for a rolled up grass mat, his alms bowl and a couple of robes. It would have taken literally less than minutes to pack up all his possessions and go. The room appeared as though there was no one living in there, which well reflected the mind of an *Arahant.* (Brahmavamso 2004, 54)

No Fear

Amongst the other impossibilities for an *Arahant* is that he can never act out of fear (AN IV 370). The interviewee felt no fear at all. He describes how, when a snake came into the almsgiving hall, he saw it nothing more than as a "rubber band" and went up to it to catch him. Later he asked himself, "how come, I am not frightened?," as previously he was frightened of snakes (Q.198). He realized that he has no fear of death (Q.199).

An *Arahant* Can Only Serve the Buddha-*Sāsana*

With regard to the question on whether the interviewee is inclined to serve others, he says he does not like to go out anywhere, he likes only the forest, he doesn't like to mingle with people. He likes to help the *Saṅgha*, to do his duty by the *Saṅgha* (Q.266–268).

As to whether he is inclined to teach, he feels that he doesn't have enough knowledge, he knows very little, he doesn't know enough *abhidhamma* etc., his retention power is also not good (Q.269–271). His responses were as follows:

Q.266 Bhante, are you inclined to help others with the Dhamma?
A. I like to actually, I don't like to go out anywhere, I like forest and I like to help *Saṅgha* only. *Saṅgha* duty, what *Saṅgha* give me, I try to do for help the *Saṅgha*.
Q.267 You like to help the *Saṅgha*?
A. Aha, aha, *Saṅgha* go smooth the way already.
Q.268 You don't like to go out?
A. I like, I don't like sleeping any way don't like enjoy, I don't desire to do this thing.
Q.269 You like to teach?
A. Actually I don't, aaah, I not really qualified to teaching, teaching yet because my knowledge very little.
Q.270 You haven't read enough?
A. Aha, aha, not read enough.

Accordingly the interviewee is inclined only to serve the dispensation of the Buddha and that too only by attending on the *Saṅgha*.

In the preceding section and in Chapter 2 we considered what an *Arahant* cannot do. The question arises as to what is it that *Arahant*s can do. Earlier we saw Venerable Dabba Malaputta who, "having nothing to do," asked the Buddha for work and chose to serve the *Saṅgha* in some way or another. Ever since he was appointed to carry out the task of assigning lodging, he carried out his duties conscientiously and tirelessly working day and night, assigning and providing lodging and alms to thousands of resident and visiting monks, even amidst many accusation against him by errant monks and nuns who were not pleased with the alms or lodging they received in the process (Vin. III 158). It is reported in the Thag.-a I, 42, that the choice of Dabba to serve the *Saṅgha* by assigning lodging was a wish that he had made in one of his previous births, during the time of Padumuttara Buddha.

The *Kassapa Saṃyutta* reports that the Buddha requested Venerable Mahā Kassapa to expound the Dhamma to the monks on three occasions and that he refused to do so on all three occasions. The Buddha says "exhort the *bhikkhus*, Kassapa, give them a Dhamma talk. Either I should exhort the *bhikkhus*, Kassapa, or you should." But Mahā Kassapa responds "Venerable sir, *bhikkhus* are difficult to admonish now and they have qualities which make them difficult to admonish. They are impatient and do not accept instructions respectfully" (SN II 203–208).

It could be inferred that though Mahā Kassapa enjoyed a position of such high esteem in the *Saṅgha* and had sufficient knowledge of the Dhamma, he was not inclined to teach the Dhamma. However immediately after the Buddha's *parinibbāna*, he came out of his jungle retreat and took over the reins of the *Saṅgha* and led the first Dhamma Assembly with a view to safeguarding the Dhamma and the *Saṅgha*. Though Mahā Kassapa was not inclined to teach the Dhamma, by this time, in accordance with the Buddha's advice, many other *Arahant*s were rolling the wheel of the Dhamma led by the marshal of the Dhamma, Sāriputta. These monks had no inclination to be restricted by the limitations of their audience, unlike Mahā Kassapa.

We can conclude that *Arahant*s, being incapable of many things that worldlings and also other noble persons are inclined to do and not being fuelled by personal "intention" any more, are inclined only to serve the Dhamma. The texts report no *Arahant* who did anything other than serving the Dhamma in some way or the other. It may be that how each *Arahant* serves the Dhamma depends on each one's past conditioning, as *Arahant*s are not generating any new "intentions" as to the mode of such service.

This state of mind is further confirmed by the interviewee's answer to our question on whether he plans for the future. He says that his mind does no planning unless to execute a duty. His "disinterest" in life and inability to motivate himself to do anything else or to generate new *kamma*s is further confirmed by the fact that, when asked whether he would like to develop *jhāna*s now, so that he would be able to abide in *nirodha-samāpatti* (cessation), he replied:

> Actually I not very like, if teacher call me to do something, aah, develop more, knowledge more, I will go to do only, like duty only, because I now like waiting die only (laugh). (Q.345)

Venerable Sāriputta in the *Theragāthā* says that he had sought liberation not for the sake of supernormal powers such as the divine eye, divine ear, knowledge of passing away and rebirth, though it is clear from the verses that he had attained at least the second *jhāna* (Thag.996–999), and elsewhere (SN III 235–238), it is said that he sometimes spent the day practising any of the four *jhāna*s, the four formless states or the state of cessation.

What Motivates an *Arahant*?

Having eliminated the sense of "I" completely, and seeing the world as impermanent, painful and as essenceless, the question arises as to whether an *Arahant* can ever motivate himself or herself to do anything constructively at all, even in serving the *Buddha-sāsana*. Ajahn Brahmavamso writes about what motivates an *Arahant* to act:

> Their behaviour consists of acts of loving kindness, compassion, sympathetic joy, and equanimity. It is these four *brahmavihāra*s that motivate every action of the *Arahant*, whether it be teaching or serving, eating or resting, or whatever else they are called upon to do.

Ajahn Brahmavamso recalls his experience with an *Arahant* who had psychic powers, who is said to have the ability to read others minds:

> in particular this monk, this great monk, was said to read minds. Suspecting this might be true, I was hesitant, and actually I was terrified, of meeting such an *Arahant*. My young monk's mind was no more fit to be read by a great monk than a raunchy novel, and certainly not in public. But when I entered the presence of such a Being, or I should say "Non-Being," all my fear evaporated in a moment. I

> felt so calm, so safe and accepted, in spite of all my faults. It is because *Arahants* don't look down on anyone, the three conceits have gone, that one feels so (much) at ease with them. All that they emanate is their compassion and wisdom. Being with a genuine *Arahants* is the most comforting and encouraging of encounters.
> (Brahmavmso 2006, 60)

It is not only the four divine abidings that motivate an *Arahant* but also gratitude. Venerable Sāriputta went in search of his mother to exhort her in the Dhamma, not fuelled by attachment to her, but motivated by gratitude. The gratitude of an *Arahant* is mainly towards the Buddha and the Dhamma he taught. Therefore he is inclined to serve the *sāsana*. This in other words is *saddhā*: *saddhā* based on understanding at its peak [*ākāravati saddhā*].

Apart from this, as discussed earlier, what motivates an *Arahant* is his or her past conditioning. An *Arahant*'s mind does not generate new *kamma*. But it can gain strength from past conditioning as in the case of Venerable Dabba who had already made a wish to serve the *sāsana* in a particular way, (i.e. by managing bedding and housing for the *Saṅgha*, pp. 180–181). This interviewee is inclined only to serve the *Saṅgha* which is motivated by gratitude to the Buddha, to the Dhamma and to the *Saṅgha*.

The *Saddhā* of an *Arahant*

When questioned whether he has s*addhā*, this interviewee says he has a lot of *saddhā* towards the Buddha.

Q.299 So you have *saddhā*?
A. Very *saddhā* to Triple Gem.
Q.300 Very *saddhā* to Triple Gem?
A. Not no thinking about, if the someone call you believe another saint, no no, because Buddha's teaching is higher in the world.

He further says that when he is passing the Buddha statue in the hermitage, he bows his head and worships the Buddha (Q.301–302).

"*Assaddho*" is used as an epithet for an *Arahant* (Dhp.97). This term is mistaken by some to mean that an *Arahant* has no *saddhā* at all, taking it to have been used in the same way as *asekha*, another epithet for the *Arahant*. "*Sekha*" means "learner" which is a term used to refer to those training for Arahantship, from those practising for stream-entry upwards. Venerable Ñāṇananda, commenting on this says, literally "*asekha*" could mean "unlearned" or "untrained." However it is used in the sense that he no longer needs any training, he is an adept (Ñāṇananda 2006, IV, 415). Similarly he says the word "*assaddho*" means; the *Arahant* no longer needs *saddhā*.

For an *Arahant*, the cognitive aspect of faith is replaced by knowledge of realization. There is no room for such faith where there is direct knowledge. Hence for the *Arahant* who has complete realization, there is not an iota of room for this aspect of "faith." However in Chapter 6 we discussed that the term *saddhā* has much wider connotation than cognitive belief. An *Arahant* does have *saddhā* in every other sense apart from this.[11] Indeed his trust in the Dhamma is even stronger, due to his direct knowledge of its truth, and in the same way he greatly trusts the Buddha, the discoverer, teacher and indeed embodiment of Dhamma.

In the *Cūlasaccaka Sutta* the Buddha says that even if someone is an *Arahant*, with a fully liberated mind, he still honours, reveres and venerates the Buddha as follows:

> The Blessed One is enlightened and he teaches the Dhamma for the sake of enlightenment. The Blessed One is tamed and he teaches the Dhamma for the sake of taming oneself. The Blessed One is at peace and he teaches the Dhamma for the sake of peace. The Blessed One has crossed over and he teaches the Dhamma for the sake of crossing over. The Blessed One has attained *Nibbāna* and he teaches the Dhamma for the sake of attaining *Nibbāna.* (MN I 235)

Further in the *Bhaddāli Sutta* the Buddha says that an *Arahant* would become a plank for the Buddha to walk across the mud, if the Buddha asked him to do so. He says:

> What do you think Bhaddāli? Suppose a bhikkhu here were one liberated-in- both ways and I told him; "Come bhikkhu, be a plank for me to walk across the mud," would he walk across himself, or would he dispose his body otherwise, or would he say "No"? (MN I 439)

The Buddha's answer that an *Arahant* would dispose his body in the mud for the Buddha to walk on, this surely also being through *saddhā.*

Arahants and Rituals

In the preceding section we saw that *Arahant*s still venerate the Buddha. Let us examine whether *Arahant*s would engage in rituals. We will consider the following verses from the *Dhammapada.*

> To many a refuge do men go—to hills and woods,
> To gardens, trees, and shrines, when tormented by fear.
> Nay, no such refuge is secure, no such refuge is supreme;
> Not by resorting to such a refuge is one released from all pain. ...
> He who seeks refuge in the Buddha, Dhamma and the *Saṅgha*, he who sees with right wisdom the four Noble Truths:
> The painful, the arising of the painful, the transcending of the painful and the Noble Eightfold Path going to the alleviation of the painful.
> This indeed is a secure refuge; this indeed is the supreme refuge. Seeking such refuge one is released from all pain. (Dhp.188–189, 190–92)

These verses indicate that people seek refuge from what they fear, in places such as shrines, where presumably they do rituals that they hope will bring protection. An *Arahant*'s mind being free from fear, there is no inclination to engage in rituals as a source of supposed protection.

The interviewee says that instead of chanting and worshipping as he did before, now his mind produces Dhamma. As a non-returner, he used to do chanting but it was more habitual. Before he started to practise the Dhamma, he chanted through fear and anxiety. Now he does not chant, but when he sees a Buddha statue he still bows his head in reverence to the Buddha. Our conversation was as follows:

Q.302 Now do you do Buddha *vandanā*, worshipping the Buddha?

A. Aaah, sometime, when I go there [pointing to the direction of the Shrine room], I will saw the Buddha, I will pay respect only.

Q.303 You pay respect by bowing your head?
A. Yeh, sometimes pay bowing.
Q.304 What about worshipping, going down on your knees, chanting, do you do all this?
A. Aaah, previous I have, but now I very less, but I in mind produce understanding, my mind is Dhamma already.
Q.305 OK, so at the third stage did you do *vandanā*, chanting?
A. little bit, less also. Because I actually, my habitual not so strong like this way previous also.
Q.306 OK, even before the first fruit it was not so strong, habitual?
A. Unless I had sick, I had fear, I will chanting at that time (laughter), but now I don't have anything, so I don't chanting or anything or the mind produce Dhamma.

Compared to his present state of mind of freedom from anxiety and fear, his state of mind before he began to practise the Dhamma was one of anxiety and fear about his future. This fear brought him to Dhamma. He expresses this as follows:

Q.329 What made you become a monk?
A. Because I had the very good way, may be the good *pāramī*, I don't want defilement.
Q.330 So you didn't try this being a layman?
A. No I don't like lay people their life. Because lay people life because in that time I very attachment. Drink or anything the bad thing I do. But after I do, I very regret, may be my *pāramī* arising, drink whisky all the time you have, but you don't have all the time your healthy, your health. I will old one day, my organs cannot function one day, I very fear this thing, anything will I fear, one day will destroy, I had money, I had anything but one day my body cannot function, money still have, but anything have, I cannot move anything, I have to find something in that time.

The Interviewee's Aim as Ending Defilements, Not Attaining Supramundane Fruits as Such

Throughout the interview from time to time it came to light that the whole aim of his practice was not to attain *Nibbāna,* but to destroy the defilements (Q.36). He says "because all the time, because my aim is, destroy all defilements."

To the question "Immediately before *sotāpatti-phala* did you wish for it?," he answered: "Aaah I don't wish anything, I my mind, my mind, only I want to destroy defilements, this my wish only. I don't wish for *sotāpatti-phala* anything, I don't think about this thing ..." (Q.36). To our question "did you wish for the Arahantship immediately before *arahatta-phala*?," he said, "I have made a wish, my wish is destroy all defilements. Not, I don't say *Arahant*, I understanding I don't want defilements (laugh)" (Q.242).

Conclusion

This interviewee has declared Arahantship. In this chapter we considered the possibility of the interviewee being an *Arahant.* First we considered our definition of an attainment of a supramundane fruit containing four elements: a) Path, b) a religious experience, c) arising of knowledge, and d) breaking of fetters.

The interviewee has been treading the Noble Eightfold Path untiringly and relentlessly for three years under the guidance of one of Sri Lanka's greatest contemporary meditation masters. A specific religious experience which marked the attainment of his *arahatta-phala* has been declared by him in the interview, with reference to a specific date, place and a meditation posture.

Having established the first two factors of the definition, we proceeded to examine the next two factors, the arising of knowledge and the breaking of fetters. With the very first experience, which he refers to as "the first fruit of the Path" (stream-entry), the interviewee understood "Path and fruition" and got confidence that if he continued the practice he would destroy all defilements. He got confidence in the Buddha's teaching (Q.16, 21). He understood that inside the body is filth and it has only four elements. He felt that his body opened up like in an operation and attachments reduced (Q.21). He understood that his body and the outside world are impermanent, *dukkha* and non-self and that this "right view" he acquired could not be changed even by his own mind (Q.54, 72). He got over lack of faith in the Triple Gem, got full confidence in the Triple Gem, will not seek another teacher (Q.71–85). He engaged in rituals only as habitual conduct and for respect to the Buddha not in fear and hope. He says now his mind produces Dhamma and he does not have to chant (Q.301–306). Hence the understanding that arose in him from this first spiritual experience seems to be in line with the understanding that arises with the release from the first three fetters, the fetters that break at the stage of stream-entry.

With the third experience, which he refers to as "the third fruit of the Path" [*anāgāmi-phala*] he felt 99% of his defilements got cut off. When someone scolds him or blames him he could only smile. He was all the time happy. But he had a "little bit of attachment" to go to "heaven" (Q.175, 208). Non-returners are reborn in pure abode [*suddhāvāsa*] *brahmā* worlds, as they still have attachment to the form and formless jhānic levels. After this experience there was no "lust" but "a little bit of delusion" was remaining in him. We analyzed his responses to sense objects. His sense-bases seem to be "de-magnetized": there seemed to be neither attachment nor repulsion for in-coming sense objects. These statements are in line with the understanding that arises with the breaking of the fetters of *kāmacchanda* (desire for pleasures of the senses) and *vyāpāda* (ill-will), the fetters that are broken at the stage of the fruit that is non-returning.

With the fourth experience, which he refers to as *arahatta-phala,* he got over the desire to be re-born in the heavenly worlds, a desire that he still had at the third stage. The interviewee has no desire to develop the "*jhānas*." He seems to have broken the fetters of craving for the form and formless levels of existence [*rūparāga* and *arūparāga*].

He sees the world as "empty," he says he has no defilements arising but only phenomena arising and ceasing in the mind. He feels he has cut off defilements 100%. He feels there is nothing more to do, he has laid down the heavy duty [*katakaranīyo ohitabhāro*] and he awaits the final passing away with equanimity. His attitude towards his body is that "it is his duty" and he feels his body has "no connection to him." He says he has no fear remaining. He cannot motivate himself to do anything other than serving the *Saṅgha.* All these statements are in line with understanding that arises from the breaking of the fetters of conceit [*māno*], restlessness [*uddhacca*] and ignorance [*avijjā*].

At times he uses conventional language such as "I, me, mine." We saw that according to the texts, *Arahants* do use conventional language, but without delusion about concepts. He has a lot of *saddhā* towards the Buddha and pays respect to the Buddha with gratitude and not with expectations or fear. Even when a person becomes an *Arahant*, he still honours, reveres and venerates the Buddha.

There are no signs of him committing or having a tendency to commit what is impossible for an *Arahant.* He is not inclined to amass material things and to plan for the future unless he has to plan as a part of his duty towards the *Saṅgha.* As a *sāmaṇera,* a monastic with just the lower ordination, he is observing the ten precepts.

We saw that an *Arahant* is defined as one "whose taints are destroyed, who has lived the holy life, done what had to be done, laid down the burden, reached his own goal, utterly destroyed the fetters of existence, one completely liberated through final knowledge, and usually dwells with a mind well established in the four establishments of mindfulness" (SN V 302). The interviewee says he usually spends most of his time observing the "emptiness of the world" or the "particles of air." For the mind to be focused on this emptiness or the "particles of air," the mind has to be well established in mindfulness.

In line with the feeling of joy of release expressed by *Arahants* of the time of the Buddha, the interviewee says he is happy and contented in life all the time because there are no defilements remaining in him. He enjoyed the cutting off of defilements just as one enjoys the fruits of a tree after planting and nurturing it.

What comes out prominently in this interview is that, though he is happy, at the same time life is very "dull" for him and he awaits his *parinibbāna* patiently. At the end of the long interview that possibly was of little interest to him, our final question to him and his response were as follows:

Q.349 Apart from what we discussed now, do you have anything else to say?

A. Actually nothing to say. If you don't ask me, I don't nothing to say, I air only look like.

The above sums up his mind-set towards existence which was highlighted throughout the interview, which in the ordinary parlance is, one of "disinterest" and in Buddhist parlance, "equanimity and forbearance" arising due to wisdom.

Contrary to the popular belief that an *Arahant* is buoyant and jubilant denoting "supreme bliss," an *Arahant* seems to spend the rest of his life happy and contended but without a sense of excitement in life and bears with equanimity the inevitable ills of the rest of his remaining short stay in *saṃsāra*. Tranquillity and joy are an essential part of the mind-set of an *Arahant*, these being factors of enlightenment [*bojjhaṅgas*]. Joy is prominent particularly in the verses of the *Theragāthā* and *Therīgāthā*, which were uttered soon after the attainment of Arahantship or recalling such a joyous moment. However the more predominant quality in the mind of an *Arahant* seems to be equanimity, it being the highest enlightenment factor. Therefore what is "supreme bliss" seems to be the fact that an *Arahant* has gained freedom from *saṃsāric* woes, never to be subject to birth and death ever again.

The interviewee has declared that he has attained Arahantship. Considering the above responses to our questions, we do not see anything in him contrary to the knowledge and understanding of an *Arahant*. Subject to the limits of recognizing an *Arahant* as discussed in Chapter 2, considering his above responses and his overall background, we could see that there is a very high likelihood of him being an *Arahant*. However the main focus of this study is first fruit of the Path, the fruit that is stream-entry. I leave it to future researchers to undertake a more detailed study of possible living *Arahants*.

Notes

1. See p. 32 for the list of ten fetters.
2. *Arahaṃ khīṇāsavo vusitavā katakaraṇīyo ohitabhāro anuppattasadattho parikkhīṇabhavasaññojano sammadaññā vimutto. So satipaṭṭhānesu supatiṭṭhitacitto bahulaṃ viharati* (SN V 302).
3. As given in the stanza "*yattha nāmañ ca rūpañ ca assesam uparujjhati... ettha esā chijjate jaṭā*" (SN I 354). See p. 100 for a discussion on this issue.
4. *Sakkāya* is defined at MN I 299 as the five *upādāna-kkhandhas*.
5. *Viññāṇaṃ anidassanaṃ anantaṃ sabbato pabhaṃ, taṃ paṭhaviyā paṭhavittena ananubhūtaṃ, āpassa āpattena ananubhūtaṃ, tejassa tejattena ananubhūtaṃ, vāyassa vāyattena ananubhūtam, bhūtānan bhūtattena ananubhūtaṃ, devānaṃ devattena ananubhūtaṃ, pajāpatissa pajāpatittena ananubhūtaṃ, brahmānaṃ brahmattena ananubhūtaṃ, ābhassarānaṃ ābhassarattena ananubhūtaṃ, subhakinhānam subhakinhattena ananubhūtaṃ, vehapphalānaṃ vehapphalattena ananubhūtaṃ, abhibhussa abhibuttena ananubhūtaṃ, sabbassa sabbattena ananubhūtaṃ.* (MN I 329)
6. See Ñāṇananda 2004, II, 41–69 for a detailed discussion on this topic.
7. *Duddassaṃ anantaṃ nāma, na hi saccaṃ sudassanaṃ*
   Paṭividdhā taṇhā jānato passato na'tthi kiñcanaṃ. (Ud.80)
8. For an analysis of Dabba's passing away, see Anālayo 2012.
9. *Yo hoti bhikkhu arahaṃ katāvī*
   Khīṇāsavo antimadehadhārī
   "ahaṃ vadāmī' ti pi so vadeyya
   "mamaṃ vadantī ti pi so vadeyya
   loke samaññaṃ kusalo viditvā
   voharamattena so vohareyyā. (SN I 30)
10. *Diṭṭhe diṭṭhamattaṃ bhavissati, sute suta mattaṃ bhavissati, mute muta mattaṃ bhavissati, viññāte viññāta mattaṃ bhavissati.* (Ud.8/as translated at Ñāṇananda 2005, III, 330)
11. See Chapter 6, pp. 131–137 for an analysis of the term *saddhā.*

— 8 —

Conclusion

In the foregoing chapters we examined the Buddhist religious experience with specific focus on the fruit that is stream-entry, based on both textual study and our field research. We also examined numerous controversies and contemporary debates around the Buddhist religious experience. It was found that amongst successful practitioners there were varied views depending on the route each one followed personally up to their goal, and some even took up the position that "that alone is the path and all others are not the path." This chapter nevertheless highlights some striking commonalities observed amongst the practioners who were interviewed with regard to the Path and its fruits and some striking observations on supramundane fruits as a whole and enumerates the reasons for the current debates and confusion with regard to the Path and its fruits. This chapter will also present a relatively simple approach to the Path based on this research and will identify some areas for future research.

The path to the ultimate Buddhist religious experience is the Noble Eightfold Path, which is unique to Buddhism. But the approach to the Path may vary depending on one's inclinations, past practices, skills, personal traits, views etc. until it merges with right view. Once the "approach" each one follows merges with right view, it is called the "stream" [*sota*] of the Eightfold Path. However, despite the numerous approaches to the Path found amongst practitioners interviewed in this research, a common ground can be established with regard to the fundamentals of their transforming experience. These fundamentals also correspond to what has been said in the texts.

All sources confirm that the fetter-breaking-experience is signless, wishless, and empty [*animitta, appaṇihita* and *suññata*]. At this point a person is not with a normal perception, nor is her perception deranged (as in insanity); she is not without perception (as in attainment of cessation [*nirodha*], and not with five-sense perception suppressed (as in formless states).[1]

Further, whilst similar non-Buddhist religious experiences generate a sense of identity or oneness with God or the universe, as discussed in Chapter 5, with the said experience the Theravāda Buddhist directly sees the true nature of existence to be: (1) dependently arising, (2) impermanent, (3) unsatisfactory, and (4) not a permanent Self or the possession of such a thing, and consequently she sees that "nothing is worth clinging to" [*sabbe dhammā nālaṃ abhinivesāya*—MN I 254]. Hence, first I conclude that the attainment of a supramundane fruit is a unique experience and the Path to such attainment is also unique.

When the said knowledge arises for the first time, marked by a specific experience, it is referred to as attainment of the "fruit that is stream-entry" [*sotāpatti-phala*]. With this attainment one is considered to have fully entered the Noble

Eightfold Path proper. From this turning point in *saṃsāra*, the vision one acquires about the true nature of existence, together with a degree of mindfulness appropriate to a stream-enterer which has an inherent tendency to look back, to probe into the mind in such a away that one sees conditionality, pushes one up-stream, against the tide of *saṃsāra* so that within a maximum of seven more births the stream-enterer makes the final exit from *saṃsāra* never again to be subject to the unsatisfactoriness and the dangers of "becoming."

Venerable Ajahn Chah, referring to his spiritual experience, writes:

> All knowledge and understanding has been transformed. Someone seeing me might have thought I was mad. In fact a person without strong mindfulness may have gone mad, because nothing in the world was as before. But it was really just I who had changed, and yet still I was the same person. When everyone would be thinking one way, I would be thinking another, when they would speak one way, I would speak another. I was no longer running with the rest of the humankind.
>
> (Chah 1987, 186)

The above account shows that this experience has led to a complete change of perception in Ajahn Chah.

Statements such as the above can give rise to doubts as to whether this is enlightenment or a delusion. In fact we often hear people being dissuaded from meditation on the basis that they would run the risk of "going crazy." Mark Epstein, a psychiatrist, professor of psychology and a meditator from New York, in his book *Psychotherapy without the Self*, writes:

> Advanced stages of insight meditation involves profound experiences of dissolution and fragmentation. Yet the practitioner, through the practice of "making present" is able to withstand these psychic pressures ... In true egolessness there could be only disintegration and such a state could manifest as psychosis.
>
> (Epstein 2007, 51)

However we already read in the introductory chapter Ken Wilber's conclusion about the religious experiences quoted by him in *No Boundary*. He concludes that we would be making a grave error if we hastily conclude such experiences to be hallucinations or products of a mental aberration, for in their final disclosure they share none of the tortured anguish of psychotic visions (2001, 1).

Striking Commonalities

In addition to the common ground identified above with regard to the fetter-breaking-experience, our field research has also observed other striking commonalities amongst the interviewees, despite the diversity of their personalities, meditative objects used by them, and experiences encountered by them. These deserve our attention, and are as follows.

1) At the time of the attainment of a supramundane fruit, all energies of these interviewees and their entire life was totally dedicated to the meditative practice. It arose during a period when there was no other distraction, no other goal that took precedence over it or shared their attention, however short a period it may have been.
2) Contrary to the modern trend, particularly in Sri Lanka, of attending *Abhidhamma* classes even before one could hardly know the fundamen-

tals of the Dhamma and meditation practice, none of these interviewees refer to the knowledge of *Abhidhamma* as a direct aid to their attainment.

3) Though there was a general determination in all the interviewees to attain *Nibbāna*, to attain a supramundane fruit, to eradicate defilements etc., none of them considered "wishing" for a supramundane fruit as a pre-condition for attaining it. Nor did they wish for a supramundane fruit just before their fetter-breaking-experience relating to a supramundane fruit.

This observation is important in the light of certain contemporary meditation *gurus* professing wishing or resolving for *Nibbāna* as an essential step on the Path immediately prior to the realization of a supramundane fruit.

In the *Purābheda Sutta* of *Pārāyana Vagga*, of the *Sutta-nipāta*, the quality of "*apihālu*" is given as one of the qualities needed for overcoming craving prior to "dissolution of the body" (Sn. v. 852). "*Apihālu*" means the opposite of covetousness. It means not longing for anything (Jayawickrama 2001, 352). The commentary to this passage explains that the term "*apihālu*" here denotes not longing for spiritual success, rather than for material things. Longing or wishing for a supramundane fruit is an obstacle for the total letting-go in the mind which is a pre-condition for a supramundane fruit. *Nibbāna* has not been fully experienced even by a trainee [*sekha*]. A stream-enterer can also only "deduce" it. Hence wishing for *Nibbāna* is only craving. Rather, what is needed is to fulfil the necessary conditions for realizing *Nibbāna*, having the eradication of all defilements as the ultimate goal. The said general determination of the interviewees to attain *Nibbāna* is *kusala chanda* which is one of the four *iddhi-padas*, or "bases of success," which are among the 37 *bodhi-pakkhiya-dhammas* (*dhammas* contributing towards enlightenment).

In the *Mahācattārīsaka Sutta*, the Buddha says:

> In one with right view, right resolve comes into being, in one with right resolve, right speech comes into being, in one with right speech, right action comes into being, in one with right action, right livelihood comes into being, in one with right livelihood, right effort comes into being, in one with right effort, right mindfulness comes into being, in one with right mindfulness, right concentration comes into being, in one with right concentration, right knowledge comes into being, in one with right knowledge, right deliverance comes into being. (MN III 76)

The above *Sutta* shows that each of these factors arise naturally and dependent on the previous factor. Accordingly, if "right view" is in place, it leads onwards to deliverance. In the above process there is no place for "wishing" for *Nibbāna*. The general determination to attain *Nibbāna* as aforesaid would fall within *sammā saṅkappa*, right resolve, which is a path-factor and would ensure progress on the Path.

4) Having attained stream-entry, these noble persons don't seem to have any other attraction or goal which takes precedence over the final goal of realization of *Nibbāna*, though the speed with which they proceed with the rest of the Path may differ. If at all, the only "distraction" seems to be their quest to serve the *Sāsana*, which is considered as complementary to the practice to some extent.

However an *Arahant* "has done his work with diligence; he is no more capable of being negligent," but a *sekha* "still has work to do with diligence," and by implication can still be negligent (MN I 477). Also out of the three types of stream-enterers, the one roaming for seven more births as against one who completes his work in that birth itself (AN I 233—See p. 90), is by implication negligent.

5) All of them are happier and more confident after attaining a supramundane fruit than they were before they started to tread the Path, and they recommend it to others unreservedly. Their experience of momentary "dissolution of the world," or their understanding of impermanence, has had no negative impact on them.
6) In the case of the lay person who was subject to our research, it was noted that she found lay life as not such an obstacle to treading the Path, though some other interviewees who had no family obligations had opted to ordain after the attainment of the first fruit of the Path. Further, all of them considered themselves as having led a successful lay life. The interviewee who was continuing in lay life as a stream-enterer was found to be totally devoted to the Path whilst fulfilling her obligations to her family, friends and society, and above all to the *Buddha-sāsana*, however with a strong inclination to renounce lay life when conditions became more conducive for this. Further, she is seen gearing up for *sīla* higher than the five precepts expected of a lay person. But outwardly these noble persons show no signs whatsoever of their deep understanding of the Dhamma other than the confidence they display in the Buddha, the Dhamma and the *Saṅgha* and their understanding of the dependent origination, which could only be fathomed by an equally knowledgeable person and by discussion with them.
7) Another striking feature which was observed in our field research is that, for the purpose of attainment of supramundane fruits, none of these interviewees seem to have strictly followed or identified themselves with a specific "meditation system" popular today, such as that of Goenka, Pa-Auk or Mahāsi meditation system, some of which seem to be highly structured and to be followed to the letter[2]. All these interviewees seemed to have followed the Path (the Noble Eightfold Path) as laid down in the *Sutta*s in general. However some of them have "experimented" with these systems in a limited way.[3]

In fact some of the interviewees, particularly those who are teachers, were rather critical of contemporary "meditation systems" which restrict students to a specific practice without regard to their natural inclinations and without recognizing their past practices. One of our interviewees says:

> Many teachers are in a rut. They have only what they have caught on to. There is a bud that opens out within the meditator herself. We don't have the insight in us to understand that we have to meddle with the bud only after it opens out. You don't see things as they are. There is an idiom in Sinhala "*wela yana vidhiyata massa gahanne,*" that is, you have to put up the structure to support a growing creeper along its natural path, that is, you have to identify the personality traits and support that. This has been completely destroyed by today's systems ... Even when

> I used to visit this place as a lay person, this place had different teachers for all these systems. The reason for this is the open mindedness of the then head monk. I am yet to see [another] such an open mind. When I think of this quality which is amply demonstrated by the Buddha, I feel sorry more for the teachers rather than for the meditators. (Interview No. 3, Q.92)

However all of them felt that all these meditation systems have some value and are not extraneous to the word of the Buddha, yet any one of these systems, by itself, is not sufficient to attain *Nibbāna*. Hence one should not become a slave to or be made to become a slave to any one of these meditation systems. Accordingly, if one is to be successful on the Path, one's mind should be open to any meditation which facilitates developing right view and seeing dependent origination together with developing of the five spiritual faculties: confidence, effort, mindfulness, concentration, and wisdom [*saddhā, viriya, sati, samādhi, paññā*] as a whole. Any meditation object which has been recommended by the Buddha backed by the Noble Eightfold Path in general would ensure this.

8) It was observed that there is a common trend in the feelings and understanding expressed by the two interviewees who had attained the fruit of non-returning [*anāgāmi-phala*]. Both of them felt that, with the attainment of the fruit that is non-returning, they eliminated "fear"—although fear is expected to be eliminated only upon reaching the final goal. Upon close examination it was found that at this point they felt that they "eliminated fear" of death. Also they both had a degree of concern for the possible eons to be spent in the *brahmā* worlds if they were unable to attain the final goal this birth itself.

Further, in the case of one of these two interviewees (Interviewee No.2), in a detailed discussion into the aspect of fear, it was found that, though he was sure that there was no fear in him for lightning and thunder, lightning and thunder did attract his attention. He finds that lightning and thunder do "register in his mind" and do not go totally un-noticed as in the case of his mind's responses to objects which are prone to arouse sense pleasure in a non-*anāgāmī*. It is possible that, though lightning and thunder do not give rise to fear in him, his mind identifies with it in some way because of the remaining, last vestiges of the "ego." Ego in technical terms is *māna*, conceit. Conceit is eliminated as a fetter only with the attainment of Arahantship. Hence his mind's responses to thunder and lightning at the stage of non-returning.

Similarly Ajahn Chah, widely believed to have attained supramundane fruits of the Path, refers to his experience of an overnight stay in a cemetery by the side of a burning corpse. He gives a vivid account of his experience of fear and overcoming fear. On this occasion, fear was so great that it filled him like a jar completely filled with water; fear built up so much within him that it reached its peak and began to overflow. However, after a long battle with fear in the middle of the night, in his sitting meditation posture itself, fear completely disappeared "as easily as turning over one's own hand." Non-fear arose in its place (Chah 2002, 71–77). However towards the morning he realized that he was passing blood with urine as a result of the fear that arose in the dead of the night, which gave rise to the thought of whether his "gut was torn," which he overcame immediately after he asked himself "What are you afraid of!". This thought process shows that fear was a point of reference in his mind, though he felt he had overcome fear. This is obviously an experience prior to the attainment of the final goal.

Supramundane Fruits

Given the numerous current debates and controversies discussed in this work concerning supramundane fruits, some issues relating to these in general, which came to light from this research, are worthy of mention.

It is noteworthy that, despite the difficulties of recognizing different categories of noble persons, the proportion of stream-enterers to non-returners and *Arahants* recognized in the fieldwork of this study reflects the proportions of such categories in the texts (e.g. SN V 406). The number I have identified as stream-enterers is much more compared to the non-returners identified in the research and rare are the *Arahants*.

Despite the heavy emphasis of this study on the four categories of supramundane fruits and the excitement, reverence and enthusiasm over noble persons displayed in Theravāda countries today, this study highlights that it is possible that a person may not even recognize himself or herself to be a particular noble person by its technical term, though in fact they have eradicated the relevant fetters that are destroyed with the attainment of a specific supramundane fruit. In fact despite having the necessary technical knowledge of the Buddha's classification of supramundane fruits, some of our interviewees refused to identify themselves in terms of these categories, on the basis that these are all conceptual mileposts on the Path and what is important is only the attainment of *Nibbāna*, the elimination of all defilements.

This argument has some validity considering Venerable Sāriputta's first encounter with the classification of the supramundane fruits. The *Navaka-Nipāta* of the *Aṅguttara Nikāya* reports an incident where Sāriputta hears some wanderers of other faiths saying that none of those who die with some "residue remaining" [*sa-upādiseso*] are free from hell, rebirth in the animal world, realms of ghosts. On this occasion venerable Sāriputta rose from there without a comment and went to the Buddha and questioned him on the fate of those who die with residue remaining. Here the Buddha refers to nine types of persons who die with residue remaining, who are free from the hells, animal worlds etc. and sets out the different types of noble persons below the level of an *Arahant:* five kinds of non-returners, the once-returner and three kinds of stream-enterers (AN IV 378).

It seems that this was the first time that the Buddha had referred to the different types of noble persons or the various stages of breaking the ten fetters:

> Sāriputta, I had not been disposed to give this Dhamma exposition to the *bhikkhus, bhikkhunīs*, male lay followers and female lay followers. For what reason? I was concerned that on hearing this Dhamma disposition, they might take to the ways of heedlessness. However I have spoken this Dhamma exposition for the purpose of answering your question. (AN IV 381)

The above *Sutta* suggests that up to this stage even Sāriputta was not aware of the various supramundane fruits of the Path by name such as *sotāpatti-phala* and *sakadāgāmī-phala* etc., as elsewhere freely referred to in the texts, except for the final goal of the Path, nor was he aware of the consequences of such fruits on the *samsāric* journey. However, obviously by this time there were many noble persons belonging to all four categories, but declarations may have been made up to such time only in terms of total eradication of defilements.

Mahānāma the Sākyan, who was a noble person, tells the Buddha that at times when he comes across a stray elephant, stray horse, etc., his mindfulness regarding the Buddha, the Dhamma, and the *Saṅgha* gets muddled and at such times he wonders, "if at this time I should die, what would be my destination, my future bourne?". Here the Buddha assures him that he is one whose mind is fortified by faith, virtue, learning, generosity and wisdom, so even if he dies under worse conditions than what he is worried about, he will go upwards like the ghee or oil in a pot being broken in water: the ghee or oil would rise up whilst only the pieces of the pot would sink (SN V 369). The Buddha further pointed out that Mahānāma's mind is fortified by confirmed confidence in the Buddha, the Dhamma, and the *Saṅgha* and possess *ariyakanta sīla* (virtue dear to the noble ones), and upon his death, his mind would incline towards *Nibbāna* just as a tree slanting, sloping and inclining towards the east, once cut down at its foot, would fall down towards the eastern direction.

Both above similes, of the pot and the slanting tree, are usually used by the Buddha to denote the destination of a stream-enterer. The confirmed confidence in the Buddha, the Dhamma and the *Saṅgha* and *ariyakanta sīla* are the hallmarks of a stream-enterer. Hence it could be safely assumed that Mahānāma was at least a stream-enterer at this point.

This same Mahānāma appears again in the *Cūḷadukkhakkhandha Sutta* of the *Majjhima Nikāya* and he complains to the Buddha that, despite him having the understanding that greed, hatred and ignorance are imperfections that defile the mind, yet at times greed, hatred and ignorance invade his mind and remain (MN I 91). Here the Buddha explains to him that, so long as one does not see the danger of sense pleasures and does not experience the joy and pleasure beyond them), he still could be attracted to sense pleasures. The commentary to this passage explains that Mahānāma was then a once-returner. A once-returner only weakens greed, hatred and delusion and has not yet eradicated them (Ñāṇamoli and Bodhi 1995, 1200, n. 206).

The above cases show that noble disciples can be ignorant about the consequences of the supramundane fruit they have attained unless they are equipped with the relevant technical knowledge to be able to identify it. Nevertheless, whether they recognize it or not, or whether they have the knowledge of its implications or not, if the defilements are truly eradicated, their destiny is certain and is not impaired by this deficiency of knowledge, as the "underlying tendencies" of their mind would naturally slant towards *Nibbāna*.

In Chapter 1, I referred to the various views expressed by contemporary meditation masters about the role of *samatha* and the *jhāna*s in the practice. Whilst some take *jhāna*s to be compulsory to commence *vipassanā*, some others profess that wisdom develops *samādhi*. Specific questions were posed to our interviewees in order to assess the role of *samatha* (deep calm, cultivated by strong concentration and mindfulness) in their practice. It was found that the majority of the interviewees were not inclined to master *jhāna*s and considered themselves *sukkhavipassakas* (dry-insight-meditators)[4]. However in their practice, which was predominantly *vipassanā*, all of them from time to time, experienced very blissful states of concentration. Whilst the majority of the interviewees had developed light-perception due to *samādhi*—sometimes referred to as the "*nimitta*" or "sign" of concentration on a meditative object—two had developed the "light of wisdom" [*vidarshanā samādhi*],[5] a bright light developed during *vipassanā* meditation (Interviewees No. 1 and 5). Interviewee No. 1 says the light which developed whilst practising *vipassanā* was so strong that it was a like a bright flash light, so much so that at the beginning he used to open his eyes to see whether there was a flash light focused from the adjacent mountain. He used it to help focus on his meditation object, this being the 32 impurities of the body. One of the interviewees had, by the time of her attainment of stream-entry, not experienced light-perception at all (Interview No. 6). Further, one of the interviewees who was obsessed with *jhānas* was prohibited by his teacher from entering *jhānas* and was restricted to *vipassanā* as he was found "playing" with *jhānas* the whole day, even skipping his meals. His teacher thought it necessary to train him to let go of even the *jhānas* (Interview No. 2).[6] From this point onwards he never developed *jhānas*. Thereafter his practice up to now is simply developing the calmness or unification of the mind sufficient to understand what his happening in his mind, namely, watching the defilements arising in his mind and applying *yoniso manasikāra* in order to dispel them. This practice has helped him to proceed to higher fruits of the Path. Interviewee No. 5 says that he has experienced the fourth *jhāna* without any light-perception. Interviewee No. 3, who is an experienced meditation teacher, observed that though light perception is very popular amongst practitioners, there are 10–20% of the practitioners to whom it does not come up in the mind. These variations in experiences seem to be conditioned by past practices, inclinations of the mind and attitudes towards *samatha* practice. Nevertheless, the said debate on the relative roles of *samatha* and *vipassanā*, and the discussion about the level of *samatha* necessary for the overall practice, which is often a focal point amongst contemporary meditators and meditation teachers, on the face of it doesn't seem to have had any real value for the practice of these interviewees, even towards higher fruits of the Path, in the sense that they don't seem to have consciously adopted any specific approach whether it be *samatha* preceded by *vipassanā* or *vipassanā* preceded by *samatha* etc. In their practice which is primarily inclined towards insight, the level of *samatha* required for a breakthrough to the respective fruits seemed to have developed naturally.

Samatha and *vipassanā* are both needed for the arising of the Noble Eight-factored Path that leads up to stream-entry. Hence it is said (AN II 156–158) that one can have any one of the following approaches:

1) *Vipassanā* preceded by *samatha*; this was later called the vehicle [*yāna*] of *samatha*, which develops deep calm, then adds insight;
2) *Samatha* preceded by *vipassanā*; called the vehicle of *vipassanā*, which on the basis of preliminary calm, develops insight then deeper calm (full "*samatha*")
3) *Samatha* and *vipassanā* yoked together; the "yoked" method, which has alternating phases of progressively deeper levels of calm and insight.
4) The mind being "gripped by *Dhamma* excitement" [*dhammuddac-caviggahītamānā*] but then settling down and attaining concentration. This seems to be referring to insight leading to the arising of various pleasant experiences to which there is excited attachment (later called

> the "defilements of insight"), then a return to composure and concentration. In time it came to be seen as the way of the "dry/bare [*sukkha*] insight worker [*vipassaka*]" (insight without the explicit need for the cultivation of *samatha*).

Similarly the texts present "*sīla, samādhi, paññā*" (moral virtue, meditation and wisdom) as a fixed course to *Nibbāna.* In most contexts (e.g. DN II 91), moral virtue, meditation, and wisdom are given in this order. This may be partly because this is the order in which people tend to work on the aspects of the ordinary Path. The wisdom derived from this, then leads to the breakthrough which is the wisdom at the start of the Noble Path. Once this is attained, stream-enterers have completely fulfilled moral virtue, non-returners have completely fulfilled meditation [*samādhi*], and *Arahants* have completely fulfilled wisdom [*paññā*] (AN I 231–232). Here *sīla* is presented as the entry point. However we saw the case of Sarakāni, who was declared by the Buddha to be a stream-enterer even though he had earlier been a drunkard. Similarly Interviewee No. 3 of this research, at the commencement of his practice until he had the fetter-breaking-experience relating to stream-entry, had scant regard for *sīla,* though he was attracted to the teaching and the practice of insight. This raises the issue of whether "*sīla, samādhi, paññā*" is actually a fixed order or whether entry to the Path is possible through any one of these. But this interviewee immediately prior to the attainment of stream-entry was staying in a meditation centre, following its daily routine and engaging in meditation which gave him no opportunity to breach the *sīla* and there is no indication that there were "breaches" at a "mental" level as he was fully committed to the practice even as an experiment. Accordingly, whilst as given in the text, *sīla* seems to be the entry point as a general rule, it seems that there could be exceptions, where one could commence from *paññā.* In fact the Path factors are grouped differently from the above order at MN I 301 (i.e. wisdom, virtue, meditation). However in order to have a breakthrough to a supramundane fruit, all three requirements of the Noble Eightfold Path, (i.e. *sīla, samādhi, paññā*), have to be satisfied.

Reasons for Debates and Confusion

This study examined several contemporary controversies and debates around the Buddhist religious experience. These may leave a novice or even a serious student on the Path much confused. Lets us examine the reasons for these debates and confusion.

The two monks Yamelu and Tekula, brothers who were brahmins by birth, once complained to the Buddha that monks who had got ordained from various clans and social strata corrupted the Buddha's word by using their own dialect [*sakāya niruttiyā*], and they wanted Dhamma to be presented exclusively in the language of an elite group [*chandaso āropemā' ti,* Vin. II 139]. The *Vinaya* commentary explains that "*chandaso āropema*" means a "way of speech according to the "honored dialect" (or vernacular, *sakkata bhāsā*), like Veda" (Horner 1952 (2000), 194, n. 2). On this occasion the Buddha forbids his words being presented in "*chandaso*" and in fact makes it a *dukkaṭa* offence (a wrong doing) saying that each one should be allowed to learn the Dhamma in their own dialect.

By this piece of legislation, the Buddha facilitated the taking of Dhamma close to the hearts of the people, expressly prohibiting converting Dhamma to a medium so technically complex that its simplicity becomes unintelligible to the ordinary person. However we can see that commentators and Dhamma preachers introducing technical terms and classifications which are not found in the *Suttas*, and this has contributed to much confusion. The word "*phala-samāpatti*" as appearing in the commentaries is a classic example of this. Also the series of "sixteen insight knowledges" found in the *Visuddhimagga* has made the path laid down by the Buddha, very complex, making it unintelligible and out of bounds to the ordinary person.

In the Āni Sutta of the *Opamma Saṃyutta*, the Buddha says:

> Bhikkhus, once in the past the Dasārahas had a kettle drum called the Summoner. When the Summoner became cracked, the Dasārahas inserted another peg. Eventually the time came when Summoner's original drumhead had disappeared and only a collection of pegs remained.
>
> So too, bhikkhus the same thing will happen with the bhikkhus in the future. When those discourses spoken by the Tathāgata that are deep, deep in meaning, supramundane, dealing with emptiness, are being recited, they will not be eager to listen to them, not lend an ear to them, nor apply their mind to understand them; and they will not think those teachings should be studied and mastered. But when those discourses that are mere poetry composed by poets, beautiful in words and phrases, created by outsiders, spoken by their disciples are being recited, they will be eager to listen to them, will lend an ear to them, and will apply their minds to understand them.[7]

In the *Kassapa Saṃyutta* the Buddha says that when a counterfeit of the true Dhamma [*saddhamma-patirūpaka*] appears in the world, the true Dhamma disappears just as much as when counterfeit gold appears in the world, true gold disappears (SN II 224). The commentary to this passage explains that there are two counterfeits of the true Dhamma: one with respect to attainments [*adhigama*], the other with respect to learning [*pariyatti*]. The former is the ten corruptions of insight knowledge and the latter consist of texts other than the authenticated word of the Buddha authorized at the three Buddhist councils (Bodhi 2000, 808, n. 312).

As the deeper concepts such as emptiness found in the *Suttas* get more and more unattractive to the majority of monks and laymen, we find the Buddhist preachers today quoting more and more poets, philosophers, scientists and even other religious leaders rather than the Buddha. Today we find even some monks from the forest monasteries practising the true Dhamma, in their Dhamma sermons, freely quoting poets, philosophers, psychologists and psychotherapists who are not associated with this practice, to the extent that the practitioners forget the true meaning of the word "mindfulness," with mindfulness reduced to "being in the present moment" as used by the western psychotherapists for mundane healing processes. These modern trends have created much confusion amongst practitioners.

In the *Mahāsāropama Sutta* of *Majjhima Nikāya,* the Buddha says that this holy life is not to be practised for gain, honour and renown, or even for attainment of virtue, concentration or the divine eye. Unshakable deliverance of the mind is its goal, its heartwood and its end (MN I 197). Mindfulness-based meditation is used today for health purposes and for relaxation. Dhamma sessions have also become an evening of entertainment without a true goal, which does not help lead towards liberation. Dhamma preachers singing away to melodious themes is not an uncommon scene; we find melodious moments even in some of the meditation sessions conducted today. By not properly understanding the goal of this Path, over the years its goal and practice has been expanded and relaxed up to the point of using talk of sexual excitement as a vehicle for enlightenment, even if only in a figurative sense. All these deviations from the practice laid down in the texts distract a practitioner and takes her further and further away from the goal of the Dhamma, which for the undiscerning may end in utter confusion.

Further, contemporary Buddhist preachers, by quoting poets and philosophers to elucidate the Dhamma, have tended to equate it with the rest of the religions in the world, thus losing sight of its uniqueness. The Dhamma is unique as, if there were no arising of a *Tathāgata,* there would not be Buddhism. The Buddha says "Truth is but one, there is no second regarding which an intelligent man might dispute with an (other) intelligent man" [*Ekam hi saccam na dutīyam atthi, yasmim pajāno vivade pajānam*] (Sn.v. 884). Hence the Buddha's teaching is unique and so is the Buddhist religious experience. There is no parallel to it, particularly with regards to its core.

In his *Nirvāna and Ineffability*, Asanga Tilakaratne, commenting on the "myth of universal identity of religion," writes:

> The Buddha rejecting the Hindu idea of Ātman and Brahman and adopting an ethical path leading to the cessation of suffering, showed that religion is possible without the Transcendental (in the sense that the ultimate Buddhist experience can be explained rationally and conceptually defined and analyzed).The traditional religion at the time of the Buddha could not believe this and grouped him with the nihilists. This difficulty is not dead. We still come across the difficulty in believing that religion is possible without such things as God, creation, eternal heaven and hell. (Tilakaratne 1993, 150)

Restricting a student to one meditation system or another and without regard to each one's natural inclinations and past practices, insisting that the path followed by the teacher "is the only path and all others are not the path" is yet another major reason for today's debates, controversies and confusion. There is only one path, which is the Noble Eightfold Path, though the mode of approach to the Path may vary from person to person. Even in the *Sutta*s, there are different approaches to developing the Path, and even different characterisations of the Path (See *Asaṅkhata Saṃyutta*, SN: 43).

Apart from these modern trends which are factors external to a practitioner that cause confusion, confusion could stem from internal factors such as misunderstandings about the *samatha* practice, for example, joy of *jhāna*s is often mistaken to be *Nibbāna.* Not only the joy of *samatha,* joy of insight too is misunderstood as *Nibbāna.* In fact joy has been listed as one of the ten defilements of insight. Also unmethodically sliding into *arūpa jhāna*s could be misunderstood as "*suññatāvimokkha.*"[8] Also suggestions made to the meditating mind by rigidly structured contemporary meditation systems may end up in the mind "projecting" *Nibbāna* rather than "attaining" *Nibbāna.* The understanding, attitudes and behaviours of those who have experienced the "projected *Nibbāna*" would naturally be different to the understanding, attitudes and behaviours of one who has "attained" *Nibbāna* (by total letting go of even the concept of *Nibbāna*). The uninquiring practitioner would never know this difference.

A Simpler Approach to the Path

Amidst much confusion and debates about the Path, compared to contemporary meditation practices, let us look at a simpler approach to the Path, based on the practice of Interview No. 2 (See pp. 227–238 for synopsis of Interview No. 2).

To the question "what is your advice for a practitioner?" the said interviewee says "looking in to the mind, that is the only thing I ask you and see how it reacts" (Q.137). He says:

> We grasp our mind or thoughts but there is nothing worth adhering to as things keep changing. You are entertaining as an actor, to establish the main character [self] because of the craving for existence. Though it is suffering, we still want editing the way we want. If you understand that and the danger of acting and editing part, then the mind will learn a lesson not to do it anymore. That is your morality or whatever... It becomes restraint by itself. (Q.136)

> Everyone knows with a little bit of intelligence our body is not ours. It decays and dies, but we think some essence is there somewhere, within and without that we can depend on. Mostly we grasp our mind or thoughts. Therefore try to understand that essence, whether it is a reliable thing. Today it says something, tomorrow another story. With this experience, that is enough for you to understand what is happening. The most unreliable in the world is your mind. Don't trust it (Q.137)... Once you understand it's cheating, it automatically letting go. That's where the Path starts. (Q.138)

He says his practice is not concentrating on anything, just watching the mind (Q.110). The crux of this interviewee's practice has been and what he is recommending is looking or probing into the mind, in a manner that one sees causes and conditions. In other words seeing cause and effect, seeing how something dependently originates, or the "relatedness of this to that" [*idappaccayatā*]. When one looks into the mind in this manner, things are known as they really are [*yathābhūta ñāṇadassana*]. When one sees things as they really are, the "grip" of the mind begins to loosen and finally one lets go totally.

In the *Bhūta Sutta* of the *Nidāna Saṃyutta*, the Buddha questions Venerable Sāriputta about the meaning of the following verse from "*The Questions of Ajita*" of the *Pārāyana Vagga* of the *Sutta-nipāta* (SN II 47):

> Those who have comprehended the Dhamma
> And the manifold trainees here
> Asked about their way of conduct
> Being discreet, tell me, dear sir. (Sn. 198)

The above verse refers to the conduct of a trainee [*sekha*]. The Buddha asks how the meaning of this, stated in brief, should be understood in detail. Venerable Sāriputta replies:

> One sees as it really is with correct wisdom: "This has come to be" ... , its origination occurs with that as nutriment" ... , "With the cessation of that nutriment, what has come to be is subject to cessation" ... . Having seen as it really is, one is practising for the purpose of revulsion towards what has come to be, for its fad-

> ing away and cessation ... revulsion towards its origination through nutriment ..., revulsion towards what is subject to cessation, for its fading away and cessation. It is in such a way that one is a trainee. [9]

The Buddha commends Sāriputta and repeats the entire statement of Sāriputta in confirmation of the practice of a trainee. The essence of this passage is, having seen as it really is with correct wisdom, "This has come to be," one practises for the revulsion, fading away and cessation of "what has come to be." Similarly, having seen the nutriments for such origination, having seen the cessation of such nutriments, one practises towards the revulsion, fading away and cessation of its origination and towards what is subject to cessation.

Accordingly he is recommending looking into the mind as the crux of the practice from the stage of the ordinary worldling [*putthujjana*] to the stream-enterer and beyond, up until the final goal. Paying attention to the "present moment" alone is not sufficient. "Being in the present moment," which is widely used by psychotherapists and some modern meditation *gurus* no doubt has a therapeutic effect and is a temporary relief from the stresses of life. However it is seeing things in terms of "cause and effect" that paves the way for deep cognitive restructuring which enables one to tear apart the shackles of the fetters that bind one to *saṃsāra*. Looking into the mind being the crux of the practice recommended by him, it should be emphasized that the total Path is eightfold and is as follows (AN V 113–117):

1. Associating with genuine people,
2. Hearing the true Dhamma,
3. Trustful confidence/faith,
4. *Yoniso manasikāra* (wise attention),
5. Mindfulness and clear awareness,
6. Guarding of the sense-faculties,
7. Right conduct of body, speech and mind,
8. The four applications of mindfulness,
9. The seven factors of awakening,
10. Release by direct knowledge.

Whilst "looking into the mind" as stated above should be practised throughout the above steps, the interviewee seems to be focusing on states of mind and mental formation (which falls within 8 above) as his main meditation object. As against practices which make a specific degree of *samādhi* compulsory (such as the fourth *jhāna* or even recalling previous births), or excluding the practice of *jhānas* altogether, or following a prescribed series of insight knowledges etc., what this interviewee is practising and recommending seems to be developing calmness and unification of the mind to a reasonable degree and looking into the mind, looking at whatever arises in the mind and whatever attracts the attention of the mind, in a manner that one sees causes and conditions (conditionality) coupled with "right view." However it should be noted that there are many other approaches to the Path recommended by the Buddha as seen in *Asaṅkata Saṃyutta* (SN: 43). This approach would lead to seeing things not only as dependently originated, but also as impermanent, unsatisfactory and non-self, thus would fulfil the practice necessary for abandoning taints "by seeing" [*āsavā dassanā pahātabbā*] as given in the *Sabbāsava Sutta* (MN: 2), which is the way to stream-entry. It also satisfies the practice of "*sīla, samādhi, paññā*" in general, leading one to higher fruits of the Path. Further, if application of right view is practised rightly, it would lead one progressively through the eightfold path factors up to right concentration (MN: 2). Whilst identifying causes and conditions for hindrances by itself weakens the hindrances and the fetters, the hindrances thus identified through looking into mind, could also be dealt with specifically, with the relevant tools recommended by the Buddha (e.g. ill-will to be dealt with through loving kindness). As per this recommendation of the practice, I reiterate; looking into mind and right view are the oars of the raft for going across to the further shore of the stream of *saṃsāra*.

Based on the foregoing chapters and our field research, I reiterate that many new trends of thought relating to supramundane fruits and noble persons and even public claims made by certain individuals with regard to the Path and its fruits, can be evaluated technically at least against the texts. In fact there is ample room to do so without having to accept them blindly or to reject them outright or even getting confused about contradictory views and opinions expressed by equally knowledgeable and known authorities. Above all, despite rampant distortions, myths and wrong views professed publicly, the true Dhamma is not limited to texts. True Dhamma is still very much alive, is taught generously and is practised diligently and discretely, even silently.

Future Research

The main focus of this study is the fruit that is stream-entry [*sotāpatti-phala*]. In this research I also found a number of cases which suggested higher fruits of the Path. I leave it to future researchers to investigate these experiences in more detail. However some of my observations warrant some comments.

This study inquired into the fetter-breaking-experience of each of the four fruits of the Path. The impact of the experience relating to the fruit that is once-returning [*sakadāgāmi-phala*] is not very prominent in the texts, to the extent that some feel that it is not an "event" like attaining the other three supramundane fruits. However from the outcome of our field research, it seems that this experience is striking enough to attract attention, to make a person look back and realize that further and significant progress was made by them on the Path or certain defilements were further reduced though not completely eliminated. Two of the interviewees felt that they drastically reduced defilements of desire for pleasures of the senses and ill-will (two fetters that reduce considerably with the fruit that is once-returning) based on a specific religious experience which occurred after the fruit that is stream-entry. One out of the said two interviewees identified this as the second fruit of the Path and the other was non-committal. Both the attainment of the fruit that is once-returning and the fruit that is non-returning could be addressed in detail in future research.

The idea of the series of the sixteen knowledges of *vipassanā* as referred to in the *Visuddhimagga* is another issue that needs further investigation. Though some of these knowledges could be distinctly identified in our interviews, the more advanced knowledges such as *anuloma ñāṇa* and *gotrabhū ñāṇa* ("conformity" and "change-of-lineage" insight-knowledges) could not be identified in practical terms, in the mental build-up of these interviewees. One reason for this could be the lack of advanced states of concentration in these interviewees as most interviewees were dry-insight meditators [*sukkha-vipassakas*] or *vipassanā-yānikas* (those using the vehicle of *vipassanā*). But just like the issue of the degree of concentration or *jhānas* necessary as a prerequisite for the practice of insight discussed above, the classification of the sixteen insight knowledges doesn't seem to have had a role in the practice of these interviewees except for Interviewee No. 3, who read a book presenting the seven stages of purification as presented in *Rathavinīta Sutta* which also presented the sixteen insight knowledges. This book helped him to make a break through to stream-entry. In fact some of our interviewees, including those who are meditation teachers (including Interviewee No. 3), reject the "sixteen insight knoweldges" approach to the Path on the basis that this series has complicated a very simple Path laid down by the Buddha in the *Suttas*. Some of them strongly feel that this approach has contributed substantially to the lack of progress in contemporary meditators.[10] All the other interviewees seem to have followed the *Suttas* directly as opposed to a secondary text such as the *Visuddhimagga*. This does not imply that they followed a path of dry insight. *Suttas* present both *samatha* and *vipassanā* as Path factors. As they proceeded with insight, they also experienced high states of concentration. Most of them seem to have adopted the approach of *samatha* preceded by *vipassanā* or both yoked together as referred to in AN II 156–158 (See p. 204). This also means that these interviewees chose not to follow a rigidly systematized Path as prescribed by contemporary meditation systems or complex texts such as the *Visuddhimagga*, but followed whatever steps laid down in the *Suttas* in general which based on their own judgement, they selected to be appropriate to their circumstances. The following incident reported by Ajahn Chah about his practice as a beginner illustrates the limitations of "systemized" or complex secondary texts. He says;

> At one time I went to see Ajahn Mun. At that time I had just begun to practice. I had read the *Pubbasikkhā* (A Thai Commentary on *Vinaya*) and could understand it fairly well. Then I went on to read the *Visuddhimagga* where the author writes on the *Sīlaniddesa* (Book of precepts), *Samādhiniddesa* (Book of mind training), and *Paññāniddesa* (Book of understanding)... I felt my head was going to burst. After reading that I felt that it was beyond the ability of a human being to practise. But then I reflected that the Buddha would not teach something that is impossible to practise. ... The *Sīlaniddesa* is extremely meticulous, the *Samādhiniddesa* more so, and the *Paññāniddesa* even more so! I sat and thought, "Well I can't go any further, there is no way ahead." It was as if I reached a dead end. (Chah 1994, 9)

Then he met Ajahn Mun and told him that he read the *Visuddhimagga* but it was impossible to put into practice. Ajahn Chah said to him that the content of these three *Niddesas* seem to be "completely impractical. I don't think there is anybody in the world who could do it, it's so detailed and meticulous. To memorize every single word would be impossible, it's beyond me." The Ajahn Mun responded; "if we were to take account of every training rule in the *Sīlaniddesa* that would be difficult ... true ... but actually what we call the *Sīlaniddesa* has evolved from the human mind. If we train this mind to have sense of shame and a fear of wrong doing, we will then be restrained, we will be cautious." Ajahn Chah says later he gradually let go all these; "when I understood more fully, I let it drop off, because it was too heavy. I just put my attention into my own mind and gradually did away with the texts." But he says when he teaches the monks, he still uses *Pubbasikkhā* as the standard (Chah 1994, 9–11). Similarly Venerable Ñāṇavīra in the *Clearing the Path* writes "My teacher, the late Venerable Nāyaka Thera, said in private that nobody had ever become *Arahant* through listening to the books of the *Abhidhamma Piṭaka.* He did not however say that they were wrong" (Ñāṇavīra 2002, 195).

The possibility of noble persons being reborn in the human world also warrants further research. A study of those who had attained supramundane fruits in this very life seems so full of obstacles, to recognize one born already with the first fruit of the Path could be harder. However it is promising that at least two of the interviewees who are experienced practitioners and meditation teachers thought they had recognized some stream-enterers reborn in this world and some of them were lay people continuing in lay life.

The Essence of this Research

In this work we discussed many debates and issues of contention about the Path and its fruits. I conclude that much of the confusion and debates about the Path and its fruits spring from lack of experiential knowledge, as against book learning. Let me quote two accounts from the texts which highlight the superiority of experiential knowledge.

The *Sumaṅgalavilāsinī,* the commentary to the *Dīgha Nikāya*, reports an incident which occurred between an erudite teacher Venerable Tipiṭaka Cūḷasumana Thero and his student Tipiṭaka Cūḷanāga Thero. There was a discussion between these two equally erudite monks as to the nature of the four *satipaṭṭhānas*. The student Cūḷanāga Thero stated that this Path is a "*pubbabhāga magga.*" The teacher, Cūḷasumana Thero expressing his opinion about the fourfold mindfulness stated that this Path is a "mixed path [*missaka magga*]."[11] When the teacher was insisting that this is a *missaka magga,* the student Cūḷanāga Thero, without contradicting the teacher, rose from his seat silently and walked away. The preceptor was much disturbed about this contradiction made by the student and was going towards a bath in deep contemplation about these issues and was considering the meaning of the *Mahāsatipaṭṭhāna Sutta*. He came to the point when he was contemplating on the meaning of the phrase "*... yohi koci bhikkhave cattāro satipaṭṭh*āne evam bhāveyya satta vassāni" (whoever develops the four applications of mindfulness in this manner for seven rainy seasons ...)At this point, realizing that he had not practised this Path for seven years and that he has not realized the *missaka magga* but Cūḷanāga Thero has trodden the Path and has realized the *pubbabhāga magga*, the teacher came back to the student and accepted publicly that the Path is a "*pubbabhāga magga*" and not a "*missaka magga*" as thought by him earlier (DN-a III 744, /*Papañcasūdanī* I (Sinhala trans., 294). This account illustrates that despite a rich tradition of book learning, when in disagreement, the tradition seems to uphold the superiority of the experiential knowledge. Hence in searching for answers to the issues discussed in this work with regard to the Path and its fruits, the experiences and opinions of successful practitioners as found in this research ought to receive due recognition.

The *Visuddhimagga* too reports a similar incident which occurred between two erudite monks in the Mahāvihāra, Anurādhapura, Sri Lanka. The elder Tipiṭaka

Cūla-Abhaya, who claimed that he had mastered the Tipiṭaka, but not its commentaries, wanted to expound the Tipiṭaka in the presence of the *Saṅgha* community. The community rejected him saying that he had not learnt the different interpretations of Dhamma from a range of teachers. Further, his preceptor wanted him to explain a particular passage and when Cūla-Abhaya did so in three different ways, he said only the first was right. So Cūla-Abhaya was directed to visit a teacher named Mahā-Dhammarakkhita and learn his interpretation of Dhamma-texts. Cūla-Abhaya proceeded to meet the teacher in the "Rohana country." Having met him and asked him to explain the Dhamma to him the teacher said, "friend Abhaya, they ask me about the *Dīgha* and *Majjhima* from time to time, but I have not looked at the other texts for thirty years. Still you may repeat them in my presence by night, and I shall explain them to you by day," and Cūla-Abhaya did so.

Next morning the villagers came to visit the teacher, as he was in the habit of expounding the Dhamma to them based on what was discussed the previous night. Mahā-Dhammarakkhita, having expounded the Dhamma to the villagers based on the previous night's discussion with Cūla-Abhaya, in the presence of the villagers themselves, sat down on the ground on a mat before Cūla-Abhaya and said to him, "friend, explain a meditation subject to me." Cūla- bhaya, taken by surprise, said "What are you talking about, venerable sir, have I not heard it all from you? What can I explain to you that you do not already know?" The teacher said to the student "Friend, as for the Path, it is different for one who has trodden it." It seems that Cūla-Abhaya was at least a stream-enterer by this time and the teacher was not. Having taken a meditation lesson from the student, before long the teacher attained Arahantship (Vism.III.53–55/Vism.97–98).

I think it fitting to encapsulate the essence of this entire research with the statement of Venerable Mahā-Dhammarakkhita Thero: *Añño esa āvuso gatakassa maggo nāma*—Friend, as for the Path, it is different for one who has trodden it!!

Notes

1. *Na saññasaññī na visaññasaññī*
   No pi asaññī na vibhūtasaññī
   Evaṃ sametassa vibhoti rūpaṃ
   Saññānidānā hi papañcasaṅkhā. (Sn. 170).
2. Interviewee No. 3 read a book called "*Satta Visuddhi*" which helped him to attain the first fruit of the Path. This is a simple book presenting the seven stages of purification as given in the *Rathavinītha Sutta* (as against complex secondary texts such as the *Visuddhimagga*) based on which certain meditation systems have evolved, (i.e. Pa-Auk meditation system). In fact this interviewee who is an experienced teacher is rather critical of the *Visuddhimagga* idea of the 16 *vipassanā* knoweldges (based on discussion with Interview No. 3).
3. It should be noted that these interviewees were not selected based on the meditation system they practised nor based on their association with certain forest hermitages to the exclusion of some others. In fact they belong to a range of forest hermitages, having different teachers (two belong to the same teacher but their practice differ from each other). In their search for the Dhamma, most of them have had a wide exposure to the Buddhist meditation systems currently practiced

in Sri Lanka and in the world. In fact one of them belongs to a hermitage which is widely known to practice a specific meditation system which he does not seem to identify with.

4. Though they identified themselves as dry-insight-meditators, two of them (Interviewees Nos. 2 and 5) were found to be in fact *vipassanā-yaānikas*, as they had also experienced *jhānas*. No.2 was barred by the teacher from engaging in *jhānas*.
5. Venerable Pa-auk Sayadaw refers to a "light of wisdom," a light that arises in the mind (not through eye-consciousness) whilst practising *vipassanā* (Pa-auk Sayadaw 1997, 25–31).
6. Even in *jhāna* practice, one has to let go of one level of *jhāna* to be able to attain a deeper level.
7. *Ye te suttantā tathāgatabhāsitā gambhīrā gambhīratthā lokuttarā suññatapaṭisamyuttā, tesu bhaññamānesu na sussusissanti, na sotam odahissanti, na aññācittamupaṭṭhāpessanti, na ca te dhamme uggahetabbam pariyāpunitabbam maññissanti. Ye pana te suttantā kavikatā kāveyyā cittakkhārā cittavyañjanā bāhirakā sāvakabhāsitā.*(SN II 266)
8. In the *Cūḷa-suññata Sutta* (MN: 121), movement through the *jhānas* and formless attainments is seen as a progressive abiding in emptiness, though are not the highest forms of emptiness.
9. *Bhūtam idanti bhante yathābhūtaṃ sammappaññāya passati. Bhūtaṃ idantiyathābhūtaṃ sammappaññāya disvā bhūtassa nibbhidāya virāgāya nirodhāya paṭipanno hoti.* (SN II 48)
10. Based on discussions (unrecorded) with the interviewees, particularly with Interviewee No. 2 and 3.
11. The relevant commentaries are not explicit about what these two types of paths are. It seems that *pubbabhāga magga is* one that develops within the first six stages of purifications of the mind, and *missaka magga* is a supramundane path.

Appendix I

The Questionnaire Used For the Fieldwork and its Rationale

The following are some of the questions used for the purposes of the interviews which gave a general guidance to the interviewer as to the approach to be used and topics to be covered. However, though it was intended to pose the same questions to all interviewees, the questions differed depending on how the discussion evolved. The questionnaire was specifically designed to investigate into the fruit that is stream-entry. However the possibility of higher fruits of the Path were also explored in brief.

Establishing the background of the interviewee

1) What is your nationality?
2) How long have you been treading this Path? (The Theravāda Buddhist Path in general)
3) When did you enter the Order?
4) How old are you?
5) What made you become a monk?
6) What made you search for this Path?

Establishing a specific significant religious experience

7) Could you describe your first significant religious experience on this Path?[1]
8) Can you describe how it happened, immediately before that what were you doing?
9) What was the thought process leading up to it?
10) Where were you when you experienced it?
11) When was it?
12) At what time of the day was this experience?
13) What was your meditation posture at that time?
14) Immediately before this experience, what was your meditation object?
15) Immediately before this, was your meditation *samatha* or *vipassanā*?
16) Can you explain your practice and your life-style in brief during this time?

Establishing clarity of mind with regard to the experience

17) How did you feel immediately after the experience?

18) Immediately after this experience what did you do?
19) Could it be that you fell asleep for a while?
20) Could it be hallucination or a creation of your mind? Why not?
21) Immediately before this, did you wish for it?
22) At the time of this experience how well read or informed were you about supramundane fruits?

Establishing the hallmarks of a stream-enterer and the knowledge realized by the attainment identified as or claimed to be the attainment of stream-entry

23) What is the essence of this experience?[2]
24) What is the significance of this experience? What is so important about it?
25) What do you think is *sakkāya-diṭṭhi*?
26) What is *sīlabbata-parāmāsa?*
27) Do you engage in *Buddha vandanā, bodhi pūjā* etc. or any other rites and rituals? Do you do these of your free will?
28) Did you engage in these rites and rituals before this attainment?
29) Do you have gratitude towards the Buddha?
30) Do you have faith or confidence in the Buddha?
31) Do you have *saddhā* in the Buddha? If so, why do you say so?
32) Do you have any doubts about the Buddha, Dhamma, and the *Saṅgha*?
33) Do you have *aveccappasāda* (unshaken confidence) in the Buddha, Dhamma, and the *Saṅgha* ?
34) Will you look for another teacher other than the Buddha for salvation from suffering?
35) What is *ariyakanta sīla* (virtue dear to the noble ones)?
36) Do you have any doubts about your *sīla*?
37) The texts refer to *ariyakanta sīla* of a stream-enterer. Do you think a stream-enterer's *sīla* is flawless? Don't they say even a white lie?
38) What is *paṭicca-samuppāda* (dependent origination)?
39) Could this experience be the experience of the supposed Creator God or the soul?
40) Could it be that it's a creation of the mind? Could it be a hallucination? Could be a mental aberration? If not, why not?
41) Did this experience lead to breaking of any fetters?
42) Did it reduce defilements?
43) What are the defilements it reduced?
44) Were you under a teacher before this experience?
45) Do you have a teacher now?
46) Do you feel you need a teacher to complete the Path?
47) Is this the experience of *sotāpatti-phala*? If so, how do you know it? What makes you think so?

48) Do you now know that the first three fetters have been eliminated within you? If so, how do you know it? Based on what evidence have you come to this conclusion?
49) Did you realize it yourself or did your teacher tell you or did you realize it yourself and got confirmation from a third party?
50) What are the defilements remaining in you?
51) Did you have any other experience, apart from this first experience, based on which the first three fetters could have been eliminated?
52) When your mind is not occupied with a specific issue or an object where does it naturally rest? Where does it return to by nature, what is the object it takes?
53) Do you plan to attain *Nibbāna* this birth itself or do you mind taking a few more births?
54) Do you think attaining *Nibbāna* is possible for you?
55) What is your concept of *Nibbāna?*

Specifically to ascertain whether there is right view

56) What is *paṭicca-samuppāda*?
57) What is your idea of view on personality?
58) Do you believe in divine worlds and hells? Are there such worlds?
59) Do you believe in gods/*devas*? Do you seek their help?
60) Have you had any encounters with gods or other non-humans?
61) Have you met any *Arahants*?
62) Do you believe that there are *Arahants* and other noble persons in this world today?
63) Could there be noble persons in Sri Lanka today?
64) Is it possible to attain supramundane fruits these days?
65) Is it possible for laypeople to attain supramundane fruits these days?
66) Is it possible to attain *Nibbāna* these days?

Investigating into the nature of the fetter-breaking-experience of a supramundane fruit

67) What was the nature of the peak moment of the (fetter-breaking-) experience? How did you feel it?
68) How did you feel at the zenith of this experience?
69) Can you describe the peak of this experience?
70) Is there sight, sound, smell, touch etc. at the peak point of in this experience?
71) Was there form, feeling, perception and mental formations at the peak of this experience?
72) Was there consciousness at the peak point?

73) A supramundane fruit is described as *animitta, appaṇihita suññata*, how do you see these in relation to your experience? Are these three similar, different or different facets of the same thing?

Differentiating this experience from the experience of *Nibbāna*

74) Is it *Nibbāna* that you experienced?
75) What is your understanding of *Nibbāna*?
76) What do you think is the difference between this experience and *Nibbāna*?
77) On this occasion, do you think even for a moment you experienced *Nibbāna*?

Inquiring into the experience of *phala-samāpatti*

78) Have you had a similar experience after that day? Has it recurred from time to time?
79) Do you experience it with prior determination or does it happen automatically?
80) Do you experience it when you are not meditating as well?
81) When you experience it, is your meditation *samatha* or *vipassanā*?
82) Is this *phala-samāpatti*?
83) Have you experienced *phala-samāpatti*?
84) Have you had similar experiences before the attainment of *sotāpatti-phala*? What is the difference between this and those experiences?
85) What is the difference between these repeated subsequent experiences and what you experienced on the day of the attainment of *sotāpatti-phala*?
86) Is *phala-samāpatti* a concrete test of a supramundane fruit?

Inquiring into the experience of higher fruits of the Path:

87) Have you continued with your meditation or taken any serious retreats after this experience?
88) Have you experienced fading away of the next two fetters?
89) Has it been experienced as a specific experience? (if so the same questions as before , posed in order to establish a specific experience) (Q.7–16).
90) Is this the attainment of *sakadāgami-phala*?
91) Is this experience similar, different or identical with your earlier experience relating to the *sotāpatti-phala*?
92) To inquire into the nature of the (fetter-breaking-) experience (the same questions as before, posed in relation to the nature of the fetter-breaking-experience (Q.67–73).

Inquiring into the possibility of the fruit that is non-returning

93) Have you cut off the next two fetters?
94) Has it been experienced as a specific experience? (if so the same questions as before to establish a specific experience (Q.7–16).
95) Do you have any attachments to the five sensual pleasures? Taste, sound, smell etc.
96) Do you exercise a choice with regard to these? Do you exercise this choice based on likes and dislikes?
97) Do you long for the sound of the Dhamma?
98) Would you like to be reborn in the *Brahmā* worlds?
99) Do you get angry?
100) Do you get irritated?
101) Are there any defilements remaining in you?
102) What are the defilements remaining in you?
103) To inquire into the nature of the peak-experience (the same questions as before in relation to the peak-experience. (Q.67–73)

Inquiring into the possibility of the fruit of Arahanthood

104) Have you experienced the fourth fruit? Arahanthood?
105) Is it based on a specific experience? (If so the same questions as before in order to establish a specific experience (Q.7–16).
106) Are there any defilements remaining in you?
107) With this new experience of cutting off all defilements, what is the difference in your view from that of the third fruit?
108) Do you feel fear?
109) Do you feel irritated over anything?
110) How do you feel? Is there happiness and joy?
111) Do you experience taste, smell etc.?
112) Do you experience feeling? Painful feeling?
113) How do you feel about your parents, family?
114) Do you feel you should serve the Dhamma?
115) Do you have *saddhā* in the Buddha?
116) Do you do Buddha *vandanā* now?
117) Are you ready to teach the Dhamma?
118) Do you plan for the future? What kind of things do you plan for?
119) Do you have any kind of attraction to anything at all?

To establish the role of *samatha* in the practice:

120) What is the role of *samatha* or *jhāna* in your practice?
121) Do you consider yourself a *samatha-vipassaka* or *sukkha-vipassaka*?
122) Did you use light-perception to develop *samatha*?

General

123) Would you recommend this Path to others?

124) Is there happiness and joy in you?

125) Are you happier now than before you started treading this Path?

126) When you started practising this, did you think that you would attain *Nibbāna* this birth itself?

127) Did you entertain the idea of "in this very life" at the beginning of your practice?

128) Do you plan to attain *Nibbāna* this birth itself or do you mind taking a few more births?

129) As a noble person, are you inclined to help others in whatever way you can or else are you inclined to go away from society and devote your time to your practice only?

130) Are you following any particular meditation system available today such as the Pā-auk, Goenka, Mahāsi systems?

131) Do you have any particular attraction or an interest other than realizing *Nibbāna*?

132) Have you come across stream-enterers by birth (those who have attained a *magga-phala* in a previous birth)?

Notes

1. This question was posed as a convenient starting point. The specific objective of the interview was to conduct research into the nature of the "supramundane fruits" of the Noble Eightfold Path. In general all interviewees had already agreed to co-operate. Interviewee was reminded of this immediately prior to the commencement of the interview. Those who were uncomfortable to answer this question either refused to participate in the research or the interview did not proceed with them beyond this point.
2. This question was posed on the assumption that the experience described by the interviewee as "his/her first most significant experience" is one related to the attainment of stream-entry. Whether the assumption was right or wrong was confirmed only based on the answers to a series of this type of pointed questions. In this process, we also found one interviewee who had not attained a supramundane fruit, but described his experience of *jhānas*. This interview has not been presented in this study.

Appendix II

Interview Synopses and Analysis

Interview No. 1

He is a 43 year old monk who is a Malaysian by nationality. He lives in a well established and well known forest hermitage situated away from Colombo, in Sri Lanka. The interviewee is not personally known to the writer. He was introduced to the writer for this purpose by his teacher, who is the chief preceptor of the hermitage. As of the date of the interview, his teacher had been closely known to the writer for over 12 years. The monk is not an *upasampadā* monk, hence was free to talk about his attainments, particularly after being requested by his teacher to have a discussion with the writer for this purpose.

The interview was severely hampered by a language barrier of the interviewee and a strong accent that was difficult to understand. Hence certain issues, though raised, were not followed up by the writer and certain other issues were never raised at all, as the writer felt that there wouldn't be clarity. Due to the same reason, transcribing was also enormously difficult, time consuming, frustrating and to that extent could have an impact on the accuracy levels. However, it is possible to follow the general trend of his thought process and understanding.

As the interview proceeded from stage to stage, it was found that he had attained Arahanthood. However as the writer was unaware of it at the early stages of the interview, answers to certain questions, i.e. regarding *saddhā*, right view etc. at the stage of the fruit that is stream-entry, may be obscured by the knowledge of his higher attainments.

The monk was a Mahāyāna monk before he came to Sri Lanka. He had got ordained five years prior to the interview and completed the Path in three years. During this time, other than talking to his teacher, the monk observed complete silence for three consecutive years and was totally engrossed in the practice.

It is noteworthy that the references to the four fruits of the Path are in terms of "percentages" (the degree) in which the defilements were reduced on attaining each fruit. Throughout the interview, the monk refers to his mind as "he." In observing his gestures, there was a regular hand movement of his bent arm stretching out in the "forward direction" indicating "going in" of the mind, as he explained the fetter-breaking-experience of the supramundane fruits attained by him. His main meditation object was "*asubha*" (the thirty two impurities of the body), subsequently combined with the meditation on the four elements. He declared that he is a *sukkha-vipassaka*, he says he has no *jhānas*, no psychic powers or other higher knowledges such as the ability to see previous births etc. and no *nirodha-samāpatti* (attainment of cessation of perception and feeling). The writer found him to be calm and collected, unassuming, pleasant and gentle in his disposition and with no barriers to smiling and laughing.

The interview was done by the writer in English in the said forest hermitage on 27th July 2006.

Attainment of *sotāpatti-phala*

1. How it has been expressed:

When he was practising *asubha* meditation, a bright light occurred within the body, two weeks after the commencement of the practice. Thereafter, when he was focusing that light on the various parts of the body, i.e. *kesā, lomā* etc. (head hair, body hair), after about one month, whilst doing walking meditation outdoor, he felt that his mind got cut off for a second or a minute, the mind "went in" to a different place, the mind didn't continue, he couldn't see anything. Immediately afterwards, he understood that 30% of his defilements had got cut off. He felt 30% of the "heavy duty" was no more, and felt very comfortable as though a 30% of heavy weight on his back has been thrown away (Q.37, 11, 13, 63, 100, and 102).

2. When, where, what time, in what posture?

In Sri Lanka, in the hermitage, when he was doing walking meditation outdoor, during day time, one month after he started to practise in this hermitage (Q.11, 29–35).

3. Does he admit that he has attained supramundane fruits?

He admits that he has attained supramundane fruits. As he is not an *upasampadā* monk, he is not restricted by rules of *vinaya* against discussing about his attainments with a layperson (Q.11).

4. The meditation object immediately before this experience:

Asubha (32 impurities of the body).

5. Did he wish for such an experience immediately prior to this experience?

No, except for the wish he had in general, to destroy defilements. He says:

> I don't wish anything, I my mind, my mind only I want to destroy defilements, this my wish only. I don't wish for *sotāpatti-phala* anything, I don't think about this thing, I think about how to destroy defilements (Q.36).

6. How long did it take for him to realize that it was an attainment of a supramundane fruit or that this experience resulted in breaking fetters?

Immediately after this experience he realized that 30% of his defilements had got cut off. But he realized that it was an attainment of a supramundane fruit only after he had the fetter-breaking-experience relating to his attainment of the *sakadāgmi-phala,* two months later (Q.52, 53, 55–57). He says:

> In that time I think I had to a few months, because I knowledge in that time, I not so very good. After the second stage, I understanding in that stage, first stage, when I go in, second stage I understand first stage, the difference (laugh).

7. Was the conclusion that it was a supramundane fruit reached by himself or with the help of a teacher?

By himself. He says:

> Actually I realized myself, but I can experience it already because I, I experience it, I don't know what is the stage because I very weak in wisdom. After that I can cut off, I saw my greedy, anger, delusion. I from that, because I all the time has the concentration. So I focused the *nāma* (name), so I understanding, reduce many already (Q.69).

8. Does he know that the first three fetters are no more in him?

Yes (Q.58–59, 54, 63, 72–73).

9. How does he know that the fetters are no more?

He understands that the defilements he had before are no more (Q.20, 49–50).

10. Was it based on this experience alone that the fetters broke?

Yes (Q.51).

11. Did all three fetters go together?

Yes (Q.64–65).

12. The nature of the fetter-breaking-experience as felt by him:

He felt that for a second, for a minute, his mind got cut off, the mind "went in" to a different place, the mind didn't continue, he couldn't see anything, he didn't feel the consciousness (Q.100–102, 105).

13.The essence and significance of the experience, knowledge that arose and effect/impact on life:

He understood "Path and fruition" and that if he continued the practice, he would destroy all defilements. He got confidence in the Buddha's teaching (Q.16, 21). He understood that 30% of his defilements got cut off (Q.11, 13, 19). He enjoyed the cutting off of defilements just as one enjoys the fruits of a tree after planting and nurturing it (Q.121–122). He understood that inside his body is filth, only four elements, felt that his body opened up as in an operation, his attachments reduced (Q.21), he understood that his body and the outside world is impermanent, *dukkha* (unsatisfactoriness) and "not-self" and that this "right view" cannot be changed even by his own mind (Q.54, 72–73).

14. Is it *Nibbāna?*

He understands this experience as the first stage of *Nibbāna* (Q.107).

> *Nibbāna* is free of suffering, I threw out 30% (Q.108). This stage is very different from *Nibbāna* (Q.114).

15. What is his concept of *Nibbāna?*

Fully no more defilements (Q.112).

16. Hallmarks of a stream-enterer:

1) Unshaken confidence in the Triple Gem:

He has unshaken confidence in the Buddha, the Dhamma and the *Saṅgha* and has no doubt in the Triple Gem (Q.74), he has gratitude towards the Buddha for showing him the Path, and will not seek another teacher (Q.81–85).

2) Does he engage in rites and rituals?

Prior to stream-entry he used to engage in these out of fear. Now he says every morning when he goes past the shrine room, he pays respect to the Buddha. He says he pays more respect now than previously, as the Buddha gave him the Dhamma (Q.76–80).

3) *ariyakanta sīla:*

He says after stream-entry his *sīla* got very strong. Now his *sīla* is unbroken (Q.86–93).

4) Right view:

With this attainment he realized the impermanence of his body and the outside world, he understood *dukkha* and *anatta* (Q.72–73). Also his views on Creator God (Q.17) and on the Buddhist cosmology (Q.21) are in line with right view.

17. Could this be the experience of the supposed Creator God or the soul? And if not, why not?

He says that he experienced it as a result of following the Noble Eightfold Path and it is not God or Soul.

> Oh no no no, this one easy, clear clear to our mind we follow the Dhamma, because the Buddha already go by this way, so we follow the Dhamma we experience it (Q.94).

18. Could it be creation of the mind, a hallucination?

He says it is not a creation of the mind or a hallucination, but a result of following the Noble Eightfold Path.

> Aaah, not creation, but we have to follow our Buddha's Dhamma, because no Buddha's teaching, we cannot go by this way (Q.95).

19. Could it be that he fell asleep for a while?

He was walking at this point of time and not asleep.

> It's like sleep, but the feeling is very different, the mind had concentration (Q.21).

20. By the time of this experience was he under a teacher?

Yes.

21. Beliefs and encounters with non-humans, gods and lower beings:

He believes in the existence of *deva* worlds, *brahmā* worlds (Q.174, 208) and the lower realms and has had some encounters with non-humans (Q.338–339).

Attainments of Higher Fruits

22. Attainment of *sakadāgāmi-phala*:

He continued to meditate on the 32 impurities of the body and after about two months from the attainment of stream-entry, in the same hermitage, whilst doing walking meditation, he attained the second fruit, *sakadāgāmi-phala*. His mind experienced a similar moment of "going in" like the fetter-breaking-experience relating to the *sotāpatti-phala*, but the feeling was different from the first experience. He felt that he had now cut off 60% of the defilements. Immediately after he attained it, he understood that it was the second supramundane fruit and it was at that time that he realized that with his earlier similar experience, he had attained *sotāpatti-phala* (Q.145–149).This fetter-breaking-experience, though similar, was stronger than the fetter-breaking-experience relating to the first fruit. With this attainment he understood that his greed and anger reduced significantly, as did delusion, his *sīla* was stronger, "right view" and the view of impermanence got stronger. The feeling was more enjoyable, more comfortable than the earlier experience.

> The defilements reduced very differently (Q.151) ... I reduced more strong greedy, previous more, now after that really less... less than 60% only, because I all the time had concentration, mind produced wisdom more already, understanding different, reduced more already, anger also reduced 60% already, delusion same also (Q.152) ... the difference is enjoy more, enjoy the comfortable, more comfortable (Q.135).

23. Attainment of *anāgāmī-phala:*

After about four months from the second fruit, in the same hermitage, in a sitting posture, he experienced a similar state of "going in" of the mind. He understood it as a supramundane fruit immediately after the experience. He realized that 99% of the defilements were destroyed. At first he thought that there were no more defilements remaining in him. The teacher had to remind him that altogether there are four stages on the Path, then, on his own he realized that he reached only the third and not the fourth fruit (Q.179–181). Afterwards he realized that 1–2% defilements were still remaining. This fetter-breaking-experience was felt as a deeper experience than the earlier two, but he experienced a similar "going in" of the mind (Q.164, 167, 175, 178).

With this attainment, there was no anger at all in him, there was a little bit of greed remaining. He felt he had no fear at all. Explaining this he described an incident where a snake came in to the *piṇḍapāta sāla* (hall where alms-food is offered) and he saw it as a "rubber band" and went up to the snake to catch him. Later he realized "how come, I am not frightened?" as previously he was frightened of snakes (Q.198). He realized that he was not afraid of death (Q.199). When someone scolds him or blames him, he can only smile. He was all the time happy. But he had a "little bit of attachment" to go to "heaven" (Q.174, 208) (*anāgāmīs* are reborn in *suddhāvāsas*, or "pure abodes," which are *brahmā* worlds, as they still have attachment to the pure form and formless states). There was no "lust" in him, but, "a little bit of delusion" remaining:

> Because now third stage go in, third stage already the defilements almost destroyed 90 more than 90%, 99% already. So I thinking at that time, may be no more already,

> after that I checked ah! A little bit delusion only 1–2% only, in there very different, because no more anger already, in that time, anger delusion greedy almost little bit only, little bit greed, anger is no more already (Q.167)... even if someone blame me, anger me, I only smile, only calm and peace only, I don't say anything, my mind not produce anger. So that stage even anything also I saw, I smiling already but attach, still little bit attachment. Ah! I would go to heaven, at this stage I was thinking, I thinking at this stage, I still go to heaven but all the time very happy, it produce happy many and no anger, anything no anger (Q.174).

As to his responses towards the five sense pleasures, he says there is no attachment to sense pleasures but there is an inclination to "habitual" things. Given a choice, the mind would reach something he is used to before, but it is not due to likes or dislikes; if something he likes is not available, it does not matter to him (Q.192–195). As to the question of whether the mind is attached to the sound of the Dhamma, he says "no, not even to the sound of the Dhamma, mind produces Dhamma" (Q.204–207).

Comparing the three stages, he says in the first stage, it's like defilements are "little bit (far from) him, like one foot away in front," in the second stage, they are further away, in the third, it's like "three feet away, in front (of him)" (Q.189). In this stage too, he did not wish for a fruit immediately before this experience; when the mind matured it automatically "went in" for a second.

24. Attainment of *arahantta-phala:*

On 28th March 2004, when he was walking up to the *kuṭī* of the chief abbot of the hermitage to attend to the duties assigned to him, half way along the walk way to that *kuṭī*, he attained the fruit that is *Arahanthood*. He distinctly remembers this date; there is no mention of a specific date with reference to the attainments of the rest of the fruits. It was after about one year from attaining his fruit that is non-returning and he was doing mediation on the 32 impurities and on the four elements, continuously observing his silence for altogether three years. Whilst he was walking, he focused on his mind and realized that his mind "went in" for one second then "*arising and stop again.*" Immediately he realized that all defilements had got cut off, he felt he had no more duties to fulfil.

> Because I thinking *deva*, want to rebirth again, I want to go to there, spend many time, so I continue because my aim is to destroy all defilements. Don't want to this, so I continually to practise more hard, more hard, more strong, ...in that time I focus 32 part. In one day very I continue even I sleep, I all the time 32 parts only (Q.232) ... I half way, I go to do my duty *Mahā Thera*, there, after that half way focus. He go in one second, he arising and stop again. I understanding "aah! No more already." All stop already, I understanding because I, I, I, in my mind. I told my teacher because I understand my teacher know my mind, I told my teacher, "teacher my duty no more, I already finished." My teacher very happy (laugh) (Q.220).

After this attainment he sees life as "empty," wherever he looks, he sees things only as "particles of air" arising and sees them like a television screen which is switched on but without an aerial. Though he can see things when he is with his eyes open, when he closes his eyes, the whole world for him is nothing but emptiness, he cannot even visualize his own face. There is emptiness all day long.

25. Psychic powers, divine eye, ability to see past births:

He has none of these. He says it is because he has no *jhānas*, specifically no 4th *jhāna* (Q.341–343). He also has no *nirodha-samāpatti* (Q.381).

(See Chapter 7 for a detailed analysis of the interview on his fruit of Arahanthood).

General

26. Does he experience *phala-samāpatti* or a state similar to that?

Yes, from time to time throughout the interview, he refers to the mind "going in" to experiencing a similar state of mind corresponding to the fetter-breaking-experience of the supramundane fruits he had attained (Q.39–44).

27. Was there a need for a teacher for him to complete the Path?

For the first fruit he needed a teacher, but thereafter, although the teacher was around he practised on his own. He says that after the first fruit, his mind was his teacher and wisdom arising in the mind can cut off defilements faster (Q.126–131).

28. Did he practise any particular meditation system such as the Goenka, Pa-auk, or Mahāsi system?

He had practised *vipassanā* in general, such as, meditation on *asubha* and on the four elements.

29. Use of *samatha*/ *jhānas* / light perception in the practice:

He is a *sukkha-vipassaka*. He says he has no *jhānas*, but he says he has developed *vipassanā jhānas* (See p. 279, n. 5) which is accompanied by light-perception. When doing *vipassanā*, he had developed a bright light, like having a spot light fixed on his heads, which he used as a flash light to direct inside his body. He could focus it on whatever part of the body he wanted to (Q.307–321) He says:

> When I sleep I don't know in that time, how come, focus intestines like torch light, torch light focused there ... Inside the intestines, my heart focused, "how come torch light?," I don't know this light, when I sleep in the mountain there "how come, they wake up, how come inside very bright?" ... because when I sleep, cannot sleep because, very very flash the mind, all the time how, the light like spot light put to my head (Q.356–364).

Interview No. 2

He is Sri Lankan monk who lives alone in a cave in a shrub jungle, away from Colombo, in Sri Lanka. He is known for his austere living. He lives under very rough conditions, in a cave without doors, windows and walls which is exposed to the wild animals and serpents day and night, with no electricity, his *kuṭī* having only a raised plank as his bed with a mosquito net. He lives on one meal a day and on his alms-round he goes to the closest village which is a few kilometres away from the cave.

He has been treading the Path for nearly 20 years, attained stream-entry as a layperson and then ordained in 1994. He has always lived alone, having refused higher ordination in order to be able to live alone. By nature very untraditional, he is very critical of current Buddhist trends, practices and traditions, contemporary meditation systems, the commentaries, practices within the *Saṅgha* community and certain rites and rituals practised by contemporary Buddhists. He is well read, has a very good knowledge of the Dhamma, a photographic memory and is able to quote the Dhamma from the texts with much ease, often with references to even the page numbers of a text. Nevertheless, he has never undertaken to deliver a formal sermon as he feels his untraditional ways and criticism of some current practices would affect the "*saddhā*" of the people. But he is constantly sharing his knowledge of the Dhamma with those who are in close contact with him.

Although he is living alone, he is from an established and well known forest hermitage of Sri Lanka. His preceptor is well known and was most respected for his realized knowledge and knowledge of the *Tipiṭaka* and is considered one of the best Sri Lanka had in the recent past.

As of the date of the interview, the interviewee has been closely known to the writer for over 12 years and he is very appreciative of the need for a research of this nature. However he refuses to admit directly his attainments as supramundane fruits, though this is not as such due to restrictions by the *vinaya* rules. When questioned as to why he is so reluctant to use the technical terms such as *sotāpatti-phala*, *sakadāgāmi-phala* etc., though he admits that certain fetters are no more in him, he thinks that all fruits of the Path less than *Nibbāna* are more concepts rather than real, and he sees the danger of concepts and that clinging to these can take one on a subtle "ego trick," so that even *Nibbāna* becomes "my *Nibbāna*."

This was the first interview conducted in this series of research interviews; hence there was a considerable amount of discussions held with him in order to formulate the queries, before the formal interview was done. Some of the questions raised in the subsequent interviews were missed out in this interview as the questionnaire developed later as we proceeded with the research.

The interview was done by the writer, in English, on 23rd May 2006, in Colombo.

Attainment of *sotāpatti-phala*

1. How it has been expressed:

His meditation system at first was "labeling," whatever he felt or that got focused on by the mind was noted by assigning a label to it such as "sitting," "standing," "feeling," "thinking" etc. One day when he was labelling in this manner for some time, the mind refused to label any more; it was tired of labelling, and at a point he experienced a "cessation," a "gap," a "gulf" a "total blankness" in his consciousness, everything stopped, he didn't feel the consciousnesses for a short while till it again appeared. This way the "consciousness" appeared and disappeared in quick succession, within a short period, for a couple of times, so that he realized he experienced something special. But at first his mind refused to accept it as having anything to do with a supramundane attainment. Much later he realized that it was "non-becoming" that he had experienced. He says:

> Something strange thing happened. I was meditating according to my teacher's instruction, but, aaah, that really I didn't accepted as, aaah, the way I want, but anyway I did whatever they asked me to do and I realized something like I was fall-

> ing asleep while meditating, everything stopped, and, aaah, my ... (Q.3). ... yes that experience is, it's like total blank, it's like dead or slept, it's a big gap (Q.8) . ... It's a gulf, something like that; I mean I couldn't label any more (Q.9). ... I was seated. They asked me to put label as much as possible, but thoughts are coming, sensations are coming, at that time so much going on picture, the only thing I can say "knowing knowing" that much, and something I can't put the exact label, but so much coming in. But after some time I couldn't do that even, then stopped somewhere, I don't know what happened, it's like the sleep, then again it came, then again it died (Q.11). I looked back and thought I was sleeping ... the mind refused to accept it as something special but still I went and reported it to the teacher (Q.3) . ... I don't think I, I still think that I slept. I couldn't label that's the thing. I, I couldn't label (Q.18). ... But later, then I realized this is something like, if it is not sleeping, it is "non-becoming" (Q.4).

2. When, where, what time, in what posture?

He was in a sitting posture. There is no mention of the place and time as the relevant questions had not been posed at the interview.

3. Does he admit attainments of supramundane fruits?

He doesn't admit directly that he has attained *sotāpatti-phala*. However he admits that in him, the first three fetters (*sakkāya-diṭṭhi, sīlabbata-parāmāsa, vicikiccā*) have been eliminated and that they have been eliminated "relative" to the said experience. Having reflected on it and upon the recurrence of it, he realized that he is on "track," on the Path, on the stream, that "cessation of becoming" has begun for him. The first three fetters are eliminated at the stage of *sotāpatti-phala*. In addition he admits that the hallmarks of a *sotāpanna*, i.e. unshaken confidence in the Buddha, the Dhamma and *Saṅgha* and strong commitment to *sīla* are present in him and these sparked off "relative" to this experience. Furthermore, there are indirect admissions of higher fruits of the Path, (i.e. the fruit that is non-returning) (Q.25, 29–36).

4. The meditation object immediately before this experience:

Labelling whatever that gets focused on in the mind, i.e. "sitting," "standing," "walking," "feeling," "knowing" etc.

5. How long did it take to realize that it resulted in the attainment of a supramundane fruit or that this experience resulted in breaking fetters?

Much later, close upon one year from this experience.

6. Was the conclusion about the attainment of a supramundane fruit reached by himself or with the help of a teacher?

First when the teacher indicated to him that he had attained stream-entry, he refused to accept it. Much later, having investigated it for nearly one year, he himself came to the conclusion that the "fetters are no more" in him and that the "process of cessation" has begun for him.

7. Does he know that the first three fetters are no more in him?

Yes.

8. How does he know that the fetters are no more?

By acquiring more knowledge about the Dhamma and having investigated and watched his mind.

9. Did all three fetters go together?

Yes.

10. Was it based on this experience alone that the fetters broke?
"Relative" to this experience (Q.51).

> I got some sort of confidence, I mean relative to that cessation, I can project the *Nibbāna*, "there can be," the assurance came (Q.51) ... not really from that experience, from that experience only I realized that personality view and all these things, very much later. Then with comparing and judging all these things, later I realized yes, that is possible, the Path is clear, not immediately after that (Q.55).

11. Nature of the fetter-breaking-experience as felt by him:

A total blankness in consciousness, as though consciousness disappeared.

12. Thought process immediately after the experience:

He thought he fell asleep or the mind was lazy. Immediately he looked into his mind. But he realized that he was energetic, he was in an erect sitting posture (Q.14–16, 21).

13. The essence and significance of the experience, knowledge that arose and effect/impact on his life:

Much later, having read books, discussed and reflected on this experience, he understood it to be "cessation of becoming." He realized that the "process of cessation" had begun for him. He realized that he is on track, on the Path, stream, (to *Nibbāna*), he realized that his "Path" is very correct. He realized that he is not the same person any more, his attachments were less, his mind started to reject "entertaining" various extraneous objects and thought processes that he had entertained up to that time. He cut down on reading, listening to music etc. for entertainment; he restrained himself by himself without anybody else's prompting. Earlier he undertook *sīla* as something "enforced" on him, but now he realized the need for it. He changed his meditation object from labelling to watching the mind and all the time started to watch his thought process.

> I started this one, looking into the mind ... That was much easier, I can see it is always the reacting and attachment and it is swinging here and there. But I learnt my own technique, mastering, let it go here and there, but I'll be an independent observer. But I couldn't, because attachments are so strong it started telling stories, thought process going on along with that. But later I realized, if my attachments cut down, giving the names and proliferating thought process also stop. So I little by little, the entertainment part cut down. That's the training what I did, my own way, stopped listening to music, reading this one, that is automatic suggestions, talking to people. Earlier I did because they asked me to do; now inner suggestion, I knew the danger. All these things, the precepts—I can't remember all these precepts now, all the ten precepts, I knew the danger now. Looking for

> comfort and all these things, I knew for sure it won't come; one day will give me the pain. Therefore I restrained myself inside. Even now you can see I won't take even plain tea. Though they call it *gilanpasa* (medicinal drink), because that conditions, such a way. Then I realized thought process, it won't ask any more. Then only I came to know this cessation is started now, I am on the track. Not the same "I am," the mind is on the track, it's trained, automatically it adjusted itself according to the environment. I need not to push any more, aaah that's the way I realized that this Path is very correct (Q.5).

He realized that when he encounters something externally, by looking within he can control his mind:

> But I trained it, "don't look! It's trouble" so I restrained it at that level, but no labelling, changed the pattern completely. Instead of seeing something, I see my mind get colourful, colourful in the sense whether it is black or white, I mean give it a some sort of feeling for the mood. Or it goes beyond that and label it, identify. For that process I cut down slowly, slowly, because, aah, I realized if I control my senses and cravings, I can stop that (Q.23).

He realized that "becoming" is the source, there is nothing called "I am," there is nothing that is not subject to change, nothing in this world that he can rely on, depend on as permanent, there is no such thing as soul or self, that the whole world system consists of projections of the mind including God and the Buddha. With this realization, the first three fetters were broken; there was no doubt about the Path, *Nibbāna* and in the Triple Gem:

> Aah later, when I realized and analyzed "becoming" is the source, "I am" is not there, whatever thought arise it doesn't matter to me, let it go as it is. So then I see, I realized there is nothing in the world either within or without to save. Everything is a constant change of, our existence itself change, constantly change, but we are craving "to be with," our mind really not "we" because it wants to exist. So I realized that there is nothing whatever you do, hear and taste (that you) can rely on. Therefore I realized, aah, there is no one. They explained the "*sakkāya-diṭṭhi*" as view on personality, but my point of view, it is [the view that there is] something permanent, eternal, essence either within or without that you can depend on, you in the sense, I know that we are getting old and die, so after that I'll be peaceful somewhere, aaah, relative to my soul or self, but that is no more exist, there is no such thing as Soul (Q.24) ... when I realized that there is no such thing as you can depend on, all the doubts and all rituals all gone. Altogether, simultaneously. Not one by one. Because they, when I asked teachers what are the doubts, they say "*buddhādiaṭatan*" (the eight doubts such as doubting the Buddha etc.), even it was not explained. Even Buddha is not a reality; that is what the Buddha found as far as I am concerned. It is not his body, neither feeling, nothing, that is his Enlightenment. There is nothing [that is an] essence inside or outside, so then if there is nothing, what is there to doubt? Buddha is Buddha that is right, what is there to save? Therefore, what's the use of doing rituals? What is, nothing to save (Q.28).

He realized that what he experienced was "temporary cessation" and relative to that he could "project" what *Nibbāna* is, permanent cessation; he got confidence that he can attain *Nibbāna*, he got the "assurance of *Nibbāna*" (Q.48–51).

14. Is it *Nibbāna?*

> Not knowing what is *Nibbāna* how I can say (laugh)? Unless I have totally eradicated or extirpated all defilements, I can't come to that conclusion (Q.50).

15. What is his concept of *Nibbāna?*

He feels what he experienced is temporary cessation, *Nibbāna* is permanent cessation.

16. Could this be the experience of the supposed Creator God or the Soul? And if not, why not?

He says what he experienced was the undefiled nature of the mind, if one can penetrate the norm of Dependent Arising, then such a person can experience the undefiled nature of the mind, not God or Brahmā.

> I think God is gone long time ago (laugh) because God, Buddha and everyone is our creation, the whole world. Mind is so tricky that it can create any damn thing if you give it a value. Even *Nibbāna* you can create. It's a concept (Q.120)... To understand this one you have to go back to what Buddha has preached about it, that is dependently arising. If you penetrate to that norm, then you can see the pure nature of the mind, undefiled, that's what you experience. Relative to that only you can judge. You can achieve to that undefiled nature, mind that is not God or Brahmā. If you cling to it you are finished, because, that is another subtle ego trick. Very subtle, but you are attached. You entertain that as "my *Nibbāna*" (Q.122).

17. Could it be that he fell asleep for a while?

First he had a doubt whether he fell asleep for a while, but he felt he was very energetic at the time. However, later he realized that it is not sleep, that it was "non-becoming" that he experienced.

18. By the time of this experience, was he under a teacher?

Yes.

19. Hallmarks of a stream-enterer:

1) Unshaken confidence in the Triple Gem

He has unshaken confidence and no doubt in the Triple Gem based on his direct experience (para.13 above—i.e. the essence of this experience). Further, he says he has hundred percent confidence in the Buddha, in Buddhahood and has gratitude towards the Buddha for showing the Path:

> I know certain defilements are no more in my mind. It never comes. I am very sure about it. So therefore I know the Buddha has following this Path, he has totally extirpated, routed out all defilements; whatever defiles your mind, colourful and I mean prejudice, bias and all these things, he hasn't got. Now I have 100% confidence [in the] Buddha, what is Buddhahood is (Q.42) ... I'll do anything, not for Buddha, [but for] who is trying to follow this Path, yes, I, I sacrifice my whole life on behalf of them, that is my gratitude to Buddha, for the *sāsana*, yes (Q.41).

2) Does he engage in rites and rituals?

He used to engage in rites and rituals before he attained stream-entry, but not thereafter. He realized that there is no point engaging in rites and rituals because he understood that there is nothing within and without worthwhile trying to protect (Q.28, 38–39).

3) *Ariyakanta sīla*

With this attainment *ariyakanta sīla* got established in him (para. 13 above). He feels that the concept of *ariyakanta sīla* can be understood only by another *ariyan* disciple and not by a *puthujjana*. He says it's a moral attitude against engaging in acts which are blamed by one's own mind, one's own conscience. He says that a stream-enterer can break his *sīla*, but he would be very mindful, he watches his mind and knows when it is broken. What is meant by "*akhaṇḍa*" (unbroken) is at a mental level, that is, he is fully aware of what is happening in the mind. Therefore he will not repeat the breach unless he would break one to safeguard against a more blameworthy situation. This interviewee admits that he says a white a lie (Q.43–47).

4) Right view

With this attainment, right view got established in him (para.13 above), that is, view on personality got eliminated. Also his views on a Creator God (para.16 above) and on Buddhist cosmology (para.26) are in line with right view.

Attainments of Higher Fruits

20. Attainment of *sakadāgāmi-phala:*

To the question on whether he has experienced the fading away of the next two fetters, he relates the following incident.

Much later [than the experience relating to his attainment of stream-entry] he was doing walking meditation in his *kuṭī* on one rainy night with thunder and lightning. Lightening struck the floor of his *kuṭī* and the floor cracked right in front of him, by his foot. For a moment he was frightened, shocked, but immediately as he had trained himself to do, he looked into his mind. For a moment the mind was totally blank, just like in the fetter-breaking-experience relating to the fruit that is stream-entry. After a while he realized that he was not walking any more but standing, and then he gave his mind the command to continue with his walking meditation: "what are you doing? You are supposed to be doing walking meditation." As he started to walk, there was another thunder bolt, but this time he realized that there was no shock and no fear in his mind. Again the mind went into a "blank." This way the mind was experiencing the "blankness" a "gap" or "not feeling the consciousness" two to three times in quick succession. When he looked within he realized that the mind was "not reacting" any more, he realized that there "was no fear in his mind or that fear has faded away." He says:

> Well I don't know the, whether next two fetters were breaking away or fading away ... much later, while I was walking alone, aaah, in thundering shower, inside the *kuṭī* there was a thunderbolt, I think I was petrified, I because of the lightning, petrified or shocked I don't know, I can't really remember, and immediately I thought I'm dead already and but my mind was trained to look in, it was trained. When it looked in, I didn't know where I was or standing or sitting, I can't remember the ... (not clear) It was totally blank, after some time, I can't say the period a thought arise "aaah, what are you doing? You are supposed to be walking." But in spite of mind's wish I tried to raise the leg, another thunderbolt blasted. So (laugh) then

> I thought no shock this time, no fear neither, when I look into the mind, but it's still and very reluctant to act for the first command, to walking meditation, ... I walked, another thunder blasted, nothing happened, I usually, normally, usually about 2–3 hours I walk and I got wet also because for the first thunderbolt it was cracked [the roof] (Q.61).
>
> I thought I was petrified...It's blank again. Total blank. Then only the thought came to reflect, because I was trained to look into the mind throughout, it automatically went and looked and again it's blank. Very much later only the thought came "you are still alive" ... Then the thought arise "What are you doing? You are supposed to do the walking meditation" (Q. 63)...It went blank once again. That is not so strong, but it was not reacting, though the command came to walk (Q. 72)...the mind went blank this way two or three times (Q.73), immediately after that (Q.74).
>
> As it recurred, the experience was not as strong as when it happened for the first time (Q.75–76). Immediately after the experience, he realized that his fear had faded away (Q.78). Unlike the attainment of the first fruit, his realization was immediate (Q.79).

Comparing the above to the earlier fetter-breaking experience relating to the fruit of stream-entry, he says it was a similar "gap," a similar state of "blankness"(Q70) but in earlier experience he had thought that he had fallen asleep (Q.77). This time, though wondering if he was shocked and petrified, he immediately realized that "the mind is not reacting" and that there was "no fear or the fear has faded away" (Q.77–79).

> Yes similar experience, earlier occasion I told you I doubted whether I was sleeping and, aaah, this occasion I suspected I was petrified or shocked or something like that. But both occasions my mind was somewhat void or blank whatever, there is a gap something like that, something unconscious state (Q.77).

But he says if he was shocked or unconscious, as he was standing, he would have fallen down (Q.70). Further, he says his immediate reaction was to look into his state of mind and realized the state of the mind as having no fear (Q.66). Hence if he was shocked or immediately after recovering from unconsciousness, he would not have been so alert to investigate his mind and to realize the state of the mind which he analyzed later as "a mind not reacting"(Q.68–69). Furthermore, he compares this state of mind with a subsequent experience and a consequent state of mind which we analyze as the fruit that is non-returning (Q.66).

During this incident he was not under a teacher and his meditation object was watching the mind, whether and how it was reacting (mindfulness of the state of mind and the thought processes). There was no wish for any supramundane fruit immediately before the incident, as both these incidents occurred unexpectedly.

21. Attainment of *anāgāmi-phala:*

As to our query about any subsequent significant experiences, he relates the following. When he was washing some dishes outside a monastery, in broad daylight at around 1 p.m., suddenly someone nearby told him that there was a huge snake coming their way. The monk told him to let it be, that he was not bothered. However this man, despite protest by the monk, took a stone and threw it at the snake. The snake hissed, put his hood up moved forward in his direction but stopped about two meters away in front of him. Just then the monk heard the sound of some dry leaves moving behind him and then he realized that there were two more snakes coming in his direction at great speed. He was surrounded by three snakes, two on either side and one in front of him. Then his training was to look within, to look into his mind. After some time a man came and shook him saying, "what are you doing?, the serpents have come and gone." Then he realized that for some time his mind had been totally "blank," he was standing but had stopped his work, his eyes were fully open and he was conscious, fully aware, but he didn't see or hear the commotion of people shouting and snakes going away. They thought that he was frightened and shocked and as a result couldn't move. But he realized that one fetter or defilement has gone forever, he got confirmation that fear was no more, "reacting power" had gone forever, there was no fear of death, the "mind is now bold enough to face death" (Q.82–89):

> Now I was surrounded by on either side two and in front one, three (snakes). Then what I trained was not to identify the snake but identify what is happening inside my mind. When I checked, I mean I looked in, now it is very conscious, totally blank and I didn't know I have already stopped my work what I was, I was washing some dishes outside and, aaah, I was not doing that. I think someone came after some time and shook me "what are you doing? Here there are serpents and they have gone away." They thought that I was panicky and I can't move my legs, really not so. I knew, awareness totally there, but I was watching my mind, its blank (Q.84). ... I got the confirmation that I have no more fear for the death or protect anything, it's gone completely (Q.86).

Comparing the previous two fetter-breaking-experiences with this, he says the mind was blank, there was no feeling, just as on the earlier two occasions, but he thinks that this experience is stronger (Q.93–94). In the earlier two experiences, initially there were doubts, however this is a "contrast," a "vivid experience" as it was in broad daylight, amidst a lot of commotion, the mind was not tired or lazy, but fully energetic, and he got immediate confirmation of the "fetter" breaking. The nature of the fetter-breaking-experience is the same as the earlier two experiences:

> It's, aah, it's really blank. non-reactive, no thought coming at all, no fear, no colourful, pain, or words, this time it is not lazy. All the time I told you it was tired and lazy. Now fully energetic, fully aware but I got the confidence one fetter is gone forever, fetter or defilement whatever there was or reacting power has gone forever. No more. (Q.89) ... Difference in the sense, aaah, earlier I didn't believe it, but this time I was very conscious and broad daylight and ... nothing was there, people are there, serpents are there, therefore it's a very vivid experience, contrast, and with that I got the confirmation also my mind is now bold enough to face the death (Q.95).

When questioned whether this is the fruit that is non-returning, he doesn't admit it as such. However there was indirect admission as the interview proceeded. When asked, "what is your current practice and what are you working towards?," he says "if I am *anāgāmī*, if I am, I don't know, if that is the stage, I'll be in real trouble. Eons and eons I have to 'be'." A non-returner does not attain Arahanthood in this birth, he is said to take rebirth in the *suddhāvāsa brahmā* worlds where the life span is for eons. He says:

> But I am very afraid of another becoming at anyway, that means any attachment I don't like, I in the sense my mind is afraid, that's what I mean (Q.112).

He adds, "it's a very critical point, if I get stuck I don't know where I will end up." The fact that this monk who is not afraid of death is worried about ending up in *brahmā* worlds shows that what he is afraid of is of the "destiny" of a non-returner, that is, rebirth in the *suddhāvāsa brahmā* worlds.

His state of mind is further confirmed by his answer to the question "what are the defilements remaining in you?": "it is conceit and *vibhava-taṇhā,*" the latter being craving for annihilation. From the discussion that follows at this point it is clear that he is very concerned about "*bhavarāgānusaya,*" the latent tendency of attachment to becoming, and that *vibhava-taṇhā* and conceit are the most prominent defilements in him at this point of time. The remaining five fetters of a non-returner which have to be eliminated to attain Arahanthood include conceit [*māna*] and ignorance [*avijjā*]. Out of the three types of cravings [*taṇhā*], i.e. craving for sense pleasures [*kāma-taṇhā*], craving to be [*bhava-taṇhā*] and craving to not be [*vibhava-taṇhā*], the *kāma-taṇhā*, the craving for all strands of pleasures of the senses, is eradicated at the stage of non-returner. However the *bhava-taṇhā* and *vibhava-taṇhā* are yet to be eradicated. V*ibhava-taṇhā* and the fetters of conceit and ignorance are highlighted in his following statements;

> Self-hatred I think, I don't want to become, and that "I" part is still there (Q.115)" ... I don't want to stop here, here is a very dangerous critical point (Q.111) ... But I am very afraid of another becoming at anyway, that means any attachment I don't like, I in the sense my mind is afraid (Q.112) ... I know the theory, but practically I can't apply. Still the attachments are there. Conceit is there. So it's a very helpless situation (Q.122) ... I know the way out is there definite, techniques are there, but some attachment to this, I think the "*bhavarāgānusaya,*" I think Q.123) ... that is because *bhavarāgānusaya*'s other side is *vibhava taṇhā*. I want to non-existing self, to annihilate. By doing this I encourage it to come up, that situation I can't help (Q.125).

When inquired into his attitude towards sense pleasures, he says that his mind now refuses to follow music, which he was very attached to previously; the mind feels "what's the use?" even the words (of a song) fade away in the mind (Q.106). Where food is concerned, he says earlier he used to select food to nourish his body but now he doesn't. No more vitamins – if he falls sick he makes a "temporary arrangement." He lives on one meal a day and eats and drinks the bare minimum to the extent of practising the *dhutāṅga*s, or ascetic practices. When *gilanpasa* (medicinal drink) is offered, his response is "for what?." He says his mind refuses to accept even irritable things, often he has to think twice of the words as the words tend to fade away in his mind due to lack of interest (Q.107). With regard to irritable things he says "when I hear something, irritable things, that also mind refuses to accept, [it says] let it go, [leave it] as it is!, leave things!"(Q.107).

General

22. Does he experience *phala-samāpatti* or a state similar to that?

On several occasions after the attainment of stream-entry, when his teacher asked him to do so, by prior determination he experienced a state of mind similar to the fetter-breaking-experience of the fruit that is stream-entry for almost the exact time period he resolved for, with the variation in time period for which he resolved and what he actually abided in, was two seconds.

23. Is there a need for a teacher for him to complete the balance of the Path?

He had a teacher only for the first fruit. Thereafter he has been practising and living on his own without a teacher.

24. Did he practise any particular meditation system such as the Goenka, Pa-auk or Mahāsi system?

He does not associate himself with any specific meditation system available today, and is very critical of them. He has followed the *Sutta*s in general.

25. The use of *samatha/jhāna/* light-perception in the practice:

At the beginning of his practice he developed light-perception and *jhāna*. He enjoyed it so much and played with it the whole day, sometimes skippng even his lunch. Because of his strong attachment to it, his teacher stopped him from entering into *jhāna*. From that point onwards, he never developed *jhāna*, his practice was developing calmness and unification of mind sufficient to understand what is happening in the mind. He says now he has no *jhāna*, in fact as his mind is afraid of being reborn in the *brahmā* worlds, the mind rejects getting absorbed in *jhāna*s, it reverts back to watching the mind.

26. Beliefs and encounters with non-humans, gods and lower beings:

He has had no encounters with non-humans, however he believes in other realms of existence such as the *brahmā* worlds. But we omitted to raise this specific question in the interview.

27. Inclination to serve/teach the Dhamma:

Though he leads a secluded life, he helps others immensely to tread the Path. He says he will sacrifice his whole life on behalf of them.

28. Whether the fetter-breaking-experience is *animitta*, *appaṇihita* and *suññata* and how he understands it in relation to his experience:

He understood these as different facets of the same thing.

> Mind has no object to hang on, it has no craving to identify, I think that's what happened. It was so fed up, it couldn't label it. So that means he didn't, never identify the object and no craving for that because of the tiredness (Q. 56)... That is void of any self, there is nothing, no essence there, always flowing, coming and going down, coming and going down, so what is there to label? (Q.57)... I think different facets of the same thing. It's not three different things (Q.59)... It's not three different paths or like that, same thing, but different perspectives of your own view (Q.60).

29. His Advice to practitioners:

To the question "what is your advice for a person who is seriously aiming at final goal?" He says:

> Then Just start right now. Leave precepts alone. You need not adhere to precepts.

> You don't need the Buddha, Buddha has laid down the Path, now Buddha is no more there, when you see your mind you can see Buddha. Nothing worth to adhere because it changes, keep on changing, you are dragging, you are entertaining as an actor. In the same character, the main actor is to get established that's because of our craving for existence. Though it is suffering still we want, editing the way we want. If you understand that and the danger of that editing part and acting part, then mind will learn a lesson not to do that anymore. That is your morality or whatever *sīla* or whatever it is. It becomes restraint by itself. (Q. 136)

When asked whether his advice is only *sīla* he says:

> Not *sīla*, looking in to the mind. That the only thing I asked you and see how it reacts. So far we think we know, everyone knows with a little bit of intelligence our body is not ours." It decays and dies but we think some essence is there somewhere within or without that he can depend on. Mostly we grasp our mind or thoughts. Therefore try to understand what is that essence, whether it is reliable thing. Today it says something, tomorrow another story, with this experience, that is enough for you to understand what is happening. The most unreliable in the world is your mind, don't trust it. (Q. 137)... Once you understand it's cheating, it automatically letting go. That's where the Path starts (Q.138).

Interview No. 3

He is a 54 year old Sri Lankan monk who lives in a well known forest hermitage situated away from Colombo, in Sri Lanka. This monk is currently the chief preceptor of the hermitage and is well known and respected as a teacher locally as well as internationally. He is very well read and well exposed to and in touch with the current academic trends too. He is known for his untraditional and outspoken nature. He is very critical about contemporary practices and rites and rituals within the *Saṅgha* community and also amongst the laypeople.

He has been treading the Path for the last 27 years. He started meditation in 1980 and had his first significant spiritual experience on this Path (fetter-breaking-experience of *sotāpatti-phala*) nearly 15 years prior to the interview, in 1988, as a layperson. Within months from this experience he got ordained as a monk as he felt he needed to serve the *Sāsana* in return and received his higher ordination in 1999. His preceptor is well known and was most respected for his realized knowledge and knowledge of the *Tipiṭaka* and was considered one of the best Sri Lanka had in the recent past.

The monk is closely known to the writer for over 12 years and he is very appreciative of the need for research of this nature. However he refuses to admit directly that he has attained supramundane fruits and refuses to identify them by the relevant technical terms, obviously due to restrictions by the *vinaya* rules. When questioned as to whether certain experiences he has had on this Path relate to the attainment of *sotāpatti-phala*, *sakadāgāmi-phala* etc., though he admits that certain fetters are no more in him, and some others have reduced, he says he sees no reason to declare it in terms of "three out of ten fetters gone" etc., and says that if the writer wants she can call it even "chocolate or ice cream." Whilst admitting that an irreversible spiritual shift took place within him based on a certain religious experience, his references to the "nature" of the experience as being "not worth a penny," "having no significance or substance," "It is not possible to even sell it in a market and buy something," are typical of his untraditional and "radical" traits which were predominant prior to *sotāpatti-phala*. All he confirms is that an "irreversible spiritual shift" took place within, a "chemical change" or a "transformation without remainder" occurred and it is on the *vipassanā* side and not on the *samatha* side. Further, that based on this shift certain fetters were gone without remainder.

He also admits that subsequently he trained to abide in *phala-samāpatti* in terms of the instructions of a teacher which is an indirect admission of having attained a supramundane fruit. He describes *phala-samāpatti* as a skill developed by him to escape from the sense bases and to abide in an "oceanic" experience. Within two weeks of his religious experience relating to the attainment of *sotāpatti-phala*, he had experienced a "series" of "qualitatively similar" and "qualitatively different" experiences to his first experience. Though he feels *kāmacchanda* and *vyāpāda* are fading away in him, he does not admit that they are totally eradicated. In response to the question on whether these two fetters have been eradicated, he says that in his *āranya* environment there is no opportunity to test his mind against them. Hence there is no confirmation in the interview about the attainment of the fruit that is non-returning (or even once-returning).

What is striking in this interview is that during the lead-up to his attainment of *sotāpatti-phala*, in general he was not "consciously" abiding in the expected a minimum *sīla* (five precepts) and in fact was ridiculing those who were abiding in *sīla*. He had the mindset of a radical wanting to break all norms and practices conducive to the attainment of supramundane fruits and was not under a teacher. However he was in a meditation centre, working as a staff member as he had just lost his job as a senior manager in the private sector and was in the company of meditators. Also he had been experimenting with the practice and engaging in discussions and reading on the subject for about three years prior to the date of his significant religious experience and was well aware of supramundane fruits. He attained the first fruit of the Path while he was reading a book, *Satta visuddhi* (*The Seven Stages of Purifications*) from chapter to chapter, and trying out the practice which was set out in each chapter. He found that what was said in each chapter of the book repeated within him as a spiritual experience as he proceeded to read the book. To him, it came as a total surprise, as he thought this state of mind was never meant for a person of his mind-set at that time. His deep appreciation of the contribution of other religious leaders such as the Christ, Prophet Mohammad and the Hindu Rishies etc. is also noteworthy, however with appreciation for the Buddha as the greatest.

His main object of meditation is *ānāpāna sati* and he considers himself more a "*sukkha-vipassaka*." He has not mastered *samatha* but experienced "*vipassanā jhāna*." He does not consider himself as following any particular meditation system available today and is critical of teachers not providing the opportunity to their students to follow their natural inclinations and having them restricted rigidly to meditation systems.

The interview was done by the writer, in Sinhala, in July 2006, in his hermitage.

Attainment of *sotāpatti-phala*

1. How it has been expressed:

It was a difficult period in his life, at a time he had been thrown out of his job and he was facing many uncertainties. He was serving as a staff member in a meditation centre, at the same time devoting a few hours a day to meditation. But he didn't have a teacher, did not have a specific meditation object, didn't know whether he was doing *samatha* or *vipassanā* and was not "consciously" abiding in any *sīla*. But he badly felt the need for meditation. A book *Sattavisuddhi*, written by a well known meditation teacher, on the seven stages of purification triggered off his interest. He started reading this book chapter by chapter, and each time he read a chapter he closed the book and tried to practise what he had read. He felt that what was written in it unfolded within him; it got activated in him as a spiritual experience. This way, he went reading and experimenting from chapter to chapter and he felt that what was in the book unfolded within him like a curled up coil opening up. At a point there was a very clear "going beyond," "a breaking of a boundary," like a river gushing into the sea, "an opening up," "a breaking up," like a river bund breaking and water gushing over the river bank, like a fever going down, like a festered boil bursting and pus being released. He felt a huge spiritual awakening. He felt that he had got caught up in a "huge operation with some fundamental principles." He felt that whilst all his problems such as not having a job, the issue of whether or not to marry, and the rest of the uncertainties in life remained unresolved, yet there was a definite solution to all his problems. He felt that his personality had gone through a change:

> What triggered it was the word called "*Sattavisuddhi*" ... The "*Sattavisuddhi*" was very clear in these. I didn't read the whole book. What I did was I read one chapter, closed the book and meditated (laugh). Nobody would believe. Because of the situation that I was in, when I read one chapter, I feel I have already finished doing it. Then I really understood that the Path has been laid for a long journey ahead of me. Because I had a lot of space in my timetable, there was complete room for it in the meditation centre. When I read the next chapter, I had already got accustomed with what I had read before. When I sit again in meditation, it works. When I was leaping like this from one to another, at a point there was a very clear "going beyond," breaking a boundary. Or else it was a like a big, like a river gushing in to the sea. I think that huge mental pressure or the issue of responsibility I had due to being without a job, likewise the issues such as, should I marry or should I enter the robes, what am I going to do next, if I am to enter the robes whom should I chose as my teacher, there were a number of problems like this, while all these problems remained unresolved, there was a huge breakthrough from another side...On the one hand it's a big spiritual awakening, on other hand, it's unbelievable(Q.5)... like a "breaking up" (*kadagenayamak*) breaking of a bund and the water gushing over the river bank. But it's not a harmful flood. This serious mental strain, no you cannot call it even a mental strain, I didn't have a mental strain at that time, even if I say a bursting of a balloon, that too is something that'll bring unhappiness to a baby, it's more like a festered boil bursting and the pus being released (Q.12)... I realized a big quake, a big difference, a big transformation, a big explosion, that a big release occurred (Q.17)... It's like a fever going down. Or else I still say I felt

> that it was a definite solution to my problems in the lay life. Yet not a single problem was solved. But I knew that I am no more at that level, that it is not a problem to me anymore. Yet the problem was unresolved (Q.6) ... I don't know, I can only say that when I was reading this, what was in that book "repeated" within me, it got activated in me. It's after that I realized that I was caught up in a huge operation with some fundamental principles. Or else that such a thing was expressed through me. But at that time I realized that my likes and dislikes, my personality had gone through a change (Q.4).

2. When, where, what time, in what posture?

He was in a meditation centre, in a sitting meditation posture, on the bed, in his *kuṭī* (Q.10–11).

3. Does he admit attainments of supramundane fruits?

He doesn't admit directly that he has attained *sotāpatti-phala*. When questioned whether it is *sotāpatti-phala,* he says he doesn't know, cannot say for sure, according to the text it has to be either a *jhāna* or a supramundane fruit. But he realized that this is an important event on the *vipassanā* side. This is an indirect admission that it is not a *jhāna* but a supramundane fruit.

When he was asked whether immediately after this experience he realized that it had resulted in a supramundane fruit, his response was:

> I don't know that. I don't know that. But I realized a big quake, a big difference, a big transformation, a big explosion, that a big release occurred. These were classified into various things much later, after I was ordained (Q.17).

However he admits that subsequently he trained under the guidance of a teacher to abide in *phala-samāpatti* (Q.16). *Phala-samāpatti* is abiding in the "fruition" relevant to a particular supramundane fruit already attained by a noble person. So there is indirect admission that he has already attained a supramundane fruit. Further, he states that immediately after this experience he started to "refine" this experience (to master the *phala-samāpatti*) according to the instructions given in the book which he read and he was surprised when he realized that it confirmed his "profound state of mind" and refers to this "profound state of mind" according to the texts as needing a teacher and a *sīla* (five precepts) as pre-conditions:

> Then what I did was, I started to refine this experience over and over again as stated in that book. When I was doing this I couldn't believe myself. The main reason why I couldn't believe myself was because I had not abided in the five precepts. Not even the eight precepts. There was no *sīla*. Similarly what I had heard was, that this is a profound thing, I had read that you need a teacher for this but clearly I had no teacher, the kind of revered teacher that is usually referred to was not there. When I got this under these conditions there arose a big doubt in me about myself, "is this a dream, am I confused?," I am not a person easily confused, no one can confuse me either (Q.5).

When he is asked whether he realized that with this incident or immediately after this incident certain fetters were gone, he says this is exactly what happened and certain clear cut changes took place in him, a "chemical change" took place (Q.20–21). He says that with these he felt enormously indebted to the Buddha and to the

Dhamma (Q.19) and wanted to surrender to a teacher. Further, in him who was up to that time ridiculing *sīla*, (though he was living in a meditation centre, where there was probably little opportunity to break any of the five precepts, even if he had not formally "taken" the five precepts) there was an irreversible change in morality to such an extent that the *sīla* that he ridiculed became the sole purpose of his life (Q.19–21). The above is a confirmation of *saddhā* or *aveccappasāda* in the Buddha, the Dhamma and the *Saṅgha* and the "*akhaṇḍa sīla*" (unbroken *sīla*) which are widely described in the text as the hallmarks of a stream-enterer.

However, when he is asked whether the first three fetters broke with this incident, the answer is "there is no necessity to declare in terms of three out of ten" (Q.22). The first three fetters are broken only at the stage of stream-entry. If he identified the fetters broken relative to the "ten fetters" (*dasa saṃyojana*s which are the fetters to be broken progressively in order to attain *Arahanthood*), it would have been a direct admission of having attained a supramundane fruit. Hence he avoids references to the "first three" fetters. However, his understanding of the Dhamma confirms the absence in him of the first three fetters (*sakkāya-diṭṭhi, sīlabbata-parāmāsa, vicikiccā*), and he will not seek another teacher for his salvation, all of which are hallmarks of a stream-enterer (Q.29–39).

It is also noteworthy that although the monk does not admit attainment of supramundane fruits, he also does not deny this outright.

4. The meditation object immediately before this experience:

It is not clear from the interview.

5. How long did it take to realize that this experience resulted in the attainment of a supramundane fruit or it resulted in breaking fetters?

Immediately after the incident he realized that certain fundamental changes had taken place in him, "certain" fetters were gone, and there was a spiritual shift, an irreversible change in morality. Later for years he examined to see whether he could break the precepts anymore and he realized that he had moved away from the concept of self etc. But immediately after the experience he had no understanding whether the "first three" fetters were broken or not (Q.19–22).

6. Was the conclusion about the attainment of a supramundane fruit reached by himself or with the help of a teacher?

He doesn't admit that it resulted in the attainment of a supramundane fruit, but refers to the experience as a spiritual shift or a "chemical" or a fundamental change which he himself realized. In any event he had no teacher for confirmation. He says:

> It comes with the incident itself. It is not something that another has to tell you or you have to think about. It's the incident itself. The incident itself creates that change. No one need impose it. No one needs to teach you. There is nothing for me to think either. It's the foundation of the thought process itself that cracks. It's the foundation of the thought process itself that reappears like a reshuffled hand of cards (Q.24).

7. Does he know that the first three fetters are no more in him?

He does not admit the absence of these in terms of "fetters." However his understanding of *sakkāya-diṭṭhi, sīlabbata-parāmāsa* and *vicikicchā* is in line with the understanding of a stream-enterer (Q.29–33).

8. How does he know that the fetters are no more?

For the last 18 years he has been examining his mind and finds that these are no more (Q.24).

9. The nature of the fetter-breaking-experience as felt by him:

He says that it is not something that can be explained in terms of the sense bases such as the eye, ear, nose, tongue etc. as several stages before you come to this experience the mind escapes from the (five) sense bases. When asked whether there was sight, sound, touch, smell etc. or form, feeling, perception, mental formations, he says there is all this yet you don't experience these through the sense bases or from outside. He says, therefore, that this is a biggest mystery to the world of the senses. He says it is like you draw two lines across and you see the point at which they cross each other and seeing that such point has no substance, no worldly importance:

> It is not something that can be explained in terms of the eye, ear, tongue nose. Several stages before coming to this stage, before about seven to eight stages before this, the mind escapes from the sense bases. (Q.8) ... There is all this yet you don't experience this through the senses or from outside. If you penetrate this there is also a light perception. There is a sound perception and a bodily, tactile sensation also. There is everything in this. But you don't experience this in any sense through the eye ear nose tongue etc. Therefore this becomes the biggest mystery to the world of senses. The sense bases cannot deny this. Yet none of the sense bases such as the ear or nose comes forward to claim that I saw, I heard etc. (Q.45).That is something that cannot be explained in terms of the eye, ear or the nose, there is nothing gained in it, It's like when you draw two lines across, you see the point at which they cross each other. You know that it has no substance, no worldly importance, no importance what so ever, having stayed in it hundred percent when you come out and look back it's like a frog having come out to the shore goes back to water and tells a fish that he had gone to the shore and come back. Then the fish ask "what exactly is a 'shore'?" "Shore" is a place where they live on air. The fish say no it's impossible. If a creature who has been born and bred in water having come out of water, goes back to water, there is no big deal in the water. Yet it lives there. What I see is something like this difference (Q.54).

10. Thought process immediately after the experience:

He realized that whilst all his worldly problems remained there was a huge breakthrough, a clear cut solution to all his problems. He realized that "this is the way forward, this is what should be done." He started to "refine" this experience over and over again in the way stated in the book. As things unfolded as stated in the book, confirming what was experienced by him, he couldn't believe it, as he thought this should not happen to a person like him who had no *sīla* nor a teacher etc. (Q.5). Thereafter he let the mind go freely and the mind was like a kite gone high up and broken off the thread. He just watched the mind fly limitlessly. It was an "oceanic" feeling, as if taking him to the *deva* worlds or like opening him to a dream world (Q.7).

11. The essence and significance of the experience, knowledge that arose and effect/impact on his life:

Certain clear cut changes took place in his likes and dislikes. There was a spiritual shift. He expresses it in the following manner:

> This is a spiritual shift that occurred through meditation which is irreversible. It is a clear reinforcement, a galvanizing. I cannot deny this because when you look at the life I led in the past, any outsider can see this. So I cannot deny this (Q.49).
>
> I first realized the power of *sīla*. That is, the *sīla* that I ridiculed all this time or that I considered as (like) being restricted to a jail, became the sole purpose of my life (Q.19) ... I who was poking fun at or ridiculing *sīla* began to worship the virtuous and also to preach to others about the importance of *sīla*. That is, there occurred an irreversible change in morality (Q.20). Later for years I examined myself: can I kill? can I steal?, can I engage in sexual misconduct? etc. and shame, fear, disgust arise towards these (Q.21) ... Before this experience, I had the desire to investigate into lust, therefore I had distorted ideas about it, that I need to experience everything about it. Similarly with hatred, to chop a creature alive knowing well that it's alive and struggling, to steal from the most heavily guarded place, to taste all the possible intoxicating drugs in the world, in cheating, to cheat even my mother and father etc. Having done all this I have been fairly successful. But there has been nothing achieved. Then when I came on to this side, the opposite happened. I wanted to stay away from even thinking of lust and hatred. Whether it happened or not this kind of transformation took place (Q.69).

He began to feel enormously indebted to the Buddha and to the Buddha *sāsana* (Q.19), in return wanted to serve the Dhamma unreservedly (Q.21). He felt a need for a teacher and entered the monkhood.

His concept of self had undergone a change, he realized that he had moved away from things like race, religion, class etc., which he grasped earlier and which restricted him and there was in general an "opening up" when it came to his dealings with the external world. He began to understand that the concept of "I" or "self" had been an obstacle to him all this time. He says "but this is not a thing you can break by thinking about it or by *sīla*. Clearly a chemical change should occur" (Q.21).

The essence of this experience was that it was absolutely void of essence, the understanding that arose is that this fetter-breaking-experience had no substance at all (Q.50–53). Great joy arose in him because he was able to match this experience with the objectives he spoke of, prior to this experience (Q.57). He was able to completely re-assess life, he got a new lease of life. He was able to discern good and the bad.

12. Is it *Nibbāna*?

He says:

> I don't know. Now you asked four such questions. I am not angry. When you ask questions you have to question this way. But you can fit in any word you like.

I have no objections (Q.47).

13. What is his concept of *Nibbāna*?

He says:

> It is something *avedaita* (which cannot be felt) that can't be experienced with the body, a state where there is no *saññā*, where the *saṅkhāra* has got "*visaṅkhāra*," and the *viññāṇa* is "*anidassana-viññāṇa*." I have this idea in me in terms of principles. This is what I have heard. So therefore "my *Nibbāna*" comes out through principles. When you look at it like this, this can never be experienced while being in this human world and nourishing *sakkāya-diṭṭhi*. It is something that you can never experience unless being desireless in life, something that can never be denied if experienced, the one who hasn't experienced can never recognize the one who has experienced, but the one who has experienced can recognize the one who hasn't experienced. It is some sort of a "non-human" [*amanussa*] experience like this (Q.48).

14. Could this be the experience of the supposed Creator God or the soul? And if not, why not?

He says:

> If you personify this, it becomes the God. If you take it without personifying, it becomes the ultimate truth (Q.43) ... personifying this is the meanest thing that man can do to mankind. Having personified they teach others also to personify. Therefore it is a dangerous thing ... But the Buddha has declared in the *Brahmajāla Sutta* that he arose to tear this apart. ... once you have an experience your skills don't diminish. It doesn't get limited. If he wants to, he can call this God, or call it Soul, but he doesn't get caught up in these, he is not obliged to prove this or to prove that this is a Catholic God or he is ten or fifteen feet tall. If you want you can call it even "ice cream" or "chocolate." The fact that you don't get caught up in designations is the biggest gain from this insight or from this leap (Q.44).

15. By the time of this experience was he under a teacher?

No.

16. Hallmarks of a stream-enterer:

1) Unshaken confidence in the Triple Gem

He referred to being enormously indebted to the Buddha and to the *Buddha-sāsana*, wanting to serve the Dhamma unreservedly and for the last eighteen years being totally committed to the practice and to the teaching of the Dhamma, having surrender to the monkhood (Q.19), having no doubt in the Buddha, the Dhamma and the *Saṅgha* (Q.31), and an irreversible shift in his morality. These are all hallmarks of a stream-enterer. See para. 11 above for the details of the knowledge that arose.

2) His ideas of *sakkāya-diṭṭhi*

He says:

> I am still investigating this. From time to time in life the "I" surfaces and there are times I get caught up and get carried away in the scheming of the "I." Whilst being carried away, if someone tells me that there is no "I" at times I even go to argue

> with them. But having gone a distance, I realize that I have started this argument with a big "Intention." The end of this episode is such that I realize that I have argued about it. Therefore still it has been placed in front of me as something to be got rid of, as a null hypothesis. I cannot say that I have got rid of it. Nor can I say that I am a person who is safeguarding this without discarding it. Still I am investigating it. That means it's a process of tapering off (Q.30).

Of course the stream-enterer still has the vague "I am" conceit, though not *sakkāya-diṭṭhi*, specific views on what I/Self supposedly is.

His ideas on Creator God (para. 14 above) and Buddhist cosmology (para. 22) conform to right view.

3) Does he engage in rites and rituals?

His concept of *sīlabbata-parāmāsa* extends beyond what is prescribed in the books to any act which doesn't realize in *Nibbāna* this birth itself, even if done with proper understanding. Before this experience, he did not engage in rites and rituals and used to ridicule rites and rituals (*Buddha-pūjā vandanā* and *bodhi-pūjā*). However, after this experience, if he has to do any of these as a monk, he can do it and in fact he spends a lot of time in the shrine room.

4) His concept of *ariyakanta sīla*

With this experience, *ariyakanta sīla* got established in him (para.11 above). He explains *ariyakanta sīla* as the sīla that is protected naturally, from within, to which *ariyan* disciples have a magnetic attraction (Q.40).

Attainments of Higher Fruits

17. *Sakadāgāmi-phala / anāgāmi-phala:*

Immediately after his first significant experience (which we identify as the fetter-breaking-experience relating to *sotāpatti-phala*), he started to refine it and to continue the practice further as stated in the book that triggered off the first experience. Then further progress unfolded as like a boulder crashing down a precipice or a wound-up coil unfolding. He had a series of religious experiences. He had no control over them. However he decided to put a stop there and to go in search of a teacher and to settle to a different life style. He says:

> That book clearly referred to a forward journey. But those instructions were not like the earlier set of instructions. It went beyond that, the answers were like some dots left here and there on a trail. When I tried to do it accordingly, it was the same. As though what was given there was meant for me. When I continued to do, it started to unfold. Then I felt it was like a boulder on top of a mountain which has been rolled down, now I have no control over it. It's crashing. On the one hand it's a big spiritual awakening, on other hand it's unbelievable. When this was proceeding, I resolved to put a stop here and thereafter to meet an elder, a revered person and to establish myself in *sīla*. Until I so resolved, it started to unfold like a suppressed coil which has begun to open up (Q.5).

To the question on whether he has experienced the reduction of the next two fetters, desire for sense pleasures and ill-will, he says that these two fetters have clearly faded to some extent (Q.67). When questioned whether this can be linked to a specific experience, he says that within the first two weeks of his most significant spiritual experience (what we identify as the fetter-breaking-experience of stream-entry), there were a series of similar "explosions," and in addition to repetitions of the first experience, some were clearly qualitatively different. These occurred at the same meditation centre. And he cannot say how many qualitatively different experiences occurred. But he doesn't want to place technical names to these, he doesn't want to explain these in terms of *sakadāgāmi* or *anāgāmi-phala* etc. But clearly some were "fresh" and some were "repetitions" (Q.70–73). Whilst similar experiences are obviously what is commonly referred to as "*phala-samāpatti*" which are fruition attainments of the supramundane fruit already attained by him, the qualitatively different experiences could be a fresh supramundane fruit. But from the interview there is no confirmation of attainments of the next two supramundane fruits, *sakadāgāmi* and *anāgāmi-phala*. He says:

> When the first main experience occurs, that person doesn't want anything else, he goes on with it. Under this circumstance when you experience something slightly more than that, then you get a little suspicious again, yet you think it doesn't have to be taken seriously. Again it develops a little more. Yet you think it doesn't have to be taken seriously. Because according to the meditation book this continues like a fire. But the fire jumps over a big notch. Without halting your effort when you continue like this. I don't understand these as "this is such and such a grade or this is a boundary or you can cut it beyond this point etc." but it continues, qualitatively better experiences occur. After some time there is a huge explosion or a huge firework. Therefore you get attracted to it joyously (Q.72) ... it is difficult to grade these, though it is difficult to grade you know that you are on the right path and that you are progressing (Q.75).

But when asked whether the next two fetters have broken off completely, he says he cannot say for sure as he is in a hermitage and there are no opportunities to test it out. But the need to test it came with these experiences itself. But when he comes out to society he feels that he is more purified than before. He says:

> I can't say it to that extent. Because this is a time that you are analyzing *kāma-rāga* and *paṭigha* which is in the mind, through the mind itself and there is no confrontation with *kāma-rāga* and *paṭigha* during this time. You are in a meditation centre in a meditating mood. Therefore it is difficult to say this. But there is a desire to see how I would behave in the event of contact with a *kāma* object, or how I would act if someone does some wrong to me. You become very sensitive to these. But there is no opportunity to test it out. Thereafter when you come out to society you realize that now I have purified more compared to those days. I feel like going to the "sick" to see whether I will contract the sickness, it is like a vaccine, having taken the vaccine I like to go to the sick to see whether I will contract the sickness. But at that time I was in a "hospital," or in a "*nirodhayana*," so I couldn't check it. The need to test this arises in the meditation centre itself (Q.77) ... so far, there has been a tendency to have miraculous escapes having almost got caught up in these. Yet I cannot say whether I will get caught up in a bigger experience than these. But I am eagerly waiting for it, before the end of this life if such a challenge with regard to *kāma-rāga* or *dosa* comes my way, I will worship such person with flowers. Because I will not get it from my relatives or from my faithful disciples. This has to come only from a Devadatta (Q.79).

General

18. Does he experience *phala-samāpatti* or a state similar to that?

Throughout the interview he referred to repetitions of his spiritual experience and also to subsequently practising for *phala-samāpatti* under the guidance of a teacher. He describes *phala-samāpatti* as an "oceanic experience" as an escape from the sensory world (Q.7, 8, 11). When asked whether *phala-samāpatti* is a concrete test of the attainment of a supramundane fruit, he says it cannot be considered a concrete test (Q.94).

19. Is there a need for a teacher for him to complete the Path?

He had no teacher for the attainment of the first fruit, thereafter he found a teacher. However currently he is without a teacher, he himself is a teacher to many others.

20. Did he practise any particular meditation system such as the Goenka, Pa-auk or Mahāsi system?

He does not associate himself with any specific meditation system popular today. He is critical about teachers restricting students to specific systems without regard to their natural inclinations and without recognizing past practices (Q.92).

21. Use of *samatha/jhāna/* light-perception in the practice:

After the series of his spiritual experiences he went in search of a teacher and practised *samatha* systematically. He is, though, more a *sukkha-vipassaka* than a *samatha-yānika*. The use of the light-perception in his meditation is very limited. He says that though light-perception is very popular there is a 10–20% to whom it does not come up (Q.88). When he was meditating outside Sri Lanka, he was trained in experiencing "*vipassanā jhāna*" and that opened up a different door altogether. He feels that if not for his attitude of lack of regard for *samatha*, he could have progressed even on the *samatha* line (Q.86–90).

22. Beliefs and encounters with non-humans, gods and lower beings:

He has had no encounters with non-humans, however he believes in other realms of existence such as *brahmā* worlds. But this specific question was not raised in the interview.

23. Inclination to serve/teach the Dhamma:

After his series of spiritual experiences he sacrifices his whole life to serve the Dhamma and to serve people treading the Path.

24. Whether the fetter-breaking-experience is *animitta, appaṇihita* and *suññata* and how he understands it in relation to his experience:

> From a *lokuttara* angle there is no breaking up in to three. It has a unitary nature. In the *lokuttara* there is no distinction as those who have experienced this and not experienced, or Buddhists and non Buddhists or those developing the Path and those who have attained the fruit. These differences are only in this world. If you look at it from a worldly angle, *appaṇihita* is that it has no value whatsoever to a man who has worldly desires. *suññata* means empty. (*animitta*?) *animitta* means

he cannot point at anything. That means it's not worth a penny. If I am to explain in my words, it means that it is not worth a penny (Q. 61)... Different facets of the same thing (Q. 62).

Interview No. 4

He is a 46 year old monk who lives in a small forest hermitage. The hermitage is in a shrub jungle about 5 km away from the closest village. He has been treading the Path for the last 20 years, having been ordained 20 years prior to the interviewee. Having lived in an established forest hermitage for some time, he has for eight years prior to the interview moved out of it and now lives mainly in solitude, though accompanied by three to four other monks. He walks a few kilometres daily for his alms-food, which is offered by the villagers at the mid-point of the jungle track that leads to the hermitage.

As of the date of the interview the monk had been known to the writer for over 12 years. Half way through the interview he felt too uncomfortable answering the questions as he felt he was transgressing the rules of *vinaya* and the interview had to be given up at that point, though some miscellaneous issues were raised after that. However there is confirmation of attainment of stream-entry, but the writer did not feel comfortable to query his religious experiences beyond this point.

His first significant spiritual attainment (*sotāpatti-phala*) was when he was around 30 years old, as a monk, four to five years after he started treading this Path. The fetter-breaking-experience relating to the fruit that is stream-entry is described as a "cessation" of the five aggregates of clinging. His first fruit of the Path is described by him in terms of the knowledge that arose. It is described in terms of dependant origination i.e. "you get the understanding that whatever arises due to conditions, all that ceases." His understanding of "self," the place and role of rites and ritual on the Path to liberation and the confidence in the Buddha, the Dhamma and the *Saṅgha* (the focus of the first three fetters broken at stream-entry), *paṭicca-samuppāda* and *Nibbāna* conform with the understanding of a stream-enterer as given in the texts. He refers to his understanding on certain issues raised in the interview such as "*sakkāya-diṭṭhi*" to be "nothing more than what he had read in the text." The "text" he refers to is *Pāli Nikāya*s and the commentaries. In addition to the right understanding of "self" or soul, his right view is confirmed by his views on Buddhist cosmology, the existence of other planes of lives, the existence of *Arahants* and other noble persons etc. In line with the confidence of a stream-enterer, he does not think he needs a teacher to complete the Path.

Though there were some references to an experience through which the next two fetters reduced, as the monk was too uncomfortable, the interview couldn't proceed in order to get confirmation about the attainment of higher fruits of the Path.

The attainment of stream-entry has been described with references to a specific day, place, time and a meditation posture, confirming that this attainment was accompanied by a striking fetter-breaking-experience. From time to time, he experiences states of mind similar to the fetter-breaking-experience described at the point of time of the attainment of stream-entry and experiences it naturally in the process of his meditation. He confirms that it is "*phala-samāpatti.*"

He is critical of those who learn the Dhamma without practice, without developing the fourfold mindfulness. He says it results in people ending up in debates and arguments and talking of supramundane fruits with doubts. He says that however much you learn the text, it leaves behind only debates and arguments. Ultimately you end up giving up the *Sutta,* also saying that it is not possible to attain supramundane fruits now, and that we have to wait until the coming of Metteyya Bodhisattva.

The interview was done in Sinhala, in his forest hermitage, in July 2006.

Attainment of *sotāpatti-phala*

1. How it has been expressed:

> I remember when I was meditating in 1992. When I was developing the meditation objects such as *kāyānupassanā, ānāpānasati* etc. from time to time, it has been possible to see, I have been able to see that whatever *rūpa, vedanā, saññā, saṅkhāra,* or *viññāṇa* (material form, feeling, perception, mental formations and consciousness) that are experienced in the meditation, these five aggregates of clinging are subject to cessation completely, without remainder (Q.7). ... That is, by meditating, through developing the four foundations of mindfulness i.e. either as *kāyānupassanā, vedanānupassanā, cittānupassanā,* or *dhammānupassanā,* we are able to see with wisdom the impermanent nature of that object or its conditioned nature, and mentally you see the release from that object. ... you are able to see the *nirodha* (cessation). You can see this cessation very clearly (Q.5)... this cessation is experienced for a very short while (Q.8). The mind arises having an object. It could be having the five aggregates of clinging such as *rūpa, vedanā* etc. as its object. Then it is the nature of the mind to arise having those as objects. Then at a given point, through our meditation, if we experience the impermanence of all these with wisdom, if we realize it, at such moment we feel the release from all these (Q.9).

2. When, where, what time, in what posture?

In 1992, in an *āranya,* when meditating alone, not in a formal retreat, in the sitting meditation posture, (Q.17–19).

3. Does he admit attainments of supramundane fruits?

After a number of attempts by the writer to confirm this, the monk very reluctantly admitted that he had attained *sotāpatti-phala* (Q.29–33). He says:

> Now when you ask this way from an *upasampadā* monk it becomes a big problem. That becomes something like us declaring the state of our supramundane fruits to the laypeople. Do you understand? Therefore if we have to answer these, there should be limits ... (laugh) (Q.29). The person who is developing the Path understands that you are developing the Path. At the end of the Path you see that you have come to the end of the Path. If it is the *phala* (fruit), you see that you have come to the *phala* (Q.31). Generally you understand it as the *phala* (Q.33). That is, anyone can understand that this ought to be knowledge, that "my mind that arose along with it, has experienced *Nibbāna*" (Q.35).

4. The meditation object immediately before this experience:

This was a *vipassanā* object (Q.7), but he also says:

> Many people ask whether it is *samatha* or *vipassanā*. As I understand, *samatha* and *vipassanā* go together. That is, contemplating on *anicca, dukkha, anatta* takes precedence. But within this you see that the mind has acquired serenity, that there are no hindrances (Q.22).

5. Did he wish for such an experience immediately before this experience?

He says:

> I have not understood attaining *Nibbāna* through any such wishing (laugh). In any event the Buddha has not declared that things happen through wishing. Therefore since *Nibbāna* is something that you cannot get by wishing, it has to be attained by following the true Path with *saddhā* as we know and understand it (Q.21).

6. How long did it take to realize that this experience resulted in the attainment of a supramundane fruit or it resulted in breaking fetters?

Immediately after the experience (Q.40). He says "normally you get such an understanding. That is, anyone can understand that this ought to be "Knowledge," that "my mind that arose along with it, has experienced *Nibbāna*" (Q.35).

7. Was the conclusion about the attainment of a supramundane fruit reached by himself or with the help of a teacher?

By himself (Q.49). He says "today usually this is determined based on what the teacher tells you. But I have not come to conclusions having asked teachers. This is my understanding. I have accepted it totally."

8. Does he know that the first three fetters are no more in him?

Yes (Q.38, 42, 43).

9. How does he know that the fetters are no more?

He says:

> You have to understand it with wisdom. You have to understand this matter. It is difficult to come to conclusions about it by asking a teacher (Q.37) ... Normally you feel, you are aware that if there was any suffering due to these in the past, that suffering is not there today (Q.39). We understand this when we meditate (Q.41).

10. Did all three fetters go together?

Yes (Q.45). He says "yes yes yes yes, if you are to see the cessation of all, you see it happening together."

11. Was it based on this experience alone that the fetters broke?

Yes (Q.42).

12. The nature of the fetter-breaking-experience as felt by him:

The fetter-breaking-experience was felt as "cessation" for a short while (Q.8). There was no form, sound, taste, touch, perception, feeling, mental formation etc. As to whether there was consciousness, the answer was "not even consciousness"

(Q.73–75). "Usually when a person experiences cessation you experience the cessation of all these. Apart from this you cannot see form or anything else" (Q.73).

13. Thought process immediately after the experience:

He says:

> At that moment what you realize is, whatever experiences you have had in your meditation, all that has ceased and there is release. This is the kind of feeling you get (Q.8).

14. The essence and significance of the experience, knowledge that arose and effect/impact on his life:

He says:

> I have been able to see that whatever *rūpa, vedanā, saññā, saṅkhāra,* or *viññāṇa* that are experienced in the meditation, these five aggregates of clinging are subject to cessation completely, without remainder (Q.7). ... the mind arises having the five aggregates of clinging such as *rūpa* etc. as its object. Then it is the nature of the mind to arise having those as objects. Then at a given point through our meditation if we experience the impermanence of all these with wisdom, if we realize it, at such moment we feel the release from all these. Then you see that this realization is neither *rūpa, vedanā, saññā, saṅkhāra,* nor *viññāṇa* (Q.9). ... The view, the right view got purified (Q.80)... you know that "all" is cause and effect and the fact that "all" that ceased (Q.56).
>
> You get an understanding about suffering. You get the understanding that whatever arises due to conditions, all that ceases (Q.82) ... If you had any suffering before due to that, now that suffering doesn't arise in you anymore. If you did anything, any unwholesome deeds under a delusion, taking it as self, now you don't commit those. (Q.83). ... If I had any kind of *dukkha* or a difficulty, a problem, this understanding has sufficed as a solution to such a problem (Q.16). Prior to this, if you had any delusions about the form, body, feeling, that the five aggregates of clinging are "me," you understand that such delusion is not there anymore. Therefore you know that there will never arise any sorrow and lamentation due to that reason any more (Q.38).

15. Could this be the experience of the supposed Creator God or the soul? And if not, why not?

There is no such thing for us who are Buddhists (Q.71). We know through our experience itself that it cannot be so. The Creator God is none other than these five aggregates of clinging (Q.72).

16. Could it be creation of the mind, a hallucination?

He says:

> Someone could say this. But this is irrelevant to me. I have not expected anything in return by proving my status or my understanding, by proving that it is true. Do you understand? If I had any kind of *dukkha* or a difficulty, a problem, this understanding has sufficed as a solution to such problem. Why? Because it solved my problem. I am not interested in solving the problems of others. If I had any delusion about the five aggregates of clinging, that it is me, I have been able to be liberated

> from that. Because after this my wisdom is, "it is not so, this problem has arisen because of my wrong understanding" (Q.16).

17.Could it be that you fell asleep for a while?

He says:

> The state of falling asleep and this state are two different things (Q.11) ... Why I say it is not so is, because a person falls asleep when sloth and topor (*thīna-middha*) arise. That is, when you lose mindfulness, when a hindrance arises, you can fall into a state of sleep unmindfully. That is one instance. In that there is a disturbance. When you wake up suddenly you get excited. This is different. Generally in meditation when you experience *nirodha* such a thing doesn't happen. There you see, you get an understanding about *Nibbāna* (Q.12).

18. By the time of this experience, was he under a teacher?

He was in an *aranya*, but he had no teacher (Q.52).

19. Hallmarks of a stream-enterer:

1) Unshaken confidence in the Triple Gem

He has no doubts whatsoever about the Triple Gem (Q.59) and will never seek another teacher for his salvation. To the question whether he has *saddhā,* and gratitude to the Buddha, his response was:

> This is not a question to be asked. ... It is just that you want it for this assignment (laugh) (Q.68). Gratitude of course was there in us in the past, it is there now, and will be there in the future too (laugh) (Q.64).

2) Idea of *sakkāya-diṭṭhi*

> That is taking *rūpa, vedanā, saññā, saṅkhāra, viññāṇa* as self and being deluded by it. If anyone realizes the conditioned nature of these, that these are *anicca, dukkha, anatta,* if anyone realizes the true nature of these by seeing its extinction, cessation, then the *sakkāya-diṭṭhi* regarding these, that is the delusion regarding these gets dispelled and any sorrow, lamentation or tension that arises due to these ceases (Q.55).

3) Does he engage in rites and rituals?

He used to engage in rites and rituals before the attainment of stream-entry, but now engage in them very little (Q.61–62). His concept of *sīlabbata-parāmāsa* is:

> The belief that you can search for *Nibbāna* through undertaking all kinds of wrong practices, wrong restraints. It is there to some extent in a worldling, in a person who has not fully understood *Nibbāna*. But once you see *Nibbāna* such a person understands, he does not accept that you can realize *Nibbāna* through these wrong practices and restraints, because of your own realization (Q.60).

4) *Ariyakanta sīla*

He feels that an *ariyan* has sufficient mindfulness not to commit a breach of the *sīla*. As to meaning of "unbroken *sīla*" he says that though an outsider may feel that a precept is broken, it may not be so, from the point of view of the *ariyan* concerned, as the factors necessary to constitute a breach might not have come together within (Q.70).

Attainment of Higher Fruits

20. Although there were indications of higher supramundane fruits, they could not be investigated as the interview had to be given up half way through.

General

21. Does he experience *phala-samāpatti* or a state similar to that?

After the attainment of *sotāpatti-phala,* from time to time, he has been experiencing a state similar to the "cessation" he experienced with the fetter-breaking-experience of *sotāpatti-phala.* He doesn't experience it with prior determination, but as a natural outcome of his meditation (Q.23–28).

He refers to experiencing two states of mind similar to the experience of the fetter-breaking-experience of *sotāpatti-phala.* One whilst meditating and the other by reflecting on the earlier experience (Q.25–26, 53–54).

22. Did he practise any particular meditation system such as the Goenka, Pa-auk, Mahāsi system etc.?

He has experimented with most of the contemporary meditation systems. But he is not following any of them (Q.135, 148). He feels that all these systems have some value and are not extraneous to the word of the Buddha, however any one of these systems, is not by itself sufficient to attain *Nibbāna.* He feels that one should not get stuck in or should not become a slave to any one of them.

23. Is there a need for a teacher for him to complete the Path?

He never had a teacher. He says "I don't feel that a teacher is essential. I feel that we can proceed with the meditation, with the help of the books" (Q.142).

24. Use of *samatha/jhāna/* light-perception in the practice:

He is a *sukkha-vipassaka.* His practice has been focused mainly on *vipassanā.* He has developed *samatha* through the practice of *vipassanā.* He has not used light-perception in his practice, though light-perception has developed naturally in his *vipassanā* practice. He has experienced *jhāna* in his practice, but hasn't mastered these or analyzed them in detail (Q.109–111).

25. Beliefs and encounters with non-humans, gods and lower beings:

He has had no personal encounters with divine beings and other non-humans. However he believes in the existence of such planes of life (Q.143–144).

26. Belief in the possibility of *Arahants*:

He says:

> I may have met *Arahants.* It is impossible that I have not met. But there is no one that I definitely understood to be an *Arahant.* But I may have met (Q.145).

27. Inclination to serve/teach the Dhamma:

He is inclined to be in solitude and to dedicate his life to his own practice rather than serving society. He says:

> I am not in the habit of devoting a lot of time for others. If someone comes to me, if there is something I can do for them, I will do something appropriate (Q.129) ... Because when we devote time for serving others often our own practice gets neglected. These two don't go together. Do you understand? It is difficult to continue with both. Because if we are to engage in benevolence we have to follow a different path. We have to mingle with the masses. Then we have to give up our own interests (Q.134).

Interview No. 5

He is a 66 year old monk who lives in a well known forest hermitage in Sri Lanka.

He has been treading this Path for 12 years and had ordained 9 years prior to the interview. His preceptor is well known and was most respected for his realized knowledge and knowledge of the *Tripiṭaka* and was considered one of the best Sri Lanka had in the recent past.

As of the date of this interview, the writer was closely associated with this hermitage for over 12 years and had known this monk though not associated with him closely. He is by nature a person of few words and his answers at the interview too were brief, mostly single words. Hence there was very little space to explore the nature of his religious experience. However there is confirmation of his attainment of *sotāpatti-phala*.

His first significant spiritual experience (which subsequently led to the attainment of *sotāpatti-phala*)[1] occurred when he was 58 years, as a monk, in his *kuṭī* at the hermitage, four years after he started treading this Path. The said experience is described by him as a "fine point" in meditation with a "tapering off of feeling" [*vedanava gevadamimak*], "feeling being nullified" [*vedanava ahosivimak*], "not feeling the oppressive nature of the five aggregates of clinging." The essence of this experience is understood by him as "the stabilizing of the eradication of the three fetters called *sakkāya-diṭṭhi, vicikiccā,* and *sīlabbata-parāmāsa.*" He understands this as the fetter-breaking-experience relating to the attainment of *sotāpatti-phala*. However he didn't have confirmation of attainment of the fruit immediately after the experience.

He understood that he attained a supramundane fruit only after about one day from this experience (Q.34). At the time of the experience, he had very little knowledge about supramundane fruits. He realized that it was a supramundane fruit only after discussing with a teacher and subsequent to similar experiences recurring over and over again (Q.43). He further states that he realized that the first three fetters were broken only after one to two months from this experience (Q.37). With similar experiences recurring subsequently, he re-confirmed that the fetters were completely eliminated. It can be assumed that originally his conclusion that this experience resulted in the attainment of supramundane fruit was not based on the understanding of absence of fetters, as the full understanding regarding the absence of fetters came much later than the date of the conclusion about supramundane fruits (i.e. two months), but his conclusion was based on the recurrence of the experience and stabilizing of it, which is commonly referred to as "*phala-samāpatti.*" However now he knows that the first three fetters have been eliminated completely, based on this experience and its recurrence (Q.39–40).

The above experience has been described with references to a specific day, place, time and a meditation posture, confirming that this is a specific experience accompanied by a peak-experience. However, compared to the expressions of the majority interviewed by us regarding their religious experiences relating to supramundane fruits, this experience though "striking" does not appear to be a "big bang."

His understanding of "self," the place and role of rites and ritual on the Path to liberation, and the confidence in the Buddha, the Dhamma and the *Saṅgha*, (being the focus of the first three fetters broken at stream-entry), *paṭicca-samuppāda* and *Nibbāna* conform to the understanding of a stream-enterer, though expressed by him very briefly. His "right view" is further confirmed by his understanding of Buddhist cosmology, the existence of other planes of lives, *Arahant*s and other noble persons etc.. He was under a teacher at the time of this attainment. In line with the confidence of a stream-enterer, he does not think a teacher is essential to complete the Path.

Soon after the experience and from time to time he experiences states similar to the fetter-breaking-experience described at the point of attaining stream-entry. He experiences it both ways, with prior determination for it and naturally, in the process of his meditation. He admits that it is *phala-samāpatti*.

The interview was done in Sinhala, in Colombo on 19th June 2006.

Attainment of *sotāpatti-phala*

1. How it has been expressed:

> When you commence the meditation, when you take your mind along the [meditation] object, right along the object, normally you experience various feelings. When you take the mind along these feelings further and further, on this object itself, along the object itself, there arises a very strong feeling. At this point when you go along contemplating this feeling, following this feeling, then thereafter you come across a fine experience, you realize that this is a "fine point" (Q.8)... generally like a "tapering off" [*gevādamīmak*] (Q.9) ... at this point of time, you don't feel the oppressive nature of these five aggregates of clinging, "the feeling got nullified" [*vedanava ahosiveemak*] (Q.10). ... With this experience, having enjoyed it for a short time, for a while, thereafter again when the mind follows the object, the mind returns to that former state again (Q.14), (the painful nature of the five aggregates of clinging).

2. When, where, what time, in what posture?

In the hermitage he is currently in, when meditating in his *kuṭī*, in the night (Q.22–24).

3. Does he admit attainments of supramundane fruits?

He admits that this experience has resulted in the attainment of *sotāpatti-phala*. He also admits that he experiences "*phala-samāpatti*" (Q.29–30).

4. The meditation object immediately before this experience:

Vipassanā meditation, in general, on all four foundations of mindfulness (Q.47–49).

5. How long did it take to realize that this experience resulted in the attainment of a supramundane fruit or it resulted in breaking fetters?

He realized that it was a supramundane fruit after about one day from the experience, after discussing with the teacher (Q.31–34). He realized that the first three fetters were broken only after about two months from the relevant experience (Q.35–38).

6. Was the conclusion about the attainment of a supramundane fruit reached by himself or with the help of a teacher?

He realized that he had attainment a supramundane fruit only after discussing with the teacher and after such experience recurred over and over again.

> When I was discussing with the teacher he said it's something like this. Later he told me to continue to meditate, when I continued to meditate, when I had similar experiences over and over again, that stage stabilized (Q.43).[2]

7. Does he know that the first three fetters are no more in him?

Yes (Q.38).

8. How does he know that the fetters are no more?

After that first experience similar experiences occurred over and over again. On those occasions, by seeing it subsequently, it was reconfirmed over and over again that those fetters which were broken were completely eliminated (Q.39). Further he says "now when those wrong deeds are not committed by you, then you realize that 'now I don't have these fetters any more'." (Q.40).

9. Did all three fetters go together?

He cannot say for sure (Q.41).

10. Was it based on this experience alone that the fetters broke?

Yes (Q.39). After the very first experience, similar experiences occurred again. On those occasions, by seeing it subsequently, it was reconfirmed over and over again that those fetters which were broken were completely eliminated (Q.39).

11. The nature of the peak experience as felt by him:

"Tapering off of feeling" [*vedanava gevadaneemak*] (Q.10), "not feeling the oppressive nature of the five aggregates of clinging" (Q.10,16), "feeling being nullified" [*vedanava ahosiveemak*] (Q.10). In this state there was no form, feeling, sound, smell, touch etc. however there was consciousness (Q.75–78)[3].

12. The essence and significance of the experience, knowledge that arose and effect/impact on his life:

> What I can say in analyzing the religious experience is, mainly it's realizing the true nature of this five aggregates (Q.4) ... that is, in general what is this life?, what are the five aggregates?, what is form?, what is feeling?, what is perception?, what is consciousness? etc. (Q.5)... [after this experience] the painful nature of the five aggregates is not so acute. You can see the changes at moderate level, the arising and falling is very clear (Q.15) ... The essence of that experience is the

stabilizing of the eradication[4] of the three fetters called *sakkāya-diṭṭhi, vicikiccā, sīlabbata-parāmāsa*. It is there that these defilements are cut off, the defilements are extinguished (Q.85) .... The understanding that arose is that eradication of the three fetters, becoming a virtuous man, developing more and more good qualities and following the Path more and more, to the end, to *Nibbāna* (Q.86).

13. Is it *Nibbāna*?

It's indeed an extinguishing [*nivimak*] (Q.79). For that stage [for *Nibbāna*] you need to go further (Q.80).

14. His concept of *Nibbāna?*

Nibbāna is the supreme state. This is to fully understand the reality with regard to these five aggregates and to be fully released from it, by this to be extinguished (Q.81) ... When we refer to *sotāpatti-phala* what occurs there is an instant extinguishing. When you refer to as *Nibbāna*, it is a long term extinguishing. *Sotāpatti-phala* is for an instant. It changes in a second (Q.83).

In that nullifying of feeling, he does not think he experienced *Nibbāna* even for a moment (Q.84).

15. Could this be the experience of the supposed Creator God or the soul? And if not, why not?

(laugh) That is not possible. Isn't it? (Q.73) ... That means, this [body] is not something created by God isn't it? (Q.74).

16. Could this experience be a mental illness?

No No. If it's an illness, such illness can come up again in the same manner isn't it?; an illness is something that affects you to a certain extent isn't it? (Q.131–132)

17. Could it be that you fell asleep for a while?

No. If I fell asleep it is not possible to know the nature of that state, it is because I was not asleep that I realized the nature of that state isn't that so? (Q.19–20).

18. By the time of this experience was he under a teacher?

Yes (Q.32).

19. Hallmarks of a stream-enterer:

1) Unshaken confidence in the Triple Gem

He has no doubt whatsoever about the Triple Gem (Q.59). He has gratitude to the Buddha "to the highest level" (Q.64). He will not seek another teacher for his salvation (Q.70).

2) The idea of *sakkāya-diṭṭhi*

Sakkāya-diṭṭhi is this ego, strong clinging as "I mine," this is *sakkāya-diṭṭhi*. In short thinking of these five aggregates which are made up of causes and effects as "I, mine" (Q.57).

3) Does he engage in rites and rituals?

He engaged in rites and rituals before the attainment of stream-entry and continues to engage in them (Q.61–63).

4) *Ariyakanta sīla*

He says *ariyakanta sīla* is the virtue which has been purified as a disciple of the Buddha, the purest virtue (Q.71). As to the issue of whether the five precepts of a stream-enterer are unbroken, he says "this is a very complex issue, it can happen knowingly and unknowingly. A stream-enterer never breaks the five precepts knowingly. It is possible that these precepts can get blemished unknowingly" (Q.72).

General

20. Does he experience *phala-samāpatti* or a state similar to that?

After the experience of *sotāpatti-phala* from time to time, he has been experiencing a state similar to the "nullifying of feeling" [*vedanava ahosiveema*] he experienced in relation to the attainment of *sotāpatti-phala* (Q.26, 39). He experiences it both ways, with prior determination for same and also as a natural outcome of his meditation (Q.26–27, 39). He admits that it is "*phala-samāpatti*" (Q.30). He experiences it both when engaged in *vipassanā* and *samatha* meditation (Q.50).

21. Did he practise any particular meditation system such as the Goenka, Pa-auk or Mahāsi system?

He did not follow any of these. He followed the Path laid down for *vipassanā* meditation in general (Q.142).

22. Is there a need for a teacher for him to complete the Path?

At the time of the interview he did not have a teacher and he does not think a teacher is essential to complete the Path (Q.138–139).

23. Use of *samatha/jhāna/* light-perception in the practice:

He identifies himself as a "*sukkha-vipassaka*" (Q.141). He has not used light-perception in his practice to develop *samatha* (Q.108). However, he has experienced up to fourth *jhāna* (Q.106) (if so, he is not a *sukkha-vipassaka* but a *vipassanā-yānika*)[5]. He does not think *jhāna* is essential for supramundane fruits.

24. Beliefs and encounters with non-humans, gods and lower beings:

He has had no personal encounters with divine beings and other non-humans. However believes in the existence of such planes of life (Q.126–130).

25. Belief in the possibility of *Arahants*:

I believe so. But I have not met, [I] cannot say (Q.134).

26. Inclination to serve/teach the Dhamma:

He is inclined to be far away from society (Q.135). As to his inclination to serve society he says "we do according to our ability, but living with society is not pleasing or agreeable" (Q.136).

Interview No. 6

She is a lay female disciple of 66 years, married housewife with two children. She has been practising meditation for over 30 years prior to the interview. At the date of the interview the writer was closely associated with her as a *kalyāṇa-mitta*, for over 12 years.

Her first significant spiritual experience [*sotāpatti-phala*] occurred when she was 36 years of age, as a married woman, when she was attending a rigorous residential meditation retreat for over a month, in a well known meditation centre in the suburbs of Colombo, 30 years ago. The religious experience relating to her attainment of stream-entry is described as "the body falling apart, part by part, reducing to a skeleton and to a heap of ash" and finally, for a moment, for a second, like striking a matchstick, the disappearance of even the dust, meditation posture and everything around and "losing awareness of feeling" [*kshanayakin daneema nathiwuna*]. The essence of this experience is understood by her as, "If anything is of the nature to arise, all that is of the nature to cease." The stanza "*ye dhammā hetuppabhavā tesam hetu tathāgato āha*" came to her mind (Q.88). She says, 'I saw impermanence there very strongly'" (Q.36). She understood that this is what happens to this body too; that it is difficult for her to retain it [the body] (Q.3), that it is not a necessary thing, not a thing she can sustain. She admits that this is *sotāpatti-phala*.

She understood that it was a supramundane fruit immediately after this experience (Q.40). At the time of the experience she had a general idea about supramundane fruits of the Path and had the confidence that it is possible to at least break the first three fetters at a retreat like the one she was undertaking. She realized that it was a supramundane fruit by herself. Later, when she was discussing and getting instructions from a teacher, the teacher also confirmed it (Q.48).

The above experience has been described with references to a specific day, place, time and meditation posture, confirming that this attainment has been accompanied by a striking fetter-breaking-experience.

Her understanding of "self," the place and role of rites and ritual on the Path to liberation and the confidence in the Buddha, the Dhamma and the *Saṅgha* (being the focus of the first three fetters broken at stream-entry), *paṭicca-samuppāda* and *Nibbāna* etc. conform with the understanding of a stream-enterer. Her "right view" is confirmed also by her views on Buddhist cosmology, the existence of other planes of lives, *Arahant*s etc. She was under a teacher at the time of this attainment. In line with the confidence of a stream-enterer, she does not think a teacher is essential to complete the Path.

After this experience and from time to time, she experiences a state of mind similar to the fetter-breaking-experience described at the point of time of the attainment of stream-entry. She describes this as a spell in meditation "without awareness" [*danimakin thora*] (Q.106), yet there is still a feeling that "you are around" [*taman inna bavak*] (Q.110). She also experiences it naturally in the process of her meditation. She is not sure whether it is "*phala-samāpatti*." She experiences this when she is engaged in *vipassanā*.

In discussing how this experience affected her lay life, she does not think that it is an obstacle to a successful lay life and does not think lay life is an obstacle to treading this Path either. She says that even after this experience, there was growth in the material aspects of her life though she was inclined to lead a quiet life. Her outer appearance changed only in terms of clothes, she was inclined towards simpler clothing. However at the time of this experience, she was on five precepts as her regular *sīla*, but after about 4 to 5 years from this experience, she found herself inclining towards a higher *sīla* and now she leads a completely celibate life. Except for celibacy, she leads a completely normal lay life discharging her duties as a wife and as a mother.

The interview was done in Sinhala, in Colombo, in March 2007.

Attainment of *sotāpatti-phala*

1. How it has been expressed:

> At that time my whole body ... all my flesh dissolved and the whole body became a skeleton. When I was watching this skeleton for a long time, even that started to fall apart, disjointed, it became like a powder and settled right at the bottom. At that time I felt it like a heap of ash. Even this heap of ash scattered all over (Q.3)... Within the wink of an eye, the [meditation] object disappeared and the feeling that it became like dust also disappeared (Q.11)..., the posture appeared again, I felt it again (Q.6–7).

It was like striking a matchstick suddenly, which lights up and extinguishes, like flaring up suddenly (Q.122). "I continued to stay on, again to focus on that same meditation object. Then gradually I began to come back to my normal state" (Q.5).

2. When, where, what time, in what posture?

In a meditation centre, during a residential retreat, early morning at around 5 a.m., when meditating in a sitting posture (Q.18–20).

3. Does she admit attainment of supramundane fruits?

She admits that she has attained stream-entry (Q.37).

4. The meditation object immediately before this experience:

Vipassanā in general (Q.22).

5. How long did it take to realize that this experience resulted in the attainment of a supramundane fruit or it resulted in breaking fetters?

She realized that it was a supramundane fruit and that the first three fetters broke, immediately after the fetter-breaking-experience (Q.38, 40).

6. Was the conclusion about the attainment of a supramundane fruit reached by herself or with the help of a teacher?

She realized that it was a supramundane fruit by herself, which was later confirmed by the teacher (Q.48).

7. Does she know that the first three fetters are no more in her?

Yes (Q.41).

8. How does she know that the fetters are no more?

With everything disappearing with this experience, she saw impermanence very strongly, the idea or feeling "I" never occurred there (Q.36); "when these things disappeared what I felt was that there are no such things [fetters]." She says that this experience itself was the fruit of the Path. There was no doubt in her (Q.35). Thereafter in her day to day activities, from the way she accepts things she knows that the fetters are gone (Q. 43).

9. Did all three fetters go together?

Yes (Q.44).

10. Was it based on this experience alone that the fetters broke?

Yes (Q.42).

11. The nature of the fetter-breaking-experience as felt by her:

At this moment, for a short while, there was no form, feeling, perception, mental formations, sound, smell, touch etc. Not even consciousness (Q.75–79). She says "the feeling that something was happening was there (Q.31) ... most probably consciousness came up subsequently" (Q.77).

12. The essence and significance of the experience, knowledge that arose/ effect and impact on her life:

> The fact that "If anything is of the nature to arise, all that is of the nature to cease." The stanza *"ye dhammā hetuppabhavā tesam hetu tathāgato āha"* came to my mind (Q.88) ... That moment itself, a little while after seeing it, it struck me: what I felt is indeed the meaning of this stanza (Q.91) ... From that I felt that this is what happens to this body too. It is difficult for me to retain this. This is not a necessary thing; this is not a thing I can sustain. This is the feeling I got at that time (Q.3) ... that there is nothing here that I can hold on to, this is what I understood at that time (Q.13) ... I saw impermanence there very strongly. When I was seeing this impermanence so strongly, the idea or feeling "I" never occurred there. It was the feeling that we are trying to grasp something that does not belong to us, the idea of "non-grasping" is what was felt (Q.36). ... we began to see the impermanent nature all the time. The view that "this is permanent, this should be sustained, this is the way it will remain" broke. "These things change from moment to moment. We cannot sustain these in this manner" is the view that came up (Q.86) ... Because of these experiences I was able to go through the rest of the time with much ease. Why? Because if there were any hurtful feelings etc, I was able to accept those with ease. In everything the feeling that things ought to happen this way and in no other way was no more, there was the ability to take things as they come (Q.167).

13. Is it *Nibbāna*?

She thinks with this experience she experienced *Nibbāna* even for a moment (Q.84).

> From that "*phala*" what we experienced is not regaining anything ... what was felt was not a state of being [*ati swabhaavayak nevei*]. So I think that is what is or what ought to be experienced in *Nibbāna* (Q.83).

14. Her concept of *Nibbāna:*

> We have finished with *saṃsāra*. *Nibbāna* is not to be reborn (Q.81).

15. Could this be the experience of the supposed Creator God or the soul? And if not, why not?

> It can't be. It is something you see from within you, not something that happens due to the influence of a third party (Q.73–74).

16. Could this experience be a delusion?

> I don't think so ... Because it was something developed over a period of time, not something that happened suddenly. By that time I had spent about three weeks at that Centre. So because that meditation was something that developed gradually it is not possible to think that it is a delusion (Q.32–33).

17. Could it be that you fell asleep for a while?

> No it was not like that. I was awake. ...There is a big difference between falling asleep and this. That is, the feeling you get when you are falling asleep and the feeling you get here are quite different (Q.14–15).

18. By the time of this experience was she under a teacher?

Yes (Q.55).

19. Hallmarks of a stream-enterer:

1) Unshaken confidence in the Triple Gem

Her right view was established through the understanding that arose with the fetter-breaking-experience. She has no doubts whatsoever about the Triple Gem (Q.59). She has gratitude to the Buddha (Q.65), she will not seek another teacher for her salvation (Q.69).

2) Ideas of right view

> There is nothing to take as "I" or to grasp as "me." This (pointing at herself) changes constantly. It's not possible to sustain this. I can't have it the way I want, this is what I understand (Q.58).

3) Does she engage in rites and rituals?

Yes, but not so much like earlier. She spends a little time for rites and rituals and more time for meditation (Q.62). Her concept of *sīlabbata-parāmāsa* is "wrong practices, to grasp wrong things, grasping and getting addicted to rites and rituals, beliefs etc." (Q.61).

4) *Ariyakanta sīla*

> *ariyakanta sīla* is the virtue that goes hand in hand with the Triple Gem. Following this *sīla* having Buddha, Dhamma, *Saṅgha* in the forefront, taking refuge in the triple gem (Q.70–71).

As to the issue whether the five precepts of a stream-enterer are unbroken, she says:

> More than by anything else, it can get flawed by a minor thing like a white lie. But he does not hide those. If a *sīla* breaks or you commit a wrong he declares it without concealing it. It is not kept in hiding. There is a tendency to openly accept the fault and ask for forgiveness (Q.72).

General

20. Does she experience *phala-samāpatti* or a state similar to that?

When questioned about *phala-samāpatti* she says she hasn't experienced it or not sure (Q.106). However she describes a state which she experiences at the end of a planned period of meditation, which seems to be same as the fetter-breaking-experience. That is, she doesn't feel form (Q.110), sound (Q.109), she is without awareness (Q.106), "feeling" "disappears" (Q.113). But there is consciousness and the feeling that she is around (Q.110). This happens when she sits for meditation resolving to meditate for a predetermined time, towards the end of such period. But she does not know whether it is *phala-samāpatti* (Q.104–117).

21. Did she practise any particular meditation system such as the Goenka, Pa-auk, Mahāsi system etc.?

She has not followed nor is currently following any of these systems (Q.143–144).

22. Is there a need for a teacher for her to complete the Path?

Currently she has a teacher, but does not think a teacher is essential to complete the Path. She says now it is not possible for her to go astray, but it is better to have a teacher to consult on any problem (Q.151–154).

23. Use of samatha/*jhāna*/ light-perception in the practice:

She identifies herself as a *sukkha-vipassaka* (Q.124). But she has experienced up to third *jhāna* (Q.126), if so, she is not a *sukkha-vipassaka* but a *vipassana-yānika.*[6] At times she experiences light-perception in her meditation, particularly when she sits for meditation having spent a quiet day (Q.125–133).

24. Beliefs and encounters with non-humans, gods and lower beings:

She has had no personal encounters with divine beings and other non-humans. However she believes in the existence of such planes of life (Q.155–156).

25. Belief in the possibility of *Arahants*:

She thinks she has met *Arahants* and has come to such conclusions observing the way they conduct themselves, specifically the lack of anger in them (Q.157–160).

26. Inclination to serve/teach the Dhamma:

She is keen to help others out of *saṃsāra*, to relieve them from suffering. She is inclined to teach the Dhamma (Q.140–142).

Interview No. 7

She is a 30 year old Chinese *bhikkhunī*, currently residing in Sri Lanka in a meditation centre attached to a well known forest hermitage. She has entered the Mahāyāna *bhikkhunī* Order in 1996. She has arrived in Sri Lanka in October 2005, having meditated in another Buddhist country for a year and a half. Ever since her arrival in Sri Lanka, she has been living in this meditation centre, practising meditation according to the Theravāda tradition. Altogether she has practised meditation according to the Theravāda tradition for about two and a half years. She is in the attire of a Chinese *bhikkhunī.*

The interviewee is not personally known to the writer. She was introduced to the writer by the interviewee's teacher, who is the chief preceptor of the said hermitage. As of the date of the interview, the teacher had been closely known to the writer for over 12 yrs. The *bhikkhunī* spoke freely to talk about her attainments, particularly after being requested by her teacher to have a discussion with the writer for this purpose. The interview was conducted through a translator as the *bhikkhunī* spoke only Chinese. Given the nature of the subject matter and the large number of questions posed within a short period, the writer felt that conversing through a third party (whose understanding of the Dhamma was not known to the writer) did have an impact on the clarity of the responses of the *bhikkhunī.* This *bhikkhunī's* whole family, i.e. mother, father, and brother, are Mahāyāna monks and nuns (Q.102). Very early in her life, she had the idea that she needed to end the cycle of birth and death, though Mahāyāna tradition does not have this as its key goal. She was very happy when she came into contact with the Theravāda tradition (Q.107).

She first undertook a Theravāda meditation practice in another Buddhist country under a teacher and later went in to a well known meditation centre in the same country. Her first significant religious experience came when she was practising at that centre (Q.21, 55). She seemed to have been practising what was taught by her first teacher and not the meditation system taught at that centre. Later she came to Sri Lanka to practise under her current teacher. She is currently following the Pa-auk meditation system.

She describes her first significant religious experience as follows; when she was watching her mind processes, watching the rising and falling of "name," observing "ceasing" of the mind, unexpectedly at the end of this ceasing she entered a "vast emptiness"(Q.18) for about 10 to 15 minutes (Q.88). Great joy and bliss arose in her as she felt she experienced the truth. When she "came out" of the "vastness" she felt like a child who has been lost wandering for years, has finally found her mother" (Q.24). Immediately after this experience, she realized that "she saw reality" (Q.64). After this experience she realized that this is the only Path to end suffering and she got 100% faith in the Buddha's teaching to end suffering and she felt she had overcome all doubts (Q.45).

She says immediately after this experience, she realized that she had broken the first three fetters, *sakkāya-diṭṭhi, sīlabbata-parāmāsa,* and *vicikicchā* (Q.56, 69). As of the day of the interview she has no doubt that the first three fetters have been eliminated by her (Q.80). Though she knows that the first three fetters are no more in her, still she is not sure whether she has attained the first fruit of the Path, *sotāpatti-phala* (Q.17, 32). Explaining the reason for her not been able to conclude whether this is the *sotāpatti-phala,* she says that once she described this experience to the teacher in the meditation centre in the country she first had the experience, he wanted her to do the practice all over again according to the meditation system taught at that centre, to see whether she could experience it through that system too (Q.20). Ever since then she has been bent on mastering that particular meditation system which includes mastering deep *samādhi* including regressing into previous births before undertaking *vipassanā* practice proper. Hence ever since then, she has devoted her total practice to mastering this meditation system, without reviewing her previous breakthrough experience.

Although she does not consider herself a stream-enterer, her understanding of self, the place and role of rites and ritual on the Path to liberation, and her confidence in the Buddha, the Dhamma, and the *Saṅgha* (indicating the absence of the first three fetters), *paṭicca-samuppāda* and *Nibbāna* conform to the understanding of a stream-enterer. Further, her right view is confirmed by her views on Buddhist cosmology, the existence of other planes of lives, *Arahants* and other noble persons etc.

This is a case where a significant religious experience has been described with references to a specific day, place, time and a meditation posture, confirming that this is a specific experience and has been accompanied by a striking peak-experience. The understanding that came from the experience is in line with the understanding of a stream-enterer. However the confidence that it is the fruit that is stream-entry is yet to arise in her. In terms of our discussion in Chapter 4 (pp. 75–82), we conclude that she has not yet attained the fruit that is stream-entry but has entered the "noble Path," thus is one "practising for the stream-entry fruit."

From time to time she experiences states similar to the peak-experience which is a vast emptiness (Q.86–89) and could enter it with pre-determination for a much longer duration such as an hour and a half (Q.43, 89). However she does not conclude that it is *phala-samāpatti* (Q.28).

In keeping with the meditation system she is currently practising, she has regressed up to the memory of six previous births, though the said system requires regressing up to the memory of a lesser number of previous births (Q.124). She says in her previous births she has found herself to be a Theravāda monk (male) and once a *deva*. She was reluctant to discuss about these in detail beyond a certain point (Q.124–130).

Her personal encounters with lower beings include appearances of them in her "dreams" and asking for merit; some claim relationship to her in the past and some do not. She says that these "dreams" are different to normal dreams, as in them she experiences a very clear mind. Then she establishes the beings in the Triple Gem and shares merit with them. At times she feels their presence as "cold energy" and feel them kneeling down by her to take refuge in the Triple Gem. After that they would go away very happy. After the said first significant religious experience referred to above, she felt them coming to her for merit more often (Q.114–118).

She is not inclined to help others right now till she masters the practice sufficiently to confirm her first fruit of the Path.

The interview was done through a translator, a Taiwanese nun also associated with the same hermitage. It was done on 26th July 2006 at the said forest hermitage.

Appendix II

First Significant Religious Experience

1. How it has been expressed:

When she was doing *vipassanā*, contemplation of the mind, watching the arising and ceasing of the mind process, at the end of this ceasing process, she quite unexpectedly (Q.39) entered a "vast emptiness" (Q.18) for about 10 to 15 minutes (Q.39). When she came out of it, great joy and bliss arose as she felt she experienced the truth (Q.24).

2. When, where, what time, in what posture?

In March 2005, in a meditation centre in another Buddhist country, in the sitting meditation posture (Q.20–23).

3. Does she admit she has attained supramundane fruits?

She believes that the first three fetters broke with this experience, though she still cannot confirm whether this is the *sotāpatti-phala* (Q. 16–17).[7] She needs more time to master her current practice, both *samatha* and *vipassanā* to be able to confirm this.

4. The meditation object immediately before this experience:

A *vipassanā* object, when contemplating on the arising and ceasing of the mind process (Q.18, 26–27).

5. Did she wish for such an experience immediately before this experience?

No (Q.34).

6. How long did it take to realize that this experience resulted in breaking fetters?

She believes that the first three fetters broke immediately after the experience referred to in 1 above (Q.63–64)—(See p. 279, n. 2).

7. Does she know that the first three fetters are no more in her?

She believes so (Q.69, 77–78). She says she knows very clearly that these three fetters are gone and day by day, she checks and it is clearer now that these fetters have gone (Q.77).

8. How does she know that the fetters are no more?

She says that it is not from this one experience of this emptiness that she had cut off these three fetters, through daily life and also through deeper wisdom that she knows that these have gone and also by checking on a daily basis she knows that these have gone (Q.77–78).

9. The nature of the peak- experience as felt by her:

The peak experience was felt as a "vast emptiness" for a short time. There was no sight, sound, taste, touch, etc. but there was consciousness (Q.29–30).

10. The essence and significance of the experience, knowledge that arose and effect/impact on her life:

She had great bliss and joy as she felt that she had found the truth, felt like a child who has been lost wandering for years who had finally found her mother. She found reality there (Q.24).

She got confidence that this is the only Path that will lead to the end of suffering and to cut off all defilements. She developed "100% faith" in the Buddha's teaching. She realized that there was no doubt in her that this Path can realize the truth about impermanence, suffering, and non-self and finally it could cut off all the defilements and suffering (Q.45).

She says the difference is like drinking a cup of juice yourself and talking about it. Now that she has drunk it herself she knows the reality. She says after this she can actually let go of this world, because there is nothing much to cling to or nothing to attach to (Q.47). And also in her daily life, she sees the breaking of the concept of "this body is mine" and she knows that and sees deeper wisdom arising; there is no such thing as self. And also she can sharply see her mind when greed or hatred arises in the mind (Q.18).

11. Could this be the experience of the supposed Creator God or the soul?

> (Laugh) actually not (laugh) (Q.70).

12.Could it be creation of the mind?

> No. ... Actually this is entered from the whole system of *vipassanā*, contemplating the mind and the body, the mind, the cessation of the mind and to enter naturally to this thing. This is a system which is a teaching taught by the Buddha, it's not by her teaching and creation of thoughts (Q.72–73).

13. Could it be that she fell asleep for a while?

Laughing, she says she was very clear, fully awake at that time, so could not have been asleep (Q.38).

14. By the time of this experience was she under a teacher?

Though she was in a meditation centre, she was not under the teacher at the centre but was practising what was thought by another teacher (Q.54).

15. Hallmarks of a stream-enterer:

1) Unshaken confidence in the Triple Gem

She has no doubt whatsoever in the Triple Gem (Q.49), she realizes that this is the only Path to end suffering and to cut off all the defilements; she has 100% faith in the Buddha's teaching. She says she will never seek another teacher for her salvation (Q.70). She has gratitude to the Buddha (Q.52). With this inexperience, she realized the truth about impermanence, suffering and non-self (Q.45).

2) Does she engage in rites and rituals?

She engages in rites and rituals due to her "respect" for the Buddha and not "expecting" anything in return (Q.51). As a Mahāyāna *bhikkhunī* she has engaged in these before also.

3) Idea of *sakkāya-diṭṭhi*

> Actually at first when you do the *nāma-rūpa vipassanā* contemplation, you do the *rūpa* first. When she did the *rūpa* contemplation she sees *kalāpas*, the particles, then she sees what's made up of these particles, then you break this concept of body and also you arouse wisdom within, you see impermanence suffering and non-self. That's the *rūpa* part. But what she mentioned that, aahm, from deeper understanding wisdom comes from contemplation of *nāma*, this mind. This mind when she contemplates that, she sees that there is *kusala* and *akusala*, the good and the bad thoughts arise, and when they arise and fall, she get deeper understanding of the reality of the mind and that's a one part (laugh) (Q.14) ... Actually when you see things as it is, as reality and you have no doubt that there is no self in this, this whole process, in this Dhamma (Q.48).

General

16. Does she experience *phala-samāpatti* or a state similar to that?

She has experienced a similar state of "vast emptiness" a few times after this experience. But she is not sure whether it is *phala-samāpatti* (Q.28). She experienced this at the end of the *vipassanā* process, whilst watching the ceasing of the mind process. Within the said emptiness she does not feel sound, smell, touch etc. (no external signs) but she feels there is consciousness (Q.28–30). Though she experienced this emptiness for the first time "naturally" in the process of meditation, subsequently she mastered the art of entering it with prior determination. The original experience of emptiness was for about 10 to 15 minutes but the subsequent emptiness is for longer periods, for about an hour and a half (Q.39–44). But ever since she started practising the new meditation system, she has not experienced it, as she has not practised her usual *vipassanā* process (Q.41).

17. Did she practise any particular meditation system such as Goenka, Pa-auk, Mahāsi system etc.?

At the time of this experience she was not practising any particular meditation system, but was practising *vipassanā* in general. But currently she is practicing the Pa-auk system.

18. Is there a need for a teacher for her to complete the Path?

She looks forward to a teacher to complete her practice (Q.109–110).

19. Use of *samatha/jhāna/* light perception in the practice:

She believes in developing *jhāna* before she engages in *vipassanā*. At the time of her first experience, she had entered the first *jhāna* and thereafter engaged in *vipassanā* (Q.24). In her practice of regressing to the memories of past births, she has obviously gone up to at least the fourth *jhāna*.

20. Beliefs and encounters with non-humans, gods and lower beings:

She has had many personal encounters with lower beings and *devas* (Q.113–120).

21. Belief in the possibility of *Arahants*:
She believes in the existence of *Arahants* (Q.70).

22. Inclination to serve/teach:
She is not inclined to help people right now until she masters the meditation practice in order to confirm stream-entry fruit (Q.103).

Interview No. 8, with Venerable Ajahn Brahmavamso

Ajahn Brahmavamso is a Western monk, of the Theravāda tradition, who is internationally renowned as an experienced teacher and a practitioner. He is British by birth, currently having Australian nationality as well, living in Serpentine, Australia, heading one of the largest monasteries in the southern hemisphere. His teacher was the most revered Ajahn Chah (1918–1992) from North-east Thailand, who is widely believed to have been an *Arahant*. At the time of this interview Ajahn Brahmavamso was 55 years, being ordained for 37 years (from the age of 18) and has approximately 32 years of experience as a teacher across the world. He insists that Enlightenment is not possible without *jhāna* (absorptions), completely rejects the teachings in the commentaries and *Abhidhamma* and accepts the *Suttas* as the only teachings of the Buddha.

This interview was done by the writer in Colombo, Sri Lanka on 31st January 2007, at a meditation retreat held in Colombo, during one of his visits to Sri Lanka.

Q.1 Venerable sir, what is your nationality?

A. My nationality is Australian, but I do have two passports. I still have my English passport. So I have two nationalities.

Q.2 How old are you?

A. I am fifty five. This is my fifty sixth year. I was born in August 1951.

Q.3 Who was your teacher?

A. My teacher was Ajahn Chah from North-east Thailand.

Q.4 How long have you been meditating?

A. I started meditating when I was 18 years. So that's 37 years now.

Q.5 How long have you been a teacher?

A. Aah, a teacher of meditation – I started teaching when I was in Thailand when I was five or six years as a monk. So that would be now about 26 years.

Q.6 What parts of the world have you been teaching in?

A. There is very few parts I haven't taught in yet (laugh). Obviously in Australia and New Zealand, Malaysia and Singapore, recently in Sri Lanka, USA, Europe and Canada, UK.

Q.7 And do you teach the Theravāda system?

A. I teach Theravāda, yes.

Q.8 Aaah, this is my first question to you. (Yes). Aaah, in the *Sotāpatti Saṃyutta*, there are certain *Suttas* which the academic world interprets to be a *magga-phala* not as a specific experience, (mhm mhm) something like the *Mirror Sutta* where you can look within and at any given point anybody can decide to declare that "I am *sotāpanna*" (yes, yes) if you have the three qualities like ... (right, right). So in that context, I am asking you is *magga-phala* a specific pointed experience which can be explained in terms of time and space, like "on such and such a day, such and such a place, such and such a posture, I attained such and such a *magga-phala*"? Is it a specific pointed experience?

A. It is a specific, pointed experience. And even though it is in the commentaries of the *vinaya*, in the *Samantapāsādikā*, it is a very important point, because, a monk is not permitted to make false claims for such things as attainments of the stream. And because that's a wrong, aaah ..., in the commentaries they gave means of finding out whether the person was telling the truth or telling lies. And there is almost like a questionnaire in the commentaries, a ... (not clear), questionnaire that we still keep, if someone says "I am stream-winner or an *Arahant.*" One of the questions we ask is: Where? And what time? Because, it is an event. And there is also another *Sutta*, which is the simile of the ship-wrecked sailors where stream-winning is looked at as [like] a person who is ship-wrecked in the sea who is floating on the surface and looks around and sees the safety of the dry land. It is an event like that. This is the Buddha's simile for the attainment of the stream-winning. Looking around in the ocean and seeing the shore, seeing dry land he knows where to go. And certainly an experience, the attainment of stream-winning is a discernible event. You know the time, you know the place. The last piece of evidence is in the *Aṅguttara Nikāya*, the Buddha actually says, "there are three places, monks, which you should revere for the rest of your life." The first place is the place where you went forth as a *sāmanera*, the first stage of ordination, where you first wore the brown robes. The second place, where you should revere for the rest of your life is the place where you attained the stream. And the last place is the third place where you defeated all the defilements and became an *Arahant*. That's in the *Aṅguttara Threes*. Buddha certainly agreed that it was a specific place, a specific time.

Q.9 How is this experience generally explained by those who attain it? Any one of the four *phalas*?

A. Any one of the four *phalas* specially the stream-winning and the *Arahant-phalas*. The stream-winning is an experience where, as a result of a deep meditation, usually a *jhāna*, which defeats temporarily the hindrances and awareness, in other words your mind is very very powerful, very very pure, where you see things very clearly and you don't see what you want to see. Nor do you deny what you don't like seeing. The first two hindrances, generally speaking the desire and ill-will are completely abandoned, that which psychologists know bends experience to suite oneself. So you have a courageous open mind. And also there is no restlessness and no sloth and topor so you are still and clear. And your doubting mind, always thinking and trying to assess is suspended for a while, gathering information rather than making conclusions. So with that degree of stillness and clarity, there is a chance, if you point the mind in the correct direction, you would actually see who the doubter is. Because it says, in the *Mahā Vedalla Sutta*, that is *yoniso manasikāra* which is work of the mind that goes back to the source, this is a *jhāna* mind. And in the words of another, being the teachings of an *aryan* those two together, if you just had a *jhāna* and your mind is free from the defilements and you point it in the areas where these enlightened beings tell you to look, the things like the five *khandha*s or the ..., who is, what is hearing this, what is doing this, the knower and the doer, about how much *dukkha* suffuses all aspects of existence. If you look at things like that, deep insights will come up the sort of insights which you think "how on earth could I not have seen that before?" that's on the side of the *aryans*, it's also obvious for the side of the *puthujjana*, the ordinary person, denial, wishful thinking simply because you want to exist.

Q.10 How would someone who would come out of that event immediately explain it to a teacher?

A. They would hardly be able to explain it. Because the event is so powerful that they are quiet, blissed out, surprised, shocked. So there has been a different state of consciousness for a while, the teacher would see that they have had a powerful experience and they would wait for the experience to settle down. And there is usually a time afterwards where the teacher would ask what had happened, what did you experience. And as I described it once, it's like a big explosion going off in your mind. When an explosion goes off, we know that some things have been destroyed. We have to wait until the smoke, the dust settles. Once the dust settles, you look to see as to what fetters, what defilements are there standing. If it's stream-winning, the things, those prominent which is destroyed is your understanding of a self. You see very clearly there is nothing, no place, no possibility of a self or anything belonging to a self or consciousness, persisting entity, there is no God, no soul, nothing, just a process.

Q.11 If we, aah, refer to this, you used the word "explosion" (yes) if we refer to this as a peak-experience, (yes) aah ... do people realize that you have attained *magga-phala* immediately or after a time gap?

A. After a time gap.

Q.12 What kind of time gap?

A. That's really, aaah, impossible to say. (Generally?) There is no general rule there. Because sometimes, specially in countries like Sri Lanka, people want to be a *sovān* (stream-enterer) so much there is so much wishful thinking. That sometimes the things that are destroyed but not fully that people give some benefit to the doubt. The hindrances come back quickly. Specially hindrances of wishful thinking and denial. I have an experience. Once this lady came up to one of the great teachers of Thailand and wanted to say that she had attained 4th *jhāna*. She said "It is 4th *jhāna* isn't it? "No it is not 4th *jhāna*" . "4th *jhāna* isn't it?," "No it is not." "It is 4th *jhāna* isn't it?," "Oh! Boy! How he never denied it, it must be the truth." She kept on asking the monk until the monk stopped saying "no" and she assumed that was a "yes." She came out afterwards, I was there in a conversation, came and told me and others "this great monk has confirmed that I had 4th *jhāna*." This is typical of wishful thinking.

Q.13 Now, as I understand for say, *sakadāgamī* or *anāgāmī* in particularly you have to take time to see whether you have eradicated lust and hatred. (Yes). But when it comes to *sotāpanna,* is it possible that people realize it almost immediately after the event without having to wait for too long? I mean those who have enough prior knowledge.

A. No you always have to wait for a long time. Not immediately.

Q.14 Could it be "yes"?

A. Could be "yes," yes. [but] you could make mistakes. You may think "yes" the self delusion has been destroyed. But you find out afterwards that it's not.

Q.15 I know you answered something similar in the Question and Answer session, but I would like to ask this here. (yes yes yes). Is *phala-samāpatti* a concrete test of a *magga-phala*? Do all *magga-phala-lābhīs* abide in *phala-samāpatti*?

A. No *phala-samāpatti* (whatever technical name you may use?) No these are commentarial terms, *Abhidhamma* terms which have no justification in the *Suttas*, no justification in real life.

Q.16 OK, aah, do people who attain *magga-phala,* aah continue to attain similar states of mind whether you call it *phala-samāpatti* or not?

A. A person who attained to be a stream-winner can always reflect on that experience and realize that he is a stream-winner again. It's a memory of that experience which the commentary calls it like a re-experience of a *magga-phala*. It's just the memory of the most powerful experience of one's life which you can recall at will. But it's a memory rather than an abiding. That's because the attainment of stream-winning is a purification of a view, the memory is always the re-experiencing of that view. When it comes to the *anāgāmī*, the fruit of *anāgāmī*, you have eradicated sensual desire and ill-will, this is an eradication of a tendency of the mind. Once you eradicate it, you don't eradicate it again. Once you blow up the twin towers, you don't blow it up a second time. They are gone once and for all. But what you can do is, recall that they are no longer there and have been eradicated.

Q.17 People, aah, tend to, aah, experience rather than believe, experience similar states of mind, what they refer to as *phala-samāpatti* or whatever (yes). What is that kind of *samādhi*?

A. That kind of *samādhi* is a little bit of wishful thinking. *Samādhi* is always *jhānas* or something higher than that. Very often what I sometimes heard is that people attain some degree of stopping of consciousness for some reason even though it is not a *nirvāṇic* state. It just like blanking out the mind. It's like something wonderful and amazing. But it is not the attainment of the path and fruit of stream-winning or not attaining of *Arahant*[*ship*]. They have not attained to a blanking out of consciousness or some sort of cessation that is gained as a result of a *samādhi* experience or a *jhāna* or even the *arūpa jhāna*. Emerging afterwards and reflecting that as an insight experience. And what that experience (attainment of a supramundane fruit) really is, it is again a powerful letting go which has always been associated with an enormous happiness and bliss. It is a bliss knowing that a huge amount of suffering is taken away from you and that itself is overcoming of hindrances. But it is not a *samādhi* state in the sense of a *sammā samādhi* or *jhāna*. It is the commentaries which have actually tried to equate *samādhi* with *magga-phala* which is not really good.

Q.18 How is it that these people who declare this, that they experience similar states, begin to experience it only after their *magga-phala*, although they had *jhānic* states before?

A. But sometimes even then you have to find out what they describe as *jhāna*. Because I know what many teachers describe as *jhāna*, but I would not agree that there is a *jhāna* state. The *jhānas* are very very recently coming to vogue in places like Sri Lanka and because they are in vogue, many people teach the states which are not real *jhānas*. As I mentioned in my talks, the *jhāna* is a state in which you cannot feel your body, the five senses completely gone, cannot form a thought. Still people say that they have attained *jhānas* when these things are still there. So it's not a full *samādhi* state yet. You'll find that this is a psychological condition of wishful thinking where people recreate what they want to experience. Too many teachers say that this cessation is an experience of *magga-phala*. Many people experience similar states, but it's not the real thing.

Q.19 Venerable sir, what is the reference in the *Suttas* to, aaah, *animitta samādhi*, aaah, you know couple of things like that? (That is). Is that also a state of *samādhi*? *Animitta samādhi*?

A. That is the way in which one experiences the state of cessation as a result of an *arūpa* state. (Sorry?) These are the states which follow the *arūpa* states. It's the same as *nirodha-samāpatti*. But this is the stage that you only get through by allowing the conscious mind to stop incrementally. You can't make such a huge jump. You go through the stages 1st *jhāna*, 2nd *jhāna*, 3rd *jhāna*, 4th *jhāna*, 1st *arūpa*, 2nd *arūpa*, 3rd *arūpa*, 4th *arūpa*, *nevasaññānāsaññā* and afterwards the mind stops. You can't suddenly jump to stopping.

Q.20 In the category of the six *samāpattis* in the *Aṅguttara Nikāya*, it clearly states, *animitta samāpatti, appaṇihita samāpatti*?

A. But that is a way through to those cessations, the means, the main objects which you enter the *jhāna* through.

Q.21 Could they be, could these people be experiencing those?

A. No because you have to go through it, through the *jhāna* to various experiences.

Q.22 Yes nevertheless, could they be ending up in *animitta samāpatti, appaṇihita samāpatti* etc.?

A. They could do that.Yes. But only way you'll be able to test is to say how they got there.

Q.23 Yes. Provided they got there through the right means.

A. That's right. You can't go to Australia without crossing the ocean. If someone says that they have been to Australia without crossing the ocean, then I'll tell them, no they have not got to Australia.

Q.24 I am talking of a person who has had a *magga-phala* already, re-experiencing a similar state.

A. Yes, *magga-phala* is not a *samādhi* experience, it's an insight experience.

Q.25 If you talk of this "peak-experience," (yes), for the four different *phala*s (yes), aah, would there be, aaah, similar states for the four different *phala*s, if you think of one person who would (No), the degree differs? Or the "peak experience" ?

A. What you mean is different for the states or different for people?

Q.26 Different for states for the same person?

A. No these are completely different. Remember these are not *samādhi* experiences. It's not cessation. Not the fact that, some people think if you experience this twice then you are *sakadāgāmī*, thrice you are *anāgāmī*, four times you are *Arahant*. That's not true.

Q.27 When you are experiencing *sotāpatti-phala* (yes), aaah, in terms of technicality what is it that occurs in the mind? Do all six senses cease? Does consciousness cease or (No ...) what happens? How do you explain this experience?

A. In the experience of stream-winning you are fully conscious. The six senses are still there, active, they are focusing on the insight, especially insight of non-self, and the mind knows that the five *khandha*s are empty of a self. That which one took to be a self, one sees very clearly is not tenable any more. You see deeply. This is not a time of suspension of consciousness. The suspension of consciousness, the consciousness only terminates properly at, after the fourth *arūpa*. You have to go through that first of all. And you should know from the *Sutta*s it's only those *Arahant*s who are liberated both ways, (who) have experiences of those *arūpa*s. Many *Arahant*s haven't experienced cessation at all.

Q.28 Now when people explain it in the sense of "I felt everything ceasing" (yes) what? Could it be that *nāma-rūpa* ceases as against consciousness?

A. Aaaaah, no because consciousness would always depend upon *nāma-rūpa*. You cannot have *nāma-rūpa* without an object of consciousness, consciousness is dependent upon objects, objects are dependants upon having a consciousness.

Q.29 Aaah, the Burmese tradition explains this; of course they believe in *phala-samāpatti* (yes yes) they differentiate between *magga-phala, phala-samāpatti*, and *nirodha-samāpatti*.

A. Yes and I disagree with them completely because they are basing their ideas on the commentaries and the *Abhidhamma* which I don't take as valid.

Q.30 Have you come across *magga-phala-lābhī*s by birth? (by birth?) *jāti sovan*?

A. Aaah, please explain what you mean by that.

Q.31 Aaah, that is a person who feels that he has got a *magga-phala* in a previous birth.

A. Yes. The only way you know that, is to re-experience that *phala* in this life. In other words if you were say a *stream-winner* in your previous life, you would not know that as a baby, you would not know that as a young man, or a young girl. There'll come a time in your life when you re-experience the same thing and you say you are a stream-winner again.

Q.32 Have you come across people like that (Yes) in your teaching?

A. Yes.

Q.33 Do they recognize on their own?

A. No, they only recognize it after they attain in this life; they recognize it in their previous life as well.

Q.34 So when you say they have attained it in this life (correct) they experience it for the first time some day?

A. As if it is for the first time.

Q.35 OK. So they feel that they have had it before?

A. Aaah, only afterwards. If they have also had the experience of stream-winning. If also they have developed the recollection of past lives, they realize that they have had that experience in a previous life.

Q.36 It's only through the recollection of past lives?

A. Yes.

Q.37 This category, previous *magga-phala-lābhīs*. Up to, aaah, what stage? –have you come across such, *sakadāgāmis*?

A. Only stream-winners.

Q.38 Only stream-winners? Not *sakadāgāmis*?

A. *Sakadāgāmi* is very hard to define. So much so that I don't take that experience as a *magga-phala* which is easy to define. *Anāgāmis* would be an event. *Arahant* would be an event. Stream-winner would be an event. *Sakadāgāmi* would not be an event.

Q.39 Aaah, you say that it is not marked by a specific experience ? (correct) Is that what you are saying?

A. Yes

Q.40 When people claim a *magga-phala,* is it necessary that it is always supported by a teacher or can a person, is it necessary for any confirmation?

A. What do you mean, necessary? Because you can't confirm it. Even in one of the great *Suttas* when the Buddha was asked, are all these people who claim this and claim that, claim to be *Arahants*, are all these people claiming what is true or claiming what is false? And even the Buddha says some are claiming true things, some are claiming what is false. Even the Buddha could not confirm it or not confirm it. So the point is that attainments are ... (Not clear) difficult to confirm, another teacher would not be able to confirm. All they could do is confirm that you are not a stream-winner, or that you are not *anāgāmī*, or confirm that you are not an *Arahant*. They would never be able to confirm that you are. And even you yourself, you could know that you are not these things and if you think you are, sometimes all it takes is for the defilements to subdue temporarily. It's immensely difficult to know except for the *Arahants*. You should if you are honest enough, and you got through the *jhānas* and you really are following the *Suttas*, and not the *Abhidhamma*, should be able to know whether that's true or not.

Q.41 In the case of a certain number of fetters to be gone at a certain *magga-phala*, say three in the *sotāpanna*, two in the *anāgāmī*, (yes) do these sets go off together in one shot? How does it go?

A. What do you mean whether all ten go in one shot?

Q.42 No no, in *sotāpanna* three fetters are supposed to break.

A. They break together, yes and the two breaks together in *anāgāmi* and five breaks together in the *Arahant*.

Q.43 This is just for the record, Bhante (laugh), I know you answered some of these already (yes) Do you have disciples who are attaining *magga-phala* today, particularly laymen?

A. Laymen, no I would pass that one because I have only some disciples and that would be, aaah, what's it called, I am betraying their confidence by saying (without any names?) what I would say is people are attaining *magga-phala* these days (yes it's OK) I am not saying my disciples.

Q.44 Do laymen attain *magga-phala* today leading a normal lay life?

A. No

Q.45 Away from normal lay life?

A. Yes. We are not saying what normal is (laugh) you got to any way answer that.

Q.46 Is a *sotāpanna*'s *sīla* unbroken?

A. No ... stream-winner can break their precepts, but they would always be able to know it, to make amends to it afterwards.

Q.47 Aaah, as a *magga-phala-lābhī*, aah, are people prone to, a tendency to serve the Dhamma or people or whatever or are they having a tendency to go away and serve themselves to complete their Path?

A. There is both types (sorry?) There is both types (both types).

Q.48 As a teacher, do you promote "in this very life"?

A. Certainly. It's very important to promote it "in this very life."

Q.49 Can *Arahants* be emotional? You know there is big controversy about, aaah ... (deleted). Yes.

A. I don't think... (deleted) is enlightened.

Q.50 The word "emotional" is attachment isn't it?

A. That's right, emotional is attachment. Yes.

Q.51– So physically ...

A. In other words, I would actually, aaah, stop that one and say something else. One can still have the positive emotions, the inspiration and joy, delight at the beautiful teaching. But one can't have the negative emotions of anger.

Q.52 Nevertheless it is attachment, ego based? (What?) Emotions? If you talk of positive emotions?

A. No. Positive emotions such as inspiration, equanimity, loving kindness, *mettā, karuṇā, muditā, upekkhā* are emotions, *pīti sukha* are emotions. So these are things that move the mind ... (Not clear) the joy in the Dhamma, these are emotions. These positive emotions would come up even in *Arahants*, ... (Not clear)

Q.53 If you are not too tired, Bhante, can you explain the five types of *anāgāmīs*? You know they talk of the five types of *anāgāmīs*.

A. Yes all that is just, aaah, first of all it shows there is an *antarābhava*. These *anāgāmīs*, there is one type of *anāgāmīs* who, after dying, before he gets into or she gets into *suddhāvasa*, becomes an *Arahant*, which actually shows that there is such a thing as *antarābhava*. That is "*antarābhava-nibbāyi.*" But this does depends upon the type of the last hindrances or last, aah, fetters. Remember the main fetters for the *anāgāmīs* is attachment to the mind specially the *jhāna* mind, aaah, *rūpa jhāna*. That's the only thing which stops them, the *anāgāmīs* from letting go completely. You remember that when they, the body ends on the death of the *anāgāmīs*, there is such a powerful letting go, there is such a force of renunciation, seeing the body dissolve, very often that's enough to trigger, to force the *anāgāmīs* to let go the last attachment to the mind, to allow that to cease. But it depends upon the attachment to the mind, how strong that is, whether the *anāgāmīs* actually does get reborn in the *suddhavāsa* and stay there for a long time or they completely let go.

Q.54 It talks of "a bit may fly up and cool down" (AN IV 70–74). (That's right, yes, it's a wonderful simile), before it is aware, before it is reborn in the *suddhāvāsa* (yes) because, so what it means is even in the *antarābhava* it can cool off?

A. Yes.

Q.55 When you say after touching the ground[8] (yes) it is after being born?

A. Just get reborn in the *suddhāvasa* (you) go immediately.

Q.56 Others are where you come back here, I mean not here (it is to the *suddhāvāsa*) *suddhāvāsa*, they go on for a long time.

A. Yes yes. There is actually the sixth type, the *jhāna anāgāmī* (yes yes)—OK that's my favourite one (laugh) (*jhāna anāgāmī*) *jhāna anāgāmī*, you know that one?

Q.57 That doesn't give ... *sasaṅkhāra*[9] ...

A. No this is the other one, there is another type. This is *jhāna anāgāmī* – is in the, aaah, somewhere, its where stream-winner, *sotāpanna* is in *jhāna*, who dies in *jhāna*, (yes, won't come back), they just get immediately reborn (yes) in the *jhāna* realms[10] and die there, they attain *Nibbāna* there, ... a person who is a stream-winner, which has a lot of *jhāna*, when they pass away, they go straight to the *jhāna* realms, the stream-winner who goes and gets their next life in the *jhāna* realms, will stay there in the *jhāna*, from there they never come back again. They fade away once the *jhāna* disappears.

Q.58 Bhante, can you comment on the Burmese tradition of *vipassanā jhāna*?

A. There is no such thing, it's a misleading teaching, it's about time they would stop that. There is no such thing as *vipassanā jhāna*. The Buddha never said such things. *Jhāna* is always first *jhāna*, second *jhāna*, third *jhāna*, fourth *jhāna*. There is no such thing as *samatha* without *vipassanā* or *vipassanā* without *samatha*, the two go together. The whole tradition of *vipassanā* being different from *samatha* or *samatha* not being necessary is wrong, is completely against the teaching of the Buddha. *Sammā samādhi* is always one two three four *jhānas*. *Gaṇaka Moggallāna Sutta*[11] only insists, the only meditation which the Buddha praises is *fourth jhāna*. There is no such thing as *suddha-vipassanā* anywhere in the Buddha's teachings, in the *Sutta Piṭaka*, there is no such thing as that.

Q. Thank you.

Notes

1. This experience by itself did not result in the attainment of stream-entry. It is after re-experiencing this number of time that he understood that he had attained stream-entry. See n. 2–4 below.
2. This interviewee, at this stage, has been identified by me as a "person practicing for stream-entry." See Chapter 4 for a discussion (pp. 81–82). Nevertheless the series of experiences which occurred (recurred) subsequently was the same as his original experience. It is after recurring of the original experience, by reflecting on them that he understood that he had attained stream-entry. It should be noted that we have defined the fruit that is stream-entry as a general state of mind (see p. 20).
3. The very first experience referred to in para 1 and 2 above and the subsequent experiences based on which he concluded that he had attained stream-entry were the same, that is, "tapering off of feeling."
4. Though the experiences were the same, this shows that the fetters were weakened first and destroyed subsequently, upon the recurrence of the original experience.
5. A *sukkha-vipassaka* is one who practises only *vipassanā* and does not experience *jhānas*. One who experiences *vipassanā* and then *jhānas* is one who practises the *vipassanā-yāna,* that is, first *vipassanā,* then *samatha*—see p. 204 for different approaches to the Path.
6. See note 5 above, and also p. 204 for different approaches to the Path.
7. I have identified her as a person "practising for the fruit that is stream-entry." See Chapter 4 (pp. 81–82) for a discussion.
8. That is, the second kind of *anāgāmī* is compared to the "bit" when it touches the ground.
9. The third to fifth types are one who attains *Nibbāna* without further activity (*asaṅkhāra*), one who attains it with further activity (*sasaṅkhāra*), and one who "goes upstream" to the highest of the five *suddhāvāsas* (pure abodes) (p. 90).
10. The *jhāna*-related rebirths are all the rebirths of the "pure form" [*rūpāvacara*] and "formless levels" [*arūpāvacara*], the *suddhāvāsas* just being part of the pure form level.
11. MN: 107. In this *Sutta,* the Buddha described a gradual training of moral restraint, guarding the sense-doors, moderation in eating, wakefulness, mindfuilness and clear awareness of all bodily movements, meditation to suspend the hindrances, then attaining the first, second, third and fourth *jhāna*.

Appendix III

Interview 1[1] (A Sample Interview)

Q.1 Venerable sir what is your nationality?

A. I am Malaysian.

Q.2 How long have you been treading this Path?

A. Treading?

Q.3 How long have you being practising?

A. I am practising here?

Q.4 Not here, in general?

A. Five year, more than five year.

Q.5 When did you enter the Order. When did you enter the robes?

A. Oh! enter the robes? Before I'm Mahāyāna. So I'm, after a five year, five year three months, I enter to Theravāda.

Q.6 Five year three months, Theravāda?

Q.7 How old are you?

A. I am 43 years.

Q.8 Could you describe your first religious experience on this Path? As Theravāda Dhamma, as a Theravāda practitioner? Can you describe your first religious experience, very significant, what is your first religious experience, mmm important religious experience?

A. Aaah important, aaah on this Path, on this Path. Theravāda Path and fruition, mmm very different what I, Path and fruition what I attained here is very, aah what I can get here in practice and finally I can get is this Path and fruition in this few years.

Q.9 I couldn't get you, can you explain again?

A. Aaah I mean is, I come to here, I can get, because I try to ... (not clear). The meditate time, meditate after that I can get Path and fruition here.

Q.10 When did you start practising here?

A. Yes.

Q.11 Can you tell me what you experienced?

A. Is it I have to describe what I experienced the practice, aah anything I practise, in at that time, I practised 32 parts, *asubha*, *asubha*, practised *asubha*, after that I continue continue practice, beginning is very difficult, because we don't have concentration.We aah no concentration. So I visualize only, visualize the 32 parts, lung, *kesā*, *lomā*, continue like this part by part, imagine only, beginning is little bit difficult, after that one week, two week more comfortable only, because a light occur, the light of wisdom occur, occur. So I focused very clearly, my lung, my heart, anything very clearly and then light focused together. After that no longer, I almost one month attained first Path only, *sotāpanna*, because almost almost close (not clear) because go in that side (the monk pointing at a particular direction), in that time, I could feel the mind defilements were reduced 30, more than 30% only. Because it was far away, 30% and anything beginning be...before is very anger, anything desire very strong come in. After that, attain that time, he very far, almost cust, cut off the 30, more than 30% only. The defilements go away. Little bit, thinking little bit far away. So attachments a little bit far, little bit far, like that it was. After that, feeling very comfortable. Because no more 30% defilements in that way at that time.

Q.12 When did you attain *sotāpatti phala*, can you describe how it happened, immediately before that?

A. Immediately actually.

Q.13 The thought process?

A. Aaah the thought process, when the thought process, when you go in that time, before he[2] continue continually produce anger, delusion many continue. After that redu... reduce after that want to continue, after that want to go in that time, he will go in, go in that time sss... in the second, in the second, the mind look like he took it far only, then the defilements automatic cut off, cut off little bit far, because the reason is knowledge, knowledge, wisdom cut off. Because aaah the Path, first Path aaah and now mutually only. So he attain, go in there. the feeling different is aaah different, different, like aaah one minute he feel he not continue, go directly go to one minute, he have to aaah one minute, second minute, thirty three minute, until sixty minute. So he slowly slowly cut off the defilements until go in that time, sixty minute, go in that time, he little bit different at that time, it's very far defilements. So he cut off understanding greedy, cut off 30%, anger, 30% only cut off only.

Q.14 So at that (time) how did you feel?

A. The feeling is aaah like the person you put down the 30% the heavy duty.

Q.15 Heavy duty (laughter), you put down heavy duty?

A. (laughter), heavy duty 30% (laughter).

Q.16 Immediately after this experience (yes) what did you do?

A. I still continue only, because I understand this Path and fruition, if I continue, would destroy all the (not clear), I am very comfort confidant, confidant to my teacher.

Q.17 Aaah that particular moment, is it a moment or is it something longer than that you experienced, *sotāpatti phala*?

A. No all the time, it is still there, cut off 30%, he not disappear anything, you all the time you disappear, all the time 30%, no more duty, no defilements, 30% cut off already, you all the time.

Q.18 You felt you cut off?

A. Aaah cut off cut off already, aaah no more.

Q.19 Could you, now you, cutting off 30% (mmm) or keeping the weight down (aaha aaha) is the effect (mmhm mmhm), was it the fruit itself, that moment or whatever, how did it lead to?

A. Actually like a person, when you plant a tree after that you can enjoy the tree, aaah enjoy the fruit, mmm that that enjoy the fruit, fruit is like a enjoy, earlier I aah enjoy the 30%, 30% is no more defilements, cut off 30% only, so I planning to try and cut off more, so carry on to continue focus 32 parts again.

Q.20 Aaah aaah again I am asking because it's not clear to me, did any particular, special occurrence (mmhm mmhm) or experience happen (mmhm mmhm) for you to feel "I cut off 30%"?

A. Oh! That means because greedy I understand, previous I very greedy, anger, very anger, delusion very strong, do anything I attachment, by my sixth sense,[3] all the time before. Before I, what my eyes see I will attach, greedy or anger will come in, after that, in that time, in that time, after the cut off 30%, what I saw aah but not really not really good also but not really bad bad, but because I cut off the 30%. I understanding, because the mind, *nāma* there reduced very greedy, defilements reduced, in this separate instance meaning different, defilement different.

Q.21 And that moment, just before that, what was your meditation, just before this moment (aaah) of cutting off, what is your meditation, what was your meditation?

A. Aaah I' m, same also, continue 32 parts only, aah continue, I focus 32 parts, all the time I focus, continue only. Because it occur wisdom, it produce 32 parts, understanding, is for the, because previous I actually I don't understand, cannot explain... (not clear) because previous I, we our ordinary person, because the Buddha's teaching, 32 parts, last 10 yrs, I already aah I know this 32 parts, but I don't know how its function go, after came to here, I understand but I think is, because the Buddha's teaching. Say if the person try to practice the 32 part, that means, the person beginning is not that, not that, different beginning, beginning like aah beginning to *Nibbāna* already, we can destroy the defilements. Actually I very confidant to Buddha's teaching. So I continue continue because understanding occur all the time, wisdom because fear are all the time, we saw sixth sense, sixth door saw outside, the attachment outside, we don't see our thing inside thing, because we don't see our inside thing, because we attachment, all the thing is a perfect one, so attachment very strong our mind. After that I focused, I continue my practice by this way understanding, is destroy because delusion because understanding, he understanding. When I open up my mind, open up my body, my inside, intestines, inside filth, inside, so you understanding, actually anything automatically the mind will understanding this... not really perfect, so because understanding you focus, continue, and open up your body, so your mind wisdom will arising, anything will destroy, open like the operation, all the time you not attachment, how beginning before you very attachment, how because you don't understand this. "How come from four elements only?," after that I when I focus, see this, wisdom will arising, understanding is different how not perfect, only ingredients, something something together, four elements, and ...your understanding is the four elements only, so understanding more and more because 32 parts give us the understanding wisdom arising. So in that time I understanding, I very happy, may be past life *kamma* also, good *kamma* ... is *pāramī* also. Because according I, I someone they checked my *pāramī* is past life, I am practice 32 parts also. So I all the time saw the 32 parts, so now will tread 32 parts very easy.

Q.22 Could it be that you fell asleep for a while?

A. Aaah

Q.23 Could it be that you fell asleep, for a while?

A. I fell asleep?

Q.24 Sleep in that meditation, at that moment could it be that you fell asleep?

A. Aah aah go in to sleep, normal normally like the same also but the feeling is different because he had, the mind had inside had concentration, had concentration. Because as concentration can produce the light and produce the aaah we are not that tired, it produce our mind very fresh, so sleep a little bit short, before is aaah can sleep whatever because very tired, easy tired, but after that, that issue little bit tired, but you feel inside a light is produce, is very light our body, concentration we feel very comfortable.

Q.25 After this experience?

A. Yes, after this.

Q.26 At what time was this, this experience, at what time was it?

A. Aaah actually is anytime.

Q.27 No *sotāpatti phala.*

A. Aha aha, almost the first month.

Q.28 From meditation?

A Yes, continue 32 parts.

Q.29 In Sri Lanka?

A. Yes.

Q.30 This *aranya*?

A. Yes yes.

Q.31 And what time of the day?

A. I little bit aaah not not very understanding, because I all the time 24 hours I almost three years I silent, I don't say anything, I don't want to disturb, because my teacher told me I don't talk, most I silent few years, but I don't say anything so I don't, the time look like not related to me also, I don't know what is the time, I don't think.

Q.32 Afternoon or morning?

A. Aaah normally I think normally is the day time.

Q.33 Day time?

A. Mmhm.

Q.34 Day time early morning or afternoon? Towards the latter part?

A. Oh yah yah, may be the morning, (morning?) yah.

Q.35 Where? In what posture?

A. Most of them, of the I walking meditation, I continued walking meditation, I still continue 32 parts also.

Q.36 Immediately before this *sotāpatti phala* (aaah) mmm did you wish for it?

A. Aaah I don't wish anything, I my mind, my mind only I want to destroy defilements, this my wish only. I don't wish for *sotāpatti phala* anything, I don't think about this thing, I think about how to destroy defilements.

Q.37 At that moment did you feel something very special?

A. Yes look like heavy thing put to my back 30 kilo, more than 30 kilo I throw away only, in that very comfortable (laugher).

Q.38 Do you experience that kind of feeling now, after that, from time to time?

A. In that time, I all the time I ... because that is my first Path so I, I don't feel that is more comfortable than now. Because now higher than that (laughter).

Q.39 But you experienced the feeling from time to time?

A. Yes yes yes.

Q.40 When you experienced that after the *phala* do you resolve and get it or does it happen automatically, do you think I should get it, resolve or in *adhisṭhāna*?

A. Aaah aaah aaah.

Q.41 Do you get it that way or automatically?

A. No no automatically, it automatically, mature, he would go in. (sorry?) When the *phala*, *magga phala* mature, it would go in, automatic go in.

Q.42 So when the *magga phala* matures you said you automatically go in?

A. Yes.

Q.43 Go in where?

A. Go in to first path.

Q.44 First path?

A. Aham ... after that mature 2nd path, mature 3rd path, after that higher than that

Q.45 When you go in, your, you say when you go in, what do you feel in there?

A. In there you feel, look like now I am very thirsty in that place had the water very fresh, that you can go to be relax, relax and really enjoy that place, before I can't enjoy this, these thing, now after I go there, I can enjoy, all the time enjoy because I don't have this thing (the monk pointing at his body), enjoy like aaah my mind duty heavy defilement throw away more than 30% in this stage, the feeling.

Q.46 Do you experience that, do you experience when you were not meditating also after that?

A. Yes yes he not disappear, all the time.

Q.47 It came all all the time?

A. All the time.

Q.48 From time to time?

A. From time to time, yes.

Q.49 How did you know it was *sotāpatti phala*?

A. Because the difference is, because aaah what I know, because I not don't know very much any Dhamma, but I, because the dha.... the produce the wisdom will arising, previous I am lay people that time, I'm monk I defilements very strong, how I cannot control, even one step only defilement occur, I very don't like this thing, but now even I go anywhere, I feel very comfortable all the time, look like the throw out .... 30 kilo, 30 the defilements, so you feel very comfortable in mind, I enjoy this thing.

Q.50 Did you realize that it was *sotāpatti phala* immediately after keeping the burden down or immediately with that special experience? (mmhm) Is it a special experience?

A. Yes for me very special experience. Why, because, I, previous I cannot, I didn't know how to throw out the defilements, now I cut but he not come back again. So I very happy, very enjoy this thing because I all the time can enjoy, previous I don't, cannot enjoy it.

Q.51 And you feel that now what you enjoy (yes) or not now, at that time, immediately after cutting off, what you enjoyed is due to that cutting off?

A. Yes yes.

Q.52 Immediately after the cutting off (mmm), or laying the burden (mmm), did you know that it was *sotāpatti phala*, immediately did you know or did you take some time?

A. Aaah In that I take some time, because my *Abhidhamma* knowledge not very good. But I, I understanding greedy anger delusion, I all the time I can focus it, he because I have the exact concentration, had light have wisdom, I can understanding occur aaah this is the ... previous I don't have this stage, greedy very strong or full time he very, after that cut off he little bit far from me, the defilements far from me, the feeling is far from me, 30% already, little bit far 30%, I understand this thing previous I don't have this thing, greedy, delusion, once cut out more than 30% already very different.

Q.53 How long did you take to understand that it was *sotāpatti phala*?

A. In in that time I think I had to a few months, because I knowledge in that time, I not so very good. After the second stage I understanding in that stage, first stage, when I go in second stage, I understand first stage, the difference (laugh).

Q.54 So can you explain, can you explain aaah what happened aaah aaah did you realize with your *sotāpatti phala* that aah there is no 'I' here, there is no I, there is no Soul (aha aha aha), did you realize that?

A Yeh of course because I, because understanding previous we attachment, the automatic the Dhamma the wisdom will arising, let me know because previous I understanding or attachment anything many thing, after that cut off this thing. we understanding this one is impermanent and non-self all the time many thing, we understanding mind all the time, in this world and outward our body and all the thing is, all the thing is impermanent and not self, so I understanding very different, is because he cannot change it, right view.

Q.55 So immediately after the first experience you realized that certain fetters, defilements were cut off?

A. Yes.

Q.56 But you got to know that it was *magga phala* after (aha aha) your second fruit?

A. Yes yeh.

Q.57 Is that correct?

A. Yes yes because I don't know how to compare. After go second stage, I will understand.

Q.58 Do you know now (mhm) that the first three fetters cut off?

A. First 3 fetters?

Q.59 Personality view (aha aha) doubt (yeh yeh) and *sīlabbata parāmāsa* (mmm) do you know that it's gone?

A. Yah yah I know.

Q. 60 Did the three fetters go together at the same time or one after the other? First fruit, first fruit?

A. Actually aaah like a, what we, when we continue, actually continually, when I continue focus 32 parts, he produce the wisdom all the time produce wisdom, wisdom that like a complete these three fetters, after complete he would go in automatically cut off by this thing.

Q.61 You you are using the word "go in and cut off"?

A. Aah because I go in, that mean I go in the path, aaah *magga phala, magga phala.*

Q.62 Go go in to *magga phala* and cut off?

A. Aha aha.

Q.63 So from time to time you go in to *magga phala* and cut off?

A. Actually is aah he will, second second, when you focus all the wisdom arising all the time, aaah minute per minute and the the three fetters slowly slowly cut off, like aaaah one minute. But we cannot say one minute, we say one second, second second 59 second, slowly slowly cut off, actually like this, after one minute you understand ah! Actually these three no more, these three fetters.

Q.64 So suddenly you understand, understand the three are no more. Is that correct?. But it went off gradually. Is that what you are saying?

A. Yes yes.

Q.65 But when you understood, you realized that all three are gone?

A. Yeh yeh yeh.

Q.66 At once?

A. Actually is, when I second stage I more understanding (laughter).

Q.67 So at this time you didn't know anything about *magga phala*?

A. What's the meaning ?

Q.68 At the first stage you didn't know?

A. Aha yes yes because previous I don't know my *Abhidhamma* or anything, very weak.

Q.69 Did you, later, did you realize it yourself or did your teacher tell you?

A. No, actually I realized myself, but I can experience it already because I, I experience it, I don't know what is the stage because I very weak in wisdom. After that I can cut off, I saw my greedy, anger, delusion. I from that, because I all the time has the concentration. So I focused the *nāma*, so I understanding, "Reduce many already."

Q.70 So when this happened you were at this meditation centre?

A. Yes yes yes.

Q.71 What do you think is *sakkāya diṭṭhi*?

A. *Sakkāya diṭṭhi*, is it wrong view? Is it?

Q.72 Yes wrong view, personality view.

A. The wrong view, our thinking our body is perfect, is impermanent, previous we are thinking like this way. This thing is my parents ... (not clear) I love it, I forever, everything is forever previous. After that cut off, it was reduced more than 30% the right view already, all the thing understanding impermanent, non-self, *dukkha*, automatically understanding.

Q.73 What do you think is personality view, personality view, *sakkāya diṭṭhi*, personality view?

A. My idea? My idea? My idea also same. I just now talked to you. previous I, what I know is aaah different is, aaah what I anything I attach to anything. After that in that time I attachment but with wisdom arising, this is impermanent anything.

Q.74 Do you have any doubts about the Buddha, Dhamma and the *Saṅgha*?

A. Oh no no no no I don't have doubt about Triple Gem.

Q.75 About *sīla*?

Q.76 What is *sīlabbata parāmāsa*?

A. *Sīla*?

Q.77 *Sīlabbata parāmāsa*, attachments to rites and rituals? Attachments to rites and rituals, *Buddha vandanā, bodhi vandanā*, do you do all that?

A. Mmm *Buddha vandanā, Bodhi vandanā*, I really really like to do this thing, like to do , but I respect.

Q.78 You like to do that? (mmm) No I mean do you do that?

A. Yes I do that. Every morning when I passing I wish, I pay the respect to Buddha.

Q.79 Did you pay respect to Buddha earlier, before your fruits of the Path?

A. Before I am same also. After I same also. More respect, because he give me the Dhamma, understanding.

Q.80 So now it's more?

A. Yes.

Q.81 So you have gratitude towards the Buddha?

A. What the gratitude? (you have gratitude? are you grateful?)
Yes yes yes because Buddha... (not clear)

Q.82 And do you have faith, confidence in the Buddha?

A. Yes very confident.

Q.83 So do you have unshaken confidence in the Buddha, Dhamma, and the *Saṅgha?*

A. Yes yes.

Q.84 Do you, will you look for another teacher other than the Buddha for salvation from suffering?

A. Aaah what's the meaning?

Q.85 Will you look for another teacher other then the Buddha?

A. Oh no no no.

Q.86 What is *ariyakanta sīla*? Do you know what *ariyakanta sīla* is? The *sīla* of a *sotapānna* (mmm) is said, is called *ariyakanta sīla* (aha aha) what is your idea about it? What do you think it is?

A. Sorry can you repeat that.

Q.87 The virtue, *sīla* of a *sotāpatti*, *sotāpanna* person, what do you think the *sīla* is? Is it unbroken *sīla* or do they break *sīla*, *sotāpanna sīla*, is unbroken?

A. Aha yeh yeh yeh.

Q.88 Do you think it is unbroken? Don't they say even a white lie?

A. That mean you say they are not broken the five *sīla* is it? Yes yes they don't they work all the time they keep five *sīla*, they don't break the five *sīla.*

Q.89 Don't they say at least a white lie?

A. What is white lie?

Q.90 A harmless lie?

A. Harmless? more harmless.

Q.91 Yah, some little little breaking somewhere?

A. Oh yeh yeh, they don't, they very fear to break *sīla*, they don't like to break the *sīla*, not like purposely, not like the, for anything he don't like to break the *sīla.*

Q.92 Even by mistake or something can it break for a *sotāpanna*?

A. What I think is normally he not purposely to do this thing. What I, what I, (not clear) by me is previous what I know is the first stage and second stage is *sīla* very strong, five precepts it won't break, because why because he very protect our life... (not clear). What I know previous is very easy to break because I don't care about. After that I very think. Because even even sometimes, the person's thing, I don't, previous I directly can move something, a person's thing (referring to stealing), now even I want to move I think about it or listen to person, personal one, to take it, to remove it. Difference is here. So they keep the *sīla* very quite strict.

Q.93 Quite strict, unbroken?

A. Yeh unbroken. Not purposely, won't broke the, not no no the mind want to break this thing, he very strict in the five precepts.

Q.94 Is that cutting off you were talking of, could it be the experience of a creator God or Soul?

A. Oh no no no this one easy, clear clear to our mind we follow the Dhamma, because the Buddha already go by this way, so we follow the Dhamma we experience it, so we can get many thing.

Q.95 Could it be that it's a creation of the mind?

A. Aaah not creation, but we have to follow our Buddha's Dhamma, because no Buddha's teaching, we cannot go by this way.

Q.96 When you cut off, when you say you go in to the *magga phala*, is there sight, sound, smell, touch, is there those in there? When you go in?

A. When you go in, in that time, the second very fast, like one second only look like. (one second?) one second. So he, the feeling is one second go in, like the person beginning it is like a defilements come from far, example the defilements like previous he is aaah my front is one foot only, after that (sorry?), after that one feet very close, after that cut it off already, cut off already, that first path go in already, he will go from 3 feet little bit far already, the defilements little bit far from me already, when you talk anything it little bit far, not influence anything directly, not directly go to influence, the difference is here.

Q. 97 So in that, at that, when you "go in" to the *magga phala* is there sound, site, smell, taste?

A. Yes same also.

Q.98 Do you feel all that in that, that "second"?

A. The second, I, because we are, we know we go in but we still has sound anything same also, but the mind mature, he go in, defilements destroy he go, different, difference is here only. But sound attachment anything little bit different attachment, difference is here.

Q.99 That is when you come out, later?

A. Yes yes.

Q.100 I am asking at that time when you are "in"?

A. Actually is the same also, like I go in, in that time, but I still can hear the sound, saw anything, sixth door still the same, but mind is difference, mind in that time one second you cannot see anything, one second you cannot see, very fast.

Q.101 So that "second" is what I am asking. (yes yes) I am asking about that "second," (yes yes) in that second mind cannot see anything. (yes yes) Is that what you are saying?

A. Yes yes.

Q.102 So mind can't see anything. Can it hear anything that "second"?

A. Actually I am not really go to that second how it happened, because may be I .... (not clear) one time only, in the second go in. but actually what the difference is, is second I could feel very comfortable to go in, go into difference place already actually.

Q.103 Do you find, is it comfortable for you to go in that second now also, after that? (after that) Can you go in to that "second"on and off?

A. No all the time, in all the time, I could feel in that time, because now I in different stage, because now I in different stage.

Q.104 Understand, I understand.

Q.105 Was there consciousness there in that "second"?

A. I don't see anything consciousness there.

Q.106 You didn't see anything consciousness there?

A. Mmm.

Q.107 Is it *Nibbāna* that you experienced?

A. Yeh can say the first stage *Nibbāna*.

Q.108 What is your understanding of *Nibbāna*?

A. *Nibbāna* like a free of the suffering, like a 30% like the *dukkha*, my duty the heavy duty (laugh), I throw out more than 30%.

Q.109 So you, at that time you felt you threw out 30% of heavy burden.

A. Yes yes.

Q.110 And what is *Nibbāna*?

A. What I know is can feel it like ... (not clear), enjoy that stage, destroy the defilements that stage.

Q.111 Destroy defilements?

A. Yes, destroy the defilements, *Nibbāna* first stage defilements, *Nibbāna* at that stage.

Q.112 *Nibbāna*, what is your understanding of *Nibbāna*, your concept of *Nibbāna?*

A. My concept is fully no more defilements.

Q.113 So what you experienced is cutting off only 30%? (I experienced yeh cutting off only 30% of defilements), *Nibbāna* is fully cutting off?

A. Yes yes.

Q.114 So there is a difference?

A. Yes very different very different.

Q.115 What happened to your view after this cutting off?

A. What that meaning, first stage in? oh, The view is it aaah.

Q.116 Did it change?

A. Yes very change.

Q.117 How?

A. When I saw anything previously compare we are not practice this thing, previous we are thinking anything we are attach anything, our idea very strong, we not think about the another person's concept or idea, some we are attachment our idea very strong, after that we changing, yeh can accept the something of good thing also not attachment anything very strong, very difference is here, to view anything, hear anything, sixth sense. (sorry?) Our six sixth sense very different.

Q.118 Sixth sense very different?

A. Yes.

Q.119 What is the essence of that experience?

A. What that meaning?

Q.120 The essence the crux of it, what did you realize, what is the significance?

A. The first Path?

Q.121 Yes, what is the significance, (significance?) I mean what is so important about it?

A. Important, I feel comfortable and no defilements in, in reduce defilements, enjoy the reduced defilements, that very comfortable.

Q.122 reduced the defilements?

A. Yes

Q.123 *Magga phala* is described as *animitta, appanihita, suññata,* do you know anything about this?

A. *Animitta*

Q.124 The signless (aha) unhankered (aha) and void, that is the way you describe a *magga phala*, do you know anything about it?

A. Aha, you talk about *Nibbāna*? That stage?

Q.125 They say *magga phala* is signless, unhankered and void, do you know anything about it? Do you feel that way?

A. I only understanding the higher stage than ... feeling, because I all the time, because my aim is destroy all defilements, my aim so I.

Q.126 After *sotāpatti phala* did you continue your meditation?

A. Yes I continued.

Q.127 Under a teacher?

A. Because the mind all the time, because in that time our mind, occur all the time occur wisdom, wisdom can produce our mind can cut off. You go by this way, better you go by this, wisdom can cut off more faster, the wisdom will arising all the time.

Q.128 No teacher?

A. In that time, some time our teacher say, "you better think yourself," in that time I thinking aaah, yeh, how come the teacher call me or I understanding mind, my mind is my teacher already.

Q.129 Your mind is your teacher?

A. Yes.

Q.130 First fruit, was there a teacher?

A. First fruit I need a teacher (laughter).

Q.131 So second fruit you don't need a teacher?

A. Yeh because wisdom arising.

Q.132 And for the future also you don't need teacher?

A. After, future I all the time because wisdom arising.

Q.133 Have you experienced the second fruit?

A. Yes.

Q.134 Can you describe that?

A. In the second fruit, in my, after one month I continually, because I all the time my duty is, I destroy all defilements is my duty. I destroy because I don't talk any more, the three years, I, my pay respect because I after that continue, defilements reduced, continue, after that may be very close may be three months, two more months, two more months, the second stage go in already. Because mature, very different is, he cut off 60% already in that time, feel the difference.

Q.135 you felt you cut off 60%?

A. Yeh yeh (laughter) because easy to compare, because 1st stage I don't know how to compare, second stage because he little bit far already 60% only noise anything, attachment cut off 60% more than 60. So I understand this stage go in already, the difference is enjoy more, enjoy the comfortable, more comfortable.

Q.136 Ealier you described that experience as the second stage?

A. Yes.

Q.137 Now?

A. Same also.

Q.138 Same?

A. Second to go in, the difference is the defilements reduced, far.

Q.139 So do you get the same experience in a bigger degree? Different degree, same experience? When you compare the two experiences (aha aha) what is the difference?

A. Difference is compare aaah more strong is. Because the right view more strong, so anything because aah this one impermanent because previous view little but may be this one not very perfect. But after that right view more strong, right view more strong, because is *sīla* more strong, because what I know I keep *sīla* more strong in that time, all the time because first stage more strong, after that second stage more strong, even the something move the personal thing (referring to stealing) I don't move the anything because the understanding is personal cannot move, can steal the someone, I don't like to steel because someone don't like it, because we very keep very strong this *sīla*, five precepts more strong.

Q. 140 Just immediately before the second experience did you wish for it?

A. Actually I no wish for it, is very natural, when you mature go in.

Q.141 So it's a natural process?

A. Yes I continue focus my my object, 32 parts.

Q.142 What was your meditation?

A. Same also. In that time I think, I continue in my walking meditation also same ... 32 parts.

Q. 143 Same, walking meditation and 32 parts?

A. Yes yes.

Q.144 Was it in the same *aranya*? This same place?

A. Yes same place.

Q.145 So this is *sakadāgami phala*, the second fruit?

A. Yes yes yes.

Q.146 After, immediately, I mean what time did you realize that it was the second fruit, is it immediately after the experience or after some time?

A. Aaah in that I already understanding. At that because very different, because I experience first time I don't know, second time I go in already because little bit defilement destroy more already and the thinking anything little bit far from me already, attachment far already, so I understanding second stage go in already, very different.

Q.147 So immediately after, you understood?

A. Yes I understand.

Q.148 The first experience, what time did you understand?

A. Aaah first stage is it? first stage little bit longer.

Q. 149 *Sotāpatti phala* what time did you understand?

A. I don't know is what time but normally I when I understand after one, a few week few week because I continually he was changing already so I understanding aah that stage produce wisdom all the time, arising. I understanding that that place I attainment the first path, is first path already I go in.

Q.150 Right, so it is when you got the second fruit you realized that you also got the first fruit at that time?

A. Yes yes yes.

Q.151 What made you think that it is the second fruit, it could have been the first fruit?

A. No no because the difference is, I already told you because the defilements reduced very differently.

Q.152 What do you think are the defilements that reduced?

A. I reduced more strong greedy, previous more, now after that really less, less already less already, I understand less than 60% only, because I all the time had concentration mind produced wisdom more already, understanding different, reduced more already, anger also reduced 60% already, delusion same also.

Q.153 Could be again a creation of the mind?

A. Aaah not actually, not creation the mind actually we are, may be our practice, understanding the, Buddha, Dhamma, *Saṅgha* so the understanding, is we follow this thing so we get path and fruition, because reduce the defilements.

Q.154 Because you follow the Path you get the fruit?

A. Yes yes.

Q. 155 So immediately before that (yes) did you wish for it?

A. Actually I not wish for it. I think very natural, when mature would go in.

Q.156 When mature would go in?

A. Yeh yeh.

Q. 157 Do you experience it now also (yes) from time to time?

A. Yes yes all the time mhm mhm.

Q.158 When you are in meditation or not in meditation?

A. No all the time I, I enjoy it, the second stage, same because he fully no more 60% defilements.

Q.159 You said that moment at the first fruit there was a "second," cutting off, in the second fruit was there a "second"?

A. Same also, same also.

Q.160 Go in?

A. You go in only.

Q.161 Now after that experience when you meditate, do you feel that "going in"?

A. Actually because I am different stage already only, higher than that.

Q.162 Yes higher, second stage, do you feel going in to the second stage, after that couple of times or when you are in meditation do you feel from time to time you go in to the?

A. Because actually now I not go in to that stage, I all the time I continue, because in that time I all the time understanding the second stage then, but now it's a different.

Q.163 OK OK now after the second stage, immediately after that second experience what did you do?

A. I continue practice, after that few months I think three four months, third stage go in already, get third stage, more easy understanding, more easy.

Q.164 Third stage?

A. Third stage go in, *anāgāmi* go in because more different is, because more deeper deeper is more different defilement very destroyed.

Q.165 So what you are saying is you experienced the third stage also?

A. Yes.

Q.166 *Anāgāmi phala*?

A. Yes.

Q.167 And how did that happen, can you tell us that experience?

A. What happen is like, compare the previous, I thought about this, world no more defilements only, I thought in that time, I thought at that time already because compare previous, I thought no more defilements already because compare the previous. Even I move one step all the defilements come in and attack me, because now third stage go in, third stage already the defilements almost destroyed 90 more than 90%, 99% already. So I thinking at that time, may be no more already, after that I checked ah! A little bit delusion only 1–2% only, in there very different, because no more anger already, in that time, anger delusion greedy almost little bit only, little bit greed, anger is no more already.

Q.168 Third experience, where did it happen? Here? In this *aranya*?

A. Yes same also.

Q.169 What was the meditation posture?

A. I think that time if I am not wrong. May be it sit.

Q.170 Sitting?

A. Yes.

Q.171 What time of the day?

A. May be day time.

Q.172 Immediately after that what did you do?

A. I continue to practice again?

Q.173 And what was your meditation at that time?

A. All the time 32 parts only continue 32 parts.

Q.174 And did you, can you describe that particular experience, third experience?

A. Third experienced, in that place, even if someone blame me anger me I only smile, only calm and peace only, I don't say anything, my mind not produce anger. So that stage even anything also I saw I smiling already but attach, still little bit attachment. Ah! I would go to heaven, at this stage I was thinking, I thinking at this stage, I still go to heaven but all the time very happy, it produce happy many and no anger anything no anger.

Q.175 Lust?

A. Lust? I think I cannot say the lust, but delusion may be I in that time I know very little.

Q.176 Delusion very little?

A. Yeh very little what I can say.

Q. 177 Again the third fruit, did you realize it yourself or did your teacher tell you?

A. Actually in that time actually I thought, I thought all the defilements no more. What I compare previous. So in that time I, I went to my teacher there, I asked teacher, actually I look like no more defilements, I asked my teacher, let him know. Actually because I compare the previous, I very different very strong, now no more look like anger anything ... (not clear) I asked the teacher, I understand the teacher is already experienced person, so I asked, the teacher, calm and peace, told me actually have four stages.

Q.178 Sorry?

A. Actually teacher said have four stages, when he say have four stages by now wisdom arising I understanding.

Q.179 What did the teacher tell you?

A. My teacher tell me actually have four stages. Had four stages that means first stage, second stage, third and *Arahant* stage. That means he don't say anything, he say have four stages. That means he don't say you in which stage, but I understanding.

Q.180 Oh! I see! he said that there are four stages. Ah oh! oh! I see.

A. Ah Ah I understand I third stage already, because I second I already know, but he don't mention anything, because he said have four stage, that means I had , I focus I had delusion little bit that time.

Q.181 So in other words the teacher helped you to correct?

A. No no he just mention had four stage I only paid respect and I go away. I understanding it's 3rd stage only.

Q.182 So you thought only third stage?

A. Aha aha.

Q.183 And now in the third fruit do you experience the same thing aah over and over again, the cutting off?

A. Yes yes yes in that time, all the time, the same also. No anger no anything so I continue to practice 32 parts.

Q.184 What about "going in"? You said in the first second fruit you felt "going in"?

A. Actually I not "going in" that stage, I all the time I continue to, continue 32 parts only. I don't "go in" anything, I produce all the time produce, focus 32 parts continue wisdom because my aim is destroy, *Arahant*.

Q.185 Now I am asking you after the third fruit did you experience that similar experience of "going in"?

A. Yes yes.

Q.186 You did? (yes yes) Automatically?

A. Yes automatically.

Q.187 Or you wished for it?

A. No no you mature, when you wisdom enough you automatically go in.

Q.188 Now what you are saying is you don't "go in" anymore, you want to cut off defilements totally?

A. Yes yes because my aim.

Q.189 So when you "go in" those days, after the third, when you go in what is the difference between that "going in" and earlier two "going in"?

A. The difference is I always say, when the second stage, first stage I destroy because my something, to me my front is little bit far, one foot only, look like one foot first stage, second little bit far already defilements come from, thirds stage already come from three feet, nothing impact to me directly, so I understand that "going in" that stage is different stage.

Q.190 So because the defilements are far you realized that "going in" is different quality, is that correct?

A. Yes yes.

Q.191 At the third fruit, now they say in the text that there is no greed anger, aversion. Five sensual pleasures, taste, sound, and all that, do you have any attachments to all that?

A. Actually not very attachment but habitual have, (habitual?) habitual because.

Q.192 What kind of habitual attachment?

A. Habitual, we cannot say no, we like to eat a fruit, we are always same same thing we like to eat, but after that we not thinking, we not desire strong, greedy want to attachment but we like to pick like same thing what we liked.

Q.193 So you exercise a choice?

A. Aah aah the difference is, in the second stage we still attachment to this one and that. I like to taste but now is no more, doesn't matter, doesn't matter because we can choose another thing, the difference is here, all the things, six sense same also.

Q.194 So you do exercise a choice depending on likes and dislikes?

A. What that likes?

Q.195 There are likes and dislikes, you like certain things, you don't like certain things.

A. Aah yeh yeh. Not not actually likes not really likes, but we still have thinking habitual, there are habitual, we like this one previous I like to take, so I continue to take, if no, doesn't matter I can replace another thing.

Q.196 Do you feel angry?

A. In third stage? no no in that no anger.

Q.197 Do you get irritated?

A. No no I irritated no irritated.

Q.198 Fear? (no) Do you feel frightened?

A. No, One example in that time *pindapata*, inside that, inside have one snake come in. Some snake come in. So I don't know my mind very calm because previous I very fear the snake, this thing. After that I go to take my bowl and go to catch them catch that, actually they always fear. Actually I looked like this one is rubber band, looked like the mind looked like rubber only.

Q.199 So you touched it?

A. I want to catch, do to them, I really fear previous. Oh! I see! I don't fear the death anything.

Q.200 So you didn't feel frightened? That's what you say?

A. Yeh yeh my mind very calm, very peace, happy, I no anger.

Q. 201 So what happened when the snake came in?

A. I want to go to catch him. He he run away.

Q.202 So you tried to catch him?

A. Yeh.

Q.203 You went up to him?

A. Yes actually after go back, how come I want to catch the snake because previous I very fear this thing. Someday I very fear. How come he catch that, I don't fear this thing looked like rubber band only (laugh).

Q.204 Do you long for the sound of Dhamma?

A. What that meaning?

Q.205 Do you, are you attached aah to the sound of Dhamma, Dhamma, you like to listen to Dhamma (previous?) Now now in the third fruit is there attachment to Dhamma, sound of *pirith*, sound of.

A. Actually anything not very attachment anything.

Q.206 Not even for Dhamma?

A. Even anything look like mind is Dhamma understanding (sorry?) mind is produce Dhamma already.

Q.207 Mind produces Dhamma?

A. Aaah.

Q.208 do you like to go to the *brahmā* world?

A. In that time I still thinking yeh I would go to *deva* world, I understand I would go, I don't know but I will 100% I will go.

Q.209 Now you know that you will go?

A. Now a different stage. So in that stage go in already, I don't like anything, no anything I like.

Q.210 So now after the third fruit you don't like to go anywhere?

A. Yeh.

Q.211 Are there any defilements remaining?

A. Aaah what's it?

Q. 212 Are there any defilements remaining in you now?

A. No I all the time clear only, coming stop, coming stop.

Q.213 Defilements come?

A. No no no defilements come, no defilements. In me I think don't want this thing. Because I all the emptiness. Air only cannot saw anything, my mind cannot saw anything, even I close the eye this world is emptiness.

Q.214 Now?

A. Yeh I all the time because all the emptiness, I cannot saw anything.

Q.215 Have you experienced the fourth fruit?

A. Yes .

Q.216 Arahanthood?

A. Yes.

Q.217 Can you experience (explain) that fruit?

A. In that fruit a little bit longer, because in that third stage I using almost 9 months or 1 year.

Q.218 Nine months after the 3rd fruit?

A. Aha, 3rd fruit, that mean, I using 1st 2nd stage, third stage, I using almost one year. Because I in that time I asked the teacher. The teacher said have four stages, I understand only, so I continually because not my stage, I don't like *deva* actually, because I thinking *deva* want to rebirth again, I want to go to there spend many time, so I continue because my aim is to destroy all defilements. Don't want to this, so I continually to practise more hard more hard more strong, all the time when I saw anything I that time almost turn, turn already in that time I focus 32 part. In one day, very I continue even I sleep I all the time 32 parts only.

Q.219 I couldn't get you.

A. All the time I focus 32 parts, continue 32 parts, (32 parts?) *asubha*, 32 parts, all the time I continue, I don't stop, I won't talking, won't anything continuing.

Q.220 After the 3rd fruit?

A. Aha aha I very up to almost 2 years, using 2 years, continuous. I half way, I go to do my duty *Mahā Thera* there, after that half way focus. He go in one second, he arising and stop again. I understanding "Ah! No more already." All stop already, I understanding because I, I, I, in my mind. I told my teacher, because I understand my teacher know my mind, I told my teacher "Teacher my duty no more, I already finished." My teacher very happy (laugh). He run away run to tell ... he told me very happy, good good good.

Q.221 So the fourth fruit, you realized it yourself?

A. Yes.

Q. 222 When you were walking up to do your duty?

A. Yes to do my duty.

Q.223 How did you feel?

A. I feel anything, look like I, I imagination, I visualize because I, I all the time I visualize, using by this way this way, because I using ...I using I imagination, I using one knife, you try put your head cut it off, how you feeling, in the 3rd path I still had little bit, little bit, fear.

Q. 224 fear?

A. little bit not fear but little bit different because he still inside have elements.

Q.225 Because you imagined you kept a knife and cut? (not clear)

A. After 4th stage the difference is, I using the knife cut it off, I cut air only, nothing already, inside all emptiness already, and here what I saw, I all the time because produce all the wisdom all the time, what I saw that anything that someone hatred me I I calm and peace only, I understand this person is hatred, hate me, anger me, because why, but I don't understanding there I but don't anger to him anything, all the time understanding only, because very far, anger for anything, attachment very far already, look like not this (the monk pointing at his body) will not connection anything, not related to me, hatred or anything same only.

Q.226 So aaah *bhante* now as an *Arahant* how do you feel? Is there happiness and joy?

A. May be I what I say I attainment this, I attainment some I saw the *sutta* some attainment they are very happy all the time, actually I am very happy but I am very dull. (very?) very dull dull dull, very boring, dull (laugh), very dull this world, because don't like this world, because I all the time I cannot saw this world anything empty only.

Q.227 You can see only emptiness in this world?

A. When I yeh I, my mind, I eye open, I can see, but I close my eyes this world is nothing. I cannot imagine how is my face look like, how is my parents how is anything, emptiness only because like air particles only, cannot see anything.

Q.228 You can see only as air particles?

A. Yeh particles.

Q.229 When you close your eyes?

A. Yeh.

Q.230 When you open your eyes?

A. When open I some time I saw particles particles there but he not gaining not reduce, not gaining not reduce, all look like, like what is it, like that television before the channel, without channel, they are seeing particles particles, all the time this world is like that.

Q.231 So do you see me like that?

A. I see you, I understanding, but sometimes have small small particles there because my attainment different so he, this attainment cannot produce concentration, concentration very low because he, what I know is *arūpa jhāna parinibbāna*, in that time, because why when in that time, I destroy, my teacher, I determination teacher know, teacher already know. In that time I happy I calm, "teacher! I no more defilements, when I die I would like to know," because I don't know I die because I, as a condition I know that this is dependent origination. I focus continue 32 parts, destroy all defilements this way, so my teacher told me, so now you attain *parinibbāna parinibbāna* already. When you 80 years time you are *parinibbāna*. In 80 years. I say very long time I have to wait 80 years.

Q.232 To die? *Parinibbāna* sorry.

A Yah so I don't like to lie, this I so I don't believe anything, I eat air only.

Q.233 You eat air?

A. Aaah.

Q.234 No taste?

A. Taste have, (taste have?) but understanding but he not attachment anything, if you like the thing you take the thing, doesn't matter. If the path and fruition, that path very different. Anything you like, OK, you want to take doesn't matter. I don't like more thing, I like less thing, less better but not attachment. If you give me anything doesn't matter, but I like very less thing only.

Q.235 *Bhante* with your new experience of Arahantship do you have feeling? Do you have painful feeling?

A. Actually painful and what I mean is I, I can describe something painful, pain. We have the body, because I am still have this body, so he has the sense, if I am not robot. I am not wood, I still have sense or anything. So he has sense like the next habitual only, habitual.

Q.236 Habitual?

A. Habitual like this thing we have our life but he cut off already 90%, 99% already the feeling anything. Normally, normally the person he cut, burn, something or fire burn something, he will anger will arising. Our but even when I burn, may be I will smile, don't have difference of this type.

Q.237 Bhante how long ago did you have this experience?

A. I already have.

Q.238 How long ago? How long ago from now? From now?

A. From that I what I know is that day 2004 (2004?) March (March?) 28th (March 28?). In that time, second I destroy all because I very understanding that time, can remember that day. So aah this day aah in that moment I walked to do my duty half way I go arising.

Q.239 Outside?

A. Yes outside.

Q. 240 That one moment you felt you cut off?

A. Yes destroy all.

Q.241 Immediately before that what was your meditation?

A. I same also I go to duty, walking, 32 parts I continue also my.

Q.242 And did you wish for the Arahantship immediately before that did you wish?

A. Already no wish. But I have made a wish, my wish is destroy all defilements. Not, I don't say *Arahant*, I understanding "I don't want defilements" (laugh).

Q.243 So now if your, cut off you will have pain?

A. Pain would normally have a little bit, but he not have the feeling anger or sad part or don't have this type .

Q.244 So no sadness?

A No no this type.

Q.245 With this new experience of cutting off all defilements, what is the difference in your view from the earlier, from the third fruit?

A. Very different is.

Q.246 Very different, is it very different?

A. Very different is. Aah the third part is only 99% only cut off. I can explain like this way. 1% only delusion. Destroy all delusion because delusion because when I anything we have thinking ah! I had parent or anything, when he destroy anything this emptiness already. I don't think about past, I don't think about future no planning now. I don't think about, no planning this thing.

Q.247 So at the third fruit you knew you had parents?

A. Yeh because because have I said have to do something to my parents, my family, anything had this thing.

Q.248 So you felt you had to do something for your family?

A. Aaha aha family anything.

Q.249 So now you don't feel you have parents?

A. Don't have no not say I have parents, actually I have, I know but not attachment to these thing, I understand is this one is our our even every person have to die every separate one day, he think about, understanding Dhamma finish but no sadness anything, don't have this thing.

Q.250 Right, no attachments.

A. Yeh attachments, friendly anything only like a duty only.

Q.251 Only duty?

A. Aha my duty is *Saṅgha* already what I do.

Q.252 So you said now, they say an *Arahant* lives in the present moment all the time, all the time mindfulness, is that how you feel?

A. Actually may be attainment is different, because attainment we cannot say, actually I don't know another *Arahant*, because he some time they have habitual, we cannot say he all the time mindful, some time he not purposely sometime he may be what I know is know is some time he has sickness or anything he cannot be mindfulness because body problem, have body problem, Not because all the time, he all the time he understanding. No defilements come in. So he very, what he done anything he can understanding all the time, all the thing you cannot say 100% some they have some told me he has habitual or may be sickness or anything, some time cannot describe 100% like this.

Q.253 Aaah in your case bhante do you see any kind of that habitual aaah kind of behavioural patterns? Do you see in you now?

A. What the habitual?

Q.254 Now after the *Arahant* experience, do you see in you any habits?

A. Habits actually habitual very less. But I try to correct (not clear) sometimes little bit not would (not clear) sometimes I thinking not good. If I not correct my behaviour some time habitual no good, If I some time little bit me want to put something of what aah..

Q.255 You want to put something?

A. No no some time, I describe something a little habitual our sometime thinking if too heavy too heavy I not have but some time habitual little I try to correct it, correct he way .. (not clear)

Q.256 I can't get you.

A. I meaning is habitual normally I have, eat the something or I like the thing I still same also. If don't have also doesn't matter. That difference is like this way.

Q.257 So habits can be for food?

A. Habit but not attachment anything now now no more doesn't matter. Some time white rice also OK no attachment, 3rd stage different totally different. Now only water only, may be I thinking, only water no rice, doesn't matter water only, no desire to this thing.

Q.258 So now if it is water only you would take?

A Yeh if no choice I would take.

Q.259 OK then in the third fruit?

A. In the third fruit still "How come no rice?" or anything still have this thing (laugh).

Q.260 3rd fruit you think "How come no rice, no water"?

A. Aaha.

Q.261 Now it's "OK"?

A. It's OK may be my my *dāna* "offer like this way" I would think this way. Because I no desire very strong.

Q.262 Now as an *Arahant* do you feel you should teach the Dhamma to others?

A. Actually for me it's a little bit difficult, why first my direct talk I had little bit concentration not strong, but Dhamma because in my mind over the word or anything aah aah like the thing image erase already, no more, I keep memory, little bit difficult.

Q.263 Sorry?

A. I keep the memory little bit difficult. May be this stage is different because I destroy from *arūpa jhāna* destroy *arūpa jhāna*, that mean in that stage in that stage I concentrate cannot develop, all the time *arūpa* only cannot saw anything. Some time I thinking word also little bit difficult. Some day I thinking "How come *Arahant* they say memory very strong?," I say I describe sometime because emptiness destroy. I all inside cannot saw anything but good is 24 hours is emptiness but is dull only, little bit dull.

Q.264 Very dull?

A. The mind is very dull.

Q.265 Dull? D..U..L....L...?

A. Aha aha.

Q.266 Bhante are you inclined to help others with the Dhamma?

A. I like to actually, I don't like to go out anywhere, I like forest and I like to help *Saṅgha* only. *Saṅgha* duty, what *Saṅgha* give me, I try to do for help the *Saṅgha*.

Q.267 You like to help the *Saṅgha*?

A. Aha aha *Saṅgha* go smooth the way already.

Q.268 You don't like to go out?

A. I Like, I don't like sleeping any way don't like enjoy, I don't desire to do this thing.

Q.269 You like to teach?

A. Actually I don't aaah I not really qualified to teaching teaching yet because my knowledge very little.

Q.270 You haven't read enough?

A. Aha aha not read enough.

Q.271 But you have enough knowledge (laugh).

A. I don't know, but for me I all time emptiness. But you ask me I understanding the mind produce understanding the very different is the path. Very different.

Q.272 Bhante after you spoke of the experience of the snake (aha yah) after third fruit, have you experienced anything like that after the fourth fruit. Anything that should have brought fear?

A. In fear actually like aaah we are at some time I imagination.

Q.273 Sorry? I Can't.

A. You talk of the 3rd stage or 4th stage, talk of the 3rd stage or 4th stage?

Q.274 I want to know the difference between the 3rd stage and the 4th stage in fear.

A. In fear I not purposely go to so that, I understanding I imagination in that time.

Q.275 Sorry?

A. Third stage third stage some time I using woman, some time using woman is greedy in woman is no more, the sexual anything. So I imagination in that time is image of woman arising anything how is my mind moving, actually my mind is no no have this thing delusion, still have but a little bit is delusion still have in 3rd stage, delusion there.

Q.276 In what sense, in what sense do you have delusion?

A. In one sense is, I little bit not remember, but try to use imagination that time, I used many way to test my mind, in that 3rd stage, I used knife imagination I use a knife, I still can feel he actually not fear but he still has the particles inside look like you cut it, you have body, you still feel have body in that time.

Q.277 You feel you still have body?

A. Aah aha in that time the different.

Q.278 After that time?

A. Destroy in that time, I using the knife, cut it and me imagination cut it off, I directly can cut it whatever I can take off, so in that time I what I know is aaah in that time, my teacher, I come to my teacher, my teacher asked me, one word only "How is your non self?" I respond, "My non self, if the person take out my eye cut it off my head piece by piece, my anger is not arise, even one word come from my mind. I don't have this thing." So I describe it to my teacher. I no more no more anger, no more anything, no more fear, that from that no more this thing.

Q.279 That was your fourth *phala* experience?

A. Aha aha compare the 3rd I still have body.

Q.280 I have body, I cut my body?

A. Aaha have this thing, I after, I now I cut anything is not my thing, I, my duty only, if no more, no more my duty only, no more my duty only.

Q.281 Do you feel now, on the fourth fruit, while you were walking up there you experienced this "going in," now from time to time do you experience that?

A. Yeh I all the time, like a even I saw, I hear, I think, sixth or anything I no defilements. Even they talk anger to me, even now describe as, even the woman take up all the thing I some time describe something all the time it takes out all because previous I greedy very strong this thing attachment, after that now I imagine all the thing they do something the bad thing in my face imagine only, I don't have this feeling or anything, my thought hear only saw only I imagination anything not this world look like not related to me.

Q.282 You feel this world is not related to you?

A. Aaah related to me, my body or anything I only particle only, I don't think particles is me also. So I don't think about now also, I don't think now.

Q.283 So the crux of that experience, if I put it to you, is like you don't feel a part of this world is that correct?

A. What that?

Q.284 You said just now this body, sorry, that you don't feel a part of this body, is that what you said?

A. yeh yeh anything when it cut it off or anything this world doesn't belong to me?

Q.285 Oh! This world doesn't belong to you?

A. Aha anything nothing because all the 24 hours saw particles only, cannot saw anything (24 hours?) aaah 24 hours, all the time emptiness, the mind *kiriya kiriya* the mind *javana kiriya* only, nothing.

Q.286 *Kiriya kiriya*? OK so you feel there is only *kiriya* all the time.

A. All the time, hear sixth or what it do *kiriya* only don't do anything.

Q.287 But *bhante* do you sleep?

A. Yes I sleep.

Q.288 In your sleep do you go in to good deep sleep?

A. Deep sleep normal is depend upon the body. Body some time healthy, sometimes health not have.

Q.289 Sorry?

A. Sometimes health is not very good, sometimes I will sleep little bit longer also because I wake up nothing to do also, so I focus I focus all the time in bed also, sometimes wake aaah little bit tired I will sleep, same like ordinary person but difference is no attachment anything.

Q.290 So you sleep like ordinary person?

A. But very short time.

Q.291 In the night how much do you sleep?

A. Normally I follow the here, 9 plus 10, after that 12 O'clock 1 O' clock wake up already, but wake up nothing to do, focus again sleep again.

Q.292 Focus where?

A. Focus particles only, nothing to do, no work to do so he wake up, he self some times to fresh the mind wake up nothing to do, all emptiness also, lay out there tired sleep again, wake up some time.

Q.293 Aaah you must be, no wonder you say you are very dull.

A. Yeh very dull because this world all the particles (laughter) sometimes I cannot accept this world, I that time "How come this world?, this world what I saw previous, still I enjoyed that *deva* anything still, after that no more" but my mind don't have no desire, dull, what is that, how to describe, I don't know how to describe the thing, like air only, you cannot see say that air is, have feeling (laughter).

Q.294 Sorry? Air?

A. Like air, air no feeling, my air, my body is like air only, I imagination. I use my hand, go to here he out come out behind already (showing with the fist that when he presses the hand against the chest, it comes out from the back) air only.

Q.295 So you feel your body is like air?

A. Emptiness all the time. Particles only, cannot saw anything.

Q.296 Now bhante do you feel you should serve the Dhamma?

A. I don't think so. But depend my teacher what teacher, what the teacher say I follow, I follow *Saṅgha* what *Saṅgha* duty give to me I will do.

Q.297 Right *bhante* now as an *Arahant* do you have *saddhā* in the Buddha?

A. Yes very strong.

Q.298 Very strong? Strong *saddhā*, can you describe that *saddhā*?

A. I don't know how to describe *saddhā* to me, but I understanding if the no Buddha I cannot attain first Path, I still may be in the hell, because I still greedy anger delusion very strong person before. In this last 3–5 years, after three year changed character fully emptiness so I cannot say, I very grate. Because because very thanks to Buddha teaching I have destroyed defilements because had the good teacher, very important also guide me.

Q.299 So you have *saddhā*?

A. Very *saddhā* to triple gem.

Q.300 Very *saddhā* to triple gem?

A. Not no thinking about, if the someone call you believe another saint no no because Buddha's teaching is higher in the this world.

Q.301 *Bhante* do you do Buddha *vandanā* now?

A. What that?

Q.302 Now do you do Buddha *vandanā*, worshiping the Buddha?

A. Aaah some time, when I go there (pointing to the direction of the shrine room), I will saw the Buddha, I will pay respect only.

Q.303 You pay respect by bowing your head?

A. Yeh sometimes pay bowing.

Q.304 What about worshiping, going down on your knees, chanting, do you do all this?

A. Aaah previous I have, but now I very less, but I in mind produce understanding, my mind is Dhamma already.

Q.305 OK so at the third stage did you do *vandanā*, chanting?

A. little bit, less also. Because I actually, my habitual not so strong like this way previous also.

Q.306 OK even before the first fruit it was not so strong, habitual?

A. Unless I had sick, I had fear, I will chanting at that time (laughter), but now I don't have anything, so I don't chanting or anything or the mind produce Dhamma.

Q.307 *Bhante* going back to your practice, what is the role *samādhi* or *jhāna* played in your practice?

A. *Jhāna*? (*Jhāna* or *samādhi*) *Jhāna Jhāna* I *Jhāna* as concentration only.

(OK for concentration only).

Q.308 Do you consider yourself *samatha* or *vipassanāyānika*?

A. I am *vipassanā*, destroy defilements, not *samatha.*

Q.309 Not *samatha, sukkha vipassanā*?

A. Yes.

Q.310 Did you use light perception? (what?) light perception, light in the mind?

A. Yes yes.

Q.311 Up to what *jhāna* did you go?

A. Actually I not *jhāna* only as concentration only.

Q.312 OK not *jhāna*, no *jhāna*, that is *vipasssanā jhāna*?

A. Yes, vipassanā *jhāna*.

Q.313 So can you describe your vipassanā *jhāna*?

A. I *vipassanā jhāna* had the light. had the any, the he very close to first *jhāna* but he not close yet, but he had light, had five faculty there inside, mmm feel body very light, very concentration strong, all the time focus anything light, when I want to open the eyes saw the particles only, particle will arising all the time, because concentration is very strong.

Q.314 Concentration is very strong?

A. I want to saw, concentration .... (not clear), all the time I can saw.

Q.315 So in the *vipassanā jhāna* is there light? Light perception, light perception?

A. What that light perception?

Q.316 Certain *samatha*, when you develop *samatha* certain people see a internal light.

A. Yeh yeh yeh yeh light yeh.

Q.317 So do you get that?

A. Yes get that, inside.

Q.318 In *vipassanā jhāna* you get it?

A. Yes.

Q.319 In *samatha* sometimes we say *rūpa jhāna, arūpa jhāna*, 1, 2, 3, 4, like that, do you get it in your *vipasssanā Jhāna?*

A. I don't have this thing, because I don't this thing because I don't have *jhāna.*

Q.320 You don't have *jhāna*, you don't consider *samatha jhāna* and *vipasssanā jhāna* to be the same.

A. Yes destroy defilements only *vipassanā.*

Q.321 So in other words for *magga phala*, for Arahanthood you don't need, necessarily need *jhāna*?

A. Yeh I don't need because I don't need *jhāna* also because we like to understanding our body because destroy defilements is wisdom not the *jhāna, jhāna* cannot produce destroy defilements.

Q.322 If I may ask you again, do you have joy and happiness and contentment in you as an *Arahant* (in now?) now as an *Arahant* do you have joy happiness and contentment?

A What that meaning, contentment?

Q.323 Are you happy with what you are?

A. Oh! If you say I happy, I happy, I happy all the time, If I say I con... (content) I con. (content). All the time but I happy I not attachment anything because the mind no defilements because happy.

Q.324 When you compare now before you got on to the Path then what is the difference?

A. First path or what?

Q.325 No as a *puthujjana*?

A. oh! As a *puthujjana* oh! very different. I don't know how to compare this thing. (laugh) I can compare you like I previous I *puthujjana* like fff... something like fff... very dirty.

Q.326 like what?

A. like faeces faeces (aha aha OK OK faeces) aha when I before very dirty defilements greedy, anger, delusion, anything. Turn to here I all the time light and comfortable, emptiness all the time like the air only, no attachments anything, so very, in that time all the thing attachments in the *puthujjana* . (Oh! You said faeces?) (laugh).

Q.327 Would you recommend this Path to others?

A. What that?

Q.328 Would you recommend this Dhamma to others? Recommend?

A. Some time every difficult, to introduce to recommend, why now the time, now the day, some time what I know, this attainment, the Path and fruition actually many were happy nobody like thinking. When I go back to home, I try to sharing the many the enjoy this this, discuss to the senior monks, because I am *sāmanera* discuss to them, some they are anger also. They are not belief, they are thinking not belief, now in this day still have *Arahant* can attain. I told them, is some anger to me. I silent only. I cannot say anything. I know they are do something bad *kamma* also. I cannot say anything why because one they even their senior monks, they don't belief have *Arahant*s now (laugh). What I say I have experienced a few times their anger to me also, sometimes scold me also so I silent cannot say anything. I know how you know, you think you want to teach someone if they thinking you say anything they don't like, anger to you, they do very bad *kamma* also. So you better, because we don't have psychic power very difficult to teach a person.

Q.329 What made you become a monk?

A. Because I had the very good way, may be the good *pāramī*, I don't want defilement.

Q.330 So you didn't try this being a layman?

A. No I don't like lay people their life. Because lay people life because in that time I very attachment. Drink or anything the bad thing I do. But after I do I very regret, may be my *pāramī* arising, drink whisky all the time you have, but you don't have all the time your healthy, your health. I will old one day, my organs cannot function one day, I very fear this thing, anything will I fear, one day will destroy, I had money I had anything but one day my body cannot function, money still have but anything have I cannot move anything, I have to find something in that time.

Q.331 Now do you have any kind of attraction to anything?

A. No I don't have, I told you my mind all 24 hours emptiness, very dull (laugh).

Q.332 When you started practising this did you think that you would attain *Nibbāna* this birth itself ?

A. Aaah previous, I will tell a story, when I came that time I defilements very strong, I came to *aranya,* I like *aranya*, actually not really like but I nowhere to go already why because previous I am Mahāyāna monk, Mahāyāna, I first teacher, I go I went there I thinking because I don't lay people go to Mahāyāna monk, I thinking to be monk very good because I want to release, very different thing. When I go to the first teacher there, first teacher is very difficult, because Mahāyāna, they want to do many thing, they need many thing, very foolish to service to opposite to my mind I very obstacle, distract, how come being a monk I want to do many thing, previous I lay people I don't want to many thing also, how come I don't catch many thing now, I want to release. So I asked my teacher "Teacher can I go to meditate?," because my mind many defilements, I persuade the person, a white person because defilement come to me all mine, I cannot, after that he said cannot if you want to go you disrobe, I said want to go to many thing want to disrobe also, I say in that time OK I disrobe, I go to second teacher 2nd teacher, 2nd teacher I go away, 2nd teacher, I want to go to another Burma, but outside to meditate. Go to there when meditate 1year, 1 ½ year come back. So my teacher said you cannot produce something, you come to here you eat and you go, you better go away. We go away and I thinking I want to meditate very difficult also, to be good monk very difficult because they don't want to meditate anything. So I thinking I better go away. So I connection, connect to the Sri Lanka, very good place, so I thinking ah! this place very good, so I came to here. So I all the time very defilements very strong. One day the teacher told me, I come from the hill, from there, hill, hill. I come down, very defilements very many, I thinking one day no more defilements, very good thought no defilements, walk no defilements, sleep no defilements, very good person that person, I, my aim is like this. After that I go to interview my teacher asked me "You want no defilement?" I say "Yes I don't want." 2 year don't silent; don't talk, so he give me 32 parts. In that time I very hard work because 32 parts may be my *pāramī* past life 32 parts. So continue. I get this benefit until now, so I very thanks to my teacher and the Buddha's teaching.

Q.333 Do you believe in gods?

A. Actually in my mind is emptiness, I don't believe mind also, my body is nothing also. How I can believe the gods.

Q.334 Earlier, earlier have you had experiences of gods and non human beings?

A. Yes actually previous I am ordinary person lay people, I was very greedy, very attachment also, I needed that power also, I very greed in any thing I will pray, blessing.

Q.335 Have you experienced gods?

A. Experienced gods, like some not experienced, my family sometimes had things problem, sometime he disturb the body shaking or anything.

Q.336 Trance?

A. Aha.

Q.337 That is all?

A. She still have something .

Q.338 Have you had experiences with lower beings (experience?) not gods, lower beings (experience?) not gods but lower beings have you experienced?

A. experienced here I many hearing in this *aranya*... hearing in my Malaysia, here also, I here also I hear quite some time disturb also, sometime they very disturb, when a monk go out have this thing, thing, kind of thing also (sorry?) he disturb sometime, the evil thing call the. Monk, disturb the monk, shake the monk up.

Q.339 Disturb the ? You have it here, have you experienced personally?

A. have have personal also.

Q.340 Bhante as an *Arahant* have you experienced *dibbacakkhu*?

A. What the *dibba*...

Q.341 Aah divine eye?

A. No actually I don't have because I don't have *jhāna* so I sometime I talk to my teacher I don't have concentration. If I concentration I will develop this thing because I don't concentration I cannot develop this thing. So sometime they criticism me that. When I want to develop, may be I according to *Vissudhimagga*, when a person destroy in the *arūpa jhāna*, emptiness destroy he cannot get *jhāna* already, that means cannot get *jhāna* cannot get can't get psychic. Can't because no *jhāna*. *jhāna* 4th normally, 4th *jhāna*.

Q.342 So without 4th *Jhāna* you won't get, what about looking at your previous births?

A. I don't have, looking my previous births, because I only practice 32 parts, destroy defilements, because destroy defilements, no need to this knowledge understanding enough.

Q.343 You have never looked at it?

A. Don't have.

Q.344 There is no, you don't want to look at it even now?

A. But I don't have *jhāna* (laugh), I everything I want to learn, but I don't have concentration, I don't have 1st *jhāna* 2nd *jhāna*. So I cannot produce this thing, now I destroy already.

Q.345 Do you like to develop it now, at this stage?

A. Actually I not very like, if teacher call me to do something aah develop more, knowledge more I will go to do only, like duty only, because I now like waiting die only (laugh).

Q.346 But you have to live till 80 years?

A. Ah?

Q.347 You have to live till 80 years.

A. yeh yeh, so dull, so very dull (laugh) so I call my teacher how is it can change, the die faster.

Q.348 What is your advice to a practitioner?

A. To a new practitioner? (to a normal practitioner) I think he, he should encourage himself, think about defilements very no good, when we have defilements we do anything attachment, if we like a person no defilements very good. Buddha's teaching so we thinking for practical do like when they reduce one first stage he destroy all the defilements 30%, second stage 60% , 3rd stage 99%, so let him choice, he want defilement together to rebirth, reincarnation together, different rebirth again, you can go by this way because all the time very defilement may be or you choose first path enough already, you destroy 30% already, so we cannot say, you have to encourage because now the person they don't like this thing, they like defilements more.

Q.349 Apart from what we discussed now do you have anything else to say?

A. Actually nothing to say, If you don't ask me I don't nothing to say, I air only look like.

Q.350 One more question *bhante*. Can you explain in detail how you did the 32 parts?

A. Oh! Explain how is the 32 part. For me I am beginning I don't have *jhāna* anything, I am like the ordinary person like any lay people come to the monastery and the teacher give me, OK you 32 part beginning, he give me 5 parts, *kesā lomā*... five parts, first five parts, I focus five parts aah! I very happy.

Q.351 How did you focus, can you explain?

A. I focused, when I imagination, if I focus my mind I visualize ah! Before I had, the book is better like hair, *kesā* how is the *kesā* look like, so we imagination visualize our *kesā* is a look like someone also can, we visualize our head had *kesā* had enough already, slowly *kesā* ... mind is produce ah! We might go this way *kesā*, *lomā*, so the mind after that one part one part mind very calm, very peace because understanding produce. after a few weeks I talk to my teacher because 5 parts I very happy, if I continue the 32 parts very good, I like 32 parts very good more parts I more happy because understanding more. So I request teacher, may be teacher know my *pāramī* ah! OK you continue your way, so I continue 32 parts, *kesā, lomā,* 32 parts some time, I tried focus, I only recite only 32 parts, *kesā, lomā*, feel very happy because understanding more inside, after that have energy, I will continue *kesā, lomā* 32 parts after that one by one, one by one share or anything intestines inside you look like very happy because all the time I because determination already in that time. I say if I not attain *Arahant* I don't want to be *bhikkhu* in that time. In that time I made a wish because the teacher told me "You want *Nibbāna* 2 year?" I say "I want." So I say "I really like *Nibbāna,* I understand *Nibbāna* as no defilements because defilements too much already, very disturb to me," so I made a wish, I continue more stronger, my view, my wish, I said if I not attain *Nibbāna* I don't whole life I don't want to be a *bhikkhu*. So I determine this one, I all the time treat this one 32 parts is my 32 friend, I treat you.

Q.352 Your friend?

A. My friend, I all the time, I talk to my friends, sleep I 32 parts, until tired sleep, wake up 32 parts only, I all the time, all time walk anything, I don't need to friend anything because my teacher is very good he know my, don't need to talk anything don't give me much duty, I think I take care the *thera* anything enough already, so all the time I continue my duty only.

Q.353 When you look at say *kesā,* how do you look at it?

A. when I *kesā,* I look imagination like the *kesā,* like the only we are before our hair we see the mirror first, we can try the mirror ah! Our hair is like this, so we saw imagination, visualize *kesā, lomā,* if we don't have *lomā,* may, doesn't matter we can imagination visualize whole body is *lomā,* because you want to more important.

Q.354 Just say *lomā* and look at it?

A. Ah! But not open eyes, using the mind, imagination, she using *lomā,* because we want to mind decide and continue focus because why, when we decide so the defilements not continue, had the ... had the *javana* group come in, he no space come, let the defilements come in, so *kesā,* If you say hair or so we continue *kesā, lomā,* so he continue continue so he don't have space for defilement come in and attack you in that space. We go by this way.

Q.355 So all 32 parts you went one by one like that, no breaking?

A. No breaking, before little bit tired until 10 already bed time, because mind produce cannot sustain some because we don't have imagination, so he mind don't like to working sometime you want to *kesā,* you don't want to go also. Because mind tired already. So he will take a rest, sometime tired, he recite 32 parts, recite by me *kesā, lomā,* continue continue him because the mind understanding more, understanding whole body is 32 parts only after that continue because this one is concentration also, when you recite you more happy, more calm, because understanding more, energy come, continue again this way my duty all the time, *kesā, lomā,* intestines.

Q.356 When you did that you got the light perception?

A. Yes yes, light one week or two week, it come as concentration, light come already (the interviewee is indicating with the hand, a flash).

Q.357 Flash?

A. Aha flash. When I sleep I don't know in that time. "How come?" Focus intestines like torch light, torch light focused there.

Q.358 Inside the intestines?

A. Inside the intestines, my heart focused, "How come torch light?," I don't know this light, when I sleep in the mountain there "How come they wake up, how come inside very bright?."

Q.359 Is it when the eyes are closed?

A. Yeh closed, because it closed a few weeks, 1 week, 2 week, because I continuously concentration very strong, knowledge very strong, no defilements, five hindrances very less, so concentration arising, so all the time "How come had this light inside?" because when I sleep cannot sleep because very very flash the mind, all the time how the light like spot light put to my head.

Q.360 Like spot light on your head?

A. Aha aha.

Q.361 So when you open your eyes what happens?

A. Open your eyes he nothing but you can saw imagine inside have bright like color, black like color (pointing the finger at the eye ball).

Q.362 Inside the eye ball? Socket?

A. Eye ball had light colour, like a black.

Q.363 when you open your eyes?

A. Ahm.

Q.364 But when you close there is light like spot light?

A. Aha yeh when I focus to there, he go to there anywhere, when I focus to there so he very good to you.

Q.365 So this is the practice you did throughout the three years?

A. Yes I continuous, until until destroy, until second year, because second almost become particles, elements already all the break already in that time, break in the 3rd stage, I already break but still have the delusion, delusion so I cannot saw actually, I cannot saw any particle only in 3rd stage but I continue also 4 elements deposit, four elements deposit.

Q.366 So after the 2nd year you got down to four elements?

A. Yeh actually 1 ½ year only turned to particles already, particles cannot saw anything my whole body. In that time I focus 32 parts mature enough already "How come the mind the heart no more already?" become particles? Oh! I cannot saw anything, "How come?, I saw intestines how come intestines no more?, head no more, I no more," I very fear, actually in that I fear, but I I could feel I don't have fear feeling "How come I fear no feeling no have this type feeling?" previous I had this feeling fear anything, emotion, "How come emotion no more?," I don't know at that stage very close already, very close go in, go in the fourth stage already, like a we are saying about 1 minute, still seconds, can go already, go in already after that use myself because mind wisdom arising all the time the mind told me you using because you 32 parts deposit very strong already, now he destroy, understanding will arising, because now wisdom very close already because particle already, now you use same also, using 4 elements, deposit deposit, deposit, deposit 4 elements whole body all my inside outside a I focused almost two years.

Q.367 Bhante it was not clear, at what stage did you cross over to the 4 elements? What stage, 4th stage or 3rd stage?

A. In third and a half almost.

Q.368 Three and a half year (laugh) half way through the *anāgāmī* you focused on four elements?

A. Aha aha all the time almost more than one and a half years all the elements because you cannot saw anything.

Q.369 So one and a half years, it was only elements, can you describe that practice? Elements?

A. Elements? (as you did it) Yah now anger no anything but I still cannot because I that stage I told my teacher "How come I cannot saw particle, 32 part no more already, how come this world I cannot saw anything?" The teacher only teacher only told me good good good continue. I saw very dull, because this world I cannot, I like the intestines because still attachment inside, delusion I don't know this thing, but I like intestines, had colour had anything. "How come don't have colour?, have to focus I very difficult, hard continue that but intestine no more, how to practice, I cannot, don't know how to practice now because no more mind wisdom because the teacher only told me you look at your mind, you understanding, you go to thought, consider yourself because he understating my mind can produce wisdom already, mind can cut my mind already, so I thought about consider this thing, the mind told me ah! Now your duty is focus element element, whole body, element, 32 parts, *kesā* element, *lomā* element, aah.

Q.370 When you say, can you describe that again, how did you concentrate on the elements? Elements is earth water, these four elements?

A. Yeh I imagination first I imagination, the I visualize, I imagination the one piece inside have four, I use my imagination only, *kesā* is small particle but understanding inside one piece inside had 4 elements inside. I imagination like this way, so *kesā, lomā,* like this way.

Q.371 So that was one and a half years?

A. Yeh more than.

Q.372 So that's what helped you to break through the last fetters, last 5 fetters?

A. Yeh.

Q.373 Thank you so much *bhante.*

A. (laugh) Actually I don't know how it is.

Q.374 Yes this is very good.

A. Is it very good. I don't know, very dull only.

(conversation not very clear).

Q.375 Can you repeat what you said just now about *Arahants* sleeping eating etc.?

A. Actually what I thinking is the way is very different in the 3rd stage and the 4th stage. Some time I show this thing, because very different, different is, some day very difficult to believe, like *Arahant* stage in, when he saw he only saw, he don't have attachment one second attachment also, he saw, stop already, *kiriya*, when he heard anything, he blame or anything, good or anything, he don't think about this thing, he will hear stop already, smell only very interesting I describe some time the faeces, some thinking faeces there, they are very anger, very disgusting will arising, but he now even from give to my front (referring to bringing it close to the face) how, very long time I don't have anger, I don't have smell, I have smell, but don't have attachment, don't have this type thing. So eat only eat only, but they will eat the thing, may be habitual little bit but he not attachment to eat anything, he because his mind no desire, sleep also, thinking also, when he thinking, he think only, when he thinking aah! good past he, thinking only, he want to consider something thinking something he do thinking only, future also he don't have planning, this thing. But he want to think, he think only, but he not attachment anything.

Q.376 So *Arahants* do plan for the future?

A. Actually not planning unless he wants to do something, have planning to something, normally he don't have planning, even I now all the time I don't think about previous, I not properly do it, *anāgāmī* thinking by this way, but when I think, that Path, all time, previous time, I don't think about yesterday is what, a *deva*, I don't think future how I can be, how I did, now I don't think also.

Q.377 *Anāgāmī* did you think about the past? (yeh yeh) You thought about the past?

A. Yes because delusion have.

Q.378 Right you planned for the future?

A. Yes.

Q.379 Right now there is no planning?

A. No planning future.

Q.380 I mean if your teacher tells you tomorrow you have to do this, don't you plan for it?

A. I plan it, but I my treat it like duty only, my duty not because my, I want to body, I want to planning, keep many thing, not this type thing, this because *Saṅgha* want, I member here, I have to do my duty, this is one more important, I no have because I planning a few years I want to go anywhere enjoy or I don't have this thing because I don't want to go out where because I don't like the city anything, very emotion, many people there, I like alone, cave or anything, but I cannot concentrate if not I want to 7th day come out eat one lunch only.

Q.381 Have you experienced *Nirodhasamāpatti*?

A. I cannot experience because I no *jhāna* (laugh)

Thank you very much *bhante*.

Interview was conducted on 27th July 2006 in a well established forest hermitage in Sri Lanka.

Notes

1. See Appendix II and Chapter 7 for synopsis and analysis of this interview.
2. The word "he" refers to his mind.
3. The words "sixth sense" refer to the mind base.

Bibliography

Anālayo. 2010. "Channa's Suicide in the *Saṃyukta-āgama*." *Buddhist Studies Review* 27(2): 3–15.

———. 2011. "Vakkali's Suicide in the Chinese Āgamas." *Buddhist Studies Review* 28(2): 155–170.

———. 2012. "Dabba's Self-cremation in the *Saṃyukta-āgama*." *Buddhist Studies Review* 29(2): 141–162.

Anuruddha Thera, K. 2004. *Dictionary of Pāli Idioms*. Hong Kong: The Chi Lin Nunnery.

Bhikkhu Bodhi. 1989. *The Discourse on the Fruits of Recluseship: The Sāmaññaphala Sutta and its Commentaries*. Kandy: Buddhist Publication Society.

———. 1996. "Nibbāna, Transcendence and Language" *Buddhist Studies Review* 13(2): 163–176.

———. 2000. *Connected Discourses of the Buddha: A New Translation of the Saṃyutta Nikāya*, vols. I and II. Boston, MA: Wisdom.

———. 2012. *Numerical Discourses of the Buddha: A Translation of the Aṅguttara Nikāya*. Boston, MA: Wisdom.

Brahmavamso, Ajahn. 2004. "Enlightenment." *Dhamma Journal*, vol.5. Perth: Buddhist Society of Western Australia (for free distribution)

———. 2006. *Mindfulness Bliss and Beyond*. Boston, MA: Wisdom.

Carrithers, M. 1983. *Forest Monks of Sri Lanka: An Anthropological and a Historical Study*. Delhi: Oxford University Press.

Chah, Ajahn. 1987. *A Still Forest Pool*. Compiled and edited by Jack Kornfield and Paul Breiter. Illinois: The Theosophical Publishing House (for free distribution).

———. 1998. *The Key to Liberation*. Ubon Rajathani, Thailand: W.A.V.E. Publications (for free distribution).

———. 2002. *Food for the Heart*. Ubon Rajathani, Thailand: W.A.V.E. Publications, (for free distribution).

———. 2013. *Still Flowing Water*. Translated by Ṭānissaro Bhikkhu. California: www.dhammatalks.org (for free distribution).

Davids, T. W. Rhys and W. Stede. 1921–1925, *Pāli English Dictionary*. 2001 edition. New Delhi: Unshiram Manoharlal.

De Silva, L. 1978. "*Cetovimutti*, *Paññāvimutti* and *Ubhatobhāgavimutti*." *Pāli Buddhist Review* 3(3): 118–145: http://www.ukabs.org.uk/ukabs/resources/journal-archives/pali-studie-review-archive/

Devasiri. A. 2008. *Papañcasūdanī*—Majjhima Nikāya *Aṭṭhakathā* (Sinhala translation), Nadimala, Sri Lanka: Buddhist Cultural Centre.

Dhirasekere, J. 1964. *Buddhsit Monastic Discipline*. Ceylon: M. D. Gunasena & Co.

Epstein, M. 2007. *Psychotherapy without Self*. New Haven, CT: Yale University Press.

Gethin, R. 1992. *The Buddhist Path to Awakening*. Oxford: One world Publications.

Hamilton, W. 1995. *Saints and Psychopaths*. St Jacinto. California: Dharma Audio Networks Associates.

Harvey, P. 1986. "'Signless' Meditations in Pāli Buddhism." *Journal of the International Association of Buddhist Studies* 9(1): 25–52.

———. 2013. "The *Saṅgha* of Noble *Sāvakas* with Particular Reference to their Trainee member, the Person 'Practising for the Stream-entry Fruit'." *Buddhist Studies Review* 30(1): 3–70.

———. 2014. "The Nature of the Eight-factored *ariya, lokuttara magga* in the *Suttas* Compared to the Pali Commentarial Idea of it as Momentary." *Religions of South Asia* 8(1): 31–52.

Horner, I. B. 1938, 1940, 1942, 1951, 1952, 1966. *The Book of the Discipline*, 6 vols. Oxford: Pali Text Society.

———. 1987, 1959, 1957. *Middle Length Sayings*, 3 vols. Oxford: Pali Text Society.

Jayatilleke, K. N. 1963. *Early Buddhist Theory of Knowledge*. Delhi: Motilal Banarsidass.

Jayawickrama N. A. 2001. *Sutta-nipāta, Text and Translation*. Sri Lanka: Post-Graduate Institute of Pāli and Buddhist Sudies, University of Kelaniya.

Johnson, R. 1969. *The Psychology of Nirvāna*. London: George Allen and Unwin.

Kalupahana, D. J. 1976. *Buddhist Philosophy*. Hawaii: University of Hawaii.

Keown. D. 1996. "Buddhism and Suicide: The Case of Channa." *Journal of Buddhist Ethics* 3: 8–31.

Khemananda Thera, P. 2007. *Cabbhisodana Sutta*. Meethirigala, Sri Lanka: Nissaranavana Forest Hermitage (for free distribution).

Kheminda Thera. 1992. *Path Fruit and Nibbāna*. 2nd edition Colombo: Balcombe House.

Kornfield, J. 1993. *Living Buddhist Masters*. Kandy: Buddhist Publication Society.

Mahā Boowa, Ñāṇasampanno. 2005. *Arahattamagga Arahattaphala*. Baan Taad Forest Monastery, Thailand: Forest Dhamma Books (for free distribution).

Mahāsi, Sayadaw. 2002. *Vipassanā Shuni Kyan* (*The Method of Vipassanā Meditation*), vol.2. Yangon, Myanmar: Buddha Sasanānuggaha Organization, Mahāsi Sāsana Yeiktha (unpublished).

Ñāṇamoli, Bhikkhu. 1956. *The Path of Purification*. Singapore: Buddhist Meditation Center.

———. and Bhikkhu Bodhi. 1995. *The Middle Length Discourses of the Buddha*. Boston, MA: Wisdom.

Ñāṇananda, Bhikkhu. 1974. *The Magic of the Mind*. Kandy: Buddhist Publication Society.

———. 1976. *Concept and Reality*. Kandy: Buddhist Publication Society.

———. 2003, 2004, 2005, 2006. *Nibbāna: The Mind Stilled*, 4 vols. Colombo, Sri Lanka: Dharma Grantha Mudrana Bharaya.

Ñānavīra, Thera. 2002. *Clearing the Path, Writings of Ñānavīra Thera* (1960–1965) vol. II, repr. Nadimala, Sri Lanka: Buddhist Cultural Centre.

Ñānārāma, Mātara Sri. 1993. *The Seven Stages of Purification and The Insight Knowledges*. Kandy: Buddhist Publication society.

Nārada, Thera. 1995. *Dhammapada*. Bambalapitiya, Sri Lanka: Swastika.

Norman, K. R. 1995. *Elders' Verses*. Vols. 1 and II. Oxford: Pali Text Society.

Nyānatiloka. 1946. *Buddhist Dictionary—Manual of Buddhist Terms and Doctrines*, repr. 1970. Kandy: Buddhist Publication Society.

Nyanaponika, Thera and H. Hecker. 1997. *Great Disciple of the Buddha*, edited by Bhikkhu Bodhi. Kandy: Buddhist Publications Society (in collaboration with Wisdom publications, Boston).

Pa-Auk Tawya Sayadaw (Venerable Sayadaw U Acinna). 1997. *Light of Wisdom*. Kuala Lumpur, Malaysia: W.A.V.E. Publications (for free distribution)

Rahula, W. 1993. *History of Buddhism in Ceylon.* Nadimala, Sri Lanka: Buddhist Cultural Centre.
Sārada Maha Thero, W. 1994. *Treasury of Truth, Illustrated Dhammapada.* Singapore: Weragoda Sārada.
Schmithausen, L. 2000. "Buddhism and the Ethic of Nature: Some Remarks." *The Eastern Buddhist.*
Shah, Sirdar I. A. 1993. *Islamic Sufism.* Delhi: Idarah-I Adabiyat-I.
Ṭhānissaro Bhikkhu (Geoffrey DeGraff). 2007. *The Buddhist Monastic Code.* 2nd. edition, 2 vols. Valley Center, California: Mettā Forest Monastery.
Tilakaratne, A. 1993. *Nirvāna and Ineffability.* Colombo: Postgraduate Institute of Pāli and Buddhist Studies.
———. 1997. "Saddhā: A Pre-Requite for Religious Action." *Recent Researches in Buddhist Studies: Essays in Honour of Professor Y. Karunadasa*, edited by Asanga Tilakaratne, Rev. Dhammajoti, and Kapila Abewardene. Hong Kong: Chi Ying Foundation.
Udita, Rev. H. 1956. *Tripiṭaka Parīkshnaya.* Colombo: Samayawardhana Bookshop.
Vajira, Sister and F. Story. 1964. *Last Days of the Buddha.* Revised edition 1988. Kandy: Buddhist Publication Society.
Vidanapathirana, G. C. 2006. *Dabba Mallaputta Hamuduruwo.* Colombo: Dayawamso Jayakody.
Walshe, M. 1996. *Long Discourses of the Buddha.* Kandy: Buddhist Publication Society.
Warder, A. K. 1980. *Indian Buddhism.* 2nd revised edition. Delhi: Mothilal Banarsidass.
Wilber, K., J. Engler and D. P. Brown. 1986. *Transformations of Consciousness: Conventional and Contemplative Perspective of Development.* Boston, MA: Shambhala.
Wilber, K. 1999. *The Collected Works.* Vol. IV. Boston, MA: Shambhala.
———. 2001. *No Boundaries.* Boston, MA: Shambhala.
Woodward, F. L. 1935. *Minor Anthologies Part II (Udāna and Itivuttaka).* Oxford: Pali Text Society.

Indices

Index of Subjects

A

a noble person in a past life, 151, 152–153
Abhidhamma, 198, 199, 212
acknowledgement, of state of mind, 62
adhigama (attainments), 206
adhigama appiccatā (fewness of wishes relating to attainments), 17
Aggañña Sutta,169
aggregates of clinging, five, 42, 150, 162, 163
  and the fetter-breaking-experience, 73, 91, 92, 98
  arising and ceasing of, 79, 92
  not feeling the, 92
  wrong view with regard to, 123
Ambaṭṭha Sutta, 162
Anattalakkhaṇa Sutta, 55
anger (*koda*), 39
Āni Sutta, 206
animal realm, 33, 138
"apihālu", 199
appanihita (wishless),
  as a gate way to liberation, 101
  contact, 108, 115
  experiences, 78, 79
  fetter-breaking-experience as, 22
  phala-samāpatti as, 65
Arahant,
  after death status of an, 69
  definition of, 22
  fetters eliminated by, 22
  powers of, 54
  questioning an, 41–44
  state of perception of an, 98
  testing the mindset of an, 49, n.6
  two types of, 87
  see also mind-set of an *Arahant*
Arahantship/fruit of Arahantship (*arahatta-phala*), 32, 63, 65, 66, 67, 74, 75, 83
  and *arahatta-phala samādhi*, 71
  attainment of, by interviewee no. 1, 172
  declaration of, 36–37, 55–56
  five ascetics attaining, 55
  five types of declarations of, 40
  of Godhika, 159
  of Mahā Dhammarakkhita, 213
  of Rāhula, 55
  one practising for the attainment of, 76
ariyakanta sīla (virtue dear to a noble person), 35, 53, 67, 78, 137, 150
  and field research, 138–141
  description of, 137
  unbroken state of, 139, 140, 141, 142
Ariyaparyesana Sutta, 164
ascetics
  and spies, 38
  five, 55
asekha (*Arahant*), 162, 190
"ash or soot", 181
assaddho, 134, 190
attainments (*samāpatti*),
  eight, 22, 114
  of *animitta*/*appanihita*, 65
  of fruition, 65
  of fruits, 55–56
  progressive, 66
avedayita, 73
āyu saṃkhāra (vital formation), 116

B

"balloon bursting", 58
barber, 55, 78
bases of success (*iddhipāda*), 199
bases of transcendence (*abhibhāyatana*), 22
bases, (*āyatana*)
  and fetter-breaking-experience, 73, 74
  five, 73, 74, 78
  six internal and external, 42, 163
  wrong view regarding, 123
batti (devotion), 133, 134
benefits (ānisaṃsa), of the Path, 65, 66, 83
Bhaddāli Sutta, 137, 191
bhava (existence/ becoming),
  cessation of, 80
  experiencing "non-becoming", 59, 97
  renewed (*punabbahava*), 36
bhavanetti (that which leads to renewed existence), 37
Bhūta Sutta, 208
birth (*jāti*), 36
  not taking an eight, 143, 149, 169, 200
  only in human and celestial realms, 149
"blankness", in consciousness, 59, 61, 93, 97, 152
bodhi-pakkhiya-dhamma, 199
"body dissolving", 152
"body falling apart", 91
bondage, 75
brahmā,
  attaining stream-entry, 168
  Baka, 176
  Mahāmoggallana's visit to Tissa, 46
  recognizing noble persons, 46
  brahmacārī (celibate), 38
Brahmajāla Sutta, 41, 123
Brahmanimantanika Sutta, 176
"breaking up a boundary", 58, 61, 92
breakthrough, to Dhamma, 34
Buddha *pujā,* 145
Buddha,
  investigating the, 132
  legitimate son of (*orasa- putto*), 169
  original word of the, 7
  sāsana, 188, 199, 200
  seeking a teacher other than the, 142, 143
  statue, 153
Buddhist cosmology and stream-enterers, 130
Buddhist cosmology, knowledge of, 81,156
Bundala, 154
burden, 172, 179
burial ground, 55, 64, n.7
Burmese tradition,
  Mahāsi Sāyadaw of, 3, 4, 47, 106
  Pa-Auk-Sāyadaw of, 3, 4, 106
  U Ba Khin of, 3
  and fruition attainment, 106–107
burning corpse, 201

C

Caṅki Sutta, 97, 132
carpenters, 35
cause (*hetu*), 65, 72, 209
"ceased to experience the word", 97
cessation (*nirodha*)
  directly seeing/knowing, 34
  of *bhava* (existence), 73
  aspect of *paṭiccasamuppāda,* as applicable to *Nibbāna,* 75
  of suffering, 75
  contemplating, 81
  of conditioned phenomena, 74, 83
  of perception and feeling , see *nirodha-samāpatti*
  of sense bases and aggregates of clinging, 163, 164
"cessation experience", 57, 59
cessation-of-perception-and-feeling (*saññā-vedayita-nirodha-samāpatti*), 22, 114
  and Citta the householder, 167
  and eradicating defilements,116
  and three types of contacts and formations, 115
  difference between death and, 116
  differentiated from fruition attainment (*phala-samāpatti*), 87, 106, 110, 108, 114, 118
  how and why, is attained and emerged from, 115
Cetiyapabbata, 16
Chabbisodana Sutta, 41–44
Channovāda Sutta, 160
clear comprehension, 77

clinging to rules and vowes (*sīlabbata-parāmāsa*), 5, 32, 81, 121, 144, 156
absence of, 142
and Buddha *pujā*, 145
and gratitude to Buddha, 145
field research on, 144–145
cognitive restructuring, 209
Commentaries, Pāli, 66, 71, 77
conceit (*māna*), 32, 36, 39, 201
underlying tendency towards (*mānānusaya)*, 43
concentration (*samādhi*),
access (*upacāra*), 3
as spiritual faculty, 32, 87, 137
blissful states of, 203
"wisdom develops", 203
conditioned phenomena (*saṃkata*), 69, 72, 74
cessation of, 72,74, 83
not compounded (*asaṃkata*), 83, 71
confusion, 8, 206
consciousness,
"a gap" in, 59, 93, 97
and supramundane path and fruit, 20
and fetter-breaking-experience, 91, 95, 117
and fruition attainment (*phala-samāpatti*), 87, 106, 108, 110, 114
and momentary path, 65, 66
and name-and-form, 96, 117
"appearance and disappearance "of , 59, 93
"ceased", 97
manifestation of, 96
non-manifestive (*anidassana* viññāṇa), 71, 176
of a noble person, 66, 75
ordinary, of an *Arahant*, 176
signless state as object of, 66, 74, 75, 83, 96
consequence (*vipāka*), of the Path, 65, 66, 83
of ignorance of supramundane fruit 202, 203
contact,
and name-and-form, 97
arising/ cause of, 97
three kinds of, 108, 115
controversies, and religious experience, 53
cool (*sītibhūta*), 36, 70, 74, 83
covetousness (*abhijjhā*), 35
craving (*taṅhā*), 96, 75
"to be" (*bhava taṅhā*), 181
to "not be" (*vibhava taṅhā*), 181, 182
Cūḷadukkhakkhanda Sutta, 203
Cūḷavedalla Sutta, 108, 114, 122
Cūḷasaccaka Sutta, 137, 191
Cūḷasuññata Sutta, 103
"curled up coil", 58

D

danger (*adīnava*), 124
dead body, auctioning a, 151
"dead to the world", 113
death bed, 55
death, 39, 40
deathless element (*amata dhātu*), 68, 71, 163
see also *Nibbāna*
debates, on religious expereice, 53
on *Nibbāna*, transcendence and ineffability, 69–75
declarations of fruits,
at a specific place, 55
at the end of a specific sermon, 55
in field research, 57–61
in terms of "feeling", 37
made in terms of fetters abandoned, 34, 36
made in terms of fundamental qualities, 35
made in terms of future destination, 33, 34
made in terms of knowledge acquired, 33, 34
of Arahantship, 36–37, 55, 56
of non-returning, 35–36
of stream-entry, 33, 35, 55
on a specific date/time, 56
questioning a monk on, 41–43
through over estimating, 10
defilements, 71, 73, 82, 172, 173,
revering the place where, were defeated, 57
state of, as a yardstick of an attainment of a supramundane fruit, 53

deliverance/ liberations (*vimokkha*), 37, 207
  eight, 22
delusion (*moha*), 36, 70, 74
dependant origination (*paṭiccasamuppāda*)
  and Dhamma, 125
  and *Nibbāna* as beyond reasoning, 75
  and *Nibbāna* as transcendental, 70
  and *Nibbāna*, 72, 75, 164
  as essential knowledge of a stream-enterer, 125
  knowledge of, 67, 75, 81, 117, 125, 129, 146, 156, 162, 163, 164, 197, 200, 208
desire for pleasures of the senses (*kāmacchanda*), 32, 36, 64, n.6, 93, 146
destination, 203
  bad, 33, 138, 148
  of a stream-enterer, 33, 149, 171
  Tusita as, 39
destiny, 33, 149
dhakkhineyya (person worthy of offering), seeking a, 143
Dhamma,
  born of (*dhamma-jo*)/ heir of (*dhamma-dāyādo*)/ created by (*dhamma-nimmitto*), 169
  gripped by, excitement (*dhamma-uddacca-viggahita*), 204
  practicing in accordance with (*dhammānudhamma-paṭipadā*), 77
  seeing/ diving into, 162
  seeing/penetrating/ understanding, 34
  uniqueness of, 207
Dhammacakkappavattana Sutta, 33, 125, 168
Dhamma-eye (*dhammacakkhu*), 33, 82, 125, 156
Dhamma-follower (*dhammānusārī*) 32, 45, 46, 77, 82, 88, 89, 138, 155
Dhamma-stream, 39
dictionary, 65
Dighāvu Sutta, 55
diligence, 200, see also mindfulness
discussion, 44
disintegration, 198
dispassion (*virāga*), 63, 98
displeasure (*domanassa*), 35
dissolution, 198, 200
doctrine,
  of inefficacy of action (*akiriyavāda*), 124
  of nihilism (*natthikavāda*)/ annihilationism, 124
  of non-causality (*ahetukavāda*), 124
  of seven bodies, 124
dry-insight-meditator (*sukkha-vipassaka*), 203, 205, 211
dukkha (suffering/unsatisfactoriness), 34, 43, 62, 75, 79
Dvayatānupassanā Sutta, 176

E

earth/ water/ wind/fire elements, 83, 69
effect, of the fetter-breaking-experience, 65, 66, 67, 69, 72, 73, 75, 83
  of fetter-breaking-experience and *Nibbāna*, 74, 83, 84
  of knowledge, 74
Eka Bīja Sutta, 90
elements (*dhātu*), 177
  Nibbāna, 75
  six, 42
  space (*ākāsa dhātu*), 95
elephant, 55, 78
emptiness,
  dealing with, 206
  experience of, 1
  "vast emptiness", 81
enlightenment factors (*bojjhaṅga*), of equanimity and joy, 194
enlightenment, 33, 149
equanimity, 77, 180, 194
escape (*nissarana*), 124
"escape from sensory world", 111
Eternalism, 123–128
event,
  and fruit of once-returning, 91
  fruits as discernible, 57, 91
explosion, 58, 61
extinction, 72

F

faculties, five spiritual,
32, 78, 87, 89, 137, 162, 201, 203
  gratification, danger and escape with regard to, 124
faith follower (*saddhānusarī*), 32, 45, 46, 77, 88, 89, 133, 138
family-to-family attainer (*kolankola*), 90

feeling (*vedanā*),
  "losing awareness of", 91
  "not having the feel of", 92
  "tapering off of", 61, 92
  three types of, 37
"festered boil bursting", 58
fetter-breaking-experience, 62, 65, 66, 67, 69, 72, 73, 78, 79, 80, 81, 82, 83, 117, 173
  and fruition attainment, 23
  and *Nibbāna* and transcendent reality, 74, 83, 84
  and simile of the adze, 56
  as a specific experience, 55, 56, 57–61
  as momentary, 73
  as signless, wishless and empty, 79, 80, 197
  at different supramundane fruits, 93, 94, 100, 117
  definition of, 22
  difference between other religious experiences and, 102–104, 117
  differentiating signless experiences from, 102–103, 117
  in field research, 91–95
  in secondary sources, 95–96
  in the *Nikāyas*, 96–100
  mysterious nature of, 72, 73
  naturalistic nature of, 70, 72
  role of sense bases and aggregates of clinging in, 73, 90–93, 118
  state of perception of an *Arahant* at, 98
fetters (*saṃyojana*), 36, 37, 109, 209
  breaking of, as a key element of a supramundane fruit, 31, 53
  eliminated at stream-entry, 5
  eliminated by a noble person, 21
  fading away of two, 60
  five, 56
  lower (*orambhāgiyāni*), 32, 35, 56
  seven, 32,
  ten, 32, 172, 202
  three, 32, 67, 77, 78, 79, 80, 81, 82, 121, 141
fever going down, 58, 92
field research,
  by William Hamilton, 15
  methodology of, 8
  on specific experience, 57–61
  selection of interviewees, 8
  impact of disciplinary rules on, 11–14
  difficulties encountered in, 9, 12–14
flood (*ogha*), 36
formless states/absorptions (*arūpa jhāna*), 22
  cessation-of-perception-and-feeling, 114, 115
  and *suññata vimokkha*, 207
  and two types of *Arahants*, 87, 88
four devine abiding, 189
four noble truths, 34, 43, 62, 79
four woeful states, 77
fragmentation, 198
fruit (*phala*), 20, 65, 83,
  as a general state of mind, 20, 66, 67
  as unique, 197
  four fruits, 74
  four supramundane, in the *Suttas*/*Nikāyas*, 32, 65, 66, 67
  momentary supramundane, 20, 65, 66, 67, 68, 75, 76, 82, 87
  "*phala*" and "*phalānisaṃsa*", 67, 68
  that is steam-entry, 121
  wishing for, 199
fruit of non-returning (*anāgāmī-phala*), 32
  attainment of, 55–56, 60, 65, 66, 67, 80, 172, 201
  one practising for the realization of, 76
fruition attainment (*phala-samāpatti*), 4, 23, 65, 73, 74
  as a reason for confusion, 205
  implicit references in the *Nikāyas* to, 107–108
  in field research, 111–113
  not a concrete test of attainment of fruits, 107, 114, 118
  Suttas differentiating cessation-of-perception-and-feeling from, 108
  Visuddhimagga differentiating, from cessation-of-perception-and-feeling, 87, 106, 110, 114
fruition, of the Path, 65, 66, 83

G

"gap"/"gulf", in consciousness, 59, 61, 93, 97
generosity,
  of a stream-enterer, 54, 141, 147
  of Isidatta and Purāṇa, 34, 35, 147

"ghee or oil", 181
ghosts, domain of, (*pettivisayo*) 33, 138
gifts, 150
Gijjakūṭa, 46, 34
giving (*dāna*), 147, see also generosity
God (Creator), 69, 117, 197
  and knowledge of dependant origination, 129
  field research on, 130, 153
gods/*devas*,
  attaining stream-entry, 55, 166, 167
  elated with stream-enterers, 150
  message from, 160
  noble persons being reborn as, 151
  recognizing noble persons, 45–46
  Sakka, 167
  stream-enterer's view on, 130
  Tusita, 39
"going beyond", 58, 92
gratification (*assāda*), 124
gratitude
  as motivation for *Arahant*, 190
  to Buddha, 135, 136
greed (*lobha*), 39, 70,
growth, in ten fields, 150

H

hallucination, 198
hānagāmī (going to deterioration), 39, 40
hatred (*dosa*), 36, 70, 74
Hattigāma, 166
"heap of ash", 91
hells (*niraya*) 33, 138, 148
higher ordination (*upasampadā*), 172
hindrances, five, 162
Hindu tradition, *Yogāstras*, 49
holi life (*brahmacāriya*) 36, 63, 72, 172
hospitality, 150

I

ignorance (*avijjā*), 32, 63
ill-will (*vyāpāda*), 32, 93
impermanence, knowledge of (*anicca*), 67, 117, 129, 163, 197, 200
implications of,
  not recognizing a religious experience, 51
  "Path, fetter-breaking-experience and effect", 69, 83
impossibilities, for
  a stream-enterer, 125,140, 142–143, 158
  an *Arahant*, 40
incapability, 77, 143, 187
ineffability, *Nibbāna* and, 69–75
investigation, of an experience 80–81
Islamic Sufism, 104
Island hermitage, Dodanduwa, 155

J

Javana, 175
Jerusalam, 153
jhāna (absorptions),
  and *animitta* states, 85, n.15
  formless (*arūpa*), 22
  four, 22
  non-returner, 49, n.3
  obsessed with, 204
  role of, 203
judgement, on fruits of the Path, 39

K

Kaccāyanagotta Sutta, 178
Kalahavivāda Sutta, 98, 104
Kālāma Sutta, 131,132
Kāligodhā Sutta, 54
kamma (action), 36, 66, 152
  six grevous (*ānantariya*) 142–143, 175
Kapilavatthu, 45, 137, 166
kettle drum and pegs, 206
khīnāsava, 62
kiriya, 175
Kitāgiri Sutta, 87
knife, 64, n.6, 157, 177
knowledge,
  and *saddhā,* 134
  appropriate to a particular fruit, 78
  as a key element of a supramundane fruit, 31, 53
  change-of-lineage (*gotrabhū*), 210
  conformity (*anuloma*), 210
  final (*aññā*), 40
  of the Buddha, to penetrate into spiritual faculties (*indriyaparopriyatte-ñāṇa*), 48
  of a trainee and an *Arahant,* 162
  of delimitation of name-and-form (*nāma-rūpa-pariccheda-ñāṇa*), 3
  of Dhamma (*dhamme ñāṇa*) 124

of entailment (*anvaye ñāṇa*), 124
of others as superior and inferior, 39
of the Buddha to assess attainment of supramundane fruits, 48
reviewing (*paccavekkhana-ñāṇa*), 30, n.11, 67
superiority of experiential, 212
three knoweldges, 36, 64, 74, 83
unobstructed, of the Buddha, (*anāvaraṇa-ñāṇa*), 48
Kosambi Sutta, 4, 162, 163, 164
kusala chanda, 199

L

labeling, 57
last body (*antima deha*), 36
lay-life, 200
liberated by faith/faith-freed (*saddhā-vimutta*), 45, 46, 88, 89, 133
liberation (*vimutti*), 62, 63, 66, 71, 98
and knowledge and vision of (*vimutti and vimutti-ñāṇadassana*), 67
by final knowledge, 172
of mind as fruit and as fruit and benefit (*cetovimutti* and *cetovimutti-phalānisaṃsa*), 68
temporary (*samāyika vimutti*), 39
life activity, (*āyu-samkhāra*), 161
light,
flash, 204
of wisdom, 204
perception, 204
lion's roar (*sīhanaāda*), 36, 186
lobhanīya dhamma, 147
logical inference, of fruits of the Path, 48
Logical positivist, 51
"losing track of the world", 112
lust (*rāga*), 36, 74
destruction of, 70, 72, 74
for formless existence (*arūpa-rāga*), 32
for pure form existence (*rūpa-rāga*), 32

M

Magadha, 166
Mahācattārisaka Sutta, 29, n.5, 199
Mahāmālunkyaputta Sutta, 129
Mahāparinibbāna Sutta, 151
Mahāsakuludāyi Sutta, 174
Mahāsāropama Sutta, 206
Mahāsatipaṭṭhāna Sutta, 212
Māhāsuññata Sutta, 157
Mahāvacchagotta Sutta, 164
Mahāvedalla Sutta, 107, 116
Mahāvihāra, 212
Mahāyāna monk, 172
Malaysian, 172
manasikāra (attending to), 74, 75, 83, 96
ayoniso manasikāra (unwise attention), 78, 146
yoniso manasikāra (wise attention), 63, n.4, n.5, n.7, 78, 79, 116, 141, 142, 146, 169
meditation,
on thirty two impurities and four elements, 172, 173, 204
sitting, 58
systems, 81, 82, 200, 201, 207, 211
walking, 60
see also meditation object in field research
mental aberration, 198
merits (*puñña*), a field of, 150
Milindapañha, 65
"mind dissolving", 152
mind,
"arose and stopped", 94, 172
as a sense organ, 174
"didn't continue", 94
general state of, of a noble person, 66, 67, 68, 76
general state of, of an *Arahant*, 75
"going blank", 153
"going into some other place", 152
"got cut off", 94
looking into the, 59–60, 209
"probing into", 208
released, 64, n.5
undefiled/pure, 57
"went in", 94, 172
"went into a different place", 94
mindfulness, 77, 87, 147, 150, 162, 201
and "being in the present moment" 206
as a spiritual faculty, 32
based meditation, 206
four foundations of, 35, 162, 172
muddled, 203

on state of *sīla,* 140, 142
mind-set of an *Arahant,*
aim as ending defilements, not attaining supramandane fruits, 192
Arahant and rituals, 191
Arahant can only serve the Buddha-*sāsana,* 188
"body as duty", 186
carrying the body with forbearance, 186
"coming stop, coming stop", 173, 174, 185
demagnetized sense bases, 183
dull, 179
"happy and contented", 178
is an *Arahant* free from all suffering?, 185
language of an *Arahant*, 182
no amassing of possessions, 187
no anger, 178
no defilements, 173
"no excitement", 180
no fear, 187
"nothing to do", 180
only phenomena arising and ceasing, 173
"particles of air", 174
perception of emptiness, 174
perception of the world, 176
saddhā of an *Arahant*, 137, 190
"television screen without channel", 174
what motivates an *Arahant*, 189
Mirror of the Dhamma Sutta 53, 62, 78
mistery, 92
momentary/moments
fetter-breaking-experience, 22
of "non-becoming", 59, 97
of supramundane consciousness, 65, 83
Path and fruit, 20
Mūlapariyāya Sutta, 179
mysterious nature, of the fetter-breaking-experience, 72, 73

N

Nalakalāpi Sutta, 96
name-and-form (*nāma-rūpa*),
and consciousness, 96, 117
and contact, 97
entangled with consciousness to form 'I', 100, 174
Ñātika village, 167
negligence/ heedlessness (*pamāda*), 147, 200, 202
New York, 198
Nibbāna
and dependant origination, 75,125
as ineffable, 69–75, 83
as object of four paths and four fruits, 74, 75, 83, 96, 162
as object of knowledge, 71
as transcendent reality, 65, 69–75, 83
definition of, 70, 72, 74, 75, 163
dhātu, 75
in field research, 73
knowledge of, as cessation of being, 162
not rejoicing in, 179
"projected", 207
signless mental concentration as path to, 102–103
stream-enterer "seeing", 161, 163
stream-enterer's slant towards, 149
wishing for, 199
Nibbāna Sutta, 72
Nigrodhārāmaya, 137
nihilism/doctrine of, 72, 123
Nikāyas, see *Suttas*
noble disciple (*ariya sāvaka*), 62, 73, 78,
well-taught (*sutavā*), 79
noble method (*ariyo ñāyo*), 33, 125
noble person (*ariya puggala*), 33, 65, 87, 117
and simile of seven types of persons, 89
definition of, 21
difficulties in recognizing a, 38–40, 46–47
in a past life being reborn in the human world, 151
language of a 142,
possibilities of recognizing a, 38–40, 143
proportions of categories of, 202
right views of a, 124
twelve types of, 32
virtue dear to a, 142, also see *ariyakanta sīla*
warning against being judgmental on, 40
wrong views abandoned by a, 123
non-returner (*anāgāmī*), 76, 165
definition of, 22
fetters eliminated by, 22
five types of, 32, 90
jhāna, 49, n.3

non-self (*anatta*), 81, 117, 129, 197
non-virtuous (*dusssīla*), 45
"not born", "not become" 69, 71, 83
"nothing is worthwhile holding on to" (*sabbe dhammā nālaṃ abhinivesāya*), 104, 117, 197
"nullification of feeling", 61

O

obstacle, 200
"oceanic experience", 111
once returner (*sakadāgāmī*)/ fruit of once returning (*sakadāgāmī-phala*), 32, 65, 66, 67, 76, 80, 210
  attainment of, 60
  definition of, 21
  Mahānāma as a, 203
  one practising for the realization of, 76
  state of fetters of a, 21
one liberated by wisdom (*paññā-vimutta*), 45, 46, 87, 88,
one liberated in both ways (*ubhato-bhāga-vimutta*), 45, 46, 87, 88, 116
one who knows and sees (*jānato passato*), 78, 82
one-seed attainer (*ekabījin*), 90
ordinary worldling (*putthujjana*), 77, 157, 209
origination (*samudaya*), 33

P

pācittiya rule viii, 11
pārājikā rule iv, 10
parinibbāna, of the Buddha, 171, 181, 188
pariyatti (learning), 206
pariyatti appiccatā (fewness of wishes relating to learning), 16
pasāda (gladness), 133, 134, 136
Path (*magga*)/Noble Eightfold Path, 20, 31, 53, 65, 66, 67, 69, 83, 171, 200, 204, 205
  as unique, 197
  different approaches to, 207
  followed by an *Arahant*, 43
  four, 74
  "mixed path" (*missaka*), 212
  momentary supramundane/noble (*ariya*), 20, 76, 77, 78
  Pubbabhāga, 212
  stream-enterer as knowing the, 144
  stream-enterer as possessing the, 121
peak-experience, 62, 78, 79, 80, 81, 117
pema (affection), 133, 134
percentages, in which defilements were reduced, 173, 179
perception
  at fetter-breaking-experience, 197
  of an *Arahant*, 98, 99, see also mind-set of an *Arahant*
  of body, 177
  of emptiness, 174, 180
  of *Nibbāna*, 99
peril, 64
perplexity, 37
persons,
  eight types of (*aṭṭha purisa puggalā*), 3, 75, 77, 79, 83, 87
  nine types of, 202
  seven types of, 89
  three types of, not easy to repay, 169
physician, 167
places,
  of misery, 33
  three, for reverence, 57
  three, to be remembered lifelong, 168
planes of misery (*duggati*) 33, 138, 148
pleasure and pain, 69
powers (*bala*),
  of a noble persons, 150
  of an *Arahant*, 54, 74
Profile of Meditative Experience (POME), 47
psychotic vision, 198
Purābheda Sutta, 199
pure abodes (*suddhāvāsa*), 45
purifications seven, 64, n.9

Q

quake, 58, 61
qualities,
  as a yard stick for determining a supramundane fruit, 147
  of a noble person, 66
  of a stream-enterer, 53, 147
  of an *Arahant*, 74
  Ugga's astonishing and amazing, 45, 166
quenched (*nibbuta*), 70, 74, 83

R

Rāhula Sutta, 55, 168
Rāhulovāda Sutta, 101
Rajagaha, 45, 151, 165, 167, (Isigili slope) 160
Ratana Sutta, 141, 157
Ratavinīta Sutta, 64, n. 9
razor, 55
reality,
  metaphysical reality, 70
  Nibbāna as transcendental, 69–75,
  "seeing *Nibbāna* as a reality", 164
re-birth, 39, 73
recluseship, 65
recommendation, 200
re-experience of fetter-breaking–experience,
  as a reality, 113, 117
  by a noble person in a past life, 151
  by an *Arahant,* 99
  role of, on the path to *Nibbāna,* 109
  see also *phala-samāpatti*
reflecting on state of mind , 62, 79, see also review knowledge
religious experience
  as a key element of a fruit, 31, 53
  as transcendental and ineffable, 2, 3
  definition, 22
  differentiating fetter-breaking-experience and non-Buddhist, 104–105
  in field research, 57–61
  of a Buddhist as unique, 70, 197
  of a Buddhist other than fetter-breaking-experience, 102–103
  of a Buddhist as non-mystic, 70
  of a non-Buddhist, 1–2, 104, 105
  of an *Arahant,* 36, 37
  transforming , 197
relinquishing (*cāga*), 147
research methodology,
  field research, 8
  textual research, 7
residue-remaining (*sa-upādisesa*), 202
restlessness (*uddhacca*), 32
results, 65, 66
reticence, to divulge attainments, 16
reverence, three places for, 57
reviewing, state of mind, 79
revulsion, (*nibbidā*) 63, 98
right resolve (*sammā-saṃkappa*), 199
right view (*sammā-diṭṭhi*)
  and seeing conditionality, 209
  and stream-entry, 121, 156
  and generosity, 147
  and signless experience, 103, 117
  field research on, 126–129
  of a noble person, 124
  twofold (mundane/supramundane), 122
river bank, 58
robbers, 177
Rohana country, 213
Roscharch ink-blot test, 47, 50–51

S

Sabbāsava Sutta, 78, 209
Saccavibhanga Sutta, 169
saddhā (confidence/faith)
  and knowledge, 134
  as spiritual faculty, 32, 87, 138
  field research on, 134–136
  groundless (*amūlika*), 131
  of Uṇṇābha, 34, 49
  rational (*ākāravatī*), 131, 133, 190
  see also unshaken confidence
sage, 69
Sakka Pañha Sutta, 167
Sal tree, 138
Samañña-phala Sutta, 29, n.5, n.6, 65, 70
samaṇahood (*sāmañña*), 89
samatha (calm)
  range of, practices, 3, 22
  and *vipassanā,* 204
  misunderstandings on, 207
  role of, 203
  vehicle of (*samatha-yāna*), 204
saṃkhāra (formations),
  and cessation-of-perception-and-feeling, 115
  bodily (*kāya*), 115
mental (*mano*), 115
  three types of, 115
  verbal (*vacī*), 115
sammā-paṭipanno (one rightly practicing), 89
Sammmādiṭṭhi Sutta, 124

saṃsāra, 73, 209, 210,
  cessation of, 80
  "temporary cutting of", 152
saṃvega, 63, n.3, 63
saṅgha,
  causing disunity amongst, 142
  entering the, 172
  sāvaka, 21, 49, n.1, 76, 83, 87
Sarakāni Sutta, 137, 142
sāsana antardhāna (disappearance of the teaching), 17
sattavisuddhi (seven purifications), 58
Sāvatti, 167
science/ non-science, 51
security, from bondage (*yogakkhema*), 75
"seeing things as they really are" (*yathābhūta-ñāṇadassana*), 208
seer-in-body/body-witness (*kāya-sakkhī*), 45, 46, 88
sekha (trainee), 162, 190, 199, 208, 209
self-confidence (*vesārajja*), 34
sense objects,
  and fetter-breaking-experience, 73, 74, 91, 92
  and signless state, 22
  declaration's of Arahnatship with regards to, 37
  non-identification with, 98, 99
  six, and *Atrahant*, 176
seven-times-at-most attainer (*satta-kkattuparaṃ*), 90
shock, 60, 61
signless state (*animitta*)
  and concentration of mind (*ceto samādhi*), 22, 23, 107, 108
  and deliverance of mind (*ceto vimutti*), 22, 107
  and elimination of fetters, 99
  and *Nibbāna*, 75, 83, 102–103
  and transcendental reality, 75, 83, 84
  animitta-phala-samāpatti, 65
  as a gateway to liberation, 101
  as not a permanent release from defilements, 102, 103
  as object of consciousness, 75, 83, 96, 117
  contact, 108, 115
  definition of, 22
  element (*dhātu*), 74, 83, 96
  experiences, 75, 78,79, 83, 95
  fetter-breaking-experience as, 22
  momentary supramundane, 20, 66
  range of, 22
silence, 57, 172
Simile of,
  a man with good eye-sight standing on the bank of a lake, 174
  a man with good eye-sight standing on the bank of a pond, 44, 70,
  a well along a dessert path, 4, 163
  clay pot of ghee or oil in water being broken, 150, 203
  distant glimpse of a splendid city, 164
  gallons of water in the ocean, 148
  horn of a rhinoceros, 146
  man struck by hundred spears, swords and axes, 148
  matinee show in a cinema, 99
  rain pouring on a mountain top, 149
  river merging with sea, 72
  seven balls of clay, 148
  seven grains of gravel, 148
  seven types of persons in water, 89
  slanting tree, 149, 203
  soil in the great earth, 148
  still flowing waters, 100
  still forest pool, 174
  the adze, 56
  two bundles of reeds, 96,97
sixteen insight knowledges (*vipassanā ñāṇa*), 4, 206, 210, 211
skeleton, 91
skeptical doubt (*vicikicchā*), 5, 32, 34, 37, 121, 125
snakes, 60
specific conditionality (*idappaccayatā*), 72, 75, 117, 129, 208
applicability of, to *Nibbāna*, 75
sphere of neither-perception-nor-non-perception (*nevasaññā-nā-saññāyatana*), 3
spiritual awakening, 58, 92
stair, building a, 72
stars, 69
stream-enterer (*sotāpanna*)
  and "vision" and understanding of *Nibbāna*, 162–163

and impossibilities, see impossibilities
and knowledge of dependant origination, 125
as not dependent on others to tread the Path, 33, 146, 163
as not seeking another teacher, 142,143
as worthy of gifts/ offerings/ hospitality, 150
blessings of a, 148
definition of, 21, 121, 131
destiny of a, 48, 171
fetters eliminated by, 21
final destination of a, 149,171
generosity of a, see generosity
knowledge appropriate to a, 67
merits of a, 148
powers of a, 67
qualities of a, 53, 67, 147
recognizing who is not a, 142–143
state of mind of a, 80, 121
strengths of a, 148, 150
suffering remaining for a, 148
three types of, 32, 90, 200
wrong views abandoned by, 122–124
stream-entry (*sotāpatti*)
attainment of, 33, 58, 59, 60, 61, 80, 155
declaration of, 33–35, 55, 78
factors of (*sotāpatti-aṅga*), 5, 35, 54, 78, 131
fetters eliminated at, 5
fruit of, 32, 65, 66, 67, 78, 79, 81
gods attaining, 55
impact of, on *sīla*, 138
one practsing for the realization of, 75–78, 82
place where one attained, 57
"striking a match-stick", 91
striking commonalities, 197, 198
Subha Sutta, 29, n.5
suicide, 78, 181
of Channa, 160
of Godhika, 159
of Ñāṇavīra Bhikkhu, 82
of Vakkali, 159
Sumangalavilasinī, 212
sun and the moon, 69
suññata (empty),
as a gateway to liberation, 101
contact, 115
experiences, 78, 79
fetter-breaking-experience as, 22
phala-samāpatti as, 65
superior people, plane of (*sappurisa bhūmi*), 77, 78
"Supreme Identity", 105
Suttas, 66, 67, 68, 73, 75, 76, 77
nature of the fetter-breaking-experience in 87, 96–100
"switching between sunshine and cloudiness", 111

T

taints (*āsava*), 37, 42, 43, 54, 55, 56, 62, 63, 78
destruction of, 172, 209
tapanīya pañha (questioned to be set aside) 70
teacher,
role of mindfulness as a, 146
stream-enterer not dependant on a, 146
texts, 197
Thai tradition,
Ajahn Brahmavamso of, 4
Ajahn Chah of, 1
theists, 69, 70
Theravāda tradition,
and *Nibbāna*, 75, 83, 96
four paths and four fruits in, 74, 83
meditation techniques of, 3
uniqueness in Path and fruit of, 105, 117, 197
thunderbolt/lightening, 60, 201
Tibetan tradition, Mahāmudra, 49
transcendence, definition of, 84, n.6
Nibbāna as, 69–75
transformation, 58
triple gateways to liberation (*tividha-vimokkha-mukkha),* 101
field research on, 101–102
Triple Gem, unshaken confidence in, 81, 131
living without reverence to, 143
true renunciant, 171

U

unanswered questions, ten (*avyākruta*), 123
underlying tendencies (*anusaya*), 77, 129, 203

uninstructed worldling (*assutavā putthujjana*), 122, 139
Universal King (*cakkavatti rājā*/ Wheel-Turning-Monach), 148, 149, 167
unsatisfactoriness (*dukkha*), understanding of 129, 197
unshaken confidence (*aveccappasāda*),
  as gladness and gratitude, 136, 137
  in Triple Gem, 35, 53, 67, 78, 131, 142, 200
unwise persons, 45
usmā (vitality), 116

V

"vacant gaze", 98
Vajjī, 11
Vesāli, 166
vicititudes, eight, 150
views (*diṭṭhi*), 96, 39
  on personality (*sakkāya diṭṭhi*), 5, 32, 121,
  sixty two wrong, 123
  twenty modes of, 122
  two extreme dogmatic, 126
view-winner (*diṭṭhipatta)*, 45, 46, 82, 88, 89, 155
village, entering a, 78
Vīmaṇsaka Sutta, 41, 132, 133
vinaya, 10, 11, 158
vipassanā,
  debate on *samatha* and, 204
  practice, 203, 204
  range of practice of, 3, 49, 65
  vehicle of (*vipassanā-yāna*), 204, 211
  ten corruptions of, 206, 207
viriya (energy), faculty of, 32, 87
virtue (*sīla*), 200 , see *ariyakanta sīla*
virtuous (*sīlavā*), 45
visesagāmī (going to distinction), 39, 40
Visuddhimagga, 20, 21, 30, n.11, n.12, 50, 64, n.9, 65, 66, 67, 68, 74, 75, 76, 206, 210, 211
  and " triple gateways to liberation", 101
  and Ajahn Chah, 211
  and cessation-of-perception-and-feeling, 114, 115
  and definition of Path and fruit, 20, 21
  and superiority of experiential knowledge, 212
  differentiating *phala-samāpatti* and cessation-of-perception-and-feeling, 106, 113
  nature of fetter-breaking-experience in, 87
  on *phala-samāpatti,* 4, 23, 105–106, 110
  role of, in this Study, 7

W

"whole world fell apart/ stopped", 97
wife or knife, 157
wisdom (*paññā*), 44
  and seventy three knowledges of the Buddha, 51
  and unshaken confidence, 136
  as a spiritual faculty, 32, 33, 87, 137, 138, 146
  directed to rise and fall of phenomena (*udayatta-gāmini- paññā*), 126, 149
  in supramundane right view, 122
world
  contacting the, 97
  deva, 49
  disgust with, 64
  disintegration/dissolution of, 56, 200
  mystery to the, of senses, 73, 92
worms, 64, n.7

Index of Proper Names

A

Abhaya (Prince), declaration of stream-entry by, 34
Adhimutta, 177
Ajita Kesakambalī, 124
Amitha Gavesi, Pallekele, 15
Anālayo, 160, 161
Ālavaka (*yakkha*), 168
Ānanda,
 and Anāthapiṇḍika, 35
 and arising of contact, 97
 and Migasālā, 38
 and Mirror of the Dhamma *Sutta*, 53
 and *saddhā*, 134
 and signless concentration of mind (*animitta ceto samādhi*), 107
 and Uṇṇābha, 49, n.3
 and lion's roar, 186
 weeping, 150–151
Anāthapiṇḍika, 33, 35, 54, 78, 147, 151,165
Anuruddha,
 ability of, to assess supramundane fruits, 48
 accused of *pārājikā* offence,10
Ariṭṭha, declaration of *anāgāmī-phala by,* 36

B

Bāhiya, 69, 71
Bhaddā *Therī*, attainment of Arahantship by, 56
Bimbisāra (King), 151, 166
Bodhi, *bhikkhu,*
 on *Nibbāna* as transcendental and ineffable, 3, 71, 72
 on unshaken confidence, 131
 on *ariyakanta sīla* /Sarakāni, 138
 on "seeing" *Nibbāna* by an *Arahant* and a trainee, 163
Brahmavamso, Ajahn,
 and *jhānic* experience, 4
 and *sīla* of a stream-enterer, 140
 and fruition attainment, 109–110
 and nature of fetter-breaking experience, 91
 on Ajahn Chah's empty kuṭi, 187
 on motivation for an *Arahant*, 189
 on persons who have become a noble person in a past life, 151
 on suffering remaining for an *Arahant,* 186
 on supramundane fruit as a discernible event, 57
Brown, Daniel,
 and field research on meditation 2, 3, 57
 on "one path and different enlightenment experiences," 105
Bucker, R.M., on "consmic consciousness," 105

C

Carrithers, Michael, in interview with a forest monk, 14
Chah, Ajahn,
 and declaration of attainments, 17
 and empty *kuṭi*, 187
 and meditation in a cemetery, 201
 and religious experience 1, 56, 95, 198
 and "still flowing water," 100
 and "still forest pool," 174
 on *Visuddhimagga*, 211

teaching technique of, 3
Channa, suicide of,160
Citta (householder), 108, 138, 167
Citta, Hatthisāriputta,
and signless experience and fetter-breaking-experience, 114
signless mental concentration of, as not *Nibbāna*, 102–103
Cūḷa-Abhaya, *Tipiṭaka*, 213
Cūḷanāga, *Tipiṭaka*, 212
Cūḷasumana, *Tipiṭaka*, 212

D

Dabba Mallaputta, 161
Dārukammika, and difficulties of recognizing a noble person, 38
Davids, Rhys, 65, 66
Dhammadinnā, *bhikkhunī*,
declaration of stream-entry by, 35
on cessation of perception and feeling, 114
on three kinds of contact, 108
Dhirasekere, Jotiya, on disciplinary rules, 11
Dīghāvu, 55,167

E

Engler, Jack, 2, 57
Epstein, Mark, 198

G

Gethin, R., on *saddhā*, 133
Godatta, and signless liberation of mind (*animitta ceto vimutti*), 107
Godhika, suicide of, 159

H

Hamilton, Williams,
about, 29, n.4
field research on enlightened persons by, 15
and virtue of noble persons, 5–6, 140
Harvey, Peter,
definition of a noble person by, 49, n.1
on first noble person, 29–30, n.6
on noble *sāvakas*, 77

I

Isidatta (chamberlain), 166,
and Migasālā, on difficulties of recognizing noble persons, 39
declaration of stream-entry by, 34
generosity of, 147

J

Jayatilleke, K. N.,
on *Nibbāna* as transcendental and ineffable, 70
on limits of knowledge, 6
on unshaken confidence,131
Jīvaka, 167

K

Kāligodhā, declaration of stream-entry by, 35, 54
Kāmabhū, on cessation of perception and feeling and signless contact, 108
Kannimahara, Sumangala, claim of, on having become a noble person in a past life, 6, 15, 151
Kappina, ability of, to assess supramundane fruits, 48
Khujjatissa, Maṅganavāsī, 16
Koṇḍañña, attainment of stream-entry of, 33,125
Kornfield, Jack, on living Buddhist masters, 3

M

Mahā Boowa, Ajahn,
declaration of Arahantship by, 17
meditation techniques of, 3
Mahā Cunda, 160
Mahā Kassapa,
ability of, to assess supramundane fruits, 48
and Dhamma talks, 188
and first Dhamma assembly, 189
attainment of Arahantship of, 56
Mahā Koṭṭhita,
and signless liberation of mind (*animitta ceto vimutti*), 107
Citta Hatthisāriputta and signless mental concentration (*animitta ceto samādhi*), 102–103
Mahā Kumara, Sosānika, 16
Mahā Moggallāna,
ability of, to assess supramundane fruits, 48

accused of *pārājikā* offence,10
and signless concentration of mind (*animitta ceto samādhi*), 108
compared to a father, 169
and lion's roar, 186
visiting *brahmā* Tissa, 46
Mahā-Dhammarakkhita, 213
Mahānāma, state of defilements of, 203
Mahāsi, Sayadaw,
meditation technique of, 3
on *phala-samāpatti*, 4, 106
research with meditators in the lineage of, 47
Makkalī Gosāla, 124
Migasālā, and how to recognize noble persons, 38
Mun, Ajahn, 17, 211

N

Nakulamātā and Nakulapitā, 167
Ñāṇadassana, *bhikkhu*, 51
Ñāṇananda, K. *bhikkhu*
on abandoning view on personality, 150
and "vacant gaze," 98, 99
and "*turiya*" in *Upanishads*, 104
and consciousness of an *Arahant*, 176, 177
and language of an *Arahant*, 182
on experience of *Nibbāna* of a stream-enterer, 71, 72, 162
on *Nibbāna* and transcendent reality, 71, 72
Ñāṇārāma, Mātara Sri, 7
Ñāṇavīra, *bhikkhu*
and *abhidhamma*, 212
attainment of stream-entry of, 82
suicide of, 154
Nārada, 162
Nighanṭa Nātaputta, 133
Nyānatiloka, in Dictionary, 65

P

Pa Auk Tawya, Sayadaw
on fruition attainment and cessation-of-perception-and-feeling, 106
meditation technique of, 3–4
on *phala-samāpatti*, 4
Pakudha Kaccāyana, 124
Pasenadi of Kosala, (King), 38, 166
Popper, Karl, theory of falsification, 51
Punabbasu's mother (female *yakkha*), 168
Purāṇa (chamberlain), 166
and Migasālā, on difficulties of recognizing noble persons, 38
declaration of stream-entry by, 34
generosity of, 147
Purāṇa Kassapa, 124

R

Rāhula, attaining Arahantship, 55

S

Saddhatissa, (King), 16
Sarakāni (sākyan), 5, 137, 142, 167
Sāriputta,
and knowledge of dependant origination, 125
and Koṭṭhita on signless liberation of mind (*animitta ceto vimutti*), 107
and questions of Ajitha, 208–209
and simile of the bundles of reeds, 96
and suicide of Channa, 160
and supramundane fruits, 202
"awaits the time," 182
compared to a mother, 169
declares Arahantship, 37, 54
like a worker awaiting wages, 181
lion's roar of, 186
as marshal of the Dhamma, 189
parinibbāna of, 150
Saviṭṭha, 162
Schmithausen, Lambert, 161
Sīha the general, 134, 166
Sirimā (courtesan), 151
Sirivaḍḍha, declaration of attainment of *anāgāmī-phala* by, 35
Sona, declaration of Arahantship by, 37
Stede, Williams, 65, 66
Subhadda, 171
Subhuti, 176
Suciloma (*yakkha*),168
Sufi Ali Ghizali (Master), 104
Sunīta, attainment of Arahantship of, 56

T

Ṭhanissaro, *bhikkhu*, on *pārājikā* rule iv, 29, n.2

and pācittiya rule viii, 29, n.3
Tilakaratne, Asanga,
on definition of transcendence, 84, n.6
and effect of fetter-breaking-experience as *Nibbāna,* 75
on *Nibbāna* as transcendental and ineffable, 3, 69, 70, 71, 207
on *saddhā,* 131–132, 133
Tungpulu, Sayadaw, 15

U

U Ba Khin, 3
Udāyi, declaration of stream-entry, 34
Ugga of Hatthigāma, and encounters with gods, 45
Ugga of Vesāli, declaration of stream-entry by, 33, 55
Uṇṇābha (brahmin),
and faith, 49, n. 3
declaration of stream-entry by, 34
Uttama *Therī,* attainment of Arahantship of, 56

V

Vacchagotta, and lay noble disciples, 164
Vakkali, suicide of, 159
Vessavana, (god), 165
Vipassi, Arapola, 15
Visākha (householder), on cessation of perception and feeling, 108, 114
Visākhā, 147, 165
Vītasoka, attainment of Arahantship of, 55

W

Warder, A.K., and the original word of the Buddha, 7
Wilber, Ken,
and "unity consciousness," 105
and Buddhist religious experience, 198
and religious experience, 1–2
on other religious experiences, 105

Y

Yamelu and Tekula, 205

Index for Findings of Field Research

advice to practioners, no.2 237
anāgāmī-phala, no.1, 225; no.2, 234
arahatta-phala, no.1, 226
ariyakanta sīla, no.1, 224; no.2, 233; no.3, 246; no.4, 253; no.5, 259; no.6, 263
background of interviewee, interviewees no.1, 221; no.2, 227; no.3, 238; no.4, 249; no.5, 255; no.6, 260; no.7, 264; no.8, 270
Creator God, no.1, 224; no.2, 232; no.3, 245; no.4, 252; no.5, 258; no.6, 263; no.7, 268
hallucination/ mental illness/ delusion/ creation of mind, no.1, 224; no.4, 252; no.5, 258; no.6, 263; no.7, 268
meditation object, no.1, 222; no.2, 229; no.3, 242; no.4, 251; no.5, 256; no.6, 261
meditation systems, no.1, 227; no.2, 237; no.3, 248; no.4, 254; no.5, 259; no.6, 264; no.7, 269
Nibbāna, concept of, no. 223; no.2, 232; no.3, 244; no.6, 258
non-humans, beliefs and encounters with, no.2, 237; no.3, 248; no.4, 254; no.5, 259; no.6, 264; no.7, 269
phala-samāpatti, no.1, 227, no.2, 236; no.3, 248; no.4, 254; no.5, 259; no.6, 264; no.7, 269
right view, no.1, 224; no.2, 233; no.3, 245; no.4, 253; no.5, 258; no.6, 263; no.7, 269
rites and rituals, no.1, 224; no.2, 232; no.3, 246; no.4, 253; no.5, 259; no.6, 263; no.7, 268
samatha/jhāna, no.1, 227; no.2, 237; no.3, 248; no.4, 254; no.5, 259; no.6, 264; no.7, 269
skadāgāmi-phala, attainment of, no.1, 225; no.2, 233; no.3, 246; no.4, 254
sleep, no.1, 224; no.2, 232; no.4, 253; no.5, 258; no.6, 263; no.7, 268
sotāpatti-phala,
  attainment of, no.1, 222; no.2, 228; no.3, 240; no.4, 250; no.5, 256; no.6, 261
  expression of, no.1, 222; no.2, 228; no.3, 240; no.4, 250; no.5, 256; no.6, 261
  fetter-breaking-experience, nature of, no. 223; no.2, 230; no.3, 243; no.4, 251; no.5, 257; no.6, 262
  knowledge that arose/significance of, no.1, 223; no.2, 230; no.3, 243; no.4, 252; no.5, 257; no.6, 262
teacher, no.1, 224; no.2, 232,237; no.3, 245, 248; no.4, 253, 254; no.5, 258, 259; no.6, 263, 264; no.7, 268, 269
three fetters, no.1, 223; no.2, 229; no.3, 243; no.4, 251; no.5, 257; no.6, 261, no.7, 267
unshaken confidence in Triple Gem, no.1, 224; no.2, 232; no.3, 245; no.4, 253; no.5, 258; no.6, 263; no.7, 268

www.ingramcontent.com/pod-product-compliance
Lightning Source LLC
Chambersburg PA
CBHW070815250426
43672CB00030B/2619
* 9 7 8 1 7 8 1 7 9 2 0 4 9 *